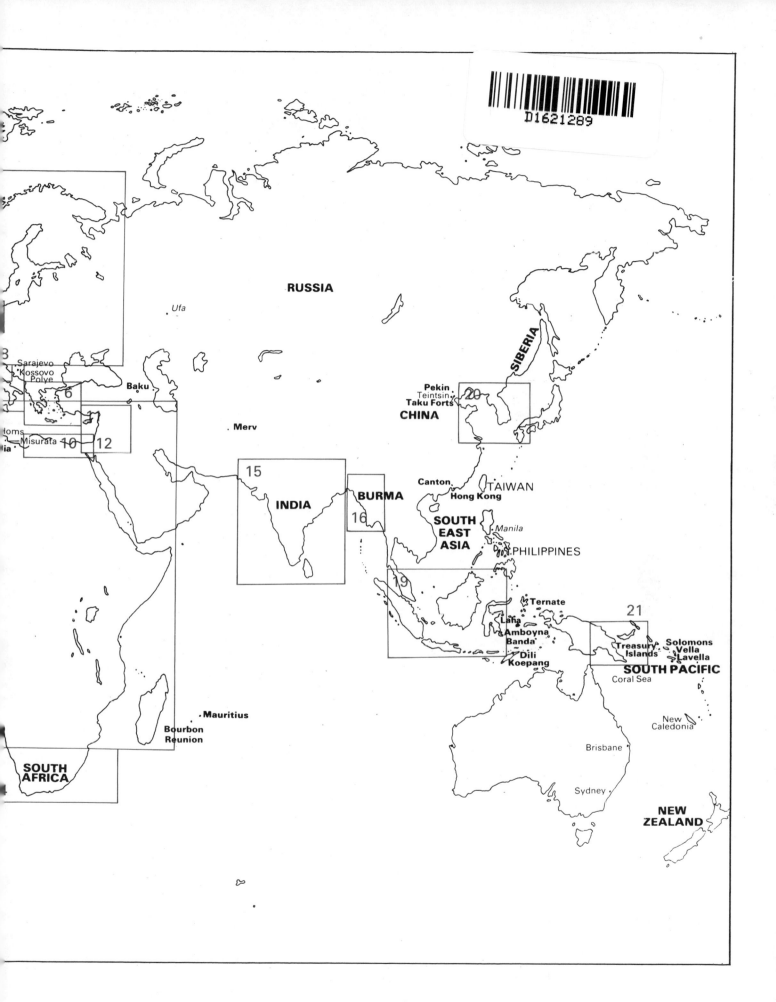

RUSSIA

Ufa

SIBERIA

Sarajevo
Kossovo Polye

Baku

6

Pekin
Teintsin
Taku Forts

20

Merv

CHINA

Moms

Misurata 10 12

ia

15

Canton

TAIWAN

INDIA

BURMA

Hong Kong

16

SOUTH
EAST
ASIA

Manila

PHILIPPINES

19

Ternate

21

Laha
Amboyna
Banda

Solomons
Vella
Lavella

Treasury
Islands

Dili
Koepang

SOUTH PACIFIC

Coral Sea

Mauritius

New
Caledonia

Bourbon
Reunion

Brisbane

SOUTH
AFRICA

Sydney

NEW
ZEALAND

Scale 1:66M

BATTLE HONOURS
OF THE
BRITISH
AND
COMMONWEALTH
ARMIES

Above: Colours of the Scots Guards. From drawings by F. W. Barry published in *History of the Scots Guards, Volume 11* (1934)

BATTLE HONOURS
OF THE
BRITISH
AND
COMMONWEALTH
ARMIES

ANTHONY BAKER

LONDON
IAN ALLAN LTD

First published 1986

ISBN 0 7110 1600 3

Published by Ian Allan Ltd, Shepperton, Surrey;
and printed by Butler & Tanner Ltd, Frome, Somerset

'Though many Battle Honours were awarded during historic campaigns, the greatest contribution which our
Regiments have made is rarely mentioned; this has surely
been the protection they have afforded to those indomitable British merchants, who in search of fresh markets
spread our influence all over the world. For some of these
Regiments this involved spending many years in stinking
garrisons overseas where their casualties from disease were
often far greater than those suffered on military service.'

I humbly pray then to admit the excuse
Of time, of numbers, and of due course of things,
Which cannot, in their huge and proper life
Be here presented.

    Shakespeare, *Henry V*

While a soldier's name is honoured,
While a soldier's fame is dear,
Nowhere shall they be forgotten,
Least of all forgotten here.

    Whyte-Melville, *Songs and Verses* (referring to Cath-
cart's Hill in the Crimea)

With him ther was his sonne, a yong Sqyer . . .
Of twenty yeer he was of age, I gesse,
And he had been some tyme in chivalrye,
In Flaundres, in Artoys, and in Picardie.

    Chaucer, *Canterbury Tales*

Below: The Battle of Inkerman as pictured in the *Illustrated Naval and Military Magazine* of 1886. *via Ian Hogg*

Contents

Lists of Plates and Maps

Maps drawn by Keith and Hazel Martin

Preface

The primary object of this book is to show in their context the battles, both Honoured and non-honoured, fought by the armies of Great Britain and the Commonwealth in innumerable campaigns and over 300 years, and to indicate the regiments that have taken part. The book is divided into four Parts.

The Parts

Part I Introduction provides a brief history of the development of the Army, and an outline of the history of Battle Honours, Colours and Regimental Dress.

Part II Battles and Campaigns of the British and Commonwealth Armies sets the scene for each battle and provides a historical background. Elaborate tactical detail has not been given, as this can be found in many other publications, although in most cases sufficient detail has been included to indicate why the battles were fought and why they were Honoured or not. Throughout Honoured battles are shown in bold type and non-honoured battles in italics.

Part III Chronology of Battles and Battle Honours is the only comprehensive list of battles fought by the British and Commonwealth Armies that has been produced. It has been devised to show which regiments were actually involved, and whether they were Honoured or not, in order to remove the confusion that can result from changes of name, title or number of regiments over the years. This section of the book is preceded by an Introduction explaining how the Chronology has been compiled and can be used.

Part IV Indexes and Maps. The Index of Battles shows each individual battle, the pages on which it is discussed in Parts II and III, the map number and the reference on that map to facilitate easy location. The Index of Place Names shows page numbers in Part II and map locations. The maps are the most comprehensive display of battles ever published. Their scale varies considerably and have been chosen as that appropriate to the situation recorded. A more detailed explanation of the Maps and Indexes is given in the Introduction to Part IV.

Sources and Bibliography

No bibliographical list has been included since it would be too vast to serve any useful purpose. Suffice to say that the sources of the majority of the material has been the Military Section of the War Office Library, supplemented by some military libraries in Canada and by the South African National Museum of Military History. From the main source virtually all the campaign and regimental histories have been consulted, including the official histories, which must total well over a thousand volumes, and unpublished material from the archives of the Library was also put at my disposal. The text of all the volumes was of great value, even though at times it was contradictory, but in almost every case the standard of maps fell far below that which would have been expected, and accurately locating the battles, even some of the better known ones, was an unexpected problem and required much research.

Acknowledgements

By far the most valuable help which I received in compiling this book was given by Mr C.A. Potts, MBE for many years the librarian of the Military Section of the War Office Library until his retirement in August 1984, who for over 20 years put his vast knowledge of military history books at my disposal, made available the archives material and was always a source of encouragement and a tower of strength at difficult times. His staff were also always extremely helpful. My thanks also go to Lt-Col Norman West, late of the King's Own Scottish Borderers, who frequently over the years commented on work as it progressed and on the methods of presentation; he also supplied many ideas and gave of his knowledge of matters military.

Not least my thanks are due to Ian Allan the publishers, for their faith in publishing a book which was such an unknown quantity.

Anthony Baker

PART I
Introduction

'The Battle of Minden or Thornhausen, where the Allied Army obtained a glorious victory over the French Army.' Tinted lithograph engraving, c1759. *NAM*

1 Introduction

In 1957 it was announced that there would be severe reductions in the strength of the British Army, and a Command Document listed the regiments scheduled for amalgamation or disbandment to accommodate the lower manpower.

It was immediately obvious that new titles would have to be invented for the amalgamated regiments, and that in any case a host of famous and honourable names would disappear. Although memories of these regiments would linger on in the minds of those who had been involved in or associated with the two world wars, their names would mean very little to future generations. Yet these were names which had helped to found a great Empire, now sadly dissipated or lost; the regiments which bore them had their own characteristics, traditions and glories. Disbandment would soon result in oblivion for some, and even in amalgamation some of the characteristics and traditions which had made individual regiments famous would die.

Looking at the Army List to see what information it gave about these Regiments, the only thing that gave any real clue to their histories was the list of Battle Honours which they bore. These Honours had been won by the indomitable courage of the British soldier, through hardship and endurance, through almost unbelievable privation in many cases, sometimes admittedly almost by accident, but always in conditions which would be hard to imagine, even in these days of films and television, by those who had not taken part in similar situations. The Honours were the result of the actions of many men, of all walks of life, living and working together in high comradeship; they represented fear and bravery, gloom and humour, desperation and elan, and now at least some of the regiments which gained them were to be consigned to the dusty archives and forgotten. Some Honours were unique and some were borne by many regiments, but now many of the regiments were to be removed from sight or merged so that individual achievements would no longer be recognisable.

Apart from the future of these regiments and their Honours, two things became apparent on reading the lists of Honours. The first was that many regiments bore Honours the origins of which, to one of the many whose knowledge of history was largely limited to a school curriculum, were totally obscure. The second was that the numbers of Honours borne by regiments varied greatly; when dates were given as part of the Honour, or when the battles themselves were well enough known to date, it seemed that some regiments had been idle for long periods whereas others had seen almost continuous action.

Taking the first point, enquiries among military men, some of whom claimed to be well read in military history, failed to produce answers which identified more than a few of the obscure battles or their dates. If they did not know, and could not point to a book which would give the answers, how could laymen or those with only a limited military background find out? It seemed almost unbelievable that no such book existed, when so many books on military history had been published over the years, even though the majority of these were produced by a regiment or written about the better-known campaigns. It was subsequently discovered that there was in fact one book, *The Battle Honours of the British Army* by C. B. Norman; but it is a selective book, not comprehensive in terms either of the battles themselves or of those who took part in them. In any case it was published in 1911, and a lot of blood has been spilt by the British Army since then in all parts of the world.

True, there are means of finding the information for those willing to carry out long and arduous research. Fortescue's *History of the British Army*, in all its numerous volumes, offers a possible solution, but this makes for a slow and tortuous task, and the book covers the tactics of battles and the participants rather than the Honours awarded for the battles. There are many other campaign and regimental histories which can be studied. But again it would not be a simple task because of both the wealth of personal detail included and because of their archaic style, as befitted the age in which they were written; and in any case they seldom figure on library shelves. It seemed then that anybody who wanted a quick, simple and easily readable answer was doomed to failure, and that the less interested or dedicated person would not be sufficiently keen to go to all the trouble obviously involved.

But although there were many ways of discovering in which country a particular battle took place, to pinpoint that battle accurately within a country was a very different matter. Many names given to battles, either by those who recognised that they should be Honoured or by those who claimed them unsuccessfully as Honours, relate to small villages, perhaps just farmsteads. In some cases even a 1:100,000 scale map does not mark them. The numerous histories have maps—sometimes. They are useful—sometimes. More often though, even where maps are provided, they do not include the battles referred to in the text, and in many cases these maps, in excuse often referred to as 'sketches', are wildly inaccurate. It is almost unbelievable, but some of the official histories of the World War II do not even mention in the text battles which have been awarded as Honours and obviously therefore do not include them on the maps. Perhaps it does not matter, but to the person who is seriously interested it is essential for comprehensiveness, and coupled with the date is often very good clue to the tactical or strategical situation which existed. Perhaps this volume contains too many maps, but at least every battle, Honoured or unhonoured, and the vast majority of the other places which occur in the narrative appear somewhere.

As to the second point, it was surely inconceivable that any country would deliberately keep regiments in being, just as an insurance policy, and not use them. The British Empire was not won by regiments which sat doing nothing, nor was the enormous task of policing it subsequently carried out by one set of regiments while the rest did all the fighting. There seemed to be two possible solutions. Either regiments had been raised mainly for policing duties, which had then absorbed such an inordinate number of them that the cost of maintaining a Standing Army must have been of doubtful benefit; or there had been a lot of battles for which no Honours were awarded for some reason or other. Again research was needed and it soon transpired that the latter theory was the answer.

So there still remained two areas about which information might be available if anyone took the trouble to find it. These were, first, the battles for which no Honours had been awarded, a knowledge of which would lead to a more complete record of a regiment's history than could be gained from, say, the Army List; and, second, the identification of the more obscure battles which had been Honoured. In both cases it might be of interest to discover why. But the books containing the information were largely out of print and inaccessible to the ordinary reader, and in any case so many would have to be consulted that, except to a student of military history, the task was bound to be at best daunting. Nevertheless it seemed possible that there were people, ordinary people who might at one time have served in a particular regiment, who wanted to know the answers. This was the genesis of the present book.

I was, perhaps am, one of those ordinary people. I certainly was not a practising military historian, for then I should perhaps have known the answers I sought, or at least have known where to look for them. But if I had realised the magnitude of the task I might never have started. What began as a relatively simple exercise of chronology and geography, with some history thrown in, gradually grew into something quite different. One thing led to another; a point would puzzle me and this led to another avenue of research. If it puzzled me, perhaps other people too; so record it. And the questions flooded in.

Why were some battles honoured and others forgotten? Were there any rules on which the decision could be based? Who took part in this or that battle and what did 'took part' mean in numerical terms? Did regiments ever try to claim Honours which had not been awarded to them, and with what result? Sometimes confusion reigned because Regiments were referred to numerically in different books on different campaigns, and although the same number was used it was clear that a different regiment was being referred to. Why was this? Did numbers change and if so why and when? The same thing sometimes happened with names, with County titles, and even worse in the early days when regiments were referred to by their Colonel's name only. Some regiments have similar badges on their uniforms or on their Colours; were these Honours too, perhaps, and what did they mean in terms of battles or campaigns?

It was also clear that the British Army as such had not fought alone, but side by side with its imperial or colonial friends and allies, and not just during the world wars. Justice would not be done unless they too were included. Battles would often only fall into perspective when the total complement of fighting troops was considered. This was particularly the case in India, so what happened to the regiments of the old Indian Presidency armies which mutinied? They had been loyal at one time and must have won Honours themselves. It might be morally sound to expunge the records, as most historians of the past seemed to have done, but it certainly did not make historical sense.

And now nearly thirty years have gone by during which other changes, disbandments and amalgamations have taken place. It would be incorrect to say that the research has taken all that time or even most of it; periods of inactivity occurred, sometimes for domestic reasons, more often because the task itself appeared to be almost too daunting after all. But in the end the desire to see not only the light at the end of the tunnel but the scenery beyond started the adrenalin flowing again and another stage was completed. It might be said that the result of the research and consolidation has been to produce yet another book, itself equally daunting to the ordinary reader. I hope not. But even if, after all, no ordinary people read it, the record exists and at least a single book is a lot less than the hundreds which were combed to produce that record.

2 The Development of the Army from 1660

When the Standing Army was first raised in 1660, and for nearly a century after that, a regiment was only known by its Colonel's name, although some attempts at unofficial numbering were made at various times. In this connection it must be understood that the Colonel equated more nearly to the colonel of the Regiment in the modern sense and was frequently not the Commanding Officer.

The Colonel was responsible for raising the regiment, and this could be a costly business, particularly if, for instance, he had extravagant tastes in dress; but at the same time, once the regiment was raised, the Colonel's position was one of honour and status and of considerable financial benefit. Frequently he was titled, usually landed, and had many other interests, even if only social ones, so that the time he was able, or willing, to spend with his regiment might well be limited; the Colonelcy became more and more a sinecure, although the incumbent was paid a salary for the job. There were many instances of Colonels who never even saw their regiments, particularly if they were engaged in a long tour abroad; and some tours were very long indeed, the record being held by the 38th Regiment of Foot, the 1st Battalion the South Staffordshire Regiment to give it its subsequent title, who spent 58 years continuously in the West Indies from 1706, only four years after their raising in 1702. Nevertheless, actively engaged or interested or not, the regiment bore, and was identified by, its Colonels' names, a habit which caused some confusion if the name happened to be a common one and was therefore duplicated. In an attempt to overcome this confusion, epithets, often relating to the facing colours of their uniforms, were added, thus giving rise, for instance, to the Buff Howards and the Green Howards. The former retained its epithet as its regimental title (The Buffs) until it was submerged in the large Queen's Regiment in 1966, and the latter still retains its epithet as its title, although many years of neglect passed between its first appearance as a nickname and its comparatively modern reuse as an official title.

The Colonel appointed the Lieutenant-Colonel, who by the 18th century had become the Commanding Officer of the regiment, as well as the other officers, but since commissions were bought, and were by no means cheap, the Lieutenant-Colonel also sometimes found better ways of occupying his time than being with his regiment. There was considerable movement of the more monied officers as vacancies occurred in regiments considered elite, and in any case the possession of the wherewithal to buy com-missions, or promotion, did not necessarily endow an officer with a high degree of military ability. It is perhaps remarkable, with hindsight, that with all the scrimshanking and corruption which undoubtedly permeated the Army in the early days, it still gained and fully deserved a reputation as the most efficient and formidable fighting force in the world. Perhaps, as is true of the present day, its reputation depended to the greatest extent on the quality of its NCOs.

Although the regiments were not numbered or placed in an official numerical order, a precedence was established from the earliest days. In 1685, for example, King James II gave the Cavalry precedence over the Infantry, a situation which has remained ever since. The first evidence of official numbering appears in the early 18th century, when regiments on the Irish establishment were actually given numbers as 'Xth Foot, Ireland'; none of these still exists. It should be remembered that at that period some regiments were held on the Irish establishment as opposed to the English establishment; this allowed more regiments to be raised than Parliament was prepared to pay for since the Irish establishment was made a charge on the revenue of that unhappy island, based on the excuse that they were needed to maintain order there, which of course was sometimes true.

The first regiments to be officially numbered on the English establishment were in fact Marines. Two regiments were raised in 1690 and disbanded by 1699, six more, of which three remained on the establishment later as the 30th, 31st and 32nd Regiments of Foot, were raised in 1702, and ten more in 1739. In 1747 regiments were officially ranked in precedence by number, although these numbers did not form part of their titles until four years later when all the extant regiments were numbered as 'Regiments of Foot'. Only a very few of the more senior with Royal connections had any additional title, and the practice of using the Colonel's name was finally abandoned.

During the next 31 years, until 1782, the precedence and numbers of many of the regiments changed, often more than once, due to disbandments. Each time it was found necessary to reduce the size of the army, the obvious solution would have been to disband the regiments with the highest numbers. But for various reasons, usually now obscure, although popularity in high places was clearly one, the process was always selective, some of the more senior regiments being reduced and junior ones, with higher numbers, remaining; the gaps thus formed in the chronological table were then closed by renumbering while maintaining the overall order of precedence. When the Army expanded, the next successive numbers were used, so that inevitably some of the higher numbers were frequently repeated. This may not have been confusing at the time, but it certainly lays the ground for confusion in present-day research.

In 1782 territorial or county titles were first used to designate the regiments in addition to their numbers. Some of the older regiments still retained their Royal titles, and all the English counties were included. The more populous counties, or those with a better reputation for recruiting, had more than one regiment allotted to them, these being numbered as 'The Xth, 1st Blankshire' or 'The Yth, 2nd Blankshire', although at that time there seems to have been little other connection between these pairs of regiments or their nominated counties. The idea was in essence a good one and it related a regiment to a particular part of the country for recruiting purposes, although in those days there were no such establishments as regimental-depots, which did not appear for nearly another 100 years. Even when regiments were stationed in England, it was only coincidence if this was in the county whose title they bore.

Unfortunately, when allocating the titles those responsible for the new system appear to have paid little attention either to the areas where particular regiments were first raised or to the areas which had, over the years, become their traditional recruiting areas. There were a number of pleas for changes of title, some of which were allowed. As an example of the extraordinary way in which titles changed, the 14th Regiment of Foot which had been raised in 1685 in Kent, around the Canterbury–Sittingbourne area, became in 1782 the 14th (Bedfordshire) Regiment of Foot; subsequently it became in 1809 the 14th (Buckinghamshire), by exchanging titles with the 15th Regiment of Foot and in 1881 The Prince of Wales's Own (West Yorkshire Regiment). Three changes in a hundred years, none of which bore any relation to the original recruiting ground. The overall result was that to most regiments their titles meant very little and to the counties the regiments meant very little, although gradually the county allegiances grew.

And so the see-saw of changes of numerical and territorial titles continued until 1881, when occurred the most fundamental change that the Army had known so far. Until this time, as has already been indicated, the history of the British Army, in terms of the units comprising it, had been a sequence of raising new regiments in times of national emergency and disbanding them once the danger was past; as the emergencies were frequent but comparatively short-lived, so were many of the regiments raised to cope with them, but the numbers involved were often large. For the Cavalry, the biggest expansion was in the period 1688 to 1716 when sixty-five regiments were raised of which only ten lasted for more than three years; never again were there any very large increases. It might be inferred from this that, 200 years before it became patently obvious for other practical reasons, it had been realised that there were limitations on the number of horsed soldiers that could be used with advantage on a battlefield. Another twenty-five years had then to pass before it was

appreciated that the concept of a lot of Cavalry was correct after all, so long as they were mounted in a practical way for the times.

For the Infantry there were four main periods of extreme expansion and reduction, which naturally coincided with major wars. These were from 1666 to 1678, when fifty regiments were raised, of which only two survived; from 1685 to 1709, from which thirty-six out of 132 regiments survived; and from 1756 to 1762 and from 1793 to 1795, from which the figures were twenty-one out of eighty-five and fifteen out of eighty-three respectively. In the last period the army included in its establishment for a short while the numerically unprecedented and unequalled 135th Regiment of Foot. Most of these regiments were raised in the British Isles, but a few were raised abroad, such as the 60th Regiment of Foot which first saw the light of day in America. An unusual instance was one regiment raised in America in 1778, the 105th Regiment of Foot, the second of that title, being formed in Philadelphia from men of Irish descent who had remained loyal to the British cause during the War of Independence and had deserted from the American Continental Army.

Although by the time of the Peninsular War the size of the Army on the basis of numerical terminology had been considerably reduced, many regiments now had two battalions, and a few more than two, and a total of active battalions existed which was not again emulated until the end of 1914. By 1818 all second and subsequent battalions of the regiments had been disbanded, with the exception of the Guards Regiments, the 60th Regiment of Foot, which had four battalions, and the Rifle Brigade, which had three. When the Army had settled down again to a peacetime role, there were eighty-three regiments altogether; most of them were employed abroad, although if Ireland is considered as a home station the split was more even. In 1826 there were fifty-one abroad, twenty-three in Ireland, four in England or Scotland and five in transit.

The emergencies which caused these sudden increases in the strength of the army were mainly ones of internal security and the possibility of invasion, and therefore very few of the newly raised regiments saw other than garrison duty in the British Isles, the home-based regiments which already existed having been sent overseas. Some, however, did, particularly a number of regiments which were specially raised for service in India and thus intended more for fighting than for the mundane occupations. These regiments gained, or more accurately perhaps should have gained, a number of Battle Honours, and the reasons why in most cases they failed to win recognition for their deeds or to leave their names in the Hall of Fame will appear in due course.

The middle of the 19th century saw the formation of a number of regiments in the colonies, as regular regiments owing allegiance to that colony to supplement the locally raised volunteer battalions. Thus in 1842 The Royal Canadian Corps was raised from volunteers from nineteen British regiments then stationed in Canada; all the volunteers had to be veterans of more than fifteen years' service. During this period, another innovation was a regimental system of giving a number to each man on attestation; this

INTRODUCTION

was only adopted as an Army system at a much later date.

In the Gladstone administration of 1868 to 1874, the Secretary of State for War was Mr Edward Cardwell. Apart from instituting a number of overdue administrative reforms, he also appreciated the need to create a better balance between the number of Infantry regiments stationed at home and overseas at any one time, and to reduce the very long periods that the men in the regiments spent out of the country. Except in time of war, the army has never been popular with the British civilian population or with its politicians; continual efforts have been made throughout the centuries to reduce its size, and thus its effectiveness, in peacetime because its cost and its comparative freedom from the controls of the bureaucratic administrative machinery were resented. As a result, it was convenient to keep a large proportion of the Army abroad, where it was not so obvious to the eye and where such bodies as the East India Company could be asked to contribute to its expenses; although there are today very few places abroad where the army can be stationed, the same philosophy exists. By 1868 there was a vast Empire to maintain and police, and in that year out of 141 line battalions only forty-seven were in England.

To improve the balance Cardwell therefore devised a system which would maintain the number of active battalions but reduce the overall number of regiments. The system was to give each regiment two battalions, the theory being that at any one time one battalion would be serving abroad and one at home. This meant that a soldier's length of overseas service could be reduced, since he could be exchanged with a man of the home service battalion even if the battalion itself remained abroad. Flexibility was thus introduced, but of course the system also meant that there would always be a number of battalions in transit, more than in the past, so that if the number stationed in the British Isles remained constant, the number available for use in overseas theatres would be reduced, and *vice versa*. This objection was mitigated by the theory that battalions in transit were always available to be rushed to the scene of any trouble more easily than if they had to be uprooted from a permanent station at home or abroad. In a sense, this was the first instance of the creation of a strategic reserve. In any case, the opening of the Suez Canal, which allowed a direct route to India where most of the overseas battalions were stationed, and the change from sail to steam power in the trooping ships meant that journey times were being much reduced, and many battalions were in fact used in a strategic concept during the next forty years.

At the time each of the first 25 regiments in chronological order of precedence already had two battalions, but most of the remainder only one; there were notable exceptions, the 60th Regiment of Foot (later The King's Rifle Corps) and the Rifle Brigade having four battalions each. In all there were 110 regiments of Foot, which included the nine battalions which had formed the old Indian Presidency Armies, and which had been absorbed into the British Army in 1862, and the Rifle Brigade, which had been denumbered in 1816 making up a grand total of 141 battalions.

In due course, in 1881, the reforms were put into effect by Hugh Childers, Cardwell having ceased to be Secretary of State seven years earlier. The outcome was that the 1st to the 25th Regiments of Foot inclusive remained independent with their existing two battalions, as did the 60th and the Rifle Brigade and, for an obscure reason, the 79th Regiment of Foot, which became The Queen's Own Cameron Highlanders and remained the only single-battalion regiment in the whole Army. The remaining eighty-two regiments were then paired off, the senior becoming the 1st Battalion and the junior the 2nd Battalion of a single new regiment. Each regiment was given a Royal or territorial title, and its number, and the 'of Foot' part of the title, was discontinued. Inevitably, such a massive shake-up resulted in happy and unhappy associations being formed. In some regiments the 1st and 2nd Battalions had known each other well in the past, had fought together and had been linked in some way before, but in some cases, through the 'exigencies of the service' and their current and future locations, the battalions were fated not to meet each other until forty years later after the Great War. An interesting example of an early link being perpetuated occurred in the South Staffordshire Regiment, where the 38th Foot (1st Staffordshire Regiment) was amalgamated with the 80th Foot (Staffordshire Volunteers), which became the 2nd Battalion. This had originally been raised by the son of the Earl of Uxbridge who had raised the Staffordshire Militia, which became the 3rd Battalion in 1908.

Territorial allegiances were broken and new ones forged; sometimes the new regiment took the old title of its 1st Battalion, sometimes of its 2nd Battalion, and often a new title was an invention that had no connection with either. In some cases the two battalions very soon buried and forgot any differences they might have had and regarded themselves as an integral part of their new regiment; in other cases they remained distinctly separate and virtually ignored their new partners, maintained their old traditions and habits, and continued to use their old numbers of Foot unofficially right up until the Great War. The old numerical system was popular, and so hard do old habits and traditions die that it is interesting to note that as a result of the most recent amalgamations some regiments have actually incorporated the combination of old numbers of Foot into their new official titles.

So there were now sixty-nine regiments which sufficed for normal policing duties and the inevitable and frequent bush-fire wars, and by 1897 they each had two battalions. Surprisingly, after a time for adjustment, the system of one battalion at home and one abroad was to all intents and purposes achieved, although the periods of service, the overseas tours, still varied considerably.

So far no mention has been made of the three oldest regiments in the Army, the Grenadier, Coldstream and Scots Guards, which at this time had respectively three, two and two battalions. They were unchanged and unaffected by the new system, but in 1897 a 3rd Battalion was authorised for the Coldstream Guards, and it was proposed that the Queen's Own Cameron Highlanders should become the 3rd Battalion of the Scots Guards. However, it was said that Queen Victoria did not approve of this arrangement, so the Camerons gained their 2nd Battalion at last and the Scots Guards had to wait a

14

further two years for their 3rd Battalion. Although the Guards battalions served in practically all the European campaigns as ordinary Infantry battalions, until the beginning of this century they had very rarely been further afield in wartime and in peacetime they were retained permanently in the United Kingdom.

No mention has been made either of the Household Cavalry, The Life Guards and The Royal Horse Guards, mainly because no significant changes occurred, and they continued that way until the Life Guards were reduced to a single regiment in 1922 (there had always previously been two) and the Royal Horse Guards suffered the indignity of amalgamation in 1969.

Militia and Volunteer forces had existed since the time of the Napoleonic Wars, some in fact claiming direct descent from forces which had existed during or in some cases well before the Civil War. These units had always had close territorial connections with county, city or town. They had already been placed on a permanent basis as a reserve force in 1860 and had been linked with regular regiments in Regimental Districts in 1874, but under the Cardwell system they became the volunteer elements of these regular regiments, the Militia battalions becoming an integral part of them, mostly as their 3rd Battalions. The Militia had already been embodied in 1745, from 1793 to 1815 during which period a large number of them had been raised, from 1854 to 1856 and from 1857 to 1860. In the future they were to be embodied between 1899 and 1902 when they saw considerable service abroad, and for the last time from 1914 to 1919.

The Volunteer Battalions, which were on a different footing under the law, were more numerous, and their numbers varied considerably from one area to another depending on the population and the military instincts of those areas; although now linked with the regular regiments they retained their independent titles for the time being and did not become an integral part of the Standing Army. Due to unrest in Europe in 1859 a very large number of Volunteer companies and other units were raised in this and the two following years. They were soon grouped by counties in Administrative Battalions for convenience, and by 1880 most of them had the title 'Xth (Blankshire) Rifle Volunteers'. After they became affiliated to the regular regiments they became 'Volunteer Battalions' of that regiment, but because they were still regarded as attached rather than as an integral part of the regiments they were numbered from '1st' onwards. To help these new allegiances regimental depots were set up and the family spirit was fostered; in this way the County regiments, the backbone of the future British Army, were born.

Not many changes took place over the next twenty-seven years. A few wars came and went, particularly the 2nd Boer War from 1899 to 1902, and it was as a result of the experiences of this war that the next major change in the shape of the Army occurred. In 1899 a few battalions were actually stationed in South Africa; with the need for massive reinforcements of both Cavalry and Infantry, other regiments and battalions were gathered from home and abroad and dispatched there as quickly as possible. As the situation went from bad to worse in the first few months of hostilities, it was realised that the regular forces alone were not enough to cope, since at the same time a presence had to be maintained in India and other parts of the Empire. Somehow the non-regular forces had to be brought into the fight. Accordingly selected 3rd Battalions, the Militia Battalions, which had already been embodied in the British Isles and in some cases were carrying out garrison duties, were sent to South Africa as well, but being composed of part-time soldiers and volunteers they could only be retained there for a year, after which they had to be replaced. By this time many regiments had acquired or raised 4th (Militia) Battalions, and these took the places of the 3rd, together with some of the 3rd Battalions which had not originally been committed. In a few cases 5th and 6th Battalions were also involved, regiments having raised extra regular battalions.

Even then the numbers were insufficient, and so the Volunteer Battalions were called upon; it was not considered practical or within the law, and in any case some of them were insufficiently recruited, to send these battalions out as complete entities, and thus Service companies were formed which became integrated with the battalions of their parent regular regiments. Again their tour of duty was limited, and the original Service companies were replaced with others until so many were used that, as Canada was to discover between 1914 and 1918, it would probably have been better to use the Volunteer Battalions in their complete form, where possible, rather than to mutilate them and produce *ad hoc* units.

Alongside the Militia and Volunteer Infantry forces, there had existed, also from the period of the Napoleonic War or earlier, Volunteer Cavalry companies and regiments known as the Yeomanry Cavalry which were also part of the Volunteer forces. They had as yet been untouched by reforms and had no specific allegiances to the regular Cavalry regiments, and so could not as easily be formed in Service companies as were their Infantry counterparts. Like the Infantry they could not be dispatched as complete units, and therefore elements of each regiment were formed into battalions of the Imperial Yeomanry; in all twenty-three battalions were formed, but not all of them took part in the war. A number of Militia Battalions did not see service in South Africa, but performed a useful and necessary service guarding Boer prisoners-of-war, eight in Malta and other Mediterranean islands, and one, shades of Napoleon, in St Helena.

The next major change, which occurred in 1908, was the formation of the Territorial Force. Although the Army administration had managed to cope with the provision of reserves for the Regular Army in South Africa, it had been done piecemeal and had been anything but easy, and it was clear that a more permanent arrangement and an efficient means of finding adequate reserves was needed in case another occasion arose. For all the numbers of troops involved, the South African war had been limited in scope, and with the developing European situation and the increasingly hostile attitude of Germany, it seemed more than possible that the occasion would arise. The wars which had been fought during the previous forty years had been bush-fire affairs, and as a result there had been no need for organised higher formations, brigades and divisions, or written establishments for them, and in South

Africa these had been hastily constructed out of the units which happened to be available, as had been their staffs. Reorganisation on a large scale was now of major importance, and the task fell to Mr Richard Haldane, who had become Secretary of War after the Liberal landslide election victory in 1906.

Haldane's reforms rationalised the Regular army without making many changes in actual regiments, but they revolutionised the Volunteer forces. Money for the army was short, as usual, and some disbandments had to be made to provide the wherewithal for building up his new organisation. But as a result there was at last a Regular Army in peacetime organised for war, consisting of one Cavalry division and six Infantry divisions.

The number of Militia Battalions was reduced, and they became Special Reserve Battalions, since their usefulness as fighting units in wartime was limited by their constitution and recruitment, on the basis of one per regular regiment with roughly a third of the regiments, whose recruiting potential in time of war was likely to be the greatest, having an extra battalion. The Volunteer Battalions had been more closely linked to their regular regiments at various dates between 1883 and 1889 and owed a greater allegiance to them. They were now converted into Territorial Force Battalions as integral parts of the regular regiments and changed their titles to battalions of those regiments; the number of battalions allotted to each regiment varied considerably according to the availability of recruits and the population, the battalions being organised into Territorial divisions. Some reform of the Yeomanry took place; they were properly constituted and designated to counties and the regiments were organised into Mounted brigades.

Apart from the Volunteer Battalions, who had for long been linked to Line battalions, there were a large number of volunteers in London who had no regular regiments with which to be linked, except for The Royal Fusiliers and the County regiments surrounding the city, who in any case had their own traditional volunteer, now Territorial, Battalions already. A new, purely Territorial Force, Regiment was formed, known as the London Regiment, which consisted of twenty-eight battalions initially and was increased to thirty-four battalions during the war. Not that this was the only regiment on the establishment which was entirely composed of Territorial Battalions. Some countries, which as a result of the Cardwell reforms had lost their County regiments, now regained them in the new form by amalgamating their Volunteer forces; and although these Territorial regiments maintained close allegiances with the same regular battalions to which these Volunteer forces had previously been linked, they were still regarded as independent and fiercely maintained their independence.

As well as the overall reorganisation of the Volunteer forces, provision was made for them to receive some training each year and to be embodied when danger threatened. This training, although not bringing them up to the standard of the Regulars, would enable them to form cadres to train recruits if and when a major expansion was needed in wartime.

And so to 1914. Much, perhaps too much, has been written about the conduct of the Great War, the strategy and the tactics, the pros and cons of the commanders and the politicians, and this is no place to add to the arguments; we are only concerned here with the development of the Army itself.

The Regular Army was ready, went to France and other theatres on the outbreak of war, and acquitted itself up to all expectations. The Territorial Force units were mostly undergoing their annual training in camp when war was declared and so could be mobilised quickly; but legally they were liable for home service only, and, whilst the majority would certainly have responded very quickly and willingly to any appeal to volunteer for overseas service, no appeal was made at this time. Instead, to start with, Lord Kitchener appealed for recruits for the New Army and these were forthcoming in very large numbers. The Reserve Battalions were employed in training this mass of manpower for their own regiments, and the Territorial Battalions continued training themselves and waited. In fact they had not long to wait.

The massive losses of the Regular Battalions in the early days of the war imposed a great strain on the replacement organisation, and it was clear that the New Army battalions could not be ready to take the field until the spring of 1915 at the earliest, partly through the time taken to train them and partly through lack of equipment. The munitions and armament factories were doing the best they could, but obviously the first task was to make good the losses in Flanders before supplies could be diverted to the new battalions. The Territorials were therefore soon called upon and the initial battalions went to France in October 1914, the first to see action being The London Scottish, the 14th Battalion The London Regiment, who took part in the Battle of Messines on the last day of that month. More followed to France and Flanders, and at the end of the year the first of the Yeomanry Mounted Brigades set out for Egypt, together with some Territorial Battalions; the Yeomanry and this Territorial division were eventually to be blooded at Gallipoli at Easter 1915, the former dismounted.

To achieve expansion the Territorial Battalions formed 2nd and 3rd line battalions, distinguished numerically as, for example, 2nd/4th and 2nd/5th Battalion, the original battalions becoming the 1st/4th or 1st/5th; these were initially reserve battalions intended to contain those men who had not volunteered for, or were unfit for, service overseas. Eventually, after re-recruiting, many of these battalions saw active service. The Yeomanry Regiments similarly formed 2nd and 3rd line units, many of the latter later becoming Cyclist Battalions; subsequently a number of Yeomanry Regiments, 1st and 2nd line, were converted to Infantry, usually as battalions of their County regiments.

During the remainder of the war, and particularly after conscription was brought in, the number of battalions in the regiments grew to immense and unprecedented proportions. It is interesting to note that, the old system of raising and numbering regiments consecutively having disappeared with the Cardwell and Haldane reforms, the new battalions were now formed, a more accurate word than 'raised' which implies some individual effort, and numbered as Service Battalions, Garrison Battalions, etc of the regular regiments. As a result the size to which some of the regiments grew was prodigious, The Northumberland Fusiliers holding the final record by forming fifty-two battalions, closely followed by The Royal Fusiliers with fifty-one.

The Cavalry generally had rather a thin time. It soon became apparent that horses were hopelessly vulnerable to machine guns; that the rapid formation of trench lines running from the sea in Belgium to the Swiss frontier, with their protective barbed-wire entanglements, precluded the use of Cavalry in the situations which they had been trained to exploit; and that in any case the ground, which had been cut up into a muddy morass of shellholes by Artillery fire, was certainly not conducive to good horsemanship or Cavalry tactics. True, the Cavalry Divisions, or parts of them, were scheduled to take part in a number of attacks in France, and the Infantry actions provided situations which would have been thought to be ideal for Cavalry exploitation, but somehow they never seemed to be in the right place at the right time, or, if they were, some snag prevented their use in anything but small detachments until the German retreat in 1918. They were used to a certain extent in Palestine in the early days, but, as in France, they mostly ended up as dismounted units fighting alongside the Infantry.

In 1916 the first tanks appeared, although it was not until later on that their full value was appreciated, particularly by the diehards who regarded them as ungainly monsters and definitely inferior to good Infantry flesh and blood in the attack. In any case they were not Cavalry and had their origins in the Machine Gun Corps; furthermore they were not regarded as fulfilling the role of Cavalry, this concept being developed by the German General Guderian in the late 1930s, but more as armoured battering-rams which would flatten barbed wire more accurately and easily than Artillery bombardments. Nevertheless the tanks had arrived, and were here to stay; by the end of the war twenty-five battalions had been formed.

After four and a quarter years the fighting was over and the task of disbanding the Service Battalions and other units began, just as massive as the task of forming them. It was not completed until 1921, by which time the regular battalions and regiments had in many cases taken up the stations which they had been rudely forced to leave in 1914. The new organisation created by Haldane only ten years before the end of the war had stood up well to its task; but while the wounds were being licked further reforms were being worked out and were to appear in 1922.

This time it was the turn of the Cavalry. The traditionalists considered an army without horsed Cavalry as no army at all and there was as yet no thought of mounting the regiments in the still much maligned tanks. Nevertheless it was clear that the 28 regiments which then existed, excluding the Household Cavalry, comprising Dragoon Guards, Dragoons, Hussars and Lancers in name but now in no way related to the types of horsemen which had given rise to these titles, were more than enough to fulfil their henceforth limited role. Initially a number of regiments were disbanded, but later in the year they were resuscitated and it was decided to reduce the total by amalgamations to twenty regiments. The seven Dragoon Guard regiments were reduced to five, only the first two remaining independent; and the twenty-one other Cavalry regiments to fifteen, the first twelve in numerical order, but excluding the 5th Lancers, of which remained independent. This was the first instance, in fact, of complete amalgamation in the British Army, since in 1881 the pairs of Infantry regiments retained some degree of independence and identity as 1st and 2nd Battalions; and even now the identities of many of the Cavalry regiments were retained by dual numbers, only the 6th Dragoon Guards and the 6th Dragoons disappearing completely by absorption into the 3rd Dragoon Guards and 5th Dragoon Guards respectively.

The case of the 5th Lancers was a curious one; they had been disbanded in 1799 as unfit for service having been infiltrated by rebels when stationed in Ireland, they had only been restored to the establishment and a junior position in the Line of Cavalry in 1858, and it was another twenty-five years before they were granted the right to all their previous Battle Honours. But the stigma remained in the War Office records, and as a result they amalgamated with the 16th Lancers, but as the 16th/5th, so hard is it to remove a black mark in the Army once it has been gained.

For the time being the remaining Cavalry regiments retained their horses and trained in their traditional role; but eventually progress could not be denied and during the 1930s most of the regiments became mechanised either as tank or as armoured-car regiments. Nevertheless the Scots Greys were only in the process of conversion and still had some horses in the latter part of 1941, and the last horsed Cavalry regiment in the army, The Queen's Own Yorkshire Dragoons, a Yeomanry regiment, did not become mechanised until the following year.

In 1917 the tank battalions had been formed into a Corps of their own which became 'Royal' in 1923. They were equipped largely with armoured cars rather than with tanks, and most of them were initially stationed in Egypt, although some served in Iraq in 1922 and subsequently a number of them were sent to India. Few changes were made to the Infantry regiments at this time, although several of them took the opportunity of changing their titles in some way or other.

Generally speaking, the inter-war years produced few changes in the structure and development of the regiments of the army. The secession of Ireland from the United Kingdom meant that the Southern Irish regiments were disbanded. Historically, even if for no other reason, this was a great loss since the Royal Irish Regiment, the old 18th Regiment of Foot, had originally been raised in 1689. Of the junior regiments, the Connaught Rangers was composed of the 88th and 94th Foot, both raised in 1793, although the latter was disbanded in 1818 and re-raised five years later; the Leinster Regiment had been formed by the amalgamation of the 100th (Royal Canadian) Foot, raised in 1858 from patriotic volunteers, descendants of old Irish regiments in Canada, and the old 3rd Bombay European Regiment; and the Royal Munster Fusiliers and the Royal Dublin Fusiliers were composed entirely of four Indian Presidency regiments which had only been absorbed into the British Army in 1862, but which had previously had a distinguished record, bearing Battle Honours which evoked the earliest days of our involvement in India.

Fate played a part in the disbandment of the 100th Foot,

since after its raising in Canada it was made over to Britain as a free gift, but in 1897 the Canadian government requested the return of the regiment to the Canadian army. This was refused by the government and by the regiment, and in the following year the request was withdrawn, as it turned out to the disadvantage of the regiment. Altogether the total number of Infantry regiments was reduced to sixty-four.

There was some rationalisation of the changes brought about by the Haldane reforms. The regimental 3rd Battalions, the Special Reserve Battalions created in 1908 from the Militia Battalions, were all renamed as Militia Battalions in Suspended Animation shortly after the war ended and ceased to exist in practice, although they officially retained a 'ghost' existence until they were disbanded in 1953. The Territorial Force became the Territorial Army; there was some adjustment in the numbers and titles of the battalions, and the battalions of the London Regiment became individual regiments. But the major changes appeared in the late 1930s when the need for anti-aircraft artillery and armoured regiments grew; a large number of Territorial Army Infantry battalions were transferred to the Royal Artillery and some to the Royal Tank Regiment.

In 1939 the Royal Armoured Corps was formed. This united at long last the Cavalry, most of which had been mechanised by now, and the Royal Tank Regiment, together with most of the Yeomanry regiments, of which those that had not been converted to Artillery were also in the process of being mechanised. Also at this time, in view of imminent hostilities, a large number of TA battalions were 'duplicated', this time many of the new battalions being given distinct numbers rather than the double numbering which had occurred in 1914. Some old titles of regiments were revived and some amalgamations, particularly among the Northern Irish regiments, were dissolved.

On the outbreak of war in 1939 the lessons of 1914 were remembered and there was a wholesale raising of new Service Battalions to meet the expected need. In the event it was found that the estimate had been over-generous and a number were disbanded again or became training regiments, and as a result the final number of battalions raised for each regiment was very much lower than in the Great War. It was a different, more open, type of warfare and there was no longer a need for massed troops to hold long lines of tenches. In the early years there was a continued concentration on anti-aircraft artillery, and later anti-tank artillery; but as the war progressed and the risk of air attack receded, so many of these regiments were converted, some reconverted, into Infantry.

Some new regiments appeared during the course of the war which identified new forms of warfare and the troops needed to operate in them. In 1940 the Special Air Service (SAS) was formed to incorporate units being raised for surprise attacks on enemy installations and various other subversive activities. In 1941 this became the Commandos. Also in 1941 the Special Boat Service (SBS) was formed for a similar purpose, the delivery of the raiding parties being by sea instead of by air. This activity had a close affinity with the role of the Royal Marines, and eventually the Commandos and the SBS became the Royal Marine Commandos, and the SAS regained its role as a separate regiment. After the war the SAS was given a TA role, as well as a regular one, by The Artist's Rifles, until the remaining regular regiment became part of the Parachute Regiment in 1970, subsequently to become independent again.

The idea of delivering picked troops to salient areas of the battlefield by parachute had also been germinating, and this method was used to great effect by the German army in 1940 and in Crete the following year. As a result a Parachute Battalion was raised in 1941 and the Parachute Regiment was formed in 1942, partly by converting whole battalions, although naturally only the volunteers for the task became parachutists and the gaps were filled by volunteers from other regiments, and partly by forming new battalions. There was no shortage of volunteers and the number of battalions had grown by the end of the war to seventeen. As well as parachutists, a proportion of the troops required for the airborne role were glider-borne and in many cases whole battalions were converted. Although the gliders themselves were towed and Air Force pilots had to be trained for this role, it was considered that the piloting of the gliders could be carried out by army personnel, trained as pilots, and from this The Glider Pilot Regiment was born; it lasted for sixteen years and was disbanded in 1957.

The final departure from old custom was also related to the air. With the greater ranges of Artillery it was found that even where some natural observation post existed the view of the Artillery officer was too limited for accurate correction of fire; the only way was to get higher up, and this meant taking to the air. Because of the complexities of Artillery fire control it was decided that it would be easier and quicker to train a gunner officer to fly than to train a Royal Air Force pilot in gunnery, and the Air Observation Post flights were formed. These remained as RAF units although the pilots were Royal Artillery officers, and therefore no new regiment as such appeared in the lineage charts until their excision from the RAF was achieved, and the Army Air Corps was formed in 1957.

Other specialist units were also formed which never reached the status of regiments and were usually referred to as 'private armies'. Examples were the Long Range Desert Group, which operated, as its name suggests, on the flanks and behind the enemy lines in the Western Desert during 1941 and 1942, and 'Popski's Private Army', which operated in much the same way in Italy between 1943 and 1945.

When peace again broke out, once more adjustments were made to the establishment. With the usual governmental desire to save money by reducing the size of the Army, the first parts to suffer were the 2nd Battalions of the Infantry regiments which were disbanded and absorbed by their 1st Battalions in 1948. In point of fact it sometimes happened the other way round, because of title or location, and the 1st Battalions were disbanded and absorbed by the 2nd; but the overall result was the same, all line regiments now having only one regular battalion. The exigencies of the service, that famous phrase that has always been the excuse for so many events, good and bad, caused ten 2nd battalions to be revitalised and restored in 1952 for a short period, but by 1957 they had all been disbanded once more, this time for good. The Grenadier, Coldstream and Scots Guards were not affected, but the Irish and Welsh Guards were reduced to a single battalion like the Infantry.

By 1954 the concept of air warfare had changed to such an extent that it was judged that the large numbers of anti-aircraft regiments in the Territorial Army were no longer needed. The few regiments still required were produced by massive amalgamations of regiments—in some cases as many as four regiments forming one battery—and there were a large number of disbandments. Although the Royal Regiment of Artillery has only infrequently been referred to in these pages so far, this point is of general interest, since most of the regiments so reduced had been converted from Infantry either before, during or after the war, and in many cases the histories of these regiments were the histories of the old Volunteer forces, going back over 150 years. A few regiments were rescued in name only by reconverting them to Infantry and amalgamating them with the TA battalions with whom they had been associated in the past. As far as the Artillery itself was concerned, the decision was devastating, since many of the regiments had regular commanding officers, most had regular training officers, adjutants, quartermasters, and senior warrant officer and NCO staffs, and the reduction of the potential for promotion and command reverberated for many years to come. The situation was further exacerbated by the disbandment, or placing in Suspended Animation which came to the same thing, of a number of regular Royal Artillery batteries, and *ipso facto* of a number of regiments which they constituted, in 1962.

But all that had happened so far was nothing compared with the event which was just around the corner. The year 1957 was the blackest for the British Army in the 300 years of its history. The decision to reduce drastically the size of the Army meant that a number of regiments were proposed for disbandment and, beyond that, all the Cavalry and most of the Infantry, were to be amalgamated. Although this time, as opposed to 1881, territorial designation and geographical contiguity were considered, the fact that two regiments came from the same county or adjoining counties did not necessarily mean that they were traditionally or spiritually compatible; once again there were to be mixed marriages, marriages of convenience, shot-gun weddings no less, which were acceptable to neither party, and the fights raged for several years to retain names which had in some cases only existed for less than eighty years, but which had seen two world wars. Of course, in the end, the bureaucrats were the only ones who won and there was no actual blood-letting, but in some cases the peace was relatively uneasy for a long time. Once again many old and revered names disappeared into limbo and are only remembered by historians, those who were members of the regiments or saw service alongside them, and by those who remember reading the gory details in the press.

One small shred of comfort remained for a while to those who fought fiercely to retain their names. The Territorial Army battalions kept their old regimental titles for a few years, although eventually these too disappeared. The amalgamations also meant that whereas in 1881 two old numbered Regiments of Foot, with their territorial titles, had been condensed into one, now in many cases four of the old regiments shared a single title and their individual traditions, histories and characteristics became even more diluted.

But bureaucratic progress in the name of rationalisation and standardisation is inexorable, and only seven years later came the first of another series of convulsions which further reduced the sovereignty, independence, individualism and historical continuity of the regiments: 'Large Regiments'. We have seen two old regiments become one, then four, but now as many as a dozen became one regiment. True, the post-1957 regiments retained some identity as battalions of the Large Regiments, but most other things they prized, other than their names, those things which meant so much to them—their cap badges for instance—vanished.

It must be understood, of course, that this view of the amalgamations and disbandments of regiments is that of an historian, and one particularly interested in the lineage and histories of the regiments and in their Battle Honours. Strategically, tactically and administratively there are no doubt excellent reasons for many of these changes, but this book is not concerned with these aspects, except in so far as they affect the traditions and history of the army. Perhaps that is a romantic and outdated viewpoint.

Meanwhile the Infantry Volunteer forces had not gone unscathed; the Territorial Army and the Army Emergency Reserve were disbanded in 1965 and a new force, the Territorial Army Volunteer Reserve, was formed, but on a much reduced scale. The principle of the reformation became clearer after the formation of the Large Regiments; one TAVR battalion was to be retained for each Large Regiment, made up of one company for each battalion (lately individual regiments) of the Regiment. This sometimes meant that several TA battalions were formed into one company, as had happened to the Royal Artillery ten years earlier, and the wastage of keen, hard-working, voluntary manpower was enormous. The reductions caused a number of complicated changes of existence and title of these units over the next 15 years but recently there has been a sign of common sense in the announcement of six new TAVR battalions although they are not due to start forming until 1986.

As a result of all these amalgamations and groupings over 86 years, the only original Regiments of Foot which retained their individual identities were The Royal Scots (1st), The Green Howards (19th), The Cheshire Regiment (22nd), The Royal Welsh Fusiliers (23rd) and The King's Own Scottish Borderers (25th). One wonders, quite impartially, why they were the ones to escape.

There have been disbandments and amalgamations since then, and most people will remember the fight put up, and won, by The Argyll and Sutherland Highlanders, the remaining junior regiment in the Army to prevent disbandment. But the ten years from 1957 to 1967 really put the seal on the traditional British Army and its more than 300 years of history.

As was said earlier, the Royal Artillery has not yet featured in this account to any extent, and a paragraph will redress that omission. Although one of the 'teeth' arms, and although present at virtually every battle, however small, since its formation, as is exemplified by its single Battle Honour, '*Ubique*' ('Everywhere'), it has not suffered many of the indignities of the Cavalry and Infantry. True, its titles and organisation changed over the years, and it too came in for amalgamation and disbandment, but to a much more limited extent. Companies and battalions were renamed batteries; batteries were formed up into brigades, which later became regiments; the functional terminologies changed as new forms of Artillery, anti-aircraft, anti-tank, coast, etc, evolved. As with the Infantry and Cavalry, old Indian Presidency Army companies and batteries were absorbed. But its character has remained, and individual batteries are still the basic unit, not the regiment as is the case with Infantry and Cavalry, and still fiercely retain a measure of independence within their regiments. When disbandments are being considered it is the batteries which cease to exist, the remainder being redistributed among the regiments. It is the batteries which have the history, not the regiments of which they form a part for tactical reasons.

Above: The Siege of Namur 1695. Etching by Pieter Persoy of Amsterdam, c1695. *NAM*

3 Battle Honours

Let this chapter begin with a quotation which epitomises much of what is to follow:

> Though many Battle Honours were awarded during historic campaigns, the greatest contribution which our Regiments have made is rarely mentioned; this has surely been the protection they have afforded to those indomitable British merchants, who in search of fresh markets spread our influence all over the world. For some of the regiments this involved spending many years in stinking garrisons overseas where their casualties from disease were often far greater than those suffered on military service.

The award of Battle Honours is primarily a system by which the Sovereign recognises the presence of a regiment at, and its contribution to, a particular battle. Secondly, it provides a means for that regiment to publicise its past glories by displaying the names of these battles. An Honour is normally the name of a battle, the word 'battle' being used in its widest sense as a fight or hostilities between opposing armies or elements of them, shown on a regiment's Colours for all to see and in such listings of that regiment's achievements as may appear in print, as for example, the Army List.

But a Battle Honour is not always just a name and can be borne as a badge either on the Colours or on regimental dress, for example a cap badge or buttons. Unfortunately such badges do not normally bear dates or names as well, and are therefore largely unidentifiable by a layman, or may not even be recognised as being the equivalent of an Honour borne as a name. Equally unfortunately, because of the various rules which have applied from time to time for the selection of battles deemed worthy of honour in this way, no listing of the Battle Honours borne by a regiment will give more than an outline of its activities in war over the centuries. Let us look therefore for a moment at these rules.

In earliest times the apparent rules were extremely simple as far as the decision about whether to make a battle merit an Honour or not was concerned: it must be a victory and it must not be a civil war. Since regiments were smaller than today and were usually committed *en masse*, the question of participation by parts of the regiment did not arise, although by the middle of the 18th century the formation of the flank companies of regiments—the Grenadier companies, which had been adopted in 1678 as picked bodies of troops, and the Light Infantry companies—into *ad hoc* battalions for particular purposes did create some problems. Both these companies ceased to exist as battalion specialists in 1858. In selecting the worthy battles, even on this basis, however, factors other than pure merit appear to have been involved. The decision was largely left to the Commander in the field, and if he was in good standing with the Court, particularly if he was a Royal Commander, his proposals were probably accepted, even if some of the battles Honoured would not be considered so important today. If, on the other hand, he had achieved some dislike or stigma his proposals would probably not be accepted. In this respect it is interesting that during Marlborough's wars, although four battles were Honoured in the north-west Europe theatre of operations, no battles in the Peninsula during eight years of warfare were Honoured; in fact few people know that there were any battles in the Peninsula since they are never mentioned in the history books.

In making his decision the Commander was probably lobbied by his regimental commanders to include battles in which they themselves had taken part, and again personalities entered very much into the matter and the outcome. Not only that, but without the hindsight of hundreds of years of history to make the addition of Honours to the Colours a worthwhile endeavour, the need to commemorate a battle, even if a victory, was perhaps not so obvious. And it must also be remembered that during the seventeenth and eighteenth centuries very large numbers of regiments were raised for a war and disbanded after it finished, and there would be very little point in the colonel of a, by then, non-existent regiment making any very great efforts to have that battle commemorated.

The battle had to have been won. But this is often a matter of subjective judgement and is not concerned purely with inflicting heavy casualties on the enemy or driving him from the field. A battle won could still reflect adversely on some of the units which took part, and a battle lost, and thus the non-award of an Honour, did not take into consideration the valour and endurance of the troops taking part. Fontenoy, for example, is today adjudged a draw; because it was not a clear-cut victory, which was obvious at the time, particularly as the French claimed it as a victory, no Battle Honour was awarded. On the other hand, a number of the battles and actions during the retreat to Dunkirk in 1940 are listed and borne as Battle Honours; but this retreat could in no way be considered a victory in the normal sense, or even a draw, although the battles did allow the British Army, and part of the French, to escape and undoubtedly delayed, and as it turned out helped to abort, Hitler's plan to invade England.

Winning is not a clear-cut, black and white event. Wars are not waged for fun or even as an exercise for the opposing armies, but for political or religious reasons. The reason why a particular battle was fought must be considered, and the effect that the result of that battle had on the reason for that war. Even a drawn or lost battle could so affect the strength and the morale of the enemy that the way is laid open for a succession of future victories to achieve the aim of the campaign; the effect on the enemy might be such, in spite of his apparent victory in the field, that he found the continued maintenance of a war impossible. Pyrrhic victories still occur in this day and age. It is equally true therefore that a battle won and Honoured might have done nothing to advance the cause for which it was fought. It becomes clear, therefore, that the winning of a battle is not a satisfactory criterion on which to base its worthiness for the award of an Honour.

Of the civil wars which were excluded, the numbers of troops involved in and the general conduct of the battles against the Scots in the 1714 and 1745 rebellions, with the exception perhaps of Culloden, and of the internecine religious battles during the period 1685 to 1691, would probably rule them out as worthy of Honour on any grounds. But the battles of the American War of Independence were also excluded, and although this can be regarded as a civil war in one sense, or as a rebellion, it was not and is not so regarded by the Americans, since they had already declared their independence and from their point of view were fighting as nationals against other nationals. Whether, therefore, it was truly a civil war may be a moot point, but there is no doubt that on other grounds many of those battles should be included in the roll of Honours. Civil wars within the British Isles are one matter, colonial wars another, and it could be argued with justification that if the American battles were not included then the battles in India against the Mahrattas and Sikhs should not be either, apart from the dubious reason that the Americans were to a large degree of British descent and white.

To a large extent the same rules for the selection and award of Honours still applied at the time of the South African War of 1899 to 1902, but a new factor and a strange situation arose. The War Office, in its wisdom, decided that twenty-six battles were worthy of individual Honour, in that the two medals that were issued, the Queen's medal and the King's medal, were provided with clasps which could be issued to soldiers who had taken part in these battles. When it came to awarding Battle Honours, however, a committee decided that twenty-six Battle Honours for one war was out of the question. Nothing like that number had been considered as worthy of inclusion in the lists of Honours before, and, since the committee in question could not foresee the holocaust only twelve years away and the number of battles which would have to be included and honoured then, it was decided that only six battles should be listed as available for claims as Honours, apart from the campaign itself. Hardly a logical conclusion, but perhaps any other is the result of hindsight.

Today there are few problems. In 1920 a Battle Nomenclature Committee was set up to evaluate all the fighting that took place during the Great War, and it not only gave names to the individual battles but categorised them in order of magnitude or importance as Battles, Actions and Miscellaneous Incidents, although it was mainly only the battles, and few of the equally important, and bloody, Actions and Incidents, which became Honoured. It also agreed the date limits of the battles etc it so categorised. Rules defining participation in terms of the headquarters and sub-units of a regiment were then laid down.

Individual claims were submitted to a Battle Honours Committee, which agreed the awards to be made. All this was apparently very straightforward, but not entirely so, since in a number of cases the only way of distinguishing battles of the same name which took place in the same year in the Nomenclature list was by a name and an ordinal number, such as the 1st, 2nd and 3rd Battles of The Scarpe in 1917, which covered a period of less than a month, and the 1st and 2nd Battles of Bapaume in 1918, which were separated by over five months. Honours which were awarded for these battles, for instance, did not include the ordinal number, so that it is not now possible to distinguish which actual battle a regiment took part in, and considerable research is necessary to identify it. Where the year could be included to distinguish battles, e.g. Somme 1916, Somme 1918, these dates were included in the Honours. Perhaps in the long run it does not matter; the name and the Honour are recorded and probably only purists and historians are really concerned with any greater detail, although in some cases regiments have claimed the distinction, usually with little success. An unusual claim, not only for an Honour but for the name of a battle, was made by the Lancashire Fusiliers, five of whose battalions landed at 'W' Beach in Gallipoli in 1915. They proposed the title 'Lancashire Landing', but presumably this was regarded as showing too much favour to one regiment, albeit one which had suffered very heavily in the battle, and it was subsequently officially entitled **Landing at Helles**.

By categorising the fighting of 1914 to 1918 into battles and actions and then only awarding Honours, except in a few isolated instances, for the battles, the Battle Honours Committee negated the work of the Nomenclature Committee, and it is clear that even then shadows of the thinking after the South African War still remained. Because of the large number of battalions which each regiment had in the field, and the fact that the individual Honours gained by any one battalion were incorporated in a regimental list, each regiment became the bearer of a large number of Honours, many of which are common to almost every regiment, certainly in the Infantry. It could be said that to bear any more Honours would be superfluous, but on the other hand it was the actions, because they were smaller, that only a handful of regiments would be able to claim and that, if they were awarded, would emphasise the individuality of a particular regiment. Some would be unique and would therefore have more intrinsic value. A number of regiments have claimed one or more of these actions as Honours, and it is these, rather than the major battles themselves, which often figure more prominently in their regimental histories.

In essence the same system was used after 1945, but this

time the categories included the Campaign as well as Battles, together with Actions and Engagements deemed to merit separate Honours within the time scale of that battle, and Actions and Engagements independent of a major battle. Although the number of possible Honours was thus increased, the regiments were smaller and never achieved the vast number of battalions they had in the previous war, and thus there is much more individuality about the Honours borne by each. One puzzling point arises, however, since actions and engagements were claimed and awarded this time; a number of battles etc. are listed for which no regiment has been awarded an Honour. One wonders who took part in these fights to make them important enough to list but not to be claimed or awarded. Perhaps the regiments themselves considered them too unimportant to claim, or perhaps the claims were turned down on some grounds; they may be cases where no single regiment participated in sufficient strength for the claim to be recognised.

This time, as in the Great War, the campaigns themselves were included in the Honours list and could be claimed. This has meant that regiments which saw action in a theatre of war, perhaps in minor actions not adjudged worthy of listing, perhaps during the static periods between battles which were often as demanding on the troops as the battles themselves, perhaps in insufficient strength during a battle to be able to claim participation according to the rules, could claim the Campaign Honour. In the past Honours had only been granted for campaigns as well as individual battles in the case of Egypt in 1801 in a very minor way, the Peninsula (1807–14) and South Africa (1899–1902). There are a few instances of comparatively minor campaigns for which an Honour had been granted for the campaign but not for the individual battles in it; examples of this are North America 1763–4 (Pontiac's conspiracy), India 1796–1819, Niagara (the American campaign of 1814–15), Abyssinia (1867–8) and South Africa 1835, 1846–7, 1851–2–3, and 1877–8–9.

The original theory regarding Campaign Honours was presumably that the award of an Honour to a regiment which took part in a particular battle was honour enough and that the campaign itself was unimportant. But there is no doubt that the number of regiments that would have been awarded the Honour only represented, in most cases, a proportion of those involved in the campaign, and that a Campaign Honour would have done justice to the unfortunates who appear from the lists to have led a comparatively uneventful life.

In the Crimean War, for example, there were just four major battles, although **Sevastopol** covers a long period of siege as well as the final onslaught, and therefore it is unlikely that any regiment would claim the Campaign Honour which did not already bear at least one of the individual Battle Honours. But in the Flanders campaigns of 1793–5 and 1799 only a small proportion of the regiments involved were awarded any of the three Honours available to the Infantry, and in the North West Frontier campaign of 1897–8 in India, which included the Malakand and Tirah expeditions, a number of regiments, British and Indian, heavily engaged in a series of actions and skirmishes against a very cunning enemy in the most ex-

hausting conditions of heat, dust and monsoon rainfall, have nothing to show for their hard work, courage and endurance because they did not take part in the expeditions.

The point is not that regiments ought to have been awarded more Honours, or that they should now start to claim them, but that the system was unfair to some. Those who appear, from the Army List, to have been unengaged were in fact unlucky, happened to be in the wrong place at the wrong time and have little to show for their efforts.

Returning to earlier wars, comparatively few Honours were actually awarded at the time of the battle, which leads to the possible suggestions that few early Commanders bothered to make recommendations or that they were all out of favour! Many of the Honours now borne have come about as a result of claims put forward by the individual regiments and the decisions of committees, such as the Alison Committee in 1882, which carried out a very useful task in sifting these claims and awarding Honours sometimes 200 years or more after the event which they commemorated. It was not until 1909 that, for example, the 2nd Regiment of Foot, by now the Queen's Regiment, was awarded the Honours **Tangier**, for service during the period 1660 to 1684, and a Naval Crown inscribed **1794** for its service as marines at the Battle of the Glorious 1st of June. It is perhaps of interest that the Alison Committee was formed with the principle that 'battles commemorated should be familiar not only to the British Army, but to every educated gentleman'; this obviously limited its scope considerably!

Even so the old rules, such as that only victories should be honoured, were used as criteria, and many bloody battles, which today would without doubt be included, were left to be forgotten. Claims were often rejected on the grounds that they belonged to a 'too remote period'; since most of them belonged to remote periods one must wonder whether the phrase was a euphemism for 'we have never heard of it and don't want to'! Some claims appear never to have been formally turned down, and still remain as possibles, as presumably rejections would also, if any future committee should ever be appointed to look into them.

The Peninsular War was an exception to the delay which accompanied the granting of most Honours, awards being made in 1817, only three years after the campaign ended. It was left to the Colonels of Regiments, few of whom had actually been involved, to claim Honours to which they believed that their regiments were entitled. Some put in many claims, but others were more modest and only claimed those Honours for battles in which their regiments had achieved outstanding distinction. The result was not only that some battles were left out because too few regiments claimed them, but a great variety in the awards made; an Honour might be granted to one regiment but not to another in the same brigade which had fought beside it. A prime example was the battle of Arroyo dos Molinos, an unexceptional skirmish in any case, but one which was claimed by, and awarded as a unique Honour to, the 34th Regiment of Foot, later the Border Regiment, mainly because during the fray it captured the French 34th Regiment. This award totally ignored the fact that two

Cavalry and five other Infantry regiments were involved, in fact far more involved than the 34th Foot which only really came into the picture after the worst of the fray was over and the enemy was on the run; but the others did not claim the Honour at this time, and in spite of applications by all the Infantry regiments they have not been awarded it since. An interesting Honour, but not a Battle Honour, was granted to three Cavalry regiments, the 5th Dragoon Guards and the 3rd and 4th Dragoons, who were each permitted to style themselves 'The Salamanca Regiment'. To a certain extent the overall situation after the Peninsular War was rectified a century or so later, but the true record still does not appear clearly on many regiments' Colours.

Some of the badges borne as Battle Honours have been granted for long periods of service abroad and others honour specific battles; sometimes the badges are borne on the Colours only and sometimes they have been incorporated in cap badges. Why there was a distinction between awarding a straightforward Honour, or a badge, or a name with a different significance, is not clear. The 'Royal Tiger', for instance, sometimes accompanied by 'India' or 'Hindoostan', was awarded for service in India between 1780 and 1826. On the other hand, the Battle of the Saints is borne by the 69th Foot as a Naval Crown with the date 1782 and the Battle of the Glorious 1st of June by the 2nd Foot and 29th Foot in a similar way with the date 1794.

The Honour granted for the Siege of Gibraltar from 1779 to 1783 was awarded in 1836 to about half the regiments who took part as the badge of the Colony, the Castle and Key, together with the motto '*Montis Insignia Calpe*'. Amongst them was the 39th Foot, from whom it was withdrawn 11 years later, being regranted in 1877. The 28th Regiment of Foot, the Gloucestershire Regiment as it was to become, wear a small badge at the back of their caps, the 'Back Badge', to commemorate their action at the Battle of Alexandria (Roman Camp) in 1801, when, being attacked from front and rear simultaneously, their rear rank turned about so that the regimental line faced in both directions. This regiment is also unique in wearing a small gold-edged blue rectangular badge on its uniform, the United States of America's Presidential Citation, for its equally valiant conduct at the Battle of the Imjin River in Korea in 1951. The 13th Regiment of Foot, The Somerset Light Infantry, incorporated the name **Jellalabad** with a Mural Crown in their badge as a more public way of displaying the unique Honour they gained for their defence of the fort of that name during the 1st Afghan War in 1842. The 19th Light Dragoons, now amalgamated with the 15th Light Dragoons as the 15th/19th The King's Royal Hussars, the 74th and 78th Regiments of Foot, later to become the 2nd Battalions of the Highland Light Infantry and the Seaforth Highlanders respectively, incorporate the name **Assaye** in their cap badges to commemorate Wellington's great victory there in 1803; there is also an **Assaye** Battery in the Royal Artillery, which the author once had the honour to command. The 34th Regiment of Foot incorporate a laurel wreath in their badge to commemorate their gallantry at Fontenoy, and the 24th Regiment of Foot carry a wreath of immortelles, everlasting flowers, on the pike above their Colours to commemorate their brav-

ery at the action of Rorke's Drift during the Zulu War, probably better known today to many people than other actions through the film *Zulu*. These are only a few examples of the Honours awarded or borne in a different form from the normal, but more details of the others will appear in later chapters devoted to particular campaigns.

Some Honours had been won by Militia and Volunteer Battalions prior to the Haldane reforms. These were mostly gained during the Crimean and South African Wars, and, since the battalions, or elements of them had generally formed a part of their regular regiments, such Honours, although awarded specifically to the non-regular battalions, were absorbed by their parent regiments in 1908 or ceased to exist. There were, however, three specific Honours awarded solely to a number of Militia Battalions, although they were not in fact for participation in battles but for much more mundane duties. These Honours were **Mediterranean**, awarded to ten battalions for administrative duties on Mediterranean islands during the Crimean War in 1854-5; and **Mediterranean 1901-02**, awarded to eight battalions, and **St. Helena**, awarded uniquely to the Militia Battalion of the Wiltshire Regiment, for guarding Boer prisoners of war during the South African War. For some obscure reason, perhaps because they were not in fact for battles, these Honours were not taken over by their parent regiments when the Militia, or Special Reserve, Battalions ceased to exist for all practical reasons in 1921, but died with them.

One other Honour awarded to the Militia is of particular interest as it is the only one for an action in the British Isles. This was **Fishguard**, awarded to the Cardigan Militia, later to become the Pembroke Yeomanry, for repelling a French invasion of South Wales in 1797. It is said that some Welsh women, wearing their traditional tall pointed hats, like dunce's caps, accompanied the members of the Militia, and that the rapid withdrawal of the French to their boats was as much because they mistook the women for witches as because of the armed action of the Militia themselves!

The practice, both in 1881 and 1957 and subsequently, has been to merge individual regimental Battle Honours when the regiments themselves have been amalgamated. As a result most unique Honours, of which there were only twenty-four until 1914 to regiments of the British Army, if one excludes those awarded to regiments of the Indian Presidency Armies which were subsequently absorbed into the British Army but disbanded in 1922, ceased to be identifiable to the Regiment of Foot which had gained and borne them. The same thing happened, of course, to the rather larger, but still limited, number of Honours which were awarded to only two or three regiments. Apart from that, with the more limited participation, in terms of numbers engaged, of regiments in battles long ago, the variety of Honours borne by each regiment prior to 1881 was quite considerable and no two were anywhere near the same. But as the present conglomerate Infantry regiments have come to incorporate more and more of the old separate regiments, so the amalgamated Battle Honours of each have become less and less distinguishable from each other.

The situation has now been reached where the majority

of Honours are common to all regiments and the lists have become virtually meaningless. The situation, of course, could be reversed if the published lists showed the Honours gained individually up to 1881, followed by those gained by the amalgamated regiments between then and 1957; none have been awarded which could be claimed by the conglomerates, because the only Honours awarded since then for the Falkland Islands battles were gained by individual regiments except for the Blues and Royals. Perhaps, however, the next step will be to award these regiments, like the Royal Artillery, the single Honour **Ubique**; it will be a sad day if, or when, that happens because then the past glories of the army will be irretrievably lost except in dusty, untouched tomes on obscure shelves of public libraries. There are reasons, perhaps, for believing that this is the real objective of some of our less patriotic fellow-countrymen now seen in high places.

Unfortunately, there are so many amongst us who have done all that they can to destroy the traditions of the British Army in some way or other, by taking the elegance and colour out of its dress, by insidiously promoting the idea that pomp and ceremony, parades (except political ones) and discipline (except the party variety) are things to be deplored, and by rationalisation for the sake of unnecessary uniformity. Having dismembered the British Empire which that Army was largely responsible for gaining, they now want to dismantle the Army itself. Trends are always difficult to reverse, but it can be done if there are those who are prepared to fight hard enough to do so. Perhaps too many of those in whose hands the future of the army now rests are unwilling to stick their necks out and fight for those traditions, which, by their service in the Army, they have accepted as part of their birthright, and of which they are the current custodians.

Having referred earlier to the Royal Artillery, some reference must now be made to the system which that Regiment employs with regard to Battle Honours. The Royal Regiment as a whole bears the Honour **Ubique**, and for long that was considered sufficient. But with the regimentation of batteries which occurred after the Great War it was proposed that Batteries themselves should bear Honours. It was claimed that this could not be done in the same way as for the Cavalry and Infantry, since the Royal Artillery batteries and regiments carry no Colours as such, but regard their guns as their Colours, and would have no way of displaying the Honours. Somewhat specious reasoning perhaps, since the Cavalry's Guidons are not big enough to display all their Honours, and individual batteries would have borne no more Honours than many Cavalry regiments. With the huge number of Honours awarded for the two World Wars even the rather large Infantry Regimental Colours became nowhere near large enough to display all their Honours; each Infantry regiment was limited to displaying ten Honours of its own choosing, from the many, on its Colours.

Nevertheless this objection was upheld, and as an alternative it was agreed that Batteries should each be allowed to claim one single Honour, from among those to which it would have been entitled under the system used in the other teeth arms, and that this Honour should be included, along with the Battery precedence number, in the Battery title. In the narrative, Honour Titles granted to Batteries are shown in bold type, as is the word 'Battery' which does not appear in the Honour Title, although 'Troop' and 'Company' does. There are some instances where Batteries were granted Honour Titles for non-honoured battles, and in these cases the battle itself is shown in italics and the Honour Title in bold. As happened in the case of the Infantry and Cavalry after the Peninsular War, a degree of modesty was shown by some Battery Commanders of the time, who, although fully entitled to an Honour, did not claim one. Modesty is perhaps a euphemism; in some cases it may have been as an objection to the principle which limited a Battery to a single Honour, in others, conversely, because the principle of battery Honour Titles at all was not accepted, and presumably in some cases from sheer inertia.

Eventually Honour Titles were granted to 66 Batteries, and are still borne today, supplemented by a number of extra ones granted after World War Two. The modesty of the Battery Commanders who did not obtain an Honour only became apparent as a problem to their successors after 1957, when a large number of batteries were disbanded. Batteries with Honour Titles, irrespective of age, were automatically retained, and of the remainder required for the establishment it was a case of 'last in first out'; consequently a number of very old batteries with long and distinguished service records were disbanded because they were untitled, to their intense chagrin.

It has already been stated that no single list exists of all the Battle Honours in chronological order, certainly not available to the general public, which also gives some idea of where the battle so honoured was fought and of which campaign it formed a part. Also, as we have seen, there have been many battles which, although they might have qualified as worthy of Honour under the present day rules, were not Honoured, and the participants in them can only by discovered by lengthy research. To fill this void in military historical knowledge such a list has been produced as Part III of this book on the battles and the Honours of the British Army. Where a battle has not been Honoured, the decision whether to include it in the list has been made on the basis of accounts of the battle in regimental and campaign histories, its strategy and tactics, and the application of the current rules to the overall picture which has emerged. Inevitably, such a decision must in most cases be subjective, although where there was a borderline case the existence of applications from one or more participants for that battle to be honoured has been taken into account. Different readers and historians may have different ideas on the suitability of a battle for inclusion, but since there is little likelihood of a wholesale series of claims for new Honours by regiments, based on the evidence of this book, the list will provide, if nothing else, a more comprehensive history of British arms and of the regiments concerned than has existed heretofore.

The Chronology of Battles and Battle Honours that forms Part III contains the names of the battles Honoured, and of those unhonoured, in chronological sequence, and of the campaigns of which they formed part; it names the regiments honoured, and those that participated in both honoured battles, to the extent which today would have merited the award of the Honour, and unhonoured battles; it also provides information about claims made by individual regiments, about Honours borne as badges or in some form other than as straightfoward names of battles, and about battles or campaigns awarded as an Honour to batteries of the Royal Artillery.

Since this is a book on the Battle Honours of the Commonwealth Armies, not just the British Army, the list of Honoured regiments and participants also includes the Commonwealth regiments concerned. In some cases it will be seen that only Commonwealth regiments were awarded a particular Honour, and in other cases that the battles have actually been given different names by the Commonwealth countries.

Part III, then, gives information from the point of view of the battle itself and those who took part in it. Information from the regiment's point of view, showing all the battles, both honoured and unhonoured, in which they took part is a subject which is under preparation.

As has already been explained, over the years regiments have been raised and disbanded; new regiments have been raised bearing the numbers of previously disbanded regiments; and at intervals their numbers, style and titles have changed. In a regimental history this presents no difficulties as there is no doubt which regiment is being referred to, but in a campaign history it presents plenty of problems, particularly if it is not known from notes or from the context whether the original numbers or subsequent ones are being used.

Today so many regiments have been amalgamated that the numbers of the individual Regiments of Foot from which they have evolved have become dim if not actually forgotten. With so much potential confusion existing, therefore, it becomes essential to distinguish and define the regimental titles being used.

The following system has been used. For the Cavalry, the titles Dragoon Guards. Dragoons and Light Dragoons are used until the early nineteenth century when 'Hussar' and 'Lancer' generally displaced Dragoon or Light Dragoon in regimental titles. Since the numbers themselves did not change until the amalgamations of 1922, and even then all but two regiments retained their identities in a single or dual form, they cannot confuse, and the reraising of regiments with previously used numbers was sufficiently rare that the historical context should make it quite clear to which reference is being made.

For the Infantry, the situation is more complex, but until 1881, when territorial titles first appeared officially, the numbers as Regiments of Foot have been used with the post-1881 titles in brackets, and after that date those territorial titles alone have been adopted. Since very few Battle Honours have been awarded after 1945, and since the regiments retained their initial territorial titles, with minor changes of style, until then, it is again hoped that the reader will not be misled. Where renumbering took place due to senior regiments being disbanded and junior ones taking over their numbers to close the gaps, these subsequent numbers have been used; the territorial title in brackets should make this quite clear. Where numbers are quoted without a territorial title it can be assumed that the regiments did not survive long enough to be given territorial titles.

In Part III where the battles, Honoured and unhonoured, are listed in chronological order, the long-standing numbers of Regiments of Foot (or of Cavalry) that were current immediately before 1881 are used, although short-lived regiments are also quoted by their numbers current at the time of the event. It is possible, therefore that a number, particularly a high number, quoted in, say, 1750 signifies a different regiment from one referred to under the same number in, say, 1850, but only because the earlier one was subsequently disbanded. As far as is known there are no occasions where two regiments, one of which was disbanded and the other assumed the same number, took part in the same battle. A case can be made out for a regiment assuming the Honours won by its predecessor of the same number, and there are prececents for this. In the list of battles in Part III of this book, where amalgamation has taken place, it is always assumed that the lower number is the senior partner of the merger (except in the case of the 16th/5th Lancers), and only that lower number is shown there rather than dual or multiple numbers; whilst this may not be always agreed or acceptable to the junior partner, it certainly saves a lot of space.

Above: Panoramic view of the battlefield on Passchendaele Ridge, showing the state of the country over which the troops had to advance. 2nd Canadian Division area, 14 November 1917. *Imperial War Museum (IWM)*

4 Colours and Regimental Dress

Having followed the development of the regiments within the army, and the evolution of Battle Honours in general terms, we must now look at what might be called the social history of the Army. There is no shortage of books on dress, medals and weapons, and detailed information can be obtained from them, but a brief account of some of the more important changes and aspects will help to keep the following chapters in perspective. Less has been written about the customs and habits of the regiments, apart from what appears in their own regimental histories, and many of these customs result from events which took place during campaigns and battles still to be related.

Its Colours have always been the proudest possession of a regiment and have always been fiercely protected, even with lives. In the earliest warfare with a congested mass of troops on a battlefield, it was essential for rallying purposes during or after the fighting to have some means of showing the whereabouts of the Colonel and the headquarters of a regiment, and no better way could be found than to raise a recognisable flag so that all could see it. At first the flag was often the family banner of the Colonel himself, and the use of the Colonel's private Coat of Arms as a device was not actually banned until 1747, and not even then for 'Royal' regiments, at the same time as King's and Regimental Colours were introduced for all regiments except for rifle regiments. Dragoon Guards still carried Standards, but Dragoon regiments now carried Guidons instead. In due course standardisation was achieved and the banner which became the Colours represented allegiance to the Sovereign rather than to the Colonel. There was normally more than one Colour, and in most cases each company of a regiment had its own, although this custom is now only continued in the Guards Regiments.

Of course, to be of any value the Colours had to be recognised by all the members of the regiment. Different colours of cloth, or later silk, were used to distinguish regiments, and the badges helped as well. But to make quite sure that everybody recognised his own, the Colours were displayed to all at close quarters by being paraded through the ranks; they were trooped, in fact, and the annual Trooping the Colour ceremony of the regiments of the Brigade of Guards is the only public memory of that traditional necessity today, although some regiments also troop their Colours on their Regimental Days.

Apart from the practical use of different colours and badges, the Colours also became a means of displaying the Honours gained by a regiment, and in 1768 Battle Honours were for the first time placed on the Colours. By this time each regiment had at least two Colours, including the King's (or Queen's) Colour and the Regimental Colour, and they were all carried into battle in much the same way as banners had been carried since medieval times. Between 1766 and 1836, when it was lost in a fire, the 5th Regiment of Foot had a third Colour, in gosling green, which was their original facing colour and was restored to them in 1950 as such. The Colour was not replaced after the fire, but the regiment was awarded **Wilhelmstahl**, which the Colour had commemorated, as a unique Honour in its place.

The King's Colour, as it was then, was a representation of the Union Flag, which helped to distinguish British troops in battles of mixed nationalities in the same Army when there must have been dozens of coloured flags fluttering over the masses of troops, and had the precedence number of the Regiment of Foot in a collar in the centre. The Regimental Colour was of the distinguishing hue and bore the badge of the Regiment. The Battle Honours were affixed to either or both of the Colours until 1844, when orders were issued that the Queen's Colour should only bear the regimental number and that Battle Honours and embellishments, i.e. badges of honour, should only appear on the Regimental Colour. An example of an embellishment is the badge of the 'Lion of Nassau', which was awarded to the 18th Regiment of Foot, disbanded in 1922, for its part in the storming of the castle at Namur in 1695. The regulations for bearing of Honours on the Regimental Colour only remained until 1919 when each regiment was allowed to bear ten chosen Honours of those awarded for the Great War on the King's Colour, probably to relieve the problem of space on the Regimental Colour which still bore the remainder. After World War II similar permission was given for ten more chosen Honours.

In 1811 it was ordered that Colours and Standards should no longer be carried into battle; this order came very shortly after the Battle of Albuhera in the Peninsula, and paintings of the last stand of the 57th Regiment of Foot, when were spoken the immortal words of he dying Colonel, 'Die Hard, 57th, die hard', which became used as a nickname for the regiment, 'The Diehards', invariably show the Colours flying above the stricken Regiment's survivors. Nevertheless, although the order was obeyed in principle in that Colours were no longer flown in battle as a rallying point, they were still carried into battle. The last time is said to have been at the Battle of the Taku Forts in 1860 by the 44th Foot, the 1st Battalion of the Essex

Regiment, although they were certainly carried by the 58th Foot (2nd Battalion The Northamptonshire Regiment) at the battle of Laing's Nek in 1881 and obviously they must still have been carried in some way until the Battle of Isandlhwana nineteen years later. Then a famous incident of saving the Colours occurred during the action of Rorke's Drift during the Zulu War in 1879. This battle was not included among those Honoured, although the only British regiment involved, The South Wales Borderers, was awarded a wreath of immortelles to be born on the pike of the Colours for the battle of which the action formed a part. The legend tells that the body of the ensign to the Colours was subsequently discovered with the Colours wrapped around him under his uniform, but this was pure romance and the true situation is narrated in due course (see page 90).

Today the Colours are seldom seen. They usually stand cased, frequently in the Officer's Mess, and only fly on ceremonial parades or when a regiment which has been awarded the Freedom of a city, marches through its streets 'with Colours flying, drums beating and bayonets fixed'.

However, in 1953, a unique event occurred, which will probably remain unique for all time, but which must be known to very few people and, so far as is known, has not previously been described in print. As many will remember, the day of the coronation of Queen Elizabeth II was wet, and the Colours that had naturally been flown by the Infantry in the procession ended up soaked. The representatives of their regiments were housed in Olympia for the occasion, and the staff of the camp offered the regiments the facility of hanging their Colours up to dry, suspended horizontally from the pikes between double-tier bunks, and properly guarded, in what was actually the Officer's Mess of the brigade headquarters which was administering the camp. Practically all the regiments took advantage of the offer and thus occurred the unique sight of almost all the Infantry Colours, both Queen's and Regimental, of the British Army hanging unfurled in one room at one time; it was a magnificent sight, and the author, who was Brigade Major of the administrative headquarters of the camp at the time, was one of the very few people to witness it. Unfortunately no photograph exists of this occurrence, much to my lasting regret. The ironical aftermath came when, after all the troops had dispersed the following day, a box was found under the bed of the Ensign of one of the regiments who had refused to trust their Colours out of their own hands; it contained the very wet Colours of a famous regiment, left behind in the rush to go home.

Through the years other Colours have been lost in unusual circumstances, particularly as a result of fire or shipwrecks. The 1st Battalion of the 89th Regiment of Foot lost its Colours and the regimental records during a shipwreck *en route* to the Weser in 1805. The 62nd Regiment of Foot were even unluckier; in 1842 their Colours were lost in the River Ganges when boats transporting the regiment were overturned. They were recovered the following year, only to be lost again in similar circumstances in 1847. A more peculiar example, which has more modern connotations, occurred to the 68th Regiment; theirs were lost in the post when being returned to them after having had a new Honour **New Zealand** sewn on!

Apart from the intrinsic value and high cost of Colours, their loss, and particularly their replacement before the due time, is no insignificant matter. The Presentation of Colours is a ceremonial event always carried out by Royalty when they have a personal interest in a regiment, both in the United Kingdom and for regiments of the Commonwealth Armies, and frequently even when the connection does not exist; and very rarely by a lesser personage than the Colonel-in-Chief or a Colonial Governor acting on behalf of the Sovereign. They are blessed during the ceremony and when they are eventually replaced they are laid up, again ceremonially, in the regimental chapel, which is frequently located in a cathedral in their county. Not so many years ago, but luckily when regiments still had two battalions, there was some interesting juggling at such a ceremony at which the presentation was made by Royalty, when it was discovered that the Colours of one battalion which were being replaced had been destroyed by fire in circumstances over which a veil had been drawn. The other battalion's Colours, which were also paraded for the occasion, were used to simulate the non-existent ones, and by consummate sleight of hand few people realised that any problems existed, even during the subsequent laying-up.

At the beginning of this century it was decreed that the central wreath on the Regimental Colours of Commonwealth regiments should be composed of leaves of a national tree, plant, etc, instead of the roses, thistles and shamrocks of the Colours of British regiments. These were to be for Canada autumnal maple leaves, for Australia wattle leaves and berries, for New Zealand fern leaves and for South Africa, proteas.

Medals were awarded comparatively late as honours for military service. The first to be awarded to all ranks who took part in a battle was for Waterloo, awarded in 1816. Chronologically, this is not the first medal, since there was an Army General Service Medal for the period of the Napoleonic Wars, from 1793 to 1814; but this was in fact an afterthought, and retrospective, since it was not awarded until 1847. Even then it was only given to survivors, and fifty-four years after the first event commemorated there were likely to be few recipients. By the time this GSM was issued another campaign medal had been awarded; this was for all participants in the 1st Afghan War and had the inscription **Cabool 1842**.

Until 1816 medals had been given on a personal or a very limited basis. Some early commanders in the field were given medals, usually gold, by the Sovereign or by parliament; on a few occasions regiments struck their own, usually only for officers or more rarely for all ranks, for a particular battle in which the regiment had distinguished itself. They were not, however worn on uniform as today but kept for special occasions. The wearing of medal ribbons, instead of the medal itself, is a modern practice which coincides with the wearing of the more utilitarian uniforms first used towards the end of the last century; but even then medals were comparatively rare, and a row of ribbons, making a splash of colour on a soldier's chest, only appeared after 1918. Such a row of ribbons, a common sight until fairly recently is now a rarity again, since even the youngest soldier who had an opportunity to win campaign medals by 1945 has now retired, and only an occasional General Service Medal and a few others, such as for the Korean and Falklands wars, are now seen.

Army dress through the centuries has been covered in depth in other books. Suffice it here to mention some of the more relevant and interesting details. In the seventeenth century and until 1747, dress, like so many other regimental matters, was largely a matter of a Colonel's whimsy; of course the basic items were similar, but the design of coats, particularly for officers, and the colours and lace were a question of individual choice. It is perhaps strange, therefore, that only one old Infantry regiment, the 10th Regiment of Foot, was dressed in a blue uniform; the Rifle Brigade, which was formed considerably later, was the one regiment until the early nineteenth century that officially wore a green uniform, with black velvet facings, which has resulted in that colour being used today for all rifle regiments.

Thus it came about that some of the facing colours, the material used on the lapels of coats and elsewhere for difference, were of odd shades, few of which have survived. The facings formed the regimental distinguishing mark when the uniforms themselves gradually assumed one basic colour, and, as stated previously, were used on occasion to differentiate between two regiments whose colonels had the same surname.

By 1767 most Infantry wore scarlet coats over white waistcoats and breeches, except for those regiments with buff facings who wore waistcoats and breeches of that colour. Drummers usually wore the colours of the coat/facings in reverse, except for the 'Royal' regiments whose drummers wore red coats with blue facings. This dress, of course, had its drawbacks when battles were fought other than in formal arrays, as General Braddock was to discover rather forcibly when his redcoats were up against Indians and forest-bred irregulars on the Monongahela River in North America in 1755. As a result a few regiments, mostly those raised for skirmishing or for fighting in wooded country, started to wear green uniforms for their camouflage effect, and this basic colour has remained to this day not only for the rifle regiments but for the fighting dress of all regiments and troops.

Thick serge uniforms, not to mention the heavy load of equipment which the unfortunate troops had to carry, were of course totally unsuited to fighting in any climatic conditions outside Europe, or even there in the summer, and the Army must have suffered terribly in India and the West Indies and in the North American summer. One of the earliest occasions when regiments discarded their equipment and outer clothing for convenience during an attack was at the Battle of Bunker Hill in June 1775 during the American War of Independence, and the unofficial and unauthorised departure from custom paid off handsomely, although it was frowned upon and did not become a common habit. But it seems that few commanders in those days had what has become known as the 'common touch', and were very hidebound.

As early as 1794 the Cavalry, when on active service abroad, wore grey uniforms, but it was a long time before the Infantry adopted anything equivalent. In the mid-nineteenth century, in 1852 in South Africa a grey jacket

or blouse was worn with untanned leather equipment, and six years later in India thin pyjama-like uniforms began to be worn on account of the heat, dyed by various means better forgotten to a drab colour which became known as 'khaki', from the Hindustani word for dust; the first regiment to do so was the 2nd Bombay (European) Light Infantry, closely followed by the 3rd Bombay (European) Regiment, which became respectively the 106th and 109th Regiments of Foot in 1862. In 1884 Queen Victoria, somewhat reluctantly because she liked the appearance of her gaily clad troops, authorised khaki uniform for active service, although the khaki service dress which became so well known between 1914 and 1918 was not authorised until 1902. The last battle in which the army fought in red coats was at Ginnis in 1885 during the 1st Sudan War.

Because of the ground conditions in India and South Africa and the preponderence of undergrowth, trousers also became unpopular and puttees were worn wound round the leg up to the knee, the name being another example of the adaptation of the Hindustani language, this time their word for a bandage. Puttees remained standard dress until 1938, when battledress was officially introduced; the change from a jacketed uniform was made partly because it was more convenient when climbing into and out of vehicles and partly because battledress used up less cloth and was therefore cheaper. But throughout the changes in fighting dress, red coats remained the dress for ceremonial occasions until 1923, when they and officers full-dress uniforms were put into abeyance, again because of cost, and were never brought back into use except for the Guards. In 1937 a blue walking-out dress, with dark green for rifle regiments, was approved in a hurry after a period of 14 years without any attire other than khaki; the hurry was caused by the somewhat belated discovery that without full dress the troops had nothing smart to wear for the coronation of King George VI. Even then it faded into insignificance before the uniforms of the Indian Army Cavalry regiments which had been maintained in all their antique splendour. Apart from that use the blue dress only made a real appearance after the World War II, when in 1947 it was slightly redesigned and became known as Number One Dress; the first regiment to parade completely in Number One Dress was The East Surrey Regiment, who wore it when acting as a Guard of Honour for an official visit of the President of France in 1950, but even then it took the 1953 coronation to make it a general issue.

Today the coloured splendour of the army of old is virtually only seen on the Guards regiments, the Household Cavalry and the King's Troop, Royal Horse Artillery, and in officers' Mess Kit, which also incorporates the regimental facing colour, and in the case of the Cavalry regiments and the Royal Artillery still includes overalls and spurs, although the horses have long ceased to exist. The facings remained largely a matter of regimental choice until the Cardwell reforms when they were standardised. After 1881 the 'Royal' regiments wore blue facings, the English and Welsh Infantry white facings, the Scottish Infantry yellow, representing the field of the Scottish Royal Arms, and the Irish Infantry green, although this was only worn by one regiment, The Royal Irish Rifles, since they and all the others were either Royal or rifles. This regimentation, like so many efforts at uniformity in the Army, was strongly resented and only remained in general use for about twenty years, after which many regiments successfully claimed the use once more of their time-honoured facing colours.

It has been mentioned earlier that some Battle Honours are borne as embellishments on both Colours and uniform rather than the name of a battle, but a number of regiments wear embellishments of one sort or another to commemorate events in their history which have been awarded to them independently of any Battle Honour as such. An Eagle is worn by both the 1st and 2nd Dragoons (later The Royal Dragoons and The Royal Scots Greys respectively) to commemorate the capture of French Eagles at Waterloo, respectively those of the 105th and 45th Regiments; The 22nd Regiment of Foot (The Cheshire Regiment) wears an Oakleaf for gallantry at Dettingen, ordered at the time by King George II but not actually authorised as an embellishment on their Colours until 1921.

A number of feathers, plumes or cockades are worn. The 5th Regiment of Foot wore a white feather in the cap for the defence against the French in 1778 of the heights of Vigie in St Lucia, although this was changed to red and white balls on the shako in 1844; the 20th Regiment of Foot (The Lancashire Fusiliers) wore a primrose yellow hackle to commemorate the defence of Spion Kop; the 35th Regiment of Foot (The Royal Sussex Regiment) wears the Rouissilon, the white plume of Henri of Navarre, for the actions of their Grenadier Company with the 'Louisburg Grenadiers' and their Light Company with the 'Light Infantry' Battalion at Quebec; the 46th Regiment of Foot wear a red plume to commemorate the conduct of its Light Company at Poole Tavern near Brandywine in 1777, and a similar coloured hackle is worn by The Black Watch to commemorate their action, as the 42nd Regiment of Foot, at the Battle of Geldermalsen in 1794. The 6th Regiment of Foot, The Royal Warwickshire Fusiliers, wear an Antelope badge whose origin is uncertain, but probably dates from 1710 when they captured at Saragossa the Colour of the Spanish 'Royal African' Regiment, which also bore this badge.

Two embellishments exist as the result of long service overseas. The 23rd Regiment of Foot (The Royal Welsh Fusiliers) wear the black collar 'flash' which was authorised as part of their dress in 1834. The flash was originally worn by all regiments in one form or another to protect the uniform from the powdered queue of the wig; when it was removed this regiment was overseas and not knowing of its removal continued to wear it for many years, then claiming it as a distinction. The 38th Regiment of Foot, more recently The South Staffordshire Regiment, wore a patch of holland material behind their badge; they served in the West Indies for 58 years consecutively from 1706 and, not having been re-equipped in that time, were wearing uniforms of holland cloth, the only available material, when they did eventually return to England. This embellishment was not authorised until 1934, however.

Some head-dresses have also originated from captures. The 2nd Dragoons (The Royal Scots Greys) wore a grenadier cap for many years in commemoration of capturing the Colours of the 'Regiment du Roi', who wore one, at

Ramillies, and the 5th Dragoons (now part of the 16th/5th Lancers) wore a similar cap; the 5th Regiment of Foot (The Royal Northumberland Fusiliers) captured a French Grenadier Battalion at Wilhelmstahl and were granted the privilege of wearing a similar head-dress, later to be modified into the Fusilier cap.

Many expressions in daily use have a military origin. One apposite here is 'Dressed up to the Nines', which was coined as a result of the smartness and sartorial perfection of the 99th Regiment of Foot when, at Aldershot in 1858, they were chosen to guard the Royal Pavilion; at the same time they also acquired the nickname 'The Queen's Pets'. As far as is known only one regiment has owned a living badge; in 1837 the 78th Regiment of Foot (The Seaforth Highlanders) brought home with them from India a young elephant but it did not like the climate and in spite of being presented to Edinburgh zoo it soon died.

In spite of the considerable effort required by every man to maintain the more colourful uniforms of the past, most males have an inherent 'peacock' attitude to dress, as is exemplified by many articles of both modern and medieval civilian wear. A soldier might have complained at having to clean and wear his scarlet full dress, but secretly it made him proud to do so, to be a 'soldier of the Queen', as the song had it, and to look the part. His girl friend admired it too! It is an old truism that to destroy something you first make it unattractive, and so unpopular. There is little doubt that the removal of the colour in dress, the flamboyance and the ceremonial of the Army, apart from the lack of overseas stations, did a great deal to reduce its attraction as a way of life; once popularity and the ability to recruit to full strength fall off it is a simple political expedient, supported by false argument, to make the shortage of numbers an excuse for further reductions and more regimentation. How well this has succeeded can be seen by any reference to the strength of the Army today compared with times in the past when the world situation was little less settled and peaceful than it is today.

A curious situation with regard to rank existed in one small part of the army from 1687 for almost 200 years. The Guards Regiments had always been regarded as elite, as they still are, and, whilst officers in Infantry and Cavalry regiments could buy promotion into other regiments where there was a vacancy, this option was not open to Guards officers who had very limited scope for promotion; they could not buy commissions into Infantry regiments and still retain their exclusiveness, and were therefore usually considerably older, rank for rank, than their counterparts in the rest of the army. Thus a system of 'double rank' was instituted, whereby these officers had one rank in their regiments and a senior one in the Army as a whole; in other words a Captain in his regiment was regarded as a Lieutenant-Colonel in the Army, and a Major as a Colonel and so on. The holders of these ranks not only received the pay of the senior rank but became available to be appointed as Brigadiers or Generals in competition with Infantry officers. This system was only abolished in 1871. A parallel system, in a way, exists to this day in the Royal Marines who always take one rank senior on board ship to that which they hold ashore, although they do not get paid for it.

Above: The Battle of Bunker's Hill, 17 June 1775. Line engraving by J. G. Miller after J. Trumbull, published in February 1798. *NAM*

Left: The 28th Regiment (The Gloucestershire Regiment) at the Battle of Alexandria 1801, at which the regiment gained its 'Back Badge'. Coloured lithograph of an original painting by Col C. J. Marshman. *NAM*

5 Regimental Customs, Nicknames and Memorable Events

Most regiments have their own peculiar customs, many of which have survived in spite of amalgamations; some, of course, have disappeared along with disbandment. The origins of many of these customs are shrouded in the mists of time, but nevertheless they have arisen from some memorable events, be it pleasant or bloody, in the long pasts of the regiments and are woven into the fabric of tradition. While they do not properly fall into the category of Battle Honours, even though many commemorate by special 'days' participation in battles for which the regiments were awarded Honours, no account of the British Army would be complete without mentioning a few of them.

A number of customs concern the wearing of swords. The 8th Dragoons (8th King's Royal Irish Hussars) wore a sword belt over the right shoulder to commemorate the capture of Spanish Cavalry belts at Saragossa in 1710. In the 15th Regiment of Foot, later The East Yorkshire Regiment, the Orderly Officer wore a sword in the Mess before dinner, to remind officers of the time, in 1689, when swords were worn at all times against sudden guerilla raids during the Scottish clan rising. The officers of the 29th Regiment of Foot, later the 1st Battalion The Worcester Regiment, wore swords at table until 1850 to commemorate a time in 1746 when they were surprised at dinner by Indians while stationed on Prince Edward Island, although after that date only the Captain of the Week and the Orderly Officer continued the practice; this event and custom also gave rise to their nickname, 'The Ever-sworded 29th'. Another curious custom of which the origin is uncertain was practised by the 29th Foot for many years; in 1759 black drummers were established in the Regiment and the custom continued until 1843, when the last one in service died.

Two examples of customs based on regimental possessions, although there are many more, concern the 5th and 91st Regiments of Foot. During the siege of Lucknow the 1st Battalion of the 5th Foot were defending the palace of the Begum Kathee who had an ivory bed; the regiment had made from it a bandmaster's baton which was used for many years. The 91st Foot, The Argyll and Sutherland Highlanders, had the misfortune of having a troop transport pierced by the sword of a Narwhal while returning home from South Africa in 1803; this was turned into a walking stick which was actually used as such during the Peninsular War.

A regimental day which is not concerned with a battle was celebrated by the 6th Dragoons; this is 'Oates Day' to commemorate the feat of Captain Oates who went to the South Pole with Captain Scott and died 'a very gallant gentleman'.

A number of customs relate to Royalty or the drinking of the Loyal Toast. The 28th Foot use the reply to the toast 'The King, Mr. President' which was used of necessity after the Battle of Albuhera when only two officers were left in the Mess. In a different vein, the 85th Foot, which became the 2nd Battalion The King's Shropshire Light Infantry, were granted the privilege of remaining seated whilst drinking the Loyal Toast, and also during the playing of the National Anthem, by King George IV in memory of their duty and service to him whilst stationed in Brighton. In yet another vein, and again concerning The Argyll and Sutherland Highlanders, the 91st Foot were granted the perpetual right to march past to the pipes in remembrance of providing the Guard of Honour for the wedding of Princess Louise and the Marquis of Lorne in 1871; it is interesting that this distinction was granted to them only a few years after they had been refused the use of the bagpipes at all between 1849 and 1864.

Many customs concern animals, particularly those used as regimental mascots. One of the more unusual was the use of a ram as a mascot by the 95th Regiment of Foot, who were presented with the first of a long succession of rams by the Rajah of Travancore in 1838; as if this were not enough, the regiment acquired a fighting ram instead of the more docile variety, if any ram can be said to be docile, during the action of Kotah-Ki-Serai in 1858, and this custom also continued for some years, one hopes not to the detriment of inspecting officers during ceremonial parades.

Regimental nicknames could well form the subject of a book in its own right. Most regiments have at least one, some have a number. They range through the descriptive, the allusive, the laudatory, the rhyming, the risible, the derogatory to the defamatory. Some were given by friends, some by foes; many concern the raising of the regiment, some the social habits, some their uniforms and some their more militant activities. Some were short-lived and some remain to this day. What is certain is that they, like the customs and the vagaries of dresss, the badges and embellishments, bring the histories of the regiments to life, translate many of the unconsidered trifles of their background and traditions into common usage. Even the most impolite references to the past, enshrined in these nicknames, are often now regarded with pride by those to whom they were applied. Some, however, are disliked by the regiments, and many of these result from the pronunciation as a word of the initial letters of their titles, a trend which in unmilitary circles becomes more and more common. We can only look at a few here, but perhaps these will whet the appetite of some military historian to treat this subject in the detail it deserves.

Let us first look at some of those which have been gained in battle, or at least through offensive action. The 11th Hussars are known as the 'Cherrypickers', which is often assumed to arise from the colour of their overall or trousers; in fact it arose from a surprise encounter with the French in a cherry orchard in the Peninsula, and their dress provided the nickname 'The Cherubims'. The 14th Lancers gained the soubriquet 'The Chambermaids' in allusion to their capture of King Joseph's silver chamberpot at Vittoria. The famous title of the 17th Lancers, 'The Death and Glory Boys', does not commemorate an action in which they took part, but alludes to their death's head badge, which was selected by their first Colonel, John Hale, and commemorates the death of General Wolfe at Quebec which was witnessed by him while serving with the 47th Foot. The same regiment have also gained two nicknames from their enemies while serving during the Indian Mutiny—'The Terror of India' and 'The Glory of the World'. In the same vein the 3rd Hussars were called 'The Devil's Children' by the Sikhs after the Battle of Moodkee in 1845, and the 19th Hussars gained the nickname 'The Terror of the East' in the early nineteenth century in India. Returning to earlier battles, the 39th Foot became known somewhat jocularly as 'Sankey's Horse' from being mounted on mules during the Battle of Almanza in 1707, and more recently the same regiment gained a short-lived nickname of 'The Norsets' in 1916 when the 2nd Battalion was temporarily amalgamated with the 2nd Battalion of The Norfolk Regiment due to heavy casualties to both battalions. The 61st Foot gained the name 'The Flowers of Toulouse' from the appearance of their very heavy casualties at that battle in 1814 lying on the battlefield in their new red coats; this regiment became the 2nd Battalion of The Gloucestershire Regiment who more recently gained a laudatory nickname 'The Glorious Glosters' for their heroic defence on the River Imjin in Korea in 1951. Another famous title was gained by the 93rd Foot at the Battle of Balaclava in 1854, 'The Thin Red Line'; they were the only infantry regiment involved in the battle remembered mostly today for the Charge of the Light Brigade.

Three regiments gained nicknames for offensive action of a rather different type. During earlier troubles in Ireland in 1798, the 89th Foot became known as 'Blayney's Bloodhounds' from their tracking down of rebels, and later the 12th Lancers were known as 'The Dungavan Butchers' after quelling a riot during the Fenian rising in the 19th century. Further west the 29th Foot gained another enemy-endowed nickname when they were involved in the Boston massacre in 1770; they became 'The Vein Openers'.

Turning to less warlike nicknames, the 16th Lancers gained the soubriquet 'Scarlet Lancers' because they were one of the first regiments of Cavalry to wear a scarlet tunic; and in similar style the 22nd Foot were nicknamed 'The Red Knights' because they not only wore a scarlet tunic but an all-red uniform including the breeches. The 13th Hussars were called 'The Ragged Brigade' from their appearance after several hard battles in the Peninsula, and the 50th Foot The Royal West Kent Regiment were called 'The Dirty Half-Hundred' for a similar reason. It may not only have been their appearance which gained the 10th Hussars the derisory nickname of 'The China Tenth'; it was also said that they were too precious and keen on maintaining their smartness to show well at dances!

Many nicknames have their origin either in the raising of a regiment or in the pre-history of a force from which the regiment grew or to which it traced its ancestry. One such is 'Pontius Pilate's Bodyguard' for the 1st Foot, The Royal Scots, who claim a direct relationship with the earlier existence of the regiment in the French Army and through that to their descent from the Scottish Legions of the Roman army. Others are more recent. 'The Cheeses', a nickname for The Life Guards, dates from the reorganisation of the regiment in 1788 which was said to have made them 'a regiment of cheesemongers not gentlemen'. The 2nd Foot, later The Queen's Regiment, gained the soubriquet 'Kirke's Lambs' from the name of their raising Colonel who commanded them at the battle of Sedgemoor and their badge, the Lamb and Flag, which was the crest of Braganza. Two regiments, the 7th and 85th Foot, share the name 'Elegant Extracts', relating in both cases to the fact that their officers had been hand-picked from other regiments. The nickname of the 9th Foot, which became The Royal Norfolk Regiment, 'The Holy Boys', has two possible origins, one of which stems from their badge, Britannia, which they gained for gallantry at Almanza in 1707 and which was said to have been mistaken by the Spanish a century later for the Virgin Mary; the other, less laudatory but still religious, is that the name recalls members of the regiment who sold the bibles, with which they had been presented, for money to buy drink, and food during one of the many lapses of commissariat efficiency.

The remaining examples are a miscellany of oddities. The 35th Regiment of Foot gained the soubriquet 'The Haddocks' during a football match from an irreverent reference to the dolphins on the Arms of the town of Brighton. The 65th Foot were called the 'Hickety Pips' from an attempt by the Maoris to pronounce their number. Smartness and the removal of speargrass from a parade ground in Burma caused the 69th Foot to be called 'Grasspickers', and an example of rhyming slang, which almost causes apoplexy among the more traditional members of the 65th Foot, is 'The Cork and Doncasters' from their title The York and Lancaster. Two nicknames appeared from a single event for the 100th Foot, The Leinster Regiment, when they sailed for India in 1911; one was 'The Innocents Abroad', because the regiment only included one officer who had been there before, and other 'The Lovesick Leinsters', because of the large number of brides travelling with them. Finally a nickname whose origin is totally obscure; the 38th Foot were known as the 'Pump and Tortoise Brigade'; this is the name of a public house outside their old barracks in Stafford, but which gave its name to which is lost in the past.

All regiments have memorable events in their histories, some famous, some notorious; quite a lot of these refer to service abroad of one sort or another and often to the regiment being the first or last regiment to do something. Few of these events have anything to do with Battle Honours, but they do help to show something of the life of the regiments, the hardships they sometimes had to endure, and the resilience and discipline instilled in them which made them the greatest fighting force in the world for so long.

In these days of air travel, and even comparatively recently of sea trooping in steamships and travel overland by train or by vehicle, both in war and in peace, one tends to forget that it has not always been like that. For 200 of the 300 odd years during which the Standing Army has been in existence, travel from one country to another was by sailing ship, and the time taken from England to, say, India was many months; these were spent in cramped and unhygienic conditions, usually in an ostensibly all male society, with poor food and a very good chance of foundering before the destination was reached. On land the only transport, except for the Cavalry, was the feet, and the commissariat was not always very successful in maintaining the supply of boots and clothing, let alone food and water. The climate frequently did not help, and little account was taken of the differing needs of troops in the tropics or in arctic conditions. Medicine, particularly tropical medicine, was in its infancy and frequently the casualties from sickness and disease, especially from yellow fever in the West Indies, far outweighed the casualties from battle; in fact regiments were often literally decimated without having taken part in any action at all.

The soldiers themselves had little contact with home during these periods of overseas service; mail was unorganised except on official business and as slow as the ships which carried it, and in any case few of the soldiers or their families could write. There must have been innumerable cases of children growing up into adults without ever knowing their fathers and many cases of whole families dying without the husband (or son or father as it may have been) being aware of the situation until many years later. Before families travelled with the troops marriages must have been almost impossible to maintain, and the size of the Anglo-Indian population on the sub-continent is sufficient evidence of the natural urges of the soldiery, the separation of families, and the inability of those who were young and single when they left England to visualise much possibility of family life for many years to come.

Nevertheless wars came, and regiments had to be moved, and the frequency of movement of some regiments united the family more often. Sometimes regiments served dual roles during their movements abroad, and most of those who went to Australia during the first half of the nineteenth century acted as guards for convicts *en route* to Botany Bay. The boredom of life in some remote stations promoted pastimes, and hockey became a national, and later an international, sport through the service of the Army in India, as did polo, while ice-hockey resulted from troops trying to play the normal game in winter conditions in Canada.

The movement of troops from one part to another of the expanding Empire was quite frequent, and there were few countries to which they did not go at some time or other. Sometimes, of course, things went wrong administratively and small units, or perhaps whole regiments, were forgotten in some far outpost where they remained for interminable years, as for example the 38th Foot whose experience in the West Indies was related on page 12. One wonders what the regimental Colonel was doing all the time in not bringing the plight of his regiment to the notice of the authorities, but it reinforces the idea that many of them had little interest in their regiments beyond receiving their salaries as Colonel; either that, or an almost unbelievably inefficient and inscrutable War Office did nothing when it remembered that a regiment had got lost somewhere, but often did not even know where it was.

Let us look briefly at some of the more memorable or odd happenings, which can again only be selective extracts from a vast number of such events.

Instances of long service overseas, or of difficult conditions during it, are the 4th Dragoon Guards, who spent 95 years continuously in Ireland from 1698 to 1793; a company of the 2nd Foot which went to Bermuda, not such a bad station perhaps, in 1701 and stayed there in a sadder and sadder condition until it was disbanded sixty-two years later; the 38th Foot, who served for fifty-eight years in the West Indies, not forgotten because they were moved about among the islands, and who in memory of that time formed an alliance in 1955 with the Antigua Defence Force; the 40th Foot, who were raised in Nova Scotia in 1717 and served abroad for sixty-six years, apart from a year in Ireland, not coming to England until 1783. We have spoken of heavy casualties from sickness; one such event relates to the 27th Foot which in 1742 was sent to Jamaica 600 strong and returned a year later with only nine of those who embarked. In 1794 several regiments landed in Flanders untrained, with very little ammunition and totally unfit for an arduous campaign; the 90th Foot was in even a worse condition since it was caught in fog and shipwrecked and landed with no clothes or equipment, and the prospect of a long cold winter. It must have been equally frustrating to the 39th Foot who twice, in 1882 and in 1885, were sent to Egypt; in both cases the fighting had ceased by the time they got there, and they were sent home again.

It has been said earlier that at the time of the 1881 amalgamations many of the affected regiments had not met each other; the 71st Foot, on the other hand, had served with their future 2nd Battalion, the 74th Foot, as early as 1790 in India in the campaign againt Tippoo Sahib. This regiment was one of the earliest to use the 'overland route' by marching from Alexandria to Suez instead of sailing round the Cape; another regiment to do so was the 69th Foot, *en route* to Burma in 1858, and they were followed by others, including the 86th Foot, who completed the march in midsummer 1861. The first regiment to do so, however, was the 80th Foot in 1801, who did it in the reverse direction and then repeated it the other way the following year when returning to India. In totally different climatic conditions, several regiments carried out long marches in Canada, particularly from the Maritime provinces to Quebec; the 85th Foot did this in midwinter in 1837/8 on foot or by sleigh. In contrast again the 17th Foot showed almost unbelievable endurance when the 1st

Battalion marched 896 miles from Lucknow to Peshawar in three months in 1874, and the 67th Foot were the first King's regiment to march right across the Indian peninsula in 1818.

In a different aspect of service, the 2nd Battalion of the 83rd Foot was the only regiment to serve throughout the Peninsula campaign as a complete unit from 1809 to 1814. The successor of this regiment, The Royal Ulster Rifles, also achieved notability when it had 11 battalions of the regiment serving on a 6-mile front in France in 1916, rivalled by the 20th Foot from whom, as The Lancashire Fusiliers, no less than twenty battalions were involved in the 3rd Battle of Ypres in 1917 and fourteen battalions were still in action in France at the time of the Armistice a year or so later. Still in terms of unusual service, only three regiments have ever served in Japan; the first to do so was again the 20th Foot from 1864 to 1866, followed by the 9th and 10th Foot respectively for similar periods. The final service record must be held by The Royal Scots Greys whose first service overseas in peacetime was in Egypt in 1920.

The 35th Foot, The Royal Sussex Regiment, have featured numerous times in these pages, and they must be acccorded two more mentions. In 1756 they surrendered Fort William Henry in the northern part of New England on Lake George in the face of overwhelming odds; during their march into captivity by the French the soldiers and their families were massacred by Indians, and this event probably formed the basis of Fennimore Cooper's famous book *The Last of the Mohicans*. Less bloody, but more unusual, is the fact that they twice received a vote of thanks from the Governor of Barbados; the first was for their services during the great hurricane of 1831 and the second for their services during an earthquake there in 1875.

An unusual honour was accorded to the 66th Foot who formed the Guard of Honour at Napoleon's funeral; it is doubtful if the 91st Foot considered it such an honour to have to exhume his body and escort it to France in 1840. Another honour of a different kind was given to the 84th Foot when they left India after the Mutiny in 1859; they are the only regiment to have been saluted by the Fort William battery at Calcutta. And talking of mutiny, but on a smaller scale, Private James Daly of the Connaught Rangers was executed in India in 1920 for mutiny due to discontent with the Black and Tan outrages in Ireland.

There is a first time for everything and a last time for many things, and this applies to the regiments as well. When Kaiser Wilhelm II became Colonel in Chief of the Royal Dragoons he was the first foreign Sovereign to be so honoured; in view of future events perhaps this was an unfortunate choice. To the 16th Foot goes the honour of being the first regiment of the British Army to fire a shot on the continent of Europe, at Walcourt in 1689. The 39th Foot, The Dorsetshire Regiment, was the first British regiment to serve in India, in 1754, and this is commemorated in their motto 'Primus in Indis'. The 2nd Battalion of the 87th Foot captured the Eagle of the French 8th Light Infantry Regiment at Barrosa, the first time that one had been captured on a battlefield. In terms of movement, the 77th Foot was the first regiment to pass through the Suez Canal, homebound from India in 1870, the 2nd Battalion of The Argyll and Sutherland Highlanders was the first and only battalion to be transported through the Panama Canal *en route* to North China in 1928, and four years later the 1st Battalion of the Northamptonshire Regiment was the first to be moved entirely by air, to Iraq.

Turning from firsts to lasts, The Royal Lincolnshire Regiment was the last to serve in the Sudan in 1955, the 2nd Battalion of the Lancashire Fusiliers was the last to serve in Trieste in 1954, The Hampshire Regiment was the last in Jamaica in 1962, and The Royal Irish Fusiliers was thought to be the last to serve in Gibraltar, in 1950, leaving the Rock without an Infantry battalion for the first time for 250 years, although a garrison battalion was subsequently reinstated. Still in the Mediterranean, the 37th Heavy Anti-Aircraft Regiment, RA, was the last unit of regimental size to serve as a permanent part of the garrison of Malta, and returned to England in 1959. The Highland Light Infantry features in the 'lasts' as well as the 'firsts'; the 1st Battalion handed over the Citadel in Cairo to the Egyptian Army in 1946, hauling down the flag which had been raised for the first time by their 2nd Battalion in 1882 after the battle of Tel el Kebir. The Lancashire Fusiliers also appear in the list again, this time their 1st Battalion; it was the last battalion to serve in Lucknow in 1947, and on the night before Indian independence it inverted the Union Jack, a sign of distress, which had for so long flown over the Residency and had been immortalized in the poetry of Tennyson, blowing up the flagpole and the base to prevent it falling into Indian hands.

A few miscellaneous events remain to be recorded here, although these are by no means of lesser stature than those that have gone before. The first bar to a Victoria Cross was awarded posthumously to Captain Chavasse who had served as medical officer with The King's Regiment at Passchendaele in 1917. During the Peninsular campaign the 88th Foot captured from the French 101st Regiment a trophy which the French had captured previously from the Moors; it consisted of a crescent and silver balls surmounted by a French Eagle and decorated with horsehair plumes, which, with the ability of the British soldier to produce nicknames, soon became known as 'Jingling Johnny'. In 1881 Queen Victoria forbade the playing of the regimental march of the Queen's Regiment, 'The Old Queen', because it included a part of the national anthem; perhaps she did not like the possible allusion and was not amused. A great honour was paid to The Black Watch in 1963 when a piper from that regiment played at the funeral of President Kennedy. In action in 1914 at Moy, the 12th Lancers became the last, as far as is known, Cavalry regiment to fight with lances in war. The need for pastimes in overseas stations was referred to earlier; many regiments formed Masonic Lodges and at least two of these remain to this day—No 570 'Charity', formed by the 5th Dragoon Guards in 1780, and one established by the 29th Foot in 1859.

Let us end on a light note. Legend has it that Duchess Jean and her daughters, mother and sisters of Lord Huntly who raised the 92nd Foot in 1794, helped the recruiting drive by visiting country fairs dressed in regimental uniform; they then placed a guinea between their lips and offered a kiss to each man who enlisted. And again, on the subject of women, there was the famous case of Harriet Snell who enlisted under the name of James Grey in the 6th Foot and, having managed not to have her sex discovered, which must have been no mean feat in the cramped conditions of those days although hygiene was not rated as highly as today, eventually deserted when she

was ordered to be flogged. She later enlisted in the Royal Marines and was only rumbled after she had been wounded at the siege of Pondicherry.

Having now introduced the British Army, with all its foibles, peculiarities and changes, let us now consider in detail the wars, battles and actions during which it gained its Battle Honours in every continent and so many countries of the world.

Top: 'Fuentes d'Onor 1811.' Norman Ramsay, Royal Horse Artillery, at Fuentes d'Onor, an incident in the Peninsular War from a painting by W. B. Wollen, RI. *NAM*

Above: 1st Afghan War 1838–42. 'The remnants of an Army. Dr Bryden, the sole survivor of the 16,000 British forces, arriving exhausted at the gates of Jellalabad, 13 January 1842.' Lithograph from the original painting by Lady Butler, 1879. *NAM*

PART II
Battles and Campaigns of the British and Commonwealth Armies

Above: The charge of the 21st Lancers at Omdurman, 2 September 1898. Photogravure after R. Caton Woodville, published 1899.
NAM

6 The Struggle with France, 1660-1793

Tangier, 1662-80

When King Charles II married Catherine of Braganza, Tangier was part of her dowry. The need soon arose to garrison it and to prevent inroads by the Moors which might diminish its potential for trade in the Mediterranean and as a port. Thus in 1662 two regiments were dispatched thither, the 1st Royal Dragoons and the 2nd Foot (The Queen's Regiment), both of which spent the next eighteen years in this rather insalubrious spot. Although there was plenty of skirmishing, and an increase in this activity led to three other regiments, The Grenadier and Coldstream Guards and the 1st Foot (The Royal Scots), being sent out during the last year of the period, there were no real battles. Nevertheless **Tangier** became the first Battle Honour, in terms of chronology, to be awarded to the British Army and is held by all five regiments with dates appended appropriate to their service there. It was the only Honour awarded for a campaign as opposed to an actual battle for almost a hundred years, until North America in 1763, in fact.

Ireland, 1689-91

Apart from Monmouth's rebellion and Dundee's uprising in Scotland, which though bloody were hardly worthy of Honour, the first fighting for the new Army against a European enemy took place in Ireland. But because the fighting took place on British soil and against an enemy nominally under the command of a deposed monarch, even though not all his troops were native to Britain, this was regarded as a civil war and no Honours were awarded. This would perhaps be an inopportune moment for regiments that can still be identified to advertise their early associations with that unhappy and war-torn land; but nevertheless a large number of regiments, of whom only four were subsequently disbanded, took part in the *Battle of the Boyne* in 1690. It is one battle, and certainly the oldest one fought by the British Army as we know it today, whose effects are strongly felt still, although from a political and a national standpoint it could not have been avoided, and had to be fought against what was in fact an invasion force. Apart from the battle itself, a few regiments took part in a number of sieges and general mopping-up operations which lasted for the next year, and which, although minor engagements, were no less ferociously fought because of that.

Flanders, 1689-97

Apart from its political implications the fighting in Ireland did provide good training for the small, and as yet inexperienced, Army, and stood it in good stead during its first taste of warfare against a foreign power. King William III has always been regarded as an unlucky, if not inept, general in the days when kings commanded their armies in battle, and this war, known rather long-windedly as the War of the League of Augsburg, no doubt provided the evidence for that assessment. Nevertheless, as was to happen many times afterwards, the Army started off badly, gradually learned its lessons and improved its skills, and in spite of losing battles on the way finally won the war.

This war saw the start of British involvement in a struggle with France, perhaps one should say the start of a new phase of the centuries old struggle with France, for European and colonial domination, which was to continue for 126 years until Napoleon's defeat at Waterloo in 1815. There were many rounds, and to be pedantically accurate the fighting was intermittent, but this is hardly the appropriate word to convey the true picture since major fighting occupied over half the years of that period, and minor actions and skirmishes kept troops in the field for many of the remainder. The first round took place in Europe, in that area which was to see so much British blood spilt, not only during this and later periods of Anglo-French hostilities, but particularly two and a quarter centuries later—in Flanders, the cockpit of Europe.

It would be an interesting study in human relations and psychology to discover why Flanders has always borne the brunt of so much warfare and suffering, but this is not the place for it. Suffice to say that the countryside is flat and this makes for ease of manoeuvre; that there are a number of major rivers which provide defensive positions and the sites on which massive fortresses could be built; and that, perhaps foremost, it was the meeting place, if you exclude the English Channel, of the three great European powers of the next 250 years, Germany (or Prussia as it then was), France and Britain, and had been the colony of a now declining power, Spain. At one time or other Britain allied itself with each of the others against the third, but interestingly France and Germany have never been on the same side.

As far as the war itself was concerned, forty-eight regiments were to be involved, of which all but eleven remained in existence, singly or in amalgamation, until the last great upheaval of reorganisation. Four major and two minor battles were fought during a six-year campaign, but of these only the last, Namur, was considered worthy of Honour, perhaps because the results were at the best draws, although none were outright defeats. Nevertheless *Walcourt*, *Steenkirk* and *Landen* were major engagements, of which the latter two gave rise to heavy casualties and much bloodshed, and the endurance and gallantry displayed by the Army was of a high order. Contrary to popular belief in recent times, it was in fact the seriousness of the casualties at Landen which originally gave rise to the myth of the Flanders poppies being nurtured on British blood. All the unhonoured battles, with the exception of *Leuse* which was a comparatively minor action in which only the Life Guards took part, have been claimed as worthy of Honour by many of the regiments which participated, but their claims have been unsuccessful, and **Namur** itself has also been claimed unsuccessfully by six regiments which formed the covering force during the siege of the fortress in 1695.

Marlborough's War, 1702–13

Only five years passed after the Treaty of Ryswyck which followed the capture of Namur before the two antagonists were at each other's throats again during a campaign which lasted for eleven years and this time involved other Powers, since part of it was fought in the Iberian Peninsula and part in Germany as well as in Flanders as usual. It is not, perhaps, strictly accurate to entitle the whole campaign as Marlborough's, since he was relieved of command in Flanders before the war finished and never visited Spain; but it is under that title that the campaign has gone down into history, he was undoubtedly the dominant figure during it, and it laid the fortunes of the Churchill family. It may be pure conjecture, but we might have had another leader in 1940 if John Churchill had not achieved preeminence in these early years of the eighteenth century, and the course of history might have been very different today.

Altogether forty battles or actions were fought, of which only five were honoured; these were Marlborough's four great battles which every schoolboy or girl knows—**Blenheim, Ramillies, Oudenarde** and **Malplaquet**—although they might have difficulty in placing them on a map of Europe, and, far removed from those geographically, **Gibraltar**, which nobody should have any difficulty in locating. Again, practically all the unhonoured battles or actions have been claimed as Honours by one or more of the regiments taking part, but at least the authorities of the day appear to have been right about the participants in the honoured battles since only one unrewarded regiment has claimed any of these; this is the 94th Foot, as a successor regiment, by virtue of the original regiment's descent from an irregular regiment in Dutch pay which fought on the side of the British. Only one of the many battles took place outside Europe, the capture of *Guadeloupe* in 1703, in which seven regiments participated, the first of the numerous occasions on which it was captured by British arms and returned to France after hostilities ceased; this has also been unsuccessfully claimed as an Honour by four of the seven regiments which took part.

Two other Honours have been claimed by regiments for naval service in which they acted as marines, *Malaga* and *Naval Service 1702–13*.

It must be remembered that war in those far off days was a more formalised and 'gentlemanly' and less all-embracing affair than it has become in more recent times. Although some fighting took place during the winter months, the habit still existed to a major extent, as it had during Caesar's wars in Gaul, of breaking off the fight when the weather got too bad and going into winter quarters, and starting up again when the weather improved in the spring and summer. This explains perhaps why only three of those forty battles took place outside the period May to September; and of these two were in Spain and the other was a siege. Sieges were common because of the strategy of holding strong points rather than defensive, or trench, lines, and although less spectacular than the set-piece battles were often a great strain on those taking part, considering the conditions under which they fought, the lack of organized supplies, the boredom and the fact that sieges, unlike battles, were carried on in winter as well as summer. The investment of a strongpoint was also often used as a means of bringing the enemy to battle, when the only way of winning was to catch an enemy army on ground of one's own choosing after months and perhaps hundreds of miles of marching while each side was trying to achieve the same end.

The official title of the campaign was the War of the Spanish Succession, but, strangely in view of this title, history largely relates this war to northern Europe; perhaps this is because it was where Marlborough and the major French army was, although a larger proportion of the forces was employed in and around the Peninsula. Sixty-two regiments were there, many of which were short-lived, against thirty-eight in northern Europe, of which nine played a part in both theatres. When one considers the almost total absence of any reference to the Peninsula in history books and the definition of a battle worthy of honour as being one of which every educated gentleman has heard, one is prompted to think of the syndrome of the chicken and the egg; it could also account for the comparatively poor record of the Army's achievements in terms of the battles borne on regimental Colours.

But nevertheless the war did start in Flanders, just, the fight at *Venloo* preceding that at *Vigo* by a mere month, six regiments having been involved in each battle and the latter having been claimed as an Honour by five of its participants. But after that opening very little happened, except for manoeuvring, for almost two years until Marlborough began his long southwards march into Germany which culminated at Blenheim. It is a significant pointer to Marlborough's greatness as a general that for the first time during this march, and for the only time for many years to come, he supplied his troops with new boots and clothing *en route*, and established an effective commissariat.

It is at this point that one of the mysteries of the award of Battle Honours intrudes itself. Six weeks before Blenheim there was fought an even bloodier battle, the storming of the *Schellenberg* redoubt. It is probably true to say that without the extreme gallantry shown by many regiments and thousands of soldiers in performing this almost impossible task, and the last-gasp success of the attack, the Battle of Blenheim would never have been fought at all, or if it had would certainly not have been the resounding success that it actually was. Yet the Schellenberg features in few accounts, other than purely military ones, of the war, and of the seven Cavalry, one Guards and thirteen Infantry regiments which took part half have claimed it as an Honour, with good justification. In fact fewer regiments took part at **Blenheim** itself, where twenty regiments were awarded the Honour, and few more took part in any other of the recognised battles.

After the success of Blenheim and Marlborough's return march to the Rhine and the Moselle valley it seemed that the war might reach a speedy conclusion, but the advantages gained were steadily whittled away. Unfortunately Britain had allies, and most of the Dutch and German commanders, particularly the Dutch generals who were closely controlled by their government, were over-cautious, dilatory and obstructive. They had their traditional interests and pride, national and personal, to consider and were not susceptible to plans which did not favour those interests and give them the opportunity to cover themselves in glory. Not that the situation has changed so much in modern times, as can be seen from the campaign in 1944 and 1945 in the same geographical area, and the reluctance of the Americans to allow Montgomery the kudos. Thus most of Marlborough's plans now and later in the war, like Montgomery's plans, which perhaps only his advanced military acumen saw as feasible, were turned down and opportunities were missed.

But in 1706 Marlborough did at last gain acceptance of a plan to attack the French in Flanders and the victory at **Ramillies** was the result; twenty-two regiments were awarded this Honour and it was claimed unsuccessfully by the 94th Foot. With the French on the run he captured a number of fortresses in the Netherlands and laid siege to others, and once more the war looked to be heading for a speedy conclusion. But once again the allied generals held back and it was not until 1708, after the French had struck at some of the Flanders fortresses, that Marlborough again managed to bring them to battle at **Oudenarde** and once more inflict on them a major defeat. Twenty-one regiments gained this Battle Honour and it was again claimed by the 94th Foot. Although France was now on the defensive, plans for an advance into its homeland were scotched as being too daring and more time was lost. It was a war of lost time and lost opportunity and for Marlborough, who could see his political enemies at home gaining the ascendancy, it was a race against time, and one that, unlike his battles, he lost. In the following year the battle of **Malplaquet** took place, and although it was not a victory of the magnitude of the previous ones, the French were driven, largely by their own ineptitude in attack and their misinterpretation of Marlborough's intentions, from a strong position, and *Mons* was captured soon after. The Honour **Malplaquet** was awarded to twenty-two regiments, the 94th suffering its usual fate.

The years 1710 and 1711 were again ones of manoeuvre, which culminated in one of Marlborough's greatest achievements, the outwitting of France's best general, Villars, by bluff and the capture of the fortress of *Bouchain*.

The battle was unhonoured, but seventeen regiments took part of which two claimed it as an Honour. It was the last battle of the war and only two fortresses remained between his victorious army and Paris, but he was removed from his command by political intrigue at the moment when total success was within his grasp.

Most of the other battles, both in Flanders and Spain, were lesser affairs in terms of numbers engaged and importance to the result of the war as a whole, although this does not mean that they were any less taxing or sanguinary as far as the soldiery was concerned. One other battle, however, does merit attention in terms of its size, and particularly because of its bloodiness. It is the only one in Spain, apart from the capture of **Gibraltar** in 1704 and 1705, for which eight regiments were Honoured, that had any real impact on events.

The battle was *Almanza* in April 1707. Twenty-nine British regiments took part, of which nine soon afterwards ceased to exist, and of which seven have applied for the Honour, making it the biggest battle of the whole war in respect of the numbers engaged. It was perhaps mainly notable, or notorious, because it was a resounding defeat, one of the very few, largely due to the ineptness of our allies there, the Portuguese, and their lack of steadiness in the face of cold steel; as many regiments surrendered in the process as at Yorktown 74 years later, even if the outcome of the disaster was less momentous. On a happier note, the badge of the 9th Foot (The Norfolk Regiment) dates from this battle, where it was awarded to the regiment for gallantry, and gave rise to one of that regiment's nicknames, 'The Holy Boys'.

Seven Cavalry, two Guards and twenty-nine Infantry regiments participated in the campaign in Flanders, of which thirteen claimed a campaign Honour, and ten Cavalry, three Guards and forty-nine Infantry regiments were involved in the Peninsula, claimed as an Honour by seventeen of them.

The War of the Austrian Succession, 1742–8

The period from 1713 to 1742 was a comparatively quiet one, during which no Honours were granted. In 1715 there occurred the Old Pretender's Rising, and the battles of *Sheriffmuir* and *Preston*, and four years later began a protracted, but not very interesting, war with Spain which was more naval than military in flavour. One small battle took place in Scotland, at *Glenshiel* in 1719, when supporters of the Stuarts backed by the French again tried to rally the Clans, one of the few against foreign troops on British soil. Another took place at *Vigo* in the same year, and the war finished with the first siege of *Gibraltar* during its British ownership which lasted for four months in 1727. Thirteen regiments participated in the siege, of which seven claimed an Honour unsuccessfully. The only other fighting during these twenty-nine years was at *Fort St Lazar* in 1741 during the curiously named War of Jenkins Ear, which again had a naval beginning, as every schoolboy knows, and was mainly naval in character throughout until the final storming and capture of the fort at *Cartagena*.

But in 1742 the scene moved back to Northern Europe

in an attempt to sort out the knotty problems of the Austrian as opposed to the Spanish succession, and it was to be a very long time before there was such a long period of peace again. It was the third round of the struggle with France and before it was over had involved 40 regiments, of which only one was short-lived. In terms of Honours granted, this war fared no better than earlier ones, only one battle out of eight justifiably meritorious actions being commemorated, and apart from one incident even this battle might not have been Honoured, although it involved twenty-five regiments and was a success, if hardly a resounding one.

This was the battle of **Dettingen** in June 1743. It has gone down into history, and was probably Honoured, more because it was the last battle in which the Army was commanded by a British king in person, George II in this case, than for any other reason; it is very doubtful whether his presence added in any measure to the success of the engagement, but there is equally no doubt that his experiences deterred him from any further appearances on the field of battle. Ten Cavalry, the three Guards and twelve infantry regiments gained this Honour.

As so often happened there was a period of maneouvring and coming and going generally before the armies could reach the same point at the same time and be brought to battle again. Then there occurred one of the most underestimated feats of British arms, and probably the battle above all others that should have been honoured and was not, *Fontenoy*. On the precepts of the day the decision not to grant an Honour was undoubtedly correct, as the fighting ended in an indeterminate draw, but in the light of later knowledge and more progressive ideas, and considering some of the battles which have been Honoured since or for which claims for Honours have been upheld, it is very strange that it has not been granted in retrospect. It seems particularly strange since nineteen of the twenty-eight regiments involved in this battle in 1745 have applied for it at one time or another, including the whole of the Household Brigade as then constituted. After these battles only two stand out, *Roucoux* and *Lauffeld* (sometimes called *Val*), in terms of the numbers participating, eleven and twenty regiments respectively.

During the hostilities in Europe a number of regiments were recalled to Britain, most of them later returning to Flanders, to parry the threat created by Bonnie Prince Charlie and the Young Pretender's Rebellion, as it was officially known. The rising did not last long and the battle of *Culloden*, which ended both the rising and Stuart hopes of regaining the throne, almost brought to an end many of the Scottish clans and resulted in their proscription and the banning of the tartan for many years. It also indirectly led to the land clearances and thus to some of the political problems between England and Scotland. The battle was of course not honoured, being regarded as a civil war rather than an invasion, but three Cavalry and fifteen Infantry regiments were involved and one of these, the 48th Foot (The Northamptonshire Regiment) claimed it as an Honour.

India 1751–5

Apart from one isolated incident, the scene of the activities of the British Army now moves for the first time out of Europe and to the Indian sub-continent, which was to be the stage for so much fighting and so many bloody battles during the next century.

British interest in India started with trading posts set up by what was to become the East India Company near Masulipatam on the east coast and north of Bombay on the west coast at the beginning of the 17th century. Gradually the number of trading posts or factories increased in spite of trading interests by the French, Dutch and Portuguese in the same part of the world, and by the end of the century they were dotted all along the coastline of India; for control purposes the Company had divided the sub-continent into three areas, even then known as Presidencies, with their individual headquarters at Fort St George in Madras, at Fort William at Calcutta in Bengal, and at Bombay, which had been another part of Catherine of Braganza's dowry to King Charles II and which he had sold to the East India Company to help defray the expenses of some of his extravagant and costly hobbies.

Meanwhile, among the indigenous population, the power of the Mogul Empire had decreased; a new Hindu power, the Mahrattas, had arisen, and the Sikhs, until then purely a religious sect, had become a military brotherhood. Apart from some posts in India itself, the Dutch had initially concentrated mainly in Ceylon and the East Indian islands, and the French in Mauritius and Réunion (Bourbon), but by the middle of the 18th century the French had established a number of trading posts on the east coast.

During the War of the Austrian Succession the French attacked and captured Madras, partly due to the greed of the Nawab of the Carnatic who had expected a handsome bribe from the East India Company in exchange for his support but did not get it, and partly due to the weakness of the Governor and his military Commander. They then fought and won a local war with the natives of the Carnatic, the strip of coast around Madras, having established and recognised the superiority of even a small force under European officers over the much larger but less disciplined native armies.

The British attacked the French fort at Pondicherry but, in spite of the arrival of Major Stringer Lawrence, an experienced soldier, and the assistance given to him by a young clerk in the Company's service, Robert Clive, who had recently become an ensign in the Presidency army, this was wholly unsuccessful. The operation was put under command of the senior officer present who happened to be an admiral, Boscawen, even whose friends admitted that he was entirely inexperienced in military matters. The situation was stalemate and peace was declared the following year.

In 1751 in the general chaos caused by the decline of the Moguls, rival claimants now appeared for the throne of the Carnatic. The French, with visions of a great eastern Empire, supported one of these claimants, from a sense of self-preservation the English supported another, and war was joined once more.

After initial reverses Clive, now a Captain in the little

Madras Army, attacked and captured Arcot, the capital of the Carnatic and the seat of the French nominee, with little opposition, but was then besieged in the fort until the besiegers attempted to storm it and were beaten off with very heavy losses. This victory was followed up and the French interests were eventually totally defeated. **Arcot** was the first Battle Honour awarded for battles in India and was unique; 'was' because it was borne by the Madras Presidency Regiment, which became first the 102nd Foot on the British establishment in 1861, later The Royal Dublin Fusiliers, and was disbanded along with the other Irish regiments in 1922. Thus, sadly, the first, and in fact a large number of subsequent, Honours awarded for service in India to the Presidency regiments, no longer appear on the Colours of any regiment in the British Army.

Between 1751 and the next important battle six years later the first regiment of the British Army, as opposed to the Presidency armies which were nevertheless composed largely of British soldiers, arrived in India. This was the 39th Foot, later to become the 1st Battalion of the Dorsetshire Regiment and to take as its regimental motto 'Primus in Indis', who with a small detachment of Artillery landed in 1754.

North America, 1755

About the same time as British interests were establishing trading posts in India, they were also establishing settlements in North America, the first being at Jamestown in Virginia in 1608. Where the British went so did the French, and in the same year the latter organised a settlement at Quebec on the St Lawrence river. Each expanded in their own way over the next century or so, the British developing colonies between the east coast and the Allegheny mountains in the fertile lands of New England, and the French extending along the St Lawrence, across the Great Lakes and down the Ohio and Mississippi rivers, in less genial climates and in the face of greater difficulties from the terrain and the native Indian tribes, to create New France. Inevitably their interests clashed as the French fortified Louisberg on Cape Breton Island as a naval base, fortified Crown Point on the route from New York to Montreal via the Hudson River and Lake Champlain and well inside the British sphere of interest, and set up a chain of forts along the western boundary of Pennsylvania which limited the expansion of British territory and trade.

When the European war broke out in 1742 it spread to North America as it did to India by virtue of French expansionist dreams (and of course British ones although these were imbued with divine right!), and when the French garrison of Louisburg attacked British settlements in Nova Scotia the British retaliated by attacking and capturing Louisburg itself in 1745. When the war finished in Europe, and Louisburg was returned to France in exchange for Madras which was considered of greater value to British merchants, trading interests caused the hostilities to continue in America, and Fort Duquesne, now Pittsburg, on the Ohio River was unsuccessfully attacked by a small force under Major George Washington, then a Militia officer of Virginia. The lack of success of his enterprise resulted in two more British regiments, the 44th and 48th

Foot (The Essex and Northamptonshire Regiments respectively), being sent out under General George Braddock to support the colonists and to complete the job which the Virginians had started.

The 40th Foot (The South Lancashire Regiment) was already in North America, and in 1755 had successfully attacked *Fort Beausejour*, when Braddock set out with his two regiments for Fort Duquesne; nearing it he was ambushed on the *Monongahela* River by a force of Indians under French officers and his force was massacred. This action was not recognised as a Battle Honour, because it was a terrible defeat and there was very little honour in it, although the troops put up a gallant resistance in impossible circumstances. But it nevertheless eventually had a significant and lasting effect on British military tactics; it was realised that the parade ground tactics employed in a set-piece battle on European battlefields, of lines and columns of troops in close order, could not be suitable when a different type of enemy was encountered in his own surroundings, inimical to European troops, and that tactics must be adapted to the terrain and the antagonist. It was also realised that the bright scarlet coats of the British soldiers and their heavy load of equipment did not lend themselves to fighting in forests where the more accustomed enemy could take advantage of the cover afforded by trees and rocks.

But the lessons, exemplified by the campaigns in the Western Desert and the Burmese jungles of 1941 to 1945, were only learnt very slowly, and it was to be another hundred years before the dictates of necessity were to influence the chairbound authorities in Whitehall sufficiently for them to appreciate that dress uniforms, which looked gorgeous and appealed to their sartorial instincts, and drill movements performed at Aldershot and similar haunts of the military, were not appropriate to fighting in parts of the world which could not by any stretch of the imagination, be likened to parade grounds.

The Seven Years War, 1756–63

The stage was now set, after a few years of nominal peace, not only in Europe but around the world, for the next round of the Anglo–French striving for power: not merely political power but the economic power which was derived from colonisation and from increasing trade in what were then, and in some cases still remain, outlandish parts of the globe.

Although the War of the Austrian Succession had led to limited and comparatively minor actions in India and North America, this was the first time that the British Army was called upon to mount major campaigns and deploy large forces in theatres other than Europe. The result was the conquest of India and Canada, as well as battles in other parts of North America, in the Mediterranean and in the West Indies.

In 1756, when war again broke out, the French, who had for some time been planning an assault on the British Isles, needed to direct the British fleet away from the English Channel and did this by an attack on *Minorca*. The attack led to an immediate success, which surpassed their intentions and expectations, and the capture of the island which was only defended by four regiments. Admiral Byng, who commanded the naval force sent to relieve Port Mahon, was too timid to take on an equally powerful French fleet supporting the landing and retired to Gibraltar, leaving the island to its fate. He paid the penalty for his temerity, being found guilty by a Court Martial of 'not having done his utmost against the enemy' and was shot, as Voltaire said, '*pour encourager les autres*'.

Europe

So the battle lines were drawn in Europe, although chronologically, as far as Britain was concerned, activity here took place later than in other areas where campaigns had been in progress for nearly three years; Pitt in fact regarded this theatre as of secondary importance to the primary objects of lopping off French possessions overseas. In 1759 a large British force moved into Westphalia; none too soon because the allied Hanoverian and Prussian forces had been forced back by a French advance from the Rhine until they held a position, albeit a strong one, on the River Weser at **Minden**. Time allowed only six British Infantry regiments and five Cavalry regiments to join this combined army, and their commander then managed to misunderstand an order from the Hanoverian Commander-in-Chief. As the battle commenced the Infantry, all alone, marched with beat of drums directly at the French Cavalry, which charged several times and each time was met with a withering fire until they and the whole French army had had enough. The regiments were described by Thomas Carlyle as 'those unsurpassable Six, in industrious valour unsurpassable'. The story goes that the regiments advanced through rose gardens and picked flowers which they stuck in their hats, so giving rise to the tradition of the Minden rose which is still worn by members of those six regiments when they celebrate the annual anniversary of their victory. The five regiments of Cavalry, together with some German horse, were in reserve under Lord George Sackville and might well have been able to reduce the considerable Infantry casualties; but although ordered to attack, Sackville ignored the order, some said because of his jealousy of a foreign Commander-in-Chief, and furthermore instructed his second-in-command, Lord Granby, not to obey it either, so that the mass of horsemen had to sit impotently by and watch their comrades being mown down. Although he was sacked, Sackville escaped such equally justified punishment as was handed out to Admiral Byng through the machinations of his aristocratic Whig friends; not only that but 18 years later he appeared again upon the scene, this time, as Lord George Germaine, as Secretary of State for War to mismanage the campaign against the revolting American colonies.

The Royal Artillery also gained what were eventually to become two Honour titles for the batteries which participated so gallantly and helped to take the place of the missing cavalry, the **Minden Batteries**. These were the earliest to be awarded for European battles, although two others were awarded for prior actions, one in India to a Presidency army battery, which later became part of the Royal Artillery, at **Plassey** and one in North America at **Louisburg**.

Perhaps other countries have the same problem as the British, although it does not usually seem so obvious in wars against them, in having so often to suffer the follies of incompetents both in the field and in the government in the early stages of any war they fight. Perhaps the British see their mistakes sooner, because somehow they manage to appoint the right men eventually and win the war if not the opening battles, although sometimes, as at Minden, the incompetence of the commanders in the early stages is negated by the gallantry of the soldiery, even though sometimes, as during the American War of Independence, the gallantry does not quite manage to negate gross incompetence.

More British regiments, Cavalry and Infantry, were sent to Germany, and buoyed by the victory at Minden an attack on the French was mounted against heavy odds at *Sachsenhausen* (or *Corbach*—as this battle was not considered worthy of Honour no specific name has been accepted for it); although the attack failed the British regiments covered the allied retreat and themselves in glory. This battle was followed by a remarkable Cavalry achievement when the 15th Light Dragoons, who had only been raised the previous year and were the only British representatives in a small force, not only helped in the defeat of the French at **Emsdorf**, but chased them for 20 miles and finally forced them to surrender; this became one of the comparatively few unique Honours on the list.

A fortnight later an ill-considered advance by a large French army left it in a position vulnerable to attack and the challenge was accepted. The Infantry was only marginally engaged, but the Marquis Granby, the man after whom so many English inns were named on account of this peculiarly British idea of an accolade, was determined to recover the good name of the Cavalry after Sackville's disgrace at Minden, and personally led the charge of twelve regiments of horse against overwhelming odds. The French were routed and suffered very heavy casualties; the twelve Cavalry regiments were awarded **Warburg** as the Honour for the battle, but the two Infantry regiments involved, in spite of subsequent claims, were not.

The final battle in a successful summer of campaigning in 1761 was again unhonoured, presumably because it was not a victory; at *Kloster Kampen* the unusual expedient of a night attack was attempted against a large french force moving to raise the siege of that town. Unfortunately it was unsuccessful and the allied army was forced to retreat in some confusion owing to the darkness; the outcome might have been a disaster but for the gallant and desperate fighting of a small British contingent of eight Infantry and four Cavalry regiments and another fine charge by the 15th Light Dragoons. After the usual winter rest it was the turn of the French to attemp to attack at *Vellinghausen* sometimes known as *Kirsh Denkern*; largely thanks to the British force, which comprised the majority of the Army in Germany, several attacks were broken and the battle was called off, once again leaving no tangible record of their achievements on their Colours.

The war in Europe was drawing to a close, largely because no outright result could be foreseen and it had been expensive in war and materials for all the contestants. Two battles remained to be fought in 1762 and the first of them, Wilhelmsthal, provided one of those irrational situations with regard to Battle Honours which have dogged the Army's history. Practically the whole British army in Westphalia was engaged and did some sterling work in attacks on the French, almost destroying one rearguard force. But it happened that one regiment in particular, the 5th Foot (The Royal Northumberland Fusiliers), greatly distinguished itself by capturing a large number of prisoners, including the French Grenadier battalion; in commemoration of this feat the Regiment was given permission to wear a grenadier-type head-dress, and was awarded **Wilhelmsthal** as a unique Battle Honour. Admittedly most, but not all, of the Infantry regiments participating were represented by their Grenadier or flank companies rather than by the whole battalion, and the Cavalry similarly was mostly represented by detachments; nevertheless precedents exist, most recently in the Falkland Islands to the Blues and Royals, for a departure from the rule book as far as these regiments were concerned, and it seems in any case to be an unreasonable discrimination against the eight cavalry regiments, the three regiments of Foot Guards and the three Infantry regiments which were fully involved that they were not also awarded the Honour, in spite of applications for it. It would not have been unduly overgenerous to have awarded the Honour to the remaining regiments which took part in a memorable battle, even in retrospect.

The final battle was a small action, only involving nine regiments, at *Amöneberg*, but the manner in which that contingent conducted and distingushed itself should have made the battle worthy of Honour. The campaign as a whole, then, provided four Battle Honours for the roll of fame, of which two are unique, little enough to show for most regiments for four summers of sometimes desperate fighting.

North America

It is now time to consider the North American campaign, which was to be one of Pitt's major efforts during the war. Eight regiments were sent out, but the only significant action in 1757 was a French attack supported by Indians on *Fort William Henry* which was defended by the 35th Foot (The Royal Sussex Regiment) and, as has been said earlier, is thought to have provided the historical basis of Fennimore Cooper's book *The Last of the Mohicans*. The campaign in the following year opened with a three pronged attack, on **Louisburg** for which an Honour was awarded to 13 regiments and *Fort Duquesne*, which were successfully captured, and on *Fort Ticonderoga* on the Champlain–Hudson route into Canada, which was a disastrous failure due to General Abercrombie's lack of adaptability to the new type of warfare and his repeated frontal attacks against an almost impregnable position. This is one of the few British battles which have been reconstructed on the actual ground, and the *chevaux-de-frise* and the breastworks protected by spiked posts on which the 42nd Foot (The Black Watch), one of the seven regiments involved, lost so many men in their very first battle clearly indicate now, and should have indicated then to any but the most bigoted General, the improbability of

the tactics used bringing success. The memorial to the battle on the site quotes the regiments which took part under their titles then current.

In spite of this British failure the French were now on the retreat in Canada, and 1759 opened with the capture of *Fort Niagara* and another attack on *Fort Ticonderoga*, which this time was conducted more expeditiously and met with success. The goal was now the demise of French power by the capture of Quebec by an army under General James Wolfe. So much has been written about the conduct and the tactics of this battle, one of the most famous British feats of arms, that it need not be repeated here; nevertheless it was a magnificent victory in the face of difficult terrain and the main French army. The destruction by Quebecois separatists a few years ago of the column raised over the place where Wolfe died, in revenge and in an attempt to expurge the defeat of the French from the minds of the inhabitants, must be reckoned as one of the most pointless iconoclastic exercises, ranking with the destruction of so many church monuments in the 17th century by Cromwell's puritans. Seven regiments were awarded the Honour **Quebec 1759** and it is a pity that the Honour for the battle was not awarded to those regiments whose grenadier companies comprised, as a regiment, the 'Louisburg Grenadiers', but again the rules of the day were rigidly observed.

But the capture of Canada was not yet complete. The French attempted to recapture Quebec the following year by a second battle on the Plains of Abraham, this time entitled the battle of *Sainte Foy*, in which nine regiments participated. This resulted in the withdrawal of the British behind the fortifications of the city, and victory was only finally assured by a multi-directional British attack on Montreal which fell on 8 September. French Canada ceased to exist. Or so it was thought, although modern history shows that the spirit of France did not die in Quebec, mainly due to the extreme moderation of the British obligations placed on the population, who were allowed to retain their own language, their religion and their customs. It is interesting to note today the large number of solely French-speaking Canadians, if such a dialect can truly be called French, with Scottish names, descendants of the troops who accepted discharge in Canada in exchange for land in an abortive attempt to lead the local people into becoming British by example, by infiltration and by peaceable means rather than by harsh rule. A good idea, but one which only too obviously failed.

Only **Louisburg** and **Quebec** figure in the list of battles deemed worthy of Honour, although twenty-two regiments were involved in the long campaign for which many have laid claim to a Campaign Honour.

India

And so to the second prong of Pitt's strategy against the French which led to the death of their aspirations in the Indias and left Britain as the major power in the East. Events there open in 1756 with a memorable tragedy, not really connected with the Seven Years War at all, known to everybody as the Black Hole of Calcutta. The ruler of Bengal was Siraj-ud-Daula, a boy of under twenty who had recently succeeded his great uncle, who was a drunkard, debauched, treacherous and a megalomaniac who hated the Europeans and lusted for power and money. He captured the British fort at Fort William and imprisoned the 146 survivors, including one woman, of the siege in a small airless room from which only a handful escaped alive. Retribution was as swift as it could be in a vast country as yet sparsely garrisoned, and it was not until early in the following year that a small force recaptured the fort after two desperate but successful attacks at the mouth of the River *Hooghli* and on the *Mahratta Ditch*, by the 39th Foot (The Dorsetshire Regiment).

Siraj-ud-Daula, although chastened, was still a problem but a plot to overthrow him by his Commander-in-Chief, Mir Jafir, helped the British as he sought their help, and Clive gave it in exchange for a promise that all the French factories in Bengal should be handed over to the East India Company if the plot was successful. In spite of odds against him of twenty to one Clive attacked Siraj-ud-Daula's army, and apart from the help given by the defection, or rather the non-activity, of the forces loyal to Mir Jafir, a torrential downpour also came to the British assistance by damping both the spirits and the powder of the Bengali forces. The fighting was in fact minimal, and the total casualties only twenty British and fifty Sepoys, but the action has a high place in British history as the Battle of Plassey, the battle which first established British power in India and the basis for the eventual empire. **Plassey** was the first Battle Honour to be won by the King's troops in India, the Honour being awarded to the 39th Foot as well as to the three Presidency regiments and one regiment of Bengal Native Infantry which subsequently mutinied.

Madras provided the setting for the next part of the campaign, and during the next three years decisive battles were fought against the French, with Indian support, at **Condore, Masulipatam, Wandewash** and **Pondicherry**, and against the Dutch in Bengal at **Badara**, described by Clive as 'short, bloody and decisive', which finally destroyed the power and influence of both these countries on the sub-continent. All these battles were Honoured, although none of them now appear on the Colours as they were awarded to Presidency regiments—a rare event but explainable. They were awarded by the East India Company and ratified a century later when the regiments which were engaged became part of the British Army, and not by the British government which, predictably, did not, either at the time or in 1861, award the Honours to the British regiments which took part, even retrospectively. Admittedly these King's regiments were themselves of short duration, but this should not have militated against them at the time when their future was unknown, and there are precedents of Honours awarded to disbanded regiments being allowed to be borne by their successor regiments of the same number.

With the foreign powers in India eliminated there now began a long struggle against the warlike races of that country; most of the accounts of these battles will occur in later chapters but the earliest clashes took place during the period of the Seven Years War, largely due to dying support of the Indian rulers by the French, ever hopeful of a lucky break and of regaining their position and influence. Taking them in chronological order and context also serves to exemplify the commitments on the still comparatively small British Army in a world-wide war.

In 1760 the nominal Mogul Emperor, Shah Alum, attempted to regain control of his Empire, but was defeated in battles at *Patna, Seerpore* and *Beerpore*, none of which were commemorated. Three years later Mir Kassim, the Nawab of Oude, rose against the British whose nominee he was in that post and precipitated a fifteen-month campaign with battles at *Kutwah, Gheriah, Oondwa Nullah* and *Patna*; that at Oondwa Nullah was particularly bloody and was the scene of heavy casualties and great gallantry by the 84th Foot, another regiment which did not survive the peace, and at Patna three regiments of Bengal sepoys were totally destroyed.

The campaign finally came to an end with Kassim and Shah Alum jointly being completely crushed at the battle of **Buxar** in 1764, the only one of the campaign which was Honoured; this was virtually a Campaign Honour, although once again only awarded to the Presidency Army troops and to Bengal Native Infantry regiments in spite of British regiments having been heavily involved in the campaign.

Before the narrative leaves the East one final action must be recorded, being the only time that British troops ever fought in the area. This was an attack on the Philippine Islands by a force provided by the East India Company as an embarrassment to Spain, and the capture of *Manila* in 1762 by the 79th Foot; this was a short-lived regiment, and so no Honour was awarded for this battle, although this was perhaps not the only reason.

The West Indies

Most of the other recognised battles of the war took place in the Caribbean and were basically the result of British naval power. In 1758 *Martinique* was captured by a single British regiment but the forces withdrew. The following year **Guadeloupe** was once again captured after a siege by a sizable force of eight regiments. In 1761 **Belleisle**, at the entrance to the Gulf of St Lawrence, and *Dominica* were taken. In 1762 **Martinique** was again captured, as were St Lucia, Grenada and St Vincent virtually without fighting and *Dominica* was successfully defended. Also in that year siege was laid to **Havannah** by a large force and after two months it capitulated; this siege provided the first example of an Honour being awarded for an action within a battle, to the 56th Foot (The Essex Regiment) who captured the fort at **The Moro**, although it was not the only regiment which took part in the assault.

So **Guadeloupe 1759, Martinique 1762** and **Havannah** were Honoured, but neither of the actions in *Dominica* were; **Belleisle** was Honoured although it is doubtful if it was any more testing as a battle than many of those through the years which were not, and in any case it is a wonder how so many troops, eight Honoured regiments and six unhonoured ones, managed to get on to such a tiny island.

The Treaty of Paris

All sides were by now ready for peace, not least among them King George III, who had come to the throne during the war, and a party of his friends. To achieve this end Pitt was overthrown, and, as was to happen 183 years later the organiser of victory was allowed no part in the negotiation of peace or the subsequent revival of the country.

In practical terms the result of the treaty was favourable to Britain in that she now held Canada and India, although both were to be troublesome in the future; but most of the remaining captures from France and Spain in the West Indies, including Belleisle, and in the Far East were handed back in exchange for the doubtful asset of Minorca. Nevertheless the nucleus of an Empire had been gained, and British regiments, who had now had experience in a variety of terrains and against a variety of adversaries outside Europe, were to carry visible evidence of that in the names **Plassey, Louisburg, Quebec** and **Minden** amongst others borne on the Colours. For all that only twelve Honours were awarded out of forty-one actions which today would probably have been regarded as meriting recognition, and there were no Campaign Honours for North America, the West Indies or for Westphalia, although India was to be covered in this respect subsequently.

Years of Peace, 1763–75

The twelve years following the end of the Seven Years War and the signing of the Treaty of Paris at Fontainebleau were again ones of comparative peace, but only in the European context. In North America there had been an Indian rising led by Chief Pontiac in 1763, which resulted in one minor battle at *Bushy Run*, and a Campaign Honour, the first such honour to be awarded by the British government unless Tangier is so regarded, of **North America 1763–64**. This was gained by two regiments, the 42nd Foot (The Black Watch) and the 60th Foot (The King's Royal Rifle Corps). The latter regiment had been raised in America after Braddock's disaster, recruited mainly among German and Swiss settlers and known as The Royal Americans, and specially dressed, armed with rifles and trained for fighting in the terrain of the eastern American colonies. The Honour was not awarded to Montgomery's Highlanders, a local regiment, which although borne on the regular strength of the Army at that time did not survive long afterwards. In the West Indies the Carib War had taken place, now forgotten but claimed as an Honour, and of course refused, by one regiment, the 14th Foot (The West Yorkshire Regiment).

In India a Muslim adventurer, Hydar Ali, had gained possession of the predominantly Hindu state of Mysore and was thus inimical to the Madras government, who mounted a campaign against him which continued intermittently from 1767 to 1771; it was indecisive and did little to curb Hydar's power, and actions took place at *Chengamah*, *Trinomally*, **Amboor** and **Tanjore**. Of these the last was the most significant but only **Amboor** and **Tanjore** were Honoured by the Madras government in favour of a single Indian native regiment in their service for the former and one Presidency regiment and seven Indian regiments for the latter. In 1774 a small campaign was mounted against

another Indian minority sect, the Rohillas, which resulted in another Honour only held by a Presidency regiment, **Rohilcund 1774**, for the campaign, the only battle of any stature being at Miranpur Katra in which seven native regiments participated.

Perhaps at this point a short explanation of the organisation of the forces in India is appropriate; there were in fact three distinct types of regiment. First there were the King's regiments, of which only one still extant, the 39th Foot (The Dorsetshire Regiment), had so far been involved in the fighting, together with a few regiments which had been mainly raised for service in that country and whose period on the roll of regular regiments was limited. Secondly there were the regiments of the Presidency armies, at this time only one to each Presidency, supported by a few batteries of Artillery, which had British, or at any rate European, personnel and were totally in the service of and controlled by the East India Company. Thirdly there were the native forces, the Sepoy regiments, also in the service of the Company, with British officers who often raised the regiments themselves and gave their names to them, with a limited knowledge of battle drill, but capable of hard fighting so long as the British regiments fighting alongside them stood firm, and dressed in white tunics in contrast to the scarlet jackets of the British regiments.

It was the Presidency regiments who were transfered to the British army in 1861 when India became an Empire, and were mostly then given Irish ititles, only to be disbanded in 1922. It was the Native forces, which over the years had become very numerous both as Infantry and Cavalry, or at least some of them, which mutinied in 1857 and whose survivors were formed into the Indian Army.

The War of American Independence, 1775–83

Because of their remoteness from Britain, the American colonies had largely been a law unto themselves since their foundation. They had raised Militia regiments, which had on occasion supported the British regiments, usually only when they could not avoid doing so, against depredations by the French and by the native Indians. Any efforts at greater control from England were resisted, as were the levies raised on them to contribute to the costs of the war against the French, which had at least partly been fought for their protection both in terms of life and trade.

Taxes were levied on imported commodities and eventually the colonials signified their grievances by the Boston Tea Party; the penal measures imposed by Britain, governed at that time by one of the most disastrous Prime Ministers that his country has ever had the misfortune to merit, Lord North, resulted in the colonists meeting in Congress at Philadelphia and drawing up the Declaration of Rights. War was now inevitable, although support for secession from more than a minority of the colonial population was by no means a certainty, and the virtually non-existent American Army would have to pit its meagre strength against the experienced professional army of the mother country. Although the war started purely and simply as a colonial struggle, before it came to an end the old enemy, France, was to take an active part on sea and land, and a renegade Frenchman, the Marquis de Lafayette, was to become one of America's most successful generals.

From the point of view of Battle Honours it was a non-event, as it was regarded by their lordships as a civil war and therefore not entitled to be recognised. In addition it was a snub to the eventual success of the infant state in worsting the British Army by refusing to consider the war as anything more than a series of local actions. Although it is perhaps a matter of judgement whether war against a colonial uprising is strictly a civil war, they were maybe correct at the time in their view, but many of the fifty-two regiments involved during the six and a half years between Lexington and Yorktown have disagreed and unsuccessfully claimed Honours for one or another of the 29 battles which could have merited recognition. And these were battles which were by no means sinecures, and during which as much or more hard action was seen than in many other wars which have been commemorated. It depends perhaps on what is being honoured; whether in fact it is the regiment, for having taken part in a battle for the aggrandisement or the defence of its motherland whatever the result, or whether it is the authorities themselves, for having achieved success vicariously through that regiment for their policies.

As a war, it was a chronicle of mistakes and missed opportunities by both sides, although the mistakes of the professional British Army were by far the more reprehensible; mostly they were the result of the low level of generalship which, with a few notable exceptions, characterise the early, if not the later, history of the war, and to the interference of politicians in London, most of who had no knowledge of warfare and were more interested in their personal prestige. It is interesting to conjecture how the face of history might have been changed if James Wolfe, who would have been less than fifty years old when the American war started, had survived Quebec.

In a large country, where the enemy could not be easily brought to battle if he chose not to be so compelled, it was difficult to achieve any very decisive engagements; there were few strategic lines or centres which, if captured and held, could influence the war. There were never enough troops for the task and no more were available through recruitment, since such service was not popular for a wage which provided little more than a starvation level of subsistence for the soldier himself and nothing for the soldier's family at home. And anyway the enemy was American, regarded basically as a sister nation, and there could be relatives, and quite close ones at that, on the opposing side.

Finally, there had been little time to learn the lessons of the war against the French in America for fighting in broken, wooded country against an enemy well used to his environment by having lived in it, and well used to firearms since they often formed his main means of subsistence. Some of the younger leaders had absorbed the new tactics, but not being in overall command had very little opportunity to impress their views on their seniors who had been blooded on European battlefields. Nevertheless, the Army was trained to fight and disciplined.

Not that in some respects the American Army was any better off, being extremely ill-supplied and being equally at the mercy of squabbling politicians. But it had in George Washington as Commander-in-Chief a man of iron will and implacable determination, who managed to hold the ragged and poorly-equipped army together, with valuable support from his wife Martha, until it could absorb enough training and discipline to make it more than a match for the British. And in the final event it must not be forgotten that the men who started the war as colonists were fighting for their freedom as an independent nation, and self-preservation is perhaps the strongest of all reasons to give of one's best, particularly in impossible situations.

At first all went comparatively well for the British, in spite of heavy casualties caused by abortive frontal attacks on *Bunker Hill* by sixteen regiments of overladen soldiery, in stifling hot uniforms, led by officers who were only too easily identifiable and could be picked off by good marksmanship, in which field the Americans had a decided edge, early in the attacks. An early attack by the Americans on *Quebec* defended by a single British regiment, the 7th Foot, failed to generate any French support and was easily defeated.

In 1776 General Howe gained the ascendent by winning the Battles of *Brooklyn* and *White Plains* and capturing *Fort Washington* and *Long Island*, and Washington and his Army were forced to retreat towards Philadelphia and to spend a miserable and starving winter among the snows at Valley Forge. Thirty regiments were involved at Brooklyn, nine at White Plains and fifteen at Fort Washington, so these were not exactly skirmishes. The following year opened with a plan for a pincer attack on the Hudson valley, General Burgoyne advancing south from Canada and General Clinton north from New York; unfortunately Clinton forgot to cancel his orders for Howe to attack Washington in front of Philadelphia. Howe carried out his attack and defeated Washington at *Brandywine*, where twenty-one regiments participated, of which eight have claimed it as an Honour followed by the indecisive battle of *Bemis Heights*, sometimes known as Freeman's Farm or Stillwater. But this meant that Clinton had no Army available for his part of the plan and Burgoyne was left with no support from the south. The result was that he found himself surrounded at *Saratoga*, or Germantown, by an overwhelming force of Americans, largely led there by Benedict Arnold, and was forced to surrender with his fourteen regiments.

The terms of the surrender were ignored by the American Congress who kept the captured British in atrocious conditions in the hope of persuading them to change sides; very few did so, but Benedict Arnold defected to the British because he did not think that he had been sufficiently well rewarded for his efforts which were so much responsible for the catastrophe. Saratoga, apart from being a military disaster, had another unfortunate side effect; the French, who until then had been sitting on the fence, now saw which way the wind was beginning to blow, and estimating the probable outcome threw in their lot with the Americans.

In 1778 the British forces withdrew from Philadelphia, which they had meanwhile occupied, and concentrated round New York; it was also decided to take advantage of anticipated loyalist sympathy in the south by sending a force to the southern States, which of course had the effect of dividing the still dangerously small army, which the politicans at home still refused, or were unable, to reinforce, and negating the principle of concentration. Nevertheless the venture was attended by success in the beginning, and first *Savannah* in 1778 and again in 1779 and then *Charleston* in 1780 were captured, but the size of the force could not be maintained in the face of a possible French attack on New York and most of the Army returned there, leaving only a token force under General Cornwallis in Georgia and the Carolinas. This small force, however, kept the war going and in 1781, although having been defeated at *Cowpens*, won the battles of *Guildford* and *Hobkirk's Hill* and fought a draw at *Eutaw Springs*.

Until then Cornwallis had, as expected, had considerable support from the loyalists, but now he decided, for no apparent reason other than to lessen the gap between the two parts of the Army and to reduce his isolation, to move northward into Virginia. To his surprise, although it should have been obvious in Washington's home state, very few Virginians joined him. He therefore established himself in quite a strong position at the mouth of Chesapeake Bay at Yorktown and waited for Clinton to reinforce him; this Clinton could not do because by now the Spanish and Dutch had also joined the enemy and the British Navy had temporarily, but disastrously as it turned out, lost command of the seas. Washington seized his chance, and mustering every available man, including a large French contingent, invested *Yorktown*. Cornwallis's position was hopeless in the face of enormous odds, having only twelve regiments with him, and no possibility of succour, and in October he surrendered.

The war was practically, and for all practical purposes, over and only a humiliating peace could follow. The American colonies were lost and the United States of America, which had been formed following the adoption of the Declaration of Independence in 1776, became a sovereign nation, able to assert its right to 'life, liberty and the pursuit of happiness' and to take its place eventually among the leading Powers of the world. During the War of Independence, between 1775 and 1782, two Cavalry, three Guards and fifty Infantry regiments took part, and of these it has been claimed as an Honour by twenty-five by various titles and for various dates.

But although the war was over on land in America it was still being fought against the combined Franco-Spanish fleets at sea, as it had been since the French entered the war. In 1778 a small force, mainly comprising the Light Infantry companies of regiments otherwise engaged in the American war, captured St Lucia against heavy odds, and in the process inflicted casualties on the French greater than their own total strength. Although the Honour was worthily gained, **St Lucia 1778** was another example of muddled and ambiguous government thinking and application of the so-called rules, since on other occasions, for example Wilhelmsthal in 1762, detachments of regiments had been refused an equally worthy Honour.

Still in the West Indies, *Grenada* was captured in 1779, *St Vincent* in 1780 and *St Kitts* in 1782, but none of these were Honoured, perhaps, illogically, because they were associated with naval actions and the regiments were serving as Marines. Illogically, because the naval battle of **The Saints** in 1782 was granted as an Honour to the 69th Foot (The Welch Regiment) and is borne as an embellishment, a Naval Crown and date; it was the first naval battle to be carried on the list of Army Honours, and to this day is one of very few.

In the European theatre *Minorca*, recovered at the Treaty of Paris, was again attacked by the French, and again the small garrison of two regiments overwhelmed by numbers and disease, had to surrender. This event occurred during a long siege of **Gibraltar** which lasted from 1779 to 1783, its second since its capture in 1704; the siege was resisted with great fortitude and expertise against very heavy attacks by the besiegers, the Royal Artillery in particular distinguishing itself and four batteries later being awarded the Honour Title of **Gibraltar**. Five infantry regiments also gained the Honour for the siege, which is not borne on their Colours but was awarded as an embellishment, and is used as a cap badge showing the Rock and the motto 'Montis Insignia Calpe'; nevertheless six other regiments were involved in some way or other in the siege and they received no Honours.

The only other Honour awarded during the period in Europe is a strange one since it is one of the few awarded solely to a Militia regiment. Early in 1781 a French force attacked the Channel Islands, and in particular Jersey, where three regular regiments were stationed as well as the Militia regiment, the three battalions of the Royal Jersey Light Infantry. The attack was beaten off and the local troops were awarded the Honour **Jersey 1781**, although the regular regiments did not get a mention.

India, 1776–94

Whilst the American colonies were being lost through governmental and military mismanagement and Britain and France were again in conflict at sea and on the American continent, sporadic, though fairly continuous, warfare was being waged on the Indian sub-continent against local chieftains who resented British interference in trade and particularly in their feudal rights, often supported unofficially by the French. It is true to say that, in under twenty years, as we lost an Empire in the West we built and consolidated another one in the East.

Pondicherry was again besieged in 1778, and although no Honour was awarded for this and a later siege in 1793, the Honour awarded to the Madras Presidency regiment for the siege of 1761 was extended to cover the remainder; which perhaps met the requirements of that regiment but did nothing to commemorate the activities of the British and native Indian regiments which were involved in the later activities. Similarly a long campaign in the Bombay Presidency from 1778 to 1782 resulted in the Honour of **Guzerat** being awarded to all three Presidency regiments, and to some Bengal native Infantry regiments, all of which ceased to exist after the Mutiny seventy-five years later; but again a number of Native regiments were left out.

But the most bitter fighting took place when Hydar Ali, after biding his time following his defeat at Amboor and Tanjore, again launched his hordes against the small

British garrisons in the Carnatic; the struggle in fact continued off and on until 1799 and became known as the four Mysore Wars. They were perhaps mostly memorable, or notorious, for the ferocity of Hydar Ali, and later for the even more extreme ferocity of his son Tippoo Sahib, and of their soldiery, and for the bestial way in which any troops unlucky enough to fall prisoner were treated; it is probably true to say that any soldier was more fortunate to be killed in action than to be captured. This fact may have accounted for the extreme determination with which the meagre British forces fought against their sadistic adversaries, who made the word 'Indian' a by-word in Britain for indescribable nastiness for years to come.

The first Mysore War opened in 1780 when a small Presidency and Native force was overwhelmed at *Conjeveram*. The situation was desperate, but a force which included one British regiment, the 71st Foot (The Highland Light Infantry), under Eyre Coote, the victor of Wandewash who was now an old man, regained the initiative the following year by defeating Hydar Ali at *Porto Novo* with very heavy losses to the enemy. In spite of the loss of another garrison at *Tellicherry* this was followed up with victories at *Pollilore*, which was close enough to Conjeveram for both battles to have been given the same title, and at Sholinghur. Of these battles only **Sholinghur** was Honoured, and this became the second Honour to be gained by a King's regiment in India; Sholinghur can perhaps be regarded as a Campaign Honour for the war, but that is inconsistent with the Honour awarded, admittedly by the Presidencies and the East India Company, for the battles of 1758 to 1761.

Both sides then withdrew to lick their wounds, Hydar Ali recognising that he had erred in attacking the British in the first place, but unfortunately dying in 1782; which left Tippoo Sahib, who succeeded him and being less able and more egotistic did not agree with him, to renew the struggle in 1782 with the 2nd Mysore War. By now several more King's regiments had arrived in India and were involved in a number of desperate struggles together with the 71st Foot and both Presidency and Native regiments, until this second phase of the war finished at the end of 1783. Only one Battle Honour was awarded, for the siege of **Mangalore**, which was gained by the 73rd Foot (The Black Watch), but the actions at *Arnee, Panianee, Hyderghur, Cuddalore* and *Cananore* went unrecognised. Even Mangalore was not awarded to the 42nd Foot, part of whom were also engaged, although this became less obvious and more confusing in 1881 when they were amalgamated with the 73rd Foot.

The 3rd Mysore War broke out after a few years of relative peace in 1789 when Tippoo Sahib again took the offensive. The British Army presence had again been considerably increased, due to the raising of some regiments especially for service in India, and to the release of troops which had been engaged in North America, although only two of these regiments, the 52nd and 74th Foot (The Oxfordshire and Buckinghamshire Light Infantry and The Highland Light Infantry), as well as the 71st Foot in the early stages only, had actually been engaged in the American War. In addition Lord Cornwallis, who had had the misfortune of having to surrender at Yorktown, was now

Governor-General in Madras and personally took command in the field. After early, if inconclusive but bitter, fighting in *Travancore* and at *Cheyoor* and *Bangalore*, the British force almost reached Tippoo's capital at Seringapatam in 1791, but was forced to retire after a battle at *Arikera*. But Cornwallis tried again later in the year and after a battle at **Nundy Droog**, which was the only Battle Honour awarded during the campaign and that only by the Madras government to its Presidency regiment, attacked *Seringapatam* early in 1792 and this time, with the aid of an army from Bombay, was successful. Unfortunately Tippoo Sahib escaped in the *mêlée*, to remain a thorn in the British flesh.

Nine British regiments as well as both Presidency regiments and a large number of Native regiments were engaged at Seringapatam, but no Honour was awarded in spite of its significance. It appears that the subsequent award of **Seringapatam** in 1799 was intended to cover both actions although by this means not all the participants in 1792 gained the Honour which was their due.

Nevertheless at this time two campaign Battle Honours were awarded, **Carnatic** and **Mysore**; both covering the period from 1747 to 1792 but not even in retrospect the 4th Mysore War which was yet to come. The geographical area covered by these Honours is not very different and a distinction between them is arbitrary, and bearing in mind the niggardliness with which Honours had been awarded in the past it is difficult to see why two were now needed to cover the same period. Nevertheless it was some tangible record at long last for nearly fifty years of unpleasant and bloody fighting. Apart from the geographical aspect, the majority of the regiments concerned in the battles of the period were awarded one Honour or the other and a large number, including practically all the Native Indian regiments which survived time and the Mutiny to become Indian Army regiments, were awarded both.

Even so, many of those that were not awarded either Honour in fact qualified for them and again there appears to have been a degree of discrimination, although the history of that period is not well documented, certainly from the point of view of the Indian regiments, and it is not easy after nearly 200 years to discover whether all or only part of largely irregular forces were engaged in any particular battle. As for the British regiments, those which survived in unbroken history were mostly Honoured, but the short-lived regiments and their numerical successors were not.

The final siege of **Pondicherry** in 1793, in which six British, one Presidency and twelve Native regiments were involved, has already been referred to earlier. The 2nd Rohilla War, fought to subdue a rising in Rampur, occurred in 1794 and provided another Honour, **Rohilcund 1794**, for the Bengal Presidency regiment, although not for nine native regiments which were also involved but did not survive the next seventy years. It was not an important engagement, but is worth mentioning because the Honour, like so many others originating in India, has now disappeared from the lists as a result of the demise of the regiment's successor, The Royal Munster Fusiliers.

Considering the wars already covered, and the Honours

awarded, one thing has now become very clear, and is further exemplified in later periods. Where an Honour was awarded at the time of the battle, and very few were, it was granted to all who took part irrespective of their future status; but where the Honour was awarded in retrospect, and this applies to the award of medals too, only those who had qualified and still survived were considered. True, it is difficult to award physically an Honour to a non-existent regiment, but at least the record, if such existed at the time, could have been maintained accurately of those meet to be Honoured, a posthumous award as it were. There is no justifiable excuse for falsifying history, even accidently, by excluding the full record of participation.

Although strictly outside the period of this chapter covering the years leading up to the start of the Napoleonic Wars, it is probably advantageous from the point of view of clarity and comprehensiveness to deal now with the 4th (and last) Mysore War in 1799 before we leave India and return to events in Europe. The time had come to remove Tippoo Sahib finally, for good and all, from the scene of history, and a large army, in terms of engagements in India, was assembled and marched on Seringapatam.

Movement in India was never easy because of the problems of supplying an army over vast distances which contained few established routes of communication, and the simplest method was to take rations, for example, on the hoof. This frequently obliged a force to move in a huge square formation, so that the transport animals and the

rations, and there were over 100,000 of them in this case, could be protected from marauding enemy cavalry. This made progress very slow, probably not more than 5 miles a day.

At least this time the army was well commanded and constituted for its task; the Governor-General was now Lord Wellesley and his younger brother, Colonel Lord Arthur Wellesley (later the Duke of Wellington), was among the officers, the army being actually commanded by General Harris who was a veteran of Bunker Hill. The mass at length reached Seringapatam, after some lesser engagements at **Seedaseer** and *Mallavelli*, the former being awarded as an Honour to three Indian native regiments and the latter ignored, although in both cases British and other native regiments took part, and although 'lesser' compared with the main battle the engagements themselves were by no means insignificant. The city and the fortress were stormed and Tippoo died in the fighting. Order was at last restored in Mysore and the territory divided between the East India Company and a member of that Hindu dynasty which Hyder Ali had deposed, who became Rajah. **Seringapatam** was awarded as an Honour to nine British, two Presidency and twenty eight Indian regiments, together with two Presidency artilleries and the Madras Sappers and Miners, but not to the other two Sappers and Miners or to six other Indian regiments. The Royal Artillery gained the Honour title **Seringapatam,** awarded to two batteries.

Above: The Storming of Seringapatam 1799. Stipple engraving by J. Vendramini from a panoramic painting by P. Ker Porter. *NAM*

7 The Napoleonic Wars, 1793-1815

When William Pitt became Prime Minister in 1784 he was faced with the ravages of many years of Whig misrule, the loss of the American colonies, and an Army reduced by the disbandment of regiments after the American war and the under-recruiting of those that remained to virtual ineffectiveness. He had little enough time to prepare for the final round of the struggle with the old adversary which, did he but know it was almost upon him. But he employed what time he had to advantage, although the pressing needs of financial and domestic affairs severely limited his attention to matters military and serious deficiencies still remained in various aspects of the Army. Nevertheless by the time the Army was needed again the War Department had taken over responsibility for pay, equipment and recruiting instead of this being left to the individual regimental Colonels, barracks had begun to be built, military manuals had been produced for drill and tactics, the Militia had been put on a more serviceable footing and the Royal Artillery and the Royal Engineers had come into being as military rather than largely civilian corps.

In 1789 the revolutionary forces in France took over power. The Bastille was stormed, King Louis XVI and his Queen, Marie Antoinette, together with uncountable numbers of aristocrats went to the guillotine and the 'Terror' was born. Fanatical hordes were prepared to carry their excesses not only throughout France but to all European countries and Britain could not stand idly by, although at first Pitt tried not to become embroiled in a European war.

The Austrian Netherlands, 1793-5

The French were short of money, as revolutionaries usually are since their activities interfere with the country's normal supply from trade and other sources of income, and in 1793 attacked the Netherlands, with an eye on the Amsterdam banks. A small British Army of two brigades, which was all that was readily available, was sent to Flanders under the command of Frederick, Duke of York, to help the Dutch.

The two-year campaign produced a higher percentage of Battle Honours to battles fought than had previously been seen, six out of 17, so perhaps a more modern outlook was beginning to take shape. The Cavalry gained the lion's share of the Honours, and of the regiments which were awarded one or more of them thirteen came from this arm, their total contribution to the Army, but only six were Infantry including the three regiments of Foot Guards. And even so the total number of regiments engaged was thirty-seven, which left eighteen Infantry regiments uncommemorated, though many of these only joined the campaign for its final four months.

The campaign as a whole was badly managed as most of those in the past, and neglect, lack of food, equipment and clothing, and the disease which emanated from these deficiencies took as heavy a toll of the Army as battle casualties. The campaign opened in May 1793 with two actions at *St Amand* and *Famars*, both of which have been claimed as Honours, by which time the government had become obsessed with the need to besiege and capture Dunkirk. **Lincelles** brought an Honour to the regiments of Foot Guards and was a brilliant engagement against a superior enemy, and a week later the battle of *Rosendahl* was fought by ten regiments near Dunkirk and under the latter name was claimed by the 14th Foot (The West Yorkshire Regiment). In falling back from Dunkirk the 53rd Foot (The King's Shropshire Light Infantry) gained one of its unique Honours when beseiged in **Nieupore**, but a small Cavalry and Guards action at *Lannoy* was unrecognised.

The campaigning season of 1794 began with three brilliant Cavalry actions, in the first of which, **Villers en Cauchies**, the 15th Light Dragoons gained another unique Honour. The British Cavalry were supported by the Austrian horsemen, and at **Beaumont**, often reckoned as one of the greatest Cavalry feats of arms, where eight cavalry regiments were Honoured, and at **Willems** where eleven regiments won the Honour, they gained fresh laurels when they charged down masses of French Infantry. But these victories did little to overcome the problems caused by the numerical inferiority of the allied forces, and to make matters worse the Austrians now withdrew their army leaving the British outnumbered by four to one. A defeat at *Turcoing* was followed by a remarkable rearguard action at **Tournay** by a single brigade of three regiments against the French hordes as the army withdrew; but no reinforcements could be provided until the autumn, when the equivalent of six brigades of Infantry arrived, and by then the army was in full retreat.

A number of actions were fought during the autumn and winter, at *Boxtel*, *Druten*, *Nimeguen*, *Geldermalsen*, *Buurmalsen* and *Tiel*, some of which have been claimed as Honours, and the gallantry of the 42nd Foot (The Black Watch) at Geldermalsen, where nine other regiments were involved, gained them the right to wear a Red Hackle in their bonnets. The winter was one of the bitterest of all time and the remnants of the army retreated across Holland and North Germany to Bremen where they were embarked, suffering untold hardships from the weather, from the complete breakdown of all supply and medical services and from the indiscipline and incompetence of many of the officers.

Such was the system at the time that commissions were virtually obtainable by anyone who could afford to buy one, training was non-existent, and in any case many of the so-called officers found 'good' reasons and pressing business needs which necessitated their return to England, and comfort, rather than remaining with their regiments during one of the most disastrous retreats in the annals of the British Army. One of the officers who did stay and accompany the Army, however, although largely untrained, was so successful that he was put in command of the rearguard. He has already been mentioned briefly in the last chapter and is to figure largely in later stages of this one and the next. Colonel Arthur Wellesley, who had purchased his promotions until he commanded the 33rd Foot (The Duke of Wellington's Regiment) at the age of twenty-four without having once heard a shot fired in anger, learnt a great deal from his experiences as was to be seen in India and later in the Peninsula. It is an ill wind...

The Mediterranean, 1793-6

Only slightly less disastrous to British prestige was the campaign fought on and around the Mediterranean at the same time as that in Flanders. A small mixed force including five British regiments occupied the French naval base at *Toulon* and, although far too small for the task allotted to it, the French forces were too raw and inexperienced to do much about it and several small actions to remove the invaders met with little success. Until, that is, a young Corsican officer was appointed to command the French artillery. Napoleon Buonaparte soon saw a means of making the harbour untenable to British ships, and after his plan had been carried out Toulon had to be evacuated, the Army taking as its base for future action the island of Corsica, which might have been thought in retrospect, but was not in practice, retribution.

But *Corsica* did not surrender without a struggle and a number of sieges were laid, during one of which, with naval support, Horatio Nelson lost his eye. Apart from an attack on *Genoa* by the fleet, during which the 11th Foot (The Devonshire Regiment) made a short foray ashore, the campaign came to an end without achieving anything worth mentioning, and the forces returned to England. No Honours were awarded for any of the nine actions which were probably worthy of inclusion in the roll of battles.

The West Indies, 1793-8

The third campaign to be mounted during these sad few years of British military history was in the West Indies, where the French revolutionary principles of Liberty and Equality had set off negro risings. The sugar islands were valuable to Britain, the policy was that they had to be held

and an army was duly dispatched thither, although the ravages of disease, in particular yellow fever, were such that many soldiers never even got into action; it is estimated that perhaps as many as 100,000 men died, of whom very few were battle casualties. But the French lost just as heavily and eventually were beaten out of the islands, only for most of these same islands to be handed back yet again at the Treaty of Amiens; a frightful cost for little result beyond the French discovery at home of a method of extracting sugar from beet, necessity being the mother of invention.

Altogether during the campaign four Cavalry and fifty Infantry regiments were involved, including one locally raised battalion of the new West India Regiment, and of them nineteen have laid claim to an individual Battle or a Campaign Honour. The campaign, costly as it was, was poorly commemorated in terms of Honours awarded, there being only two, **Martinique 1794** and **St Lucia 1796**, out of a possible total of twenty-five and even in these cases not all the participants were Honoured; at Martinique eleven out of twenty-eight and at St Lucia only two out of thirteen. Apart from those two noted, *St Lucia* was also the scene of battle in 1794 and 1795, and four individual battles could be recorded for which the 1796 Honour was awarded; *Guadeloupe* in 1794 involved twenty-four regiments and two individual battles; battles occurred in *St Domingo*, the modern Haiti, in 1794 and 1796, *Grenada* in 1795 and 1796, *Jamaica* in 1795 (*the Maroon War*), *St Vincent* in 1795 and 1796 and *Porto Rico* in 1797. A remarkable lack of imagination and gratitude was thus displayed by the government, which sent so many men to unnecessary death.

No Campaign Honour was awarded to any of the regiments which took part. Apart from Guadeloupe and Martinique, however, all these islands remained in British hands after the peace and helped to lay the foundation of the British West Indies.

Miscellaneous Engagements, 1794-1801

Outside the continent of Europe but still in that geographical context, a number of raids took place by both sides which were largely unhonoured. But the period is mainly notable for three Honours which were awarded to Regiments serving as Marines in naval engagements. In 1794 Lord Howe's engagement with the French fleet off Cape Ushant, which became known as **'The Glorious 1st of June'**, resulted in an Honour, in the form of a Naval Crown and date, being granted to the 2nd and 29th Foot (The Queen's Regiment and The Worcestershire Regiment), although the 69th Foot (The Welch Regiment) were also involved and disputed their lack of recognition. The Queen's Regiment still celebrate the Honour as a regimental occasion.

In 1797 the 69th Foot were more successful, being awarded **St Vincent 1797** for the naval battle off that cape, although this time the 11th Foot (The Devonshire Regiment) were the unlucky ones and unsuccessfully applied for the Honour subsequently. Finally in 1801 came Nelson's great victory at **Copenhagen**, the Honour for which was awarded to the 49th Foot (The Royal Berkshire

Regiment) and the Rifle Brigade, both as a named Honour in the usual way and as a Naval Crown with date as an embellishment to be worn on their accoutrements—a unique case of two Honours for the same battle.

In 1798 the British carried out a raid on *Ostend* with five regiments, of which one has applied for it to be Honoured, and later in the same year *Minorca* was captured by a small force of four regiments. In 1800 an attack was mounted on the French base in Malta, occupied by them during Napoleon's journey with his army to Egypt, and resulted in the island changing hands although the Knights of St John remained in overall charge, the British occupancy lasting until very recently. The first permanent troops on the island after its capture were batteries of the Royal Artillery and their presence was maintained continuously until the last full regiment of artillery serving there left the island in 1959. **Malta** was awarded as a Battle Honour to the Royal Malta Regiment, and the 35th Foot (The Royal Sussex Regiment) bear the date as an embellishment on their badge, but the services of the 30th and 89th Foot (The East Lancashire Regiment and The Royal Irish Fusiliers), which were also involved, were not recognised.

In the opposite direction the French also carried out raids. One of these in 1797 on South Wales resulted in **Fishguard** becoming the only Honour ever awarded for an engagement in the British Isles, and that to a Militia regiment, again a rarity, The Cardigan Militia which later became The Pembroke Yeomanry. Apart from the action of the militia in dispersing the raid, two apocryphal stories are told concerning the local female population. One is that a group of Welsh women dressed in their scarlet cloaks, who were watching the engagement from the hills surrounding the port, were mistaken by the French for a body of English redcoats, and the other that women appeared in the port wearing the tall conical hats of the period and were mistaken by the French for a coven of witches. Whatever the truth, if any, of the matter this small affray has gone down into the history of the British Army as a unique occasion.

The other raid was carried out in Ireland, where rebellion was seething, inspired and abetted by the French, and where accounts of activities written at the time bear a remarkable similarity to accounts written in the press today. It resulted in an action at *Castlebar* when the 6th Foot (The Royal Warwickshire Regiment) removed the menace, which was also applied for as an Honour by the 17th and 29th Foot (The Leicestershire and Worcestershire Regiments), by the latter not so much as an Honour to themselves but for the restoration of the badge of the 'Irish Harp' awarded to the Worcestershire Militia which subsequently became part of that regiment.

Apart from the European zone two captures were made which were of significance for the future. The Netherlands having been occupied by France, Dutch colonies were regarded as legitimate prey and in 1795 a small force landed at the southern tip of Africa and seized the Dutch trading post at Cape Town. This was handed back at the Treaty of Amiens only to be attacked and recaptured, this time for good, eleven years later. A larger force of mixed British and Indian regiments attacked and captured *Ceylon*, also

in 1795, although the new colony did not fall into British hands until the following year, and even then only the maritime provinces, although the first Kandian War in 1803 subdued most of the rest of the island. It remained in their possession as a valuable coaling and naval base in the Indian Ocean until the Empire was dissipated and the island became an independent member of the Commonwealth in 1948 as Sri Lanka.

The Helder Campaign, 1799
Once again, in 1799, an attempt was made to drive the French out of the Netherlands, this time with support from the Russians, of all the unlikely allies; it was said that this arrangement came about because the Tsar was annoyed at Napoleon's seizure of Malta since he himself wanted to become Grand Master of the Order of St John.

Success attended the landing and the subsequent occupation of a bridgehead with an action at *Groete Keten*, but in September the Duke of York arrived as Commander-in-Chief, which did nothing to improve the management of the campaign, and an advance southwards met with less success because of the nature of the country, intersected with dykes, and the incompetence of the large force of Russians. An action took place on the *Zype Canal* and a major engagement at *Schoorl-Oudkarspel* involving twelve regiments was claimed by the 40th Foot (The South Lancashire Regiment) as an Honour under the title of *Alkmaar*. A second attempt to push forward the following month showed some improvement, and victory at the Battle of **Egmont op Zee** resulted in this Honour being granted to nine regiments, although it was subsequently claimed unsuccessfully by six of the remaining fourteen regiments which participated. Individual actions during this battle were fought at *Bergen* and *Schoorldam* and a few days later at *Alkmaar* again, but the onset of winter and the miserable condition of the troops, apart from the uselessness of our allies, made any further campaigning out of the question and the army was embarked for England. It was lucky that the French did not realise the plight of the army, or what was merely an ill-managed operation might have been a total disaster.

Both the campaigns in Flanders, in 1793 and 1799, were anything but successful and the trials and tribulations of those taking part were extreme, largely owing to weather and the lack of efficient administrative services, but also to the inadequacy of those in command. Most of the Army took part in one or the other, or both, for little tangible reward, and a Campaign Honour, applied for in fact by thirteen regiments as 'Flanders' and by ten regiments as 'North Holland' or 'Helder', out of the fourteen Cavalry and forty-four Infantry regiments which participated, would have been little enough recognition of their suffering. At the same time it must be accepted that the few victories were commemorated, but remembered that Dunkirk was not a victorious campaign either and yet it was covered by the campaign Honour of **North West Europe 1940**.

This campaign also saw the first engagement of an Artillery battery as a military entity, the Chestnut Troop of the Royal Horse Artillery.

India

In the years 1800 and 1801 a number of minor actions were fought in Mysore against native rulers who were backed by the French. At *Arrakaira* two British and three Indian regiments were in action, and the largest of these battles took place at *Bednore* and *Conagul* against the forces of Dhoondiah Singh in which two British and three Indian Cavalry and two British and seven Indian Infantry regiments participated. Other actions took place against the Polygars in Tinnevelly and the ceded territories in 1801—*Panjalamcoorchy*, *Caliarcoil* and *Ternakul Fort*. The 77th Foot (Middlesex Regiment) claimed 'Southern India 1800–02' as an Honour but this was refused.

Egypt, 1801

For the first time during this account of the Napoleonic Wars a real success story can be recorded, and one moreover that was reasonably well served for Honours, with a Campaign Honour, although this was in the form of an embellishment, as a badge or date on accoutrements, rather than as a clear title to be placed on the Colours, and two individual Honours for battles.

It was a short campaign lasting only five and a half months altogether, with most of the action crammed into the first seven weeks. Napoleon's invasion of Egypt in 1798, and the capture of Malta *en route*, was a hazardous adventure, and it is possible that it was accepted by the French Directoire as much as a means of ridding themselves of the general, who was becoming a thorn in its side and a danger to it, as of gaining military advantage. It is also possible that it was seen as a threat to Britain's new Empire being built in India and the East. In any case the enterprise was made more difficult by the British naval victory at Cape St Vincent, and doomed by Nelson's victory at the Battle of the Nile which annihilated Napoleon's fleet and left him cut off from France. However, Britain could not entertain a huge French force remaining in Egypt, even if it was helpless, and decided to attack it there.

The initial landing at *Aboukir* was not recognised by an Honour, although it was made in the face of a desperate French defence; the British force of twelve regiments was under the command of General Abercrombie, who had commanded the successful landing at the Helder, and General (Sir John) Moore.

A few days later several other sharp engagements took place which drove the French back to the outskirts of Alexandria; the battle of **Mandora** was granted as an Honour to the 90th and 92nd Foot (The Cameronians and The Gordon Highlanders), but those at *Roman Camp*, and at the *Mareotis Bridge* which only involved the 44th Foot (The Essex Regiment), were not. The Army then dug itself in among the sand dunes, one of the first examples of this type of defence; it turned out to be a wise precaution because a week later the French counter-attacked. A confused and desperate struggle ensued during which the 28th Foot (The Gloucestershire Regiment) gained their famous 'Back Badge', a miniature cap badge worn at the back of their caps, when they turned their rear rank about, and fighting literally back to back, drove off repeated attacks by French Cavalry.

Unfortunately Abercrombie was killed during the battle, and a memorial and a barracks for the British battalion stationed in Alexandria for the next 150 years was built on the site. Why *Alexandria* was not awarded as an Honour is even more inexplicable than the exclusion of Fontenoy, since to the seventeen participating regiments, of which four claimed it, this battle was at least a victory, and since it was recognised by the first general issue of a medal to all those who took part, although the percentage of participants who actually received it was somewhat limited because the issue was not made until thirty-eight years later!

The campaign came to an end with the storming of the fort at **Marabout** which was awarded as a unique Honour to the 54th Foot (The Dorsetshire Regiment). One interesting feature was the presence of a small Indian contingent, the first time Indian regiments had been in Egypt or in fact anywhere very far from the bounds of India itself; they arrived too late to take part in the fighting but were recognised by the Campaign Honour. The campaign also added to the Honour Titles of batteries of the Royal Artillery and subsequently there emerged a **'Sphinx Troop'**, two **'Sphinx Companies**, and two **'Sphinx Batteries**, although all five now use a common Honour title, **Sphinx Battery**.

More Miscellaneous Engagements, 1803–10

One of the problems of recording the events of the Napoleonic Wars is that they consisted of a number of clear-cut campaigns, such as those in Flanders, in Egypt and later in the Peninsula and at Waterloo, but also in a large number of minor engagements, raids and assaults. It is difficult to fit these latter events into a comprehensive story without resorting to headings such as that above, which inevitably gives the impression of unimportance. Undoubtedly some of these actions were relatively unimportant, but many of them had a lasting influence on army experience and training and on the gradual accretion of the British Empire.

In 1803 another attack was made on St Lucia, in the West Indies, handed back to France after the Treaty of Amiens which followed shortly after Napoleon's defeat in Egypt but which only resulted in a year's peace. Another Honour named after this small island, **St Lucia 1803**, came from this minor engagement, awarded to the 1st and 64th Foot (The Royal Scots and The North Staffordshire Regiment) although the 68th Foot (The Durham Light Infantry) and the West Indian regiment were also involved. This was followed in the next year by an attack on, and an Honour for, **Surinam** and in 1805 by the capture of **Dominica**; the former was awarded to the 16th Foot (The Bedfordshire and Hertfordshire Regiment) and the 64th Foot, and the latter to the 46th Foot (The Duke of Cornwall's Light Infantry) and to the West India Regiment, which thereby gained its first Honour. Although Surinam was subsequently returned to the Dutch, the other two islands were to remain permanently in British possession.

The capture of Cape Town and its return to the Dutch has already been mentioned. Once the war had restarted the threat of French interference with our communications with India occurred again, and increasing sea traffic necessitated a base *en route* to the East. Thus another expedition was mounted in 1806 and was again successful. This time Cape Town was not handed back, **Cape of Good Hope 1806** is carried on the Colours of six regiments and claimed by another two, and the foundations of an expansion of Empire in South Africa, and subsequently in East and West Africa, were laid.

In the Mediterranean, too, a British presence was maintained in support of some of the then independent Italian kingdoms, and Sicily was occupied as a base for a number of years. Although French influence in Italy was strong, King Ferdinand still ruled in Naples and with the object of bolstering up his resistance a force was landed on the mainland and advanced towards that city in 1806. It met a superior French force at **Maida** but vanquished it, mainly owing to the tactical advantage of the British line over the French column. Owing to Neapolitan feebleness and quarrels between the British land and sea commanders there was no ultimate success from the venture; seven regiments were awarded the Honour, although it is interesting to note that among these the 61st Foot (The Gloucestershire Regiment) were only represented by their Grenadier company, whilst the 56th Foot (The Essex Regiment), who were represented by their Light company, were not awarded it. Another expedition to Italy was made in 1808 when *Scilla* was beseiged but no Honour resulted.

Between these two enterprises a second expedition was sent to Egypt in 1807, much smaller and less well prepared than that six years earlier. After the removal of the Napoleonic threat Britain had withdrawn in 1803 and Egypt had returned to its nominal Turkish rule; but Turkey being now under French influence it was decided to reoccupy the country. The force captured Alexandria and then advanced towards *Rosetta* where it was defeated; a second attack also failed and the small battered Army was evacuated, having lost the prestige that had been gained in the Eastern Mediterranean in 1801.

The comparative nearness of the Cape of Good Hope to South America made British trading eyes turn in that direction and particularly towards Argentina. As it was already a rich country, it was believed that its capture would provide valuable prize money for the poorly paid sailors and soldiers, and that an expedition could be justified on the basis that most of the continent was held under the domination of France's ally Spain. A preliminary attack on the north side of the River Plate resulted in the Battle Honour **Monte Video** being awarded to four regiments after a gallant night attack. When reinforcements arrived from England an attack was mounted on *Buenos Aires*, but this involved street fighting to which the British troops were not accustomed, and the Argentinians, who were strongly advocating independence and were in no mood to exchange their Spanish yoke for a British one, fought desperately among the barricaded streets and houses. The attack failed, as it was almost bound to do from the start and General Whitlock, the Commander on the spot, was rather unfairly made the scapegoat for an ill-conceived expedition and cashiered on his return to England.

Nearer home an expedition was launched against *Copenhagen* in 1807, because, Denmark being under Russian influence and Russia temporarily supporting Napoleon, it was felt that British influence in the Baltic might be difficult to maintain in the face of the combined Russo-French fleets and much of the wood for the ships, and particularly the masts, of the British Navy came from the forests of Sweden and Finland. The Danes were defeated and the danger was removed, although against such a pitifully weak adversary little pride can be taken in the action; nevertheless eight of the fifteen regiments involved have claimed it as an Honour without success.

In 1810 raids were also carried out against *Santa Maura*, which resulted in the capture of the Ionian Islands, and *Mili* on the coast of Sicily, but the force employed was only one regiment in each case and as these successes were not recognised as Honours.

Finally in this mixed bag of engagements two more exploits in the West Indies must be noted, both concerning islands which had figured prominently in the fighting over the past fifty-odd years, Martinique and Guadeloupe. In 1809 a successful attack on the former gained the award of **Martinique 1809** as a Battle Honour for ten regiments including the West India Regiment once again, although two contributory battles were included under the same heading; it also resulted in two more Royal Artillery Honour Titles, **Martinique** Battery and **The Battle-Axe Company**. In the following year **Guadeloupe 1810** became an Honour for five regiments after the capture of that island yet again, although in this case six regiments which were also involved in some degree were not commemorated. Inevitably neither of the islands remained in British hands after the eventual peace, although this was the last time either of them were to figure in the battle record of the Army.

The Peninsular Campaign, 1808–14

In any war on as grand a scale as the one against Napoleon, the final round of the long struggle with France, and in spite of the small campaigns, the expeditions, the raids and the general nibbling at the edges, sooner or later must come the major clash of arms, the battle or series of battles which finally decides the issue. At different times and for different reasons, for most of the time one side or the other tries to avoid, or is unable to achieve, the major conflict, but eventually it must come. The Iberian Peninsula was perhaps not the choice of either Britain or France for the scene of Armageddon, but the French precipitated a crisis and Britain, at first almost by accident in answer to pleas for help and later by appreciating that the moment had arrived for final action and that Spain was as good a place as any to bring the major French armies to battle, accepted the challenge.

On a trumped-up pretext Napoleon had sent an army into the Peninsula, occupying first Lisbon and then Madrid. The King of Portugal escaped to South America with British help, but the King of Spain was initially treated as a welcome ally, and with his Queen and heir was invited to visit Napoleon in France to discuss matters of mutual interest; once out of Spain it was announced that he was a captive, and the Spanish rose in anger. Although they had some initial successes they were no match for the French armies, and appealed for help from Britain with whom they had been on friendly trading terms for some years.

Help was willingly given and a force was assembled to land in Portugal under the command of Sir Arthur Wellesley whose victories in the Mahratta War in India (see Chapter 8) had made him an obvious choice. Unfortunately there were generals senior to him, including Moore, who considered that they should be in overall command but in most cases had an inflated view of their own competence, and, such was the situation in those days, were able to sail to the Peninsula under their own steam and once on the spot could not be outranked. The fact that there were in reality two Peninsular campaigns, separated by the evacuation at Corunna and the later reinforcement of the small Army which remained in the Peninsula after the evacuation, was the direct result of this squabble for command, which was also, incidently, largely responsible for the need for the retreat to Corunna itself.

In terms of Battle Honours the army was well rewarded during the campaign; all the major battles were Honoured, although some of the lesser ones were not, and a Campaign Honour was awarded which is borne by eighty-seven regiments. Even that figure does not truly reflect the magnitude of the struggle or the size of the forces engaged, since during that period the majority of regiments raised two battalions and in many cases both battalions fought in the Peninsula. This was a forerunner of the situation a century later when existing regiments raised large numbers of battalions instead of new regiments being raised as had happened in the past; it was an interesting innovation and was carried out in spite of the fact that only a few years earlier thirty-odd extra regiments had been raised, mainly for home service against the risk of invasion by France, and then disbanded. Well-founded organisation instead of panic-station expediency had at last triumphed.

The first battle, which was incidently the last in which the army fought in powdered wigs and pigtails, occurred at **Rolica** soon after Wellesley's landing when a small French force was defeated. Wellesley outnumbered the enemy, for once, and attacked before the French could be reinforced. He tried to outflank them by a pincer movement but in this was thwarted. A gallant but uncessary charge by the 29th Foot almost upset Wellesley's calculations, but he ordered a general advance and now the French had to retreat. The battle was awarded as an Honour to thirteen regiments and claimed by the 20th Light Dragoons who only had detachments present.

The main French force then attacked four days later at Vimiero while Wellesley was covering the landing of reinforcements. For the first time Wellesley employed the tactic of placing his army on a ridge lying down out of sight; the French attacked in several columns led by a mass of skirmishers, but as they crested the ridge they were met by intense musket fire and rapidly retreated again. The same tactics were repeated against further attacks with the same result until the French spirit was broken and they were defeated outright. For some reason the spelling of the Honour become **Vimiera** and it was awarded to twenty-one regiments, although one participant was unhonoured.

The way was now open for a general advance on Lisbon, but it was at this point that the fruits of victory were thrown away as the senior generals appeared on the scene, and instead of insisting on a French surrender, which could have been easily accomplished, overbore Wellesley's strategy and allowed the mass of French prisoners to be repatriated. Not only that but as a final example of foolishness the prisoners were carried back to France on British ships!

This left the way open for Napoleon to dispatch another army to Spain, which first annihilated the Spanish army and then forced Moore, who was by now in command, to retreat towards the coast at Corunna. Two Cavalry actions of note, both gallantly carried out and successful, took place during the retreat; the first at **Sahagun** provided yet another unique Honour for the 15th Light Dragoons, but the second at *Benavente*, although equally meritorious, brought no recognition to the 7th, 10th and 18th Light Dragoons which participated in it. It was now winter and the bitter weather added to the hardships of the retreating British Army, which so often seems to have retreated in the middle of winter rather than in the better summer weather, and which, as Moore appreciated, would be decimated by cold and hunger if it could not reach Corunna quickly.

It was an epic march and the rearguard fought some brilliant small actions when the pursuing French got too close. Unlike many previous retreats, as for example in Flanders nine years earlier, the morale of the troops remained high and although hungry, shoeless and sometimes almost without clothes, discipline was maintained and embarkation was completed in January 1809. The action was only marred, as at Quebec, by the death of the Commander-in-Chief, Sir John Moore, at the moment of success. Nevertheless it was still a retreat, and to that extent a failure of arms, but it was not without compensating success, for it allowed the Spanish Army to recover by drawing off the French forces, and left the French themselves ever after nervous of any manoeuvre which could cut their lifeline with Bayonne. **Corunna** was awarded as an Honour to thirty Infantry regiments but strangely not to the three Cavalry regiments which had accompanied the retreat. The Royal Artillery commemorate the retreat with two more Honour Titles.

Not the whole of the British Army had in fact retreated to Corunna, and a small contingent had gone southwards into Portugal. It was on this nucleus that Wellesley, who had returned to Lisbon a few months later with some reinforcements from England, built a new Army. He had two opponents, Marshall Soult on the River Douro and Marshall Victor on the River Tagus. He decided to deal first with Soult so as to relieve the fertile area in which his army was quartered and force the French into the barren country of north-west Spain, meanwhile leaving a small force to protect Lisbon from Victor. The Army advanced rapidly northwards towards Oporto and drove Soult back across the river where he felt secure, having destroyed the bridges and the boats; but Wellesley crossed secretly in a few old wine barges which he had found, slowly because he could only ferry thirty men in each boat at a time. The first party across entered the Bishop's seminary and fortified it. Soult, who was asleep at the time, was totally surprised, and in spite of his attempts to rally his troops was routed. The crossing of the Douro was reckoned as one of the most daring exploits of British arms and resulted in a Battle Honour, **Douro**, for one Cavalry and three Infantry regiments which carried out the actual crossing, although nine other regiments took part in the engagements leading to the crossing and Soult's retreat, and a further four which were only marginally engaged have claimed the Honour unsuccessfully.

Having put Soult out of action, Wellesley now turned south again rapidly to deal with Victor, who had retreated towards Madrid. Unfortunately for Wellesley a combined attack with the Spanish troops had been planned, but they did not materialise and by the time they were ready Victor had retreated again. A unique chance had been missed and Wellesley determined to fight him alone. But Victor had turned again and realising that Wellesley on his own had a disadvantage in manpower attacked a British brigade which had gone to sleep without posting proper sentries, believing that they were far from the enemy. The battle which took place when they met was not one of the great General's best.

The armies were roughly equal in numbers, although the British force was supported by a large number of Spaniards whose boastfulness was not matched by their achievement, and who eventually departed somewhat precipitately leaving the British by now heavily outnumbered. Cavalry charges met with little success since the ground had not been properly reconnoitred in advance, but the Infantry, and particularly the Light Division which arrived on the scene after a remarkable forced march, fought bravely against a number of heavy French assaults and Victor had to retreat again towards Madrid. **Talavera** was awarded as an Honour to twenty-two regiments, but once again there were seven others which were involved in some way of whom several have claimed the Honour. The battle also provided the Honour Title of **Talavera Battery** for the Royal Artillery.

There was now a year of inactivity in the Peninsula which Wellesley, who had been created a Viscount after Talavera, used to reorganise his forces, to prepare a more efficient commissariat and supply system and to fortify his base at Lisbon by constructing in-depth fortifications, the Lines of Torres Vedras. The French seemed reluctant to attack him while they too reorganised and prepared for the next move, which turned out to be Napoleon's order to drive the British, or as he called them the Leopards, into the sea.

But meanwhile, in northern Europe, the army had suffered another disaster resulting from a well-conceived but badly executed plan to occupy Flushing and Antwerp while Napoleon's back was turned, and to divert some of his forces from the Peninsula. An expedition sailed in the autumn of 1809 for *Walcheren* in the Scheldt estuary and captured Flushing, but it became bogged down on the waterlogged island while the French managed to get together enough troops to fortify Antwerp and make the objective of the foray unattainable. It was obvious that the force had to be withdrawn, but such were the arguments between the two totally incapable commanders of the land and sea forces that by the time the evacuation was carried out thousands of men, who should have been reinforcing the army in the Peninsula, had died of fever and other effects of the soggy conditions.

In the Peninsula in 1810 Wellesley took the only opportunity to deliver a blow against the French, whose main army was now commanded by Marshall Massena; the Light Brigade with Cavalry support forced a crossing of the river *Coa*, although the action did not merit an Honour, and Wellesley then advanced to meet Massena and took up his position on a steep ridge at Busaco. Believing that their Portuguese allies were of little value, Massena attacked the British with only part of his force in the mist at dawn and gained the front part of the ridge. But Wellesley had again made use of a reverse slope and the Light Division drove them back down the hill. The French attacked again but were every time repulsed. **Busaco** was awarded as an Honour, but only to eighteen Infantry regiments of the twenty-four which took part. Wellesley, who had always realised that Busaco could be no more than a holding action, then withdrew to the security of his Lines of Torres Vedras, and the limited campaign of 1810 came to an end.

The first three years of the Peninsula campaign had resulted in a lot of manoeuvring, some long marches and retreats by both sides, and very little decisive action. But in 1811 the war was to get into top gear. In the south of Spain Cadiz was being blockaded by the French and operations commenced to free the port; a combined Anglo-Spanish army under Spanish command was used, but the commander, not having sufficiently appreciated the ground or carried out any reconnaissance, was ambushed and his troops were thrown into confusion. The day was only saved by prompt action by the small British contingent, and the Spanish were never again trusted with a command which would endanger the British Army. Seven regiments were awarded the Honour **Barrosa** and three other applicants for it were refused.

In the north Wellesley was besieging the fortress of Almeida and the French under Massena marched to relieve it. The armies met head on in a bloody fight which badly damaged the new 7th Division. A lull occurred. When the battle began again next day Wellesley's position was desperate. But he used the Light Division to cover the retreat of the battered 7th Division, and after some fierce fighting by the Scottish battalions and a charge by the Connaught Rangers another British victory resulted, largely as a result of the gallantry of the Light Division, the Cavalry and the Royal Horse Artillery, and the French retreated, together with the garrison of the fort, towards Salamanca. **Fuentes D'Onoro** was a major engagement awarded as an Honour to twenty regiments, although again a number of participants were excluded. The Artillery battery which fought with the Light Division did not use the actual name of the battle when granted an Honour Title but commemorated the name of its battery commander under the title of **Bull's Troop**. Between these two Honoured battles, Barrosa and Fuentes D'Onoro, three more engagements had taken place, at *Casal Nova*, *Campo Maior* and *Sabugal*, but none of them was deemed worthy of recognition.

It must be appreciated that the whole area over which the campaign was fought was very large and that there were no fixed lines which could be attacked or key points taken which would materially inhibit the enemy. To this extent the situation was similar to that which had obtained in America during the War of Independence thirty years earlier. Wellesley could not be in two places at once, and therefore had to delegate one area to subordinates who were in the main incapable of conducting major independent battles, certainly not to his standards, although they were perfectly competent when acting under his direction.

Beresford, in the south while Wellesley was in the northern area, was one of these, and learning that the French were marching to relieve his siege of Badajoz marched out to meet them. But he was out of his position when the French attacked him, and let down again by his Spanish allies he was in a desperate situation when the Fusilier Brigade was ordered into action. This counterattack, and the gallant and spirited defence by the rest of the British force of an untenable position, halted the French advance but at a cost of 60 per cent casualties. The battle of **Albuhera**, awarded as an Honour to fifteen regiments with this time only two excluded, became a household word largely through the famous words of the commander of the 57th Foot (The Middlesex Regiment) which gave rise to their nickname, 'The Diehards'. Beresford was replaced and the *siege of Badajoz* was resumed, but when the resulting assault failed it was raised, and not being a success no Honour was granted for the action by only five regiments, nor for the engagement by three Cavalry regiments at *Usagre*. Wellesley, in the north still, retired towards *El Bodon*, where a brilliant action in open country against French cavalry and a small engagement at *Aldea da Ponte* allowed his army to complete its passage safely.

The year's campaigning came to an end with a small but nevertheless sparkling action against an isolated French division at Arroyo dos Molinos. The enemy was surprised and routed with the loss of many prisoners, but the action, which but for one particular incident, or perhaps accident, might well have gone unrecognised, again resulted in a peculiar anomaly in the granting of Honours. One of the regiments in the British detachment was the 34th Foot (The Border Regiment) and in the confusion of the retreat it captured part of the French regiment, including its drums, which was also numbered the 34th. To commemorate this coincidence the regiment claimed and was awarded **Arroyo dos Molinos** as an unique Honour. But the anomaly lies in the fact that the 34th Foot was only lightly engaged, and even then only in the closing stages of the engagement, whilst the remaining five Infantry regiments, who bore the brunt and who all applied for the Honour, and the two Cavalry regiments involved, were refused the award. The similarities in discriminatory practice between this and the award to the 5th Foot of **Wilhelmsthal** are very apparent.

The campaign in 1812 began unusually early, in January, and this departure from custom which totally surprised the French accentuates Wellesley's strategic genius. He had already several times threatened the French stronghold of Ciudad Rodrigo in earlier years without success, but he now decided to besiege and capture it before the French could be reinforced. The investment was an unpleasant business as trenches and parallels had to be dug in frozen, snow-covered ground, and the working parties themselves froze at night. The breaches were stormed, a task which was made easier by the exploding of a French mine which caused the defenders more damage than the attackers. The fortress was captured, albeit with heavy losses, and the town sacked, which in those days was the normal fate of captured towns. The Honour of **Ciudad Rodrigo** went to eleven regiments, although once again six others which assisted in the assault were ignored. At the same time a small action was taking place at the southern tip of Spain, not far from Gibraltar, which resulted in the award of **Tarifa** to two regiments, although this was only half the detachment involved.

The French threat in the north was now reduced sufficiently for Wellesley to move his army southwards and lay siege once again to Badajoz. This fortress was more strongly constructed and more stubbornly defended than Ciudad Rodrigo and its capture was a much more difficult undertaking. Instead of attacking the main fortress, as had happened twice before, Wellesley this time decided first to breach the city walls from the other side. The main forts were stormed with a stream of rockets, but he dared not wait for more favourable circumstances for the main assault as Marshall Marmont was marching to the relief of the fortress. The main attack was launched in impossible conditions of weather, exploding powder bombs, mines and inundations prepared by the defenders, but nevertheless continued to progress. In spite of appalling casualties and with unparalled heroism, the assault was successful this time and the impregnable fortress was captured, and twenty regiments added **Badajoz** to their Colours.

Subsequent to the capture of Badajoz two small battles were fought. The first was an entirely cavalry action at *Llerena* in which five regiments participated, and which was applied for unsuccessfully by two of them under the name of 'Villa Garcia'. The second was honoured as **Almaraz** and this was awarded to three Infantry regiments although one Cavalry and two further Infantry regiments also took part, and it was claimed by two regiments.

Wellesley now turned again to concentrate in the northern area. He planned to carry the war into the French camp by attacking Salamanca, but, learning of large reinforcements coming up for the enemy, began to retire again to cover his communications with Ciudad Rodrigo. The French attacked him as soon as the reinforcements arrived and before Wellesley could retire any further, but were bluffed by the sight of the dust clouds raised by the supply and baggage wagons being sent back to Ciudad Rodrigo into thinking that the main retreat had started, and detached part of their force to cut the road. This opened a gap in their line which Wellesley was quick to exploit and by a sudden assault routed the whole French Army. This is often regarded as the shortest major battle in military history as it lasted only forty minutes, during which time 40,000 French troops were defeated by a smaller army and lost nearly half their strength in casualties. **Salamanca** was a famous victory and is borne on the

Colours of forty-two regiments, and, remarkably enough in this case all applications by regiments not originally awarded the Honour were eventually approved, although many had been initially refused.

Wellesley now entered Madrid in triumph, but was unable to remain there for long through lack of resources and the distance from his main base in Portugal, and moved northwards. He invested *Burgos* but was unwilling to risk another heavy casualty list by assaulting the fortress and, learning of a strong force advancing against him, withdrew to the Portuguese frontier, with a small cavalry rearguard action being fought *en route* at *Torquemada*. Neither of these actions was recognised as worthy of Honour.

The year, a turning point in the war, came to an end, Wellesley having achieved much and having been able to unite his whole army for the first time, now that the French threat to southern Spain had been eliminated by their need to withdraw those forces northward to join the rest of their army to contain him. But outside the Peninsula Napoleon had been encountering problems, in particular the failure of his dubiously viable attack on Russia and the long winter retreat from Moscow with its heavy casualties. Napoleon was forced to fight a battle in Germany towards the end of 1813 at Leipzig and was defeated. The only British unit present was an artillery battery known as The Rocket Troop, but no Honour was awarded to it. A month prior to that a small engagement involving one British regiment, the 73rd Foot, had been fought a few miles away at *Göhrde;* again no Honour was awarded although the regiment claimed it unsuccessfully. Napoleon's Russian campaign had necessitated the withdrawal of some of his force from Spain and at last left Wellesley with a roughly comparable force. The situation had now changed dramatically.

The way was open for an advance northwards to try to block the gap at the western end of the Pyrenees which was the French lifeline with home. Wellesley therefore advanced north-eastwards through Spain in the spring of 1813 and the French had to withdraw from Portugal to avoid having their army there outflanked and cut off. The French vainly attempted to stem the advance and at last turned at bay at Vittoria, only 60 miles from the frontier, so certain that they would defeat the British that they erected stands so that the townspeople could watch the battle. Wellesley's plan depended on a left flanking movement to cut the road of retreat, and a strong feint on the right, with the main attack in the centre. The key to the position was the hill of Arinez which was captured by Picton's 3rd Division by a camouflaged attack, and in spite of strong French counter-attacks they held their ground. The final attack captured the village of Margarita, the centre of the French defences, and the battle was over.

Wellesley's tactics and his attack had been decisive, and apart from defeating the demoralised French army under King Joseph, Napoleon's brother, captured all their guns and all their baggage, including the loot accumulated over the years. The townspeople had their spectacle after all! **Vittoria** was awarded as an Honour to eight Cavalry and forty Infantry regiments, although this time the anomalies of the past again crept in and three Cavalry regiments and two regiments of Foot Guards were left out. Wellesley was

made a Field Marshal for his part in the campaign so far, to add to his Marquessate awarded after his victory at Salamanca, and his title of Generalissimo of the Spanish Army granted after the same battle.

San Sebastian was now besieged and although, as in the case of all the major fortresses, its final assault after an initial failure was accompanied by heavy casualties, it eventually fell. The Honour of **San Sebastian** was awarded only to the six regiments which participated in the assault and not the other eleven regiments which took part in the siege. Meanwhile a French counterattack towards Pamplona had been beaten off, and **Pyrenees** was awarded as an Honour to cover all the battles of this phase, although particular actions at *Roncesvalles* and *Maya* were claimed independently by three regiments.

Minor actions took place at *San Marcial*, claimed by one regiment as 'Lesaca', and *Ordal*, and in October Wellesley crossed the river *Bidassoa* into France. For some peculiar reason the latter was not awarded as an Honour, although it was a significant occasion and eighteen regiments took part in the attack, of which a number have claimed it, the members of the original Light Brigade doing so under the title of 'Vera'. The French fell back again, defending unsuccessfully the rivers which barred Wellesley's progress, and first **Nivelle** and then **Nive** were added to the list of Battle Honours, both of them having a large number of recipients but producing a number of unsatisfied applicants. An individual action by three regiments at *St Pierre* during the crossing of the Nive is also uncommemorated.

Now there was no reason for the army to go into winter quarters; Wellesley was sweeping forward and nothing was to delay him. A brilliant little action was fought by the three regiments of Foot Guards at *St Etienne*, followed by another small one by two regiments at *Garris*, on the way to the next major battle at **Orthez** in February 1814, awarded as an Honour to thirty-eight regiments. It will be seen that in the major engagements towards the end of the war most of the regiments comprising the army were engaged in all of the battles; irrespective of this high degree of participation, which must have meant that some regiments were only lightly engaged, the majority were awarded the Honours, which makes it all the more strange that each time a few were missed out for no apparent reason.

The final battle, apart from another small engagement at *St Etienne* against a remnant of the French which had been cut off, took place at **Toulouse**, and although the outcome could be categorised as a draw, and was actually claimed by the French as a victory, perhaps because of the heavy British casualties, Wellesley was still able to take the city and a week later armistice was signed. Napoleon's resistance in northern Europe had already come to an end; he abdicated and was exiled to Elba, and the long struggle, certainly in the Peninsula and apparently everywhere else in Europe, was over.

Peninsula was awarded as a Campaign Honour to twenty regiments of Cavalry, the three regiments of Foot Guards and sixty-four Infantry regiments, by far the largest number of recipients of any battle up to this time as far as British participation is concerned. This was to remain a record until the 2nd Boer War, although 132 regiments were honoured for Afghanistan 1878–80 but over 100 of these were Indian regiments. Furthermore the campaign as a whole produced more Honours for many individual regiments than they had gained in any earlier campaign, and in many cases more than they had been previously awarded in their whole existence. As a campaign it also provided two more Honour Titles for the Royal Artillery, the **Chestnut Troop** and **Lawson's Company**. Three regiments were denied the Campaign Honour; none of them had spent very long in the Peninsula nor been involved in any engagements of note, but at least under modern rules they would have qualified. In addition to the Honour all regiments which served in the campaign were granted the right to include a laurel wreath on their badges in memory of the fallen.

The Far East, 1810–11

While the war was continuing in the Peninsula some small operations were being carried on against the French and the Dutch in the Far East. An expedition was sent to the East Indies in 1810, which resulted in the capture of **Amboyna**, **Banda** and **Ternate** and these three unique Honours for the Madras Presidency regiment, which was the only one involved. At the same time another larger expedition was sent from India in the other direction which captured the island of **Bourbon**, now known as Réunion and for long a French colony as it was returned to them after the war. It resulted in an Honour for the 69th and 86th Foot (The Welch Regiment and the Royal Ulster Rifles) and three Indian regiments, together with the Madras Artillery and Engineers, although three other British regiments were involved in the expedition.

It is perhaps interesting to note here that Honours in the Presidency armies were not limited, as in the case of the British, to Cavalry and Infantry only but were awarded to the Artillery and Engineers either on a corps basis or to individual batteries, and that for the Engineers this practice continued through World War II.

The capture of Bourbon was followed up a few months later by a descent on Mauritius, another French island and a trading post, but this was a much bigger operation and involved fourteen British and eight Indian regiments. Strangely, since one was granted for Bourbon, no Honour was awarded for *Mauritius*, although the island survived until comparatively recently as a British colony, and the Honour was claimed by five of the regiments which took part, one of them under the title of 'Ile de France', which was its name under the French.

The following year **Java** was invaded by a force of five British and two Indian regiments, who together with the Madras Artillery and Engineers were granted the Honour; a British Cavalry regiment, the 22nd Light Dragoons, who were represented only by a detachment, were not honoured, but the Royal Artillery gained another Honour Title, **Java Battery**. After the capture of the island, in which the whole enemy force of 17,000 was destroyed or captured, Stamford Raffles was made administrator, and strongly opposed its return to the Dutch after the peace. As compensation he obtained Singapore from the Sultan

of Johore and established British influence in Malaya instead; one wonders who was right. Being a persuasive man he might, of course, have achieved both.

North America, 1812–15

Although the activities in the Far East were comparatively unimportant, those in North America were much more serious. The blockading measures of Britain against the French had interfered with American trade; based on the grievances that this caused, a little prompting from Napoleon convinced the Americans that they had a good chance of getting their own back on the British by capturing Canada. In addition there was still a strong faction in the country that believed that anything that did harm to Britain was to be encouraged, since the reasons for which the War of Independence had been fought only thirty years before were still well remembered. In 1812 America declared war on Britain.

Due to commitments in Europe and the East the garrison in Canada was small, backed up by some largely untrained Militia; but the British cause was strongly supported by the Loyalists who had been driven from the United States at the end of the war and were bitterly anti-American, and it was clear to General Brock, who was a very competent officer, that defensive action would achieve little. He therefore soon attacked the American garrison of Detroit and captured the town, and followed this up quickly with successful attacks on Queenston and the area around Brownstown, Frenchtown and Maumee. Only two British regiments were involved, the 41st Foot (The Welch Regiment) in all three and the 49th Foot (The Royal Berkshire Regiment) in the second one only, and they received the appropriate Honours. Apart from **Detroit** there appears to have been some doubt over the spelling of the other forts and the Honours for these were published as **Queenstown** and **Miami**, and the latter, in view of its present day connotations, can easily lead to confusion as to the locale of the fighting.

The Americans had started the war with a hastily contrived army and poor generals, but by 1813 they had managed to achieve improvements; the year thus produced a number of sharp engagements along the frontier line from Lake Erie in the west, around Lake Ontario and up the St Lawrence river towards Montreal. No Honours were awarded for any of these engagements which were mainly fought to check American incursions into Canada, although only that at *Moravian Town* was a defeat and the victory at *Chateaugai* was due to a Canadian Militia regiment, The Voltigeurs, who were the sole participants. Half a dozen British regiments were involved, and as well as The Voltigeurs the Canadians were represented by The Glengarry Light Infantry Fencibles and The Stormont Militia; *Chrysler's Farm*, after which the American attacks could be said to have definitely failed, was claimed as an Honour by the 49th Foot in 1850, but this was refused. Finally at the end of the year the British took the offensive again and captured *Fort Niagara* and *Buffalo*.

By the following year, with the Peninsular War at an end, more troops were available, much to their disgust since they were looking forward to going home after several years of hard campaigning, and the war was carried into the American heartland by an attack on Washington. The invasion force sailed up Chesapeake Bay and the Potomac River, and, having landed, defeated the Americans at **Bladensburg** and carried on to sack the city and set fire to public buildings, including the White House, in retaliation for the American destruction of Fort York, now Toronto, the previous year.

Meanwhile fighting was still going on on the Canadian border with battles at *Street's Creek, Lundy's Lane, Fort Erie, Niagara* again and an abortive expedition on and around Lake Champlain. Only one Honour was awarded, **Niagara**, and this became in effect a Campaign Honour for the whole war on the frontier. It was awarded to eight regular regiments and, contrary to normal practice, to two regiments, the 103rd and 104th Foot, whose existence was to be very limited; in addition one Canadian Militia regiment, The Glengarry Light Infantry Fencibles, received it and another Battery of the Royal Artillery gained the grounds for a future Honour Title as **Niagara Battery**.

There the war should have ended, with Canada secure and the Americans left in no doubt after the expedition against their capital that the British Army was more of a force to be reckoned with than thirty years earlier. But enough was not enough and it was decided to teach the Americans a further lesson at the beginning of 1815 by capturing New Orleans. Unfortunately, the British general left much to be desired in respect of competence, and he came up against one of the few really high-class American generals in Andrew Jackson, 'Old Hickory' as he was known probably from his flexibility and resourcefulness. A frontal attack was a disaster and resulted in heavy casualties, including General Pakenham himself; more than that, it tarnished the reputation which had been gained on the frontier and at Washington and deprived the British of a number of regiments which could have been more valuably employed in Europe at Waterloo.

Several regiments applied for an Honour for the American campaign under different titles. The 1st Foot (The Royal Scots) wanted 'North America 1812-14', the 58th Foot (The Northamptonshire Regiment) 'America 1814', the 39th Foot (The Dorsetshire Regiment) 'Defence of Canada 1814' and the 49th Foot (The Royal Berkshire Regiment) the same but with the dates '1812-1814', but all these were refused. Before leaving the American theatre it should be recorded that in 1815 *Guadeloupe* was once more attacked and captured but it was a very minor affair.

Flanders 1814-15

Whilst success was attending the British Army everywhere else in the world in 1814, Flanders was once again the graveyard of hopes and of the unfortunate troops who formed a small force which tried to take advantage of Napoleon's fading star and bring the war to a rapid close. Acting in conjunction with their allies, a landing was made in Holland and, following a successful encounter at *Merxem, Bergen op Zoom* was attacked *en route* to Antwerp; but the French resistance was not entirely over and although the British forced an entry into the town a counter-attack drove them off again with heavy casualties.

A month later the war was over, and the small force, remaining in Flanders for the time being, was able to form the nucleus of Wellington's army for his last and greatest victory the following year.

Napoleon's exile on Elba had lasted less than a year when on 1 March 1815 he escaped and landed in France with a detachment of his Guards. He moved northwards, joined by members of his old armies who were still loyal to him and who saw a chance of vindicating their defeats of the past two or three years; he reached Paris later in the month with a considerable army behind him. Once again the bogeyman was loose and it seemed that the struggle was about to begin all over again just as the world was licking its wounds after twenty-three years of strenuous and bloody fighting.

Napoleon now had to be defeated for good and removed once and for all from the world stage, and Flanders once more was chosen, inevitably, as the scene of battle for several reasons. It was the nearest point to Britain and thus the easiest place to assemble an army, and also the most convenient place where she could combine with her Prussian allies; and, since the Congress of Vienna had decreed the amalgamation of Holland with the old Austrian Netherlands (Belgium as it now is) as the Kingdom of the Netherlands, it appeared to be an obvious objective for Napoleon, particularly since the Belgians were not happy with Dutch masters, preferred to have the French, and would therefore be likely to join him in significant numbers.

Wellington could not attack immediately or in France, since for political reasons it was essential that Napoleon should be seen to be the aggressor and the allies seen to be supporting the will of the French people. Nevertheless he assembled his army in Flanders and waited; his army was not as large or as well trained as he wished because demobilisation and the disbandment of regiments had followed the peace, and with the American adventure still continuing only six of the regiments ultimately with him in the Peninsula were initially available to him. Apart from this, the Prussian force was much smaller than had been promised and slow in mobilising. He had not long to wait, and in June Napoleon made a rapid and well concealed advance towards Brussels, which housed Wellington's headquarters, outflanking the British and Prussian outposts on the way.

The strategy and tactics of the battle which ensued are too well known and too well documented for any need to reiterate them in detail here; strangely enough, in view of the history of the previous twenty years, it was the first and only time that the two great generals met each other in battle. In brief, Wellington occupied a strong position but was heavily attacked and only just managed to hang on, the Prussian main force under Marshal Blucher arriving late but just in the nick of time, and Napoleon, having staked his all, failed in his final assault and suffered the penalty of all power-seekers by being exiled, this time permanently, on the island of St Helena.

The fighting was hard and desperate, and as Wellington is supposed to have said was, 'a close run thing', and the battle of *Quatre Bras* two days before the main battle was claimed as an Honour by six regiments which participated.

Waterloo was awarded as one of their most prestigious Honours to fifteen Cavalry regiments, to the three regiments of Foot Guards and to twenty Infantry regiments. The Royal Artillery eventually added to its list of batteries with Honour Titles the names of **Mercer's Troop, Ramsay's Troop, Sandham's Company, Rogers's Company**, and **Lloyd's Company**, all names of individual commanders, and the battle is celebrated by **Bull's Troop**. Strangely enough there is no Waterloo Battery.

In the final event twelve Cavalry and nineteen Infantry regiments, including the Foot Guards, were awarded both the Honours of **Peninsula** and **Waterloo**, and that period of our history known as the Napoleonic Wars came to an end, as did the centuries-old struggle with France. Most of the territory that Britain had captured was handed back because it was felt that the war had been fought against Napoleon, the usurper, rather than against France, and

only Malta, the Ionian Islands, the Cape of Good Hope, Ceylon, Mauritius, St Lucia, Trinidad, Tobago and a few small West Indian islands were retained.

Furthermore, the large loans of money made to our allies were not called in and the cost of the war was not made good by reparations, so that Britain was left with a huge National Debt. To paraphrase a much later *bon mot*, never has so much been owed and so little repaid by so many. Nevertheless, of all the countries involved Britain, as before and since, was the only one which had not been invaded or fought over and in many cases devastated; the trade which resulted, partly from the need to repair the destruction in Europe and partly because any competition from other countries, except America, was for many years negligible, went a long way to make up the deficit. It was perhaps the one tangible gain from so many years of fighting and was to serve Britain in good stead for a century to come.

Above: General Wellesley leading the bayonet charge at the Battle of Assaye, 23 September 1803. Engraving by Thomas Williams after James Godwin. *NAM*

8 Foundations of the Indian Empire, 1800-19

Whilst the various campaigns of the Napoleonic Wars described in the last chapter were being fought in Europe and elsewhere, Britain was also engaged in the East in building an Empire in India, by strengthening the somewhat flimsy foundations which had been laid in the second half of the eighteenth century. During that period the task had been to defeat and eliminate as competitors the French, Dutch, and to a limited extent the Portuguese, for trading rights and control over the vast sub-continent; now this had been achieved and the task was to convince the Indian states, races, nations, or whatever they may be called, that organised British rule would bring them greater benefits than the feudal strife which had gone on for centuries past. The method of convincing them was to be conquest if diplomacy failed, as it was almost bound to do since one can rarely sit down and discuss niceties and the future with tigers who can see very little beyond where their next meal is coming from.

India contained a large number of independent states, of all sizes, shapes, creeds and religions, but of all these the most significant, certainly after the demise of Tippoo Sahib and his Mysoreans and the acceptance by Hyderabad of British protection, were the Mahrattas. They were not so much a nation as a loose federation of semi-independent princes, held together by mutual greed and a love of war, but still capable of fighting among themselves when there was nobody else outside the confederation who could be conveniently or usefully ravaged. The main principalities were Poona, Gwalior, Indore, Nagpore and Baroda, the last of which took little part in the hostilities to follow, situated in the western and northern part of central India, and using as bases almost impregnable fortresses set on rocky crags in the Western Ghats.

The Mahrattas were brilliant horsemen and had imported Europeans, mostly Frenchmen, to train their forces after having witnessed the effectiveness of well-organised troops in earlier encounters with the British; they were a power to be reckoned with, unlikely to submit to foreign rule without a desperate struggle, and the situation was ripe for a trial of strength. Luckily we had in India at that time two commanders of exceptional ability in Lake and Wellesley, and it was during the years 1803 to 1806 that the latter displayed his military genius and laid the foundations of his own fame.

The traditional campaigning season in India was the dry period from October to March, when of course the mounted Mahrattas could cover great distances at high speed and would be difficult to bring to battle. Wellesley therefore decided to open his campaign during the monsoon, when rivers became raging torrents which the Mahrattas would find impenetrable barriers, whereas he, with his pontoons, could cross over comparatively easily, although the conditions for his troops would be far from pleasant.

A short digression is necessary before the account of the battles starts, on the subject of spelling. The Indian, as with the Arabic, languages are never easy to transliterate into English, and even today different people use different symbols for doing this; in addition the dialects themselves result in different local pronunciation. The outcome is a wide divergence of spelling of most of the Indian towns, and certainly of the smaller ones which usually give rise to the names of battles and Honours, since many of the historians of the period had had no contact with the natives of the country and there were of course no accepted atlas spellings of the names. The spellings used here are basically those which occur on the regimental Colours as Honours, and those which appear in documents of the same era for battles not honoured, but where other spelling has become commonplace since those far-off days the modern name has been indicated as well for clarity.

The war thus opened in August 1803 by the capture of the fortress of *Ahmednuggur* by one British Cavalry and two Infantry regiments and a slightly larger force of Indian troops under Wellesley; the assault was rapid and the outer fortifications were captured before breakfast. The fort was pounded by guns for four days until it surrendered, but in spite of this early and brilliant success no Honour was awarded. At about the same time a small action took place at *Broach*, near Bombay, again unhonoured, and further north Lake stormed the fortress of **Ally Ghur** (Aligarh); this provided an Honour for the 76th Foot (The Duke of Wellington's Regiment) and for three regiments of Bengal Native Infantry which have not survived, and a disappointment for the 24th Light Dragoons who were presumably not awarded it because of their ephemeral existence. Lake followed this success with an attack on a large force of Mahrattas outside Delhi, and won the battle, with the capture of most of the enemy Artillery, largely by marching the British Infantry directly at the line of guns which they took with one volley and a charge in spite of heavy casualties from the cannon fire. **Delhi 1803** was awarded as an Honour to the 76th Foot and to a larger force of Indian troops, of which only one Infantry regiment has survived, two Cavalry and a further eight Infantry regiments disappearing after the Mutiny; again the 24th Light Dragoons were unlucky.

But now in the south Wellesley was to win one of his most famous victories. Trying to effect a junction with another British force he came across the Mahratta camp in an angle between two rivers, and in spite of being unsupported and the strength of the enemy position decided to attack; his force was only 7,000 strong with a few guns whilst the enemy numbered around 50,000, supported by over a hundred guns and a horde of irregular horsemen. His little army had to cross over a ford and then came under heavy cannon fire, as the Mahratta army changed front and he had to conform. His tactics were brilliant and again it was a matter eventually of charging the gun line and then holding off massed Cavalry counter-attacks, but the British and Indian troops fought magnificently against overwhelming odds, although losing nearly a quarter of their numbers in casualties, until the Mahrattas, who had a number of well-trained regiments but mainly relied on the strength of their irregulars, had had enough. Unfortunately, because he had had to commit his reserve Cavalry early in the battle to save the right wing which had strayed off course, Wellesley had no force to follow up the retreat. **Assaye**, Wellesley's first major victory and perhaps one of his hardest battles, was awarded as an Honour to one British Cavalry and two Infantry regiments, the 19th Light Dragoons and the 74th and 78th Foot (The Highland Light Infantry and The Seaforth Highlanders), to batteries of the Madras and Bombay Artillery, the Madras Sappers and Miners, and to three Indian Cavalry and five Infantry regiments. As an Honour it is borne by the British regiments on their badges rather than on their Colours, and one of the Bombay batteries which was subsequently absorbed into the Royal Artillery translated the Honour which it was granted at the time, and which it lost in 1861 on absorption, into an Honour Title as **Assaye Battery** sixty or so years later. This completed technically the first phase of the Mahratta War, but the second was to follow almost without a break.

Shortly after the victory at Assaye small actions occurred in the north at *Barrabatta* and *Asseerghur*, and Lake captured *Agra*, the key to Hindustan, but no Honours were awarded although Asseerghur was claimed by the 94th Foot (The Connaught Rangers). He finally brought the Gwalior forces to action at **Leswaree** and defeated them, once more by charging the guns. Two British Cavalry regiments, the 8th Hussars and the 25th Light Dragoons, and one Infantry regiment, the 76th Foot again, were awarded the Honour, although the 24th Light Dragoons were left out; it was also awarded to five Indian Cavalry and seven Infantry regiments, but of these only three survived, being entirely from Bengal, in which Army most of the mutinous regiments were eventually to be found. Wellesley had meanwhile been engaged in the south and had defeated the Nagpur army at *Argaum*. A large mass of enemy horse and foot were on the plain in front of the village, and to make things difficult Wellesley's force had to advance through a sea of tall grass, only emerging and seeing the enemy when very close and being assailed by massed guns. There was some confused and panicky

retreat, but Wellesley brought the crisis under control. The final attack was made at dusk and the casualties among the Mahrattas were huge although the British force suffered only very lightly. In spite of its significance and an application for an Honour by two of the three British Infantry regiments involved, it was not recognised; a large force took part consisting, apart from the three regiments mentioned, of one British and five Indian Cavalry regiments and twelve Indian Infantry regiments. A fortnight later he also fought a major engagement at *Gawilghur* which has also gone unhonoured. Gawilghur is a massive, impregnable fortress, which for some reason was inadequately defended; it was assaulted by the easy route and capitulated, but if the main bastion had had to be assaulted the outcome might have been very different.

By now Lake, having routed the less able of his adversaries, was up against the Holkar of Indore, who employed the traditional Mahratta tactics of Cavalry fighting and mobility. Delhi was besieged by the Holkar and only a desperate cavalry charge on his camp at *Farrakhabad* at dawn by three British and three Indian Cavalry regiments, supported by three Infantry regiments, saved the situation. Lake's army also fought another hard battle at **Deig**, and then besieged and finally captured the fortress six weeks later; the Honour for the whole engagement was awarded to one British Infantry regiment, the 76th Foot, to the Bengal Presidency Regiment (The Royal Munster Fusiliers), and to two Indian Cavalry and six Infantry regiments of which only one remained. One British Cavalry and one Infantry regiment, and one Native Infantry regiment, were not recognised for the Honour, although it was claimed by the 22nd Foot (The Cheshire Regiment).

Bhurtpore was now besieged at the beginning of 1805, but although he assaulted four times with heavy casualties Lake was unable to capture it; nevertheless, by small Cavalry actions at *Combir* and *Afzalghar*, he managed to drive the Holkar's forces into the northern Punjab, and the Mahrattas knew that the time had come to hide their light under a bushel for a while. So ended the 2nd Mahratta War and for a time peace reigned.

Inevitably a few minor actions took place during the next few years; one was at *Chumar* in 1807; another occurred two years later when a rebellion in Travancore was put down by one Indian native regiment, which later became the 93rd Native Infantry and was awarded the Honour **Cochin** by the Presidency, and by one British Infantry regiment, the 12th Foot (The Suffolk Regiment), which was not; and in 1815 a campaign was waged in *Ceylon* by three British Infantry regiments, of whom one claimed an Honour covering the period of action there from 1796 to 1820, which finally delivered the whole island under British rule.

The next major engagements, however, were fought over an eighteen-month period from 1814 to 1816 against a nation which was later to provide one of the staunchest fighting forces of the British Indian army, the Gurkhas. They originated in the Himalayan foothills and being a warlike race, whose only real interest in life appeared to be in fighting, had established a Kingdom in Nepal; several attempts had previously been made to annex their territory without success and now a more determined effort was launched. It was a very difficult little war, fought in most unfriendly mountain terrain, but gradually the British troops managed to advance through the passes, captured the capital, Katmandu, and forced the Gurkhas to sign a treaty. They agreed to surrender their territory so long as they were left alone in peace and on the undertaking that they would not wage war against the British, and the treaty has been honoured ever since; only in recent years has Nepal itself been known to the world as anything but a country of mystery and the place where Everest expeditions start.

The most valuable outcome of the war and the treaty which followed was that the Gurkhas themselves began to cross the frontier and enlist in Indian regiments, and in due course were formed into their own regiments; they were never actively recruited by the British, who were not allowed to enter Nepal, but gradually grew in size until at the end of the World War II they comprised ten regiments each of a number of battalions, of which only three remained on the British Army strength after Partition in 1947 when the Indian Army regiments were shared out between India, Pakistan and Britain. No Honour was awarded for the campaign in *Nepal*, but one British Cavalry and six Infantry regiments, of which four have claimed the Honour, took part, supported by four Indian Cavalry and no less than twenty-eight Indian Infantry regiments.

After their defeat in 1806 many of the irregular followers of the Mahratta armies had been banded together as the Pindari, who were little more than a robber band, although of great size, which had been terrorizing the Punjab and central India and committing horrible atrocities. Their name was hated and cursed by the Indians themselves who had suffered most from them, and it became necessary to remove this menace. A large army was assembled and in 1814 began systematically sweeping the countryside, destroying the gangs and their power, until three years later the job was done, the leader of the Pindari, Chitu, having been eaten by a tiger while hiding in the jungle! But the Pindari had been secretly supported by the Mahratta chiefs, and inevitably the business of destroying them escalated into another war against the Mahrattas themselves.

The 3rd Mahratta War, also known as the Pindari War, began at the end of 1817. The Residency at Poona was destroyed by fire, but the Peishwa of Poona was defeated a few days later by an army a tenth the size of his at **Kirkee**; this was an all-Indian engagement and the Honour went to the Bombay Presidency Regiment (The Royal Dublin Fusiliers), a battery of Bombay Artillery, which subsequently came to the Royal Artillery and was granted the Honour Title of **Kirkee Battery**, and to four Indian Native Infantry regiments. A further battle at *Poona*, although not honoured, removed the Peishwa from the scene, one British, one Presidency and eight Indian regiments of Infantry being involved. The Bhonsla of Nagpur was the next to be engaged and he was defeated at **Seetabuldee**, another all-Indian engagement, the Honour going to the Madras Artillery and to one Cavalry and three Infantry regiments who between them had vanquished a force of 18,000 men. A further battle at Nagpur itself finally destroyed the power of the Bhonsla himself, and, transliterated into the Battle Honour **Nagpore**, became

added to the Colours of one British regiment, the 1st Foot (The Royal Scots), the Madras Artillery and Engineers, two regiments of Indian Native Cavalry and ten of Native Infantry.

Now came the turn of Indore and at the end of the year the Holkar was beaten into submission at **Maheidpore**, and a single British regiment, the 1st Foot, again gained an Honour, together with the Madras Presidency Regiment, the Madras Artillery and Engineers, a Hyderabad Artillery battery, three regiments of Native Cavalry and eight of Infantry. Unfortunately the part of the 22nd Light Dragoons in the battle was not recognised, nor was an irregular and transitory Cavalry regiment, The Mysore Horse. To all intents and purposes the war was over but inevitably some minor engagements occurred before the end of the struggle. At **Corygaum** on New Year's Day 1818 a minute British force, consisting of a troop of Madras Artillery, the much attenuated Madras Presidency Regiment and an understrength Native Cavalry regiment, later to be The Poona Horse, totalling only 750 men, almost unbelievably won the day against a Mahratta force of 20,000. A few months later a minor action was fought at *Mulligaum* by eight regiments; in January 1819 a small battle was fought and Honoured at **Nowah**, the recipients being three Indian Infantry regiments and a battery of Hyderabad Artillery; finally at *Asirgarh* in April, where Lake had won a victory sixteen years earlier, one of the largest forces of British troops assembled during the war, thirty regiments of which three were from the British army, brought the conflict to an end.

It had been a long and bitter struggle against a desperate, hard-fighting and competent enemy, but had again demonstrated the enormous advantage that a well-disciplined force, even though small, had over largely untrained, irregular troops which might have a superiority of numbers of anything up to 20 to 1. The individual battles were mostly honoured, although usually through the action of the Presidencies and the Governor General rather than through the British authorities in London, to whom these activities in India were a small and unimportant distraction compared with the major problem of defeating Napoleon and then winning the peace in Europe. The campaign as a whole was not Honoured, such action not being the habit of the Presidencies, but Britain could well have done so for the benefit of not only her own but also the supporting Indian troops whose loyalty she was anxious to win, since three British and fourteen Indian Cavalry regiments, and nine British and fifty-five Indian Infantry regiments who had taken part in the gruelling campaign had not received any of the individual Battle Honours and therefore gained no recognition at all for their arduous work.

Apart from the Peishwa of Poona whose territory was annexed, and whose capital became one of the main British administrative bases in the sub-continent and a by-word for British Indian army customs, manners and morals, the other princes were allotted fixed territories to rule and in exchange for their loyalty became immensely richer than any of the men who had fought to subjugate them and calm their appetites for plunder and rapine.

British power in India was now unassailable, although this is not to say that other sects and races did not try during the next forty years to wrest some of the power back to themselves, to their eventual discomfiture and realisation that this was not possible. But it had taken seventy years since Plassey to achieve such power, creating in the process not only an Empire for the British, which lasted another 130 years and provided a source of great strength through the Indian Army in the major wars which were to follow in the next century, but saving India itself and its inhabitants from the regimes of anarchy and terrorism and the internecine struggles which had plagued the country for centuries. The battles which had been fought in achieving this end had been some of the hardest and bloodiest in military history, usually fought against appalling odds, and against men to whom the taking of life was not merely an inevitable adjunct to warfare but something in which they took great delight and pleasure outside actual warfare.

One history of the period written more than half a century ago says that these wars and battles are little remembered, forgotten save by the regiments of the British and Indian Armies which bear the Battle Honours. Unfortunately that is not so today; the wars and battles are still forgotten, but now even by those regiments as well. The British Indian Army has not existed for a generation and it is doubtful whether those regiments which still remain as part of the Indian and Pakistan Armies would wish to remember the feats of their so-called oppressor and their predecessors who fought for the British Raj. The Presidency regiments which became Irish regiments in course of time were disbanded in 1922, and most of the King's regiments have now been either disbanded or amalgamated and their individual exploits and contribution to the Empire blurred or deliberately expunged by those who no longer believe in tradition or Great Britain. Perhaps the Indian wars are best, perhaps only, commemorated today in the Honour Titles of those Batteries of the Royal Artillery which were Indian units at the time; the names of **Assaye** and **Kirkee**, and from earlier occasions **Plassey** and **Seringapatam** still live, and their 'days' are still celebrated by these Batteries. [But perhaps the author is biased because he once commanded **Assaye Battery**!]

Before we leave India mention must be made of a general service Honour which is held by eight British In-

fantry regiments. This is the single word **India**, with all that that implies, which in one case, the 84th Foot, is accompanied by a date, and which in four cases, the 14th, 65th, 67th and 75th Foot, is borne as a badge together with the 'Royal Tiger' and covers service in India for various different periods during the years 1787 to 1831. The eight regiments are:

12th Foot (The Suffolk Regiment)   for the years 1798–1809
14th Foot (The West Yorkshire Regiment) for the years 1807–1831   with Royal Tiger
65th Foot (The York and Lancaster Regiment) for the years 1802–1822   with Royal Tiger
67th Foot (The Hampshire Regiment)   for the years 1805–1826   with Royal Tiger
69th Foot (The Welch Regiment)   for the years 1805–1825
75th Foot (The Gordon Highlanders)   for the years 1787–1813   with Royal Tiger
84th Foot (The York and Lancaster Regiment)   for the years 1796–1819   including the date
86th Foot (The Royal Ulster Rifles)   for the years 1799–1819

Application for a similar Honour has been also made by the 1st Foot (The Royal Scots) for the years 1815 to 1819, which is virtually the period of the Pindari War; by the 47th Foot (The Loyal Regiment) for the years 1807 to 1829, in both cases with the inclusion of the dates in the title; and by the 22nd Foot (The Cheshire Regiment) for the years 1803 to 1819.

Another general service Honour was also awarded to cover roughly the same period in India. This was **Hindoostan** which covered the period from 1780 to 1823. Eight different regiments bear it for specific dates, in two cases with embellishments. The regiments are:

8th Dragoons   for the years 1802–22
24th Light Dragoons   for the years 1803–8
17th Foot (The Leicestershire Regiment)   for the years 1804–23   with 'Royal Tiger'
36th Foot (Worcestershire Regiment)   for the years 1790–3
52nd Foot (Oxford & Bucks LI)   for the years 1790–3
71st Foot (Highland Light Infantry)   for the years 1780–1800
72nd Foot (Seaforth Highlanders)   for the years 1782–93
76th Foot (Duke of Wellington's Regiment)   for the years 1790–1805   with the badge of 'Elephant and Howdah'.

9 Expansion of Empire, 1818-60

By 1818 Britain was at peace, if only temporarily. The Napoleonic War in Europe, with its extension into North America, had been won and the Mahratta threat to India had been subdued; the occupation of France following Napoleon's banishment had come to an end and the troops had returned to England. Economy, after nearly thirty years of costly warfare, was the watchword; the army suffered severe reductions, and industry which had produced the material with which to fight the wars was largely idle, although being slowly turned over to peacetime production to meet the needs of a war-ravaged Europe.

But for the time being at least thousands of soldiers had been discharged and had no employment, nor were they trained for anything except fighting even if work had been available, and industry had laid off men as well.

Until the time of the American revolution forty-odd years before, much of the surplus or out-of-work manpower had had a ready outlet as settlers in North America, and, whilst Canada was still keen to take in emigrants to a limited extent, the vast unsettled areas of America were largely lost as a place for the unemployed or dissident to go to. The problem now was how else to dispose of the surplus. Two immigrant areas only remained, South Africa, which during the last decade or so had begun to build itself up as a nation, and Australia, which had barely started to exist.

Apart from the reduction in size of the Army, the conditions in which the soldiers lived were hardly conducive to making it an attractive form of peacetime employment. The soldiers were poorly quartered, poorly fed and poorly paid. Crime and drunkenness was rife because there was little else to do and little time was spent in training. Delays in bringing the law up to date, caused by the preoccupation of governments with war, meant that many crimes which today would be considered quite minor ones were still punishable by death, transportation or flogging.

It was in this context that commerce began to look for new markets abroad, often needing the assistance of the Army to protect the trading posts and in fact to make trade at all possible, and the British Empire began, almost unnoticed, to expand. Not that the wars covered in this chapter are all to do directly with the actual expansion of Empire; two wars in Burma, several in South Africa and one in New Zealand certainly were, but those in India, against other sects which replaced the defeated Mahrattas as thorns in the flesh, were a matter of consolidation of territory that had already been captured and thus were only indirectly expansionist; those against the Arab pirates in the Persian Gulf and in China were fought purely for reasons of trade, and the Afghan war was defensive. Nevertheless even these latter contributed to establishing Britain as the major world Power, and this reputation was based on the Empire which was being established.

South Africa

The present position in Southern Africa, and the glib statements that minority white governments are overbearing the blacks whose homeland it is, are rarely seen in proper perspective or context. At the time of the Dutch settlement of the Cape, and even after its capture by the British at the beginning of the nineteenth century, the indigenous black population, the Bantu, was very small, scattered in tiny pockets across a vast empty land and primitive in habit. There was also a very few Bushmen and Hottentots who were entirely indigenous. The Bantu were cattle-owners and had started to migrate into Southern Africa, from as yet not fully identified areas in the northern part of the continent, probably as early as the 10th century, always searching for new grazing grounds. But it was only during the latter part of the 18th century that native ingress started to gain momentum. Most of the natives percolated from east Africa into the eastern coastal areas, many of them to escape the slave raids by the Arabs from the lands around the Persian Gulf, and they were largely warlike by nature. By this means it became their adopted homeland, but only subsequent to white occupation and colonization, and the latter therefore have a fair case for also claiming the southern part of the continent as their land which has been infiltrated, rather than vice versa.

The Dutch emigrees, who had settled in the Cape in the second half of the 17th century, were mainly farmers, and they too were constantly searching for new grazing and moving along the southern coast and further inland to find it. Inevitably, at the end of the 18th century the Bantu and the Dutch settlers met and started to dispute ownership of the same territory. But the Dutch settlers believed that an average sized farm was about 6000 acres and that their children, of whom there was no lack, should not divide this land but should each have the same for themselves.

And this, it must be remembered, occurred in a huge land where it might have been assumed that ten times the population could have existed happily and peaceably. But there was really not that much good arable and grazing land available for each nation to have all that they wanted, a great deal of it being desert, mountainous or thorn veldt. The British, after their occupation of the Cape, tried to fix boundaries, but the Dutch did not accept colonial rule and regarded themselves independent and outside British law.

Settlement of surplus population from Britain began in about 1820, mainly in the eastern part of Cape Colony and nearer therefore to the immigrant natives. Like most colonisation the task of establishing themselves was immensely hard and was not made any easier by native cattle-stealing. It was to control the black immigration and to deter their frequent incursion into the white settlements that a number of wars, initially of minor significance but gradually growing in size, violence and importance, were fought. They became known as the Kaffir Wars, 'kaffir' being originally a derogatory term applied by the Dutch settlers to the indigenous population, and later being applied generally to all the native population, both indigenous and immigrant. To an extent it is this all-embracing use of the word Kaffir which has helped to cloud the present situation.

Just how many Kaffir Wars were fought is a matter of conjecture and depends to a large extent on the definition of a war. Understandably the South African enumeration differs from the British, and the first major encounter in 1834, which is usually known in Great Britain as the 1st Kaffir War is known to the South Africans as the 6th, and for clarity it is this latter numbering which is used here. Thus the first wars which are of interest in this narrative, because of participation by British forces, are the 4th Kaffir War of 1811–12 in which only one South African regiment, The Cape Mounted Riflemen, took part and the 5th Kaffir War which lasted sporadically over several years culminating in 1819. Two British regiments, the 38th and 72nd Foot (The South Staffordshire Regiment and The Seaforth Highlanders), took part in the latter war, of which the former applied for it as an Honour, and the Cape Mounted Riflemen were again involved.

The 6th Kaffir War started right at the end of 1834 and continued for nine months. It was a series of battles between the invading tribes and the European settlers supported by small military forces, and was sparked off, an opportune word, at around Christmas time by the burning and pillaging of about 800 farms and an enormous loss of stock. The official policy was 'settlement', a sympathy with the Kaffirs and the abandonment of disputed areas to the marauders. But the outcry from the settlers was sufficient to modify this policy over the years, and the skill of Sir Harry Smith, who had taken part in the siege of Badajoz so many years before, was largely responsible for maintaining South Africa within the Empire. Three British regiments, the 72nd Foot again, supplemented this time by the 27th and 75th Foot, were awarded the Honour **South Africa 1835**, but the two irregular South African regiments, The Cape Mounted Riflemen and the Cape Mounted Yeomanry, which also took part, were not.

But there was also another deep-seated reason for the conflicts in South Africa than occupation of settled territory by marauders. Two years before the 6th Kaffir War the British had declared slavery illegal and freed all slaves, and the Dutch settlers, who had employed a large number of these, considered that they had been paid insufficient compensation when they had had to give them up. They regarded all blacks as servants and slaves. Very religious and Calvinistic in outlook, they regarded themselves, and only themselves, as God's chosen people, and that anything or anybody who acted against their interests was acting against God's will. When Lord Charles Somerset arrived as Governor in 1814 he further upset the Dutch by making them subject to the laws, held courts in English which the Dutch did not, and did not want to, understand, and even worse considered that the blacks should have equal rights.

Thus this British interference with what they believed were their rights was the last straw to their numerous real and imagined grievances, and a large party of farmers, 'Boers' in Afrikaans, left the Cape and moved northwards in 1834 and the following years beyond the Orange, and eventually the Vaal, Rivers and over the mighty Drakensburg range into northern Natal, where they thought that they could escape the dictates of the British government and carry on in their old ways.

This became known as The Great Trek, but it was to a certain extent out of the frying pan into the fire since the Boers soon came into contact in Natal with the Zulus, who were by now a formidable fighting force. Piet Retief, one of the Boer leaders, invited Dingaan, the Zulu ruler, to sign a peace treaty allowing the Boers to settle on, own and farm some of the territory occupied by the Zulu. After discussions a treaty was signed, but before the Boer party could leave they were treacherously attacked and the party massacred by the Zulus. The Boers vowed vengeance and crushed the Zulu impis at the Battle of Blood River in 1838. They thus discovered that they had military as well as farming skills and attacked a small British settlement near Durban. There were no British troops in the vicinity to help the settlers, but reinforcements were sent in due course and the Boers retreated inland. The central part of the country thus passed almost entirely into their hands.

Next the territory between the Orange and Vaal Rivers was declared British and the insurgent Boers were attacked and defeated at Boomplaats in 1848. But beyond the Vaal, the Transvaal as it now became known, the rebellious Boers would not be reconciled and under the British policy of appeasement, which led to another and infinitely more costly war nearly a century later, the Boers were granted an independent state in 1852. This divided South Africa into British and Dutch spheres of influence and laid the foundations for political and military conflict which resulted in two Boer Wars and is still reverberating even today. Apartheid, in its universal but not Afrikaan interpretation is no new policy; it was virtually introduced in 1833 because the Dutch farmers insisted on maintaining slave labour and continued to do so for more than a century both in South Africa and in the East Indies, in opposition to the policies of most of the rest of the civilised world with the major exception of the Americans, who did not accept abolition until they had fought a costly civil war 30 years later, and even then, in the southern states, considered blacks inferior for another hundred years.

But to return to the Cape, for a few years the situation was relatively quiet, but in 1846 the 7th Kaffir War broke out and lasted until the end of 1847, the reasons for it being much as before; this time eight British regiments were involved and Honoured, but the part played by the same two South African regiments was still not recognised.

The 8th Kaffir War started at Christmas in 1850 and was a much larger affair, not being concluded until March 1853, bringing a second Honour of **South Africa** to four regiments and the first to six more. Two other British regiments, the 45th and 72nd Foot, were not Honoured and neither were three South African ones, the same two as before plus Armstrong's Horse. The country was rugged and forested and unsuited to scarlet uniforms, both from the camouflage and climatic aspects, and for the first time the British Army fought in loose, nondescript uniforms with untanned leather equipment, the forerunner of the modern khaki. The fighting was as rugged as the country and it was a misfortune that the lessons learned were so soon forgotten and had to be relearned fifty years later, against a much more formidable adversary than the Kaffirs, during the 2nd Boer War.

Burma

British power was extended eastward beyond the Indian borders during this period as a result of Burmese aggression rather than British aggrandisement. The boundary between the two countries was delineated by rugged mountains and forests, with virtually no communications, and as has been found in more recent times these formed an effective barrier to mass attack while being desperately unfriendly terrain in which to fight. The Burmese themselves were ethnically of quite different stock from any of the various Indian peoples and there had never been much contact between them; certainly no Indian ruler had ever attempted to extend his influence into this land of dense jungles and vast rivers.

But now a new Burmese dynasty had arisen with delusions of grandeur and laid claim to eastern Bengal; infiltration began across the border, albeit in small numbers but nevertheless with aggressive intent. War became inevitable and a small Indian force spent the year of 1824 on the Indian side of the border doing its best to keep the infiltration in check. Two Bengal Native regiments were awarded the Honour **Assam** for these actions, but two others which also participated, one of which subsequently became the 6th Gurkha Rifles, were not so Honoured. At the same time a force was transported by sea to southern Burma and captured Rangoon; this force was initially largely British, and most of the Indian regiments came from Madras since the Bengalis had a rooted aversion to crossing water, and one regiment actually mutinied rather than accept this form of travel.

But the capture of Rangoon was of comparatively little significance since the seat of government was at Ava, far inland on the River Irrawaddi, and had to be eliminated before victory could be claimed. As soon as the army moved northwards into hostile country it was faced with a type of warfare new to it, since the Burmese were adept at building stockades and sangars and digging in. The first battle took pace at **Kemendine**, with which one Native Indian regiment was Honoured although the Madras Presidency Regiment was not, and it was then discovered that in spite of the strength of the positions they raised the Burmese were not very resolute in defending them.

During 1825 a number of encounters took place as the force moved towards Ava. A British force of three regiments together with the Madras Presidency Regiment defeated the enemy at *Donobyu*, which was however not considered worthy of an Honour. In the west of the country some ferocious fighting, in which the Burmese gained some success, took place in the **Arracan**; an Honour was awarded to one Indian Native Cavalry and five Infantry regiments, although it was denied to the two British regiments, the 44th and 54th Foot (The Essex Regiment and The Dorsetshire Regiment), of which the latter applied for it as an Honour, and fourteen other Indian regiments. A sharp affair at *Napadi*, where a small force of five regiments, four British and one Indian, was engaged, also went unhonoured.

Eventually the Army reached the outskirts of Ava early in 1826 and the Burmese capitulated without any further fighting, agreeing to withdraw from the Indian frontier if they were allowed to retain their autonomy. The end of the campaign came in the nick of time since the British strength was fast evaporating, more from sickness, from which nearly 90 per cent of the force became casualties at one time or another, than from battle casualties; the British regiments which originally landed at Rangoon had been practically wiped out. The Honour **Ava** was awarded for the campaign to ten British regiments, the Madras Presidency Regiment, the Madras Artillery and Engineers, and to seventeen Indian Native regiments; no British regiments went unhonoured but twenty-five Indian regiments did, although a number of these were irregular units and may not therefore have been considered to qualify. In addition one Indian regiment was awarded the Honour as **Burmah** instead. The Royal Artillery gained another Honour Title, **Arracan Battery**.

But in spite of their defeat and their promises the Burmese gradually returned to their old ways and continued their arrogant and aggressive behaviour, and it became clear that sooner or later they would have to be taught another lesson. Thus the 2nd Burma War began with another expedition which reached Rangoon and stormed the Shwe Dagon Pagoda in April 1852; luckily the lessons of twenty-seven years earlier had not been forgotten this time and the Commander made sure that sufficient transport, supplies and medical facilities were included along with the fighting troops. Once more the army advanced northward to Ava and the Burmese government again surrendered. This time the British government did not make the mistake of allowing the Burmese continued independence on the basis of worthless promises and Rangoon and the province of Pegu were annexed to the Empire, leaving Ava and Upper Burma completely cut off from the sea and virtually impotent.

Again a campaign Honour was awarded, **Pegu**, which was granted to three British regiments, the Bengal and Madras Presidency Regiments, the Madras Sappers and Miners and to eleven Indian regiments. Once again, inevitably it would seem, six Indian regiments participated without recognition.

New Zealand

The scene now moves a few thousand miles further eastward to Australasia. Since Captain Cook's survey of the coast of New Zealand in the third quarter of the eighteenth century land settlers, sealers and whalers had appeared on the two main islands but in comparatively small numbers. But there was an indigenous population, the Maoris, who had a Stone Age mentality and a primitive life style, and few efforts were made by the settlers to understand them. The Maoris were fiercely warlike, had cannibalistic tendencies and were very possessive of their tribal lands; as a result they continuously fought among themselves, and the advent of the European weapons, which they found that they could obtain by barter from misguided settlers, soon created a situation in which wholesale slaughter and revolting massacres threatened to wipe out the race altogether through internecine strife.

The New Zealand Company had bought vast tracts of land from the Maoris for distribution to the settlers, but the Company now discovered that because of the peculiar Maori customs the written agreements on the land had no meaning. They bound nobody but the signatory himself and the rest of his tribe felt at liberty to carry on warfare against settlers or Maoris for land which they still believed that they owned.

It was clear that something had to be done, and done quickly, and that the British government, partly because their nationals had helped to create the situation and partly to forestall French interest in the area, had to do it. They therefore annexed the whole territory of the islands to New South Wales in 1840, and the Treaty of Waitangi which was signed with the natives vested sovereignty in Britain, the Maoris still being allowed to own the land but to sell it only to the government. This angered the New Zealand Company, which saw its authority being undermined, and it promptly increased its settlements in the North Island, where most of the Maoris lived, and soon came into bitter conflict with them. The settlers claimed land which the Maoris, under the Treaty, were not allowed to sell to them, and the Maoris as a result attacked some of the settlements now held under the Crown.

Few troops were available to keep order, but war was inevitable and a small force was sent from New South Wales in 1845. The little army came up against stockade warfare which had been previously experienced in Burma; the Maori *pa* was usually very strongly fortified and even heavy guns could do little against it, and the Maoris themselves were more resolute than the Burmese. Being more interested in fighting for fighting's sake than in holding land, the Maoris retreated from *pa* to *pa* as each became too battered, and the lot of the Infantry against these savage fighters in thickly forested country, with no roads and no transport, was unenviable. Gradually, however, the British gained the upper hand and peace was made in 1847; the Treaty of Waitangi was invoked again and the Maoris were allowed to retain the lands for which they had fought.

Only three regiments took part, the 58th, 96th, and 99th Foot (The Northamptonshire, Manchester and Wiltshire Regiments), and all received the Honour **New Zealand**. Unfortunately no date was included in the Honour and there is no obvious way of distinguishing these regiments from those which fought in the 2nd Maori War twenty years later.

China

For centuries past China had been virtually isolated from the rest of the world; the Chinese still considered themselves the centre of the universe, surrounded by barbarians who were allowed to trade with them only if they were sufficiently humble. Until now the East India Company had had a virtual monopoly of the Chinese trade, and a very lucrative trade it was, largely financing the rest of the Company's operations. But the Chinese officials were rapacious and extorted vast sums 'on the side'; thus it became almost impossible to trade in commodities which showed only a moderate profit and the only goods which really provided sufficient profit to allow the Chinese their 'squeeze' were varieties of Indian opium, which the Chinese bought in large quantities.

In 1833 the British government, not really understanding the situation, ended the East India Company's monopoly, but was not prepared to submit to the arrogant Chinese merchants; and when the Chinese, in 1840, seized a large quantity of opium being imported for sale in Canton, the government was forced to take strong measures. So began the 1st China War, otherwise known logically enough as the Opium War.

A force was sent from India to the China seas which first seized Hong Kong at the mouth of the Canton river, and, since this did nothing to subdue the Chinese, then attacked Canton itself, forcing its evacuation. A number of the actions took place on and around the Yangse Kiang River, until the Chinese, realising that their weapons and tactics were no match for the British, came to terms in 1842. Hong Kong was annexed to the Empire, posts were opened in China for trade and British merchants were recognised, albeit reluctantly, as of equal status to the Chinese themselves.

The Honour **China Coast** was granted, borne on the badge of the British regiments and on the Colours of the Indian. Five British regiments gained the Honour, and six Indian regiments plus the Madras Engineers; four Indian regiments went unhonoured. The Royal Artillery did particularly well out of this small war, the Honour Titles resulting from it being the **Dragon Troop** and, creating lasting confusion in the Regiment, three **Dragon Batteries**.

For a number of years trade continued peacefully, but gradually Chinese arrogance reasserted itself and negotiations concerning the ensuing disputes started in 1856. In 1857 the 59th Foot (The East Lancashire Regiment) was sent to restore order in Canton, and after a short, sharp affair which only lasted a week was awarded a unique Honour. This was **Canton**.

The Treaty which followed allowed British and French ministers to be received in Pekin, but when eventually these officials arrived *en route* at Taku near Tientsin their landing was opposed and an expedition had to be sent from India to sort matters out and enforce the Treaty. The force attacked the **Taku Forts** in August 1860 and was awarded an Honour for doing so; this was gained by one British

Cavalry and seven Infantry regiments, and by two Indian Cavalry and two Infantry regiments and again the Madras Sappers and Miners.

The force then advanced on Pekin itself, in conjunction with a French force, and at first it seemed that their presence was sufficient to ensure that the negotiations would be settled amicably. But the Western diplomats had still reckoned without the Chinese, who in the middle of the ceremonies seized and imprisoned them, subjecting them to atrocious tortures. The Army then proceeded to attack the city which quickly surrendered, but not before the Emperor's Summer Palace had been destroyed. Perhaps this one act more than any other brought home to the Chinese that they were in the presence of powers greater than they; at any rate the right to trade was firmly established, Tientsin was opened to British ships and the 2nd China War was brought to a successful conclusion. The Honour **Pekin 1860** (without the date in the case of the Indian regiments) was awarded to six British and four Indian regiments, mostly the same ones as had been granted **Taku Forts**.

A Campaign Honour was awarded, **China 1858-62**, but only to the Indian Infantry regiments which had not taken part in other Honoured engagements. Seven regiments gained this Honour, but two were omitted. No Royal Artillery Honours emerged from this encounter, and the significant thing about the campaign was that—unusually—all who participated, except for the Indian Campaign Honour as stated above, received the Honours awarded.

Persian Gulf

For many years the countries around the Persian Gulf, including Arabia and Persia itself, had been a major trading area for European countries, and shipping had always been subject to raiding by Arab pirates operating in and around the Gulf. As early as 1809 a small expedition had been sent from India to destroy some of their strongholds and had had some success; but in such a large area the potential for piracy was immense, and, although the incursions were limited for a time, they soon built up again.

Accordingly in 1819 another force, strangely enough of almost identical composition to the one ten years earlier, was sent to the Gulf and again met with considerable success. No Honour had been awarded for the first expedition and, presumably because of the similarity of the forces, the Honour awarded for 1819 was stated to cover both. From the point of view of both British and Indian regiments this was unsatisfactory; only the 65th Foot (The York and Lancaster Regiment) was awarded the Honour **Arabia**, whereas the 47th Foot (The Loyal Regiment) had also participated both times and applied for the Honour without success. On the Indian side the Bombay Pioneers (as they became later) were awarded the Honour but as **Persian Gulf 1819**, whilst the one other Indian regiment in 1809 and the two others in 1819 were not recognised. Yet another case of injustice leading to confusion.

Two years later, in 1821, another series of actions in the same area resulted in another Honour, with the rather unusual title of **Beni Boo Alli**; again confusion seems to have reigned in the Honours department, since the Bombay Presidency Regiment, the Bombay Artillery and seven Indian Native regiments were awarded it, but the 65th Foot, who were also there, and applied unsuccessfully for it, and the Bombay Sappers and Miners were not.

A number of years passed, although the piracy continued, until the next expedition in 1839 captured the port of Aden, which remained a British colony, trading and coaling base for almost 130 years; it was only a small force which took part and received **Aden** as an Honour, the Bombay Presidency Regiment, the Bombay Artillery and two Bombay Native Infantry regiments.

Finally in 1856 occurred the final war in the area, known as the Persian War, and, perhaps to make up for previous deficiencies, considerably over-Honoured for the degree of fighting which took place, but as usual with confusing illogicality. The opposition was not heavy and the campaign only lasted for five months, but it produced the individual Honours **Reshire**, **Bushire** and **Koosh-Ab** and the Campaign Honour **Persia**. Of these one British regiment, the 64th Foot (The North Staffordshire Regiment), and the 2nd Bombay European Regiment (later The Durham Light Infantry), two Indian Cavalry and three Infantry regiments and the Bombay Sappers and Miners gained all four; the 78th Foot (The Seaforth Highlanders) and one Indian infantry regiment gained the last two, although the Indian regiment had participated in the first two as well; the 14th Light Dragoons only gained the Campaign Honour although they applied for **Koosh-Ab** as well; and one Indian Cavalry regiment, the Madras Sappers and Miners and nine other Indian Infantry regiments gained the Campaign Honour. Six other Indian regiments participated for no Honour at all.

Afghanistan

Apart from Britain, looking far and wide to expand her trade and at the same time her Empire, the major Power in Europe after the fall of Napoleon was Russia, and, being of an expansionist nature although not geared to overseas expansion, the Russians started to look eastwards. They had considerable influence in Persia already and had made progress with Afghanistan by supporting Dost Mohammed, the usurper ruler of that country. The British foresaw the possibility of Russian hordes descending through Afghanistan into the plains of India and decided that they should forestall this nightmare by replacing the old dynastic ruler, Shah Shuja, on his throne, if necessary by force.

Unfortunately any knowledge of the terrain of the country and its mountainous and rough nature was scanty, and, to make matters worse when contemplating a march into the country, India as it then was and Afghanistan were not contiguous. A wide strip of land lay in between, with the Punjab, ruled by the Sikhs, in the north and the Sind in the south; and the Sikhs, although quite agreeable to supporting the venture in principle, refused to allow the passage of British troops through their territory. This meant that to mount an attack on Afghanistan an enormous detour across the Sind Desert and the River Indus was necessary before the ascent of the passes could even begin.

Nevertheless in the summer of 1839 the Army carried out this manoeuvre with the blessing of the ruler of Sind, and marched on to Quetta and Kandahar, which surrendered without resistance, and then to Ghuznee, which was expected to follow suit. But it did not; the siege guns were far back down the baggage train, rations were running short and the fortress still held out. As disaster threatened a 'do or die' attempt to breach the walls with a mine succeeded, the city was stormed and fell. Dost Mohammed lost his nerve and fled, and the British force was able to enter Kabul, the capital, in triumph.

The Honour of **Ghuznee 1839** was awarded to two British and four Indian Cavalry regiments, the Bombay Artillery and Engineers, the Bengal Presidency Regiment, and three British and four Indian Infantry regiments, which all in all was a small force to have achieved so much.

Another engagement was fought at **Khelat** later in the year, which was awarded as an Honour to two British and two Indian regiments together with the Artillery and Engineers as before. This was apparently the end of the affair; Shah Shuja was installed on the throne and Kabul started to be developed as a typical Indian peacetime station. In fact at this point a Campaign Honour, **Afghanistan 1839**, was awarded to those who had participated, and one of the Bombay Artillery batteries, later a part of the Royal Artillery, was one day to gain the Honour Title of **Shah Shuja's Troop**.

Unfortunately there was one major problem, which did not appear to have occurred to the Indian government, and as a result it had done nothing to try to find the answer. The problem was that the Afghans much preferred Dost Mahommed as their ruler and in 1841 broke into revolt, not only against Shah Shuja but also against the British who had brought him back. One Indian Infantry regiment had already been involved in putting down a rising the previous year in **Kahun** for which it was awarded a unique Honour, but now the fate of the whole force in Kabul became critical.

The ineptness of the military commanders and the politicians was such that for a while nothing was done; the citadel could have been provisioned and defended until a stronger force could arrive to help, but before anybody reached a decision the unprotected provision depot was destroyed by the insurgents. Shah Shuja was assassinated; Macnaghten, the political resident, was murdered while acting as an envoy to the Afghans; and the Army Commander, old, infirm and incapable, agreed to hand over the treasury, his guns, and officers and their wives as hostages as a condition of safe conduct back to India of the remainder of the Army. At the end of 1841 the Army set out in retreat, but as might have been expected the Afghans did not honour their agreement and attacked it continuously; only one British regiment had been left in Kabul, the 44th Foot (The Essex Regiment) together with four Indian regiments and a vast horde of camp followers, so their capability for defence against the tribesmen was limited. Their strength dwindled and dwindled and the final 200 stood and were overwhelmed at Gandamak; one survivor only, Dr Bryden, struggled on to the fortress of Jellalabad in January 1842, and thus the whole force from Kabul, families and all, barring a very few prisoners, perished. No Honour was awarded for the *Retreat from Kabul*, perhaps because it was not a pitched battle.

Jellalabad was defended by one British regiment, the 13th Foot (The Somerset Light Infantry), together with some Engineers, part of an Indian Cavalry regiment of which the remainder had been lost in the retreat from Kabul, and a very low strength Indian Infantry regiment. In spite of being surrounded by Afghans and surviving an earthquake which damaged the walls the 'Illustrious Garrison', as it became known, held out. Khelat was bravely defended by a single Indian regiment, which gained the Honour **Khelat-I-Ghilzai** thereby, but Ghuznee was forced to surrender. However Kandahar was held by two British regiments, the 40th and 41st Foot (The South Lancashire Regiment and the Welch Regiment) and twelve Indian regiments under General Nott, and when given his orders to retire to India he ignored them and gallantly marched to relieve beleaguered Jellalabad, then advanced on Kabul to rescue the hostages instead of retreating to Quetta. He relieved the garrison of Khelat, captured Ghuznee and destroyed it, and reached Kabul at the same time as a relief army, which had crossed the Punjab and come up the Khyber Pass.

The prisoners were released, the bazaar blown up and the whole force returned to India late in 1842. Although the reappearance of the Army in India was treated in some quarters as a victory, as was Dunkirk in 1940, the whole campaign had been a disaster on a grand scale, only mitigated by the heroic defence of Jellalabad and Khelat and Nott's return to Kabul against heavy odds and orders.

A number of Honours were awarded. The 13th Foot with the two Indian regiments were awarded **Jellalabad**, to be carried on the cap badge with a Mural Crown. The 40th and 41st Foot were awarded **Candahar 1842**, together with eight Indian regiments, and the Bombay Artillery and the Bengal Engineers who were also in the garrison, although the four remaining Indian regiments were not. The same two British regiments were awarded **Ghuznee 1842**, as were eight Indian regiments of Nott's force, and **Cabul 1842** was awarded to the members of the joint armies, going to six British and seventeen Indian regiments and the Bengal Sappers and Miners, although five other Indian regiments were excluded. **Kabul Battery** was eventually added to the Royal Artillery Honour Titles.

The campaign was a tragedy resulting from over-confidence, lack of planning and supplies, and perhaps above all from political incompetence and political control of the military who had warned in advance of the dangers of the enterprise. As a result British prestige was considerably lessened and Dost Mohammed was restored to the throne. The original reason for the war, the possibility of Russian infiltration into India, seems to have been forgotten, but it was never a real threat in any case.

India

The first action in India during the period concerned the redress of an old wrong, at least from the British point of view. In 1805 Lake had been unable to take the fortress of Bhurtpore which for twenty years thereafter had remained a challenge to British supremacy, particularly since it was rumoured among the Indians that the British were afraid to attack it for fear of being repulsed once more. In 1824 a usurper seized power, and since the issue could no longer be dodged there occurred at the end of the following year the so called Jat War, although since it only lasted a month and included one major battle the merit of such a title is doubtful.

A large force, very strong in Artillery, advanced on the fortress, battered and mined it. When the mines were exploded with considerable effect the impregnable fortress was stormed and captured with a surprisingly light casualty list. The action added enormously to British prestige. The Honour **Bhurtpore** was awarded to four British regiments, the Bengal Presidency Regiment, the Bengal Engineers, twenty-three Indian regiments, of which only six survived the Mutiny, and also to two Gurkha regiments, the first time that they had been in action as part of the British Army. The Royal Artillery eventually added **Bhurtpore Battery** to its list of Honour Titles.

Apart from a minor action to put down a rising in *Coorg* in 1834, undertaken by three British Infantry regiments of which one, the 55th Foot (The Border Regiment), applied for it as an Honour unsuccessfully, the Scinde became the next scene of hostilities. Operations had taken place between 1839 and 1842 in the area of **Cutchee**, when an Honour had been gained by two Indian Cavalry regiments, one of which subsequently took the title of The Scinde Horse; but now it was thought necessary to put down the Baluch chieftains who misruled the area and take it under British control. A small force under General Sir Charles Napier therefore advanced into the region and soon came face to face with ten times his numbers at Meeanee early in 1843. The 22nd Foot (The Cheshire Regiment) was the only British regiment in the force together with half a dozen Indian regiments, and they sat at the top of a dry nullah while the much larger force of Baluchis milled about at the bottom, unable to get at them but exchanging fire at very short range. Eventually the heavy casualties of the Baluch forced them to withdraw. A similar battle was fought five weeks later at Hyderabad, after which the Baluchis surrendered and their country was annexed.

The campaign became famous because of the legend of Napier's single-word punning telegram sent to the Queen after the event, in which he stated 'Peccavi' meaning 'I have sinned'. Three Battle Honours were awarded, for the two main battles and for the campaign. The 22nd Foot was awarded all three, but the Indian recipients varied. The Bombay Artillery, Madras Engineers and six of the seven regiments involved gained **Meeanee**; nine out of the fifteen gained **Hyderabad**; but, oddly, only four Cavalry regiments gained the Campaign Honour of **Scinde**, presumably because in their case it was treated more as a general service and mopping-up Honour, separately from those awarded for the individual battles, than for the campaign as a whole. The 28th Foot (The Gloucestershire Regiment) applied for the Honour although there is little evidence of their involvement, and the Royal Artillery subsequently gained another Honour Title from Hyderabad — the **Eagle Troop**.

Later that same year trouble recurred with the Mahrattas. During the war nearly forty years earlier Gwalior, although part of the Mahratta Federation, had not been actively engaged. Now, as a result of a dispute over the succession of the Maharaja, there occurred a military *coup-d'état*, although the phrase had not then been coined. The disturbances that this produced could not be countenanced by the British and the Army moved in to sort things out.

A large force was divided into two wings which, by coincidence, each encountered a part of the Mahratta army on the same day, 29 December 1843. Two battles were fought simultaneously and both were won, although with considerable losses, and **Maharajpore** and **Punniar** entered the list of Battle Honours. The former was awarded to one British and seven Indian Cavalry regiments and to two British and seven Indian Infantry regiments, together with the Bengal Sappers and Miners; one Indian Infantry regiment was omitted from the award, and subsequently **Maharajpore Battery** commemorated the event for the Royal Artillery. In the latter battle one British and four Indian Cavalry regiments, two British and four Indian Infantry regiments and again the Bengal Sappers and Miners were awarded the Honour; strangely, however, in the circumstances some regiments of the Gwalior Contingent, troops from the state who had become part of the Indian Army as opposed to the Maharaja's Army, were also present and the Honour additionally was granted to two Cavalry and seven Infantry regiments of the Contingent.

The opposition of the Sikhs to British entry into the Punjab has already been mentioned in connection with the Afghan War; but until now, as well as keeping others out they had been content to stay in their own territory. In recent years they had been under the strong rule of Ranjit Singh, but in 1839 he had died and there followed the customary Indian problem of succession; there were several members of Ranjit's progeny in contention and a power struggle by weak but ambitious men had allowed their army to get out of hand. The new leaders, partly to distract attention from their own inadequacies and partly to occupy the army, decided to attack British India, with the treasure of Delhi as the target, and late in 1845 they crossed the Sutlej. The situation was dangerous because the Sikhs were naturally stubborn fighters and had been drilled into well-disciplined troops, closely copying the East India Company's sepoys, under French officers who had served in the Napoleonic armies. There is little doubt that they were superior soldiers to the British sepoys who faced them and therefore an additional burden fell on the British regiments.

The first battle came when the British attacked the Sikhs in a belt of jungle at **Moodkee** and drove them back, although with heavy losses; one British and six Indian Cavalry regiments, and four British and nine Indian Infantry regiments gained this Honour, although three Cavalry and five Infantry regiments in the Indian part of the force were not awarded it. The Sikhs had withdrawn to a strong position at **Ferozeshah**, not far away, and three days later the British again attacked them, this time into such a hail of Artillery and musket fire that even the British regular troops at times fell back in confusion with very heavy casualties. In most previous engagements against native troops a few volleys of musketry at close quarters had been enough to make them retreat, but not so the Sikhs, who were made of much sterner stuff and only gave way when their regiments were nearly decimated. Eventually a charge by the 3rd Light Dragoons on the enemy guns was successful, largely perhaps because this was a tactic not previously experienced by the Sikhs, and the day was won.

But in the darkness part of the Sikh force had been able to withdraw and the British were in no fit state for another encounter immediately. Nevertheless General Gough advanced at daybreak and captured the Sikh encampment, and the other wing of the enemy force, which had been on the point of advancing against him, drew off. It had been a close run thing as far as the actual battle was concerned but it had also brought British supremacy in India close to destruction. One British (The 3rd Light Dragoons) and eight Indian Cavalry regiments, together with six British, one Presidency and fourteen Indian Infantry regiments and the Bengal Engineers were awarded the Honour, and one further Indian Cavalry regiment and four Infantry regiments were engaged with no tangible evidence of their presence.

A month only elapsed before the next encounter in January 1846. A small force covering a baggage train ran into a superior Sikh force on the banks of the Sutlej, and, realising that retreat would be difficult for the Sikhs with the river at their backs, decided to attack them. Largely due to a gallant charge by the 16th Lancers the Sikhs were broken and forced to withdraw across the river with heavy losses of men and guns. **Aliwal** became a Battle Honour for one British and five Indian Cavalry regiments and for three British and seven Indian Infantry regiments, which included two Gurkha regiments.

The Sikh effort was now almost expended and they fell back on Sobraon, their last position on the British side of the Sutlej. A fortnight after the battle of Aliwal, Gough attacked their position with his main Army. Charging with bayonets, followed up by Cavalry, he soon took the Sikh entrenchments, the bridge of boats was destroyed and the enemy was driven into the river, with losses estimated at nearly 70,000 men and many guns. **Sobraon** was awarded to three British and seven Indian Cavalry and eight British, one Presidency and twelve Indian Infantry regiments, and to the Bengal Sappers and Miners. Inevitably some who were present did not receive the Honour, this time one Indian Cavalry and ten Indian Infantry regiments.

The British Army marched into Lahore with the Punjab at their feet and the 1st Sikh War, otherwise known as the Sutlej campaign, was over. The Punjab was not annexed but a Council of Regency was set up, and it was hoped that after his defeat the Sikh ruler would accept this arrangement; but his pride had been hurt but not broken and an uneasy peace reigned for a short while only. Two months later two British officers accompanying the newly appointed Governor of Mooltan were murdered at the instigation of the Mulraj, the man he was replacing, and the south-west Punjab was once again in revolt. A small force of Pathans under a British officer overcame Mulraj, and in due course a British force including a supposedly loyal Sikh detachment reached Mooltan; but the Sikhs soon deserted to the Mulraj, the British force had to fall back and on this signal the whole of the Punjab prepared again for war.

Gough marched from Lahore in October 1848 and first encountered the Sikh force at *Ramnagar*, the enemy being driven back, with heavy losses to both sides. This battle was not awarded to the four British and seven Indian regiments involved, and the next engagement at *Sadulapur* six weeks later was similarly omitted from Honour although five British and eleven Indian regiments took part in the battle. Meanwhile the Sikhs had fallen back on the river Jhelum to await reinforcements, and there, at **Chillianwallah**, Gough attacked them in January 1849. But the Sikh position was in dense jungle and very strong, and when it started raining fighting became impossible and the battle was left in an indeterminate state. Nevertheless the Honour was awarded to three British and six Indian Cavalry regiments and to three British, one Presidency and twelve Indian Infantry regiments, for once all who took part.

The British force at Mooltan had been engaging the enemy for four months, and a week after Chillianwallah eventually captured the town; **Mooltan** was awarded as an Honour to eight Indian Cavalry regiments, a battery of the Bombay Mountain Artillery, the Bengal and Bombay Engineers, and to three British, one Presidency and nine Indian Infantry regiments. Terms for peace were proposed, but rejected by the Sikhs whose reinforcements had by now arrived, and they took up a position at Goojerat on the River Chenab; and there in February came the final trial of strength.

Although Gough was outnumbered by more than two to one, he now had plenty of artillery and the battle opened with a steady bombardment of the Sikh guns before the British line moved forward. The relentless advance of major British forces overcame all resistance and the Sikhs were put to flight; they were pursued until the whole of the Punjab was in British hands, and the power and will of the Sikh ruler was at last broken. **Goojerat** became a Battle Honour for three British and thirteen Indian Cavalry regiments, the Bengal and Bombay Sappers and Miners, and seven British, two Presidency and nineteen Indian Infantry regiments, the largest force by far to take part in any of the battles.

The 2nd Sikh War, the Punjab campaign, unlike the 1st, was also granted a campaign Honour, **Punjaub**, and this was awarded altogether to thirteen British and sixty Indian regiments, including Engineers and Artillery.

So the Sikh power was finally crushed and this time the Punjab was annexed, the experiment with a protectorate having failed. Apart from the gain of territory and the removal of the final tribal threat in India, the main tangible evidence of the victory was the great Koh-i-Noor diamond, the Mountain of Light, previously owned by Shah Shuja and surrendered by him to Ranjit Singh, but now sent to England to find a permanent home, set in the Imperial Crown.

To most British leaders of the day the struggle for a unified imperial India was now at an end. But to achieve this end a vast native force had been raised, five times the size of the British force in India. This position of strength revived the ideas of freedom from foreign rule in the minds of some of the Indian chieftains, and the results of their ideals and the events which led to their final defeat and to India becoming the pearl in the crown of the British Empire must wait until the next chapter.

10 The Crimea and the Mutiny, 1854-9

In the last chapter two factors were mentioned which materially affect this period and its wars—the situation in the British Army after the defeat of Napoleon and Russia's expansionist ambitions. We saw that the Army, or part of it, was kept busy in colonial wars, although because of the lack of news media as we know them today comparatively few people in England had very much idea of what was going on. This in any case was part of the policy of the Army leaders; Parliament was still as anti-Army as it had always been and only grudgingly provided the money to pay for it. This meant that to retain any semblance of a fighting force a number of regiments which were not actively engaged in campaigning were kept in garrisons abroad, on the basis that what the governmental eye did not see its heart would not grieve over. An additional advantage of this was that, since reinforcements took so long to reach the far-flung outposts from Britain, it was obviously practical to have reserves nearer to the possible scene of action.

But it was still not an army in modern terms, not even in terms of the Peninsular War, but a collection of regiments; auxiliary services and logistical support barely existed and training, except on-the-job training in battle, did not exist at all. The endurance and courage were still there in the fighting troops, as witness the battles in Afghanistan, India and elsewhere; but although the troops may have served against native armies, however numerous, this experience would not be of much account against a European enemy, particularly in terms of strategy and tactics. Not that this worried the government, if it ever thought about it, because a European war had become almost unthinkable; the opening of the Great Exhibition in 1851, after 36 years of peace, seemed to most people to presage the continuation of universal peace. But those parliamentary ostriches who had the courage to take their heads out of the sand occasionally would have seen that revolution was in the air in Europe, in Poland and in Austria, particularly, and that in other areas all was not as well as might have been thought.

Louis Napoleon, nephew of Bonaparte became Prince-President of France in 1848, and four years later in emulation of his uncle was proclaimed Emperor. He was determined to prove himself as great a man as his kinsman and set out to avenge his overthrow by subduing and humbling the powers responsible for it—Britain, Russia, Austria and Prussia. But he was not stupid, and saw that to achieve his aims he would have to use one of them as an ally, and decided to choose Britain—at least until he had defeated the remainder when he could then turn on Britain herself.

The Crimean War, 1854-6

Napoleon III, as he now was, first looked for a good reason to attack Russia with British support, and Tsar Nicholas I unwittingly helped him in his designs. After the overthrow of Napoleon Bonaparte Russia had become the dominant Power on the continent of Europe, dictatorially ruled by the Tsar who was also head of the Orthodox Church and had extended his influence into contiguous countries on the pretext of protecting Christians. His description of Turkey as the 'sick man of Europe' sowed the seeds of suspicion, and when he demanded a protectorate over all Christians in the Turkish Empire, which would have given him a foothold on the Mediterranean, the Russian goal for centuries past, this was refused. Russia therefore attacked Turkish territory in what is now Romania, and followed this up with the destruction of the Turkish fleet in the Black Sea by the Russian fleet based on Sevastopol in the Crimea. Britain was alarmed for her own Middle and Far Eastern spheres of influence, and could not sit idly by; on her own initiative, but to Louis Napoleon's great joy, she joined France in declaring war on Russia early in 1854, and this action was supported by Turkey.

It was clearly impractical for the allies to attack the vast land bulk of Russia, but command of the sea enabled them to attack the Crimea. If this could be denied to the Russians, Turkey and the Middle East would be safe, and the Russians themselves could only reinforce the Crimea by transferring troops and supplies over hundreds of miles of country virtually without any communications. But the climate of the Crimea, very hot in summer and bitterly cold in winter, was not conducive to long campaigning and it was therefore essential to make a quick and decisive attack to secure the only Russian fortress and base at Sevastopol.

The British force sent from England was small, but was largely composed of long-service troops who were well drilled and experienced in battle since many of the regiments had already been proved in other parts of the Empire. Unfortunately it was still not an army; there was no properly organised staff, transport or supplies, and medical facilities were rudimentary in the extreme. The command was vested in Lord Raglan, who had had a long and distinguished service career at the 'Horse Guards' but had no experience of commanding large bodies of troops.

The force landed temporarily, to organise itself, on the coast of Bulgaria and immediately began to suffer casualties from cholera and dysentery, so that when it eventually set sail again for the Crimea its strength, limited even to start with, and vitality were much reduced. Nevertheless it landed in good order on the west coast of the peninsula, some way north of Sevastopol, and the Russian commander, seeing the danger of being cut off by an allied advance across the Crimea, marched out to meet it and took up a strong position on the heights overlooking the River Alma with one flank on the sea. Here, in September 1854, the Allies attacked him.

The British forces may have been weak but they did not lack the glitter and colour of the parade ground, and this was probably the last deliberate battle fought in full dress with all the panoply of the old style of warfare. The British line tried to advance across the river and up the hill in parade formation as it had been taught, but the terrain did not allow this for long and soon order and dressing was broken in an attempt to press on. Their fire was heavy and accurate and the tight-packed Russian formations were no match for them. With the French finally successful also in reaching the top of the hill on the right of the British, the Russians broke and then fell back under heavy Artillery fire. The battle was won, and the first Victoria Cross was awarded after the battle to Sergeant Luke O'Connor of the 23rd Foot (The Royal Welsh Fusiliers). The action proved that the Allies were more than a match for the Russians so long as they were in open country and away from their fortresses.

Alma was awarded as an Honour to five Cavalry and thirty Infantry regiments, although in the case of ten Infantry regiments and the whole of the Cavalry their participation was extremely limited and they played largely a watch-and-wait role. The Royal Artillery gained another Honour Title, **Alma Battery**.

The Russians now fell back towards Sevastopol and Lord Raglan wanted to attack them again while they were still vulnerable; but the French, still very traditional in approach, objected since the army had no established port until Sevastopol itself was captured and the opportunity of destroying the Russian armies was lost. Instead it was decided to establish a base on the port of Balaclava and thither the army marched, although the camp was eventually set up some miles from the port which presented problems of manhandling supplies with little transport and no roads.

As a result of this extraordinary and stupid allied manoeuvre the Russian forces retreating from the Alma were allowed complete freedom of movement into the fortress of Sevastopol; in fact the two armies almost met by accident, crossing each other's tracks on the march, but each was too surprised and disorganised to do anything about it. The flair of a Wellington or a Stringer Lawrence was missing, and as a result the character of the war changed because now the allies became besieged in their base. Nevertheless, after a heavy Artillery bombardment, the opportunity to attack Sevastopol presented itself, but again the French refused to co-operate, and this last chance of

a speedy end to the war was lost.

A Russian force now attacked the redoubts near Balaclava occupied by the Turks and captured them, which only left a single British regiment between the Russians and the undefended port. The 93rd Foot (The Argyll and Sutherland Highlanders) formed quickly in two long lines and after a few volleys the enemy withdrew; the 93rd gained the soubriquet 'the thin red line' and Balaclava was saved. At this point, as the Russian cavalry withdrew, the Heavy Brigade of the British Cavalry launched a courageous attack although greatly outnumbered, and if the Light Brigade had joined in as its commander, Lord Cardigan, was ordered to do (shades of Minden!) the Russians must surely have been destroyed. Shortly afterwards the famous charge of the Light Brigade on the enemy guns took place; this has gained fame from the gallantry with which it was executed, and notoriety as the epitome of purposelessness and the useless wastage of human life owing to poor command and to imprecise and badly issued orders. Quite apart from which, if Cardigan had obeyed orders, instead of allowing his pride to require the lion's share of any publicity, the casualties could have been avoided and the Russian Cavalry destroyed. The charge is so well known in detail that it is unnecessary to describe it here, but as the French general who witnessed it said '*C'est magnifique, mais ce n'est pas la guerre*'.

The net result of this lack of co-ordination and opportunism was the loss of another chance to end the war quickly and the establishment of the Russian position more strongly than ever on the British right. Nevertheless **Balaclava** became one of the most famous and universally known of British battles and the Honour for it was awarded to ten Cavalry regiments and only one Infantry, the gallant 93rd Highlanders. For the Royal Artillery, although no Honour Title was claimed or awarded for participation in the battle, it is celebrated by C Battery, RHA.

Few British reinforcements had arrived since the initial landing and the losses had been quite heavy, but a large number of Russian regiments had trudged from Moscow across the steppes and now their forces in and around Sevastopol had a considerable superiority in strength. In November 1854 they attacked again on the British right and this was a much more serious threat; their advance started in the darkness of early morning in fog and rain, and before he had the opportunity of deploying his forces Raglan found himself opposed to massive enemy forces. The British troops joined the battle piecemeal and took up their formations as and how they could, and only their dogged courage and determination and the lack of Russian initiative save them from annihilation. In the fog nobody really knew what was happening but on every possible occasion the British attacked the dense Russian formations and eventually they were forced back and suddenly broke in retreat.

It was hardly a good example of how a battle should be conducted, any more than Balaclava, but it proved once again that the British training and methods of warfare were infinitely superior to the Russian. **Inkerman**, which became known as the 'Soldier's Battle', was awarded as an Honour to five Cavalry regiments, although their part in the battle was very slight, and to twenty-seven Infantry regiments. The Royal Artillery gained another Honour Title, but as with that awarded for the China War to what were eventually to become three Dragon Batteries, three Batteries later claimed **Inkerman** in their titles. The 46th Foot (The Duke of Cornwall's Light Infantry) claimed the Honour unsuccessfully, although only part of the regiment was present as it had been at the Alma.

The war now came to a halt as winter set in. It was one of the worst winters the British Army ever experienced, exposed as they were on a bleak upland plain with no shelter from the elements and virtually none of the essential comforts needed to sustain life. Perhaps only the fate of the army in the winter of 1794 in Flanders bears any real comparison. The commissariat had again failed to appreciate the needs of the fighting troops, partly because the 'Horse Guards' had not anticipated that Sevastopol would not have been captured quickly and partly because the organisation for an army just did not exist. The Army almost perished from cold, hunger and sickness and by the end of the winter there were more men in hospital than there were fit for duty; a storm had destroyed the shipping in Balaclava harbour and the tracks to the camp became impassable.

The years of parliamentary parsimony had produced the inevitable result, and only the bitter weather itself prevented the Russians from taking advantage of the situation and attacking. News of the disaster slowly reached England because for the first time there were newspaper reporters with the Army, and the public raised an outcry. The government had to take action at last and supplies were sent out; medical resources, until then notable only by their total inadequacy, were assembled, and a small group of nurses under Florence Nightingale set off, practically by their own efforts, to take over the base hospital at Scutari where the situation was so appalling that men preferred to take their chance in the field rather than be sent to almost certain death at the so-called hospital.

As well as supplies, reinforcements were also sent out, together with siege guns, and eventually as winter passed the Army regained its lost strength; but the losses had been of experienced soldiers and the reinforcements were mostly young, new recruits. The French had also been reinforced, and now they became the largest national force in the Crimea, and the situation was reversed from the previous autumn because now they wanted to attack and the British were in no position to do so. Nevertheless, against Raglan's better judgement, they fell in with French plans and in June 1855 co-operated in an attack on the two great redoubts, the Malakoff and *The Redan*, the British share being the latter. The attack failed with heavy casualties and Raglan became the scapegoat for governmental inefficiency and was recalled.

A further attack was mounted in September and this time the French were successful although the British attack failed again. No Honour was awarded for the attacks on the Redan, presumably because of the lack of success, but altogether twenty-four Infantry regiments were involved. With the French now dominating the fortress of Sevastopol, the Russian position was untenable, and in any case they had had enough, and they withdrew. This was the real end of the war although peace was not made until the following year.

Sevastopol was awarded as a Campaign Honour for the Crimean War; it was gained by thirteen Cavalry and forty-nine Infantry regiments, and the only regiment which participated in any way without any award was the 6th Dragoon Guards. Of those awarded the Honour only thirty-five had been engaged in any of the four major battles; nevertheless the remainder had taken part in the siege of Sevastopol and had suffered the hardships of the campaign and fully deserved the award.

Napoleon had partly achieved his plan to avenge the French retreat from Moscow, although perhaps not very convincingly, and had gained in prestige after the final battle; the Russians had been humbled to a certain extent, and signed a number of agreements which they soon broke. But British prestige had suffered badly; the Army had fought bravely and to the best of its ability given the appalling conditions and lack of organisation and supplies, but the Navy had failed to bring the Russian fleet to battle and had achieved little. But if the military image had been tarnished, the administrative debacle led in due course to many reforms which prevented such avoidable tragedies as the Crimea, particularly the medical one, from happening again.

One Battle Honour awarded in connection with the war has not yet been mentioned, and was the first of its kind and in fact one of only three such Honours granted. In order to free fighting troops as reinforcements in the Crimea a number of Militia Battalions attached to the regular regiments were sent out to the Mediterranean, as volunteers, to carry out garrison duties in the islands, mainly Malta and Corfu. These ten battalions were awarded the Honour **Mediterranean**, but it was regarded as an Honour to those individual battalions, and was never borne officially by their parent regiments, unreasonably perhaps when those battalions eventually became a permanent and integral part of the regular regiments, but then it was not actually a Battle Honour either. With the eventual disbandment of the Militia Battalions, in practice in 1922 but officially not until 1953, the Honour died with them.

The Indian Mutiny, 1857-9

Although the war in the Crimea was over, the need for reinforcements had further reduced the small British force in India to a dangerous level. The reports which had filtered back to India of the heavy losses and the mismanagement of the campaign had lowered the prestige of the Army among the very large Indian forces which had been raised for the Crown to cope with the emergencies and risings of the past 30 years. In addition the misplaced trust in the loyalty of the Sepoy regiments, many of whose members had in recent memory fought against those same British regiments, and a lack of understanding of them, had lowered the level of discipline and given the Indians the feeling that the British were not after all as powerful as they had once thought.

Because of the general unpopularity of service in India, particularly with the Sepoy regiments, compared with that at home, the system had grown up of officers exchanging their postings with officers already in India, officers who were poor enough to need the purchase price for the exchange and were prepared to put up with the conditions for the extra money, which would either enable them to keep pace with their richer brother officers or put something aside for when they retired. As a result many of the officers in the country had grown old, tired and uninterested in the service and were less and less able to exercise proper command over their native troops. Also the pensions paid by the Indian Presidency governments, particularly Bengal, were pitifully small and inadequate and in many cases officers were not eligible for them until an advanced age. This meant that the higher ranks were filled by men who could not afford to retire, and while decades earlier they may have been good, efficient officers they no longer had the energy or will to take decisive action.

The real cause of the Mutiny, like that of so many wars, is impossible to relate to a single factor but arose through a host of minor reasons which together produced enough grievances to persuade the dissidents that the time had come to drive their British masters out of their country. A tense and uneasy feeling had existed in India for some time. Some of the contributory factors were the technological progress in the creation of the railway and telegraph systems, the institution of education among the Indians, a curtailment of certain religious practices, such as suttee, and the destruction of some temples which stood in the way of the new railway lines, all of which seemed to indicate to unsophisticated minds that Britain was trying to turn them into Christians. Other factors were land dispossession, salt and grain taxes, a loss of privilege for the common man, particularly in Oude which had only recently been annexed, and two curious prophesies, first that British rule would end on the centenary of Plassey—23 June 1857—and secondly that a major catastrophe was imminent.

All in all the old order was changing, from a native point of view not for the better, and perhaps the government did not act with sufficient sympathy towards Indian tradition or with the delicacy which progress demanded in a largely illiterate country. But early in 1857 there occurred the spark which became the popular reason, although now often discounted in favour of the reasons already stated, for the explosion which was shortly to come.

The cartridge of the new Enfield rifle, which was just then appearing in India, could be opened by hand but was normally bitten open and the bullet was said to be greased to allow an easy passage of the barrel. Some were undoubtedly greased but most were waxed and the grease story was spread to undermine further British rule. The story first spread was that the grease was cow fat, which may well have been true and would certainly not have occurred to the authorities at home as any sort of problem. But to the Hindu the cow is sacred and in no way would Hindu native troops lose caste by biting the greased cartridges. The next story to spread, almost certainly put around by Hindu dissidents, was that some of the grease used was pig fat, and this had the same effect on the Muslims as the first story had on the Hindus. The two stories had the effect of uniting the two, otherwise inimical, factions and religious divisions of India against the British, who it was said had been so lacking in understanding, if not deliberately insulting, as to create the situation and, it was rumoured, were intending to discipline the Sepoy regiments for refusing to accept the new cartridge.

Administration was lax and stereotyped, nothing could be acted upon or shown to the Governor General unless it was written and in any case took months to percolate through the bureaucratic systems, so that the Governor General knew nothing of the situation or had any warning of its implications. In the outpost stations many of the commanders had made no efforts to understand the Sepoy mentality and often made matters worse by bombastic and autocratic attitudes.

At this point it is perhaps necessary to give some idea of the Native Army in India and thus of the size of the problem which confronted Britain. In the three Presidencies together there were approximately eighty-eight Cavalry and 253 Infantry regiments; 'approximately' because there were a number of irregular regiments and local levies and the records of these are not comprehensive. Of these regiments by far the majority, sixty-one Cavalry and 144 Infantry, were in Bengal, and this was the seat of the trouble. Not all the regiments actually mutinied at the start of the trouble, although most of them did within a short while, but in the end twenty-four Cavalry and sixty-seven Infantry regiments joined the flag of revolt in Bengal together with two Infantry regiments in Bombay, but no complete regiments in Madras or in the Hyderabad contingent which was nominally also part of the Bengal Presidency.

There were few British troops in northern India, most were in the Punjab, and only four battalions in the whole of Bengal, an area equivalent to France and Germany together. It was summer time and many British officers, including those of the Sepoy regiments, were in the hill stations on leave, and it took time to recall them and to get the British regiments on the move once the Mutiny broke out. At Barrackpore a young Sepoy named Parde was cut down during a disarming ceremony of the 19th Native Infantry and became the symbol of rebellion. At Meerut, where eighty-five Sepoys who would not accept the new cartridge had been court-martialled and publicly humiliated, the first major outbreak took place on 10 May, when the whole Sepoy garrison mutinied during Sunday church parade when the British troops were unarmed. Officers were murdered, barracks and houses were set alight, and the mutineers then moved towards Delhi, which was still the spiritual capital of the country. The city, together with huge quantities of arms, ammunition and gunpowder, fell the following day to the Native troops in the city, who also mutinied and imprisoned the British officers in the Palace, and to the advance guard of the mutineers from Meerut.

Shortly after this mutinies of significant proportions also occurred at Cawnpore and at Lucknow. At the former place the British commander, having heard what had happened at Meerut and having no illusions about the loyalty of his Sepoys, constructed a defensive area outside the city to which the Europeans could withdraw. When the mutinous force did attack them in overwhelming numbers the few British troops beat off the attacks so well that eventually the Sepoys withdrew. But living nearby was a man called Nana Sahib, who had for a long time born a grudge against the British. He was an adopted son of the last Peishwa of Poona, whom they had removed, and he felt that he had a right to what he believed were his possessions. This barbarous and embittered man, who had nevertheless enjoyed a social relationship with the European community, now offered them safe conduct by the Ganges to Allahabad. As soon as the Europeans had emerged from their defensive area and were embarking the Sepoys treacherously attacked them, and later put to death all who escaped the murderous close-range fire, except for some women and children who were imprisoned in Cawnpore itself.

At Lucknow Sir Harry Lawrence, the Chief Commissioner of Oude, also seeing the danger, hastily fortified the Residency and installed the Europeans there, defended by his one British regiment, the 32nd Foot (Duke of Cornwall's Light Infantry). He then attacked the rebel force which had assembled, but was repulsed, and this was the signal for a general rising in the area. The Residency was besieged, Lawrence was killed and his successor, with thoughts of the tragedy at Cawnpore, determined never to surrender.

It must be remembered here that the mutineers were not a few men from here and there, but whole regiments, Cavalry and Infantry, which remained as trained and ordered formations, now led by senior Indian NCOs, and were thus a force to be reckoned with. At this point at any rate the planning of the leaders of the Mutiny was in general noticeably superior to that of their masters, who, in spite of numerous pieces of evidence that something big was breaking, had steadfastly refused to accept or put any credence on the intelligence. Shades of Malaya eighty-four years later!

For reasons of both strategy and face the massacre at Cawnpore had to be avenged and Delhi had to be recaptured, and a small force was immediately sent to Delhi from the Punjab. It took up a position outside the city and soon found itself being heavily assailed by the mutineers from within. More reinforcements came from the Punjab, men who had been only recently won over to the British side after the Sikh Wars, but who nevertheless respected them as fighting soldiers, and despised the troops from the eastern parts of Bengal who formed the bulk of the mutinous regiments.

But it was not until September that the force was large enough to consider an assault on the city; by this time also many of the older officers had gone sick or died, at any rate had left the field, and their replacements were younger, more mentally alert and prepared to redress the situation. Breaches were opened in the walls but losses were heavy and only about 5,000 men were available for the assault against ten times their number in the enemy ranks. Nevertheless the attack was successful and by the end of the month Delhi was again in British hands, although only after further heavy casualties.

The titular head of the Mogul dynasty, around whom the mutineers had rallied was captured and subsequently died in exile, and his sons, who were accused of the murder of European women and children, with good reason, were shot out of hand. This finally brought an end to the dy-

nasty which had ruled India actively or only in name for centuries. The Honour of **Delhi 1857** was awarded to two British and seven Indian Cavalry regiments and to five British, two Presidency and nine Indian Infantry regiments, plus the Bengal Sappers and Miners. The Royal Artillery gained another Honour title, **Tomb's Troop**, named after the Battery Commander.

Meanwhile another small force had been assembling at Allahabad as reinforcements arrived, mainly from the Calcutta area, and was put under the command of General Henry Havelock. In July he moved out with less than 2,000 men up the Ganges towards Cawnpore; it was a grim march but in a week he reached his goal, only to find that he was too late to save the women and children, who had been butchered by the Nana's orders and their bodies thrown down a well, which was later sealed and became the centre of a garden of remembrance.

The defence of the Residency at Lucknow had been courageously continued by the single British regiment and one loyal Sepoy regiment, with the inevitable casualties, sickness and shortness of food. Havelock now set off thither from Cawnpore and slowly progressed, joined by a few more reinforcements and General Outram, who was now the Chief Commissioner of Oude and, although Havelock's senior officer, refused to take over command from him. Eventually Lucknow came in sight and on 25 September the little force of six British and one Sikh regiments attacked the besiegers and fought its way into the Residency to reinforce the heroic garrison, executing all the mutineers that they captured, mostly by blowing them from the guns. But this was in no way a relief since the siege continued; there were many more mouths to feed, although by this time large stores of grain, which Lawrence had concealed against such an emergency under the Residency, had been discovered, but the larger force made the defence easier than before.

Relief was still essential as soon as possible and this became the first priority of the new Commander in Chief in India, Sir Colin Campbell, who was one of the few senior officers to have fought in the Crimea with distinction. A force was assembled, partly from the victorious troops from Delhi, and, leaving only a minimum guard at Cawnpore, it moved towards Lucknow which it reached towards the end of November. The besieging mutineers were attacked by one British and five Indian Cavalry regiments and seven British and three Indian Infantry regiments who showed no mercy on the enemy and eventually joined hands with the garrison. Lucknow was relieved and the women and children evacuated, but Havelock died soon afterwards of dysentry outside the city which will always be linked with his name.

Meanwhile things had been getting worse back at Cawnpore, where the Gwalior Contingent, previously considered loyal, had now joined the mutineers, and with other Sepoys, all under the command of Tantia Topi, attacked the city. The small detachment there fought back to defend the city and the bridge of boats which Campbell had constructed across the Ganges, which it succeeded in doing with heavy loss. Campbell, having relieved Lucknow, now returned and crossed the bridge; the civilian refugees, women and children whom he had brought with him were sent on to Allahabad and he was now free to attack the rebels. *Cawnpore* was captured and the mutineers were routed; this was the decisive battle because the British were now in the ascendant and instead of struggling to survive against the mutineers were now able to concentrate on putting down the rebellion. One British and five Indian Cavalry and thirteen British, one Presidency and one Indian Infantry regiments took part in the capture, but in spite of its importance no Honour was granted for it.

It might be supposed that only the British troops supported by a small number of loyal Indians had been able to carry out the defences, reliefs and captures so far during the war, but there were also instances of individual loyal Sepoy regiments heroically carrying out defensive operations on their own. *Saugur* was defended by a single Bengal regiment, and Honours were awarded to a Sikh regiment for the defence of **Arrah** and the capture of **Behar**, the former of these two being applied for by the British regiment which took part, the 5th Foot (The Royal Northumberland Fusiliers).

The time had now come to reoccupy Lucknow, where Outram was still holding out with a small force, and a large force was assembled for the purpose early in 1858. Campbell arrived there once more in March and battered his way through the enemy defences, finally capturing the city; but unfortunately he failed to cut off all the mutineers, many of whom escaped into the surrounding countryside to set up more areas of resistance, although by now they were fighting for their lives. Also in March the fortress of Jhansi, where the Ranee had thrown in her hand with the mutineers and had ordered the garrison to be massacred, was attacked by a force of three British and five Indian regiments; before it could be taken, however, Tantia Topi, at the head of a large army, advanced to its rescue with the intention of attacking the besieging force in the rear. Sir Hugh Rose, in command of the British force, left a detachment to continue the siege and with the remainder turned and attacked; Tantia was routed and Rose then turned back and assaulted and captured *Jhansi*, again with little mercy being shown to the defenders.

Tantia and the Ranee, who had escaped from Jhansi, now turned to Gwalior and when the loyal Maharajah moved out to attack them his whole force went over to the enemy and he was forced to flee. Rose now reassembled his troops and marched on *Gwalior*; there he defeated the rebel army. The Ranee, disguised as a cavalryman, was killed and Tantia, having been pursued all over India and eventually captured, was tried and executed. What happened to Nana Sahib, who had been declared Peishwa of Gwalior by Tantia, nobody knows, but he certainly escaped and lived in hiding for some time afterwards.

In the meantime Campbell had roved the countryside and in April and May had put down a rising in *Rohilcund* with nine British and thirteen Indian regiments. The end was now in sight, although for another year forces were employed hunting and capturing the bands of mutineers, and the war was over. It was now necessary to re-establish British rule and authority, and to base it this time on a more stable footing.

British military strength had been more than doubled during the crisis and was maintained at this level; although the Presidency Armies of Bombay and Madras had remained loyal, the regular regiments of Bengal had virtually ceased to exist since all the Cavalry and all but 13 of the seventy-four Infantry regiments had mutinied. The government of India was transferred to the Crown at the end of 1858, and the Presidencies established under the East India Company, as well as the Company itself, ceased to exist. The British Presidency Regiments, which by this time had been increased to four Cavalry and nine Infantry, were transferred to the British Army as the 18th, 19th, 20th Hussars and 21st Lancers, and as the 101st to 109th Foot, which continued in their own right until the Cardwell reforms twenty years later when some became the Royal Dublin Fusiliers, the Royal Munster Fusiliers and the Leinster Regiment and others were made into the 2nd Battalions of the new county regiments. The Presidency Artillery Batteries became part of the Royal Artillery, although a few Mountain Batteries remained on Indian Army strength. The Indian Presidency Regiments, Cavalry and Infantry, became part of the Indian Army and also came under the Crown, and at the same time were reorganised, first being renumbered, still by Presidencies, to fill in the gaps caused by the Mutiny and other changes, and later being numbered in a single system throughout in the sequence of Bengal, Sikh, Punjab, Madras, Hyderabad and Bombay finishing up with the Gurkhas.

Apart from those already mentioned purely for Indian regiments, very few Honours were granted for the campaign, which is quite extraordinary when the small Persian war which had but shortly preceded the Mutiny was granted three Battle Honours and a Campaign Honour. **Delhi** has already been mentioned. **Lucknow** was awarded to three British and six Indian Cavalry regiments, the Bengal and Madras Sappers and Miners, and to twenty British, two Presidency and six Indian Infantry regiments. But this single Honour covered a number of quite distinct battles, separated by time and circumstances, which could well have been appropriately Honoured as the *Defence*, the *Reinforcement*, the *Relief* and the *Capture of Lucknow*; in fact the 32nd Foot applied for 'The Defence of Lucknow' and the 10th and 93rd Foot (The Royal Lincolnshire Regiment and The Sutherland Highlanders) applied for 'The Capture of Lucknow', instead of the general Honour but without success. The only other Honour was **Central India**, which was awarded for the mopping-up campaigns outside the Battles for Delhi and Lucknow, to four British and eight Indian Cavalry regiments, to the Madras and Bombay Sappers and Miners, and to nine British, two Presidency and twelve Indian Infantry regiments and to three field batteries of the Hyderabad contingent. Four British, one Presidency and eight Indian regiments or levies were omitted and two British regiments applied unsuccessfully for the Honour.

No Honours were awarded for *Cawnpore*, *Jhansi*, *Rohilcund* or *Gwalior*, and there was no Campaign Honour, which was particularly hard on the ten Cavalry and eighteen Indian Infantry regiments involved, who had remained loyal but received no recognition of the fact. The Royal Artillery gained some more Honour titles from the batteries which participated. **Middleton's Company** and the **Residency Battery** arose from the battles for Lucknow, and

136 Battery also celebrates these battles. **Eyre's Company** dates from the defence of Arrah, and **Strange's Company** was claimed and awarded for an action at Doadpur in October 1858 after most of the fighting was over.

It had been a very bloody and hard fought campaign, one which is known to virtually everybody as 'The Mutiny' without qualification, although probably to comparatively few in detail; it had brought the names of Havelock, Outram, Campbell and Rose to undying fame, but like so many previous wars the tangible evidence of the struggle, the hardships and the bloodshed in terms of Battle Hon-

ours carried on the Colours of the regiments, is remarkably scant.

It brought the end of an era in India, which had lasted just a hundred years from Clive's victory at Plassey in 1757 and which had seen the gaining of a vast Empire. But it also brought to the fore, to reinforce the lessons of the other war of the decade in the Crimea, the need for the reorganisation of the army on to a better footing to tackle such emergencies and the need for administration, support and medical services, all of which came to fruition just over twenty years later.

Above: 'The Storming of Delhi'. Fighting on the bridge during the attack on the Kashmir Gate, 14 September 1857, during the Indian Mutiny. Line engraving by T. Sherratt after M. Morgan, published 1859. *NAM*

11 Small Wars, 1860-1906

In this twentieth century everybody has got used to wars on a very large scale, in terms of both the area covered and the millions of men involved, compared with even major wars of past centuries. Although the wars covered in this chapter were small in stature and, with the exception of the 2nd Afghan War and the Burma War of 1885, the number of men was limited, they were of immense importance in the expansion of the British Empire, the extension of British trade and influence, and in raising Britain to the status of a, if not the, major Power in the world. Although these wars were scattered geographically over four continents, they rate a comparatively small space in the history books, but the spread itself indicates the improvements which had been made in the administrative machinery of the Army, without which the problem of transporting and supplying the troops would have been insoluble.

During this period the Cardwell reforms took effect and the Army was totally reorganised, with an upheaval in 1881 only rivalled before or since by the reorganisation and mass reductions of 1957 and the years following. The conditions of service life were greatly improved with the building of barracks and significant increases in pay, rations and general welfare facilities. Queen Victoria's interest in the army and Rudyard Kipling's books and poetry, which enabled the ordinary reader for the first time to appreciate both the hardships and the lighter side of service life, played their part. Uniform was made less burdensome and more fitted to the conditions of modern warfare, small arms were radically improved, the machine gun appeared and rifled breech-loading guns came into service. All in all the Army and its methods changed very considerably over this fifty-year period, and it was these small wars, even if this title is to some extent a misnomer, that contributed as much to this as anything.

New Zealand

Although the Constitution of 1852 had brought a measure of peace to the country the old strife over land claims was always threatening to break out again; the colonists wanted more and the Maoris, not having all that much anyway in a small island, objected. The Maoris attempted to strengthen their position by electing a 'king' of their own who would see that the terms of the Treaty of Waitangi were maintained; but the Governor objected to this move, and when the Maoris refused to withdraw he decided to teach them a lesson and war broke out early in 1860 in the area of Mount Egmont.

The British Commander advanced slowly in difficult country, battering the *pas* (stockades) as he went, but with little effect as new ones were being built all the time. When Sir George Grey, who had negotiated the previous peace and was a friend of the Maoris, returned as Governor the war, which had been going on for a year ceased. But the Maoris had been let down too often by the 'word' of the Europeans and even Grey was not now fully trusted; two years later in 1863 the war broke out again.

The campaign was fought on much the same lines as before, from *pa* to *pa* through difficult terrain; the authorities in London wanted to withdraw the troops as a lesson to the colonists, but as this could not have achieved a lasting result Grey himself took field command of a force which included some loyal Maoris and colonists, and four regiments of Australian militia, known as the Waikato Militia, and by degrees drove the enemy into an ever smaller area until finally they gave up. The main battle took place at Rangariri in November 1863, in which only British regiments participated, but the Australians, originally only in a policing role, took part in the final major attack at Te Ronga in June 1864. The fighting ended in 1866 but the last British regiment did not leave until 1870.

The regiments which took part were awarded the Honour **New Zealand**, the same as for the previous Maori War, but still unfortunately without dates, so that from the Army List and the Honours borne on the Colours of these regiments it is impossible to tell whether they took part in the 1st Maori War of 1845-7 or the 2nd Maori War of 1860-6, which in any case was split into two distinct parts, 1860-1 and 1863-6. None of the participants in the first war took part in the second; four Infantry regiments took part in the first instalment of the second war and the same four plus another six took part in the latter instalment. It was notable for being the first Honour gained by a New Zealand regiment, or for that matter any Commonwealth regiment other than Indian, as the Taranaki Regiment traces its ancestry back to the colonists who took part in Grey's force. The Royal Artillery gained another Honour title from the 1860-1 fighting, **New Zealand Battery**.

Canada

For fifty years after the end of the war of 1812-14 all had been quiet in Canada and the work of colonization had steadily progressed. But during the American Civil War Britain had sympathised with the Confederate States, and after it was over the American government allowed, if not actually encouraged, raids over the border into Canada from 1866 onwards by disbanded Irish soldiers who had formed a large part of the strength of the North during that war. There were also elements in the United States who saw this as a means of achieving a North American dream of a union which included Canada. The Fenian Raids, as they were called, were not very serious but they did provide the first Battle Honour for a Canadian Militia regiment, **Eccles Hill**, which was granted uniquely to the Victoria Rifles.

The immediate outcome of the raids was the confederation of the provinces of Canada into a Dominion to give them more strength against such raids and to deter the Americans from any attempts against taking over the individual provinces piecemeal. The new Dominion government then bought out the Hudson's Bay Company rights to land, although allowing it to remain as a trading organisation; this annoyed the French-Canadians in the Fort Garry (the modern Winnipeg) area who rose in revolt in 1869 under Louis Riel, a half-breed trapper, imprisoning settlers and murdering those who had incurred their ire.

Colonel Wolseley, later Sir Garnet Wolseley, who had been sent to Canada at the time of the Fenian raids, set out with a tiny force of one British and two Canadian regiments to struggle through the wilderness and almost impossible country. The force reached Fort Garry after a month's travelling in August 1870 and dispersed the rebels with virtually no opposition, Riel fleeing to the United States; the Red River expedition, as it became known, was entirely successful. No Honours were awarded during this four-year period in Canada, apart from the one to the Canadian Militia already mentioned, but altogether nine British and fifteen Canadian Militia regiments participated, which at least might have merited a Campaign Honour.

Over the next fifteen years the vast country was gradually opened up; the Canadian Pacific Railway, uniting eastern and western Canada, was built and settlers slowly spread into the areas which had previously been the hunting grounds of the trappers. Once again there was conflict between the French-Canadians, the half-breeds and the Indians on one hand and the new European settlers on the other, and Louis Riel returned from exile to lead another rebellion. This time only Canadian troops took part in the expedition to quell the rising, and after some fighting it was put down and Riel was captured and hanged. Three individual Battle Honours and a Campaign Honour were awarded. **Saskatchewan** was granted to the Royal Canadian Regiment, **Fish Creek** and **Batoche** were awarded to The Fort Garry Horse, The Royal Grenadiers and The Royal Winnipeg Rifles, and **North West Canada 1885** was awarded to five Cavalry and sixteen Infantry regiments. At the time these were all Militia regiments but in due course three of them became regular. The North West campaign was the last fighting to take place in Canada.

East Africa

Towards the end of the period, when large areas of Southern Africa were being added to the British Empire, the British East Africa Company was formed to administer territories in this area. In 1890 an agreement was reached with Germany, who also claimed large areas of territory in the region, on the way in which East Africa should be divided between them. Under this agreement Uganda and Kenya became part of the British zone of influence, which greatly annoyed Karl Peters, the leader of the equivalent German company, who had always looked upon this rich area as his own. Peters therefore used some subversive tactics, and in 1896 some of the native troops in Uganda, mostly Sudanese who were unhappy at being so far from home, mutinied and raised a revolt.

The British forces locally were very small and a number of Indian regiments were sent to quell the rising, which they did successfully although slowly; but this still left an irate German army on their borders, which in due course was to cause considerable trouble. An Honour, **British East Africa 1896–99**, was awarded to three Indian regiments but two others, together with local regiments, the Uganda Rifles and the East African Rifles, were not recognised for their part in the campaign.

One other campaign must be recorded, the operations which began in 1901 and, although completed for all practical purposes by 1904, dragged on until 1921. This was in the area of British Somaliland against the tribes which supported the 'Mad Mullah'. Few troops took part in the campaign, and most of these were Indian, but there was some severe fighting in 1904 which finally routed the Mullah. Honours were awarded as **British East Africa 1901** to one Indian regiment, later the Mahratta Light Infantry, and as **Somaliland 1901–04** to five Indian regiments and the Bombay Sappers and Miners and to one African regiment, The King's African Rifles. Two British regiments, of which one has claimed the Honour, and one other Indian regiment qualified for the latter Honour.

West Africa

During the eighteenth century and subsequently, British trading posts had been established on the West African coast, initially as places from which to operate the notorious slave trade. Although at various times expeditions had penetrated inland, only the ports themselves and a small area on the coast were colonised to any extent.

In Ashantee, later to become the Gold Coast and later still Ghana, the coastal posts were hemmed in by a very warlike tribe, the Ashanti, who practised human sacrifice on a large scale; early in the century an attempt had been made to subdue them and stop their heathen rites, but without success, and the Governor of the time had been killed and his skull taken to their capital Kumasi, as a drinking bowl. Their depredations and assaults on the more peaceful tribes got worse, and in 1873 Wolseley was instructed to take a force and quell them. With three British regiments, supported by local troops from Ashantee itself and Nigeria and a West Indian regiment, he advanced inland and having defeated them in some very bloody battles, bloody that is from the Ashanti point of view, particularly at Amoufu, eventually reached Kumasi which was entered by the Black Watch on 5 February 1874. The Ashantee made little effort to escape from the captured city, even shaking hands with their conquerors. But the conditions were such, both in the city and in the surrounding countryside, where several thousand human sacrifices had taken place, that Wolseley collected everything worthwhile to take back to the coast with him and burnt the city. Honour **Ashantee 1873-74**, was awarded to all the regiments which took part.

Actions of one sort or another continued throughout the last quarter of the 19th century and the early years of the 20th, particularly in Sierra Leone and in Nigeria where the French were interested in colonisation and had already restricted British expansion by penetration inland of the coast down the rivers from the north. There were very few British troops available and most of the actions were carried out by local levies and by West Indian regiments. Four Battle Honours were awarded during the period, **West Africa 1887, West Africa 1892-3-4, Sierra Leone 1898-9** and **Ashanti 1900**; the first three were granted to the West India Regiment, the last two to the West Africa Regiment, and the final one to the Nigeria and Gold Coast Regiments and to the King's African Rifles. No British troops were involved in these actions.

Abyssinia

A curious little campaign took place at the beginning of 1868 in Ethiopia, as it was then known and is again now in spite of the title of the Honour granted for it. The mad ruler of the country, Theodore, apart from committing many atrocities on his subjects, had also imprisoned a number of Europeans, and it was necessary to mount an action to free them. A combined Anglo-Indian force landed on the coast, but before taking any offensive action it had to clear up the chaos of animals which had been brought as pack transport on account of the virtual non-existence of any roads. Having sorted this out the force advanced, and as soon as it reached the capital, Magdala, which was only achieved after monumental administrative problems, Theodore committed suicide and the prisoners were released. The force then returned to India, more or less without any fighting at all.

Nevertheless a campaign Honour, **Abyssinia**, was awarded, another of the totally illogical examples of such awards, to one British and four Indian Cavalry regiments and to four British and nine Indian Infantry regiments, together with an Indian Mountain Battery and the Madras and Bombay Engineers. Only one Indian Infantry regiment which participated was omitted.

Egypt and the Sudan

A series of much more serious and significant campaigns took place in the extreme north-east of the African continent during the last two decades of the century. In spite of their defeats in Egypt during the Napoleonic Wars, the French had retained strong influence and become even stronger following the opening of the Suez Canal, which had been designed by a Frenchman, de Lesseps, and constructed with French capital. Nevertheless the Egyptian ruler, Ismail, owned a large batch of shares in the Canal, but largely through his personal extravagance had run up enormous debts; his shares were his only asset and had to be sold to clear the debts. They were bought after secret negotiations by the British Prime Minister, Benjamin Disraeli, in 1878 on behalf of his country. This gave Britain a considerable interest in the operation of the canal and was a blow to French domination and influence in the area.

This activity was followed in 1882 by the deposition of Ismail and a rise of nationalism and anti-foreign feeling in the country, much as happened again 70 years later. A massacre of Europeans took place in Alexandria, and French and British warships were sent thither; but the French, fearful of further conflict with Germany following the war of 1870, did not want to tie up a force in Egypt, and left the job of tidying up the mess to the British whose sailors landed and occupied the city.

A major force was now dispatched to Egypt under command of the man whose name has already appeared several times in this chapter, Garnet Wolseley. Having 'leaked' the information that the force would land at Aboukir it actually sailed on into the Canal, much to de Lesseps' wrath at his Canal being used for British military purposes, and landed at Ismailia. The Egyptians promptly fortified Tel el Kebir and Wolseley advanced on them; because of the strength of the Egyptian position he considered that a daylight attack would be suicidal and the largest night advance to date was launched, direction being kept by a Naval officer steering the line by the stars and a sextant. At daybreak the Egyptians were surprised and routed at a very small cost in British casualties, and by nightfall the army had reached Cairo, mainly due to an inspired cavalry advance, where the remainder of the native army surrendered. Britain now had the dominating influence in the country. British officials were employed to reorganise the government and British officers took over the organisation, training and, practically, the command of the Egyptian army.

Two Honours were awarded, one for the campaign, **Egypt 1882**, and one for the battle, **Tel el Kebir**, and the majority which took part gained both. Five British Cavalry and thirteen Infantry regiments and three Indian Cavalry and three Infantry regiments were awarded the Honour for the battle, and a further nine British Infantry regiments gained the Campaign Honour only. The Royal Artillery gained another Honour Title, **Broken Wheel Battery**.

While this activity was going on in Egypt, further south in the Sudan there was also trouble. The Egyptians had for centuries treated the Sudanese abominably and used them freely as slaves, and a revolt now arose under Mohammed Ahmed, who was known as the 'Mahdi' and who proclaimed a Holy War or *jehad*. Although she was trying hard to eradicate the very wrongs about which the Sudanese were rebelling, Britain's assumption of responsibility for Egypt inevitably involved her in the situation. A force of Egyptian troops was sent to Khartoum, but on the way it was surrounded by the Mahdi's forces and annihilated; now the main objective, since it was not considered politic to employ British troops, became to extricate the remaining Egyptian garrisons and administrators, and this task was given to General Gordon.

But the situation had really become too serious and difficult for one man to solve. Although he eventually reached Khartoum he was besieged there by the Mahdi's forces, by now known as the Dervishes. Meanwhile there had been another revolt at Suakim on the Red Sea and another Egyptian force sent there had also been overwhelmingly defeated by a Dervish army half its size. There was now no alternative but to use the British army and a small expedition was sent to redeem the situation; this it did, defeating the Dervishes at El Teb and Tamaii early in 1884. This campaign was known as the Suakin Expedition and an Honour was awarded, **Egypt 1884**, to all who took part, two Cavalry and five Infantry regiments. One of these regiments, The York and Lancaster Regiment, unsuccessfully applied for the Honour to be changed, to commemorate the battles themselves, *El Teb/Tamaii*.

Meanwhile Gordon was still locked up in Khartoum, maintaining its defence with very limited resources, and the British government began to realise that if it did nothing it would be justifiably accused of leaving its emissary to his fate at the hands of the Mahdi. Wolseley therefore set out up the Nile with a relief expedition, but the distance was great, the country and the climate anything but friendly, and, with the cataracts on the river making steamer travel impossible, progress was slow and by the end of 1884 it was clear that the force probably would not reach Khartoum before it fell. One chance was to cut across the great Nile bend and save time that way; even a few British troops in Khartoum might stave off the day until the main army arrived. It would be impossible to maintain an army by this route and the only hope was to mount some troops on the few camels available. The small force set out and in January 1885 it was attacked by an overwhelming number of Dervishes at **Abu Klea**. Although it was touch and go for a time and the Mahdist forces penetrated the British 'square', they were eventually driven out and the little force continued on its way. An Honour was awarded to the 19th Hussars and the Royal Sussex Regiment (35th Foot), but detachments of the three regiments of Foot Guards also represented in the Camel Corps were not so honoured. The one Artillery battery present claimed the Honour eventually and **Abu Klea Battery** was added to the growing list of Honour Titles.

The Nile was reached again at last and the expedition embarked on the last stage of the journey to Khartoum, but only after an unexplained delay of nearly a week which probably cost Gordon his life. When the steamers reached the city in January 1885 the Egyptian flag was no longer flying over the citadel; Gordon had been savagely done to death two days earlier. The force was withdrawn down the Nile and *en route* had another encounter with the Dervishes at **Kirbokan**, which was awarded as an Honour to two Infantry regiments, with the 19th Hussars, who were present but in less than the required strength, being unlucky. An Honour was also awarded for the campaign, the Khartoum Relief Expedition, as **Nile 1884–85**, to the 19th Hussars and to nine Infantry regiments, one only participant, The Green Howards, being left out.

Meanwhile, although intervention in the Sudan was still banned by the government at home, a force had been operating in the area of Suakim since the previous year. It had won a battle against the Mahdi's forces at **Tofrek**, also known as McNeill's Zariba, which was awarded as an Honour to the Royal Berkshire Regiment (49th Foot), who also gained the prefix 'Royal' for their conduct during this battle, and to three Indian Infantry regiments and the Madras Sappers and Miners. Another battle at *Hasheen*

was fought by six British and four Indian regiments, again with the Madras Engineers, but this was not honoured. The campaign, if it can be called that, was also recognised with an Honour, **Suakin 1885**, which was awarded to eight British and five Indian regiments, and also, the first time that they had been employed as part of a British force, to three Australian Infantry regiments.

Back in the north the new Egyptian army was steadily improving in training and morale, and at the end of 1885 a battle was fought on the Nile just south of the Sudanese frontier at *Ginnis* by a mixed Egyptian and British Army; no Honour was awarded to the five British Infantry regiments which took part, but, for a small affray, it has an important place in the history as it was the last battle in which the British Army fought in red coats.

In England there was a General Election in 1896 and a change of government, and, the Conservatives having gained power and being less inhibited about the use of force, an advance into the Sudan was authorised to put down the Mahdi's rising once and for all. General Kitchener was now Commander-in-Chief of the Egyptian Army and resolved to start the campaign with this alone, only bringing in the British Army when he had established forward bases in the Sudan from which to mount the final attack. This policy worked well and, apart from an engagement on the Nile which gained the North Staffordshire Regiment (the 64th Foot) the Honour of **Hafir** in 1896, the Egyptian Army by its own endeavours established the bases needed by early in 1898 and all was ready for the final encounter.

The advancing Army, now consisting mainly of British regiments, first met a portion of the Mahdi's army which was trying to establish a defence on the River Atbara. They had constructed a *zeriba*, or stockade, thorn bushes being used instead of barbed wire which had not then been invented, and this was attacked. The Dervishes were routed although they fought desparately with many hand-to-hand engagements. An Honour, **Atbara**, was awarded to four Infantry regiments.

Kitchener now advanced on Khartoum itself and eventually came into contact with the main Dervish army a few miles from the city at Omdurman; it was dark and after a long march the Army was very vulnerable to attack, but luckily the Mahdi missed his chance. But he did attack the following morning in vast numbers compared with the British force, although the withering rifle fire never allowed his army to get to grips and they were mown down in their thousands. They were finally routed by a charge by the 21st Lancers, of which Winston Churchill was a member, which suffered considerable losses; it was the last time that British Cavalry charged unbroken Infantry. The power of the Mahdi was broken and henceforth for more than half a century the Sudan was governed as an Anglo-Egyptian Condominium.

Khartoum was awarded as an Honour for the final battle, instead of Omdurman, the name under which it is commonly known, and since the whole British force was engaged it also serves as a Campaign Honour. It was granted to the 21st Lancers, the Grenadier Guards and seven Infantry regiments; although no Royal Artillery Honour title traces back to the battle 80 Battery celebrate the event.

India

The scene now shifts eastwards, once more to the great Indian sub-continent and its neighbours, an area which has taken up so much of the previous chapters. During this period however it is not the main part of the country, where the troubles had finally come to an end following the Indian Mutiny, which takes one's interest but the Frontier regions.

The North West Frontier of India has figured in innumerable boys' and adult stories and films, and consequently most people can visualise the warring tribes, particularly the Pathans and Afridis, perched on rocky outcrops and ambushing the plodding columns in the valleys below, the rugged scenery of the Khyber Pass, and the hardships of fighting in this part of the world. Kipling's stories of the British Army particularly come to mind. Although in some areas or periods of time which have been written about or filmed on many occasions, such as the American West, the factual situation has been embellished to suit the audience, this cannot be said of the North West Frontier, and most of the stories told are either based on fact or could well have happened. It is, after all, difficult to embellish the ultimate. This even applies to the slightly bizarre stories of the guard fixing bayonets and charging the latrines at Razmak at dawn, the very unpleasant reason for which does not need to be elaborated.

It is also true that the Frontier is a name to be treated with much respect in the annals of the British Army and few are the regiments that have not served there at some time or other during the century of years up to the Partition of India. It became a problem naturally after the Sikh wars when the boundaries of India, and of British responsibility and influence, were extended through the Punjab to the rocky wilderness on the borders of Afghanistan, Baluchistan and Kashmir. No Honour was awarded, however, to cover this early period of tribal warfare from 1849 to 1868, but nine British regiments and no fewer than fifty-five Indian regiments, eighteen of them Cavalry, did their duty during these years. Nor was one awarded for the first of the punitive expeditions which occurred in 1863 in *Umbeyla*, in the hill country north of Peshawar, which was also the first fighting in which the Indian regiments newly formed after the Mutiny took part; the fighting was difficult and craggy outposts often changed hands many times. Those that took part, seven British Infantry regiments, of which two applied for it as an Honour, and fifteen Indian regiments aquitted themselves well.

Although intermittent fighting continued all the time, the Frontier next came into prominence at the end of the century with the Chitral expedition. This was caused by the traditional Indian problem of a disputed succession, and the usurper besieged the British garrison, a small force of Sikhs and the Kashmir Rifles, who were virtually local police, in the fort at Chitral in 1895. For this gallant defence the Sikh regiment was awarded the Honour **Defence of Chitral**. A relieving force, whose problems were caused more by the terrain than by the tribesmen, was sent, consisting of seven British regiments and nineteen Indian, including two Cavalry, and the Bengal and Madras Sappers and Miners. They were awarded the Honour **Chitral**, but an engagement in the *Malakand Pass* in which four of the

British and four of the Indian regiments took part was not considered worthy of separate Honour.

In 1897 and the following year, however, there occurred a war of greater significance since the main dread of the authorities, a general rising of all the frontier tribes, was only just prevented. This time the Afridis were the main enemy. After a brief encounter at *Maizar* in which two Indian regiments were involved, more serious fighting took place again in the Malakand Pass for which the Honour **Malakand** was awarded to nine Indian regiments, although four others and four British regiments, of which one subsequently applied for it, were denied the Honour. An engagement at *Chakdara* in which six Indian regiments participated was not recognised. The Khyber Pass was closed, the whole Tirah area was in revolt, and a very large expedition was sent to restore order out of chaos.

The *Mohmunds* were quelled by a force of four British and fourteen Indian regiments without an Honour; *Dargai*, also unhonoured, was successfully stormed by five British regiments, of which one applied for it as an Honour, and by four Indian. But in the event the force, large as it was, was not strong enough to quell the whole of the rebellion, and having penetrated into the most inhospitable territories and subdued most of the tribal risings it was forced to retreat, leaving behind it a vacuum which was eventually to lead to further bloodshed.

There were two Campaign Honours awarded. The first was **Tirah**, which was granted to nine British and eleven Indian regiments, together with three Mountain batteries and the three regiments of Sappers and Miners, although seven other British and eight Indian regiments were involved but omitted from the award. The second was a wholly Indian Honour, **Punjab Frontier**, and was awarded to nine Cavalry and twenty-three Infantry regiments and the three regiments of Sappers and Miners. Nevertheless nineteen British regiments and a further eight Indian regiments participated in the area covered by the Honour.

Whilst sporadic fighting with a few major battles had been continuing on the North West Frontier, trouble had also been experienced on the North East Frontier. A rising, in *Bhutan* in 1864 was eventually put down after a campaign lasting sixteen months; no Honour was awarded for the campaign which added this small country to the Indian Empire, but two British and thirteen Indian regiments took part, including three Gurkha regiments who should at least have felt at home in the savage terrain.

A more serious outbreak of trouble occurred in 1888, which resulted in a punitive expedition being sent to *Hazara*, and a smaller force to subdue and annex *Sikkim*. Neither action was Honoured, but five British and eleven Indian regiments took part in the former and one British and three Indian in the latter. After two years of relative peace revolt flared again, resulting in a second expedition to *Hazara* and one to Samana: the former involved two British and seven Indian regiments with the Bengal engineers, and the latter resulted in an Honour, **Samana 1891**, being awarded to a single Sikh regiment, although a further two British and twelve Indian regiments, including the Engineer regiment again, also participated. The campaign also included expeditions to Manipur and against the Chin Lushai and involved quite a large force, fighting, as always on the Indian frontiers, in difficult country against ambushes and sniping from native bands which were more at home in the terrain than were the British regiments or the Indian regiments which mostly originated on the plains. Two British and forty-one Indian regiments, including Artillery and Engineers, took part on the North-East Frontier. Another expedition also took place to Samana in 1897, involving the same Sikh regiment which had previously gained an Honour there, and this time they gained a second one but without a date, **Samana**.

Another event occurred on the borders of India in 1904. It was suspected that intrigues were fostering trouble in *Tibet* which would put the Russians, who it was thought in many quarters still had expansionist designs on India following their war with Japan, on the Indian frontier. A small force under Colonel Younghusband entered the country and surmounted enormous problems of supply and communications, operating across the Himalayan passes in cold and snow at the highest altitude at which British troops have ever fought, before entering Lhasa. The Dalai Lama abdicated and his successor signed a treaty with Britain. No Honour was awarded, but the Royal Fusiliers (the 7th Foot) applied for it and the 8th Gurkha Rifles were the only other regiment involved.

Afghanistan

Ever since the end of the 1st Afghan War in 1842 relationships with the Afghans had been uneasy and they still bore a grudge against Britain in general and the Indian government in particular. The Russians meanwhile had been steadily expanding eastwards and, having now reached the frontier of Afghanistan, had sent a mission to Kabul which had been amicably received.

To the Afghans this was a way of showing that they had powerful allies, and to the Russians it represented another move against the British who had so far bedevilled all their major efforts at expansion, remarkably enough by diplomacy except in the case of the Crimea. To the Indians Afghanistan had always been part of the Mogul Empire and therefore was regarded still as rightfully a part of their country. To the British it was a threat which could only be removed by establishing a balancing mission in Kabul; the Afghans were not receptive to the idea, the atmosphere was explosive and the government decided to insist by sending an envoy supported by a force of arms late in 1878. The mission was stopped at the fort of Ali Masjid in the Khyber Pass and war became inevitable.

The British army was divided into three wings, called Field Forces, the Kurram, the Peshawar Valley and the Kandahar, commanded respectively by Generals Roberts (later Lord Roberts, VC, of Boer War fame), Sam Browne (Originator of the belt) and Stewart. The three forces were scheduled to enter Afghanistan by the Kurram, Khyber and Khojak Passes, which were in fact virtually the only entries into the mountainous and rugged country. Browne attacked and captured the fort at **Ali Masjid** in November 1878 and an Honour was awarded to five British and ten Indian regiments together with an Artillery battery and the Bengal Engineers, although one British regiment was excluded. At the same time Roberts was attacking **Peiwar**

Kotal which was taken at the beginning of December, the Afghan defenders being routed; another Honour was awarded for this battle, to two British and six Indian regiments, again including a Mountain battery.

The way was now open to Kabul and the Afghan leader fled to Russia. He was succeeded by his son, Yakub Khan, who immediately agreed to all the British demands, and the envoy plus an escort from the Corps of Guides reached the capital in the summer of 1879 and established the Residency there. But Yakub Khan had little control over his people, and mutinous Afghan troops, still opposing the British presence, poured into the city and attacked the Residency; in spite of a desperate defence the tiny garrison was overwhelmed. It was hardly an action for which an Honour could be awarded, but The Guides bear as a distinction on their appointments 'Residency, Kabul'. Retribution had to follow.

The Kurram Field Force was reconstituted under General Roberts and renamed the Kabul Field Force; it advanced once more towards Kabul, and in October met a very large force of Afghans a few miles from the city. The Afghans stood in a strong position, but Roberts outflanked them and when they started to retreat he put in a cavalry charge and pursuit. Kabul was soon re-entered. **Charasiah** was awarded as an Honour to one British and three Indian Cavalry regiments, a Mountain battery and the Bengal Engineers, and three British and four Indian Infantry regiments.

Yakub Khan abdicated and Roberts took over the administration of the area. But his comparatively small force was similarly placed to one 37 years earlier, a long way from home with difficult communications through the Khyber Pass which could virtually be cut at any time by fanatical tribesmen. During the period of a fortnight in the middle of December a number of actions were fought around Kabul; the mistakes of the 1st Afghan War were not repeated and the British force was concentrated inside the cantonments. When the massed tribesmen finally attacked the city they were mown down by rifle fire and routed by the Cavalry. **Kabul 1879** was granted to one British and four Indian Cavalry regiments, four British and eight Indian Infantry regiments, the Bengal Engineers and three Mountain batteries.

Another force under General Stewart had also entered Afghanistan. It had had to fight its way through the Khyber Pass and then defend it while the main force advanced to Kandahar. No Honour was awarded for this eight months of very arduous duty in the *Khyber Pass* but seven British and thirteen Indian regiments were employed there over the period. Having cleared the pass the main force met the Afghans at **Ahmed Khel** and defeated them, and an Honour for the battle was awarded to three Indian Cavalry regiments and two British and five Indian Infantry regiments. They moved on to Kabul, but it soon became apparent that a major Afghan army was advancing on Kandahar where a small British detachment had been left.

Another detachment under General Burrows was sent back to help, although even the combined forces would be still greatly outnumbered; in July 1880 this detachment found that the Afghans were at *Maiwand* preparing to advance to Ghazni to cut the Kandahar-Kabul road, and

Burrows immediately moved to intercept them. The Afghans were in overwhelming numbers and their guns pounded away at the British line; when the British guns started to run short of ammunition the Indian regiments gave way and only the British regiment, the 66th Foot (The Royal Berkshire Regiment) was left to cover their retreat. Their numbers were gradually reduced until only eleven were left alive, and this 'last eleven' made a desperate charge and died fighting to the last man. This was only the second time that a British force had been annihilated in Asia, the other being the 44th Foot in the retreat from Kabul in the previous Afghan War, and the only time they had been defeated in a face to face fight. Like the fight of the 44th Foot no Honour was awarded, and as well as the 66th Foot five Indian regiments had fought in the earlier part of the action; however, the Royal Artillery were eventually to add another Honour title, **Maiwand Battery**.

The survivors from the Indian regiments at Maiwand reached Kandahar and with the small force of troops already there were besieged in the city. There were few troops available to relieve them, and General Roberts decided on a most dangerous plan, to march his force from Kabul; he was not strong enough to leave communications garrisons so would be totally cut off and defenceless until he reached Kandahar and could only survive then if he could defeat the besiegers. His 10,000 troops reached the invested city on 31 August and attacked the Afghan force under Ayub Khan the next day; they inflicted a decisive defeat on them, capturing their camp and all their guns. The Honour **Kandahar 1880** was awarded to six British and twenty-one Indian regiments and to a Mountain battery and the Bombay Engineers.

By the following spring Afghanistan had been evacuated and the Commander of the British force had been elevated to the peerage with the title of Lord Roberts of Kandahar by a grateful government. Apart from the disaster at Maiwand the campaign had been a success since it had given the British a foothold in the Khyber and Bolan Passes and protection for the plains of the Punjab. A campaign Honour was awarded, **Afghanistan** with dates between 1878 and 1880 inclusive, to five British and twenty-eight Indian Cavalry regiments, five Indian Mountain batteries and the three Indian corps of Engineers, and to twenty-four British and sixty-seven Indian Infantry regiments. Up to this time it was the largest number of regiments awarded any Honour—128 altogether.

Burma

After the 2nd Burma War in 1852 the northern part of the country had been left in the hands of the native rulers; this had presented few problems in the intervening years up to the early 1880s, but then a weak and vengeful young man, Thibaw, ascended the throne. Dominated by his wife, he committed a horrifying massacre of members of the Royal family and then started persecuting British trading interests in both the north and the annexed south, aided and abetted by the French from their adjoining territory in Indo-China who still, in spite of everything, had their eyes on India.

This situation clearly could not be allowed to continue, and in 1885 the Indian government sent in an army to protect their interests. It took little action to cause Thibaw's power to collapse, and this time Upper Burma was also annexed; nevertheless it took some years of occupation by British and Indian troops before the robber bands, which had multiplied under the late King's misrule, had been put down and peace returned to the country.

The fighting had been minimal but a campaign Honour, **Burma 1885-87**, was still awarded to eleven British regiments, and to forty-nine Indian regiments which included all the fighting arms. One British regiment which participated was not awarded the Honour.

China

It will be remembered that two wars had been fought in China, the first from 1840 to 1842 and the second from 1858 to 1861, both of them largely the result of the Chinese hatred of foreigners. After nearly forty years of peaceful trading with China another rising occurred in 1900, once again directed against foreign influence; it was led by a secret society with the delightful name of 'The Harmonious Heavenly Fists', which was soon nicknamed 'The Boxers'. Murder and assassination were rife, the Chinese government took no action to put down the rising, and the foreign diplomatic communities were forced to fortify the Legation Quarter of Pekin. An international army was assembled at Tientsin, and, led by British and Indian troops, reached Pekin after some hard fighting and relieved the siege of the Legations.

The rebellion died out, and China was ordered to pay indemnity for the havoc caused. The Kaiser persuaded the other powers to agree to the appointment of a German Commander of the so-called peace-keeping force, although the German element of the army had not arrived until the fighting was over; 'so-called' because the German troops interpreted too literally the Kaiser's orders to eliminate the Boxers and their supporters as Attila's Huns would have done.

Pekin 1900 was awarded as an Honour to The Royal Welsh Fusiliers (the 23rd Foot) and to four Indian regiments, and a purely Indian campaign Honour, **China 1900**, was awarded to a further seventeen Indian regiments and the three regiments of Sappers and Miners, although three regiments of Indian state troops were omitted.

Conclusion

This has been a long chapter covering a variety of fighting in widely different parts of the world. It was a period vital to the establishment of the British Empire and Britain's predominant position in the world, but such a rise to power could not have been achieved without creating opposition from other major countries. Outstanding among these was Germany, united during the period into one country under an Emperor, the Kaiser, from a large number of principalities. It was largely German support for their cause which decided the Boers to attack the British and precipitate the 2nd Boer War, which is the final subject of the next chapter, and their pique culminated in the invasion of Belgium and the Great War, only twelve years after the South African War ended.

12 South Africa and the Boer Wars

South Africa

By the mid 1870s South Africa contained two semi-autonomous Boer-governed republics, the Transvaal and the Orange Free State, and they were both in considerable difficulties. They were in constant dispute with the warlike native tribes in and around their territories from which they were always trying to extract more tribal lands, and administratively and financially they were in even greater trouble.

In 1873 a curious incident occurred which is worth recording. The chief of a splinter group of the Amahlubi tribe which had been slaughtered by the Zulus, Langalibalele, had moved from the Zulu lands to the Bushman River area of the Natal hinterland as one of the tribal buffer states set up by the British in 1849. Some of his tribesmen worked in the Kimberley diamond mines, were often paid off in firearms and made him think of times past and of independence. He was ordered to hand over the guns but refused, and such defiance had to be punished. It was rumoured that he meant to flee to Basutoland and it was decided to close the passes over the Drakensberg to prevent this with a group of local militia under the command of Major Durnford, who subsequently appears in the narrative as the officer in command at Isandhlwana. The going up the passes was indescribably difficult and few of the force reached the top; but those who did found that Langalibalele had beaten them to it and surrounded them on their arrival. The whole affair was mismanaged, but a few managed to escape while Langalibalele fled into Basutoland as he had planned. For fear of the consequences on other tribal groups a detachment of 86th Foot with other militia detachments was sent into Basutoland to capture him. The terrain was very rough and unmapped but eventually they were successful and Langalibalele was brought back to Pietermaritzburg to stand trial. The trial was rigged, a disgrace to British justice, and he was banished, although later allowed to return to his tribal area.

The Bantu tribes had of course often risen against the British, and in 1877 the 9th Kaffir War began through the latest attempt, this time of the Gaikas and Galekas, to throw off the foreign yoke and regain the land which they believed was their own. The fighting was as furious as usual, but by 1879 the war was over. Eight British Infantry regiments had been involved, but most of the fighting had been undertaken by South African Militia regiments. One or other of these local regiments, The Cape Town Rifles, Prince Alfred's Guard, The First City Regiment, The Kimberley Regiment and the Kaffrarian Rifles claimed Honours for the battles in the *Transkei*, *Gaika/Galeka*, *Gaikaland* and *Griqualand West*, but all were refused. As far as British participation was concerned a Campaign Honour was granted to cover all the actions in the years 1877–79 and more will be said of this later, but only one South African regiment was Honoured, which was not in fact one of those already mentioned.

Because of the situation between the Boers and the native tribes the British government first granted the Basutos, Bechuanas and Swazis British nationality as Protectorates, and then annexed the Transvaal, at which the Boer population protested strongly but unavailingly. But by so doing the British had to take over the Boer problems, and the gravest of these was the attitude of the Zulus, bloodthirsty towards their own people as well as their enemies, who claimed most of the Boer territories as their own. Action had to be taken and in 1879 a British force crossed from Natal into Zululand.

The Zulu War

In January 1879 the main force under Lord Chelmsford crossed the Buffalo river at Rorke's Drift, where he left a small detachment to guard the ford, and camped at *Isandlhwana*, which was the name of a craggy mountain rising out of a wide plain below the Nqutu Hills. The following day all but a strong camp guard moved out to search for the Zulu army. The force did not find them, but unfortunately while they were gone the Zulus found the camp and the detachment at Rorke's Drift. The camp was not disposed for defence; the troops left behind, from the 24th Foot (The South Wales Borderers), the Natal Carbineers and a large force of native troops, which broke and was of little help during the battle, were not expecting trouble and the result was a massacre.

Of the 1,800 men in the camp only fifty-five Europeans and a small number of native troops escaped, and the 24th Foot were killed to a man. Although a number of messages had been sent to Chelmsford, with the main force, they were not couched in such a way as to indicate the peril in which the camp lay. Some messages did not arrive, and in any case the force could not have been back in time, and the massacre was only discovered by the main force on its return to camp. But at the same time the detachment at *Rorke's Drift* managed to fight on against appalling odds until even the Zulus had suffered more casualties than they could stomach and eventually, after a day and a night of desperate fighting, they withdrew before Chelmsford's force could appear.

The battle, and the apocryphal story of the discovery of the Colours of the 24th Foot wrapped around the dead ensign's body, has become too famous in print and film to need detailed description here, but it was one of the outstanding examples of gallantry above and beyond the call of duty as evidenced by the eleven Victoria Crosses awarded. In fact the story of the Colours was a myth as the ensign in question had been carrying the Colours from Isandhlwana, still on their pike, and in crossing a river had lost his grip on them and they had floated away downstream. He was killed by the Zulus shortly afterwards, and subsequently both his body and the Colours, which were some distance away, were recovered, and the Colours were carried for another fifty years still in their tattered state.

The receipt of the news in England once again raised a public outcry against inadequate military command and Sir Garnet Wolsely was sent out as Commander-in-Chief. But before he could get there the war was over. The Commander was not inadequate but had been caught napping, and a main cause of the massacre was the colonel who had been left in command of the camp and the initial slackness of the troops themselves who suffered death as a result. The force was now reorganised and set out to exact revenge.

A small column advanced from the Lower Drift of the Tugela River and captured the mission station at Eshowe, but was cut off by the Zulus and eventually had to be extricated. Another column, operating eastwards from the Transvaal frontier under Colonel Evelyn Wood with Redvers Buller in command of the mounted units, undertook a disastrous expedition to *Hlobane* Mountain, but most of them managed to escape and in due course the main part of the Zulu army was defeated at *Kambula*. At last reinforcements had been sent to Chelmsford from England and he set out once again to subdue the Zulus, this time with a large force which advanced on *Ulundi*, the royal kraal of Cetshwayo, and annihilated the rest of the Zulu Army there. The Zulus, armed mainly with assegais, were no match for British rifles on more nearly even terms of manpower and were mown down in heaps. It was during this advance that the Prince Imperial of France, serving with the army officially as an observer, was caught while taking an unauthorised part in a patrol and was killed.

The Zulu power was broken for good and their military organisation destroyed. Bearing in mind what had been done in India in similar circumstances with, for example, the Sikhs, it is perhaps odd that the Zulus were not recruited into the British colonial forces, but perhaps the authorities had the Sepoy mutiny too fresh in their minds and were too fearful of violence if the Zulus were ever given the wherewithal to achieve power.

A single Campaign Honour was awarded to cover the 9th Kaffir War and the Zulu War, **South Africa** with the dates **1877**, **1878** and **1879** appended to it as appropriate. It was granted to two Cavalry and 14 Infantry regiments of the British Army and to one South African regiment, the Natal Carbineers, and thus the emphasis was placed on the latter rather than the former war. This meant that twelve South African Militia regiments received no official credit for the hard fighting which they had undergone. Isandlhwana and Rorke's Drift were not separately honoured, but the 24th Foot were granted the right to bear a wreath of Immortelles on the pike of their Colours in memory of their gallantry and their losses during the battles.

The 1st Boer War

With the defeat of the Zulus and the Bantus the Boer's enemies had been removed and they now started agitating for their independence again; when the British refused to grant this they raised the flag of revolt in December 1880. The British garrison in the Transvaal was small and scattered and was attacked, besieged and ambushed. A force advancing to relieve Pretoria from Natal was defeated at *Laing's Nek* and another small force repulsed at Ingogo. An attempt was made to outflank the Boers by seizing the hill of Majuba overlooking their camp. Unfortunately it was not appreciated that from the summit there was a great deal of dead ground, and from this the Boers attacked, swarming up the hill while the defenders' heads were kept down by fire from a neighbouring hill, and overwhelmed the few men on top. Small actions ranged over Basutoland, the Transkei and Natal and a larger force was assembled to redress the balance and teach the revolutionaries a lesson. But before it could take the field the British government capitulated again and in 1881 signed a dishonourable peace granting the Boers their independence once more.

So ended the 1st Boer War, having paved the way for the second and larger one less than twenty years later. No Battle Honours were awarded either for the campaign or for any individual engagements, although it must be admitted that none of the actions was of a size really to warrant recognition. Native wars had also occurred during this period and four South African regiments claimed the Honour of **Basutoland 1880-81** and two claimed **Transkei 1880-81**, and these were later partly granted by the South African Government and one British Cavalry and four Infantry regiments and seven South African Mounted and Infantry regiments and three Artillery batteries were involved in the short campaign.

Matabeleland, Mashonaland and Bechuanaland

The northern part of Southern Africa, around what was then Matabeleland and Mashonaland, next came into prominence. The Matabele were a sect of the Zulus and inhabited an area north of the Transvaal and Bechuanaland. They were equally ferocious as their parent race, and one of the impis, to prevent being 'disciplined' by wholesale execution for not carrying out its orders, broke away and ravaged Mashonaland. The Boers were talking of taking action and to forestall this and an extension of their territory, Cecil Rhodes, who was the Commissioner of Bechuanaland, in 1890 sent a small force into the area which was eventually to be named after him, Rhodesia. It occupied Mashonaland and added a further huge slice of territory to the Empire, with very little cost or effort, but lots of imagination.

While the British were occupied in Mashonaland, the Matabele also rose in revolt and besieged Bulawayo. A small British force of one Cavalry and two Infantry regiments was sent thither and, since an all-out attack on the Matabele strongholds would have been too expensive in men and material, the Commander, Colonel (later Field Marshall Lord) Plumer, negotiated with them and eventually pacified them. No Honour was awarded for this or any other actions in the area.

At roughly the same time as the events just related there had also been a revolt in Bechuanaland in 1896-7. This had been put down by an entirely South African force of nine regiments and three Artillery batteries after fighting a significant battle at *Langeberg*, which was claimed as an Honour by some of the participants but disallowed. The Honour **Bechuanaland 1896-97** was granted to five South African Infantry regiments.

The 2nd Boer War, 1899–1902

By 1895 Rhodesia, as Matabeleland and Mashonaland together became, had been added to the already vast possessions in South Africa and only one obstacle remained to the union of all these territories; this was the attitude of the Boer burghers, mainly farmers, in the Transvaal and their uncompromising leader, Paul Kruger. By the annexation of the northern territories the Boers were now almost enclosed and resented the fact. But Kruger had succeeded in isolating the Transvaal from the more moderate Afrikaaner settlers in the Cape and other parts of South Africa by making admission into the state difficult and imposing heavy tariffs on goods entering it. More seriously from the British point of view he was fraternising with the Germans, who it must be remembered were still sore at being ousted from parts of East Africa, and had been acquiring weapons.

In the Transvaal, on the Rand, the large mining population, the Uitlanders, mostly of British origin, were refused any political rights, although they had to contribute to the running of the country by payment of taxes, and Kruger had attempted to make them subject to military service. So intense was the feeling that when Kruger visited Pretoria the Uitlanders covered his carriage with Union Jacks, in his eyes an insult for which he never forgave them. They talked of revolt and it was said that Cecil Rhodes encouraged it in order to be able to use force against the Boers. Whatever the truth, a raid was made into the Transvaal in 1896 under the command of Dr Jameson who had been installed as administrator of the new territories by Rhodes. But this was a costly mistake as the Uitlanders did not rise in concert with the raid and the whole episode resembled a damp squib. It did however result in closer accord between Kruger and Germany and an anti-British telegram of support for Kruger from the Kaiser. It also gained Kruger support from the Dutch in the south and from some elements in Britain. However anti-German feeling swept England, particularly when the Kaiser talked of making the Transvaal a German protectorate.

Kruger's totalitarian attitude towards the non-Boers was not acceptable to the British government. In Johannesburg a boiler-maker who had committed no crime was killed by the police, his murderer being acquitted by a jury which was commended for their verdict by a Boer judge, and the Uitlander population, being incensed, appealed to the Queen. War was imminent.

To solve the problem diplomacy was tried and failed, and fears grew that the example of Kruger's intransigence in the Transvaal might spark off Boer risings elsewhere in South Africa. To guard against this possibility reinforcements were sent to the weak British garrisons, only 12,000 troops spread over the whole of Southern Africa, and Kruger made this a pretext for an ultimatum to the government that if the reinforcements were not withdrawn he would declare war on Britain. The Orange Free State, also under a Boer President, Steyn, took Kruger's side, and Britain, having no intention of complying with the ultimatum, therefore found herself at war on 10 October 1899.

Many of the oldstagers in Whitehall and the Army saw this as just another bush-fire incident, a fight against untrained and undisciplined troops, notwithstanding the fact that they were white instead of the usual black. It was not even realised that the Boers were experienced horsemen and excellent shots, necessary adjuncts to their life and survival in the wide veldt. But there were some, not only in London, who appreciated that the situation might not be so simple.

As well as the British Regulars, Australia immediately offered to send troops, and colonial troops and Volunteers in South Africa were also available. This was a new situation with the nations of the Empire, because eventually Canadian and New Zealand troops took part, uniting in support of the motherland, and it may be said to have been the start of the concept of the Empire as a family, as it certainly was until the late 1940s and as it remains to a certain extent today. Equally certainly the War Office did not consider the offers of help and believed that only regular troops were capable of fighting a war.

The war, as it developed, consisted of three phases. First there was the Boer invasion of British territory, the investment of some towns which were to become household names and early disasters. Second, there was the strengthening of British forces, resources and command structure, which enabled the Army to relieve the beleaguered garrisons, to carry the war into the Transvaal itself and to deny the Boers their bases. Third, perhaps the most difficult and frustrating phase, was the searching out of small pockets of Boer resistance and wearing down their strength and spirit, over a vast area of rugged terrain, until they were prepared to sue for peace. And the key to the overall strategy was control of the railways, the only reasonably quick means of communication over the enormous distances.

War against native forces, however formidable they were, was one thing; war against a European type of enemy, particularly a cunning one who was fighting in his own environment, was quite another one. In the end the British forces actually outnumbered the Boers by five to one, which says a great deal about the Boer tactics of hit and run, cause as much damage as possible and melt away into the bush and open veldt.

Such a large force, nearly half a million men in all, needed quite different tactics, methods of command and administration from those which had sufficed for the past forty years, and because of the lack of opportunity for pitched battles for long before that. Few of those engaged had had any previous experience of warfare, many were virtually untrained Militia and Volunteers. New organisations and their staffing had to be devised, and until this was achieved by the more far-sighted of our senior officers of the time the British forces had to suffer defeat and humiliation such as they had not known for a very long time, in fact since the American War of over a century earlier which at one stage appeared to be going to be repeated.

The area of the fighting was vast, considerably larger than the beaten zone in Europe in 1914 to 1918; lines of communication were immensely long where they existed and frequently they did not exist at all. The country was eminently suitable for defence, a plateau broken mainly by small hills—kopjes—and ridges, but also by some high and rugged mountains, which dominated a wide area around them and made frontal attack suicidal. The climate was hot by day and, because of the altitude of over 5,000 feet, cold at night and very cold during the winter months, which not only increased the hardships of the troops, but produced transportation problems because of the need for tents and adequate clothing. The army was at last beginning to regard the welfare and morale of its troops as important. Maps were largely non-existent and the native guides who were frequently used instead were very unreliable, and, even when they were not deliberately leading forces into Boer positions and ambushes, were often just as lost themselves as those they were supposed to be guiding.

Not that the Boers had it all their way. Although they were excellent horsemen and crack shots as their livelihood demanded, and they used the terrain to advantage, militarily they were short of artillery and their leaders were largely untrained in command. In fact, because of their way of life and of their independent natures, very often in the early days command was more of a soviet.

The war began on 12 October 1899 with the Boer investment of Kimberley, which included Cecil Rhodes among its population. This was followed eight days later by a projected attack on the British garrisons in the coal-mining area of northern Natal. The Boers rode into Natal from the Transvaal in a host and found no opposition. The mountains were undefended, and tunnels, bridges and the railway line were left untouched. They were soon at Newcastle and moving towards Dundee and Ladysmith, and their advance guard captured Elandslaagte, which was only a minute settlement, but its capture severed all communications between Dundee and Ladysmith. Dundee was a small mining village, dominated by the hills of Impati and Talana, which General Symons discounted as being capable of being occupied by the Boers. However, the following morning after a rainstorm and when the clouds lifted, the hill tops were seen to be crowded with the enemy, who quickly opened fire with their guns on the British camp. But the Boer guns were soon silenced and a frontal attack on *Talana Hill* was successful, although General Symons was killed and the casualties were heavy. It was reported as a great victory since Dundee was saved, but the situation was still critical.

Three new, and subsequently famous, names now arrived on the scene. The first was Sir George White's cavalry commander, General John French, and the second was his chief of staff, Major Douglas Haig. French was ordered to recapture *Elandslaagte*, the Infantry Commander being Colonel Ian Hamilton. After a fierce battle which lasted all day the village was captured, and a subsequent Cavalry action succeeded in cutting off and annihilating an escaping Boer force, which created in the Boers an undying hatred of the British cavalry. One British and one South African Cavalry and three British Infantry regiments were involved. Three VCs were awarded, but the recommendation for Colonel Hamilton was refused on the grounds that a senior officer should be valorous and did not need to be decorated for doing his duty!

No Honour was awarded for either of these actions, although the latter was unsuccessfully claimed by three of the regiments which took part. Nevertheless those men who took part were entitled to a clasp to their war medal for each, a situation which was to be repeated many times during the course of the war. But these were comparatively small affrays and it became clear that the isolated salient in northern Natal could not be held. Sir George White now abandoned Elandslaagte and Dundee and retreated to Ladysmith, when he had the Boer force at his mercy, leaving the camp with its tents, supplies and food behind. During the retreat the force demonstrated against Rietfontein, but this was a minor action.

White's intention was to tie up a large part of the Boer forces by inviting investment so long as the city was not too closely besieged. He attacked part of the Boer besieging force at Pepworth Hill and *Lombard's Kop* with five Cavalry and seven Infantry regiments of his force. Unfortunately the Boers had outflanked them and unleashed a murderous fire, which caused a retreat which became a rout, although it was mitigated by a brilliant fighting withdrawal by the Artillery. At the same time the troops attempted to occupy the pass of Nicholson's Nek, but first occupied the hill of Tchrengula, or at least half of it while the Boers had an advantage by occupying the other half. There they were overwhelmed and surrendered, 1,000 men being lost, and the two battles emphasised that in a fairly matched battle the British were a poor match for the Boers. These defeats allowed the Boers to close in and the whole Natal force was thus shut up in the town where it was to remain for four months.

Mafeking, a small town in the endless wastes between the grassland of the veldt and the Kalahari desert, whose only claim to fame was that it was the largest railway depot between Kimberley on the Orange Free State border and Bulawayo in Rhodesia, was also besieged, the commander there being a Major Baden Powell who, by organising the local boys into troops of scouts to help him in carrying messages between the defenders, laid the foundations of his eventual world-wide movement. The initial Boer plan was achieved. With three main towns invested the British would now have to try and relieve them, which meant attacking the Boers where they had all the advantages, in prepared positions, held in strength but which they could abandon when they wanted and operate as guerillas against the more stereotyped British.

The Boers now moved to a limited offensive. President Steyn's forces crossed the Orange Free State border into the Cape Colony towards Stormberg. A group under Louis Botha moved south from Ladysmith and overran Colenso on the Tugela river, an armoured train sent to the relief of the town was ambushed, and Winston Churchill, then a correspondent for the *Morning Post*, was captured although he soon escaped.

The available British forces were still small, and apart from those invested were split into four portions reaching from Kimberley in the west to Natal in the east, none of them being of sufficient size or strength for the tasks which they were required to carry out. But a move had to be made and this started in the west. Under Lord Methuen a force of one Cavalry and seven Infantry regiments drove the Boers from *Belmont* and two days later four Infantry regiments captured a position at *Graspan*. The force now came up to the Modder river, and crossed it after some severe fighting. Although the first two battles were not recognised, an Honour was awarded for the last, **Modder River**, and was granted to one Cavalry and eight Infantry regiments, including the three Foot Guards. The Loyal Regiment (47th Foot) applied for the Honour but were denied it. In only five days the force had made a major advance towards Kimberley and only the hills around Magersfontein now barred its way. At the end of November everything looked rosy.

But in the second week of December the picture changed dramatically and disastrously. These few days became known through the press to the British public awaiting news of the war, perhaps the first time in our history that the civilian population really felt involved in the military activities of the Empire, as 'The Black Week'. It all started when one of the central forces under General Gatacre attacked the railway junction at Stormberg. The guides lost their way in the dark and at daybreak presented the flank of the column, which had advanced into enemy held territory without advance or flank guards and without any reconnaissance, to a strong Boer position on higher ground. The outcome needs no explanation, it was not even worthy of being called a battle. It was a massacre, and after losing a very large number of prisoners, apart from the other casualties, the force retreated.

Two days later Methuen, pressing on towards Kimberley, attacked the Boers at Magersfontein at night. Again there had been no reconnaissance and an initial bombardment had warned the Boers to expect the attack. No attempt was made to outflank the position which was assaulted frontally. The Highland Brigade found itself at dawn almost on top of the Boers, held up apparently by what in the dark appeared to be a barbed-wire entanglement but which in the event turned out to be only a fence, and by a belt of thick bushes, and was engaged by devastating rifle fire at point-blank range. The British force had not expected to find a strong defensive position on the plain in front of the hills, being prepared for defences on the hills themselves. The regiments took cover and remained pinned down all day, suffering heavy casualties every time they tried to attack or to withdraw until darkness offered them relief, and they retreated to the Modder River. Two Cavalry and nine Infantry regiments were involved at *Magersfontein*, for which no Honour and not even a clasp to the medal was awarded.

Finally, four days later in the east in Natal, General Redvers Buller made his first attempt to relieve Ladysmith. He tried to cross the Tugela River at *Colenso* by frontal assault, although a flanking assault would have been more practical and prudent, but once more the attack was delivered without proper reconnaissance and with very little decisiveness. The guides led the force to a bend in the river where there was no ford and which was enfiladed by Boer fire. The guns had to be brought into action within rifle range and most of them were lost, although they fought gallantly, and the attacks, having to be mounted from exposed positions, collapsed wherever they were made. The Royal Artillery gained another title, **Colenso Battery**.

Three heavy defeats and high casualties, which could be ill afforded in such a small army, made it indeed a black week, one of the blackest in our history. Nevertheless not all was lost since General French, between Methuen and Gatacre, had had some small success around *Colesberg*, and his force of five Cavalry regiments including the Household Cavalry and nine Infantry regiments managed to capture some positions, and at least tied down the Boers and kept them from sending reinforcements to their other armies over the next couple of months. The New Zealanders were in action here for the first time. The Royal Artillery commemorated this engagement with another Honour Title, **Cole's Cop Battery**. At the same time a raid was made from Belmont on a rebel commando at Sunnyside which succeeded and allowed the Australians and Canadians to go into action for the first time.

The British defeats brought in their train hostility from most of the rest of the world, delighted to see the British Empire brought to its knees, and shook the Empire to its very core. The Boers were adulated for their achievements by the small countries who were pleased to see an equally small power humbling the great, and by the great powers because of their jealousy of British success in colonisation and world trade. The countries which vilified Britain most urgently sought her help fourteen years later. Nobody actually declared war on Britain, but it was probably only the power of the Royal Navy, and the unpreparedness of some of the countries which most wanted to see British power destroyed, which prevented this happening.

Clearly a dramatic change of heart and policy on the part of Britain was urgently necessary. Not all the generals in South Africa were by any means incompetent, but they lacked direction and leadership. The change was initially achieved by a new Commander-in-Chief, and Lord Roberts, who last appeared in these pages during the 2nd Afghan War twenty years earlier, was appointed, although he was then 68 years old and his son had recently been killed trying to save the guns at Colenso. Lord Kitchener became his Chief of Staff. Reinforcements were sent to South Africa in large numbers, Militia and Volunteers as well as regular troops, and in particular cavalry, including the Yeomanry and many regiments of mounted Infantry hastily trained for the purpose, to combat the mobility of the Boers and to add a facility for reconnaissance which up to now had been sadly lacking. Roberts' main objective was to secure Cape Colony, and a secondary but still vital aim was to increase his transport so that he could move and manoeuvre independently of the railways.

The Boers were very sensitive about Ladysmith, still besieged but a thorn in their flesh in the rear. The British were equally sensitive about the town and made its relief a priority. The Boers however made the first move, and early in January 1900 attacked *Caesar's Camp* and *Wagon Hill*, two of its main defensive positions. The attacks were beaten off after desperate fighting and a courageous charge by the Devonshire Regiment (11th Foot). No Honour was awarded to the four Cavalry and five Infantry regiments involved.

Nevertheless the garrison had become short of food and was beset by sickness, and another major attack could well be fatal. General Buller decided to cross the Tugela River again and used a large force for his attack. From the first slowness, lack of appreciation of the situation and poor command doomed the endeavour. The river was crossed and the hill of Spion Kop was occupied, but the flat summit of the hill limited the number of troops who could be deployed, and in any case the top was under fire from Boer positions in neighbouring hills. Communications failed, no attempt was made to quieten the Boer positions and the commander was too far away to know what was going on. During the night the gallant force abandoned the position and returned across the river, ironically not realising that the Boers were doing the same thing themselves having suffered heavy casualties from the fire from Spion Kop. The relief of Ladysmith was no nearer.

Another attempt was made to capture the hills of Vaalkrantz and Doornkop, a little to the east of Spion Kop, which would open and guard a pass which could lead to Ladysmith. Buller was in command again, and showed an incredible degree of indecision and changes of plan. The result was that after a fierce but fatuous battle the British again retreated in the face of heavy Boer fire and the third attempt to breach the *Tugela Heights* had failed.

Lord Roberts now took over personal command on the Kimberley front, having French as his Cavalry Commander. He planned to advance across country, with his increased mobility, towards Bloemfontain, which might relieve the pressure in Natal and on Ladysmith, and would certainly, if successful, by-pass Kimberley and thus automatically relieve it since the Boers could not retain their investment without being cut off. The Boer Commander, Cronje, did not realise that the British could now advance free of the railway, and anyway despised them. When the advance was discovered a small force attempted to bar the way near Magersfontein, but this was easily brushed aside by a Cavalry charge and that night, 15 February, Kimberley was relieved, a patrol of mounted Australians being the first to enter the town. The **Relief of Kimberley** was awarded as an Honour to eight Cavalry and seven Infantry regiments, the part taken by two more Cavalry regiments not being recognised, and applied for by the South African Light Horse Regiment. The Infantry were not actually involved in the relief but had played their part in the action leading up to it.

Next the principal Boer commander in the Orange Free State, Christian de Wet, attacked a supply convoy near Kimberley; but Roberts decided not to abandon his plan, sacrificed the convoy and placed his forces on half rations. Cronje meanwhile had set off eastwards along the Modder River towards Bloemfontain, but had been unwilling to abandon his own supply train, moving in cumbrous ox-wagons, and therefore made slow progress. He managed to bypass the British force, but the dust of his march was visible from far off, French's cavalry chased him and he was soon forced to fight a series of rearguard actions. He eventually tried to cross the Modder River near Paardeberg, but again his transport proved a hindrance as the oxen had to be allowed to graze, and the British had their opportunity.

Cronje was surrounded, and, in spite of attempts by de Wet to relieve him was continually attacked and suffered heavy casualties, particularly among his oxen. Finally on 27 February, the anniversary of Majuba nineteen years earlier, Cronje surrendered. Seven Cavalry and eighteen Infantry regiments were awarded the Honour **Paardeberg**, as was also the Royal Canadian Regiment, the first Honour awarded in South Africa to a regiment which was not an actual part of the British Army.

Meanwhile Buller had been reinforced again and made yet another attempt to relieve Ladysmith. After hard fighting he crossed the River Tugela once more, with his whole force this time, and on the same day that Cronje surrendered at Paardeberg Buller's Cavalry entered Ladysmith and that siege was raised. Unfortunately, perhaps after so many reverses, Buller's main concern was the relief, and it is said that he ordered the cavalry not to pursue the retreating Boers, although in fact they were too exhausted to go very far. Had he followed them up the Boers, with a heavy defeat and the raising of two sieges in a fortnight, might well have sued for peace.

The **Defence of Ladysmith** was awarded as an Honour to four Cavalry and eight Infantry regiments of the British Army and to three Cavalry regiments of the South African; one British Infantry regiment and one South African Mounted regiment were unrewarded. The Honour for the **Relief of Ladysmith** was awarded to three British Cavalry and twenty-three Infantry regiments and to two South African Cavalry and one Infantry regiment, although one other South African Cavalry regiment participated without recognition. The *Cape Colony* was now freed from potential Boer attacks and, with the change of fortunes achieved in only two months by resolute and efficient command on the British side, the Boers were forced on to the defensive.

Lord Roberts's strategy and skilful use of the troops at his disposal had produced the first real successes of the war. His next move, which changed the whole face of the conflict, was to capture Bloemfontein, the capital of the Free State. He advanced towards the town and the Boers attempted to stand at *Driefontein* from which position they were driven with significant losses. Nine British regiments took part in the battle, supported by one of Australian Cavalry, The New South Wales Lancers, the first time that troops of that Dominion had been engaged in a major battle in South Africa. Three days later Bloemfontein was entered and the Boers fled northward into the Transvaal.

After two months of heavy fighting the Army needed to draw breath and to be resupplied, no easy task with only a single railway line. During this phase, at the end of March, two batteries of Artillery escorting a convoy were ambushed at *Sannah's Post* by de Wet. Very heavy casualties were suffered with the loss of seven guns although the convoy was saved, and one of the batteries involved, Q Battery, later claimed and was granted the Honour Title of **Sannah's Post Battery**, one of the very rare instances of an Artillery Honour where no other Cavalry or Infantry regiments gained one during the same action.

In a vain attempt to stem the tide which was now flowing so strongly against the Boers, de Wet next besieged the small town of *Wepener* on the Basutoland border which was desperately defended by one Canadian and two South African regiments. After a fortnight a relieving force appeared and de Wet raised the siege; this small action had a greater significance than would have been expected from its size since it allowed Roberts to prepare for his next advance without having to take overt action himself while the Boers' attention was drawn elsewhere. This was the start of the march towards Johannesburg and Pretoria, which soon made progress, crossed the Sand River and captured the Free State replacement capital of Kroonstad.

It will be remembered that a third town had been besieged at the beginning of hostilities, Mafeking, far to the north on the western Transvaal border. For some time a small mixed force of Dominion troops had been vainly trying to move towards its relief, and now another small force of South Africans joined them. Although still outnumbered they were now able to break through and raise the siege, the Kimberley Light Horse entering Mafeking on 17 May. When the news reached London the capital erupted in exultation after the grim news of the early part of the war and the recent successes. Crowds thronged the streets and throughout the country festivities and bonfires, often bearing effigies of Kruger and other Boer leaders, marked the culmination of the change in British fortunes. It was strange, in view of the popular feeling, that the *Relief of Mafeking* was not honoured as was the end of the other sieges, although three South African regiments were involved in the final assault and regiments of other countries had been engaged in the advance which made relief possible.

Lord Roberts now announced the annexation of the Free State under the name of the Orange River Colony and his force crossed into the Transvaal. Minor battles took place at the end of May at *Doornkop* near where Jameson had surrendered, seven British and one Canadian regiments taking part, of which one applied for it as an Honour, and on the Klip River. Another small action at *Biddulphsberg* near Bethlehem in the Orange Free State on the same day was fought by three British regiments, two of them Guards battalions, but like so many of the actions of this war no Honour was granted. Two days later *Johannesberg* and Germiston fell but the victorious army gained no recognition for this feat either; it was composed almost entirely of British regiments, three Cavalry, three Guards regiments and thirteen Infantry regiments, and the 16th Lancers unsuccessfully applied for it to be Honoured.

But for all the recent successes the war was by no means over. Just as on the British side the earlier, less competent generals had been replaced, so on the Boer side the most able were becoming apparent, mainly de Wet, Botha, who had held Buller in his first attack on the Tugela, and de la Rey. They were under no illusions as to their fate in defeat, and saw clearly that the British were still thin on the ground for the enormous amount of territory which they had to control, particularly the long single railway line. They also saw that they were now no match for the British in set-piece battles, and decided, as their only alternative and hope, to rely entirely on guerilla warfare which, with their mobility in the open country, would enable them to attack isolated garrisons and to cut the railway more or less at will. In spite of the considerable action the war had only been going on for eight months and was yet to drag on for a further two years.

Early attacks brought the Boers some success, but Roberts, with his usual foresight, could see that the essential requirement was to drive the enemy from the vicinity of their capital, Pretoria. He entered the capital on 5 June 1900. An engagement was fought at *Aleman's Nek* in June by six British Infantry regiments, of which one applied for it as an Honour, and by the South African Light Horse. Another much larger action took place at the same time at *Diamond Hill*, in the hills through which ran the railway to Delagoa Bay, about 30 miles east of Pretoria. The Boers were in a strong position and the fighting was fierce, but eventually the Australian New South Wales Mounted Rifles, fighting for the first time as a regiment instead of being broken up into detachments and attached to British regiments as were most of the Commonwealth troops, captured the hill and the Boers retreated down the railway. The battle was one of the last major actions of the war, in which twenty-four British regiments, one Australian and one South African took part, and Botha's force was driven towards the Portuguese frontier.

Most of the Boers, and Kruger himself, were in the eastern Transvaal, but before Roberts directed his forces thither, assisted by an advance by Buller northwards from Natal, he decided to try to destroy the Boer forces in the Orange River Colony, and set off towards Bethlehem and Bloemfontein. The Boers had established a defensive position in the Wittebergen (White Mountains) in the centre of which was the Brandwater Basin, with almost all the Free State troops. The British Commander made little effort to press an attack or to close the passes through which the Boers could escape, and very quietly under cover of darkness a large number of the enemy moved out. Those left in defence were slowly dislodged by local actions until the majority were in the centre of the basin. In spite of indecision and near panic some got away but the majority were captured. The engagement at *Wittebergen* involved thirteen British and one South African regiments.

West of Pretoria, in the Magaliesberg mountains the Boers under De La Rey carried out some successful raids and Botha tried to draw Roberts away from any action in the area by attacking in the east, at Edendale near Diamond Hill, but after a heavy engagement was forced to withdraw. However De La Rey kept up his successful raiding tactics in the Magaliesberg until pursuit got too hot and he slipped away to fight another day. Another small but tenacious outpost encounter at *Geluk* in the south-east of the Transvaal in August involved only the King's Regiment (8th Foot), and was inconclusive. The two armies eventually met up at *Belfast* on the Delagoa railway in August. A major engagement involved thirteen Cavalry regiments, including the Household Cavalry, the three Guards regiments and four other Infantry regiments. Again it was not Honoured, as in fact no battles had been since the Relief of Ladysmith in February and as no further battles of the war were to be.

The final major battle was fought the next day at *Bergendal*, twelve British regiments, of which the Rifle Brigade applied for it as an Honour, taking part; Buller distinguished himself here, his last battle probably being his best. The Boers, although still full of fight, were politically finished as they had no firm bases and no towns which they could call their own for more than a few days at a time. Kruger went to Europe to try to drum up help, but found that the support given to his cause when he was winning had evaporated once it was seen that there was little hope for him.

The British forces had now forced a hole in the Boer defences and poured through into the eastern Transvaal. On 1 September Roberts proclaimed the annexation of the Transvaal. But the remaining Boers largely escaped and fled northwards. In November a small engagement was fought on the *Komati River* by three British and one Canadian regiments, and in the middle of the next month there was an encounter at *Nooitgedacht* when two British Infantry battalions ran into a Boer force. But the main fighting was now over and Lord Roberts handed over command to Kitchener. He had taken over himself in the darkest days of the war, achieved success and rendered perhaps his greatest service to the Empire in a lifetime of memorable service. The name of General 'Bobs' would live on with the heroes of past generations.

Kitchener now had three tasks; to protect British communications, to prevent the Boers gaining access to supplies and resources, and to harass them until they gave up the struggle. He established blockhouses, bullet-proof and linked together with barbed-wire entanglements, the first major use of this defensive weapon to become so important and to claim so many lives on both sides in the trench fighting of the Great War. He also established, more distastefully, concentration camps, which were to play so great a part in a very differently developed form in World War II. Into these he brought thousands of the white population, destroying in many cases the farms from which they were evicted to prevent them from being used as shelter by the roving Boer guerilla bands. The burning of the farmhouses was a very unpopular and much-resented move because they represented so many years of hard work to the farmers. Also the conditions in the camps, although everything was done to run them as humanely as possible, were far from good and the mortality rate was high. The enemies of Britain made much propaganda at the time, as they have more recently, out of this action.

Beyond that Kitchener harried the Boer forces with drives into the blockhouse and barbed-wire defences, which gradually sapped the will and the numbers of the

guerillas. Prisoners were difficult to hold and many were released on giving an oath not to fight again; most of these broke their oaths, because they felt that they had been given under duress, and sometimes were captured several times, and eventually, to prevent this, the prisoners were deported, mostly to St Helena and some to the Mediterranean Islands, India and Ceylon.

De Wet now moved south and crossed the Orange River into the Cape Colony, and at the same time other guerillas moved down from the north into the eastern Transvaal again and caused considerable havoc. British troops trying to surround the Boers and capture their leaders were frequently ambushed, and apparently still had not understood the principles of guerilla warfare or how to cope with the Boer bands. The hunt for de Wet occupied a lot of men for a long time with little success.

So the war dragged on throughout the whole of 1901 and well into the following year. There were innumerable encounters, some of them ferocious, only three of which were of a size or significance worthy of note. The first was at *Lake Chrissie* in the eastern Transvaal in February when a Boer force under Botha attacked a British camp, threw it into confusion and then achieved his purpose of getting past the British cordon. Two British regiments took part although a third claimed it as an Honour. The second was at *Moedwill* near Rustenberg across the Magaliesberg where again the Boers threw a cordon camp into disarray, although without achieving anything, again with two regiments participating, one of which, the Scottish Horse, unsuccessfully claimed it as an Honour. The third was at *Baakenlaagte* at the end of October, again a two-regiment affair, but was a much more fiercely fought battle in which the Boers over-ran a British position and caused very heavy casualties. It was claimed as an Honour by the Scottish Horse, although in this case an Artillery battery without an Honour Title, 166 Battery, also celebrate the battle for their devotion to the guns when fired on at point-blank range.

Overtures for peace were made when the Boers were at last in an impossible position. But the main requirement of the peace terms, that there should be only one South Africa, and that a part of the Empire, was a stumbling block to Boer thinking. Eventually after much argument they accepted the terms and the war came to an end with the signing of the Treaty of Vereeniging on 31 May 1902.

South Africa was at last united, but at a heavy cost, particularly in financial terms, to Britain. British casualties had not been high, less than 6,000 killed in action, but deaths from wounds and disease, particularly enteric fever, accounted for nearly three times that number. There were adverse opinions among the Boers to accepting British sovereignty, but their leaders realised that there was no alternative and that the country must unite in the face of the growing Kaffir population. Twelve years later Britain's erstwhile enemies provided a major contribution to the next great war in which she was involved.

The War in South Africa, the 2nd Boer War had also united the rest of the Empire as never before with a large number of Dominion troops participating. A Campaign Honour was awarded to the largest number so far of any one Honour. Including Cavalry, Infantry, Militia, Volunteers and Yeomanry 196 British regiments gained **South Africa** with appropriate dates between 1899 and 1902. It was also granted to twenty-two Canadian, thirty-seven Australian, twenty-three New Zealand and twelve South African regiments.

A departure from normal was the award of Honours to certain Militia Battalions in their own right instead of as part of a parent regular regiment, which were not borne by the parent regiment unless it already had the Honour. Also a number of Militia Battalions were granted Honours in their own right in recognition of their tasks of guarding Boer prisoners and for garrison duty. An Honour **St Helena** was granted to Militia Battalions of the Gloucestershire and Wiltshire Regiments, and **Mediterranean 1901–02** was granted to eight other Militia Battalions.

But apart from the Campaign Honours and the two Militia Honours, there were only six individual Battle Honours. At the same time clasps for seventeen individual battles were awarded to those troops who took part in them. It seems indefensible that, if these seventeen battles were considered sufficiently worthy for them to be commemorated on the chests of the soldiers themselves, only six of them were considered worthy of being borne on the Colours of the regiments with whom the soldiers had served. Although for the first time some effort had been made by their Lordships to classify the engagements which merited recognition in their eyes, in the end they lost their nerve because of the large number. It was a great pity, particularly in view of the number of Honours which had to be granted only a few years later, although even then many of the recognised battles, actions, etc were not allowed to be awarded.

Natal

The final war in this period in South Africa occurred again in Natal in 1906 when there was a Zulu rising. For quelling the revolt, and in contrast with the war over only four years, an Honour was awarded to five South African regiments as **Natal 1906**, including the Zululand Mounted Rifles. Three other South African regiments, and one British, the Royal Warwickshire Regiment, were refused it, and one other South African regiment, The Light Horse, claimed it as 'Native Rebellion, 1906.'

Above: Men of the Cape Garrison Artillery with 15pdr BL guns at the Modder River, South Africa, 1900. *via Ian Hogg*

13 The Great War: Part 1, 1914-15

The Build-up, 1902–14

During the two and a half centuries up to the beginning of the twentieth the British Army grew from a handful of regiments, raised and largely owned and paid for by their appointed Colonels, into a major fighting formation. It was largely responsible for the accumulation and growth of the British possessions overseas into the greatest Empire the world had known, operating in support and defence of the intrepid traders who had opened up posts in all parts of the world in spite of all the odds against them and of their sometimes bitter experiences. It fought numerous wars and many battles, apart from the innumerable skirmishes and minor actions, against European and native forces, at one extreme against highly trained armies commanded by excellent generals and at the other against untrained rabbles incited by their equally untrained leaders to a bloodlust.

Shortly after the turn of the century, as has been seen, the long and arduous Boer War came to an end, and the country and the army hoped to return to the pleasures and prosperity of the peace. They were assured by the politicians that they would do so; they were promised, as they were again and equally unreliably thirty-odd years later, 'peace in our time'. But the peace which had been heralded with relief and euphoria was not to last for very long, and shortly the Army would have to look to the laurels of its long existence, would be faced with the greatest trial of strength that it had ever encountered, would nearly go under, but in the end would survive and would once more emerge victorious.

In 1914 the Great War, as it was known until the onslaught of another equally great war, the so-called 'war to end war', began. But before the narrative of that great event and its relationship to the Battle Honours of the British, and now also the Commonwealth, Armies can unfold, it is necessary to put its origins and cause into perspective, and to see some of the significant events during the twelve years after the end of the Boer War which led up to it. So much has been written about these events by all manners of men, in so much more detail than is possible here, that it is difficult to know how much needs to be covered. This book is not a history of wars but a history of the Honours associated with those wars; nevertheless, to the majority of those who will read it the events happened so long ago, and have in some cases become so glossed over with legend or shrouded with mist, that the meaning of the Great War and its place in that history of

Honours will be equally misty or legendary unless some attempt is made to describe Europe during those years, and the personalities and events which led up to the catastrophe and made it inevitable.

Britain had suffered a lot of hostility, as has been related, during the Boer War from most European countries, and, although the worst of it had died down before the peace treaty was signed, much remained. The government was determined to change all this and so, at first, took a conciliatory line to regain friendship.

Probably the major achievement was by King Edward VII himself, who, being a francophile before being a politician, saw the value of friendship with the traditional enemy, the French, in the prevailing climate in Europe, and personally promoted this. The result was the Entente Cordiale which ended, at least overtly, hundreds of years of antagonism. France had already entered into an alliance with Russia, and although Britain's own ties with Russia were more tenuous and were largely based on family connections rather than political strategy, this alignment of the three major powers on the extremities of Europe left Germany and her allies surrounded and isolated in the middle.

The family ties between the rulers of a number of the European countries should have prevented wars if it were true that blood is thicker than water; unfortunately, as so often happens in families, it is the petty antagonisms and jealousies which in the end prove to have the stronger influence. Queen Victoria's progeny were established through marriage, dynastic marriages mainly, in the major countries involved in the European struggle for supremacy. The Tsar of Russia was cousin to King George V since their respective mothers, the Empress Maria and Queen Alexandra, were sisters, daughters of the King of Denmark. The Empress of Russia was a granddaughter of Victoria, being the daughter of Alice who had married the Grand Duke of Hesse and was thus also a cousin of George V. Kaiser Wilhelm II of Germany was a grandson of Victoria through her eldest daughter Victoria, and was thus a cousin to both George V and the Tsar. There were numerous connections as well with the German princely families, as well as with Spain and Greece, but these were of less importance in the overall political situation.

The greatest hostility to Britain had been shown by Germany, led by a blustering bully, Kaiser Wilhelm, unsure of his hold on his people, obsessed by pomp and ceremony, conscious all the time of his physical infirmity and the need to hide it, willing to take the advice of his ministers when it fed his own ego and denigrating those countries which he believed stood in his way of achieving by divine right domination in Europe and throughout the world. Germany was extremely jealous of Britain's position in world trade and of the Empire which she had amassed, most of it before Germany herself had become a nation and was still a collection of principalities and minor kingdoms. As has been seen this jealousy had already caused colonial clashes in Africa. The Kaiser's first overt action was to try to drive a wedge between Britain and Russia.

In 1902, two years before the signing of the Entente Cordiale, Britain had signed a treaty of mutual aid with Japan; this was advantageous to the former because she wanted a friendly nation willing to help her in any possible attack on her Far East possessions, and to the latter as a guard against possible Russian advances in Manchuria and Korea. Such Russian advances were being encouraged by Germany, mainly because they would occupy the Russian Army and draw it far away from Germany's eastern frontier and thus, so she thought, prevent any adverse build up of power which might be a danger to her, particularly with a large French army on her western frontier.

But the Russian Army was able to be transported to and fro fairly easily and quickly on the newly built Trans-Siberian Railway and in any case her involvement in the war with Japan which began in 1904 was mainly, and disastrously, naval. Britain did not go to the help of Japan, such help not being asked for, for two main reasons; ostensibly because Japan had actually started the war to eliminate the Russian presence on her doorstep, and more practically because the British treaty with France and the French treaty with Russia would have created some awkward internal situations—which of course the Kaiser realised full well. Although Germany did not succeed in driving in the wedge through the direct action of this war, she made some propaganda, without achieving any significant success however, out of the Dogger Bank incident when the Russian Baltic fleet, *en route* to the Far East, accidentally fired on some British fishing vessels in the dark and sunk one of them.

In 1906 the European Powers began to take up sides as a result of the Algeciras Conference which was held to try to decide the future of Morocco. France claimed that this comparatively unimportant country came within her sphere of influence, and Britain supported her in exchange for being allowed a free rein in Egypt, as did Russia because of her treaty obligations. Germany raised objections and was supported in this by Austria-Hungary. Meanwhile Italy, although officially a member of the Triple Alliance of central European countries, remained neutral. Although the Conference decided nothing it brought Britain and France closer together which was not what Germany had intended and was to her disadvantage. Russia was in any case getting tired of Germany's attempted domination and interference in her domestic affairs, or perhaps it is more accurate to say that the Tsar was getting fed up with Cousin Wilhelm's patronising attitude towards him.

Two years later the next phase of the build-up to war occurred in Turkey. The Turks had been oppressing and occasionally massacring the Orthodox Christian minorities ever since the 'Bulgarian Atrocities' of 1876, and Britain and Russia, belatedly though not jointly, refused to accept the situation any longer; the former because they were Christians and the latter because they were Orthodox. But the atrocities in themselves meant very little to Germany and the Russo-British action provided an excuse for the Kaiser to step in as a friend of Turkey and make her his ally. The immediate result, and a major cause of the Great War, was the Austrian occupation of Bosnia and Herzogovina. This was objectionable to the Serbs as these countries had at one time been Serbian provinces and they were currently trying to reach agreement for a union between them again. Although Britain did not recognise the annexation it was to Russia that the Serbs appealed for help; Russia herself was affronted by the annexation, since discussions were in progress to allow Austria more control over her Slav minorities, and was prepared to assist, but Austria at once threatened Serbia with an ultimatum unless Russia advised her to give way and accept the situation, which Russia promptly did in the hope of protecting the Slavs.

While these events were proceeding on land, the balance of power at sea was shifting towards Germany, who was building ships as fast as possible, since Russia had lost both her Far Eastern and Baltic fleets in the Russo-Japanese War, had not replaced them and now had negligible power. In Britain there was agitation for a rapid expansion of the Royal Navy in order to keep pace with Germany and maintain the balance. In 1911 Morocco was again in the news when Germany flexed her muscles and sent the gunboat *Panther* there, precipitating the so-called Agadir Incident, on the pretext of protecting the interests of a non-existent German population; she demanded a major portion of the French Congo in exchange for its withdrawal. This was barefaced blackmail and the French stood firm, supported by Britain; Europe was on the brink of war but Germany was not yet ready for the conflict and eventually withdrew without the Congo.

In the same year Italy abandoned her neutrality and declared war on Turkey. She attacked Tripoli, on the pretext of the Turkish mistreatment of Italians there, but actually because this was the only part of North Africa which was not under the control of one or other of the Great Powers. She wanted her share and was afraid that Germany might forestall her. The affair was soon over, but it put Germany in a dilemma because Italy was still officially part of the Triple Alliance, and Germany was openly friendly with Turkey and had encouraged her as an ally. The outcome was that Germany cultivated Turkey more strongly and gradually dropped Italy from her reckoning.

In October 1912 a complicated and unexpected series of events started in the Balkans, the real powder keg of Europe. First Bulgaria, Serbia, Montenegro and Greece joined together, attacked Turkey and drove her out of Europe. Germany and Austria were both shocked; the former because Turkish Army officers were being trained in Berlin and had failed, and as a result found it necessary to maintain a physical presence in the Turkish Army from then on; the latter because she had never considered the Serbs to be a threat to her and was now worried about the Austrian Slav subjects in the northern Balkans.

But the Balkan alliance was not very strong and Bulgaria, Austria's protégé, then attacked Serbia and Greece with disastrous results to herself. Next Roumania attacked Bulgaria, shortly followed in the attack by Turkey who thus regained a foothold in Europe, in Macedonia. Austria herself planned to attack Serbia to gain a long-wanted outlet to the Aegean Sea and the Mediterranean through Salonika, but the Serbs stood firm against the threat and the Italians unexpectedly rallied to the support of the Serbs. The eastern alliances were being drawn, with Turkey becoming closer to Germany, and Bulgaria agreeing to support Germany and Austria in any attack on Serbia.

The European armies were now being organised for war. Four years earlier, in 1908, the British Army had undergone a major overhaul and Richard Haldane, the Minister of War, had set the pattern for the next 60 years by the introduction of the Territorial Force, the forerunner of the Territorial Army. By this means each Infantry regiment gained one or more battalions of Volunteers, not just affiliated as had been the Volunteer Forces but actually a part of the regiment. No longer were the volunteers just a good social club, an excuse for showing off a uniform and spending a few weeks at camp each year; now they were to be integrated with the Regulars and brought up to a degree of training which in only a few years was to be a complete surprise to the rest of Europe. The Yeomanry became the equivalent of the Territorial Force as an adjunct to the Cavalry, but were not integrated with them. The Staff College was extended in scope and the Officers Training Corps was formed to provide a nucleus of officers both for the Regular and Volunteer forces and as a reserve for war. The Commonwealth Armies were similarly organised, although in the case of the Canadian, Australian and New Zealand Armies the organisation was abandoned as soon as the war started, for no apparently good reason. In 1912 the Royal Flying Corps was established with Naval and Military wings, although progress was slow and by 1914 there were still only about a hundred aircraft available.

On the continent Germany forged ahead with her preparations for war, but although the French found it hard to keep pace they were still a threat to German plans. It was essential for Germany to gain a massive numerical advantage over the armies of the west, because Belgium too had to be invaded to gain a wide enough front for a tactical advantage for the number of troops they needed to deploy and to allow the Schlieffen Plan to develop; and to this end she prepared to reduce her troops on the Russian frontier. She felt safe in doing this because she thought that Russia's internal problems would prevent her from taking much part in a war, and that Austria would be strong enough to counter any likely threat from the east. The German plan relied on an initial conflict against France whose western allies, Britain and Italy, she thought would be too weak, or too slow in coming to her support, to be of any value.

Austria now became the key which was to unlock the door to war. She was virtually surrounded by enemies who all wanted slices of her territory; Russia wanted Galicia, Roumania wanted Transylvania, Italy wanted the Tyrol and the Adriatic coast and Serbia wanted the south Slav

kingdoms. The Emperor, Franz Josef, was very old, a survivor from a dead age. It was a tradition of the Habsburg dynasty that they only married royal blood; his son had committed suicide in sordid circumstances and his heir was his nephew, the Archduke Franz Ferdinand, who had broken the rule by marrying the Countess Sophia Chotek, a Czech and therefore a Slav. Apart from the traditional aspects this created a problem, since the Austro-Hungarian alliance depended on the suppression of the Slavs. Franz Ferdinand had been forced to sign an oath that his children would not succeed him, but the Emperor feared that when the time came he would break it. The Archduke was ostracised in Austria and he hated the Kaiser, but the latter, appreciating the internal situation, set out to curry favour with the Archduchess Sophia and with her help gained Franz's confidence and supported him.

In June 1914 Franz Ferdinand, as Inspector of the Army, visited Bosnia with his wife, and the 28th was chosen for a review of the Army in Sarajevo; this was a bad choice on somebody's part because this was the day known as Vidovdan when the Serbs remembered and brooded upon their defeat by the Turks at Kossovo Polye, 'The Field of Blackbirds', in 1349. It was known that there were assassins in the crowd, but the Archduke ignored the threat; a bomb was thrown which missed him, but still he continued his progress through the streets until he and his wife were shot at point blank range by a Bosnian Serb, Gavril Princip, who thereby not only precipitated the Great War but removed the one man in Austria who might have done something for the Slavs for whose sake the killing was ostensibly carried out. There was suspicion that the Archduke might have been 'set up', à la Chicago a decade later, because of his unpopularity with the Habsburgs and as a pretext for Austrian action against Serbia, and this was enhanced by his quick and unceremonial burial.

Germany seized on this 'act of God', as the Kaiser put it, as a perfect pretext for the war for which she was now ready and started mobilising. While Austria tried to lay the blame for the assassination on the Serbian government the world waited for a month to see what would happen.

On 23 July the Austrians issued an ultimatum to Serbia, which the Serbs accepted, much to the surprise and chagrin of the Germans. But by deliberate mischance the Kaiser did not see the Serbian note until it was too late for him to retract, and the Austrians decided that the Serbian reply was inadequate and declared war. On 30 July Britain introduced mobilisation, the speed of which was helped because much of the Territorial Force was already embodied and under arms at annual training camp. In spite of the Tsar's desire and efforts to maintain peace, the inevitable Russian mobilisation was also ordered, and in reply Germany declared war on Russia on 1 August. Germany offered France the opportunity of remaining neutral but somewhat naturally she refused because of her treaty obligations and Germany declared war on her two days later. The Kaiser then contravened his treaty with Luxemburg, next threatened Belgium, who appealed to Britain under the terms of a Treaty concluded in 1839, and to France to protect her neutrality, unavailingly as Germany declared war on her too and invaded both countries on the same day. Of the Great Powers only Britain was not yet involved; she did not wait for the inevitable ultimatum but took the step herself, and having received no satisfactory reply from Germany Britain and the British Empire declared war on Germany on 4 August.

France and Flanders, 1914

Thanks to the Haldane reorganisation the British Army was in a comparatively good shape. By calling up the regular reservists one Cavalry and six Infantry divisions could be put into the field straight away, although they were not all immediately deployed, and behind them were fourteen Mounted brigades and fourteen First Line Infantry divisions of the Territorial Force. The training of the TF was not yet up to regular standards, nor were regiments yet up to full strength, but they were probably as fit for action as the German and French reserve formations which were deployed. However, the terms of their contracts were for home service only, and although an appeal for volunteers would probably have been answered by the vast majority, as in fact it was later on, if it had been decided to send them abroad, they were deployed to defend the coast.

Lord Kitchener was now brought into the government as Minister for War, and immediately realised and made it clear to his colleagues that the British Empire must prepare itself for a long struggle, which could only be ended by major battles in Europe to destroy Germany, in which she needed to play a major part in relation to her world power and resources. But for all his undoubted abilities he was a traditionalist, had not been involved in the creation of the Territorial Force and did not appreciate its potential. This may have been because he misunderstood the terminology; he had seen French Territorial troops, aged conscripts in the last stages of their service, in action in 1870 where they had played a very undistinguished role, and did not appreciate the differences between these formations and the young British territorials.

Kitchener therefore decided to create six more Regular Divisions (two Cavalry and four Infantry) and to raise the New Armies, initially six Infantry divisions but soon increased to twenty, by calling for volunteers from the civilian population; the poster appealing for volunteers was probably the most famous one ever seen and there was certainly no shortage of men answering the call. But of course they had to be trained from scratch and many months elapsed before they were ready for action. In the meanwhile two Indian divisions, totally unsuited to the conditions in which they later found themselves fighting, were earmarked to be sent to France to support the five Regular divisions which formed the original British Expeditionary Force. The Regulars undoubtedly acquitted themselves magnificently, but their losses in the first year of war of trained officers and NCOs were so heavy that by 1916, when their experience was badly needed and many of them would probably have held senior positions in the New Armies, they were dead, killed in subordinate posts. The early use of the Territorial divisions, if it did not reduce the overall carnage, would have undoubtedly

spread the losses more thinly and preserved a greater proportion of the highly trained Regulars.

The BEF started crossing to France on 9 August and the first stage was completed by 22 August, with great smoothness and efficiency, and with equally great secrecy. Only two days before the first contact between the BEF and the German army the High Command did not believe that any landing of British troops on a large scale had taken place. And even later the Kaiser referred to the BEF as 'that contemptible little army', a title which has been used by the survivors of those early days with pride ever since.

Mons and Le Cateau

When the British army arrived in France the situation of the French was desperate; they had totally underestimated the strength of the German armies and the width of the front on which they were advancing, and their plan to attack the invading Germans on the frontier met with complete disaster. The British, one Cavalry and four Infantry divisions, concentrated in Belgium south-west of Mons, on the left of the French, in a position which according to the French dispositions and plan should have left them clear of the German right wing, but which in fact placed them in the path of one German army and outflanked by another. They were ordered to advance, and what were generally believed to have been the first shots of the war fired by British troops occurred when a patrol of the 4th Dragoon Guards met a German picquet near Soignies, 10 miles north-east of Mons. It was at this point that the French formation immediately on their right was penetrated and withdrew, leaving the British isolated; they withdrew to the line of the canal through Mons where the first assault of the German armies fell.

The British had two advantages; first, the Germans had not expected to find them there at all, believing that they would take much longer to take the field than was in fact the case, and secondly the standard of the British Infantry rifle fire was so high that the Germans believed that they had come up against an incredible number of machine guns. These two factors enabled the BEF, under Sir John French, to extricate themselves from a perilous situation, but not before they had suffered heavily. The battle opened on 23 August, but there was never a hope of the Army standing its ground. It tried hard for a couple of days, then slowly retreated. General French was determined that he would not be left in the lurch again and to make sure that his next position was tenable the Army had to cover nearly 100 miles, until by 5 September it stood on the river Marne south-east of Paris.

Three Battle Honours were awarded during this period. **Mons** was gained by eighteen Cavalry and forty-four Infantry regiments, and **Le Cateau**, fought when the 2nd Corps turned and stood their ground for a day during the retreat because they were too tired to retreat any further, was gained by fifteen Cavalry and thirty-nine Infantry regiments, many of the regiments gaining both Honours. The Honour **Retreat from Mons** was awarded to virtually the whole of the British Army then deployed, nineteen Cavalry, one Yeomanry and sixty Infantry regiments, which was only eleven Cavalry and fourteen Infantry regiments short of the establishment of the Regular Army. An Honour was claimed, but not allowed, for *Audregnies* by the Cheshire Regiment (22nd Foot). The Royal Artillery gained two more Honour Titles, **Le Cateau Battery** and **Nery Battery**; the latter Honour was unique to the Royal Regiment, and notable for the three Victoria Crosses gained by the Battery during a fight between it, with some support from the Cavalry, against overwhelming odds. The 5th Dragoon Guards and 11th Hussars unsuccessfully claimed *Nery* as an Honour, and the 2nd Dragoon Guards and six Infantry battalions were also involved in the fray.

The Marne and the Aisne

German losses had also been heavy, unexpectedly so as far as they were concerned, and they had had to leave garrisons, siege troops and flank guards as they advanced; thus, although they had enjoyed a 50 per cent advantage in strength at the start of the war the two sides were now more or less evenly balanced numerically. The Schlieffen Plan had gone wrong, because the total strength had been below that originally envisaged, and because as the two German Armies on their right wing advanced a gap opened up between them, and the far right had to swing in to pass to the east rather than the west of Paris as the plan required.

Now the British on the Marne, in support of the massive French armies, began a counter-offensive into this 30-mile gap between the German armies; the latter had outrun their supplies and they were now forced on to the retreat, much to their chagrin and dismay, eventually taking up a strong position on the River Aisne. If only the BEF had been a little bit quicker they might not have reached it. The first Battle of the Marne may be considered as one of the most significant, if not one of the great, battles of world history, the one which in due course was mainly responsible for winning the war, and the one which if it had been lost would have meant the end of the war, with a German victory, in a few weeks. It was recognised as an Honour for a large number of regiments, as was to be the pattern throughout the next four years in France and Flanders in the majority of cases, inevitable with the large armies involved and the attrition caused by trench warfare which often required a whole division to be replaced after only a few days in the line, thus bringing into action in one battle two or three times the number of regiments than had been the case in earlier wars. The pattern was also partly caused by the curious situation whereby the Battle Nomenclature Committee had listed a large number of battles and engagements in which comparatively few regiments participated, but the majority of these were not accepted when claimed as Battle Honours.

The Honour, **Marne 1914**, was granted to nineteen Cavalry, one Yeomanry and sixty Infantry regiments which, perhaps not surprisingly, were the same ones as those granted the Honour of the Retreat from Mons.

The German position on the Aisne proved too strong to be taken, although some advances were made, bearing in mind the exhausted state of the British and French Armies

after three weeks of continuous heavy defensive fighting over long distances and the cold wet weather. It signalled, although nobody realised it at the time, the start of trench warfare and the stalemate which was to exist in the west for the next four years; the line held by the British remained virtually unchanged for the next three years no matter whether the British or the French were the incumbents. The first Battle of the Aisne was awarded as an Honour, **Aisne 1914**, to nineteen Cavalry, one Yeomanry and seventy-one Infantry regiments; only two Regular Infantry regiments were now not involved in France, although they were to be within a month.

Antwerp, La Bassée, Messines and Armentières

Apart from the main actions of the armies in France and Belgium, other operations were carried out to give support to the hard-pressed Belgians and to create a diversion. At the end of August, whilst the armies were retreating from Mons, three battalions of Royal Marines landed at Ostend, confused the Germans as to their strength and intentions, and were withdrawn again after about a week. In September a brigade of Royal Marines, supported by a regiment of Yeomanry, were mounted in London omnibuses and ostentatiously showed themselves in various parts of Belgium for about a month. A larger and more important operation was the despatch of the Royal Naval Division to Antwerp, late in September, to defend the port and to keep the Scheldt open (shades of 1809!) in co-operation with the Belgian Army. The city was soon under siege by the Germans, and within a short time, in spite of plans to reinforce the garrison with British Infantry and Cavalry divisions and French troops, the Belgians collapsed and the Naval Brigade was withdrawn.

The only way in which the stalemate in France could be broken was by one side or the other being able to increase its forces sufficiently to upset the balance. The French were already virtually totally committed as were the Germans, although the latter might be able in time to increase their strength in the west by eliminating the threat in the east. Thus it remained to the British to try to fulfil its potential with the New Armies. But first the possibility of outflanking the Germans, or at any rate protecting the Channel ports, had to be tried by extending the allied line northwards to the coast. Unfortunately the Germans had the same idea.

Four fresh and newly-formed German Army Corps were concentrated in northern Belgium and drove for the coast where they reached Zeebrugge and Ostend. But by then the Belgians were on the line of Nieuport and Dixmude, had breached the dykes and had caused inundations on and around the River Yser; their Army then formed the extension on the left of the British line to the sea. The British divisions which had been landed to try to defend Antwerp were now diverted to join up with the rest of the BEF moving northward from the Aisne, forming a line from north of Arras to Ypres; in addition they had now been joined by the Indian divisions. On this line they met the full force of the German onslaught aimed at capturing the Channel ports of Dunkirk, Calais and Boulogne.

The area of Flanders, in which so much heavy fighting was to take place until the end of the war, is most unsuitable for modern warfare. Most of it is below sea level and any hole, dug as a trench or blasted out by a shell, fills with water in a very short time making winter conditions, in particular, appalling. The roads had shallow foundations and soon broke down under the heavy traffic making it difficult for supplies to be brought up to the front; cross-country movement, especially for Artillery, was almost impossible because of the use of the land for agriculture interspersed with factories and mines.

The major battles opened around La Bassée on 12 October after a British advance, but when the German defences proved too strong the troops pushed northwards where they were counterattacked near the village of Givenchy which caused a limited withdrawal until a further attack regained the village. But in the face of heavy German attacks and heavy British losses it was decided to withdraw and concentrate on the line of Armentières–Wytschaete and open a new attack further north still at Messines. German attempts to break the line at Armentières were met with further stiff resistance and more heavy losses.

La Bassée was notable as the first battle in which Indian troops were engaged in Europe. Messines was perhaps even more notable for the fact that here for the first time the Territorial Force was engaged, represented by one Infantry regiment, The London Scottish, and by one Yeomanry regiment, The Oxfordshire Hussars, which was also involved along with The North Irish Horse at Armentières. Territorial Force and Yeomanry involvement was continued at Ypres with the addition of the North Somerset Yeomanry, the Northumberland Yeomanry, the Leicester Yeomanry and The Hertfordshire Regiment.

Three Battle Honours were awarded during this period, which in fact overlapped the first battle at Ypres. **La Bassée 1914** was gained by five British and two Indian Cavalry regiments, the Bombay and Bengal Engineers, and by thirty-one British, nine Indian and four Gurkha Infantry regiments. **Messines 1914** was gained by seventeen British Cavalry and one Yeomanry regiments and eighteen British and five Indian Infantry regiments, and **Armentières 1914** by fourteen British and one Indian Cavalry regiments, two Yeomanry regiments, the Bombay Sappers and Miners, and forty-one British, eight Indian and two Gurkha Infantry regiments.

The 1st Battle of Ypres

By now the main part of the BEF was concentrated around Ypres and decided upon an offensive, still with the objective of turning the German right flank. But it was still not realised that the German Army opposite them was building up to overwhelming strength of around four to one, and the only advantage to the allies was that the British force was of first-line, highly-trained and disciplined troops, whereas the Germans were mainly reservists; many times in the forthcoming battles this discipline was to save them from annihilation.

The British were holding a salient in front of Ypres, always a dangerous defensive position, and it became an obsession with the Germans to pinch it out. Any detailed account of the battle must be very involved as the fighting was continuous on an extended front. The fighting during the whole period up to 22 November was extremely desperate largely because it opened with an attempted advance, which created the salient and never stood any chance of success from the first; the casualties were appalling but the superb training and the incredible musketry fire of the Regular regiments frequently saved the day when all appeared to be lost.

The flower of British youth and the Regular Army perished on these Flanders fields, but although the line nearly broke on numerous occasions the front was maintained more or less intact, and the British commander, Sir John French, made the prophetic statement that 'the Germans will never get further west'. They did not, and the Ypres salient in particular was the scene of some of the fiercest fighting of the war during the next four years. The Menin Gate, the huge edifice erected where the road from Ypres east to Menin leaves the city, serves as a memorial for all those unbelievably brave men who fought and died there; it is in fact a piece of British soil, ceded by the Belgians after the war, from which even now, over seventy years later, the Last Post is still sounded daily in memory of those who died, thousands of whom, whose names are inscribed on the Gate, have no known grave.

Three individual battles during the 1st Battle of Ypres were honoured. They were **Langemark 1914**, on the northern junction of the salient, awarded to seven Cavalry and twenty-nine Infantry regiments; **Gheluvelt**, on the Menin road, to eleven Cavalry, thirty British and one Indian Infantry regiments; and **Nonne Boschen**, in the centre of the line, a battle fought on what was to become the day of the armistice four years later, to six Cavalry and thirty-five Infantry regiments. The campaign Honour **Ypres 1914** was gained by nineteen Cavalry, three Yeomanry and forty-three British and one Indian Infantry regiment, and it must be remembered in all these Honours that the Cavalry regiments were almost always fighting dismounted as Infantry. One action, *Hollebeke Chateau*, which was not separately listed by the Battle Nomenclature Committee, was claimed as an Honour by the 1st Dragoons, but unsuccessfully; most of the Cavalry corps was engaged here, as well as an Indian brigade which was sent to reinforce them, in a particularly desperate engagement.

These battles, however, were not the end of the fighting in 1914. There was a defensive action at **Festubert** towards the end of November where there was only a limited British involvement; the Honour was granted to one British Cavalry regiment, and to three British, eight Indian and four Gurkha Infantry regiments together with the Bengal and Bombay Engineers. Late in December another defensive action was fought at Givenchy, but unfortunately in terms of clarity of Honours this battle was linked with another action at the same place in January 1915 although more or less the same regiments were engaged at each; the Honour **Givenchy 1914** was awarded to two British and four Indian Cavalry regiments, and nineteen British, nine Indian and six Gurkha Infantry regiments, supported again by the Bengal and Bombay Engineers. One other engagement, the attack on *Wytschaete* which took place in mid-December, was unsuccessfully claimed by The Liverpool Scottish.

Australasia, 1914

While these great and momentous events were going on in France, the armies of the British Empire were also involved in other remote parts of the world. In the Pacific, on 30 August, a New Zealand expedition occupied the island of Samoa and destroyed the German wireless station on the island of Nauru. Early in September an Australian expedition attacked German New Guinea. Detachments landed at Port Moresby in New Guinea, at Rabaul in New Britain and at Herbertshohe in the Bismark Archipelago (later named Kokopo), and after a brief but bloody encounter captured the islands. The Honour, **Herbertshohe**, was granted to two Australian regiments. Australian forces subsequently occupied New Ireland, the Admiralty Islands, Nauru and the Solomon Islands. In China the German naval base of Tsingtao, on Kiaochow Bay, was blockaded by the Japanese fleet, Japan having declared war on Germany eleven days after Britain; a land attack was launched against it by a combined British/Japanese force and the fortress surrendered early in November. One British regiment, The South Wales Borderers (24th Foot), and one Sikh regiment of the Indian army were awarded the Honour **Tsingtao**.

West Africa, 1914

In West Africa, only a few days after the war had started and before any British troops had moved to France, an attack was mounted on the German colony of Togoland by a single native regiment of the British Empire in Africa, The Gold Coast Regiment. In the space of under three weeks the colony capitulated and the regiment was awarded the unique Honour **Kamina**. A month later another attack on a German colony was launched, this time on the Cameroons; again native regiments were employed, almost alone, but here the campaign was not so successful and much more protracted, and in fact did not come to an end until early in 1916. The first battle for which an Honour was awarded was **Duala**, which was gained by four regiments, the West Africa Regiment, and the Regiments of Nigeria, Gold Coast and Sierra Leone.

East Africa, 1914

In November an Indian force landed and attempted to occupy Targa, 130 miles north of Dar-es-Salaam. The Germans had established strong positions manned by African troops inland, and the leading Indian troops (13th Rajputs) broke under heavy fire; it was not entirely their fault as they had not been trained for anything beyond ceremonial duties, and they retired in confusion and panic. The expedition had been defeated, and the evacuation of the force was haphazard as no plans had been made for it. It was one of the more notable failures in British military history, owing to thoroughly bad staff work and planning, and no further offensive action was taken in East Africa until 1916.

France and Flanders, 1915
Neuve Chapelle and Hill 60

After the Ypres battles of 1914 the BEF was in no condition to take any offensive action until some reconstruction had taken place; the Regular Army as such had ceased to exist and now what was left of it had to absorb and to train thousands of new troops. But the ground that it occupied could not be held by purely defensive action and during the winter local actions were carried out which became known as raids, the first of which is thought to have been made by a patrol of the 1st Battalion The Worcestershire Regiment (29th Foot) at the beginning of February. Raids were then, and throughout the war remained, an unpopular activity; they were carried out for various reasons, perhaps to harass the enemy, perhaps to take prisoners for intelligence purposes, but whatever the reason they always incurred casualties, sometimes heavy, particularly to junior officers but always to trained men who could be ill spared and only replaced with difficulty.

The French took the offensive in the early months of 1915 and by March the British decided to follow suit with an attack on the German positions at Neuve Chapelle; the theory behind the attack was the need to keep pressure on the Germans whilst they were still heavily engaged on the Russian front. Historically it was the first battle which had been deliberately planned in advance and preceded by a concentrated bombardment, and although there was no breakthrough it at least achieved its objective of keeping German troops on the western front and inflicting heavy casualties on them. The battle was fought on a wide front of nearly 12 miles from La Bassée in the south to near Armentières in the north; the village of Neuve Chapelle was soon captured but the attack on the Aubers Ridge failed and the casualties were heavy. The Germans themselves attacked a day or two later at St Eloi, but had no success and a British counterattack recaptured the small amount of ground lost; it was in this action, not considered a part of the main battle and not honoured, that the first Canadian battalion, of the Princess Patricia's Canadian Light Infantry, saw action in France.

The Honour for the battle, **Neuve Chapelle**, was gained by five British and three Indian Cavalry regiments, by the Bengal and Bombay Engineers, and by thirty-seven British, ten Indian and six Gurkha Infantry regiments. The British contribution included two Yeomanry regiments and four Territorial Force battalions, one of which fought alongside its regular colleagues.

Early in April intelligence began to come in that the Germans were intending to use poison gas; the sources were a prisoner, Belgian informers and the German press, which started to accuse the allies of such usage, a sure sign that this was something that they intended to do themselves. Nevertheless, in spite of this, the High Command discounted the evidence, but because of the possibility of a conventional attack decided that Hill 60, a couple of miles south-east of Ypres, should be captured. It is a good indication of the flatness of the countryside that a man-made mound, constructed from earth from a railway cutting, only 60 feet high should be of such importance. It overlooked, and allowed enfilade fire on, the British trenches, and in the middle of April it was assaulted and captured; it was the scene of heavy casualties and great bravery, four Victoria Crosses being won during the initial assault including the first awarded to a Territorial Force officer. The summit changed hands a number of times, latterly as the result of a gas attack, finally remaining in German possession with British trenches on its flanks. The Honour for the battle, **Hill 60**, was awarded to nine Infantry regiments, and an unsuccessful application for the *Hill 60 Counterattack* on 4 May by the Cheshire Regiment (22nd Foot) was made.

The 2nd Battle of Ypres

But the attack on Hill 60 soon became a small element in a much larger battle as the 2nd Battle of Ypres broke out. The lack of action by the British after Neuve Chapelle had indicated their weakness, and the Germans had decided to reinforce the front and to attack, although their strength depended less on Infantry troops than on Artillery and the new weapon of destruction, poison gas. The use of gas was, of course, dependent on the wind being in the right direction and this meant that attacks using this medium of frightfulness often had to wait for long periods; in point of fact the Allies found it even more difficult to use as the prevailing winds favoured the Germans. At Ypres the wait for the wind to be in the right direction became too long and tedious, and the Germans decided eventually to launch an attack against the right flank of the French line north of Ypres, in which direction the wind happened to be blowing instead of towards the British, which was held by a French colonial division with a Canadian division on their right, whose flank, if the Zouaves broke, would then be turned. There was no defence against the gas, chlorine, and the French troops either had to retreat or die where they stood, with the Germans, wearing gas helmets, following up the attack. The Canadians were now in extreme danger for a gap had opened, but their line held and they even put in a counterattack which caused very heavy casualties by being unexpected.

An outpost line was formed, and reinforcements were coming forward; a general advance was then made, but as it was over open ground, in full view of the enemy and without proper artillery support the result was inevitable and no ground was gained. These opening stages of the battle became known as the Battle of **Gravenstafel** and the Honour for it was awarded to thirty-nine British and eighteen Canadian regiments.

But there was no respite from the fighting and there began a series of actions which gained the name of the battle of St Julien. The battle started with a German attack against the Canadians supported by gas; although protection against the gas was still only rudimentary the attack was held. More attacks followed and eventually the Canadians drew back; counterattacks tried to restore the position, but with only limited success and the whole battlefield became a scene of seesaw action, of attack, counterattack and defensive actions. **St Julien** was awarded as an Honour to sixty-eight British regiments, of which

sixteen were Cavalry, to eleven Indian and eighteen Canadian.

The next few days were quiet and a time for reorganisation. It seems that the view of the British Command was that a withdrawal to a more easily defended line which reduced the salient was the best strategy, but the French were violently opposed to such action and determined to retake the ground lost. But the French attack did not take place and eventually a British retreat to the Frezenburg Ridge began; the first stages were uneventful with no enemy interference, but suddenly a heavy bombardment accompanied by gas erupted. The German attack was held and at night the withdrawal continued. But the new position could not be developed quickly under continuous bombardment, and more German assaults were only held after heroic resistance; the actions continued unabated, ground being lost, regained and lost again and always with heavy casualties. At the end of six days of fighting the Germans had gained about 1,000 yards. The Honour **Frezenberg** was awarded to sixteen Cavalry and fifty Infantry regiments of the British Army and to one Canadian regiment.

The final battle of 2nd Ypres occurred towards the end of May and came to be known as the Battle of Bellewarde Ridge. A massive German attack, supported by the largest wave of gas so far, was launched on a 5-mile front, and slowly it made ground, but very little, and in the face of desperate British resistance it petered out. **Bellewarde** was gained by seventeen Cavalry and forty-five Infantry regiments, and again one Canadian battalion, the PPCLI. One other British regiment applied for the Honour, but for dates later than the official battle, and this was not accepted. During this action the Royal Flying Corps first took a major part in support of a land battle and gained its first VC.

So ended the 2nd Battle of Ypres, and a desperate and bloody battle it was. In spite of their advantages in heavy Artillery and their surprise use of chlorine gas, the Germans in fact only gained about 2 miles of ground at the deepest point of the Salient and the general flattening of the bulge was on the whole to the advantage of the British. The battle had lasted nearly seven weeks, and the Honour for it, **Ypres 1915,** was awarded to twenty-seven British, including six Yeomanry, and four Canadian Cavalry regiments, and to fifty-seven British, ten Indian and thirty-eight Canadian Infantry regiments plus the Bombay Engineers. It was applied for unsuccessfully by one British Cavalry regiment and should also have been awarded to the Liverpool Scottish who had gained the Honour of Bellewarde, one of the individual Honours covered by the general Honour.

Aubers, Festubert and Hooge

While the battles of Ypres were still engaging the 2nd British Army in mortal combat, the 1st Army, further south, was co-operating with the French, partly to reduce the pressure at Ypres and partly to try and capture Lille with its coal mines. Early in May an attack was made on the Aubers Ridge, the stumbling block during the battle of Neuve Chapelle, supported by a heavy Artillery bombardment, which had comparatively little effect since shrapnel shells were mainly used instead of high explosive because of a shortage of the latter. In the lull in this area since Neuve Chapelle the Germans had improved their trench defences, and strengthened the wire of their entanglements, so that ordinary wire-cutters were useless, and climbing over the wire in the face of machine guns was not a healthy or profitable procedure. Initially the Indians had some success, but the enormous strength of the Germans in machine guns made failure inevitable. This unsuccessful battle demonstrated again that Battle Honours were no longer reserved for victories, and the Honour **Aubers** was granted to fifty-two British, ten Indian and five Gurkha regiments with the Bengal and Bombay Engineers.

To help reduce pressure on the French another attack was launched a week later in front of Festubert. The German position appeared to be in bare, flat ground with ruined cottages dotted about, but in reality there was a network of sunken water-filled ditches and to make matters worse the German Artillery had the whole area registered and covered. A night attack was launched with the Indians in the van but the Germans were ready and immediately sent up flares and opened up with machine guns; but the British were more successful with two further thrusts and broke into the German front line at the point of the bayonet, and then took the second and third lines before the Germans could recover. In a short time they were $\frac{3}{4}$ mile behind the German defences at two points with a narrow, but heavily defended, gap between; the following day an all-out attack was made on this area and the Germans started to withdraw. At last there had been a successful attack, and if Artillery support had been stronger and more ammunition available and if a method had then existed for maintaining telephone communication between the front and the headquarters, and more particularly between the gunner OPs and the guns, an even greater success might have been attained. The ten-day Battle of **Festubert 1915** was awarded as an Honour to forty-eight British, twelve Indian, five Gurkha and forty Canadian regiments.

Actions took place in June at Givenchy and at Bellewarde, and some ground was gained, but no Honours were awarded for them. The only Honoured battle during the summer of 1915 in France was **Hooge 1915** and this in fact covered three quite separate actions in July and August. This village on the Ypres–Menin road, a desolate place even in peace, had been captured by the Germans during the 2nd Battle of Ypres and an effort was now made to recapture it; some ground was gained but not the village itself, and during the battle, apart from gas, the British suffered for the first time from another German weapon which was forbidden by the Rules of War—the flamethrower. The Honour was awarded to twenty regiments.

Loos

Probably the German-occupied town which the French most wanted to recapture was Lille, and as a preliminary to this they wanted the British to attack the coal-mining area of Loos in concert with a French attack in Champagne. Sir John French was not keen to comply because

he could not achieve in the time available the superiority in Artillery which was needed to destroy the German wire defences which were being steadily strengthened all along the Front. But the British were over-ruled, largely because the French wanted the attack to take place before the Germans could transfer more artillery from the Eastern Front; but in the event the French were unlucky because the fall of several key towns, such as Kovno, released the guns, and it was said that Hindenburg had sacrificed large numbers of German troops in the attacks in order to achieve this.

The British share of the attack took place between the La Bassée canal and Loos, while the French planned to attack Lens and Vimy Ridge. Historically the battle was of interest for two reasons; it was the first time that the New Army divisions were used in attack, rather than in defence, and it was also the first time that poison gas was used by the Allies. The latter was, in fact, more of a hazard than an asset, since the front was curved and the wind that would suit the British would not suit the French, and vice versa, and the attacks were timed to coincide on 25 September; in the event the French were more favoured, but they still had their troubles, totally unexpected, because a German engineer had reversed the flow of a river on their front and produced a bog right in their path. The British attack was supported by attacks on the front from north of La Bassée to Ypres.

The day of the attack dawned in heavy rain which turned the ground into a chalky quagmire; but the mist caused by the rain, mixed with a British smoke screen, helped to mask the advance. The German Artillery fire was intense and casualties were very heavy, but nevertheless the advance prospered, reached Loos itself and Hill 70, and the Scotsmen in the centre actually advanced 4 miles across heavily fortified ground to the suburbs of Lens, whilst the London Territorials on the right wing kept up with them and manned the defences for the inevitable counterattack. They were completely cut off by German Artillery fire and nothing could be brought forward to them, but luckily the trenches which they had captured were well supplied with food and the only thing that they lacked was water, although the rain, caught in ground sheets helped to alleviate their thirst. On the left, although some ground was captured, the advance was held up by the Hohenzollern Redoubt, one of the most formidable defence works of all time. The French attack met with only limited success.

The fighting went on for another fortnight and in spite of heavy German counterattacks the ground captured at the beginning of the assault was held. Nevertheless the main objective, Lille, was not reached. The Battle Honour, **Loos**, was gained by ten British Cavalry regiments, the majority of them Yeomanry, and seventy-two British and twelve Indian/Gurkha regiments of Infantry, together with the Bengal Engineers. Two individual Honours, *Bois Grenier* and *Pietre*, were unsuccessfully claimed by the Rifle Brigade. Two regiments were also denied their applications for Loos since they had been involved only at a later date than that allocated for the battle.

Egypt, 1915

At the end of 1914 the Germans had put considerable pressure on their Turkish allies to invade the Middle Eastern countries at the eastern end of the Mediterranean, with the ultimate objective of capturing Egypt. The main reasons for this move were to force the British to keep a major garrison in Egypt, which would reduce the manpower available for the Western Front, and to provide the Turks with some, hopefully, comparatively easy and early successes to encourage the population, which was in general hostile to Turkey's involvement in the war.

There was nothing to hinder the Turkish advance which was launched until their Army reached Egypt itself and in particular the Suez Canal. Luck was then with them, since on reaching the Canal in February 1915 they found that the *khamsin* was blowing, this being a strong, hot desert wind which is normally so full of particles as to represent a sand fog, and they hoped that the wind and the sand would hide the sound and sight of their attack. Under cover of this, on 3 February, the Turks attacked the Canal, but the storm did not provide sufficient luck to overcome the lack of reconnaissance and they came up against a highly-trained and well-prepared British army, composed of a Lancashire Territorial division, an Indian division and strong Australian and New Zealand contingents. The result was a foregone conclusion; the Turks were soundly defeated, with many casualties and the loss of their entire bridging train, the British only suffering minimal losses.

Although this was not the end of the fighting in Egypt, either on the eastern frontier against the Turks or on the western against the Senussi, the first assault had been parried with ease and a large part of the garrison was able, later in the spring, to be sent to Gallipoli without danger of reprisals. The Turks could only record a dismal failure instead of the success for which they were looking, but this situation was soon to be reversed in Gallipoli.

An Honour for this *Defence of the Suez Canal* was unsuccessfully claimed by the Duke of Lancaster's Own Yeomanry. Eventually, as will be seen, Honours were awarded to cover the whole campaign on the Suez Canal and for the campaign in Egypt over the period 1915 to 1917, but ironically The Duke of Lancaster's were not included in either of these awards because they were only in squadron strength, although again they applied.

The Persian Gulf and Mesopotamia, 1915

In the years just before the war the British had been instrumental in discovering large deposits of oil at the head of the Persian Gulf, which by 1914 were being worked by the Anglo-Persian Oil Company At about this time, too, the change over from coal- to oil-burning ships had largely been completed by the Royal Navy and these oilfields were essential to the maintenance of supplies and mobility of the Navy in Middle and Far Eastern waters. The Germans also had their eyes on this area for the same reason.

At the end of 1914 an Indian force, which included several British battalions, had been landed on the Persian Gulf coast to protect these interests which were being threatened by Turkish arms with Arab support. A number of engagements were fought and the threat to the oilfields themselves was largely removed; the force then turned its attention to Basra, which had in fact been evacuated by the Turks although they still held the town of Qurna nearby. Attacks on this town were at first unsuccessful, largely because of the problems of crossing the River Tigris, but eventually this was achieved and the town was surrounded, and soon surrendered in December 1914. No Honours were awarded, or indeed claimed, for any of these actions.

But in April 1915 the Turks were seen to be preparing for an attack to recapture Basra and the small British force was reinforced. The immediate threat was soon removed after an action at **Shaiba** which was recognised as an Honour for three Indian Cavalry regiments, the Bombay Engineers and three British and ten Indian Infantry regiments. **Basra** was also awarded as an Honour for the period preceding the action at Shaiba, including the capture of Qurna, and was gained by one British regiment, The Dorsetshire Regiment (39th Foot), eight Indian Infantry regiments and the Bombay Sappers and Miners.

The ultimate objective was the capture of Baghdad but it was a very long way away and there were very large Turkish forces which would have to be defeated before this could be achieved. The Turks had retreated from Shaiba and concentrated with other forces at *Nasiriya* on the River Euphrates; it was a strong position and the attacking troops were met by a fusilade of fire. The town was captured, but the sharp action was not awarded as an Honour, although it was claimed by The Royal West Kent Regiment (50th Foot) whose 2nd Battalion had distinguished itself and was largely responsible by its example under fire for the success of the attack.

The next obstacle which General Townshend had to overcome was the town of Kut-el-Amara, where the Turks had been reinforced by fresh troops. The British reached the outskirts of the town in September, and when it was found that the south bank of the river was mined Townshend changed his place of attack, left his tents up as a decoy, crossed the river and attacked from an unexpected direction through gaps in the marshes. After a day of heavy fighting and much marching in extremely hot weather, a final charge broke the Turks and captured all their guns; but the troops of both sides were so exhausted that the British could not press home their advantage or prevent the fortress and the town from being successfully evacuated. Nevertheless **Kut el Amara** had been captured, only 120 miles from Baghdad, and the Honour for the battle was awarded to two Indian Cavalry regiments, the Bombay and Bengal Engineers, and four British and thirteen Indian Infantry regiments.

The British force was really too small to attempt the final advance to Baghdad with any hope of success, the troops were worn out having advanced nearly 300 miles from Basra during the heat of the summer, and no reinforcements were in sight during the apparent indifference of the British and Indian governments to the campaign or the plight of the soldiers. Nevertheless it was decided to take the gamble with Townshend's tiny force against the Turkish strength, which was overwhelming.

In order to fortify Baghdad the Turks had left only minimum forces as a rearguard, and these were attacked, although the planned enveloping move did not succeed the Turks did not stay to fight, and fled. The British and Indians pressed on, using whatever river craft they could to ease the burden of the troops from having to march, although the nature of the river made for slow progress; nevertheless by late November they had reached the main Turkish defence position near the ruins of Ctesiphon, only 20 miles from Baghdad itself.

The attack on Ctesiphon was a complete success, wiping out large numbers of Turkish troops and taking many prisoners; it was carried out with such ferocity and vigour that German reports afterwards put the British force at 170,000 men when in fact not more than 12,000 could have actually made the attack. They held off Turkish counter-attacks for a couple of days but then their lack of supplies, and particularly of water, robbed them of the glory of their remarkable achievement in getting so far, and they had to retire by night to the River Tigris a few miles away. The position there was too weak, and the troops themselves had suffered heavy casualties and were too exhausted to resist further attack; fighting rearguard actions all the way the force had to retreat to Kut-el-Amara. The Honour of **Ctesiphon** was gained by three Indian Cavalry regiments, the Bengal and Bombay Engineers, and three British and fourteen Indian Infantry regiments.

The pursuing Turks were not far behind when the weary troops reached Kut at the beginning of December and put its defences in order for the siege which they knew must follow, the Cavalry having been sent back downstream before the investment was complete.

Thus began one of the most heroic and gallant defences under siege in the annals of the British and Indian Armies. The Turks made repeated and furious attacks and sometimes made small gains, always however being counter-attacked by the defenders, until they decided to give up the struggle and starve out the defenders instead. Rations were short until in January 1916 a large store of grain was found hidden in the town, and, being too much for the one mill to grind, aircraft were persuaded to drop millstones to the beleaguered troops; this helped for a while but eventually all the horses and mules were slaughtered for food. A relieving force was being assembled but it was to be some months before it could arrive.

Meanwhile the gallant garrison held out and the year 1915 came to an end for the long-suffering troops, who had almost achieved the virtually impossible task of capturing Baghdad. Over a year was to pass before this objective was achieved with a force three times the size of the original one.

Gallipoli, 1915–16

Early in 1915 it has already become clear that, with the onset of trench warfare, the possibility of either side in France being able to achieve a decisive victory was unlikely. Apart from problems with the Germans and Austrians on the Eastern Front, Russia was in difficulties with the Turks in the Caucasus; there was a shortage of war material generally and some sort of diversion was needed to give her any help possible. A tempting area for attack was the Dardanelles; if a passage could be forced there,

and then through the Bosphorus, the way would be open to the Black Sea. Turkish activities in the Middle East would thus be severely curtailed by her need to defend her homeland, subversion and intrigues in Persia and Afghanistan would be reduced, and the Balkan countries would be stimulated to a more pro-British attitude. A tempting idea indeed, and its chief advocate was the First Lord of the Admiralty, Winston Churchill.

But there was also a politically dangerous aspect, as any land attack which was not successful could reduce Britain's standing in the Moslem world; and the possibility of failure was always present because the Turks had been for some time strengthening the Gallipoli defences and had troops standing by to stem any assault.

It was already recognised from the evidence of earlier attempts, however, that a purely naval expedition would be very hazardous because of the narrowness of the channel guarded by forts on the northern side on the Gallipoli peninsula. The best answer was a landing on the peninsula to capture the forts and open the way for the ships, but the shortage of trained troops available meant delaying the operation; if anything was to be done quickly therefore a purely naval action, in which the forts would have to be bombarded and put out of action as the ships advanced along the waterway, would have to be resorted to in spite of the dangers.

There was no shortage of ships for the purpose because the Royal Navy had available a number of heavily-armed older battleships that would not be suitable for a running fight in the North Sea or the Atlantic. The decision was taken, therefore, to carry the passage by unsupported naval gunpower. Fifteen battleships were sent to the Aegean Sea accompanied by the Navy's newest warship, the *Queen Elizabeth*, which it was decided could be spared from the Grand Fleet; apart from strengthening the attack on the Dardanelles this, it was hoped, would indicate Britain's great sea power and increase the confidence of neutral countries in an eventual allied victory.

In spite of heavy bombardments in February and March the attack failed, mainly through the effect of a combination of guns, torpedoes and mines in a very narrow waterway, which left little room for manoeuvre for the great ships.

Before the naval attack had finally failed plans were being made for a seaborne land attack and General Sir Ian Hamilton was chosen to command the operation. The force consisted mainly of the 29th Division, the East Lancashire Territorial Division and the Australian and New Zealand Infantry at that time in Egypt, and with a small French detachment was assembled at Mudros. Unfortunately the Turks, and their German allies, knew well that the attack was being planned and that probably the only practical place for a landing was on the tip of the peninsula in the area of Cape Helles, and were ready for it.

Luckily the Turks did not know, although it probably soon became obvious to them, that the planning for the landing and the subsequent follow up and advance was virtually non-existent. Those who should have carried it out were criminally responsible for the horrendous casualties which occurred largely owing to this failure.

No attempt had been made to gain any knowledge of

the enemy positions, and in any case there were no adequate maps on which to indicate them. There were no engineers included in the force to prepare the beaches. The landings were delayed because the ships had been loaded in Britain with little thought for the needs at the other end and had had to be reloaded in Alexandria. There was a shortage of guns, very few mortars and no hand grenades, and the fact that each division was issued with a different type of rifle needing its own particular ammunition made the problem of resupply well nigh impossible. It is difficult to think of any comparable action in history, before or since, on land or amphibious, which was more notoriously lacking in the necessities to make it even minimally viable.

Anzac Cove and Cape Helles

What the Turks also did not know in fact was that an additional landing was planned, north of the main Turkish position, at Gaba Tepe and this task was assigned to the Australians and New Zealanders, or as they came to be known, the ANZACs. The Australians of the Anzac Division landed here just before dawn on 25 April and were met with heavy fire from Turkish trenches on the beach and on the steep brush-covered hillside behind; undeterred, the troops stormed ashore and up the cliffs, using only the bayonet, and by dawn had gained the first ridge, finding that there was no depth to the Turkish positions.

It was then realised that a mistake had been made in the darkness and that the landing had been made at the foot of a great sandstone mount, Sari Bair, and not at Gaba Tepe which was a neighbouring beach; in the event this was a fortunate mistake because the enemy was completely surprised. The landing place was nicknamed Anzac Cove. By mid-morning the Australians had captured the hill and, now being under heavy fire, moved out to try to silence it. Such was the impetuosity of the attack that by rapid advances and great bravery they got within a few hundred yards of the other side of the peninsula at Maidos, the key to the Narrows; if they had had the strength to advance that little bit further they would have opened the road northwards to Constantinople in a few hours of fighting, but they had outrun themselves and, in spite of now being supported by the New Zealanders, had to withdraw to Sari Bair. Despite heavy counterattacks the Turks could not dislodge the Anzacs, who were supported by the fire of the battleships which caused terrible losses. Further attacks were made by the Turks with no more success and the Australians and New Zealanders were able to dig trenches and to fortify their position. The Honour for the assault, **Landing at Anzac**, was gained by sixteen Australian and sixteen New Zealand regiments.

Meanwhile at the southern tip of the peninsula the British landing was taking place. Because the beaches were dominated by some batteries on the Asiatic shore at Kum Kali, the small French contingent was directed there to quieten the guns; they landed on that most historic of all battlefields, the plain of Troy, and were successful in their endeavours, rejoining the British on Gallipoli the next day.

But at Cape Helles, unlike Anzac Cove, there was no surprise because the landings had to be carried out in day-light, and the beaches and the high ground beyond were all under observation and direct fire from the Germans and Turks. True, on Y Beach on the left flank of the attack, and at S Beach on its right, the landings were almost unopposed and the troops quickly reached their first objectives; W Beach was more difficult, but the hills around the beach were eventually won after heavy casualties, particularly in the Lancashire Fusiliers who later asked for it to be Honoured as 'Lancashire Landing'. The most difficult and bloodiest landings were at X Beach and at V Beach which was heavily defended; it was here that the old collier, the *River Clyde*, was used as an armoured transport and beached, but this only carried a part of the landing force and the casualties among the remainder, in particular the Dublin and Munster Fusiliers at V Beach and the Royal Fusiliers at X Beach, were horrendous and only the greatest gallantry allowed a foothold to be gained and, eventually, the first objectives on the hills around the beach to be captured.

After twenty-four hours, as a result of heroic attacks by the landed troops, the Turks had fled from their positions in the hills and the beach could be declared reasonably safe. A strong Turkish counterattack, which hoped to push the British back into the sea by sheer weight of numbers, failed and in spite of further counterattacks the positions were consolidated and the campaign, like that on the Western front, degenerated into trench warfare. The Honour for the assault, **Landing at Helles**, was awarded to twelve British Infantry regiments.

For the next two months the fighting continued unabated; battle casualties were heavy and those from disease would have been even higher if the spread of pestilence from flies, rats and rotting corpses, which had been common in earlier wars, had not been prevented by modern methods of hygiene. But the fighting achieved little except more casualties, in spite of reinforcements, particularly by Indian troops and the Naval Division.

Krithia

There were three separate battles at Krithia, all of which were eventually covered by the same Honour; the first was in reality the Turkish counterattack referred to above. The second battle began on 6 May with an attack by the 29th Division and the French, but made little progress even when the Lancashire Territorials joined in; now an Australian brigade was deployed and joined the attackers but even then progress was slow and after two days, when the attack was called off after ground had been won, lost and won again, the British had gained only between 400 and 600 yards. The third Battle of Krithia occurred at the beginning of June with a deliberate assault on the fortifications of Achi Baba; the attack this time additionally included the 42nd East Lancashire Division and the Naval Division. In spite of the increased strength little progress was made although once again great bravery was shown in the face of overwhelming rifle and gun fire and the casualties were heavy. The Honour **Krithia** was awarded to fourteen British, three Indian, three Gurkha, four Australian and sixteen New Zealand regiments.

At the time of the 2nd Battle of Krithia the Anzacs were

fiercely attacked at Sari Bair; the surprise Turkish assault initially gained some ground and as a result the opposing forces were in places only a few yards apart, but the Anzacs could not be overcome. Another massive Turkish attack was launched but with no more success, and eventually the lines returned more or less to their original positions. **Defence of Anzac** was awarded as an Honour to eleven Australian and twelve New Zealand Mounted and sixteen Australian and sixteen New Zealand Infantry regiments.

Over the whole of Gallipoli the fighting had now reached a stalemate and by the end of June the first phase of the campaign came to an end; the initial hopes for success, which depended largely on a quick breakthrough, were not entirely dead, although they were dying, but after two months of constant heavy fighting a time for reorganisation and rehabilitation was necessary before any new attacks could be launched. Two Honours, what might be called semi-Campaign Honours, were granted for this phase. **Helles** was awarded to fifteen British, two Indian, three Gurkha, four Australian and sixteen New Zealand regiments, although why the Indian 69th Punjabi Regiment was excluded, since it was awarded Krithia, is not clear. **Anzac** was awarded to thirty-four Australian and twenty-eight New Zealand regiments. It should be pointed out here that the Anzac forces had formed expeditionary force battalions which were sent overseas, rather than the basic Territorial or Militia regiments themselves, and as a result the EF battalions often represented more than one Militia regiment; thus the numbers of Honoured regiments frequently exceeds the number of battalions actually employed in the fighting. The same situation occurred with the Canadian forces.

For a month comparative peace reigned. Strong Turkish defences stretched across the south of the peninsula in front of Krithia and the British could not attack them frontally, and the Anzacs were similarly placed facing an impenetrable ring of trenches. The only way that any progress could be made and a really damaging attack be made against Turkey, who had already had to withdraw a large number of troops from Egypt and Mesopotamia to maintain her Gallipoli defences, was by a mobile war, and the only way that mobile warfare could possibly be achieved was by a further landing with fresh troops further up the coast.

Suvla Bay

The place chosen for the landing was Suvla Bay, only a few miles from Anzac Cove but potentially much better protected from submarine attacks on the approaches and the anchorage, which had already proved a problem earlier in the campaign and at one point had reduced the troops to a dangerous shortage of food and ammunition. If this attack could be kept a surprise, and thus draw off Turkish troops to counter it from the nearest point rather than from the mainland, and if the massif of Sari Bair could be captured and the narrow waist of the peninsula controlled, Turkish communications with Krithia and Achi Baba would be cut; if this happened the pressure on the British would also be reduced. A lot of 'ifs', but it was a case of

achieving these ends or admitting failure and withdrawing altogether from the peninsula.

The Anzacs were reinforced by the Indians from Helles and by two New Army divisions, and the landing was entrusted to two New Army and two Territorial divisions; just prior to the landing a feint attack was made by the Greeks, supported by British warships, on the Turkish mainland to prevent the early movement of reinforcements.

The landing was made on 6 August and achieved complete surprise, but little else. At the same time a desperate holding attack was made in front of Krithia and once more the casualties to the 29th and East Lancashire Divisions were devastating in frontal assault. Simultaneously the Anzacs and Indians moved forward from Anzac Cove to attack Sari Bair and a plateau ridge from it known as Lone Pine; in both places casualties were also high as progress was made, by a flanking rather than a direct attack as the Turks had expected, and at Lone Pine the first wave of attackers was virtually annihilated. But progress nevertheless was made, and Lone Pine and most of Sari Bair was captured; but by then the Anzacs were exhausted and the New Army battalions lacked the experience to hold all the ground that the Australians had captured. A Turkish counterattack was at first successful but then ran into a barrage from the British warships, controlled for the first time by wireless from observers ashore, and the Turkish carnage was such that they lost about 12,000 men in half an hour. By nightfall the counterattack died away and the mixed British, Indian and Anzac force was able to retain much of the ground that it had initially won.

But meanwhile the landing had run into trouble. The attacking force consisting of a whole army corps supported by warships was faced with a defence of no more than one brigade, but formations were inexperienced, command was poor at most levels and there was almost unbelievable mismanagement by the generals; the administrative plan had not anticipated the climate and there was a grave shortage of water. With the benefit of surprise it was a golden opportunity to move forward quickly and cut the peninsula, but nothing happened, not even patrols had been sent out, and the Australians from Anzac Cove, who had taken their objectives against desperate opposition and pushed forward, found none of the Suvla troops with which they should have joined up and advanced.

Sir Ian Hamilton went with all speed to Suvla to see what had gone wrong and ordered an attack, but the Divisional Commander concerned declined to carry out a night attack because his division was too scattered; one brigade, however, was found to be concentrated and ready and was ordered forward, but even so it took ten hours to get on the move and by the time it reached its objective in the Anafarta Hills the Turkish Army had already begun to come up and the brigade was forced back. Eventually a full-scale attack was launched, but by then it was too late and in spite of the courageousness of the Territorial divisions they suffered greatly and the attack failed.

On 21 August another attack was launched on the Anafarta Hills. This time the by now famous 29th Division was brought round from Helles in support of the 11th Division; the latter again failed to take its objectives, largely through going in the wrong direction, and the 29th Division, trying to make good the failure, was caught on a spur known as Scimitar Hill. The English Yeomanry division, fighting dismounted, was sent to their help and behaved magnificently but still could not take the position in the hills. The last real chance for a breakthrough at Gallipoli had gone, thrown away with the loss of thousands of lives by incompetent staff work and generalship.

The final battle was an Anzac one against another Hill 60, of almost as bloody memory as the one in Flanders. The New Zealand mounted rifles reached the summit of the hill and held it against all that the Turks could do to dislodge them, thus providing an outlook, and an artillery observation post, over a wide stretch of the peninsula.

Six Battle Honours were awarded for the period of the Suvla battles, including another semi-Campaign Honour. **Landing at Suvla** was awarded to thirty-four British Infantry regiments. **Sari Bair** was awarded to eighteen British, one Indian, three Gurkha, twenty-three Australian and twenty-eight New Zealand regiments, about half the Anzac contingent being made up of dismounted Cavalry. **Sari Bair-Lone Pine** was granted to six Australian regiments and **Hill 60 (Anzac)** to twelve New Zealand Mounted regiments. **Scimitar Hill** was gained as an Honour by fourteen Yeomanry and forty Infantry regiments, all British. Finally **Suvla**, the semi-Campaign Honour, was awarded to sixty-four British regiments, including the Yeomanry, one Indian and three Gurkha regiments, thirty-three Australian and sixteen New Zealand regiments. For some peculiar reason the twelve New Zealand mounted regiments were not granted this Honour, although all the other regiments which gained one or more of the individual Battle Honours were; it is true that Hill 60 was outside the date period for Suvla, but the period could have surely been adjusted, being arbitrary any way, and in any case the Mounted regiments had also been present at Sari Bair.

The Evacuation

From now on the battle stagnated, and in spite of the continued confidence of the troops on Gallipoli, and Sir Ian Hamilton himself, that success could be gained once sufficient reinforcements had arrived to make good the appalling losses, the decision was taken to evacuate. The reasons quoted were that the troops had suffered greatly from casualties, particularly among officers, and were constantly under heavy fire; they could not be withdrawn from the line for rest because they only held a fringe of ground on the coast and there was nowhere for them to go; they were weakened by sickness, the climate and general exhaustion; there was little hope of any successful attack and nothing was likely to be gained from tying up a very large force where it could serve little purpose in furthering the war effort against Germany.

But it was also appreciated that withdrawal in the face of a strong enemy would be almost as hazardous as staying on the peninsula, and plans for this had to be carefully made. Meanwhile the weather deteriorated to add to the problems of the soldiers, and a rain storm in November was so devastating that in some places trenches filled up with water and troops had to swim for their lives. This was followed the next night by a blizzard and heavy frost which froze the soaking clothing to their bodies, and for many of the Anzac and Indian troops it was the first time that they had ever seen snow. In fact the plight of the Turks was even worse as they had little or no personal protection against the elements and any plans that they had for driving the British off the peninsula were given up.

Although out of strict chronological order, as it did not take place until January 1916, the evacuation must be covered here to bring this unhappy episode to its logical and inevitable conclusion. The plan was to thin out the front-line positions gradually by night in the hope that the enemy would not notice, and this objective succeeded, partly because the Turks were too busy repairing their defences and roads after the storms to pay much attention. Warships were standing by to blast the Turkish positions if they suspected what was happening and launched an attack. The sick and wounded were evacuated first; this was followed by the total evacuation of Suvla and Anzac covered by a diversion at Helles, but still the Turks did nothing although they were now able to concentrate their entire forces against the few men left there. The Turks were clearly in a bad way, from hindsight, and perhaps the men on the spot had judged the situation better than the experts in Whitehall, and one final concerted effort would have achieved the success which all had been striving for for so long.

The Turks made some weak assaults which were repelled and finally the last troops left on 9 January, finishing with a grand firework display when all the remaining stores, including ammunition and explosives, which had been piled on the beaches were set on fire. This was perhaps the only really celebratory episode during the whole eight and a half months on Gallipoli. The great ideal for which so many men had sacrificed their lives was over.

A Campaign Honour, **Gallipoli 1915-16**, was awarded, and apart from the Campaign Honour for the Boer War, was granted to the largest number of regiments up to that time. It was gained by twenty-eight Yeomanry and fifty-eight Infantry regiments of the British Army and the Newfoundland Regiment, three Indian and four Gurkha regiments, twenty-one Cavalry and twenty-eight Infantry regiments of the Australian Army, and twelve Mounted and sixteen Infantry regiments from New Zealand; a grand total of 171 regiments, many of which had been represented by more than one battalion. One solitary regiment, the Glasgow Yeomanry, applied for, but was refused the Honour.

South West Africa, 1915

Whilst the better-known battles were proceeding in France and at Gallipoli, fighting was also taking place in various parts of Africa.

In the late nineteenth century Germany had annexed a large slice of territory on the west coast of Southern Africa, which was given the name of German South West Africa; the vast country was arid and sparsely populated, but rich in minerals particularly diamonds. There is no doubt that the Germans were hoping for a Boer rising in South Africa on the outbreak of war which could fully occupy the

British troops and allow the Germans themselves to invade. But no Boer rising took place, although de Wet and Maritz assembled a force of dissident Boers to fight the Union forces. The rebellion lasted three months but no fighting took place and the only effect was to delay the operations in South West Africa slightly.

Some fighting had occurred in 1914, the South African seizure of the entrance passes to South West Africa and the British naval seizure of two of the colony's ports. But in early 1915 an advance into the colony began from several directions and slowly the German forces were driven back. A number of actions were fought, but only one was considered of sufficient merit to warrant a Battle Honour; it is doubtful if this particular affair, little more than a skirmish, was really more worthy of an Honour than many of the other actions. The action, in April, was at Gibeon, where, after an initial rebuff, an all-out attack was launched by the Union forces who very quickly outfought the Germans and pursued their broken formations for many miles over difficult country. **Gibeon** was awarded to five South African Cavalry regiments.

Actions continued and the capital, Windhoek, was entered in May. This was the beginning of the end, the German position was now hopeless, and the capture or destruction of their army became only a matter of time. On 9 July the Germans surrendered unconditionally. The campaign was notable for the few battle casualties caused, although at one time or another several thousand prisoners were taken by one side or the other; during the nine months of the campaign the Union losses were less than 2,000 and the German ones probably not more than a few hundred, less than could be expected from one normal day's fighting on the Western Front. The Campaign Honour **South West Africa 1914–15** was awarded to eighteen Cavalry or Mounted rifle regiments, four Artillery batteries and eighteen Infantry regiments of the South African Army, and to the Northern Rhodesia Regiment.

West Africa, 1915

In spite of the British capture of Duala in 1914, the Germans in the Cameroons had a very high opinion of their invincibility and had fortified a number of mountain strongholds from which they could carry out raids into the surrounding countries. But they had maltreated the natives who now hated them, and the British gained from this as they could always rely on accurate information about the German positions and movement.

Two of their strongholds were at Garua and Banyo with a line of communication between them. The first was assaulted at the end of May and its fall was partly attributable to a mutiny of the black forces impressed by the Germans, and partly to a change of direction of attack by the British; they had made their presence known and the native spies sent out by the Germans refused to relay the information back to them. Actions continued all over the country, but the next main attack was directed at Banyo. It was a difficult assault against a steep mountain, which became very slippery when it rained, with strong defences; there was initially a shortage of Artillery ammunition on the British side which put the attacking troops into a dangerous situation, but supplies of shells arrived in time and a barrage enabled the troops to reach the summit and capture it. From then on it became a mopping-up operation, not simple or without incident by any means, and with the Germans withdrawing from one fortified position to another, but the result was inevitable and the German army surrendered on 18 February 1916.

Two unique individual Battle Honours, **Garua** and **Banyo**, were gained by the Nigeria Regiment, and the Campaign Honour, **Cameroons 1914–16**, was awarded to five West African and one West Indian regiment.

Below: 1st Battalion 39th Garhwal Rifles breaking through wire uncut by artillery barrage at Neuve Chapelle, 10 March 1915. Modern sepia tone print after a painting by Frederick Rose, 1938. *NAM*

14 The Great War: Part 2, 1916-17

The Background

The year 1916 started off in France much as 1915 had finished, with a number of local actions but with no major battles. In fact between the end of the Battle of Loos and the start of the Battles of the Somme, a period of about nine months, the Battle Nomenclature Committee only listed one battle, which was almost entirely fought by Canadian forces, and four actions in which, again, the Canadians were largely involved. This does not mean of course that the armies were idle or that life was pleasant; the conditions were the same, mud, cold, wet and death always lurking round the corner. Innumerable raids and minor incidents took place, but compared with the great battles fought or to come they faded into insignificance for the historian if not for the participants. The armies were licking their wounds and girding up their loins for the next stage of hostilities.

In other theatres fighting continued; in Macedonia, Egypt and Mesopotamia the armies faced each other and in East Africa a new campaign started, but the fighting, as in France, was on a comparatively small scale. However, before describing these actions of the British and Commonwealth Armies and those in France, attention must be paid briefly to other events of considerable moment.

The most important of these, because of its effects on their Allies and the war as a whole, must be the valiant and sacrificial fight of the French at Verdun, a name which in France still conjures up visions of past glories. The Germans needed victories to appease a population grown restive after eighteen months of lack of any real success and they realised, as did the Allies, that any attempt to break through in the trench complex could be disastrous in terms of the casualties which would inevitably be suffered. But they also appreciated that the strain on the French Army had been immense, that civilian morale was at a low ebb after seeing their Eastern Frontier regions occupied for a year and a half, and that the Army was very near to breaking point; if they could draw the French into a major battle on their own, unsupported by their Allies, they might be able to cause such heavy casualties and a further lessening of morale that if the battle did not destroy the French Armies it would force them to surrender.

The place selected for the battle had to be one which was significant to the whole of France, which they would be prepared to defend, at least initially, to the last man and which emotionally would require such a sacrifice. General von Falkenhayn, Chief of the German General Staff, divined that such a place would be Verdun, an ancient city, a key fortress in the defence system, regarded with pride and veneration by Frenchmen and far removed from the area of operation of the British and Belgians. Falkenhayn had judged the situation accurately, but what he had not reckoned on was the fanatical courage and tenacity with which the French would mount its defence; he had in fact selected a place which fulfilled his conditions too well.

Against massive attacks the French, commanded by General Petain, only gave ground very slowly and the German casualties turned out to be almost as heavy as the French. The fortress did not fall and eventually, after nearly six months, the British attack on the Somme, largely mounted for the purpose, compelled the Germans to call off the assault in order to stem this other assault on them. By the end of the year, when the battle virtually finished, the French had counterattacked and had retaken nearly half of the ground that they had lost in the first six months.

By the beginning of 1916 it had at last become clear to practically everyone in Britain that the war was unlikely to finish in the near future. It was also clear to the military leaders and even to the politicians that the supply of volunteers to the forces, which was decreasing rapidly, was insufficient to make good the battle losses already suffered and that there would inevitably be more losses. There was only one answer—to introduce conscription, which already existed in all the other European countries. A bill was passed by Parliament, in spite of strong opposition from certain sections of the population, particularly from the Trade Unions and, perhaps understandably, from those who would be conscripted, and by the autumn the first conscripts were already under training.

Although the Irish were excluded from the conscription bill its implications for the future caused many men to join the Sinn Fein to avoid having to fight for the hated British. Nationalist feeling was rising in Ireland, and the seeds of rebellion were fostered by rising prices and the shortage of commodities caused by a war in which they did not believe; arms had been obtained from Germany, more to tie up British troops than to encourage revolution, and arrangements had been made for a series of 'manoeuvres' at about Easter whose real purpose could be guessed. It was decided by the British authorities to arrest the leaders of the potential rising but before they could do so, on Easter Monday, the first shots were fired and the rebellion, which was eventually to lead to the division of Ireland, the secession of the South from the British Commonwealth and the troubles today, had begun.

The last major non-military event of 1916 occurred at sea. Having captured the German naval code books early in the war the Naval Staff was able, at the end of May, to warn Admiral Jellicoe of the imminence of German naval action which enabled the Grand Fleet to raise steam and concentrate before the Germans left port. Both fleets were very large, the British having the advantage in strength and speed; they came into contact in the North Sea 100 miles or so off the Danish coast, and so began the Battle of Jutland, the only large-scale naval battle of the whole war. It became a battle of tactical movement, fought partly in and partly out of a fogbank, the British objective being to cut off the German High Seas Fleet from its base and destroy it. In this they did not succeed, although they sunk eleven ships while losing fourteen themselves. After two days the inconclusive action, for the handling of which Jellicoe was strongly criticised, came to an end and the Grand Fleet retired to Scapa Flow; the German fleet had also sailed unopposed for its home port from which it never emerged again before the end of the war.

France and Flanders, 1916

The Canadian forces had been reinforced during the winter and had received back the brigades and the battalion of the PPCLI which had been on loan during 1915 to British divisions, and as a result were now able to field two divisions on the front at Ypres. They attacked the German positions near *St Eloi* by mining their line which reduced the already boggy ground to a quagmire; although they initially gained ground it was soon recovered by the enemy. The battle was claimed by the Canadians as an Honour but without success although it was officially listed.

At the beginning of June the newly-formed Canadian 3rd Division was in action just south of the Menin Road in the area of Mount Sorrel; the Germans attacked after a heavy bombardment but did not exploit their early successes. A quick counterattack failed, and after a few days the German offensive was resumed, getting within sight of Ypres before being stopped. A new and better-planned Canadian counterattack then regained nearly all the ground lost in the last eleven days. The Honour of **Mount Sorrel** was awarded to fourteen Cavalry and Mounted rifle regiments and to fifty-five Infantry regiments of the Canadian Army and to five British Infantry regiments.

The Battle of the Somme, 1916

In early 1916 Sir Douglas Haig had assumed command of the British forces and immediately began to investigate the possibilities for a major British offensive; of various possibilities open to him an attack astride the River Somme in conjunction with the French seemed to offer the best chance of success, and would also help to relieve the pressure on the French at Verdun. The Somme is a winding river and its valley is undulating but with higher ground to the north; the area, Picardy, had not seen any previous large-scale action and the British, who had extended their

line southwards from Arras during the winter, had had a comparatively quiet time.

The German positions in the chalk hills, said by Winston Churchill to be one of the strongest natural defensive positions in Western Europe, had been fortified and been made immensely powerful. Small gains would be of no value in this country because of the overlooking high ground, and the planned offensive had as its objective a complete breakthrough. The British front was about 20 miles long, with Albert in the centre and about 2 miles behind the front, and initially it was intended to make a series of attacks at different points rather than a concentrated assault on the whole German position. This was at first considered impractical with the limited forces available, even after a week long and heavy softening-up bombardment, but in the event the opening attacks ranged across the whole front. During the bombardment the Germans kept their heads down in their trenches and their batteries remained silent so as not to give away their positions and invite counter battery fire.

Early on 1 July the assault of the 4th Army, made up of some nineteen divisions, began, covered by smoke screens; the smoke, as usual, was a mixed blessing since it blinded the attackers but did not hinder the Germans who had carefully laid out their machine gun lines and their Artillery targets, and the waves of troops were met with a withering fire. The attack met with mixed success, in some areas succeeding beyond expectations and in others being bogged down, but in general it failed to reach its main objectives. The casualties were the worst ever suffered, before or since, by the British Army in a single day—in the region of 60,000.

After the horrific first day of the battle bad weather intervened, but at the end of the first week the Army, reinforced by another Army Corps, moved steadily forward in the face of strong opposition and almost impregnable defence works at Contalmaison, the Quadrangle, Mametz Wood and Trones Wood. Further major attacks were launched on the first three of these strongholds, preceded by a bombardment of such unbelievable intensity that it was too much for the Germans, even for the Prussian Guard, who had been ordered to fight to the last man. All these objectives were captured and the first phase of the battle was deemed to have ended by 13 July, although to the troops engaged on whom the pressure was unrelenting, this would no doubt have been hard to believe.

Although the individual battles were listed, for the purposes of Honours they were linked under the title of **Albert 1916**; the Honour was awarded to five Cavalry and seventy-six Infantry regiments, all but a handful of the Infantry regiments of the Army, including the independent Territorial Force regiments, being represented. The Royal Newfoundland Regiment was awarded it uniquely as **Albert (Beaumont Hamel) 1916**. It was also awarded to three batteries of South African Artillery. Two individual Honours were claimed unsuccessfully, *Beaumont Hamel* by the Royal Fusiliers (7th Foot) and *Schwaben Redoubt* by The Royal Ulster Rifles (83rd Foot).

At the same time an attack had been made on Trones Wood from the other flank. The fighting was desperate and frequently hand-to-hand. A detachment of the Royal

West Kent Regiment (50th Foot) was cut off in the wood and held out for 48 hours under intense enemy fire, as well as a British Artillery bombardment since it was assumed that they had perished, until the wood was finally captured. This attack formed part of the assault on the Bazentin Ridge which was opened with an Artillery bombardment which, according to those present, made the prelude to 1 July appear like routine firing. Five fresh divisions had been brought into the attack, position after position fell and eventually the ridge was carried. The Honour of **Bazentin** was granted for this stage of the attacks and was gained by two Cavalry and fifty-nine Infantry regiments of the British Army, five Indian and three Canadian Cavalry regiments, and four South African Artillery batteries.

Before this phase had finished the next series of attacks on High Wood and Delville Wood had begun. The initial assault on the latter was accomplished with magnificent courage by the South Africans, shortly followed by Scottish battalions, and gradually the rest of the German positions were taken and held in spite of counterattacks. The carnage in Delville Wood was said by survivors to be the worst that they had ever experienced, but the South Africans and Scotsmen hung on, cut off and without rest for a week. Longueval and Fromelles were captured. By the end of the month the objective had been captured in entirety. As an Honour, **Delville Wood** was awarded to forty-nine British and four South African Infantry regiments, together with an Indian Cavalry regiment and a South African Field Ambulance. *Fromelles* was unsuccessfully claimed as an individual Honour by The Oxfordshire and Buckinghamshire Light Infantry (43rd/52nd Foot).

Meanwhile, and it will have been seen how each of the new attacks overlapped the previous one and therefore increased the strain on the defenders, an assault had been directed at the Pozières Ridge. Again the struggle was desperate and for the first time on the Somme Australian troops were involved; Pozières itself was captured and the line was stabilised from the now non-existent village to the now open ground of the erstwhile impenetrable Delville Wood. An Honour was awarded for **Pozières** which was gained by fifty-four British, fifteen Canadian and thirty-seven Australian regiments, and five batteries of South African Artillery.

On 3 September the allied front pressed forward again. First Guillemont and then Ginchy were captured. **Guillemont** was awarded as an Honour to forty-four British and three New Zealand regiments, and **Ginchy** to twenty-eight British and the same three New Zealand Mounted rifle regiments.

After a few days a new attack began all along the front; although it followed the established succession of attacks it had a fundamental difference which was eventually to change totally the concept of warfare. The 'Machine Gun Corps, Heavy Section' had arrived from England in the greatest secrecy and emerged from hiding for this assault; but their 'machine guns' had an unusual shape and a colloquial name which still remains to this day their official title—tanks. To say that their appearance on the battle ground flabbergasted the Germans would be a gross understatement and they caused more than a little surprise to the Allies as well as their development had been a very

well-kept secret, and they gave the British a great psychological advantage in the continuing battles. Except for the right flank the new attack met with success; the Canadians captured Courcelette, the New Zealanders, led by a single tank, captured Flers, and other objectives were taken. An Honour was awarded for the battle, **Flers-Courcelette**, to eleven British, five Indian, fourteen Canadian and three New Zealand Cavalry regiments, and to eighty-four British, twenty-six Canadian and seventeen New Zealand Infantry regiments, plus six South African Artillery batteries and a Canadian machine gun squadron. This remains one of the highest numbers of recipients of an individual Battle Honour, as opposed to a Campaign Honour. This was the first major action by New Zealand troops in France, who had only been minimally involved at Guillemont and Ginchy.

There was a break of a few days in the battle and then on 25 September an attack opened on Morval, and on the following on Thiepval, where ferocious fighting developed around perhaps the most sophisticatedly defended of all the German positions. Within three days both were captured, again assisted by those queer, waddling ungainly monsters of the battlefield, the tanks. The keys to the capture of Morval were Combles and Bouleaux Wood. The Germans had filled the wood with machine guns and mortars, but by a masterstroke the British avoided attacking the wood; they captured some enemy trenches on the edge which they then transformed into a wall which shut the enemy into the wood and out of the battle unless they were prepared to attack in the open in the teeth of British gunfire. Combles, when it fell, was the first major town, as distinct from villages and hamlets, to be captured from the Germans in two years of trench warfare.

Morval was awarded as an Honour to seventy-two British, six Indian and twenty New Zealand regiments and a South African Artillery battery, and **Thiepval** to thirty-one British and twenty-two Canadian regiments and five South African batteries. It was also applied for without success by two other British regiments, but in these cases it was for dates earlier than those officially listed.

During the first three weeks of October the advance was continued towards Bapaume; more ground was won and the positions on the whole of the great Transloy ridge in front of the town were consolidated, but the capture of Bapaume itself had to wait until early the next year. These actions were recognised by the Honour **Le Transloy**, although it was the ridge rather than the town which was the scene of the fighting; it was awarded to seventy-three British, the Royal Newfoundland, twenty New Zealand and four South African regiments and to one South African battery.

The weather was now deteriorating as winter drew on, with almost continuous rain by day and frosty nights, and, even though keyed up by success, the British and Commonwealth Armies had been fighting against the desperate defence by the pick of the German Army for four solid months and were tiring. One final assault was made, this time switched to the northern end of the front astride the River Ancre. Officially the battle for Ancre heights had begun in parallel with the attack on the Transloy ridges since the clearing of the Schwaben and Stuff redoubts was considered part of the former battle. But the crucial fighting in fact lasted for ten days in the middle of November. It was a defensive rather than an offensive attack, designed to engage the German army on this front and prevent it from reinforcing the crumbling forces in front of Bapaume. The terrain was attrocious as the incessant shellfire had created innumerable craters, some very deep, in the chalk which were all now filled with water and formed literal death traps for friend and foe alike.

On both sides of the river the fighting was severe and casualties again became very heavy. Beaumont Hamel was at last captured, having been first attacked on the opening day of the battle by the Newfoundlanders whose regiments were broken in the attempt. One man who shewed extreme bravery in the attack was Colonel (later General Sir Bernard) Freyberg, then commanding a battalion of the Naval Division and in World War II to command the 2nd New Zealand Division in the Desert and Italy with great distinction, who, though wounded in four places, still led the assault on the now extinct village and was awarded the VC. At the beginning of November the Durham Light Infantry suffered very heavy casualties in an abortive attack on the *Butte de Warlencourt*. Two separate Battle Honours were awarded for the two parts of the battle. **Ancre Heights** was awarded to fifty-four British and fifty-one Canadian regiments and to six South African batteries. **Ancre 1916** was awarded to fifty-eight British and twelve Canadian regiments and again to five South African batteries. Both Honours were unsuccessfully claimed by the Yorkshire Dragoons.

This fighting brought to an end the great battle of the Somme and the fighting in France in 1916. It had been a major success for British arms and had proved that the Germans were not unbeatable even when supported by extremely strong defence works; it also proved the immense advantage that massed Artillery, particularly heavy Artillery, could give to an attacker. But success was not gained lightly and the stubborn defence of the German armies proved even more expensive to life and limb; the British casualties, in round figures, were 500,000 and the German ones half as many again. When French losses were added the battle had claimed a million and a half victims not all dead by any means, but put out of the fight and needing to be replaced.

The Honour for the whole series of battles, **Somme 1916**, virtually a Campaign Honour, was awarded to a vast number of regiments. Altogether one hundred and nineteen British, the Royal Newfoundland, nine Indian, eighty Canadian, forty-nine Australian, twenty New Zealand and four South African Cavalry and Infantry regiments and to the ubiquitous six South African Artillery batteries, a South African Field Ambulance and a Canadian machine gun squadron. And even this total does not indicate the real size of the forces engaged when it is remembered that most of the British regiments had more than one battalion engaged. The Royal Fusiliers had twenty-one battalions in France at this time, although not all on the Somme, The Kings Royal Rifle Corps had fourteen battalions and the Lancashire Fusiliers twelve battalions involved in the battle, and at one time the Royal Ulster Rifles had eleven battalions in action on a 6-mile front.

Egypt, 1916

As related in the previous chapter the main activity during 1915 had been the defeat of the Turks on the Suez Canal. The British had not followed up the retreating Turks, mainly on account of the summer climate and lack of water, but with the coming of winter some actions were taken against the Turkish outposts. The Turks were not entirely idle themselves, and at Easter 1916 heavily attacked a British outpost at the Qatia oasis; on the point of retreat the British force was saved by an air attack and the Turks retired instead. During the summer the Turks increased their strength in front of the British outpost force at Rumani and at the beginning of August they attacked. The assault was soundly defeated and again a Turkish attempt to invade Egypt had been repulsed. The Honour for the battle, **Rumani**, was awarded to six British Yeomanry and sixteen Infantry regiments, and to fourteen Australian and nine New Zealand Cavalry and Mounted rifle regiments. It was also claimed unsuccessfully by one other British Yeomanry regiment.

After the utter failure of the second Turkish attempt to invade Egypt the British objective became to clear them out of the Sinai peninsula. Only slow progress could be made because of the climate, the terrain and a lack of transport, in spite of a vast camel train for supplies, and the need to build up a strong enough force for the purpose. By December the Anzac troops in the force had captured El Arish and reached Magdhaba; although the Turks were dug in and fought strenuously, they had been surprised by the speed of the final part of the advance and were surrounded and captured. The force, now with its Yeomanry element, pressed on to Rafah and early in January 1917 attacked and captured it. This victory and the surrender of the entire Turkish force meant that the objective had been achieved and Sinai was wholly in British hands. Two Honours were awarded, one for the Anzac forces and one for the British. **Magdhaba-Rafah** was gained by nine Australian and nine New Zealand Mounted regiments, and **Rafah** by three British Yeomanry regiments and the Honourable Artillery Company.

Whilst the fighting had been going on on Egypt's eastern frontier across the Suez Canal another, less publicised but no less arduous, campaign had been fought on the western frontier against the Senussi tribesmen. Although the Senussi had no quarrel with Egypt or the British and were reluctant to get embroiled, they were eventually pursuaded by the Turks to take action against them late in 1915. In December a small British force at Matruh was attacked and successfully defended itself, but the Arab army was growing. The Western Frontier Force was therefore formed, mostly composed of Yeomanry regiments, Indians and New Zealanders, and fought its first battle against the Senussi in *Wadi Majid*, which was won although the enemy defended strongly in terrain which was much to their natural advantage. Towards the end of January 1916 a Senussi force at *Halazin* was attacked and although it was forced to retreat the horses of the attackers were too exhausted for a pursuit. Neither of these battles was Honoured but both were unsuccessfully claimed by the Duke of Lancaster's Yeomanry, who claimed Honours for most of the battles in Egypt, east and west, and the Campaign

Honour, with equal lack of success.

By the end of February the Senussi Army had retreated half way from Matruh to Sidi Barrani and was encamped at Agagiya. A charge by the Yeomanry supported by South African Infantry swept the Arabs from their defences, although suffering considerable casualties. The Senussi had had enough of fighting the British and fled. It was not the end of the campaign, however, and minor actions were fought westwards along the coast and eventually inland to the oases of Dakhla and Siwa, and to Gyuba in the Sudan against the Sultan of Darfur, all of which entailed crossing some extremely inhospitable terrain, much of which became better known to the same troops and many others during the Second World War. Finally after Siwa had been entered in February 1917, the campaign came to an end, the power of the Senussi broken and no longer a threat. Of these various actions only **Agagiya** was awarded as an Honour, to the Dorset Yeomanry and to two South African Infantry battalions; and this was another case of discriminatory Honours, since the Royal Bucks Hussars were also engaged but neither claimed nor were granted the Honour.

And so the campaign to protect Egypt against Turkish incursion which had begun in January 1915 came to a successful end just over two years later. The Honour **Egypt 1915-17** was granted to thirty-eight Yeomanry and fifty-seven Infantry regiments of the British Army and the Newfoundland Regiment, to two cavalry and thirty-three Infantry regiments, including eight Gurkha, of the Indian Army, to twenty-three Australian and twelve New Zealand Light Horse and Mounted Rifle regiments, to forty-eight Australian, seventeen New Zealand and four South African Infantry regiments, together with the Madras Engineers and a South African Field Ambulance. Comparatively few of these regiments had been actively engaged in the twelve actions listed during the campaign, but they had been part of the defence force and therefore vital to the campaign. They fully deserved the Honour if only for their presence in the unpleasant conditions under which they existed while in Egypt during the two-year campaign, and it must not be forgotten that many of these regiments also served in Gallipoli during this same period, going from and returning to Egypt.

Mesopotamia, 1916

Kut had been besieged at the end of 1915 and even by early 1916 the small British force in the town was steadily getting more desperate; over the next four months several attempts were made to relieve the garrison. This should not have been too difficult a task as the Turkish force was not large and the Army at Basra was being rapidly reinforced, but the planning for the relieving force had largely neglected the logistical aspects and as a result there was no adequate transport or supplies. So the relieving forces had nearly as many problems as the besieged.

Three unsuccessful relief attempts were made, in January, March and April, of which the last was the most strenuous; it was the rainy season, the Tigris was high and because of the position of Kut in a deep and narrow bend of the river any assault on the besiegers had to be a frontal one. Briefly, neither could the siege be raised nor could supplies be got into the town via the river. The garrison was starving and saw no hope in continued resistance; on 29 April, after 143 days, it surrendered.

An Honour, **Defence of Kut Al Amara**, was awarded to the four British and twelve Indian Infantry regiments, and to the Bengal and Bombay Sappers and Miners, which had suffered the siege; the Royal Hampshire Regiment (37th Foot) were not recognised for the Honour although they claimed it. An Honour was also awarded to the troops of the unsuccessful relieving force, **Tigris 1916**; it was gained by one British and four Indian Cavalry regiments, twenty-four British and twenty-nine Indian Infantry regiments and all three Indian Engineer regiments.

Macedonia, 1916

In October 1915 a combined Franco-British force had landed at Salonika at the request of Venizelos, the Greek Prime Minister. He had in fact resigned the day after he issued his invitation because the King would not support his policy, having pro-German tendencies. The object of the expedition had been to help the Serbs in their fight against Bulgarian aggression; in this the expedition was too late as the Serbs had been virtually beaten before the force arrived. But, the force having landed, it was decided to maintain a base there for future operations which were bound to be needed in spite of official Greek opposition to it.

It set out to fortify an advanced defensive line and in so doing in December the British element had fought a battle at **Kosturino**, north of Lake Doiran, after retreating from Serbia, which gained an Honour for nine Infantry regiments. But apart from this action there was little further activity until the end of the summer of 1916, by which time the Franco-British troops had been reinforced and Serbians, Russians and Italians had joined this very international army. Then the Bulgarians began an invasion of Greek territory and came into contact with the British near Lake Doiran, and a number of sharp engagements occurred. In August there was some fierce hand-to-hand fighting in an attack on *Horseshoe Hill*, and the battalion which captured the hill repulsed all efforts to remove it. The battalion concerned, of the Oxfordshire and Buckinghamshire Light Infantry (43/52nd Foot), claimed this as an Honour but it was not granted.

At the beginning of October the British, in conjunction with their allies on other parts of the front, began operations on the River Struma towards Serres. The advance was successful, initially against stubborn resistance and counterattacks, and by the end of the month had reached the entrance to the Rupel Pass, the fort controlling which had been surrendered by the Greeks to the Bulgarians earlier in the year, and had got within a few miles of Serres itself. The Honour **Struma** was awarded to four British Yeomanry and twenty-six Infantry regiments.

East Africa, 1916

The final campaign to be recorded during the fighting in 1916 was a new one. From the early days of the war the Germans in their East African colony had carried out raids across the border, particularly into Uganda and around Lake Victoria, and had had a number of skirmishes with the British; since the end of the Cameroons campaign German East Africa was the only colony which they still possessed. It was therefore decided to eliminate the threat and clear Africa of the enemy, a decision which was strongly supported by the vociferous parties in England who had little idea of the difficulties of fighting in a tropical country a campaign which could never be anything but a sideshow. The small British force was reinforced and reorganised, and the command of the expedition was given to General Smuts, who had been one of the more successful commanders of Boer forces during their war against the British less than twenty years before.

In February it was decided to occupy the area around Mount Kilimanjaro, and haste was needed if this was to be accomplished before the rainy season started. Two columns set out, and the German Commander, who knew all about the preparations being made, appreciated that he would have great difficulty in holding the area, although he did not intend to give up lightly, in spite of the problems which the attacking forces would face. The force was a mixed one consisting of a small British element and larger South African and Indian ones. There were few actions of any significance but the advance and occupation of the region was a major achievement in itself.

The first Honour of the campaign, **Kilimanjaro**, was awarded to two British Infantry regiments, the Royal Fusiliers (7th Foot) and the Loyal Regiment (47th Foot), which were the only ones engaged during the whole campaign which did not in fact finish until after the war in Europe. It was also awarded to the Kings African Rifles, to two Indian Infantry regiments and the Bombay Engineers, and to two Cavalry and eight Infantry regiments, and five Artillery batteries, of the South African Army. A large number of actions and skirmishes took place during the remainder of the year, both inland and on the coast, but none of these, despite the difficulties of fighting against a determined enemy, was recognised as an Honour.

France and Flanders, 1917

At the beginning of 1917 the attack on the Ancre defences was reopened with limited forces in spite of the winter weather accompanied by snowstorms and deep mud. Some German positions were captured there, and then the attack was switched to the Bapaume front. Miraumont, Gommecourt and Thilloys, among other villages, were taken, until by the middle of March the British troops were poised on the threshold of Bapaume itself, and the Germans were preparing to withdraw all along the front to their prepared and strongly fortified Hindenburg Line. On 17 March the attack on Bapaume was launched and by the end of the day the town was in British hands, and this was followed by the capture of Le Transloy with practically no opposition. On the next day Mont St Quentin and Peronne were occupied. These actions were recognised by the Honour **Bapaume 1917**, which was gained by seven British and thirteen Australian regiments and two South African batteries, and was unsuccessfully claimed by two Yeomanry regiments.

The scene was now set for an advance on the sector east of Arras on a fourteen-mile front. On 9 April two parallel attacks began, the northern one on Vimy Ridge, which had for so long defied assault by the French, and the southern one along the River Scarpe. The force employed at Vimy was preponderantly Canadian, although British troops played a valiant part, and at first they met little opposition in most areas; but then a large German force emerged from underground between the first and second lines after the first waves of Canadians had passed, which forced them to stop and destroy the enemy shooting at their backs. In spite of intermittent snowstorms the advance continued and quickly the great ridge was captured, and the troops could look down on the group of villages and hamlets which were to be their next objectives. The Honour **Vimy 1917** was awarded to twenty-five British and fifty-five Canadian regiments, eleven of the latter being Cavalry regiments fighting dismounted.

On the Scarpe the battle had gone equally well, here mainly British regiments being employed supported by Canadians and South Africans; within a few days Monchy Le Preux and the Wancourt ridge were taken, and held against heavy German counterattacks, and the Hindenburg Line had been breached. The advance had been made with comparatively few casualties, particularly in relation to the holocaust on the Somme, but the German armies had been shattered. The battle on the Scarpe, officially the First Battle of the Scarpe, was not separately Honoured, but the three quite separate battles there, officially recognised as such, within a period of a month, were combined into one Honour, and as a result it is almost impossible now to discover which regiments were engaged in any or all of these battles.

The second Battle of the Scarpe followed after a ten-day break, and the initial success was maintained. Guemappe and Gavrelle were captured, then recaptured by the Germans and finally captured again, the Germans being too exhausted by now to offer the same degree of resistance which they had exhibited during the counterattack. Before the third and final Battle of the Scarpe was fought Arleux was captured. Oppy was attacked but without the same success; it held out for another two months and became an individual Battle Honour. The capture of **Arleux** was a particularly gallant and brilliant action which ended in hand-to-hand fighting in the village; the Honour was awarded to forty-three British and twenty-three Canadian regiments and to two South African batteries. Perhaps it should be explained, since it has been recorded a number of times now, that of the Commonwealth countries only the South Africans and the Indians, in respect of Mountain batteries only, awarded Honours to the Artillery, although of course British Artillery batteries were subsequently awarded Honour Titles.

The third Battle of the Scarpe took place at the beginning of May. The Germans thought that the Canadians had been in the line for so long, perhaps not realising that there were now four divisions of them, that they must be tired and weak, and they prepared to counterattack from Fresnoy; but before they could do so the 'weak' Canadians, having made a very early start, had encircled the village, captured it and the whole counterattack force and repulsed several attacks. The Honour **Scarpe 1917** was eventually awarded, as has been said already to cover all three battles, to twenty-three British Cavalry regiments, to seventy-four British, the Royal Newfoundland Regiment, twenty Canadian and four South African Infantry regiments, to two of the ubiquitous South African batteries and to a South African Field Ambulance, the latter being another unusual case in the award of Honours. The Cheshire Regiment (22nd Foot) in fact applied for the three battles to be recognised separately, as *Monchy Le Preux*, *Gavrelle-Guemappe* and *Fresnoy* respectively, but this was refused.

In addition to those individual ones already recorded, an overall Honour was awarded for the period of the Arras battles as **Arras 1917**. This was gained by twenty-four British, twelve Canadian and one Australian Cavalry regiments, by the Tank Corps, by seventy-five British, seventy-nine Canadian and four South African Infantry regiments, and the Royal Newfoundland Regiment, and by four South African batteries and the Field Ambulance. One of the Canadian regiments honoured was that of McGill University in Montreal, one of the very few occasions when a university contingent has gained an Honour.

Meanwhile on the right flank of the Arras front a new offensive had developed which first, at the beginning of May, captured the village of Cherisy and then opened out to the south. The Australians were custodians of this part of the front and had been picking away steadily at the German positions whilst the great Arras offensive had been continuing. The fighting which now ensued was fierce, with attack and counterattack from both sides, the Germans particularly having very heavy casualties, but by the middle of the month Bullecourt had been captured and the front had been driven to within a few hundred yards of Queant, the key position in the Hindenburg Line. The Honour of **Bullecourt** was awarded to eighteen British and forty-eight Australian Infantry regiments and to one South African Artillery battery. It was applied for unsuccessfully by one other British Infantry regiment and one Yeomanry regiment.

Finally in the series of battles on the Arras front severe pressure was directed towards Lens and in particular Hill 70 which Sir John French's offensive in 1915 had failed to capture. The capture of Lens, regarded as one of the most formidable fortresses, would also enable the northern end of the Hindenburg Line to be turned. The Canadians carried the battle to the environs of Lens by capturing Avion and some villages on the River Souchez which ran just south of the town. In concert with this a small British force launched a violent assault on Oppy which had been holding out for two months and captured all its objectives. **Oppy** was awarded as an Honour to eight Infantry regiments and four South African batteries.

In the middle of August the Canadian army corps assaulted Hill 70 by a very early surprise attack preceded by only a minimal bombardment. Although the defences were strong and intricate the surprise allowed the capture of the hill to be made unexpectedly easily, although there were inevitably fierce actions at some points. At one stage it appeared that the Canadians might outflank Lens itself but the German defence stiffened and, in view of the other major offensive which was now gaining ground on the Ypres front and the fact that the indomitable Canadians were at last tiring, it was decided to keep the pressure on but not to make any further advances. **Hill 70** was awarded an Honour to eleven Cavalry and seventy-three Infantry regiments, again including the McGill University contingent, of the Canadian Army and to four British Infantry regiments and to two South African batteries.

Three weeks after the battle of Bullecourt, whilst the battles on the Arras front still continued and before the German Army had had a chance to recover from the mauling it had received on Vimy Ridge and elsewhere, a new offensive was opened further to the north, in Flanders. On the southern edge of the Ypres salient two high ridges, Wytschaete and Messines, dominated every movement of troops in the neighbourhood of Ypres itself, and no attack on the main German position could be made until these menacing observation posts were removed. The attack on the ridges was preceded by a massive bombardment which lasted for a fortnight, Messines ridge was mined, and the whole operation was planned with great care and thoroughness.

Early in the morning of 7 June nineteen mines were exploded, and the British, Australian and New Zealand troops advanced up the slopes behind a creeping barrage. Although they had to avoid the mine craters because of the fumes from the explosives, they made steady progress on a 9-mile front, the British mainly on Wytschaete and the New Zealanders on Messines. As a result of the bombardment the ridges were taken with comparatively little trouble and by nightfall the troops had crossed them and advanced into the lower ground beyond. During the next few days the gains were consolidated and a further advance was made which carried the whole of the German first and support lines. The Honour of **Messines 1917** was awarded to cover the attacks on both ridges and was gained by sixty-five British, twenty-five Australian and twenty New Zealand regiments and one South African battery.

The Germans still had some observation from ridges overlooking the Salient and inevitably made their own preparations to counter the attack which they knew was imminent; in particular they manufactured a large number of small concrete forts which became known as pillboxes, and reinforced the defences with troops and guns from the Russian front. The British similarly had some knowledge of the German activities and trained for attacks against the pillboxes. Six weeks after Messines was captured the main offensive, which became known to history as the third Battle of Ypres, began with one of the heaviest Artillery bombardments known up to then and heavy attacks against the German aircraft, supported by the French on the British left flank.

The objective was a range of hills which ran in a curve between Houthulst Forest in the north and Gheluvelt on the Menin road in the south, the centre of which was the rather higher ground of the Passchendaele Ridge. The Germans were well aware of the importance of these hills which gave them observation over the British positions in the swamps around the river close to Ypres, whither they had been driven in 1915 and kept penned ever since; they also knew well that if those ridges were lost and the Allies were able to break through them on to the Flanders plain there were few good defensive positions available to them and none prepared to meet the advancing enemy. A breakthrough of this sort was obviously in the minds of the allied high command, but this was not the only objective of the campaign. After the bloodbath of Verdun the French Army was on its knees and in some cases very near to mutiny; the only way of saving not only the French army but also the entire allied position on the Western Front was to take the pressure off them, even if this meant the sacrifice of British lives in an offensive which eventually dragged on long after there was any hope of achieving the tactical objectives. As a result the generals responsible for the offensive and for the appalling loss of British and Commonwealth lives during it gained an opprobrium which was certainly not justified, mainly because the condition of the French Army had to be hidden from the enemy at all costs, and the true object could not be disclosed at the time.

The main British attack began on the village of Pilckem and the area around it, supported by the Anzacs east of Messines. Against furious opposition the first objectives were soon taken, including famous villages which had been the scene of such desperate defensive actions two and a half years earlier, such as *St Julien*, Frezenburg and Hooge, and a large number of prisoners and weapons were captured. Strong counterattacks were mostly repulsed, and even where ground had to be relinquished it was soon regained. A week later a minor action captured the village of Westhoek. **Pilckem** was granted as an Honour to sixty-seven British and one Canadian regiments and was unsuccessfully claimed by the Yorkshire Dragoons. The Cheshire Regiment (22nd Foot) applied for *Westhoek* as an Honour but was also refused.

It was a few days before the offensive could be resumed, and then it was aimed north and east of Ypres. The assault took the British divisions to the outskirts of Langemarck but on this occasion the nature of the ground and the wet and misty weather slowed down the attack and the enemy machine gunners took a heavy toll. Counterattacks developed; because of the bad visibility there was often little warning and no artillery support, and some of the ground was lost. An Honour was awarded, **Langemarck 1917**, to seventy-two British regiments, the Royal Newfoundland Regiment and one Canadian, the York Regiment, which was attached to the British force for the campaign.

The first two battles of the campaign had been separated by a fortnight but had gained enough ground for the main thrusts to be launched; another month passed before the necessary concentration of men and Artillery had been built up. But by then the enemy had an ally in the weather which was unusually wet for the time of year; days of continuous rain in early August had turned the shell-torn ground into a quagmire, and although by mid-September the weather had improved a little it was still very muddy under foot. The next attack was centred on the Menin road in an attempt to take that section of the curving ridge which it crossed; the attackers were successful all along the front although the fighting was desperate, and they managed to keep the counterattacks at bay and consolidate on the ridge during the next few days thanks to the accuracy of the Artillery bombardment which was now being directed from the air on the enemy concentrations. The Honour **Menin Road** was awarded to sixty-eight British, one Canadian, one New Zealand, forty-eight Australian and four South African regiments, plus three South African batteries and the Field Ambulance.

The attack along the Menin road was further exploited by an assault on Polygon Wood, but to make this finally successful and capable of being defended after its capture it was necessary to attack the high ground around the village of Broodseinde, from which observation could be gained over the area of the wood. The attack on the shattered wood, where a large Anzac force was engaged in company with British regiments, met with strong opposition, because the German commander knew as well as Haig the value of the ridges, and the defence was stiffening. As each objective was captured waves of counterattacks had to be beaten off by Artillery and machine gun fire. With the successful attack on Broodseinde, whither most of the army which had captured Polygon Wood was directed, and its capture by the Australians, sometimes held to have been one of the most crushing defeats inflicted on an enemy by British arms, the whole of the ridge south of the Passchendaele sector had been taken. An interesting feature of the attack on Broodseinde was that the Germans had by coincidence planned to attack at the same moment and the two masses of advancing troops met in the open, more like an eighteenth- or nineteenth-century battle than a twentieth-century one. But the Germans were surprised and broken by the artillery barrage accompanying the British attack. **Polygon Wood** was awarded as an Honour to seventy-four British, one Canadian, seventeen New Zealand and fifty-nine Australian regiments, and to three South African batteries; the Australian recipients represented all but one of the entire Australian Infantry contingent in France. **Broodseinde** was gained by fifty-three British, one Canadian, twenty New Zealand and thirty-seven Australian regiments and by the same three South African batteries.

But by now the weather had turned wet and cold again, and not only were the swamps in front of Ypres virtually impassable but the higher ground had become churned up and littered with water-filled shell holes and larger craters, which made any advance very hazardous. In the event Haig had to decide whether it was worth continuing the attack. The factors were first that a French attack was to be launched on the Aisne at the end of October and it was essential to retain the maximum German forces on the Ypres front in order to weaken them in front of the French, and secondly that another British offensive was being planned to capture Cambrai and there too it would be advantageous if the comparatively weak German defensive forces there were kept that way. So the battle for the Passchendaele Ridge had to be continued, although subsequently Haig was criticised for the enormous losses suffered on this front while obtaining very few objectives.

But it must be pointed out, as it was in the House of Commons nearly a year later, that other considerations had also entered into the decision-making. These were the virtual collapse of the Russian armies, which would shortly release hordes of German divisions for the Western Front and the need therefore to gain as much ground as possible before this happened; the heavy defeat suffered by the Italians at Caporetto; and the inability of the Americans to give any help on land. In effect therefore the only allied army which could conduct any offensive operation was the British, and the only place that they were poised and ready to do so was in front of Ypres.

In spite of the continuous rain the next stage of the attack was directed at the northern end of the ridge, centred on Poelcappelle, which gave its name to the battle, but in fact on a wide front which stretched as far north as the Houthulst Forest. The Germans were in course of a relief, were taken unawares and suffered heavily. By nightfall Poelcappelle and the northern objectives had been captured in the face of fierce counterattacks, but no progress had been made on to the Passchendaele Ridge itself, even though the Australians supported with an attack from Broodseinde. The Honour **Poelcappelle** was gained by sixty-three British, the Royal Newfoundland, one Canadian and fifty-one Australian regiments and a single South African battery.

The final phase of the battle was now about to commence, and on 12 October, three days after the capture of Poelcappelle, the bloodiest of the battles in front of Ypres began. And still it rained, the mud deepened and it became colder, to add to the burden of the now tiring troops. The Anzac troops were mainly involved in this first attack of the two Battles of Passchendaele, which were eventually, as on the Scarpe, to be covered by a single Honour, and were reasonably successful. The weather then suddenly improved and the Germans daily expected a resumption of the attack; but it did not come for a fortnight by which time the weather had deteriorated again. The Canadians had now come into the line again in the centre of the front around Passchendaele village and their problems were increased by the mud, which was now thicker than ever, and by the very heavy German bombardment and machine gun fire; their only advantages were that the mist helped to screen them and that in the mud the enemy shells lost quite a lot of their effect. Not that the conditions on the Canadian front were any different from those elsewhere; in the north the supporting Belgian troops actually poled their way across the marshes in flat bottomed boats.

So the great battle for the ridge went on and slowly the attackers inched forward; it finally ended in the middle of November with both sides still on the ridge. Whether the offensive should have continued after the weather had made it almost impossible to achieve success, whether it achieved its strategic success in drawing in and holding German troops from other fronts, will always be debated. It certainly crippled the British and Commonwealth Armies engaged for months to come, possibly even contributed to the German success in the spring of 1918, and it certainly gained the unenviable reputation of one of the most destructive battles in terms of the loss of British life in history, where as many men drowned in the mud as

were killed by enemy weapons. By the time that they were relieved in front of Passchendaele the Australians had suffered 30,000 casualties during the battles, and the Canadians who relieved them were to suffer 16,000 casualties before the desperate battles for the ridge were over.

Passchendaele was awarded as an Honour to eighty-seven British, fifty-two Canadian, one South African, twenty New Zealand and sixty-one Australian regiments including their entire Infantry force, five South African batteries and their Field Ambulance. The battle brought to an end the third Battle of Ypres, and a Campaign Honour was awarded for this to cover the three and a half month period, **Ypres 1917**. It was gained by the vast total of one hundred and twelve British, the Royal Newfoundland, eighty-seven Canadian, four South African, sixty-two Australian and twenty New Zealand regiments, by six South African Artillery batteries and their Field Ambulance; and it must again be remembered that most of the British regiments, and many of the Canadian, were represented by a number of battalions.

But the fighting in 1917 was not yet over, although the conditions were now anything but conducive to further campaigning, and in earlier wars the contestants would have long since retired into winter quarters. Haig now needed to take the pressure off the Passchendaele Ridge and he could only do that by an offensive somewhere else; because of the exhaustion of the troops this had to be where a surprise attack might meet with the required success quickly. Cambrai was chosen because it was being used as a rest area for German troops recovering from the *mêlée* in front of Ypres; nevertheless the Germans believed that with the Hindenburg Line defences even this position was easily tenable, and that they would get enough warning from the preliminary bombardment to bring up fresh troops. This was therefore a suitable place for a surprise attack, without any preliminary bombardment, but supported by tanks, which the Germans had not appreciated had been much improved technically since they had first been used sixteen months earlier. The preparations were made in the greatest secrecy. It was to be almost entirely a British battle, certainly in the early stages, although later small Canadian and Indian Cavalry forces were brought into the battle.

On 20 November the tanks attacked and only when they were on their way was a heavy bombardment opened. Behind came the Infantry and in spite of some savage fighting the German positions were over-run, in some cases to a depth of four miles. Behind them again came the Cavalry, mounted now for the first time for months. The success of one small part of the Cavalry force, by now excluded in most generals minds from having a useful role in warfare as it had developed on the Western Front, showed what effect might have been achieved if only the whole of the available force, or even a larger force, had been employed, which could have exploited the initial tank and Infantry success, broken into the German rear areas and perhaps have captured Cambrai itself. But this was not to be.

The comparatively small British Army was by now exhausted and had done all that could have been expected of it, although Cambrai was not captured. The Germans were now rapidly bringing forward fresh reserves and throwing them into the battle. The attack still went on, Bourlon Wood now being the objective, and finally captured it; but by now the opposition was too strong for troops who had been fighting offensive actions almost non-stop for the best part of a year. Strong counterattacks developed and despite gallant defence some of the ground was gradually lost. The British withdrew to a strong defensive position and by the middle of December both sides had had enough and the fight was called off for the winter.

Cambrai 1917 was awarded as an Honour to twenty-six British, the Royal Newfoundland, nine Indian and four Canadian Cavalry regiments, to the newly formed Tank Corps, and to eighty-seven British Infantry regiments. One of the Indian cavalry regiments, Hodson's Horse, was presented with a Guards Bugle for their support of 1st Guards Brigade. The Honour was also gained by two South African batteries and a Canadian machine gun squadron. An individual Honour, *Gouzeacourt*, was claimed by the five British Guards regiments for a brilliant action on the opening days of the battle, but was not recognised.

So ended the fighting in France and Flanders in 1917, the Year of Attrition as it became known because of the continual nibbling away at the German positions, the only year of the war when there was continuous combat throughout. It is true that no great gains were made, no breakthrough was achieved, but in the context of trench warfare, with two massive armies of roughly equal strength facing each other and prepared to fight for every foot of territory, nothing further was really to be expected. At least the British and allied armies went forward rather than backwards and even a few miles in the circumstances was an achievement. The Allies were worn out and had suffered heavy casualties, particularly at Passchendaele, but the Germans had suffered much more heavily and because of their increasing weakness their attack in the spring of the following year was a last-ditch attempt to sway the outcome of the war by a sudden breakthrough; and when that had failed the way was open for the conclusion of the fighting and an allied victory.

Macedonia, 1917

There was comparatively little fighting, at least on the British part, in the Salonika theatre during 1917; in fact most of the activity in Greece was political, culminating in the enforced abdication of King Constantine, and his replacement by his second son Alexander, and the return to power of Venizelos. What fighting there was occurred in the area west of Lake Doiran where the line was adjusted several times by each side early in the year. In April this was followed by a British attack; a considerable amount of ground was taken and defended against formidable counterattacks. A fortnight later the Bulgarians attacked the new British positions in force but were heavily repulsed; this action formed the catalyst for a series of attacks by the Allies all along the front, known as the Battle of Vardar, but these form no part of this account as British troops were not significantly involved. An Honour, **Doiran 1917**, was awarded to cover the two actions, and was gained by forty British regiments and refused to one Yeomanry regiment which claimed it.

Palestine, 1917

The advance into Sinai, which had achieved its objective with the capture of Rafah at the beginning of 1917 and had removed the Turkish threat to Egypt and the Suez Canal, had provided a springboard for the next stage of Middle Eastern operations, the invasion of Palestine. The most practical route for an advance was initially along the coast and then fanning out; the first objective, therefore, was the ancient city of Gaza which from time immemorial had been regarded as the key to southern Palestine. The country was undulating and cut by water courses across the line of the road; it was highly cultivated, including olive groves, and many cactus hedges made natural defences which the Turks had utilised to the full. The British force was comparatively small and the available resources did not allow for large-scale operations, so the attacks had to take maximum advantage of the ground and the isolated positions of the Turks, supported by the maximum use of mounted troops.

The first attack on 26 March was on the Turks defending Gaza itself, a combination of a direct assault with an encircling movement to prevent both Turkish escape and reinforcement. No sooner had the assault started than a thick sea-fog rolled in and all was confusion for a while; but when it cleared the attack proceeded vigorously. A fierce fight developed among the cactus in which a New Zealand Mounted regiment particularly distinguished itself, and by nightfall Gaza had been surrounded. Unfortunately there had been setbacks in the outlying country which had not been communicated to the headquarters, and the situation was not as hopeful as it first seemed.

A withdrawal took place over the Wadi Ghazze south of the city, as a result of counterattacks by Turkish reinforcements after the troops sent to hold them back had failed to do so, and the whole British position was now in jeopardy. A month later the second Battle of Gaza was opened, but it soon became clear that in spite of local successes this attack, too, had been a failure; the troops were exhausted, and water and ammunition were running short. As the very hot summer weather approached the condition of the troops worsened; but reinforcements were arriving at last, and in June the command changed, General Sir Archibald Murray handing over to General Sir Edmund Allenby, lately the Commander of the Cavalry Corps in France.

Allenby's task was straightforward, to capture the Gaza–Beersheba defence line and then advance to capture Jerusalem. It may have been straightforward but it was by no means simple. The Turks had been strongly reinforced as a result of the collapse of Russia and the availability of numerous Turkish divisions which were no longer required on the Caucasus front, supported by senior German commanders, and were now planning an offensive of their own to recapture Sinai, although in the event this was forestalled. British preparations were progressing apace and this time the main attack was to be directed against Beersheba; the preparations had been carried out with absolute secrecy and the Turks were persuaded by deception that Gaza was again the objective.

At the end of October the third Battle of Gaza began with a holding attack on Gaza itself to mask the Cavalry attack on Beersheba. With great flair the mounted Anzacs swept into the latter town and the supporting Infantry completed its capture by nightfall. The advance continued to the north of Beersheba in rugged and broken country and the Turks now feared that their line would be rolled up from the east towards the coast. But in front of Gaza the holding attack had been translated into a full-scale assault once Beersheba was captured and by early November had proved successful, although heavy casualties had been suffered. The Turks retreated precipitately and the first part of the offensive was completed.

Gaza was awarded as an Honour to cover the six-month period of the three battles, and as had happened several times in France it produced the problem of lack of identity or distinction between the participants in each. It was gained by thirty-three British Yeomanry regiments, one Indian Cavalry and one New Zealand Mounted rifle regiment, by the Tank Corps and the Madras Engineers, by fifty-two British and six Indian Infantry regiments and by three South African Artillery batteries. It was applied for unsuccessfully by one other Yeomanry regiment. A separate Honour **Gaza–Beersheba**, covering the third battle only, was awarded to the Mounted Anzac troops and was gained by fifteen Australian and eight New Zealand regiments. As in the Scarpe battles in France, the Cheshire Regiment (22nd Foot) applied for Honours to cover each battle severally, under the titles of *Gaza, Mukhadem* and *Beersheba* respectively, but this was refused.

On the day following the official ending of the Gaza battles a brilliant action took place at *Huj* where Austrian batteries defending the retreating Turkish columns were charged and destroyed by a detachment of the Warwickshire Yeomanry in an action reminiscent of Balaklava; they lost over half their number in this gallant attack, but in spite of this their application for an Honour was refused, presumably because less than half the regiment was engaged.

A few days later an Infantry attack on Junction Station, where the Beersheba railway line joined the Jaffa–Jerusalem line, and a Cavalry attack on the El Mughar ridge were both successful and opened up a gap in the Turkish defences which resulted in further retreat. An Honour, **El Mughar**, was awarded to cover both these actions which was gained by fifteen Yeomanry and fifteen Australian Cavalry regiments, by thirty-six British and two Indian Infantry regiments and by the three South African batteries. It was claimed by one yeomanry regiment, the ubiquitous but unlucky Duke of Lancaster's Own Yeomanry, but their application was again refused. The capture of the station was a serious blow to the Turks, because it contained large quantities of stores and also gave the British control of the main railway network, and their positions for the defence of Jerusalem itself were in imminent danger.

Allenby's advance continued up the coast and on 16 November the Australians captured Jaffa; his plan was then to advance eastward to cut the Jerusalem–Nablus road behind the Turkish defences and so avoid a battle which might cause damage to the Holy City. Although the weather turned wet and the going became difficult this advance met with comparatively little resistance, but inevitably heavy local fighting developed. The main battle was fought on the Nebi Samwil ridge, the site of the biblical Mizpah which was said to contain the tomb of the prophet Samuel, where the fighting was fierce and strong counterattacks developed from the ridge, the last Turkish defensive position of any real significance before Jerusalem. Although not all the objectives were taken, the majority were, and a position was achieved from which the final advance on Jerusalem could be launched. An Honour was awarded to cover the period of the advance from Jaffa to the capture of the ridge, **Nebi Samwil**, and this was gained by fourteen British Yeomanry and fifteen Australian Cavalry regiments, thirty-two British and three Indian Infantry regiments and the same three South African batteries; it was claimed, again unsuccessfully, by the Duke of Lancaster's Own Yeomanry.

During the ten-day period of reorganisation another force had moved northward from Beersheba and captured Hebron, and it was from there in the event that the advance on Jerusalem began. The weather turned wet again but the advance continued and the Turkish positions steadily fell although not without some sharp fighting and significant casualties. But when the British troops were poised for the final stage it was found that the Turks had withdrawn during the night towards the Jordan valley, and Jerusalem fell into allied hands unscathed on 9 December.

The city had been captured many times in its long history but never before by the British, and this capture marked the end of the first phase of Allenby's Palestine campaign. It soon became apparent, however, that the Turks were not beaten yet and were preparing a large counterattack to recapture both Jerusalem and Jaffa; but when it came the defenders were well prepared and the Turks were beaten back time after time until they were exhausted and at the end of the year they were once more in retreat.

The Honour **Jerusalem** was awarded, to cover both its capture and its defence, to twenty-two Yeomanry, fifteen Australian and nine New Zealand Cavalry or Mounted Infantry regiments, and to forty-six British and three Indian Infantry regiments. The Honour **Jaffa** was awarded for its defence to four Australian Cavalry and nine New Zealand Mounted Infantry regiments and to fifteen British Infantry regiments, the Duke of Lancaster's again being refused the Honour.

Mesopotamia, 1917

The surrender of Kut in April 1916 had raised a storm of indignation in England and the authorities at last set to work to produce an army worthy of the operations before it, by reorganising it and reinforcing it with men, munitions, transport and supply services. General Sir Stanley Maude took over the command, but he had no easy task. The Turks had strengthened their defences, in depth in front of Kut and on the right bank of the River Tigris, but the British were still occupying their trenches on the left bank, both lines, strangely, being in elongation of their lines of communication. By the end of 1916 the British concentrations for the attack on Kut were completed, the main objective being the Turkish position on the River Hai, although the position on the Khadairi bend of the

Tigris had to be captured first since it menaced the flank of the attack.

Heavy rain did nothing to help the operations but nevertheless the British trenches were gradually advanced under heavy bombardment. Early in January 1917 Indian troops attacked and captured the position which put the Turks in danger of being outflanked, but they counterattacked strongly and the fighting carried on for two days until the Turks abandoned their position in the darkness.

The British and Indian forces then began to cross the River Hai at the beginning of February, supported by an intense bombardment; after several days during which the battle swayed to and fro, the Turkish line was taken and the Turks retired into Kut, occupying the liquorice factory made famous during the siege; this factory, too, was stormed and taken. Pressure was now put on the Turkish position in the Dahra bend, which was soon occupied, and it was clear that the Turks were getting weaker. By the middle of the month the Sann-i-yat position was attacked and gradually reduced. The river was crossed in boats, and the Gurkhas were involved in a fierce action before a bridgehead was established; from this base the Turks were eventually surrounded and on 25 February the remains of the Turkish army was destroyed.

The various actions were covered by a single Honour, **Kut al Amara 1917**; it was awarded to two British and five Indian Cavalry regiments, and to twenty-four British, twenty-seven Indian and six Ghurkha Infantry regiments, and to the four Indian Army Engineer regiments, Madras, Bengal, Bombay and Burma.

Without pause the victorious Indo-British troops followed up the broken Turkish Army in the advance to Baghdad; a rearguard near Kut was destroyed and on 6 March the furthest point reached by General Townshend was passed. Turkish reserves were drawn in from Persia, but General Maude was too strong for them.

The battle for Baghdad opened with a frontal attack against the main Turkish position in concert with an enveloping movement by the Cavalry and an Infantry column, similar tactics to those employed at Kut. A strongly contested river crossing followed, which resulted in hand-to-hand fighting, but a bridgehead was established; a major force crossed and two days later Baghdad was occupied to the intense joy of the inhabitants, freed at last from the Turkish yoke. The advance continued beyond the city to consolidate its capture, and on 2 April the Indian Cavalry joined up with Cossacks of the Russian army advancing southwards.

Baghdad was awarded as an Honour to two British and three Indian Cavalry regiments, to the four Indian Engineer regiments, and to twenty-one British, twenty-two Indian and six Gurkha Infantry regiments.

The summer heat and the need to rest his troops made Maude leave the enemy undisturbed for a while, and during this period the German General Falkenhayn took over the command of the Turkish forces. His main problem was that the Turks were more than willing to fight to reoccupy the Caucasus and to battle with the Russians with religious fervour, but they were not particularly keen on fighting the British; thus the gradual fading away of the Russian Army was of less value to the German commanders of the Turk-

ish Army than might have been expected. His intent, nevertheless, was to strike back at the British; but his intention was forestalled by further advances up the Euphrates and Tigris, made possible largely by the development of railway communications and the use of river boats.

On the Euphrates in July an attack was made on a Turkish outpost at Ramadi, which was being used as a concentration point for a counterattack on Baghdad, but a severe sandstorm prevented it from being brought to a conclusion; another attack was mounted in September by a small force which captured the town more by manoeuvre than by a proper attack. *Ramadi* was unsuccessfully claimed as an Honour by the Dorsetshire Regiment (39th Foot).

In parallel with operations on the Euphrates, and shortly after the affair at Ramadi, operations were opened on the Tigris. An attack was made on a Turkish position at Tikrit, which fell remarkably easily, perhaps because some of the attackers were from Scottish regiments and the Turks had experienced the kilted warriors before. Because the position could not be held safely a further advance was made on the Jebel Hamrin, from which the Turks were also driven largely by manoeuvre, and a firm base was now held on the Tigris. No Honours were awarded to individual regiments for these various actions although they were recognised jointly as an Honour, **Tigris 1917**. Mesopotamia was nearing its conclusion as a theatre of war by the end of the year.

East Africa, 1917

Penultimately in the events of 1917 the scene moves to German East Africa, where it will be remembered that a series of actions the previous year had steadily driven the Germans back and were threatening to encircle them. Similar actions occurred in 1917, but few of them, although by no means insignificant, were to be recognised for Battle Honours. One that was took place in the first few days of the year during General Smut's advance to secure a crossing of the Rufiji River. An attack captured a camp at Wiransi but the enemy escaped because of the weakness of the British force; they were then attacked again and severe hand-to-hand fighting resulted, but in spite of all that the attackers could do the Germans again slipped through the net. An Honour was awarded for these actions, **Beho Beho**, and was gained by the Royal Fusiliers (7th Foot), the Nigeria Regiment, four Indian and two South African regiments.

As the year wore on the German forces suffered more and more from sickness, shortage of materials and the desertion of native troops, and were being pushed back towards the Portuguese East African frontier and the sea. The terrain was broken and covered with dense bush, quite unsuitable for normal fighting, but the advance continued and in July the Germans were attacked in a major position south-west of the small port of Kilwa. The fighting was indecisive and again the Germans managed to retire but, nevertheless an Honour was awarded; **Narungombe** was gained by the King's African Rifles, the Gold Coast Regiment, and three Indian and two South African regiments.

In October another major action was fought at **Nyangao**

which was awarded as an Honour to the Royal Fusiliers, the Kings African Rifles, the Nigeria and Gambia Regiments, to two Indian regiments and four South African, one of which was a Mounted regiment. This action virtually sealed the fate of the German forces and to all intents and purposes the battle in East Africa had finished by the end of November 1917.

India

Many theatres of war have figured in the fighting of the Commonwealth Armies so far in this narrative, but one has been overlooked, perhaps because it had been the scene of sporadic actions and semi-continuous warfare for so long that it was not recognised specifically as part of the Great War. This was the North West Frontier of India. But in spite of the more memorable battles elsewhere the troops that fought there and in Waziristan also served their country although the enemies were not directly Germans

or Turks but the same as they had always been, the warring tribes of Tochi, Mohmand, Bunerwal and Swat, and the Mahsuds. It is not practicable to single out any particular actions, although a number, mainly punitive expeditions, were listed by the Battle Nomenclature Committee.

Two Honours were awarded, one specific and one as a general Campaign Honour. **Waziristan 1917** was awarded for operations against the Mahsuds to a single Indian regiment, the 15th Lancers. **North West Frontier 1914–18** was the Campaign Honour, although as far as dates were concerned it primarily covered actions up to the autumn of 1917, and it was gained by one British, the 21st Lancers, and seven Indian Cavalry regiments, the Madras, Bengal and Bombay Engineers, and by eight British and twenty-three Indian Infantry regiments, together with the British Cyclist Corps. Four other British Infantry regiments participated in the general fighting but were not recognised for the Honour.

Above: Flanders, during the Great War. *via M Fall*

15 The Great War: Part 3, 1918-19

France and Flanders, 1918

Most of the year 1917 had gone very much the way of the Allies in all theatres of war until the protracted fighting in front of Ypres at Passchendaele, and the appalling casualties suffered there, which destroyed the euphoria created by the earlier victories in France. Therefore, the collapse of the Russian Army, more from subversion as a result of the rise of Bolshevism than from German pressure, and the subsequent Treaty of Brest Litovsk, and the defeat of the Italians at Caporetto, made the new year of 1918, which eventually after many dangerous moments proved the year of victory, open under a dark cloud.

The year started quietly; a period of rest and reorganisation was needed after the 3rd Battle of Ypres and in addition the British line had been further extended southwards. During the first months there were repeated warnings of a new German offensive which was not in any way being kept secret but almost advertised, except for the date. Thus Haig's main object during this period was to strengthen his defences as well as rest his depleted divisions, and the German object was to build up a massive offensive force. Many raids were carried out by both sides mainly to take prisoners and to obtain identification of units.

Picardy and the Somme

The German plan was based on four groups of armies; from north to south the first was directed at Arras to act as a flankguard against any counterattack, the second was directed at Croisilles and Bullecourt, the third at Bapaume and Peronne and the most southerly at St Quentin. Against this huge offensive force were ranged on the British side only nineteen divisions in the line and thirteen, including three Cavalry, divisions in reserve. The weather favoured the Germans; on 20 March it was raining with low cloud, which precluded air observation, and on the following day the rain combined with the warm spring weather to produce dense mist and fog all over the battlefield; in these conditions, and supported by a heavy bombardment which drenched the British forward positions in poison gas, the great German offensive, which was intended to drive through to the Channel ports and finish the war with one major thrust, achieved complete surprise, which it would not have done in clear weather.

All along the line the Germans broke through, although the pressure varied from place to place, and the main weight initially fell on the area of St Quentin; most importantly it managed to break the hinge between the British and French parts of the front line. As the day wore on the situation became increasingly grave as allied formations were decimated and gaps appeared in the defences. Nevertheless the harassed troops reacted with great courage and defensive skill and in all areas managed to retreat to new positions and plug the gaps. On 23 March Peronne was captured and the following day the main offensive switched to Bapaume, followed by attacks on Rosières, just south of the Somme, and on the area in front of Arras in quick succession. In the southern part of the front the assault was then concentrated at the beginning of April along the line of the Rivers Avre and Ancre, both thrusts having the railway junction of Amiens as their objective. But by then the weary British and French troops, who had never lost heart or spirit, had formed a strong defensive position in front of Amiens and Arras; by 6 April the Germans had been fought to a standstill, and they themselves considered that they had thereby suffered a strategic defeat in spite of the ground which had been gained.

In spite of this Sir Hubert Gough, the Commander of the 5th Army, which had suffered terrible losses, was blamed for the retreat and dismissed from his command and by implication his troops were also blamed for retreating too precipitately. Most of the blame was levelled by those who had not been there to see what the conditions were like and would probably have retreated much faster if they had been. In any situation of this sort a scapegoat had to be found and Gough was made to suffer; but in fact the troops behaved magnificently against overwhelming odds and time and again turned to delay their pursuers by stubborn defence and counterattack, and when necessary died to a man rather than surrender. In point of fact the strength of the 5th Army was totally inadequate for its task and it had insufficient reserves, apart from which it had only recently taken over this part of the front and did not yet know the ground well.

The first phase of the German attack from 21 March to 5 April was officially known as the offensive in Picardy, and six individual Battle Honours and a Campaign Honour were awarded. Typically, however, three of these, the Campaign Honour and those for the Battles of Bapaume and Arras, were combined with battles which eventually took place during the British advance in the early autumn, with the resulting confusion as to which regiments had gained the Honour for which period. The exception, slight enough, is that when the Honour for Bapaume is borne after Amiens on their Colours it is clear that these regiments were only present at the later battle, although when it is borne after St Quentin it could apply either to the earlier battle or to both, and of course it could be borne without either of them.

The Cheshire Regiment (22nd Foot), as they had done for previous occasions of similar stupidity by the authorities which had decided on the Honour, unsuccessfully applied for the Honours to be separated. They proposed that 'Somme 1918' should be used for the earlier battle and 'Picardy' for the later; that 'Bapaume' should be divided into 'Bapaume 1918', the name taken for the double Honour, for the March battle, and 'Mont St Quentin', the name used in any case by the Australians who were not engaged there in March, for the autumn battle; and that the Honour of 'Arras 1918' should apply only to the March battle with 'Quéant' for the later one. Sensible proposals indeed, but ones which fell on the deaf ears of those who considered economy of Honours more important than historical exactitude and clarity.

Of the Honours, then, that were awarded the Campaign Honour **Somme 1918** was awarded to one hundred and fifty-one British, twenty-one Canadian, sixty-one Australian and twenty New Zealand regiments, one Canadian machine gun squadron and three South African Artillery batteries. **St Quentin** was gained by one hundred and twenty British regiments, roughly a quarter of them Cavalry and Yeomanry, and by five Canadian and their machine gun squadron. **Bapaume 1918** was gained by one hundred and nineteen British regiments, and by two Canadian and seventeen New Zealand regiments, all the New Zealand regiments having been Honoured for the autumn battle. **Rosières** was awarded to sixty-one British and one Canadian regiment. **Arras 1918** was awarded to the largest number of all; to seventy-four British, eighty-five Canadian, four Australian and twenty New Zealand regiments and to three Canadian machine gun squadrons and the three South African batteries. **Avre** was gained by thirty-two British, one Canadian and seven Australian regiments and **Ancre 1918** by thirty-nine British, twenty-five Australian and seventeen New Zealand regiments. Two individual Honours were claimed, but not awarded, during the period—*Fontaine-les-Clercs* by the Royal Inniskilling Fusiliers (27th Foot) and *Cugny* by the Royal Ulster Rifles (83rd Foot).

Flanders and the Lys

But although the offensive had been stemmed in Picardy the German strength had not been much diminished and a new offensive began after a few days in Flanders, between Ypres and La Bassee. This attack on 9 April was directly aimed at the Channel ports, with St Omer and Hazebrouck being the initial objectives, and became known as the Battle of the Lys. Again the weather favoured the Germans as it had been an unusually dry spring and much of the marshy ground in the area had more or less dried up.

The first assault was made towards Estaires from the ridge in front of Lille which had defied all the allied

attempts at capture; although considerable advances were made Givenchy held out for nearly a fortnight. On the following day the assault was switched to Messines under a heavy bombardment; again the British were forced to retreat and during the day both Messines and Armentières fell to the enemy. The situation became more critical still as Bailleul and Kemmel fell, towns which had been held by the British since the early days of the Ypres offensive. Reserves were thrown in to stop the attack at all costs but often there was virtually nothing but a thin outpost line between the German and the Channel ports which they craved.

But although numerous attacks were launched towards Béthune and Hazebrouck the defences somehow managed to hold out due to the sacrifice and gallantry of the hard-pressed troops. But by now reserves from the Amiens battlefield were also coming in and helped to defend the Forêt de Nieppe in front of Hazebrouck. The German losses were terrific and their attacks were made without any apparent regard for the casualties being suffered, but the Commander, Ludendorf, could not accept, after his successes on the Eastern Front, that victory was not within his grasp.

And then, after just over a fortnight, the weather at last began to favour the British because it rained and the combination of mud and British gunfire proved too much and the offensive began to waver. The final attacks were made on the Scherpenberg positions on 29 April, but they failed to break through and the Battle of the Lys came to an end. As in front of Amiens, the Germans had gained a lot of ground but had not achieved their intended break-through. But right at the end of this period another major attack took place in the south, on the Somme front, on the village of Villers Bretonneux; although the village was lost initially, and then partially regained by British troops, an Australian brigade launched a strong counterattack which drove the Germans well clear of the village and captured a large number of prisoners. This was a welcome victory among all the defeats of the past few weeks. It was during this battle that British and German tanks first met in conflict.

A campaign Honour and eight Battle Honours were awarded during this phase. **Lys** was gained by seventy-nine British, the Royal Newfoundland, thirteen Australian, three New Zealand and three South African regiments, and by three South African batteries. **Estaires** was gained by thirty-seven British regiments and the three South African batteries, **Messines 1918** by one Yeomanry and thirty-four British Infantry regiments and three South African Infantry regiments, and **Hazebrouck** by fifty-eight British and twelve Australian regiments. **Bailleul** was awarded to forty-one British, the Royal Newfoundland and three New Zealand regiments. **Kemmel** was another Honour which covered two periods, although this time within a week of each other, which the Cheshire Regiment again proposed should be divided into 'Kemmel 1918' for the former and 'La Clytte' for the latter; however, it was awarded, without distinction of actions, to fifty-two British, the Royal Newfoundland, three Australian, three New Zealand and three South African regiments, and the battle is celebrated by 166 Battery Royal Artillery although not as an Honour

Title. **Béthune** was awarded to twenty-seven British regiments and three south African batteries, and **Scherpenberg** to thirty-one British and three New Zealand regiments, although it was claimed unsuccessfully by the Hertfordshire Regiment. One individual Honour was also claimed without success; this was *Pacaut Wood* and the unlucky regiment was the Royal Hampshire (37th Foot). Finally **Villers Brettoneaux**, which properly belongs to the Somme Battle, was awarded to twenty-three British and twelve Australian regiments.

The Aisne

In spite of the failures and the heavy casualties the German offensive was not yet over and after a month's rest, during which the British tried to reorganise their shattered forces and moved some of the worst-hit divisions to a quiet area on the Aisne, the next phase of the assault opened in the very area which had been deemed quiet and almost impregnable. Once again the German attack was initially successful even though the terrain was very difficult, with wooded hills and deep valleys, but the experienced divisions were by now able to cope more effectively with the onslaught, giving ground but not losing cohesion.

The brunt of the assault fell on the 50th Division, which on its formation as a Territorial Force division in 1908 had been commanded by Lord Baden Powell, of Mafeking and Boy Scout fame, and which held a position on the Chemin de Dames ridge. Alongside them was a French division which was forced to retreat, leaving the men from Tyne and Tees totally exposed and isolated; the division was over-run and virtually destroyed suffering over 5,000 casualties during 27 May, and the remnants, in spite of a gallant defence, were forced into a rapid retreat also to avoid being surrounded. The battle went on for ten frantic days; on the flank the city of Reims was ably defended by a Franco-British force, and the Allies managed to hold their fall-back positions on the line of Villers-Cotterets and Château Thierry on the Marne, where American troops played their first major part in the war.

Once more the German offensive had been fought to a standstill despite all that they could do to break through, and, by a strange coincidence, on the Marne where the initial offensive in 1914 had also been finally broken. Only a Campaign Honour and two individual Battle Honours were awarded for this phase; the number of British regiments involved, all Infantry and the only Commonwealth forces to see action here, was far smaller than on the Somme and the Lys, since this was essentially a French sector of the front and the British troops were only there more or less by accident. **Aisne 1918** was awarded to thirty regiments. The two individual Honours were, perhaps surprisingly, both unique, the only ones to be awarded in France and Flanders. **Bligny** was gained by the Kings Shropshire Light Infantry (53rd Foot) and the battalion, the 4th, was also awarded the French Croix de Guerre for its exploits; the Cheshire and North Staffordshire Regiments (22nd and 64th Foot) were also both involved in this fierce action although for some obscure reason they were denied the Honour despite applying for it. **Bois des Buttes** was awarded to the Devonshire Regiment.

Before the next phase of the offensive started another isolated battle took place in front of Amiens on the Somme front. It was an all-Australian affair and their attack captured the village of **Hamel** which was awarded as an Honour to twenty-two regiments.

The Marne

After the repulse of the Aisne offensive and with the arrival of American troops in the field Ludendorf was faced with a problem; the one thing that he could not do was stand still, which gave him the options of retreat, which was anathema to him, or attack. He therefore decided on the latter and launched the last great German offensive of 1918, and in fact of the war, in the area south-east of Château Thierry. The main attack fell on the French who employed a ruse as old as the hills which took the Germans completely unawares. The main French forces were withdrawn, without the enemy realising it, from the hills of Champagne which they had won after so much heavy fighting, so that the massive German bombardment fell on a countryside empty of all but outposts; these retired slowly, realistically representing large formations, before the advancing Germans. Once they were buoyed up with success and in the open the French hit them with machine guns and gunfire; the havoc that this caused was so absolute that the German losses were of the same order as the British on the first day of the Somme in 1916.

No British troops were involved in this action or the subsequent counterattack by a Franco-American force which broke through the German line near Soissons. But then a small force did arrive and immediately went into the attack south of Reims; it made significant advances but the primary effect on the enemy was amazement that any British troops at all could be spared from the other fronts. It brought home to the Germans the strength and endurance of the British Army as nothing else had done; and this single stroke virtually stopped the German attack in its tracks, threw their Army on to the defensive and changed the whole complexion of the war. It is almost unbelievable that just two British divisions could have had this effect.

But the battle was not yet actually over. The Germans had pulled back across the Marne but were still defending the Hartennes plateau and the Tardenois hills, although this was becoming increasingly difficult for them. Allied attacks were launched north of the River Ourcq and across the Soissons road, the 51st Scottish Division now being attached to the French Army; in spite of a heavy German bombardment and murderous machine gun fire the Scots won through and captured the heavily defended position near Fère-en-Tardenois. Their gallantry was such that the French erected a monument to them on the heights. By the beginning of August both battles were over, the German forces were in demoralised withdrawal and the great spring offensive was defeated at last.

Two Battle Honours and a Campaign Honour were awarded, more or less the same regiments gaining each of them. **Soissonais-Ourcq** was gained by fourteen British regiments; **Tardenois** by twelve British Infantry and one Australian and three New Zealand Mounted regiments.

The Campaign Honour **Marne 1918** was awarded to twenty-one British Infantry regiments and the one Australian and three New Zealand Mounted regiments.

The Advance in Picardy

The Germans now expected an allied assault but were not unduly worried by the thought; after all the position was not very different from that facing von Moltke in 1914 and he had nearly broken the British at Ypres only a month after being defeated on the Marne, and Hindenburg would not admit that he could not also defeat the hated enemy, even though nearly four years of strenuous fighting had intervened.

All along the front the German armies in their defensive positions were being reinforced and their strength was still formidable. The British had been weakened by months of fighting to halt the German offensive and many untried troops had been brought into the reformed divisions with little opportunity for training them; only the 1st Army on Vimy Ridge was reasonably intact. But a number of changes in the command of the major allied formations had assembled the majority of the generals experienced in offensive warfare, and particularly in the type of offensive that came to be known in the next great war as the *Blitzkrieg*.

The essence of the allied plan for an attack was surprise and the achievement of local concentration without alerting the Germans; the chances of success were of course increased because of the German estimate of allied, and especially British, weakness. The area chosen for the assault was, as in 1916, the Somme and the main force to be used was the Canadian Army Corps, which was moved south from Arras to Amiens with great speed and secrecy. The Australians were already concentrated there as they had been holding this part of the line for some months, and a large British force was also moved in to relieve them for the attack. Not that all the preparations went smoothly because at the beginning of August a German shock division decided to recapture the high ground between the Ancre and the Somme; in a fierce action they took their objectives but were driven off again by a counterattack the following day. This battle was not honoured, nor even officially listed.

The Germans expected the main assault further south and therefore the attack which began on 8 August was regarded by them as a local diversionary action; but it was in fact the real thing and took place in thick fog, which had been forecast by the meteorologists, supported by a massive Artillery bombardment which devastated the German positions. The assault achieved complete surprise and by midday one Australian battalion had advanced nine miles with only three casualties. German reserves were being captured before they had time to get into position, so rapid was the advance, nearly all their Artillery was captured and the roads leading to Peronne were jammed with retreating troops among which complete chaos reigned after they were attacked by machine gun fire from low-flying aircraft. The Canadians forced the River Lure and during the day their Infantry, supported by mounted Cavalry and armoured cars, advanced eight miles.

The Somme defences had been broken and the great German salient created in front of Amiens in March had been destroyed, and in a week the line was back in its original 1914 position between Albert and Lassigny. The tables had been turned with a vengeance. And now the next phase of the offensive was being planned. The Honour of **Amiens**, which more accurately should have been suffixed by the date 1918, was awarded to twenty-nine British, one Australian and seventeen Canadian Cavalry regiments, to the Tank Corps, to thirty-eight British, eighty-one Canadian and fifty-five Australian Infantry regiments, and to a Canadian motor machine gun brigade and three machine gun squadrons. It was applied for by the Norfolk Yeomanry, but for dates later than the official ones, and refused. Two individual Honours were also unsuccessfully claimed; by the 5th Dragoon Guards for *Harbonniers* and by the South Lancashire Regiment (40th Foot) for *Mont Vidaigne*.

The next phase as far as the British were concerned consisted of a two-pronged attack on Bapaume and St Quentin. On the morning of 21 August the British 3rd Army attacked, again under the thick fog for which it had been waiting and which had been forecast, preceded by tanks, as part of an allied line of attack 90 miles long from Arras to Soissons. The outposts were soon driven in, and although the battle which developed was desperate at times the advance continued; the Albert–Arras railway was crossed, Albert itself was entered and two days later the advance had reached a point only 2½ miles from Bapaume. The offensive swept over the Thiepval-Pozieres ridge to Courcelette, and the Australians captured the ridge of Chuignes on the south side of the River Somme; other villages made famous two years before, La Boiselle, Contalmaison, Bazentin and Mametz Wood, were taken.

The Germans counterattacked and the struggle covered the old battlefields of Flers, Delville Wood, Montauban and Combles, but although this stopped the advance temporarily and even drove it back in places, the losses suffered by the Germans were such that it could only be a delaying action against the inevitable. On 29 August Bapaume fell to the New Zealanders.

Several Battle Honours were awarded for this period of fighting. **Bapaume** has already been mentioned as having been combined with the earlier battle in the previous March. **Albert 1918** was awarded to ninety-eight British, fifty-one Australian and seventeen New Zealand regiments. Four Australian regiments were awarded a separate Honour for this operation, **Albert 1918 (Chuignes)**.

Second Battles of Arras

After the first few days of the offensive in front of Albert the Germans were preparing to withdraw into the strong defences of the Hindenburg Line; had they been allowed to do so the British advance would inevitably have been considerably hindered and slowed down. In parallel, therefore, with the attack on Bapaume a new attack, initially mainly by Canadian troops, was opened along the River Scarpe, and this officially began the campaign to be known as the breaking of the Hindenburg Line, which occupied the next six weeks. This move took the Germans again by surprise and met with instant success, taking villages further advanced than had previously been reached and for which desperate struggles had gone on the year before.

The impression should not be gained that the advance was without stiff opposition, and the Germans put in a number of counterattacks, but the strength and endurance shown by their troops in even the previous year had lessened. Nevertheless reinforcements were brought up and the intensity of the fighting increased; Bullecourt was captured, lost and recaptured. The Australians stormed the key height of Mont St Quentin; at the beginning of September the Canadians and British advanced through the Drocourt-Queant switch line with remarkable ease and speed, and in one village captured the German town-major and his staff asleep. The Germans began a general retreat and for the first time the Allies entered undamaged hamlets and villages where the only British troops seen by the French civilian inhabitants since the beginning of the war had been as prisoners.

Again several Honours were awarded. **Scarpe 1918** was gained by fifty-one British and fifty-five Canadian regiments, the Canadian motor machine gun brigade and three squadrons, and three South African batteries. **Mont St Quentin** was gained by thirty-five Australian regiments and **Drocourt-Queant** by forty-four British and forty-one Canadian regiments, by the Canadian motor machine gun brigade and two squadrons, and by three South African batteries.

The Hindenburg Line

The battles for the Hindenburg Line proper were now about to start and after a week of reorganisation the offensive again swung into motion. In early September limited advances took place as the Germans retired into the main Hindenburg Line system. When they fell back from Ham a new form of warfare was employed; they placed charges in all the houses which were later electrically detonated and the town was almost entirely destroyed. American troops were now taking a major part and having reached the Meuse started to bombard Metz.

The new British offensive began on 12 September when the 62nd Division advanced on Havrincourt and repeated their victory of nearly a year earlier; they were counterattacked and had to withdraw from the town, but later the Germans were driven out again. This was the last serious reaction to the British advance between Douai and St Quentin. The Honour **Havrincourt** was awarded to twenty-seven British and nine New Zealand regiments.

The next attack was made in the area of Epehy, where a very strong German defensive system had been rapidly constructed and their Commander hoped that an attack on it would fail and allow him to break the British Army employed. On 18 September the British and Australians attacked, supported by tanks which were less effective than usual owing to heavy rain; the defence was desperate but could not stem the advance, which went on all day and all night, with some regiments taking more prisoners than their own strength, until it was within 2 or 3 miles of St Quentin and threatening to outflank it. The Yeomanry

division still so called although by now the Yeomanry regiments had been amalgamated in pairs and converted to Infantry also took its objectives, and although the resistance increased at Epehy itself and counterattacks developed, rapid aimed fire broke them before they reached the British line. The Honour of **Epehy** was gained by the Life Guards, twenty Yeomanry regiments, the Tank Corps and fifty-four British, one Canadian and twenty-two Australian Infantry regiments.

For a week it rained and the chalky ground became very muddy, but then the sun came out again hotly and the ground soon dried; now the assault could go on all along the front. In the north a weakened army attacked near Armentières towards Neuve Chapelle and the Aubers ridge; the German front was broken where it crossed the Menin road, the Messines ridge was turned and by the end of the first day the Army was close to Menin itself. The last Battle of Ypres and in Flanders was rapidly turning into a pursuit.

Further south the Canadians attacked along the Cambrai-Douai road; they were heavily counterattacked and had to withdraw for the night, but the following day pushed on into the outskirts of Cambrai. Further south again the Scheldt Canal was reached where it became the St Quentin Canal and was crossed, as was the Canal du Nord and the southern defences of St Quentin were turned. Everywhere the Germans were on the retreat, the Hindenburg Line was passed and the Allies were entering country untouched by war; the German commanders were at last considering suing for peace in the hope that this would keep the German Army intact.

Beaurevoir was reached and when this was taken the German communications were in grave danger, because Le Cateau, through which ran the main German railway line supplying the front, was only a few miles away. On 8 October Villers-Outreaux, which outflanked the stiffening resistance around Cambrai, was entered; by now it was too late to delay the advance and on 9 October the Canadians entered the town. The Germans had no alternative but to retire towards the River Selle and Le Cateau. The objective, the Hindenburg Line, had been captured although the casualties had been heavy.

Four Battle Honours were awarded for the period from 27 September to 9 October. **Canal du Nord** was gained by seventy-two British, fifty-six Canadian and seventeen New Zealand regiments and by the Canadian motor machine gun brigade and three machine gun squadrons. **St Quentin Canal** was won by sixty-five British, four Canadian and twenty-three Australian regiments, and one Canadian machine gun squadron. **Beaurevoir** was awarded to fifty-four British, four Canadian and twelve Australian regiments, a Canadian machine gun squadron and the South African field ambulance. **Cambrai 1918** was awarded to thirty-one British and thirteen Canadian Cavalry regiments, to seventy-six British, nineteen Canadian, seventeen New Zealand and three South African Infantry regiments, to the Canadian motor machine gun brigade and three squadrons and to three South African batteries.

Further north the 2nd Corps had battled across the Passchendaele ridge; the German general von Armin hoped, with the optimism of desperation, that he might win a defensive victory in Flanders, but it was not to be. The German line north of Menin was broken. This allowed the Belgians and French to advance to capture Ostend and Zeebrugge, and demonstrated Haig's strategic skill in his attempt to take Passchendaele and break through here in 1917. **Ypres 1918** was gained by sixty British regiments and the Royal Newfoundland Regiment and unsuccessfully claimed by the Yorkshire Dragoons.

The overall Honour for the breaking of the **Hindenburg Line** was awarded to a very large number of regiments, in fact most of those in France. It was gained by the Household Cavalry, twenty-three British Cavalry, twenty-seven Yeomanry regiments and the Tank Corps, and by the five Guards and eighty-six Infantry regiments; by sixteen Canadian Cavalry and seventy-two Infantry regiments and four machine gun regiments; and by fifty-seven Australian, seventeen New Zealand and three South African Infantry regiments and by three South African artillery batteries and a Field Ambulance—a grand total of 310 regiments or the equivalent.

The Final Advance

By now of course trench warfare was a thing of the past and had given place to field warfare, supported by tanks, smoke screens and Artillery barrages; one problem encountered by the change was the forward movement of the heavy guns, which had been stationary for so long, often not having had to change position by much even during the major battles, that new skills had to be rapidly learned. After the fall of Cambrai, and with the Germans withdrawing to Le Cateau and the River Selle, the British steadily moved forward, reaching the river the following day. In the south of the front Bohain was taken and, to the north of Cambrai, Douai was being rapidly outflanked and was captured on 17 October. On 11 October the first passage of the Selle was made between Le Cateau and Solesmes.

At the northern end of the allied line the Belgian Army under King Albert took Bruges on 19 October and drove on to the Dutch frontier. By this time the British, advancing in front of Ypres, had reached Courtrai, but were then checked; the city was outflanked by the capture of Roubaix and the drive towards Tournai, which also outflanked Lille and this city and Courtrai were evacuated without any serious fighting. These advances were honoured by the award of **Courtrai**, gained by seven Yeomanry and forty-four Infantry regiments, all British; and the Royal Newfoundland Regiment. An individual Honour, *Tieghem*, was claimed, but refused, by the Norfolk Yeomanry.

On the River Selle the Germans had strengthened their defence of the river line north from Le Cateau through Solesmes towards Valenciennes, and there had been some fierce fighting. After a week's delay needed to bring up the heavy guns the offensive opened again on 17 October in heavy rain. The river was forced in a number of places. Bridgeheads had to be established to allow bridges to be built so that the tanks could continue to support the advance; this was accomplished under heavy enemy bombardment and it was very much an engineer's battle.

Le Cateau was captured. The enemy counterattacked and were held although it was a very hard-fought action; the Germans appeared to have recovered some of their resolution and spirit. South of Le Cateau the army, which had been moving towards Guise, turned northwards and attacked towards Landrecies. The advance across the Selle continued into the Forêt de Mormal, and all the time the fighting was very hard and only the great spirit of the attackers still gave them the edge over the defenders. The outskirts of Valenciennes were reached, the intensity of the fighting increased and the New Zealanders joined the attack; they provided enough extra strength to break the defence and establish the position for the final advance.

This operation was covered by an Honour, **Selle**, which was awarded to seventeen British Cavalry and Yeomanry regiments, seventy-three British, seventeen New Zealand and two South African Infantry regiments, and a South African field ambulance. One individual Honour was claimed unsuccessfully, *Le Cateau 1918* by the Scottish Horse.

The advances to the Selle in the south and Courtrai in the north had left an enormous German salient 30 miles deep between Tournai and Valenciennes. Eventually the Canadians attacked and captured Denain, classically connected with Marlborough's campaign, on the southern flank of the salient, and a fierce action took place near Tournai. In spite of desperate defence the Germans now had to draw back, until the British line was straightened and Valenciennes was directly threatened. The battle for Valenciennes began in the last few days of October; the Germans had destroyed the sluices on the Scheldt Canal and inundated miles of countryside, which left only one narrow strip of solid ground south of the city on which to mount the attack.

Famars, scene of a battle in 1793, was taken and the southern suburbs were entered; street fighting took place as the city was gradually overcome. The city was now being outflanked by the Canadians who had found a dry patch and worked round the north, but finally Valenciennes had to be taken by direct assault. The Germans threw in every available man in a desperate rearguard action; they counterattacked the British south of the city but the gunfire was intense and they broke under it. The British advanced again and this was the decisive moment of the battle. The Germans just did not have the strength to resist any further and the city fell to the Canadians on 2 November. The Honour, **Valenciennes**, was awarded to thirty-five British and twenty-two Canadian regiments.

Pressure from the Belgians north of Tournai, which threatened to outflank Ghent, and from the British south of the city striking up from Valenciennes contained the German forces so that they could spare no reserves for the final battle of the war which took place in and around the Forêt de Mormal. Further south the French attacked between Guise and Rethel, which also caused a German withdrawal towards Mormal. The British objective was now Mauberge, which would outflank Mons and enable them to capture the Mauberge-Cologne railway which was the main German supply and transport route.

There was no delay after the capture of Valenciennes and the final battlefield stretched from Le Quesnoy in the north to the River Sambre in the south. The river was forced at Catillon and Ors, and Landrecies fell; meanwhile in the centre the troops advanced through the forest against determined and gallant German defensive actions, and in the north Le Quesnoy was captured by the New Zealanders, under heavy bombardment, some of the troops actually scaling the walls of the fortress. The Germans counterattacked *en masse* but their attack was devastated with heavy losses. The Honour of **Sambre** was awarded to ninety-four British, ten Canadian and sixteen New Zealand regiments and a South African field ambulance. A separate Honour, **Sambre (Le Quesnoy)** was awarded uniquely to one New Zealand regiment.

The advance now continued towards Bavai and the main road to Mons. The German Army was broken, disorganised and in full retreat; it was still holding a deep salient to Tournai, but this was so far outflanked to the south that at last they had to withdraw there as well. On 7 November the Guards entered Bavai and advanced towards Mauberge, which was carried two days later after heavy fighting. This was the fortress into which the Germans in 1914 had hoped to drive the British army and encircle it, but by refusing its shelter and retiring towards the Marne Sir John French had saved his army and France as well; it was appropriate that it should have been captured right at the end of the war.

The end now came very quickly. Ath was taken and on the evening of 10 November the Canadians were close to Mons itself; early on the morning of Monday 11 November 1918 troops of a Montreal battalion entered Mons. The scene of the first battle of the war in August 1914 was also the scene of the final battle four years and three months later. On the previous day the Armistice had been signed in a railway carriage in the Forêt de Compiègne and at 11 a.m. the cease fire brought the war to an end.

The Honour covering the last week of the war, **Pursuit to Mons**, was gained by thirty-nine British and nine Canadian Cavalry and Yeomanry regiments, and by fourteen British, one South African and fifty-nine Canadian Infantry regiments, by the Canadian motor machine gun brigade and three squadrons and by six South African batteries. It was refused to one other British Infantry regiment, and not awarded to the Guards despite their presence and capture of Bavai.

The whole four and a quarter year campaign in the theatre was covered by an Honour, **France and Flanders 1914–18**; as can be imagined practically every regiment in the British and Canadian Armies and in the Australian and New Zealand Infantry were awarded this Honour and it is almost easier to note those regiments which did not gain it rather than those that did. In the event it was awarded to twenty-seven Cavalry and fifty Yeomanry regiments of the British Army and to twenty Canadian, fourteen Indian, two Australian and three New Zealand Cavalry or Mounted Infantry regiments; it was awarded to six South African Artillery batteries, to the Tank Corps and to the Madras, Bengal and Bombay Sappers and Miners; it was awarded to one hundred and five British, the Royal Newfoundland, forty-one Canadian, seventeen Indian, six Gurkha, sixty Australian, seventeen New Zealand and four South African Infantry regiments; it was also awarded to two Canadian motor machine gun brigades and four machine gun squadrons, and to a South African field ambulance.

For some inexplicable reason fifty-two Canadian regiments, Infantry and Cavalry, which had been awarded numerous and various individual Battle and Campaign Honours in the theatre, were not awarded the overall theatre Campaign Honour. Most of these however, bear the Honour **Pursuit to Mons.** A formidable number of regiments indeed from the British Empire; each British regiment represented a large number of battalions, and in these and the Commonwealth regiments the personnel must have changed many times over during the course of hostilities.

The British regiments which did not gain this Honour, and thus did not serve in France and Flanders during the war, were three Regular Cavalry and nine Yeomanry, together with a few battalions of the London Regiment of the Territorial Force. The Cavalry regiments were the 7th Hussars, who were in India and Mesopotamia, the 14th Hussars in Mesopotamia and Persia, and the 21st Lancers who spent the whole of the war in India, perhaps the unluckiest, or luckiest depending on how you look at it, of all the British Army. Eight of the Yeomanry regiments were variously in action in Egypt, Gallipoli, Palestine and Macedonia, and the ninth, the Inns of Court Regiment, saw no active service as it became an Officer Producing Unit.

One remarkable fact emerges from the fighting in France and Flanders. In spite of the length of the war and the fact that the front stretched from the sea to near Nancy for a distance of about 300 miles (further south it virtually never moved), the lateral movement, because of the immobility of trench warfare, was very limited indeed. After the initial German advance to the Marne and the subsequent establishment of a trench line in September 1914 until the German offensive in 1918, not much more than 25 miles on a front of only about 70 miles was gained by the Allies; in front of Ypres where some of the heaviest and most continuous fighting took place the lateral movement was less than 10 miles. The maximum depth of the fighting zone, taking into account the German 1918 offensive, the deepest they managed to penetrate, and the final allied line at the Armistice, virtually the German frontier from where they started the invasion of France and Belgium, was only about 80 miles in a couple of places. Thus the fighting was intense over a small area of countryside, which as a result was devastated and even the terrain itself in some places bore little resemblance to its original form; virtually all the villages and woods in the area were totally destroyed.

And now it was all over and peace had to be achieved and then maintained, because at this stage it must not be forgotten that there was only an Armistice which had to be renewed every three months. But before the activities of the peace the events of 1918 in the other theatres of war which led up to the final ceasefire in these theatres must be narrated.

Italy, 1918

During 1917 the only British participation in Italy had been by some Heavy Artillery brigades, no Infantry divisions being able to be spared from France. The Italians themselves had suffered the catastrophe of Caporetto and had retreated to the River Piave. The year 1918 opened quietly. Although the Austrians planned a new offensive they were having problems with their Slav troops who were becoming increasingly rebellious; but at the same time the German offensive in France had still made it difficult for any of the allied troops to be sent to Italy.

The Austrian offensive did, however, open on 15 June along the line of the Piave, the objective being the Venetian plain, with a gas bombardment which had little effect as the allied troops all now had efficient respirators. The small British force now in Italy, just two divisions, held a strong pivot position in the mountains on the left wing of the front near Asiago; the Austrians had underestimated the British strength and their assault was repulsed with heavy losses after some fierce fighting. All along this part of the front the attack was held, although in some places some ground had to be given up.

On the allied right flank the attack had more success, crossing the low-level Piave, capturing many guns and threatening Treviso and Venice; a counterattack was successful except near the coast. But it then started raining and the river rose rapidly; in addition many trees, which were brought down from the mountains on the flood, destroyed the bridges which were the main enemy supply routes and trapped his army against the river. Then the rain stopped, the river dropped again, the Austrians escaped across the river and the Italians were able to counterattack again. The Honour **Piave** was awarded to twenty-two British Infantry regiments.

During the rest of the summer Austrian domestic problems increased; they would have liked to sue for peace but the Allies were not interested in a separate peace with them. Because of the lack of action on the Italian front the British force was ordered to be reduced in size in September in order to strengthen the army in France; but this reduction never took place because of a new and rapid concentration of allied forces on the Piave for the delayed offensive. On 24 September the attacks began, the British having to cross the river, which was very wide on their part of the front, and having first to capture an island in the river with the aid of Italian manned boats. The next phase, which involved wading the river by a human chain and storming the Austrian positions on the far bank, was also successfully achieved and the main assault opened. Throughout the front the Allies advanced and when the 48th Division entered Vezzena it became the first British division on enemy territory; the pursuit continued, hundreds of thousands of prisoners being taken, and on 4 November an armistice was signed.

The final battle was recognised by the Honour **Vittorio Veneto** which was gained by the Northamptonshire Yeomanry and twenty-one Infantry regiments including the Honourable Artillery Company. A Campaign Honour was also awarded, **Italy 1917–18**, and this was gained by three Yeomanry regiments and thirty-five Infantry regiments, which included two Yeomanry and thirteen Infantry regiments which had not been awarded either of the individual Battle Honours.

Macedonia, 1918

At the beginning of 1918 the troops at Salonika were preparing for the last major offensive which was to end the war in the Balkans. The Greek Army had been reorganised and now joined the Allies as a formidable fighting force. The offensive began in July, but the British contingent did not take any significant part until the beginning of September, and then attacked a number of fortified hills and captured them; one of these was *Roche Noir*, which was claimed as an Honour without success by the Gloucestershire Regiment (28th Foot). Ten days later, in another local operation, *P Ridge* was captured after heavy fighting, another Honour claimed, without recognition, by the Cheshire Regiment (22nd Foot).

The culminating assault began along the whole front on 15 September with a series of violent battles. The British part of the line was still astride the Lake Doiran area. In spite of desperate fighting by the Bulgars and Austrians the Allies advanced rapidly in the extremely rugged and mountainous country, and within a few days a gap had been opened in the Bulgarian line and they were in full retreat. The British Cavalry entered Kosturino and Strumitsa and the Allies had won an overwhelming victory; the Bulgarians sued for an armistice.

The Battle Honour, **Doiran 1918**, was awarded to one Yeomanry regiment, the Lothian and Border Horse, and twenty-two Infantry regiments, and unsuccessfully applied for by two additional Infantry regiments. A campaign Honour, **Macedonia 1915–18**, was also awarded and gained by ten Yeomanry regiments and fifty-nine British and four Indian Infantry regiments.

Palestine, 1918

After the capture of Jerusalem it was believed that one more major defeat in Palestine would discourage the Turks to such an extent that they would rebel against their German masters; but it is doubtful if this belief was fully thought out or correct at that time, certainly after the German successes in France in the spring. Based on this policy, therefore, an offensive was planned with Damascus and Aleppo as the final objective, but this had to be delayed for several months because of the reduction of Allenby's force by divisions being sent to France from March onwards.

Nevertheless a more limited offensive was launched in February towards Jericho and the Jordan valley. Despite the rough and mountainous terrain an advance was made against determined resistance during heavy rainstorms; two rocky hills, El Muntar and Jebel Ektief, fell, the line approaching the cliffs overlooking Jericho, and meanwhile the Anzacs mounted troops were making an encircling movement up the Jordan valley to take the Turks in the rear. There were checks and counterattacks, but all were brushed aside and on the night of 20 February the Turks evacuated Jericho, which the Australians entered the following morning, going on to establish themselves on the banks of the Jordan. The capture of the town was a strategic success for the future, and the Honour **Jericho** was awarded to seven Yeomanry, four Australian Cavalry and nine New Zealand Mounted rifle regiments, and to seventeen British Infantry regiments.

Next the high ground covering the Jordan approaches had to be taken. The main objective was the dominating height of Tell 'Asur, which the Turks had entrenched and defended with massed machine guns. After heavy fighting the mountain was captured and defended against all counterattacks. The advance continued astride the Jerusalem–Shechem road and the fighting was intense; but the objectives were taken and the way was now open for an advance across the Jordan. The Honour **Tell 'Asur** was gained by eighteen Yeomanry regiments, by five South African batteries, and by thirty-six British, one Indian and one Gurkha Infantry regiment.

Shortly after the capture of Tell 'Asur a raid was made across the Jordan; it was directed at Amman, the purpose being to disrupt the Hejaz railway in conjunction with Arab attacks. The attack met with surprisingly strong resistance in crossing the river, because the Turks had moved in a large concentration of troops to curb the Arab raids on the railway. After four days marching in hard country and worse weather conditions Es Salt was entered and the railway was reached at several points, damage being caused to it. But in spite of everything the British could do Amman itself remained in enemy hands, and with enemy reinforcements pouring in the raid was abandoned. But the raid had at least succeeded in maintaining the Arab position for harassing the Turks in the east and on the railway, and a second attack was made on Es Salt at the end of April. Again it was repulsed by the Turks with German assistance, the British troops were almost surrounded and had to beat a hasty retreat across the Jordan.

Three Battle Honours were awarded for these actions. **Jordan** was awarded to twelve British Infantry regiments. **Jordan (Es Salt)**, covering both actions, was awarded to fifteen Australian Mounted regiments, and **Jordan (Amman)**, another exclusively Australasian Honour, was awarded to nine Australian and nine New Zealand Cavalry and Mounted rifle regiments.

For the next four and a half months Allenby could only attempt local actions since the withdrawal of a large part of his force inhibited any more positive advances, and the replacements, Indian troops largely from Mesopotamia, had to be trained for their role in the new conditions. A strong Turkish attack was mounted in July but it was routed by encircling movements by Australian and Indian cavalry. The Turkish troops were clearly becoming demoralised, living under frightful conditions and ravaged by disease; by September they were in a poor condition to maintain their defence against British forces which, in spite of their disappointments early in the year, were now rested, reorganised and ready to finish off the battle for Palestine.

Allenby's front now ran roughly in a north-west to south-east direction; on the coast his left wing was on the plain of Sharon which led, through the Musmus Pass, into the plain of Esdraelon, whilst the right wing was more or less where it had been all the year, on the Jordan north of Jericho. The plan now put into operation had as its main objective the total defeat of the Turkish Army, and to this end the very complex but masterful plan for the assault was based on two attacks directed at Megiddo and Nablus.

Elaborate deception manoeuvres were employed to indicate that the main attack would take place in the Jordan valley; a vast camp of empty tents was established and all movement was made at night under cover of gunfire to cover any noise.

The attack began on 19 September after a short but intense bombardment, and the Turks were completely surprised. The Turkish line was broken and the Cavalry advanced rapidly, cutting off large bodies of the enemy, and it was soon clear that a sweeping victory was in the making. Although there was heavy fighting here and there, Turkish resistance had almost come to an end with their armies over-run and in full retreat. Bombing attacks from the air created complete chaos among the fleeing Turks and their communications were destroyed.

The biblical and historical battle of Armageddon, identified with Megiddo, was being fought all over again. By 25 September the battle was over, with the British troops having occupied Haifa and Acre and reached the Sea of Gallilee; Palestine was now captured.

Three Battle Honours, all for the same dates, were awarded to cover the different areas and phases of the battle, most regiments gaining at least two of them. **Megiddo**, the mini-campaign Honour, was awarded to seven British Yeomanry, ten Indian, fifteen Australian and nine New Zealand Cavalry or Mounted rifle regiments, to five South African Artillery batteries, to the three Indian Engineer regiments, and to twenty-seven British, twenty-seven Indian, four Gurkha and one South African Infantry regiments. **Sharon** was gained by six Yeomanry, ten Indian and six Australian Cavalry regiments, by five South African batteries and the three Indian Engineer regiments, and by twenty-one British, twenty-four Indian and four Gurkha Infantry regiments. **Nablus** was awarded to one Yeomanry, nine Australian and nine New Zealand Mounted regiments, to the Bombay Sappers and Miners, and to six British, thirteen Indian and one South African Infantry regiments. The Duke of Lancaster's Yeomanry applied unsuccessfully for all three Honours.

The advance now switched eastwards. Amman was captured and on 1 October Damascus was entered. During October the advance continued through Syria to Aleppo; there was very slight opposition and no Honour was awarded or merited, although the Duke of Lancaster's Yeomanry claimed one, *Syria*. The campaign in Palestine was over and the Turks had suffered an unparalleled disaster. Out of an army of nearly 3 million less than half a million remained; probably half had deserted but the remainder of the losses, less prisoners, were represented by those that were killed or died of disease.

The Campaign Honour, **Palestine 1917–18**, was awarded to thirty-four Yeomanry, ten Indian and twenty-two Australian Cavalry, and nine New Zealand Mounted rifle regiments, to five South African Artillery battieres, to the Madras, Bengal and Bombay Engineers, and to fifty-three British, twenty-nine Indian, four Gurkha and one South African Infantry regiments, and to the West India Regiment. Inevitably it was unsuccessfully claimed by the Duke of Lancaster's Yeomanry.

Mesopotamia, 1918

After capturing Baghdad and then consolidating the hold on the area beyond it at the end of 1917, the British did not immediately press their attacks as the Turks were no longer a menace, but had to maintain their strength on this front which reduced their effort in Palestine and elsewhere. A patrol advance in March caused the Turkish forces to withdraw towards the village of Khan Baghdadi; being exhausted by the difficult retreat they halted at the village where they suffered heavy casualties from air attack.

With some delay in following up, the British and Indian troops attacked on 26 March, the Cavalry cutting off further retreat after a long and arduous cross-country encircling movement, which the Turks had assumed to be impossible because of the nature of the terrain. More than 5,000 prisoners were taken and the Turkish remnants fled towards Aleppo. **Khan Baghdadi** was awarded as an Honour to one British and three Indian Cavalry regiments, to the Bengal Engineers, and to three British and twelve Indian Infantry regiments.

The advance continued, without any action which merited an Honour or even the claim of one, throughout the summer and early autumn. A part of the force was sent to Palestine to replace troops withdrawn to France, but this was of little consequence as most of Mesopotamia had now been won and little was required but a holding position to prevent any Turkish counter move, unlikely as this appeared to be in the circumstances, or a withdrawal of forces.

The Germans, however, were not finished yet in this part of the world and opened operations on the northern frontier of Persia and Afghanistan around Merv, and on the Caspian Sea around Baku. The object was to gain support for the Turks from the Muslim inhabitants of these areas, and for the force, supported by Bolshevists, to attack towards the Khyber Pass and into India. A small British/Indian force was raised and set out for Baku to forestall this move; the terrain was difficult and progress, which could not be rapid anyway, was further delayed by the need to help local inhabitants who were starving after Turks and Cossacks had lived off the land and devastated it.

After enormous difficulties the little force reached Baku in August where, supported by some supposedly loyal Russians and Armenians, they had to withstand a number of Turkish attacks. The Armenians turned out to be treacherous and the British were left exposed and only maintained this position by extreme gallantry and endurance; but the situation was now hopeless and they had to withdraw from the town, nevertheless foiling the German intentions. The Honour **Baku**, little known but well merited, was awarded to three British regiments, the Royal Warwickshire, Worcestershire and North Staffordshire Regiments (6th, 29th and 64th Foot). The actions around **Merv** gained this Honour for two Indian regiments.

In October the final battle was fought in Mesopotamia near the ruins of the ancient Assyrian city of Asshur. The Turkish forward position in the mountains was naturally very strong, and the British being short of transport there was no alternative to an attack along the Tigris. A frontal assault would have been suicidal and a turning movement was tried, which because of Turkish observation over the area could achieve little surprise. Strong raids misled the enemy as to the direction of attack and caused him to concentrate in the wrong area, which allowed the encircling movement to take place as planned. The Turks abandoned their stronghold in the night and the main attack could now take place.

The fighting was hard and the terrain appalling, steep mountains and deep gorges with only goat tracks for movement and communications, but the attacking troops pressed on. A Cavalry detachment discovered a shallow part of the river through which horses could just walk, which gave it access to the enemy's rear, and made full use of the advantage. With the Infantry and Cavalry attacks the Turks could not move forward or back and fought desperately, but their resistance could not last and on 30 October they surrendered.

The four-year campaign was at last over, with the British victorious in the part of the world in which Alexander the Great and the Romans under Julian and been overcome. The Honour from the last battle, **Sharquat**, was awarded to two British and five Indian Cavalry regiments, to the Bengal Engineers and to four British and eight Indian Infantry regiments. It is also celebrated by 'W' Battery Royal Horse Artillery, but not as an Honour Title. The Campaign Honour **Mesopotamia 1914–18** was awarded to three British and thirteen Indian Cavalry regiments, to all four Indian Engineer regiments and to thirty British, fifty Indian and ten Gurkha Infantry regiments. Three other Indian Infantry regiments participated in the campaign but were not awarded the Honour.

The troops which served in Persia, including the expedition to Merv, were awarded the Honour **Persia 1916–19**. It was gained by one British and two Indian Cavalry regiments, by the four Indian Engineer regiments, and by five British, thirteen Indian and two Gurkha Infantry regiments.

India and East Africa, 1918

There is little to add to the previous narrative about these campaigns. In India there was some fighting during an expedition to Baluchistan against the Marri and Khetran tribes, and an Honour **Baluchistan 1918** was awarded to one Indian Cavalry regiment, the Bengal and Bombay Engineers, one British, one Indian and two Gurkha Infantry regiments and the Cyclist Corps.

In East Africa there was virtually no fighting beyond mopping-up operations in Nyassa, Mozambique and Rhodesia after the action at Nyangao, although the final German surrender did not occur until 25 November. The campaign Honour **East Africa 1914–18** was gained by one Indian and five South African Cavalry regiments, by six South African Artillery batteries, by the Madras and Bombay Engineers, by two British, twelve Indian and ten South African Infantry regiments, and by the West India Regiment, the King's African Rifles, the Nigeria, Gold Coast, Gambia and Northern Rhodesia Regiments and the Nyassaland Rifles.

Russia, 1918-19

During the war the Allies had provided vast quantities of stores, mainly munitions, for Russia, and much of these had been accumulated in the Murmansk and Archangel areas in the northernmost part of that country. With the Russian collapse the Germans were naturally keen to get their hands on this material, and had already arranged with the Bolshevist provisional government for the Kola peninsular, on which Murmansk lies, to be included in Finland, which had virtually become a vassal state of Germany with the election of Prince Frederick of Hesse as King. The Bolshevist government had repudiated any debt for these stores and the Allies therefore believed that they had a right to regain their property.

Early in 1918 a British naval force landed at Murmansk and in the late summer an international force, including British troops, landed there as well and reached agreement with the local soviet to defend and maintain the territory. The agreement was soon abrogated by the Bolshevists and as a result the British force moved into the White Sea and occupied Archangel; they then attacked and defeated the main Soviet forces in the area and also occupied Onega which maintained the communications between Murmansk and Archangel. Now thousands of Russians joined the Allies to fight against the Bolsheviks.

The winter passed fairly quietly, although heavy Bolshevist attacks on Shenkursk, nearly 200 miles south of Archangel, and Tarasovo resulted in these towns being abandoned. By the summer of 1919 most of the stores had been removed and it was decided that the local Russian forces should be equipped with the remainder and trained, to allow the withdrawal of the allied presence, by now almost entirely British. The withdrawal could only be undertaken under cover of an offensive and this was undertaken by the Russians with some British support in the Troitsa area late in August; the Bolshevists were defeated at Yemtsa and the evacuation was completed without further incident. The evacuation of the base at Murmansk then began and was completed by October.

Several Honours were awarded. **Troitsa** was gained by the Royal Fusiliers (7th Foot), **Archangel 1918-19** was gained by eight regiments and **Murman 1918-19** was awarded to four regiments, all Infantry.

On the outbreak of war a body of Czechs had joined the Russian Army and fought with it; when Russia signed the Treaty of Brest Litovsk the Czech army, with Russian agreement, asked to be transported to the Western Front so that they could continue fighting, and the simplest, though hardly the most direct, route for them was across Siberia. With the Bolshevist rise to power this agreement was rescinded, and the Czechs declined to give up their arms, took possession of stations along the Trans Siberian Railway and arrived at Vladivostok, where they also took control. In July it was decided to send an allied expedition to their support and this, including two British battalions, marched along the railway westwards.

The only action of any note took place at **Dukhovskaya** and this Honour was awarded to the Middlesex Regiment (57th Foot). A campaign Honour, **Siberia 1918-19**, covering the period until the withdrawal in June 1919, was awarded to the Middlesex Regiment and to the Royal Hampshire Regiment (37th Foot).

Conclusion

So the Great War came to an end with the Allies victorious all over the world. It had been called the 'war to end war', but the idea of having been defeated in battle never really entered the minds of the senior German commanders, by whom the Armistice was regarded as only a break in hostilities, the war over being just the first round in the campaign to achieve their ideal, the German domination of Europe.

The casualties had been on a scale never before experienced or ever imagined, and were to affect every aspect of life in the participant countries for decades to come. On the Western Front alone those of Britain, France and Germany, killed, wounded and prisoners, were of the order of 10 million. But perhaps the most significant event for the future was the overthrow of Imperial Tsarist rule in Russia and the rise of Bolshevism.

Now peace had come after the holocaust, although this was a relative term as fighting and civil wars continued in Europe and elsewhere for a number of years. The British involvement in these events between the great wars of the first half of the twentieth century leads us to the next chapter.

Above: 'The Canadians at Ypres 1915.' Men of Princess Patricia's Canadian Light Infantry defending a trench against charging German infantry. Print taken from painting by W. B. Wollen. *NAM*

Left: The Menin Gate, Ypres. *IWM*

16 Between the Wars, 1919-39

After the victories and defeats, the hopes and disappointments, the excitement and boredom, and the almost continual action all over the world during the Great War, it is inevitable that what followed must be an anticlimax, although a welcome one. During the next 20 years the British and Indian Armies were often in action but the wars were of the 'brush fire' variety. Nevertheless they provided plenty of opportunity for developing new organisations and equipment, and the tactics to go with them, which was to prove so valuable in the next great contest of strength.

Right at the end of the war in Europe, when it was clear that all was lost, Soviet style revolution was brewing in Germany. The Kaiser, who had engineered the war for German aggrandisement and had gradually during its progress become little more than a puppet of his Prussian General Staff, fled to the Netherlands having lost the faith of his people.

Under the terms of the Armistice the Allies established bridgeheads across the Rhine, the British at Cologne, but no further occupation of Germany was allowed. The advance into the bridgehead areas was accomplished slowly, partly to allow the Germans to remove their armies into Germany to avoid clashes with the allied armies, and partly because many of the communications had been destroyed deliberately in the last few days of the war and had to be repaired before the movement of troops could take place.

The Peace Conference in Paris, at Versailles, began in January 1919 and lasted a year. Not that all that time was taken up in settling the Peace Treaty with Germany, as is often thought, as this was in fact signed in June 1919; but the rest of the defeated Central Powers, Austria, Hungary, Bulgaria and Turkey, also had to be dealt with. By the terms of the Treaty Germany lost Alsace and Lorraine to France, the Saar and Danzig to international control, and other areas to Belgium, Denmark, Lithuania and Poland; and thereby were sown some of the seeds which matured 20 years later, as the ethnic minorities so returned within the boundaries of their native lands contained a fair number of Germans as well who now became, in their turn, ethnic minorities.

The German colonies were also distributed to the Allies, euphemistically as Mandates or Protectorates. Their Navy and Air Force were abolished and the cost of the war, estimated at the then astronomical figure of £20 billion, although it seems now quite a normal sum, was made a German liability. Germany's allies were similarly penalised, and apart from the division of the Austro-Hungarian Empire into its integral parts, two new countries, Yugoslavia and Czechoslovakia, emerged. Finland and the three Baltic states of Estonia, Lithuania and Latvia became independent of Russia. The map of Europe had been redrawn, and although some problems were removed a lot of new ones were created.

Outside Europe the Turkish Empire was also dismembered. Palestine eventually became the national homeland of the Jews under British Mandate as a result of the Balfour Declaration of 1917, Syria and the Lebanon came under French mandate, and kingdoms were created out of Mesopotamia and Arabia, and Hashemite Princes installed as the Kings of Iraq, Transjordan and Saudi Arabia. Egypt became independent although Britain retained treaty rights for military bases to protect the Suez Canal, and the Sudan became a British–Egyptian condominium. As in Europe new problems were to grow out of the solutions of the old.

In Britain the main problem was the employment of the demobilised troops, thousands of whom had known no other employment than military service and were now in their early twenties and untrained; the problem had previously existed after the Napoleonic Wars, when emigration and colonisation had proved a solution which was now only available to a much lesser extent. Within the Army the Royal Corps of Signals was formed out of the Royal Engineers in 1922, the Tank Corps became 'Royal' in 1923, and the Territorial Force became the Territorial Army on the basis of being a part-time extension of the Regular forces rather than purely a home defence force.

As so often had happened in the past after a long war, the government was all for cutting costs as rapidly as possible and the Army, praised in war and shunned in peace, suffered as usual. Under what was known as the 'Geddes Axe', from the Minister for War, the Cavalry was reduced by eight line regiments by amalgamation, and the Infantry regiments were reduced to two battalions each, apart from the disbandment of five Irish regiments for quite different reasons. The Cavalry suffered most because of the total disappearance of two regiments, the 6th Dragoon Guards and the 6th Dragoons, and the loss of independence of the others.

Some reorganisation also took place in the Indian Army, inevitably based on a reduction of cost of its maintenance, of all arms by amalgamations and disbandments. A rationalisation had taken place in 1902 when all the separate

Presidency armies were brought into a single numerical system rather like the old British system of numbered regiments of Foot. Now large ethnic regiments were formed, each of six battalions, numbered from 1 to 5 and 10, the regiments themselves being numbered from 1 to 20 with a territorial title. The Gurkhas had been separated in 1901 but now became part of the British Army rather than the Indian.

As a result of the Locarno Pact, under which Britain, France, Italy, Belgium and Germany mutually guaranteed the Belgian and French frontiers with Germany fixed at Versailles, British troops left Cologne at the beginning of 1926, although some of them moved to Wiesbaden where they remained until the end of 1929.

The Third Afghan War

In 1919 the Amir of Afghanistan, who had been friendly to the British during the war, was murdered and succeeded by his third son, who it was hoped would follow suit. But the new Amir had made rash promises to the Afghans in order to gain the throne, including the annexation of Karachi, and to extricate himself from an impossible situation he declared a Holy War and attacked the Indian frontier at several points.

There was no shortage of troops in India and a force immediately advanced into the Khyber Pass, defeating the Afghan irregulars there, and the revolt began to evaporate. The Amir sued for peace and this was signed after just six months of hostilities. The Honour **Afghanistan 1919** was awarded to one British and nineteen Indian Cavalry regiments, to the Madras, Bengal, Bombay and Burma Engineer regiments, to twelve British, fifty Indian and eleven Gurkha Infantry regiments, and to the British Cyclist Corps. Two other British and nine Indian regiments took part but were not Honoured; a massive force against comparatively few irregular troops.

Mesopotamia

The Arab tribes of Mesopotamia, or Iraq as it had become, had been used to a large degree of independence under the lax Turkish rule before the war, but now a mandate had been granted to the British and they could see themselves being 'governed' to an extent that they did not welcome. They had been able to salvage quantities of arms and ammunition of various sorts from the wartime battlefields and were now a formidable power.

In 1919, and again in 1920, some of the tribes revolted, taking a town near Mosul and killing an armoured car detachment stationed there. The town was recovered a few days later and a mobile striking force prepared, very small in spite of the large number of troops in the country because of the large numbers needed to guard strategic points and Turkish prisoners and to look after a mass of refugees. Several other towns were attacked or besieged, some were regained and some evacuated, and ambushes caused a significant number of casualties.

Luckily not all the tribes had risen in revolt and gradually the situation was brought under control; reinforcements had arrived, and in early 1921 the tribes were de-

cisively beaten and the rebellion crushed. Two Honours were awarded, **Haifa-Aleppo 1919** and **Iraq 1920**, but each only to one regiment of the Indian Army, although a large number of British and Indian regiments were involved; why this should have been is not clear. It was claimed unsuccessfully by The Royal Ulster Rifles (83rd Foot); a separate Honour, *Mesopotamia 1920-21*, was applied for, also without success, by The East Yorkshire Regiment (15th Foot).

Ireland

While small wars continued around the world, not always involving British troops, a much more vicious affair was going on much nearer home in Ireland. Since the Easter 1916 rising nationalist extremists had gained a lot of power, and in 1919 they declared Ireland a republic and raised the Irish Republican Army from the most desperate and fanatical elements that they could find.

British law virtually ceased to exist and those who tried to abide by it were terrorized; soldiers were murdered, although the Irish called these deeds legitimate acts of war. An attempt to counter the IRA by a British auxiliary force, known as the Black and Tans and made up of demobilised and unemployed officers and men, made the situation worse as the auxiliaries were as ready to commit murder and terrorism as were the Irish.

The British Army in Ireland was in difficulties as it could not aid a civil power which no longer existed. The opposition at Westminster was strongly against any punitive measures being taken, and the Americans, to whom the Irish vote was important in an election year, exerted pressure against any action, using the enormous British war debt as their weapon. Faced with internal and foreign opposition there was little left to the government but abject surrender; a treaty was signed giving Ireland, except for the six mainly Protestant counties of Ulster, independence and the garrison was quickly withdrawn. A side effect that has been mentioned many times before, particularly in relation to the Presidency regiments in India, was the disbandment of five regular Irish regiments of the British Army, and the obliteration from the list of Battle Honours on the Colours of these regiments of the large number of Honours unique to them through their service in India.

India

Ever since the first involvement of the British in India by the East India Company over 300 years before, trouble had never been far below the surface, and the inter-war years proved no exception, although the fighting was mostly limited to the North West Frontier.

In 1919 a notorious incident occurred due to the unrest and rioting caused by a civil disobedience campaign led by Gandhi and his Congress Party. Amritsar, the Holy City of the Sikhs, was one area much involved, and after a number of murders of British civilians the garrison was reinforced under the command of Brigadier Dyer. The Riot Act was invoked, but in spite of this a large crowd assembled one day in April and failed to disperse when ordered to do so, partly because of the congestion in the narrow streets surrounding the assembly area, and the situation looked very dangerous. Fire was opened without a proper preliminary warning and over 400 members of the crowd were killed. Dyer was severely criticised, but as a result the rules for Aid to the Civil Power were overhauled.

In 1921 the strongly Muslim Moplahs, who inhabited an area on the Malabar coast, were being incited by Congress Party agitators to revolt against the government. Some civilians and troops were murdered and strong reinforcements were sent in, which by the use of punitive columns eventually restored the situation. No Honour was awarded to the three British, three Indian and two Gurkha regiments involved, but the Dorsetshire Regiment (39th Foot) claimed one as *Malabar*.

Waziristan, for the umpteenth time over the past 75 years, became a trouble area again even before the 3rd Afghan War was fought. In spite of strong punitive expeditions against the Mahsuds and Wazirs the fighting continued for the next two years, and it was finally decided to establish permanently garrisoned fortified posts, and a proper camp was established at Razmak in 1923. It was at this camp that the 'thunderboxes' in the latrine lines were charged with fixed bayonets by the guard every morning in case there were tribesmen hiding underneath who had slipped into the camp during the night—which goes to show that life on the Frontier was not very peaceful! A large number of troops were used over the period, six British, forty-four Indian and nine Gurkha regiments. The Queen's Royal Regiment (2nd Foot) applied unsuccessfully for an Honour, *Waziristan 1921*.

During the 1930s the North West Frontier was the scene of almost continuous minor fighting, which erupted periodically into more serious outbreaks. In 1930 agitators caused riots in Peshawar which spread along the frontier among the Pathans, the Mohmands and the Afridis in Tirah; operations to quell the uprisings continued from June to September, when the continuing pressure created dissensions among the different factions in the warring tribes, which was the usual end to periods of hostilities on the frontier. An Honour was awarded, **North West Frontier 1930**, but only to the 5th Gurkha Rifles, in spite of the participation of one British and three Indian Cavalry regiments, and eight British and a large number of Indian and Gurkha Infantry.

Two other Campaign Honours were awarded for later serious outbreaks of trouble. **North West Frontier 1936–37** was again gained by the 5th Gurkhas, and **North West Frontier 1937–40** by the same Gurkha regiment and by the Indian 13th Lancers. Once more many other regiments actually participated; nine British Infantry regiments were involved each time, although not all the same ones in each case, and a large number of Indian Cavalry and Infantry regiments.

Another episode of importance between the wars occurred further east, in Burma in 1930. At this time Burma was still politically a part of India and moves by the British government to separate it were opposed by Indian agitators, who thought it might cause unemployment among Indian labourers who frequently crossed the border to find work. It had always been an unruly area and it was not

the first time that British and Indian troops had been sent there to put down rebellions. Only a small garrison was stationed there and when the revolt broke reinforcements were sent in from India, all Indian regiments. It was a difficult country to fight in, as was to be proved only a few years later against a more determined and organised enemy, but gradually the rebellious tribes were driven into limited jungle areas where they could obtain few arms and little food. By the end of 1931 the worst was over and by early the following year peace was again restored. No Honour was awarded for what was in any case largely a police action, although there were spasmodic sharp actions, but seven Indian regiments participated.

Palestine, 1936–9

Since the McMahon Letters of 1915 proposing a great Arab State, the Balfour Declaration of 1917 viewing 'with favour the idea ... of a national home for Jewish people in Palestine' and the end of the Great War which freed the Arab people from Turkish bondage, events had been few in the Middle East. Jewish immigration had continued, but the objectives of Zionism—to establish a Jewish state—had largely been hidden, except perhaps from the drafters of the British Mandate for Palestine in the League of Nations, who had favoured and raised the hopes of the tiny minority of Jews in its clauses which excluded Arab rights in the land in which they had lived for centuries.

But in 1933 Jewish immigration increased dramatically as the result of Nazi persecution and by 1936 even the legal immigration figures caused consternation to the Arabs. The Arabs still had a large majority, but the Jews would not accept any democratic institutions while they were still a minority, and had been buying up land, much from absentee landlords, and evicting the Arab villagers who lived there.

Terrorism grew and turned into sporadic murder and retaliation. The Arabs, led by the Grand Mufti of Jerusalem, called a general strike and asked for a halt to immigration and land sales. The British government ignored them and added injury to insult by increasing immigration quotas. Full-scale revolt broke out and British troops were brought in to keep the peace, which at least deterred surrounding Arab states from taking part.

Attempts by a Royal Commission to find an acceptable solution failed, basically because the Arabs would not accept any partition of their land. More disorders followed, and after the Munich crisis more British troops were sent out. Their task against guerillas operating in their own country with good intelligence would have been difficult enough without the authorities, incredibly, requiring the troops to go back to barracks every night and allowing any gangs that they might have surrounded by five o'clock to escape in peace!

The British government at last woke up to the fact that a serious situation existed, limited immigration again and made it clear that they had never intended a Jewish state to be set up in Palestine. Although this did not satisfy either side the Second World War started and grievances were shelved—for the time being.

No Battle Honours were awarded for this campaign;

there were no real battles, although conditions were not very pleasant, and this attitude on Honours was to prevail, apart from the war, for the next forty years. Perhaps it will never again change. A large number of regiments participated over the three-year period.

Reorganisation

By 1935 it was becoming clear that, even if another European war could be avoided, there was a pressing need to reorganise the structure of the army which had existed with few changes since 1908, and to recognise officially many of the changes which had been tried out unofficially.

It was appreciated that greater mobility and firepower was the key, and the main change was mechanisation and the phasing-out of horsed Cavalry, regiments being equipped with either armoured cars or tanks. Infantry brigades were reorganised to include a support battalion, which contained machine guns, anti-tank guns and a reconnaissance company. To this end thirteen regiments and two battalions of Guards were turned into machine gun regiments. The main effect of this was for the first time to have two different types of Infantry regiments in the army, which could make interchange and reinforcement of each type difficult in an emergency.

The Situation in Europe

Apart from the territorial changes, which in fact did little damage to Germany as a nation, and the economic sanctions, which were in any case an impossible condition of the Peace, the Allies imposed on Germany a democratic constitution, with the government established at Weimar. This requirement was largely made at the instigation of the Americans, who, having arrived very late in the theatre of war when the heaviest fighting had already taken place, nevertheless took great credit on themselves for the victory and sought to impose their terms on the peace, and were supported by Lloyd George. The latter was not particularly pro-monarchic and the former were strongly anti-monarchic. This left a power vacuum in Germany, whose people by their very nature needed a strong figurehead to look up to and in any case regarded this as yet another act of vengeance by the victors.

Instead of a constitutional sovereign, who could have been found without much difficulty, to satisfy their German militaristic and feudal outlook, Hindenburg was venerated for a time but, ageing, left the way open for a more unscrupulous leader. Political and economic problems had in 1923 led to a collapse of the Mark and a high level of inflation, incredible even in these days when inflation is the norm, through the indiscriminate printing of paper money; at one time the Mark reached 43,000,000 to the pound sterling on the foreign exchange.

France was in an equally difficult political situation, and having failed to persuade the Peace Conference to place the Franco-German frontier on the Rhine, marched into the Ruhr. In spite of the victory France still feared Germany and her policy during the next twenty years was to do anything to prevent or pre-empt another German attack. The League of Nations had been created to provide a forum in which all nations could join to try to prevent future hostilities by discussion and negotiation rather than aggression; although it was the brainchild of President Wilson of the USA, his own country immediately executed an act of infanticide by refusing to join it herself and not allowing Germany to do so, thus destroying its purpose before it had even had time to become established. Thus it never achieved its aim.

Although she had been disarmed, Germany was surprisingly allowed to retain an army of 100,000 men; conscription and a staff corps were however forbidden. This limited army of course could, and in fact did, form the cadre for a much larger army once the peace treaty had been abrogated, and allowed the military tradition to be maintained. But in spite of the military restrictions Germany did manage to make preparations towards a future renewal of the conflict; members of youth organisations were trained on military lines, civil airports were developed in such a way that they could be quickly converted to military use, the coastal defences in Heligoland and Kiel were not dismantled as they were supposed to have been and some U Boats were being built covertly and illicitly. In addition factories were being built, largely with funds provided for that purpose by the United States and Britain, which contained machinery, not the purpose of the funds, which could easily and quickly be converted to the manufacture of weapons and munitions. All of which indicated that the Allies were not supervising the Peace Treaty very assiduously.

In 1925 Hindenburg was elected Chancellor of an impoverished Germany. In 1929 Ramsay MacDonald became British Prime Minister, and one of the aims of the Labour government which he headed, supported by the Liberals, was for total, if possible but failing that unilateral, disarmament, although Churchill had proposed a dictum that the redress of the grievance of the vanquished should precede the disarmament of the victors. Also in 1929 came the crash on the New York Stock Exchange, the consequences of which were felt world-wide and trebled unemployment in Britain.

While these events were occupying the minds of the allied politicians, an unemployed house-painter, who had suffered from chlorine gas poisoning in 1918 on the Western Front and who had come to the conclusion during the early 1920s that the defeat of Germany had been largely caused by Jewish businessmen and profiteers in league with the Bolsheviks, associated with extremist nationalist groups in Germany and Austria. Supported by a group of like-minded men who abhorred the shame of defeat, Adolf Hitler eventually emerged as a national figure and the leader of the National Socialist or Nazi party. By vigorous electioneering his party gradually gained seats in the Reichstag, reaching 230 by 1932; his following in the country increased and he eventually gained the grudging support of the military chiefs.

In January 1933 Hitler succeeded Hindenburg as Chancellor of Germany. Any opposition to his policies was dealt with harshly by his secret police. In February 1933 the Reichstag building caught fire; this was undoubtedly arson, and although the true perpetrator will probably never be known, but could well have been organised by the Nazi party, the deed was blamed on the Jews and Communists. Now Hitler really had Germany behind him.

In 1934 Britain and France could, without much difficulty, have called on the League of Nations to control the Nazi party in Germany, which still had only a bare electoral majority and which was still opposed by a sizeable part of the population. But weak governments did nothing, relying on Hitler's word that he had no intention of territorial expansion and wished to have an agreement with Britain to abolish submarines. Italy now allied herself with Germany, or perhaps more accurately Mussolini with Hitler, and, rightly regarding the British and French governments as spiritless and vacillating, broke her agreement with the League of Nations and invaded Abyssinia. Although the League voted by 150 to 1 to take collective measures against Italy and impose sanctions, very little was actually done; certainly no overt action was taken to prevent the invasion or limit it, and although an embargo was put on certain imports the most vital one, oil, was still allowed to flow freely. The lack of honour of the British government and its absolute weakness was exemplified by the fact that the fleet lay at Alexandria, reinforced and ready for action, and did nothing to prevent Italian troopships using the Suez Canal.

To such a low ebb had Great Britain sunk; at the root of it was Stanley Baldwin, the Prime Minister and the man who said that there must be no war, and who, having won the election on an anti-aggression platform, was prepared to keep the peace at any price which kept him in power. It is said that a nation gets the government that it deserves, but what had Britain done to deserve such a collection of ineffective, self-centred, spineless egoists as it now had at its head? The Foreign Secretaries of Britain and France, Hoare and Laval, now went so far as to agree a pact to partition Abyssinia between Italy and the Emperor Haile Selassie, which meant in fact allowing Italy to have complete control. What perfidy!

Since there had been no active resistance to the rearming of Germany, Hitler now decided to make more positive moves and in March 1936 he reoccupied the demilitarised zone of the Rhineland, thus breaking both the Peace Treaty and the Locarno Pact; not that the breaking of treaties worried Hitler, particularly when he knew that the major Powers in Europe would be totally ineffective to do anything about it and the Americans were sheltering behind isolationism and refused to have anything to do with world affairs. The French were naturally worried but the British government persuaded them to take no action, and the Labour and Liberal leaders issued sufficiently misleading statements, even saying that Hitler had been provoked, to allay any martial instincts in the population, which was anyway still in a pacifist mood.

Hitler again said that he had no further territorial ambitions, everyone believed him, and after a short period of waiting to make sure that there would be no action he set about fortifying the Rhineland that he had occupied. His next step was to deny any intention to interfere in Austria, which should have been enough in itself to arouse suspicion; the Chancellor, Dollfuss, had been murdered by Nazi sympathisers two years earlier, and Hitler signed a friendship pact with that country and at the same time drew up secret plans for invading and annexing it.

Meanwhile civil war had broken out in Spain between the communist-influenced government and the right-wing, fascist, military faction led by General Franco; this put Britain in a quandary since she could not overtly support either side, but it gave the Germans and Italians, particularly their air forces, good practice and training by allowing volunteers (sic) to fight in support of Franco. A number of British volunteers, defying governmental neutrality, less valuably joined the International Brigade.

In Britain the most serious event in 1936 was the abdication of King Edward VIII; Baldwin, supported by the Archbishop of Canterbury, handled the abdication crisis with skill, but little honour, because he sensed the view of the majority of the population, just as he had done earlier when, knowing Germany to be rearming, he refused to go to the country on a rearmament platform because he knew that he thereby would lose the election.

Germany's position was being made abundantly clear. She said that she must have what she called *Lebensraum*, living space, for her burgeoning population, and suggested covertly that Britain should allow her a free hand to annex Poland, Danzig, White Russia, the Ukraine and Austria; this proposal was put to private parties, not to the government, and needless to say it was not agreed as there were still some people in authority with integrity, nor was the proposal made public.

In February 1938 the Austrian Chancellor, von Schuschnigg, was summoned by Hitler and ordered to allow members of the Austrian Nazi Party to join the Austrian cabinet; under duress he agreed but refused to allow any further German interference in Austrian affairs and proposed to hold a plebiscite to gauge the feeling of his people. The Germans took this as an affront, mobilised and marched into Austria in March, annexing the country to the German Reich. Although the British government complained, no further action was taken.

At this point Britain signed an agreement with Italy allowing her a free hand in Abyssinia and Spain in exchange for goodwill in central Europe, a rather doubtful exchange at the best of times. The situation in Czechoslovakia was now grave and it became apparent that this would be the target of the next German outrage. In May Hitler started his run-up to the invasion of Czechoslovakia by insisting on a settlement of the Sudeten problem, the Sudetenland having been German territory before it became part of the Austro-Hungarian Empire and was ceded to the Czechs at Versailles; of course he said that it was only this area that interested him, not the whole of the country. Lord Runciman went to Prague to try to resolve the situation with the Czech government and the German ambassador but the negotiations soon broke down as he could not satisfy the Czechs.

Neville Chamberlain, having succeeded Baldwin as British Prime Minister, now took a personal hand and went to Munich to meet Hitler; he was convinced that if he agreed to the session of the Sudetenland and could persuade the Czechs to agree as well, Hitler would not invade Czechoslovakia, and that neither Britain, nor France who had treaty obligations to that country, could do anything practical in any case to help the Czechs. He accepted Hitler's word and his assurances of friendship and having no further territorial claims. Nevertheless the Czechs began to mobilise and the French, partly, and the British Navy were also mobilised. At the end of September 1938 Chamberlain returned to Germany for a further meeting with Hitler; this time they signed a note agreeing that Germany and Britain should never go to war with each other.

Chamberlain thought, naively, that he had won; on his return to England he spoke of 'peace with honour' and 'peace in our time', and waved his copy of the note to the crowds which greeted him. Whether the Czechs agreed with the honourableness of the so-called peace is another matter which did not apparently worry him, perhaps because he believed the remark attributed to him that it was a little country of which nobody had ever heard. The French had in any case left their ally to her fate, and seven months later Germany declared Bohemia and Moravia, the two western provinces of Czechoslovakia, a German protectorate and marched in.

Meanwhile in April 1939, just before the occupation of Czechoslovakia, the Italians invaded Albania as a springboard for action against Greece and Yugoslavia, both of which countries they subsequently attacked. Britain at long last appreciated that action had to be taken and, realising that Poland was probably the next state on Hitler's takeover list, guaranteed to the Poles that she would give them all possible support if Polish independence were threatened.

As the summer of 1939 continued most of Europe was girding itself for a war which had now become virtually inevitable. Conscription was introduced in Britain, opposed by both the Labour and Liberal parties which thus once more failed in their duty to their country by supporting pointless pacificism. The French were already manning outpost positions in front of the great forts of the Maginot Line, and in Britain preparations continued apace.

Since the crisis in 1938, and in view of the threat of air attack, the anti-aircraft defences had been strengthened and a number of Territorial Army Infantry battalions, one or more from almost every regiment, had been converted into AA regiments. Many had been replaced in their original regiments by raising duplicate battalions as reserves following a recruiting drive to which volunteers now flooded in. The key parties for the anti-aircraft and radar sites now started to assemble and reservists were called up; the Navy and the Army were mobilised. As far as possible, given the limited time for preparation since the pacifist role was abandoned, Britain was ready for war.

17 World War 2: Part 1, 1939-41

To a large part of the population of Britain the Second World War is barely classed as history, not only because it occurred well within living memory but because millions of men and women who took part in its events are still alive to tell the tale. To many others of the young, however, it is very much history and those of us who reminisce about it are looked upon as Methuselahs. The books that have been written on the strategy, the tactics, the politics, the aftermath and the personalities are legion; to repeat these in a history of Battle Honours would be an act of supererogation and little therefore needs to be said in the narrative on the conduct of the various campaigns beyond an outline that gives some reason for the actions that occurred and which links together the Honours awarded.

As far as the award of Honours was concerned the same rules applied as for the Great War, which now became known as the First World War, in short WW1; the number of battles and actions named by the Battles Nomenclature Committee was of the same order for both wars, but this time there were fewer inhibitions about granting them to applicants than there had ever been before. The result was that more than twice the number of Honours were awarded than for all the previous wars put together. Until 1914 there had been 235 Honours, from 1914 to 1939 there were a further 190, mostly during the Great War, and from 1939 to 1945 during World War II 929 were awarded. Many of these were unique and this is sufficient indication of the mobility of the forces engaged, the number of small, isolated actions and their enormous geographical spread. Of course, the number of regiments to which each was awarded was very small compared with the Honours awarded during the France and Flanders campaign, with the exception of the Campaign Honours themselves. There was also a more general and comprehensive participation by Commonwealth armies.

The text, therefore, will largely cover the major Honours where a number of regiments were involved, apart from exceptional circumstances, and it will be necessary to consult the Chronology of Battles and Battle Honours (Part III) to obtain the complete details. During this war the Australian and New Zealand regiments were still numbered as Expeditionary Force units and only related later to their parent units for the grant of Honours, but the Canadian and South African regiments fought under their proper titles.

North West Europe, 1939-40

On 1 September Germany attacked Poland, the British guarantee was invoked and an ultimatum was sent to Germany to withdraw, followed by a second ultimatum on 3 September. No satisfactory answer was received and Britain declared war on Germany that day. Now began what was to become known as the 'Phoney War', although it was unexpected. The British Expeditionary Force moved to France, but although it was anticipated that the main German threat would come, as in 1914, through Belgium on the lines of the old Schlieffen Plan, the Belgians wanted to remain neutral if possible and no troops were allowed to cross the Franco-Belgian frontier to take up defensive positions.

Air raids on British towns and installations were expected, in fact a false alarm was sounded virtually at the moment that war was declared, and the German land attack was awaited. But in the west nothing happened. Poland was over-run, the Russians also advancing from the east under the terms of their non-aggression pact with Germany, but the Germans made no attempt to attack France or Belgium, or in fact Britain by air. And 'nothing' continued to happen during that bitterly cold first winter of the war; the most offensive action during that period was the dropping of leaflets on Germany by British aircraft.

More divisions, Territorial Army this time, were sent to France and the Army improved its defences even though it knew that when the attack came it would probably have to leave them and move to new, unprepared positions in Belgium. The oddest things about the eight months of quiet were that no exercises were held to practise the anticipated move and that the communications of the Army were not improved, the inter-Army communications still being via civilian telephone exchanges. But the calm could only be the calm before the storm, and inevitably it had to break.

Norway, 1940

Germany's main supply weaknesses were iron ore and oil, much of the former coming from Norway and Sweden and being shipped through the port of Narvik. Norway being neutral, this was legitimate although the German use of Norwegian territorial waters to transport ore was not. Britain therefore decided to mine the inshore waters and to land a force at Narvik and other ports to seal them off and halt the flow, justified by information that Germany was planning to occupy the Norwegian peninsula.

But although mining had gone ahead the delay in landing the force, a result of French objections, resulted in a *coup de force* by the Germans who occupied Norway on 8 April; but they had to fight their way overland from the south of the country and this still left the possibility open for the occupation of the ports, now entirely legitimately. Small forces were landed at Namsos and Andalsnes with the intention of supporting a major attack on Trondheim which could then be a base for further operations; but the Chiefs of Staff changed their minds about the viability of such an attack due to the risk to the fleet, perhaps with Gallipoli in mind, and the capture of Trondheim was therefore left to the forces already ashore. But these were too small for the task, and after an initial advance were forced to retreat in the face of growing German pressure and bitter snow conditions; after some hard fighting in limited actions Namsos was evacuated on 28 April and Andalsnes three days later.

The policy now reverted to the landing at Narvik, which had also originally been judged too dangerous by the Commander on the spot; the landing took place at the mouth of the fjord on 13 May and the port was captured a fortnight later. But by now other momentous events had occurred in France and all available troops and warships were needed in Britain. Narvik was therefore evacuated on 8 June, considerable quantities of stores as well as guns having to be destroyed, and the brave Norwegian venture came to an end.

Five individual Battle Honours were awarded, all unique. **Vist**, **Kvam**, **Otta**, **Stein** and **Pothus** were gained respectively by the Royal Lincolnshire Regiment (10th Foot), the King's Own Yorkshire Light Infantry (51st Foot), the Green Howards (19th Foot), the Scots Guards and the Irish Guards. A Campaign Honour, **Norway 1940**, was awarded to these five regiments together with four others.

France and Flanders, 1940

On 10 May the storm broke with cataclysmic force with the German invasion of Holland, Belgium and Luxemburg; a minor storm broke in Britain as well, a benevolent one, when Chamberlain resigned and was succeeded as Prime Minister by Winston Churchill. The British and French forces moved rapidly into Belgium and Holland in accordance with the French plan of defence, the former taking up positions on the River Dyle in the area of Louvain. With hindsight this was undoubtedly a mistake, as the promised Belgian defences had been inadequately prepared and planned and were incomplete, the Belgian Army positions in front of and to the north of the Dyle had already been over-run, and the French army had deteriorated during the winter through Communist subversion and the general malaise of inactivity. On the other hand the defences on the Franco-Belgian frontier were well-prepared and joined up with the Maginot Line, which could have caused fearsome casualties to a German frontal assault, although the defences in the Ardennes were only rudimen-

tary as it was believed by the French that large modern armies would not be able to advance through the area.

But the die had been cast and the battle began in earnest with a massive German assault led by ten armoured divisions, the effect of the armour being much more shattering to the Allies now than it had been to the Germans when tanks were first used against them in 1916.

The British Expeditionary Force was under the command of the French. There were three main reasons for this, first that the French believed that they were pre-eminent in the art of war and that it was their right, secondly that the British armies had been under command of Marshall Foch during the Great War and they saw no reason why it should not be the same again, and thirdly that the small British force was only a fraction of the size of the French army which numbered over 2 million men. Not that it was a happy arrangement. There had already been acrimonious debate between the two governments on the subject of the Ardennes front, which was poorly manned and was in any case the shortest route to Paris, and the route that had been used in 1870 and on many previous occasions.

To start with everything went according to plan and the new defence positions were manned within two days, but by the next day a tense battle had developed although the French did not appear to be sure where the main thrust was being developed. By 14 May the Germans on the Dinant-Sedan front on the Meuse had destroyed the French Army there and were advancing towards Paris between the Aisne and the Oise, and the Belgian and French armies in the Netherlands were in rapid retreat. Although the BEF was still in position on the Dyle and fighting strongly against heavy attacks it was rapidly being out-flanked and left in an isolated position. The Royal Air Force was suffering heavy casualties trying to support the French on the Meuse, and the fear arose that if the losses continued at this rate the air defence of Great Britain would be seriously at risk.

By 15 May the French had already decided that they had lost the battle, their Army in Flanders had been destroyed and the enemy had advanced 60 miles through a wide gap on the Ardennes sector; to make matters worse they had committed their entire force and left no reserves to plug the gaps. On this day also the Dutch capitulated leaving the northern flank wide open. The BEF and the one French Army remaining intact in Flanders were now ordered to retire towards the Escaut (the Scheldt). The Honour, **The Dyle**, was awarded to three armoured and eleven Infantry regiments including two battalions of Guards.

The British now had to extend their line and form an *ad hoc* force to defend Arras, and it became clear that withdrawal to the coast might become a necessity, although the preferred policy of the French was, somewhat naturally, a retirement south-westward to the Somme to join up with the remnants of the French Armies. In England the Local Defence Volunteers, later to become the Home Guard, began to form in every town and village. The army reached the Escaut on 19 May after a fighting retreat and remained there until the 22nd. The Honour **Withdrawal to the Escaut** was awarded to four armoured and five Infantry regiments, and **Defence of the Escaut** was awarded to twenty-five Infantry regiments.

In the meanwhile a forlorn effort was made to stem the German advance at **Amiens**, for which a unique Honour was awarded to the Royal Sussex Regiment (35th Foot), and at Arras. There, parts of two Infantry divisions and a tank brigade attempted to break out south and west from the town to occupy the area around Cambrai and Bapaume. But the German resistance was much stronger than expected and they soon counterattacked, and although Arras was held for a time the force eventually had to withdraw. An Honour for **Defence of Arras** was awarded to one armoured and nine Infantry regiments and another for the **Arras Counterattack** to one armoured regiment, the Royal Tank Regiment and two Infantry regiments.

It was now decided that the Channel ports of Boulogne and Calais should be defended in case they were needed for evacuation as well as Dunkirk, and garrisons were sent from England to defend them. The German armoured thrust had already reached the sea and now advance on the ports, which were soon surrounded. Boulogne was evacuated again after only 36 hours, but it was decided to defend Calais to delay the German advance on Dunkirk, until it was over-run after a desperate and gallant defence. The Honour **Boulogne 1940** was gained by the Irish and Welsh Guards, and **Calais 1940** was awarded to the Royal Tank Regiment, the Kings Royal Rifle Corps (60th Foot), the Rifle Brigade and a Territorial Army battalion, the Queen Victoria's Rifles.

Any idea of a breakout southwards across the Somme was now just wishful thinking and the only policy open to the British Army, which might enable at least some of them to escape, was a rapid withdrawal to the sea at Dunkirk and evacuation. The Germans had swung northwards and the big question was whether a corridor could be kept open north of the line La Bassée-St Omer to allow the withdrawal to take place; and to do this were only five regular and five TA divisions, which then had to be themselves lifted off the shore in the teeth of enemy air and ground attack. A monumental task indeed.

Attacks along the La Bassée canal were very heavy and the British force withdrew to the Ypres–Comines Canal where the fighting again was very severe, while the Belgian Army on their left was rapidly being broken. The troops at the base of the corridor near Lille were now in danger of being surrounded and had to make a rapid retreat. The fighting to stem the German armoured attacks was fierce and the British army fought magnificently. But by 29 May the German pincers had closed and only the Dunkirk area was left in allied hands; much of the British Army had by then escaped together with a number of French troops. But the Belgian Army had surrendered.

A number of Battle Honours were awarded to cover the period between 23 and 29 May. A unique Honour, **French Frontier 1940**, was awarded to the East Yorkshire Regiment (15th Foot); **St Omer-La Bassée** was awarded to two armoured regiments, the Royal Tank Regiment and twenty Infantry regiments. **Wormhoudt** was gained by four Infantry regiments, **Cassel** by one armoured and three Infantry regiments and **Forét de Nieppe** by two regiments. **Ypres–Comines Canal** was awarded to one armoured and fifteen Infantry regiments. The Royal Artillery gained another Honour title, **Hondeghem Battery**.

The period at Dunkirk and the final evacuation by the little ships is so well known that it needs little further account here. As the troops, British and French, were embarked and left, some from the port and most from the beaches, so the perimeter shrank because there were fewer troops left to defend it. The beaches were under heavy air attack and gunfire and the crowded shipping suffered heavy casualties, but the evacuation went on, and on 4 June the operation was completed with over 330,000 of the army saved, although virtually all the equipment and weapons had been lost. The Honour **Dunkirk 1940** was awarded to those troops who had defended the bridgehead, rather than all those who passed through; it was gained by four armoured and twenty-seven Infantry regiments.

But this was not the end of the battle of France. When the main army had retreated to Dunkirk the 51st Highland Division had still been in the Maginot Line area and was now behind the Somme, together with part of the only British armoured division, because it had been unable to rejoin the main army. Furthermore the 52nd Lowland Division was landing in Normandy with other troops, and a Canadian division was earmarked to land at Brest. The French troops evacuated from Dunkirk and some which had returned from Norway were also returned to France.

The objective was to try to bolster up the French, who in reality, and with hindsight, were already beyond help, physically and morally. Not that the whole French army had yet been beaten, because three Army Groups, on the Rhine, in the Maginot Line and on the Somme, perhaps a million and a half men, had not even been engaged so far. On 5 June the next German assault was launched between Paris and the sea, the small British force being compelled to retreat to the Seine in the area of Rouen.

The chances of holding the assault, with the French still in confusion, were as small as they had been in Flanders, and in spite of gallant defensive actions Rouen was taken and the Highland Division was driven into the coastal area between Rouen and Dieppe and the lower Seine. This was a disaster which could have been avoided if the French command had viewed the situation with any realism and ordered a withdrawal while there was still a route open into Brittany. The troops fought their way to St Valery to await evacuation on 12 June, but thick fog prevented ships from reaching the beach and picking them up, and virtually the whole division was captured. The troops of the Lowland Division and the remaining British troops, about 135,000 in all, were evacuated from the Brittany ports after heavy fighting. The Battle of France came to an end when the French asked for an armistice on 17 June, and surrendered.

Five Battle Honours were awarded for this period. **Saar** was gained by two regiments for the defeat of a heavy German attack on a section of the Maginot Line, **The Somme 1940** by four armoured regiments, the Royal Tank Regiment and seven Infantry regiments, and **Withdrawal to the Seine** by three armoured and three Infantry regiments. **Withdrawal to Cherburg** was awarded to one Infantry regiment and **St Valery en Caux** to one armoured and seven Infantry regiments. The campaign Honour for the

Battle of France, **North West Europe 1940–42,** was extended from the period narrated to cover the Dieppe Raid and the raids on the radar site at Bruneval and the harbour installations at St Nazaire. It was awarded to eleven armoured regiments, the Royal Tank Regiment, sixty-one Infantry regiments, the Parachute Regiment and the Commandos, and to eight Canadian regiments. Two regiments awarded individual Honours were for some reason excluded—the Irish Guards, who had helped to defend Boulogne and gained the Honour for it, and the Royal Irish Fusiliers (87th Foot) who had gained the individual Honours of the **Withdrawal to the Escaut** and **St Omer-La Bassee.**

The Middle East and East Africa, 1940

At the beginning of the war there was no immediate threat on the African continent, but there was nevertheless a strong potential threat from the Italians whenever they should decide to become participants. There was not long to wait after the fighting began in earnest in Europe, and on 10 June, before the fall of France and once Mussolini could see that there was no longer any danger to his western frontier, Italy declared war.

But in the intervening period of the 'Phoney War' Britain had not been idle and her strength in the Middle East had been augmented to the equivalent of about four divisions, with the Yeomanry Cavalry Division and parts of Australian and New Zealand divisions in Palestine. Further south on the Italian–Abyssinian border with the Sudan there was a small force, and there was a South African brigade and two of West Africans in Uganda and Kenya. Nevertheless there was still a shortage of troops compared with the very large Italian forces.

Somaliland

The first action of the war in East Africa and the Middle East was unexpectedly in British Somaliland, where a small force was defending the Protectorate at the Tug Argan Gap near the frontier with Abyssinia. The Italians attacked at the beginning of August at Hargeisa and ten days later captured the Tug Argan position mainly due to an outflanking movement; the British had to withdraw to prevent a disaster and Somaliland fell into Italian hands, which was to prove to be the only British defeat by the Italians during the war.

Three Honours were awarded. **Tug Argan** was gained by the King's African Rifles and the Northern Rhodesia Regiment, **Barkasan** was gained by the Black Watch (42nd Foot) for a rearguard action to allow the force to embark at Berbera, and the Campaign Honour **British Somaliland** was awarded to the three regiments already mentioned and to an Indian battalion which subsequently became the 1st Indian Parachute Regiment.

Egypt, 1940

In spite of events in East Africa the most dangerous area was the Egyptian/Cyrenaican frontier. The Italians had developed their North African colonies and had built a road along the coast right up to the frontier, no doubt with a future conflict in their minds, which now enabled them to concentrate a large force on the frontier near Bardia and Sollum. The glittering prize of Egypt lay before them and a very long and tenuous supply line stretched behind. On the Egyptian side the communications were much more limited with the road from Alexandria stopping at Mersa Matruh, and only a small mechanised force covered a possible Italian advance.

Within 24 hours of the Italian declaration of war this small British force took the offensive, much to the surprise of the Italians who did not even know that there was a war on. Within a few days it had captured Fort Capuzzo and was roving more or less at will over the desert; but this situation was not to last for long as enemy reinforcements arrived and re-established their frontier defences. An Honour for these actions, **Egyptian Frontier 1940,** was awarded to three armoured regiments, the Coldstream Guards and to two rifle regiments.

On 17 September the long-expected Italian attack began, on Sollum and through the Halfaya Pass, their troops arrayed as if on an exercise in perfect formation, and the British covering force made a fighting withdrawal to Mersa Matruh, with the Artillery taking a heavy toll of Italian vehicles since these were offered to them, as it were, on a plate. But there the Italians stopped and settled down, apparently content with their efforts. An Honour, **Withdrawal to Matruh,** was awarded to the 11th Hussars, although the Coldstream Guards, who had taken the brunt of the delaying action were not recognised for it.

Whilst the next Italian move was awaited, and plans were being made to forestall it with a British advance, across the Mediterranean Mussolini declared war on Greece, attacked across the Albanian/Greek frontier and was repulsed. The British guarantee of aid to Greece was invoked, and although this could not be immediately honoured on land the British Navy helped by redressing the balance of naval power in the Mediterranean with an airborne torpedo attack on the Italian fleet in Taranto harbour, which disabled half of it for some months. The British also began the occupation and defence of Crete.

In great secrecy the scene was now set for a British attack on the Italians in the desert, using to our advantage the fact that their supply route ran beside the sea and was therefore capable of interdiction by the Royal Navy. Although the advance began in December most of the action took place in the following year and the early attacks will more logically be narrated as part of 1941 rather than splitting the account into two parts. There was, however, a sharp action before the assault, at **Bir Enba,** which was successfully claimed as an Honour by the 11th Hussars, although the 3rd Hussars and the Royal Tank Regiment also participated.

Abyssinia, 1941

At the outbreak of war the Italians had a large Empire in Africa. Apart from their North African colony of Libya, made up of Tripolitania and Cyrenaica, the whole area of East Africa between the Sudan and the British colony of Kenya, consisting of Eritrea, Abyssinia, Somaliland and the Juba, was in Italian hands. If the British Empire were to collapse, which Mussolini saw as highly probably after the fall of France, the evacuation of the European continent and the single-handed British defiance of Hitler, it would leave the greater part of the African continent under Italian control. Hence the first effort at domination, which has already been recorded, in British Somaliland.

The campaign in Abyssinia which now opened was most unusual because of the large number of unique Battle Honours which were awarded, three quarters of the total number; this indicates better than anything else the small size of the Empire forces employed compared with the very large Italian Army stationed there. The Honours which were awarded, unique or not, were even so still less than 40 per cent of all the actions listed for the campaign.

In July 1940 the Italians had crossed the border into the Sudan and occupied Kassala and Gallabat. This area had to be cleared before an advance into Eritrea and Abyssinia could be launched and **Gallabat** was retaken in November 1940, the Honour being awarded to the Royal Garhwal Rifles of the Indian Army. The initial advance into Eritrea in January 1941 went well until the almost impregnable position at Keren was reached.

Several unique Honours were awarded for this phase. **Jebel Dafeis** was gained by the West Yorkshire Regiment (14th Foot) for an attack on an enemy post north-east of Metemma, **Jebel Shiba** by the Highland Light Infantry (71st Foot) for an intercept action on retreating Italians in which a large number of prisoners were taken and 4/10th Baluch and 3/18th Royal Garhwal Rifles also participated, and **Gogni**, for another successful attack on rearguards protecting Italians retreating on the Barentu road, to the Worcestershire Regiment (29th Foot), an action in which the 3/8th Punjab Regiment and the Sudan Regiment also took part.

Heavier opposition was encountered at **Agordat** where a frontal attack by 4th Indian Division was made, the Honour being awarded to the Royal Fusiliers (7th Foot), the Queen's Own Cameron Highlanders (79th Foot) and three Indian regiments, although another Indian regiment and a squadron of 4th Royal Tank Regiment also participated. Severe fighting took place in the Barentu Gorge, followed by an advance by 5th Indian Division against strong opposition before the town itself fell, and **Barentu** was awarded as an Honour to the Worcestershire Regiment, the Highland Light Infantry and the 3/18th Garhwal Rifles, with three other Indian regiments also involved in the action.

An attack in strength began in the Juba region where the port of Kismayu was taken with little opposition; the advance continued towards Gelib, where the enemy was routed, and the way was now open to Mogadiscu which was entered a week later. Six unique Honours were awarded. **Beles Gugani** was gained by the King's African Rifles. **Yonte** by a South African regiment, the Duke of Edinburgh's Own Rifles, **Bulo Erillo**, **Gelib** and **Alessandra** by the Gold Coast Regiment and **Goluin** by the Nigeria Regiment. **The Juba** was gained by the King's African Rifles, the Nigeria and Gold Coast Regiments, and by three South African regiments, the Royal Natal Carbineers, the Duke of Edinburgh's Own Rifles and the Transvaal Scottish.

In front of Keren a number of new attacks were mounted during February and early March; the Italians were defending desperately and made a number of counterattacks. Four unique Honours were awarded for **Karora-Marsa Taclai**, **Cubcub** and **Mescelit Pass**, all to the Royal Sussex Regiment (35th Foot), an Indian regiment also being involved in the last. At the end of March a more determined effort was made by the 4th Indian Division and after a prolonged and fierce battle Keren was captured after one of the battalions had scaled the cliff on which the town stood. Casualties were heavy on both sides and the Honour **Keren** was awarded to six British and eight Indian regiments.

The advance continued and Asmara and Massawa both fell during the first week in April with the capture of a large number of prisoners. Unique Honours for **Mount Engiahat** and **Keren–Asmara Road** were awarded, as well as **Ad Teclesan** to one British and two Indian regiments for an attack on a strong rearguard position, and **Massawa** to two British and one Indian regiments with the tank squadron also taking part. The Italians retreated to Amba Alagi another very strong position, followed by the 5th Indian Division, which with the 4th had played the major part in Eritrea so far until most of the 4th was sent to Egypt, its task in East Africa finished and there being a need for it in the Desert.

A South African brigade reached Addis Ababa, pressed on to Amba Alagi, and, in company with a brigade of the 5th Indian Division, attacked the Italians from the rear; the position fell at the end of May and practically the whole of northern Abyssinia was now free from Italian domination. The Honour **Amba Alagi** was awarded to one British, two Indian and the three South African regiments.

Meanwhile, in the middle of March, troops from Aden landed at Berbera in British Somaliland and quickly recaptured it. The advance which now began rapidly recovered the rest of the country, crossed the border into Abyssinia and captured Harrar and Diredawa before also marching towards Addis Ababa. Several more unique Honours were awarded. **Berbera** was awarded to an Indian regiment, **Marda Pass**, **Babile Gap** and **The Bisidimo** to the Nigeria Regiment, **The Awash** to the King's African Rifles, and **Diredawa**, a purely South African Honour, to the 1 Transvaal Scottish.

Commonwealth troops had also been active in western and northwestern Abyssinia; the Honours **Afodu**, **Gambela** and **Fike** were awarded uniquely to the King's African Rifles, **Dadaba** was gained by one South African regiment, an armoured car company and a light tank company, and **Colito**, during which a Victoria Cross was won posthumously by a sergeant of the King's African Rifles, by two African regiments.

So far only the campaign in the northern part of Abyssinia and Eritrea has been referred to, but action had also been going on in the south from across the Kenya border. Since the time that the first attacks had been made to clear Kassala and Gallabat a force of South African and African troops had been steadily advancing. A number of raids in strength had been carried out and in July 1940 the Honour of **Moyale** was gained by the King's African Rifles, in September **Wal Garis** was won by the Gold Coast Regiment, and at the end of that year **El Wak** had been gained by three South African Infantry regiments, an armoured car company and a light tank company and the Gold Coast Regiment, and **El Yibo** by two South African Infantry regiments and an armoured car company. In February and March 1941 three more Honours were awarded; **Mega** to five South African regiments and two armoured car companies after a fierce battle and **Todenyang-Namaraputh** and **Soroppa** to the King's African Rifles. For the fighting from April to June **Giarso** was awarded to the Northern Rhodesia Regiment, **Wadara** to the Gold Coast Regiment after prolonged fighting in heavy jungle, **The Omo** to two African regiments and **Lechemti** to the Nigeria Regiment.

The final acts of the war in Abyssinia again switched to the north where the last Italian troops had been holding out. **Combolcia** was awarded to the three South African Infantry regiments and an armoured car company in April, but the rainy season curtailed most further action until the end of the year. Finally **Gondar** was captured and awarded as an unique Honour, as were adjacent battles at **Ambazzo** and **Kulkaber**, all to the King's African Rifles, and the campign came to an end on 28 November 1941.

Two campaign Honours were awarded, since the South Africans, and sometimes the Indians, awarded Honours with names of their own choosing instead of those selected by the Battle Nomenclature Committee. **Abyssinia 1940-41** was gained by the Royal Tank Regiment, seven British Infantry regiments, four African regiments and fourteen Indian regiments. **East Africa 1940-41** was gained by six South African Infantry regiments and the armoured car and light tank companies.

Iraq, 1941

Under the terms of the 1930 Anglo-Iraqi treaty Britain was granted the right to maintain bases in Iraq and in time of war to have all possible facilities. But when hostilities began against Germany Iraq did not declare war, although she broke off diplomatic relations, but did not even go this far when Italy entered the fray. There was a strong pro-German, or perhaps anti-British, party in Iraq and in March 1941 this began to influence affairs to such an extent that Britain was forced to take action to eliminate it and to protect her interests, in particular the port of Basra.

A small force which had been embarked in India for Malaya was diverted to Iraq and landed at the end of April; more troops were sent to reinforce it, but resources were still very limited. The Iraqis concentrated their troops against Habbaniya, where a British battalion had been landed by air a few days earlier to protect the base there. The Iraqi troops were attacked from the air and responded by shelling the cantonment, but no Iraqi attack developed. British patrols were sent out and after a few days the Iraqis had had enough and their army dispersed. An Honour for

the **Defence of Habbaniya** was awarded to the King's Own Royal Regiment (4th Foot).

A mechanised brigade group now reached Habbaniya from Palestine and attacked the Iraqis holding the bridge over the Euphrates at Falluja. In spite of inundations the bridge was captured and the Honour **Falluja** was gained by the King's Own and by the Essex Regiment (44th Foot). The way was now open for an advance on Baghdad, but it made slow progress, owing to the blown-up bridges over the waterways and the active presence of German and Italian Air Force squadrons, although it reached the outskirts of the city at the end of May. The British presence near their capital was too much for the rebel Iraqis whose leaders fled to Persia. Baghdad was entered and an armistice signed. **Baghdad 1941** was awarded as an Honour to the two Household Cavalry Regiments and the Essex Regiment, and a Campaign Honour **Iraq 1941** was awarded to the Household Cavalry regiments, two Yeomanry regiments and the two British Infantry regiments already noted, and to four Indian regiments.

The Western Desert, 1940-1

In December 1940 the British Army was on the Egyptian frontier, planning an assault on the Italians, using great secrecy in order to achieve the surprise which was so necessary when a small force was to attack a very much larger one. On 6th they moved forward quietly and took up positions ready for the assault on Sidi Barrani; the armour outflanked the town and cut the coast road to the west, and the garrison was isolated. The attack on the town was a 'set piece' battle and it fell after three days of hard fighting, assisted by naval bombardment, a hoard of prisoners was taken and eight Italian divisions were annihilated. The armour had meanwhile entered Buq Buq. At the same time as the assault on Sidi Barrani the Coldstream Guards at Mersa Matruh fiercely attacked the Italians' position there and took a large number of prisoners, which in their report they said that they had counted by the acre rather than by heads. **Sidi Barrani** was awarded as an Honour to four British armoured and ten Infantry regiments, and to one Indian Infantry regiment. **Buq Buq** was awarded to three armoured regiments.

The rest of the campaign was a pursuit of the fleeing Italians, with every now and then a battle thrown in when the fugitives decided to stand and fight. The 4th Indian Division was sent off to Eritrea, as has already been seen, and replaced by an Australian division which had recently arrived in the theatre. The storming of Bardia in early January 1941 was very similar to the battle at Sidi Barrani, the armour isolating the town before the main attack took place, and again the fighting was severe. A fortnight later Tobruk also fell to the same method of assault, and in six weeks the Desert Army had advanced 200 miles and captured 100,000 prisoners. **Bardia 1941** was awarded as an Honour to one British and one Australian Cavalry regiments and to eight Australian Infantry regiments. **Capture of Tobruk** was awarded to the same two Cavalry regiments and to one British and nine Australian Infantry regiments.

The advance continued both along the coast and inland across the Cyrenaican highlands, the Djebel-el-Achdar. On

7 February Benghazi was captured, and the armoured formation reached the coast south of the town at Beda Fomm where a large enemy column was surprised and captured. The Italians were in desperate straits, and after a small counterattack had failed their army surrendered. The advance then continued as far as Agheila on the Tripolitanian frontier. No Honour was awarded for the actual capture of Benghazi, which had occurred with very little fighting, but two others were awarded during this phase. **Derna** was gained by one Cavalry and four Infantry regiments of the Australian Army, and **Beda Fomm** by five British armoured regiments and the Rifle Brigade. **Giarabub** was awarded to one Australian Cavalry and one Infantry regiment.

The advance was halted for reorganisation and the building-up of supplies for the next long run to Tripoli. But now several things happened to mar the smooth progress of the desert war. First, the main formations which had achieved the successes, 7th Armoured Division and 6th Australian Division, had been withdrawn to re-equip and rebuild their strength and had had to be replaced by formations which were not fully trained and not yet fully used to desert conditions. Secondly, much equipment and transport, and some fighting troops, had been withdrawn to be sent to Greece and Crete. Thirdly, German troops had started to arrive in Tripolitania under one of the greatest German commanders of the war, General Rommel, and it was appreciated that they would be a different proposition in battle from the Italians.

Although the position at Agheila was a strong one, guarding a defile, shortage of trained troops and the length of the supply lines meant that it could be only inadequately defended. Rommel's attack began on 31 March and the British army slowly withdrew. Mersa el Brega and Agedabia were lost after heavy fighting with serious losses, and the evacuation of Benghazi became a necessity; a British division earmarked to attack Rhodes now had to be retained as a reserve, and at a stroke the situation in the Middle East once again changed for the worse. The retreat from Benghazi began, and a disaster occurred when General Neame, VC, and General O'Connor, his nominated successor, were both captured while driving back along the coast road.

The German advance, like the British one, depended on two prongs, one along the coast and one across the desert uplands; in both they made rapid progress, although there were some desperate rearguard actions, and within eight days they had reached Tobruk, which the British had decided to fortify and try to hold, even if it were surrounded and bypassed, as a thorn in the enemy's side. It was bypassed and soon the German and Italian forces were streaming through the Halfaya Pass, and by early June the Desert Army was back on the Egyptian frontier at Sollum. The British retreat along the coast was successfully accomplished, but inland the situation was different. At Mechili an armoured divisional headquarters and three Indian regiments were surrounded and forced to surrender; near Derna an armoured brigade was ambushed and destroyed. Tobruk was heavily attacked but the rudimentary defences held.

A number of Battle Honours were awarded to recognise the gallant but unavailing British rearguard actions. **Mersa el Brega** and **Agedabia** were both gained by the Rifle Brigade and one of their TA battalions, the Tower Hamlets Rifles, and **Derna Aerodrome** by the same two regiments and the King's Royal Rifle Corps.

The hastily, but eventually strongly, defended fortress of Tobruk held out against all that Rommel could throw against it from 8 April to 10 December; the garrison was mainly Australian, with some British armour and artillery. The perimeter was long and air attacks were frequent and severe; supply could only be maintained dangerously by ships at night, none being able to remain in port in daylight hours without risk of damage or destruction from dive bombers.

The main German assault began on 13 April. A small force broke through at one point and dug in, but was later thrown out by a patrol, of which one member, Corporal Edmondson, was posthumously awarded the Victoria Cross, the first Australian to be so decorated in the war. Next day a bigger attack was made on the part of the perimeter near the German occupied airfield of El Adem, and German tanks and infantry reached the El Adem crossroads where they were engaged by a British tank regiment and two regiments of the Royal Horse Artillery, and desperate fighting took place. The Australians manning the perimeter closed the gap, reserves were committed and the Germans realised that they were in a trap and withdrew while they still could. The enemy was astonished as he believed that once tanks were through the defences nothing could stop them. The Germans now moved on towards the Egyptian frontier and Tobruk was isolated. The next attack came on 30 April in what became known as the Battle of the Salient. The pattern of the assault was as before, and as before the breakthrough was stemmed by British artillery fire, the accuracy and power of which contributed greatly to the successful prolongation of the siege. On 1 May the Australians launched a counterattack, which gained very little ground in spite of heavy casualties, but at least it forced the Germans on the defensive and they made no further major attacks during the siege. The defence will go down in history as one of the great examples of an unsuccessful siege by overwhelmingly superior forces. **El Adem Road** was awarded to four Australian Infantry regiments, and **The Salient 1941** to seven Australian Infantry regiments and a pioneer battalion. **Defence of Tobruk** was awarded to one British and one Indian armoured regiment, to one British and twelve Australian Infantry regiments and to the Australian pioneer battalion.

General Wavell, commanding in the desert, decided not to allow the Germans to settle down on the frontier, become reinforced after their advance and prepare for a further assault, and he also wanted to relieve Tobruk as soon as possible, as a long defence of the port did not at that time appear to be very feasible. A small force, therefore, was ordered to attack without delay and on 15 May armoured Guards and Infantry troops advanced along the escarpment and captured Fort Capuzzo and Sollum. They were immediately counterattacked and withdrew to the Halfaya Pass. Ten days later Rommel attacked the position at Halfaya and the small force had to retire rapidly to avoid capture; the German position there was to be a considerable problem to the next British attack. The Honour **Halfaya 1941** was awarded to one British and one Indian armoured regiment, to the Coldstream Guards and Scots Guards, the former of which had suffered heavily at Halfaya itself, and to the Durham Light Infantry (68th Foot) who had suffered very severe casualties both in the capture of Cappuzzo and in the counterattack against it later the same day.

Still Wavell did not give up the possibility of inhibiting a German build-up on the frontier or of the relief of Tobruk. On 15 June another assault was made by 7th Armoured Division, 4th Indian Division, now returned to the desert from Eritrea, and the Guards Brigade. There were early successes when the Guards took Capuzzo and moved towards Sollum, and the armour captured Sidi Suleiman and moved towards Sidi Omar; but the position at Halfaya held out against repeated Indian attacks. Two days later, no progress having been made, a powerful German armoured force counterattacked; against their heavy guns the lightly armed and armoured British tanks had little chance, and in spite of air support the whole force had to retreat back to where it had started. The Honour awarded for this unsuccessful episode, **Sidi Suleiman**, was granted to three British armoured regiments and to two British and two Indian Infantry regiments, although one British and one Indian Infantry regiment were not recognised for it.

Tobruk remained a thorn in Rommel's side and during the summer posed a strategic threat which prevented him attacking Egypt, thus having fulfilled its objective. His aim was to remove the threat, and the British aim was to relieve the town with the Desert Army, now known as the 8th Army and commanded by General Auchinleck. In fact the British acted first and began an assault, with complete surprise in heavy rain, on 18 November, just four days before Rommel's own offensive against Tobruk was due to start. The Indians and New Zealanders on the coast swept around the German positions at Sollum, Bardia, Halfaya and Fort Capuzzo; the armoured division and the South Africans further inland pushed forward towards Sidi Rezegh, a lone hill dominating the German communications route and the key to the relief of Tobruk, meeting very little resistance other than at Bir el Gubi, Saleh and Gabr. An Honour **Gabr Saleh** was awarded to the 11th Hussars and the Sharpshooters (Yeomanry), and **Gubi I** to the same two regiments plus the Royal Gloucestershire Hussars (Yeomanry).

But at Sidi Rezegh the 7th Armoured Brigade ran into the German armour and a confused and ferocious struggle began; eventually almost all the armour of both sides was sucked into the battle, and the British, having lost two thirds of their tanks, were forced to withdraw. **Sidi Rezegh 1941** was awarded as an Honour to four British armoured and two Yeomanry regiments, and to two British, thirteen New Zealand and six South African Infantry regiments. Two other South African regiments were involved but not recognised, one reconnaissance battalion and one armoured car regiment. The Royal Artillery gained another Honour title **Sidi Rezegh 1941** Battery.

On the coast the New Zealanders advanced rapidly from Bardia and almost regained Sidi Rezegh the day after it had been lost, but failing to do so concentrated nearby.

The Indians were fighting at the Omars to contain the enemy with great gallantry, particularly in a gun-to-gun battle between twenty-eight German tanks and a British 25-pounder regiment which in the end got the better of the exchange although suffering heavy casualties for their temerity. Meanwhile the garrison of Tobruk made a sortie south-eastwards, also towards Sidi Rezegh although it did not quite manage to break through to the New Zealand position. Both sides had suffered very heavy losses and the battle hung in the balance. The Honour **Tobruk Sortie 1941** was gained by one armoured and five Infantry regiments all British.

Rommel now counterattacked at night against the 4th Armoured Brigade, which held most of the fit British tanks, and a South African Infantry brigade, practically annihilating the latter. He followed this up with a raid in strength which carried him via Gabr Saleh to the frontier again. He wrought havoc in the rear areas until he came up against the Indian division and his eastward movement was stopped; he therefore turned northwards towards Bardia and then back towards Sidi Rezegh, pressed by British armoured forces. In five days he had circumnavigated practically the whole of the 8th Army, and although in the event the raid did not have the effect that he wanted it was a close-run thing.

While Rommel was careering around the desert with his Afrika Korps, the New Zealanders persisted in their attacks on Sidi Rezegh and after two days of desperate fighting captured it. On 26 November the troops joining in the Tobruk sortie established contact with the relieving force, and it was this situation which brought Rommel rapidly back from Bardia to recapture Sidi Rezegh once more, inflicting very heavy losses on the New Zealanders. **Taieb el Essom** was awarded to the 11th Hussars, but four South African regiments who took part were not recognised for the Honour; **Belhamed** was awarded to the Royal Tank Regiment and to three British, one Australian and thirteen New Zealand Infantry regiments; **Zemla** was gained by seven New Zealand regiments.

The whole army now regrouped and bypassing Sidi Rezegh advanced on El Adem. Rommel made a final effort to relieve his beleaguered frontier garrisons, but one at the Omars had already been eliminated by the Indians and another at Sidi Aziez was in the process of being eliminated. He was repulsed and forced to begin the long retreat back to the Gazala line. **Omars** was awarded to one British, one Indian and four New Zealand regiments and **Sidi Aziez** to twelve New Zealand regiments.

On 4 December the Indians attacked Bir el Gubi after a long approach march by night over unreconnoitred country; the opposition varied, in places being very weak and in others very strong. Against the latter the battle raged for three days, the Infantry being counterattacked by German tanks, and eventually the force had to withdraw. **Gubi II** was awarded to the 11th Hussars and to one British and one Indian Infantry regiment, although another Indian Infantry regiment and three South African regiments also took part. On 10 December, after an attack from El Adem, the South Africans and Indians were able to join up with the garrison of Tobruk and the siege was lifted after eight months. The value of the siege had been inestimable. The Honour **Relief of Tobruk 1941** was gained by three British and one Indian armoured regiments and by the Durham Light Infantry, although a number of other Indian regiments were also engaged.

Once the main objective, the relief of Tobruk, had been achieved, the secondary object of pursuing the retreating Axis forces could be undertaken by the seasoned desert veterans, the 7th Armoured Division on the desert flank, the 4th Indian Division on top of the escarpment and a New Zealand Infantry brigade along the coast to hold the enemy at Gazala. After a sharp action with heavy casualties at Sidi Breghisc, which was not honoured, the main fight took place at Alem Hamza against strong opposition. One British battalion, the Buffs, was almost wiped out, but the German casualties were also very heavy and eventually they withdrew. **Alem Hamza** was awarded as an Honour to the Buffs (3rd Foot), one Indian and ten New Zealand Infantry regiments, and one other Indian regiment was involved but not Honoured.

The advance continued rapidly, Rommel was not able to stand at Gazala as he had hoped, and Benghazi was entered for the second time on 24 December. Right at the end of the year, after a furious battle, an Honour **Chor es Sufan** was gained by one armoured, two Yeomanry regiments and two Infantry regiments, all British.

To finish off the desert war for 1941 mention must be made of a number of Honours which were awarded to or claimed by South African regiments under their own Battle Nomenclature arrangements, mostly their own names for battles already narrated. In December **Marsa Belafarit** was awarded to one armoured regiment and several Honours were claimed but not recognised—*Bir Sciafsciuf* by two regiments, *Halfaya* by ten regiments and *Agedabia* by three regiments.

Greece, 1941

After the swings and roundabouts of the desert war, two disastrous episodes must be recounted, first in Greece and second in Crete. It will be recalled that after the Italian attack on Greece the British guarantees to that country were invoked; it was not possible to provide ground forces immediately but in March 1941 an expedition was sent, consisting of one Australian and one New Zealand division and a British armoured brigade. In spite of the predominately Anzac nature of the force a British general was appointed to command, but the command structure was overcomplicated and produced its own major problems in addition to those caused by the enemy.

The objective was to hold a line in the north of the country from the mouth of the Aliakman River, through Veroia and Edessa, to the Yugoslav frontier near Monastir, in conjunction with some weak divisions of the Greek Army, whose main force was on the Albanian frontier, and whose competence was in any case suspect. A large German Army, comprising ten Infantry and two armoured divisions, had now joined the Italians, thus outnumbering the allied army very considerably, and invaded the country through the Monastir Gap on 6 April. They also invaded Yugoslavia, whose Army was rapidly broken and retreating in confusion, capitulation soon following.

The first contact was on 10 April when German forces probed the positions at Veve in a heavy snowstorm. An Australian brigade and the British 1st Armoured Brigade held on desperately for two days, but the British left flank was now threatened and, in spite of a bitter rearguard action, had to withdraw to the Olympus-Aliakmon line where the New Zealanders were holding a position around Mount Olympus itself. During this period the Greek Army ceased to be a fighting force and the expeditionary force was on its own in its defence of Greece.

The New Zealanders defended the area around Mount Olympus for some days until the whole force had to retreat again, this time to the line of Thermopylae, Brallos and Delphi. A number of Honours were awarded for this phase. **Mount Olympus** was awarded to four Australian and fifteen New Zealand Infantry regiments and an Australian machine gun battalion; **Aliakmon Bridge** was awarded to one New Zealand regiment and the **Servia Pass** to thirteen New Zealand regiments and the Australian machine gun battalion. **Veve** was gained as an Honour by two British, two Australian and one New Zealand Infantry regiments.

At this stage 1st Australian Corps, commanded by General Blamey, was redesignated the Anzac Corps, to reduce command chaos which by now existed, reminiscent of the situation not so very different over a quarter of a century earlier. The main threat during the retreat to Thermopylae was expected from the left flank but in the event came from the east where an Anzac force defended the Tempe Gorge and the Olympus Pass for three days with great gallantry against overwhelming odds until the rest of the force had reached Larissa. This was the key point and, because of the lack of roads, all communications had to pass through this town; it was obviously a major German target and the New Zealanders defence was thus of utmost significance and importance. Honours were awarded for the **Platamon Tunnel** to four Zealand regiments, for the **Olympus Pass** to ten New Zealand regiments, and for the **Tempe Gorge** to two Australian and five New Zealand Infantry regiments.

Meanwhile the part of the force on the left flank was also falling back, in good order but under very heavy attack, from both ground and air and with the fighting of many rearguard actions, to straighten the line at the narrowest part of the Greek peninsula through Thermopylae and Larissa. **Soter** was gained as an Honour by a single Australian regiment, **Proasteion** by the 4th Hussars and one British Infantry regiment, and **Elasson** by ten New Zealand Infantry regiments.

Larissa was safely, if hazardously, passed while the rearguard actions were delaying the German advance, but the cost was very severe. The underlying hope was that the exploits of Leonidas and his Spartans would be repeated, but it was not to be and once more an evacuation loomed ahead, only a week after the initial battles, this time with no little ships to help and with a much larger stretch of water to cross than the English Channel. The modern motor road does not go through the Pass of Thermopylae but over the Brallos Pass, a very steep scarp on the northern side but a gentle slope, albeit with deep gorges, on the southern. Even this strong defensive position could not stop the Germans, in spite of courageous Anzac resistance against overwhelming opposition to allow the retreat to take place towards the possible evacuation beaches. The Honour **Brallos Pass** was gained by three Australian regiments and **Molos** by thirteen New Zealand regiments.

The evacuation could only take place from the southern beaches of the Peloponnese and, the expeditionary force having retreated past Athens, the British armour attempted to hold the bridge over the Corinth Canal, but without success, and the Germans captured the town of Corinth. **Corinth Canal** was awarded to the 4th Hussars and eventually the beaches were reached without further incident and the evacuation was completed on 29 April.

Out of a total of more than 62,000 originally in the country 50,000 men were taken off, and the casualties were remarkably light in view of the ferocity of the fighting, only 750 being killed but 10,000 being taken prisoner. But the casualties still amounted to over 20 per cent of the Expeditionary Force, and of these the British troops, only a small proportion of the force, suffered more than half, although their share of the Honours awarded does not indicate accurately their true involvement in the efforts to stave off disaster. Although the operation was a catastrophe it had one valuable overtone in that the German invasion of Russia was delayed for a month, and that month made all the difference in that they were unable to defeat the Russians before the winter set in.

A Campaign Honour, **Greece 1941**, was awarded, and was gained by the 4th Hussars, the Royal Tank Regiment, the New Zealand Scottish armoured car regiment, and by two British, nine Australian and fifteen New Zealand Infantry regiments and the Australian machine gun battalion.

Crete, 1941

Crete was a most important strategic point in the Middle Eastern war, being a base for warships engaged in the protection of Malta. But it was also vulnerable to air attack from enemy bases on Rhodes, although well defended against this form of attack. It will be remembered that there had been a plan to attack Rhodes, but that Rommel's counter-offensive in the desert had caused this to be abandoned to provide immediate and necessary reserves. Nevertheless there was no real need for a large permanent garrison in Crete all the time that the Allies held Greece, but unfortunately there was no plan to reinforce it once Greece was lost, and Crete would clearly become the next German target.

Many of the troops evacuated from Greece were sent directly to Crete, so that the island was now held by a British brigade and the equivalent of two brigades each of Australian and New Zealand troops, together with a lot of Greeks who were to prove as generally incompetent as they had on the mainland. But this was not enough and most of the garrison was tired after their experiences on the mainland, and they could only achieve *ad hoc* defences in the time available to them. There were airfields at Maleme, Retimo and Canea and the base was at Suda Bay.

On 20 May the Germans launched a massive air attack on the island using dive-bombers and parachute and glider-borne troops. The attacks were mainly directed at Maleme airfield and Canea, which were defended by the New Zealanders who were completely overwhelmed by the troops and the extremely heavy air bombardment. German casualties were enormous but still more troops poured in. Everywhere the British and Anzacs resisted with a ferocity which surprised the Germans. A German seaborne convoy was heavily attacked by the Royal Navy and suffered terrific losses; but as with the airborne attacks the Germans seemed to have a complete disregard for their casualties.

Small groups of New Zealanders were still fighting at Maleme, but they too were now exhausted after 48 hours of heavy fighting following the battles in Greece. They withdrew to Galatos and eventually from there to the evacuation beaches. Meanwhile the defenders had had to retire from their positions around the other airfields, and established defended localities which were virtually cut off from each other; but being hopelessly outnumbered thoughts again turned to evacuation as the only solution. After a most gallant defence the garrison of Retimo was forced to surrender when the troops were totally exhausted. Heraklion, further to the east, was attacked at much the same time as the other areas and here too the defence was spirited and determined and took a terrible toll of the German attackers. But the Germans were too strong and eventually the small garrison managed to break off the engagement and was evacuated.

A number of Battle Honours were awarded for the first phase of the battle. **Maleme** was gained by fourteen and **Galatas** by fifteen New Zealand regiments; **Canea** was awarded to two British, two Australian and eleven New Zealand regiments, **Heraklion** to four British and one Australian regiments and **Retimo** to one British and two Australian regiments.

The small force had reached the limits of its endurance and could now only withdraw to the coast and hope to be taken off, fighting a strong rearguard action all the way and suffering heavily all the while. Two Honours were awarded during the withdrawal. **42nd Street** was gained by two Australian and fifteen New Zealand regiments, and **Withdrawal to Sphakia** was gained by one British, two Australian and fifteen New Zealand regiments. But at last even the evacuation was brought to a standstill by intense air attacks on the naval vessels, and about 6,000 men had to be sacrificed and abandoned on the island. Of the Commonwealth force of about 16,000 men over half were lost during the campaign, the majority as prisoners. The campaign had lasted for just twelve days. But whatever the British and Anzac casualties and losses, the German ones were probably very much higher and their experimental and only Airborne Division at that time was destroyed in the encounter.

The Campaign Honour **Crete** was awarded to the 3rd Hussars, seven British, five Australian and sixteen New Zealand Infantry regiments, to the Commandos and to an Australian machine gun battalion.

One thing was very clear. The attempt to honour the obligations to Greece had been a disaster and a terrible waste of badly needed manpower and should never have been made. If those troops had been used to carry on the advance in the desert from Agheila to Tripoli, as they could have done without too much difficulty, apart from supplies, against the defeated and retreating Italian Army before the German forces landed, the whole aspect of the Desert and the Middle Eastern War would have been very different.

Syria, 1941

Following the occupation of Iraq, the next two months were spent in clearing hostile elements from Syria, which posed a much more serious threat. After the collapse of France, Syria, which since 1918 had been under French control, was infiltrated by Germans and Italians who succeeded in arousing considerable anti-British feeling among the Arabs. There was a possibility of more overt German action which would create serious problems for our vital interests in the Middle East, and German and Italian Air Force units were already operating from there.

Elsewhere in the Middle East, as has been seen, Greece had been evacuated after a short but bitter battle, and coinciding with the end of the Iraq episode and the mounting tension in Syria the Germans had attacked Crete and after a bloody battle the British force had again had to evacuate. In the desert Tobruk was besieged and the German and Italian forces were back on the Egyptian frontier. All in all, apart from in East Africa, the situation was very much in the enemy's favour, which of course aided his efforts at sowing discord.

British resources in the Middle East were still very strained, but action had to be taken rapidly, and one Australian division, part of the British 1st Cavalry Division, now motorised, and an Indian brigade were moved into northern Palestine to be ready for any eventuality. The objective was to capture Damascus and Beirut, after which it was thought that the revolt would collapse.

British troops crossed the frontier into Syria on 8 June and although the initial opposition was slight, it soon grew more determined as the enemy realised what a weak force was being employed, and counterattacks developed, one of which overwhelmed a British battalion at Kuneitra. On the coast the River Litani as crossed, Merjayun besieged, although it was to hold out for nearly three weeks, and Adlun taken. Inland the British/Indian force had reached the perimeter defences of Damascus, but nearer the coast there was bitter fighting at Jezzine where the advance was held up. The Vichy French counterattacked at Merjayun and Kuneitra and both towns were recaptured. The Indian brigade was severely mauled in an attack on Damascus, but in a subsequent attack the city fell to the Free French who had been fighting alongside the British and Indians. But more strength was needed to achieve any results and the force in Iraq was now directed towards Palmyra.

The Battle Honours for the period were mostly gained by the Australians. **Syrian Frontier** was awarded to four Australian Infantry regiments, **The Litani** to the Commandos and two Infantry regiments and **Adlun** to one Cavalry and two Infantry regiments. **Merjayun** was gained by one British and one Australian Cavalry regiments, and by one British and five Australian Infantry regiments. **Sidon** was gained by two Cavalry and two Infantry regiments and a machine gun battalion and **Jezzine** by two Infantry regi-

ments and the machine gun battalion, all these being of the Australian Army. The Honour of **Damascus** was only awarded to one Australian and one Indian Infantry regiments in spite of the heavy fighting there.

The rest of the campaign was by no means a walk-over, as had been hoped, and heavy fighting took place on the other route of entry, along the pipeline to Palmyra and the coast north of Tripoli and up to the line of the Euphrates from Iraq. This successful campaign was completed on 12 July after five weeks of fighting. Of the Honours for the actions in this phase only one was all British, **Palmyra**, which was awarded to the Life Guards, the Royal Horse Guards, one Yeomanry regiment and one Infantry regiment. **Jebel Mazar** was a combined effort, being awarded to one Yeomanry and two British Infantry regiments and to one Australian Cavalry regiment and the machine gun battalion, several other regiments having been involved in earlier attempts to capture it. Two Honours were gained solely by one Indian Cavalry regiment, the 13th Lancers, **Raqaa** and **Djerablous 1941**, and **Deir ez Zor** was gained by the same Cavalry regiment and the Gurkha Rifles.

All the rest of the Honours were all-Australian affairs. **Wadi Zeini** was gained by one Cavalry and one Infantry regiment, **Dimas** and **Chehim and Rharife** uniquely by Infantry regiments, and **Damour**, a much larger battle, by one Cavalry, eight Infantry and one machine gun regiment. **Mazraat ech Chouf** was awarded to two infantry regiments, and **Hill 1069** and **Badarene** also uniquely to Infantry regiments. All in all a lot of Honours for a short campaign.

The Vichy French now sued for an armistice and hostilities ceased on 11 July. Although British and Indian casualties were high, the Australians had as many casualties in Syria as in Greece and Crete combined, which showed that the Syrian campaign was not the 'sideshow' that it has often been made out to be.

The Campaign Honour **Syria 1941** included a number of regiments which had not gained individual Honours, and was awarded to four British, two Australian and one Indian Cavalry regiments, to six Yeomanry regiments, to the Madras and Bombay Sappers and Miners, to six British, eight Australian, one Indian and two Gurkha Infantry regiments, and to an Australian machine gun regiment, a Pioneer regiment and the Commandos. The situation in the Middle East was improving but still very dangerous, and the Indian brigade had suffered such heavy casualties that it was virtually out of action for six months when it could ill be spared.

Persia, 1941

Once the Russians had entered the war there was an urgent need to supply them with munitions, and because of the difficulties and uncertainties of the Arctic sea route the only practical route for the large quantities required was from India through Persia. There was also a need to protect the Persian oilfields for British use. But as elsewhere in the Middle East the Germans had established an active mission in Tehran, about which the British authorities had done absolutely nothing, but which had persuaded Persia to support the German cause. British approaches to the Persian government for right of passage and the expulsion of the German mission were received coldly, and the only alternative was quick action and occupation, even though the forces in the Middle East were already fully stretched and only a minimal number of troops could be spared.

Arrangements were made with the Russians for co-operation by an invasion in the north if that should prove necessary, while Britain concentrated on the south, the first objective being the oilfields around Abadan. The invasion began on 25 August and captured Abadan and Ahwaz with little opposition. The force then advanced on Kurmanshah but on 28 August, before an attack could be launched, the Persians surrendered and the campaign was over. Teheran was occupied on 17 September and the Shah abdicated in favour of his son. Three Honours were awarded for the campaign by the Indian government, the Battle Nomenclature Committee not listing it at all. They were all gained by the same Indian regiment, the 13th Lancers, and were **Ahwaz 1941**, **Qasr Sheikh** and **Persia 1941.**

The Far East
Strictly, the start of the war against Japan, which began with the attack on Pearl Harbor and first affected British troops in Malaya and Hong Kong, should also be included under the events of 1941. But since the attack only took place in the second week of December, and the denouement of that attack and the escalation of the war into Burma and the Pacific the following year, it is considered more practical to narrate these events in the next chapter.

Norway, 1941
At the end of December a successful raid was carried out by Commandos to destroy fish oil facilities and shipping. Severe fighting occurred on the islands of Vaagso and Maaloy and heavy casualties were inflicted on the German defenders. An Honour, **Vaagso**, was awarded to the Commandos.

Conclusion
So ended 1941, which had seen some successes for the British and Commonwealth Armies, primarily in East Africa, but also in Syria and Iraq and to some extent in the Western Desert, where after all Benghazi had been captured twice at the end of a 500-mile advance and Tobruk had maintained a long siege. But on the debit side were the disasters of Greece and Crete, as well as the events in the Far East still to be narrated. The year had shown the ruthlessness and the power of the German attacks, as well as the weakness of the Italians, and a glimpse of the strength of the Japanese, but it had also brought the great powers of the USSR and the USA into the war at last. Now Britain and the Empire were not alone and the allied strength more than outmatched the Axis in manpower, if not yet in fighting experience or callousness.

Below: Bren gun carriers moving an infantry company in Cyrenaica, 1941. *via Ian Hogg*

18 World War 2: Part 2, 1942-3

Nearly two and a half years of war had passed when 1942 opened, and it cannot be said that they had been very encouraging months for the allied cause. At least not on the surface. On the debit side western Europe had been evacuated, apart from an unoccupied part of France which nevertheless could not take any overt action against Germany. Greece and Crete had been evacuated, and Malta was isolated and under heavy air attack. The battle had flowed back and forth in the Western Desert and Egypt was still in danger, although the rest of the Middle East and East Africa had been cleared of the enemy. Japan had entered the war with a murderous air attack on Hawaii and was attacking Malaya and the Pacific islands. Britain itself had been under immensely concentrated air attack.

But there were some distinct credits as well. First Britain and the Empire had withstood the German onslaught and had not given in as some other countries had done. German attempts to invade the British Isles had been stemmed and abandoned after the successes of the Battle of Britain. In spite of numerous evacuations which had been necessary, in all cases the majority of the troops concerned had been extricated to fight another day. In the desert the lightly armed and armoured British tanks had surprisingly shown themselves a match for the Germans under Rommel, and more than a match for the Italians. Perhaps, most significant of all, the USA and the USSR had now entered the war.

The year 1942 was to be one of change, with some successes and the first signs of the possibility, nay the probability, of eventual victory, although the new nations in the battle and Britain were to receive some grievous blows before the year was over in Eastern Europe and in the Far East.

South East Asia and Malaya, 1941–2

At the same time as the Japanese attack on Pearl Harbor, and without a declaration of war, Singapore and Hong Kong were attacked by air and landings were made on the Malayan coast. Britain then declared war on Japan. Two days later Britain was shocked to learn of the sinking of the two great battleships, *Repulse* and *Prince of Wales*, off the coast of Malaya by air attack.

It was accepted that the small garrison of Hong Kong would have no chance of holding off the impending, overwhelming Japanese attack, and after carrying out demolitions in the port of Kowloon it withdrew to the island. The Japanese landed on 18 December, and quickly drove back the defenders, who suffered heavy casualties until they were over-run and surrendered on Christmas Day. Some fighting continued in Borneo for some months but everywhere in South East Asia the Japanese were successful.

The islands of the Dutch East Indies fell one by one until only Java was left. Massive Japanese convoys were approaching and naval battles developed during which almost all the allied warships were sunk; it was decided that no further reinforcements would be sent, and that the Australian battalions and a squadron of the 3rd Hussars should fight to the last against an estimated four or five Japanese divisions. The finish could not be long delayed and the island surrendered on 8 March.

Java 1942 was awarded to two Australian regiments, one a machine gun and one a pioneer. The Honour **Hong Kong** was awarded to one British, two Canadian and one Indian regiment, and the Hong Kong Volunteer Defence Corps, and **South East Asia 1941–42** was awarded to two British, two Canadian and one Indian regiment.

Meanwhile the Japanese had landed on the northern coasts of Malaya on 8 December and again the garrison was inadequate to hold them back. During the month landings were made progressively down both the east and west coasts of the Malay peninsula, an Indian division fighting rearguard actions all the way, and by the end of the year the fighting had reached Ipoh and Kuantan. A number of Battle Honours were awarded for this first period of severe fighting with its heavy casualties. **Kota Bahru** was awarded uniquely to one Indian regiment, as was **Grik Road** to one British regiment, the Argyll and Sutherland Highlanders (91st Foot). **Jitra** was awarded to one Indian and two Gurkha regiments, and one of the Indian Mountain Batteries was granted this as an Honour Title. **North Malaya,** covering the first two weeks of the attack, was awarded to one British and two Indian regiments, one of them dismounted Cavalry, and one Gurkha regiment.

The 9th and 11th Divisions, both composed of British and Indian troops, were defending the east and west coasts respectively, with behind them an Australian division and part of another British-Indian division, the remainder of which was expected to arrive shortly. The 11th Division held a position at Kampar against heavy attack until another Japanese landing behind them on the Perak River forced them to withdraw to the Slim River. There, a few days later, they again suffered a massive assault and, thrown into confusion, were to all intents annihilated, and only small detachments managed to get away. Their withdrawal exposed the flank of the 9th Division at Kuantan, still in contact with the enemy and also suffering repeated assaults.

Ipoh was awarded to one British and two Indian regiments. **Kuantan** was awarded to two Indian regiments and the Bombay Sappers and Miners, **Kampar** to the Bombay Engineers and to two British, one Indian and two Gurkha Infantry regiments, and **Slim River** to one British, one Indian and one Gurkha regiment. **Central Malaya,** for the overall battle, was gained by one British, two Indian and one Gurkha regiments.

General Wavell, who was now in command of the Far Eastern battle, ordered a deep withdrawal to take the hard-pressed and tired troops out of reach of the Japanese for a few days, and to allow fresh troops to take over the defence of Johore, where the next battles were expected to take place. An Australian battalion fought a bitter delaying action at Gemas while the new position on the Muar River was being established, and the battle there raged fiercely for a week, until the four battalions were attacked by a whole Japanese division and assailed by seaborne landings as well. They stood no chance, were surrounded and eventually some of them, about 20 per cent, fought their way out in small groups, all the senior officers being killed.

The defensive line was further withdrawn and was now rapidly approaching the tip of the peninsula and Singapore. The next major attack was delivered on Batu Pahat where there were only three British battalions; after five days of assault they were surrounded and the survivors were taken off the beaches by the Navy. All the while the Japanese were being reinforced and by now strongly outnumbered the original force, let alone what was left of it after five weeks of desperate fighting. The Australians were heavily attacked on the east coast near Mersing, and the Indians in the centre, until it was clear that the only hope of survival was to withdraw to Singapore Island. Rearguard actions were fought with severe losses to allow troops and vehicles to cross the causeway, and by 31 January all those that had survived had crossed on to the island and the causeway was blown up.

Several more Honours were awarded for this third phase of the withdrawal. **Gemas** was gained by one Australian regiment, **The muar** by one British, one Indian and two Australian regiments, **Batu Pahat** by three British regiments, **Niyor** by one Indian regiment and **Jemaluang** by one Australian regiment. **Johore,** awarded to cover this phase and the rest of the fighting other than the individual battles, was awarded to three British and six Australian regiments, and 2nd Gurkha Rifles.

The withdrawal had been stubborn and desperate with severe losses, and brought great credit on the outnumbered troops who took part. But now the remainder, who had been earmarked for its defence but who had had to be used on the peninsula, were concentrated on a small island, and it was hoped that they might be able to resist until reinforcements could arrive. Unfortunately the defences of Singapore had been planned with a seaborne attack in mind and none of them were of any use against a land attack as the heavy guns were emplaced and could not be

brought to bear. The air force only had a fraction of its planned strength, some of these aircraft were obsolete, and it was totally inadequate against the Japanese air strength. Nevertheless the troops were disposed in the best defensive positions that could be created in the time available and with the general shortages.

The Japanese attacks came on 8 and 9 February and were directed against the Australians on the north-west coast of the island. Although they fought gallantly and desperately the enemy was too powerful for them and rapidly broke their positions; British troops were brought from other coastal positions to support them but with no success. Within six days the attack had reached the outskirts of the town and port itself and it was obvious that the position was untenable. A few troops were evacuated in small local craft, but most of these were sunk or captured. It was decided to put an end to the needless slaughter and to capitulate. Singapore surrendered unconditionally on 15 February.

The Honour **Singapore Island** was awarded to nine British, one Indian, one Gurkha, six Australian regiments and an Australian machine gun regiment, the Malay Regiment and the Singapore Volunteer Corps. An Honour was awarded for the campaign which had lasted just ten weeks, a most prestigious Honour. **Malaya 1941–42** was gained by ten British regiments, including both battalions of the Cambridgeshire Regiment which thereby ceased to exist until after the war, to six Australian Infantry and one machine gun regiment, to the three regiments of Indian Engineers and to ten Indian regiments, one of which was a Cavalry regiment fighting dismounted, to three Gurkha regiments, to the Malay Regiment and to the Singapore Volunteer Corps.

Burma, 1942

Having started 1942 in the Far East and swallowed one bitter pill, it might be better to get the swallowing of the second bitter pill over and done with as soon as possible, and then turn to other pleasanter things. Although it was expected that the Japanese would attack Burma as soon as possible, it was not generally believed that this would happen until the Battle of Malaya was over. This belief was proved wrong, with air raids on Rangoon in December 1941 and a land attack through Siam in the middle of January 1942. The Japanese quickly captured Kawkareik and Moulmein against spirited resistance by an Indian formation, although none of the regiments concerned claimed either of these as an Honour.

The withdrawal began across the Salween River and it was clear that the first strong defensive position would be on the Sittang River. Unfortunately the bridgehead troops were attacked by the Japanese before the main force, the 17th Indian Division, could reach it. In the belief that the division itself had been attacked as well and largely destroyed, as it had not yet reached the river, the single bridge was destroyed. Thus when the division eventually fought its way back to the river disaster faced it, with over ¼-mile of fast-flowing water ahead of it and few means of crossing it. Nevertheless part of the force did manage to cross, although most of the weapons and equipment were lost. The Honour **Sittang 1942** was awarded to two British and three Gurkha regiments of which 7th Gurkha Rifles also subsequently was granted the Honour **Sittang 1945** and an Indian Mountain battery was also granted it as an Honour Title.

The only remaining defensive position before Rangoon was the Pegu River, and the remnants of the 17th Division were joined there by three more British infantry battalions, and an armoured brigade which had been sent from the Middle East to Java and diverted to Burma.

It was at this point that problems arose with Australia. Australian divisions had already been much involved in the war in the Middle East, in Greece and in Malaya, and following the Japanese attack the divisions in the Middle East were being returned to Australia in case of an escalation of the war to that continent. The situation in Burma was desperate and the only reinforcements which could possibly arrive in time was the leading Australian division at sea in the Indian Ocean. Requests were made to the Australian Prime Minister for it to be diverted, and these requests were refused point blank. In spite of arguments from Churchill and the American President, Australia was adamant and the refusal was maintained; the British and Indians were left to fight on, alone and outnumbered. The only change was that Wavell now became Commander-in-Chief India and General Alexander took over the command in Burma; it was intended that he should command all the troops in Burma, but the American General Stilwell had arrived to command the Chinese army in the north of Burma and the Americans would not agree to his being put under Alexander's command.

Meanwhile the small force had been unable to stem the Japanese advance on the Pegu River and withdrew to Rangoon. When the Japanese reached Rangoon they planned to encircle it and to mount their attack from the west, and while this movement was taking place they blocked the northward road to Prome. After destroying the oil refinery the British tried to get out but were repulsed; having gathered their full strength they tried again and now found that the blocking force had been removed, as the encircling Japanese had now reached the position for their attack, and the way was open—for a very short while. They were thus able to escape with all their Artillery and transport. **Pegu 1942** was awarded as an Honour to one British armoured regiment and to two British and two Gurkha Infantry regiments, and **Taukyan** to one British regiment, both actions occurring during the withdrawal. The retreat was not pressed immediately by the Japanese who now needed to reorganise after the heavy fighting and casualties.

There was now no way for the British force to be reinforced and to all intents and purposes the fall of Rangoon, with its air and port facilities, meant the loss of Burma. All that was left for the tired and hard-pressed troops was a 600-mile walk out of Burma, through the jungles and mountains, into India, pursued by the Japanese and threatened by the onset of the wet season.

So the troops moved slowly back towards Toungoo and Prome. The Japanese attacked a Chinese division at the former place, defeated it and their main force moved up on the Irrawaddi, thus cutting off all contact between the British and the Chinese. The retreat continued towards Kalewa with a number of rearguard actions being fought, the army being accompanied by the civil government of Burma and by thousands of refugees. At length, after two months, and two days before the rains began, the almost impossible feat was accomplished and Alexander's Burma army reached the Indian frontier at Imphal, although by then all the remaining vehicles and tanks had been lost. It was a defeat of the first magnitude, but, like Dunkirk two years earlier, it was a magnificent achievement, and at least the Japanese were now barred from their passage into India.

A few Honours were awarded for this period, all for rearguard or protective actions during the retreat. **Paungde** was gained by one armoured and three Infantry regiments, all British. **Yenangyaung 1942** was gained by the Bengal Sappers and Miners, and by three British, one Indian and one Gurkha Infantry regiments, and the same Indian Mountain battery was also granted this as an Honour Title. **Kyaukse 1942** was gained by three Gurkha regiments, **Monywa 1942** by one British, one Indian and one Gurkha regiment and **Shwegyin** by 7th Gurkha Rifles.

The Western Desert and Malta, 1942

We left the situation at the end of 1941 with Benghazi having been captured for the second time and the British forces pushing on towards El Agheila. But the initial successes of a year before were not to be repeated as, unlike the Italians, Rommel avoided being cut off at Antelat by strongly defending it and withdrawing during the delaying action to El Agheila himself. Ascribed to bad weather and air attack, which might be thought to be mutually exclusive, but mainly due to the difficulty of getting the port of Benghazi working and the need to ferry supplies all the way from Tobruk, few troops could be taken forward, and only the Guards Brigade and 7th Armoured Division, shortly to relieved by 1st Armoured Division which had recently arrived in the theatre, were able to be maintained facing the enemy.

Meanwhile, at the turn of the year, the enemy garrisons which had been holding out at Bardia, Sollum and Halfaya were heavily attacked and after a hard battle they surrendered. There were thousands of prisoners, and at the same time over 1,000 British prisoners were released. Two Honours were awarded. **Bardia 1942** was gained by one New Zealand and five South African regiments, with two other South African regiments unhonoured. **Sollum** was gained by one South African regiment with another one unrecognised, although this was the South African name for it and the official British name **Clayden's Trench** is not found in the list of Battle Honours carried by any regiments.

But General Auchinleck had miscalculated the enemy situation at the western end of the front. Due to disasters to British ships at sea, and the inability of the RAF in Malta to give its previous support because of heavy German air attack on its bases, Rommel was being supplied with munitions and troops without difficulty.

On 21 January, Rommel carried out a reconnaissance in

force, and finding little opposition pressed forward. Weak rearguard actions were fought by armoured forces with heavy losses at Saunnu and Msus, which did little to delay the inevitable. The 4th Indian Division was diverted from its proposed offensive to contain what started out as a feint with a weak force towards Mechili, while Rommel's main force attacked Benghazi, which was once more hurriedly evacuated.

The Desert Army fell back with apparently very little little control by senior commanders, and without the Guards Brigade and 4th Indian Division being allowed to stand in defence as their commanders wanted and considered possible, and the showing of 1st Armoured Division was nothing to be proud of. Several companies of Guards discovered abandoned tanks which they collected and drove back, making good use of them in defensive actions during the retreat. Why they were abandoned and where their units had gone is not part of this narrative. The Desert Army retreated to a line through Gazala and Bir Hacheim, which was in fact the line which Rommel had intended to hold, facing the other way of course, in the previous November.

Several Honours were awarded for this period. **Saunnu** was gained by three armoured regiments and the Rifle Brigade, **Msus** by three armoured regiments and the Coldstream Guards, **Benghazi** by two Infantry regiments and **Carmusa** uniquely by the Cameron Highlanders (79th Foot). A South African Honour, **Agedabia**, was claimed by two recce regiments and an armoured car battalion.

The two armies faced each other on the Gazala line for three months, while General Auchinleck slowly planned another offensive and appeared to be avoiding overt action.

Further heavy air attacks on Malta had inhibited the allied means of preventing convoys taking reinforcements and supplies to Rommel, and had caused the island itself to be near to starvation because of the difficulty of British convoys getting through and the damage caused to them in harbour even when they did get through. However, in May a large force of aircraft, Spitfires, was delivered to Malta from two aircraft carriers, one British and one American, which redressed the balance of air power, and the heavy attacks abated. It was too late however to prevent Rommel being resupplied, and supplies to the island were still a problem and the food crisis continued.

The defences of the Gazala line had been laid out as a series of fortified points named 'boxes', covered by minefields and themselves held by Infantry with armour held in reserve. The 2nd South African Division held defensive positions around Tobruk supported by an Indian brigade. Rommel attacked on the night of 26/27 May at Bir Hacheim with the intention of outflanking the British positions and taking them from the rear. The British armour resisted stoutly, Bir Hacheim itself was held tenaciously by a Free French division, and his plan was foiled. But he retreated into the minebelt which now helped him more than the defenders, and prepared for the next assault.

Early in June Rommel concentrated his attacks on the bridgehead in front of the 'box' held by 50th Northumbrian Division and at Bir Hacheim. The former area, because it controlled a gap in the line through which any

movement in either direction must take place, became appropriately known as the 'Cauldron', and massive armoured battles took place in it. Eventually the British had to withdraw, but not before inflicting enormous casualties on the enemy armour and guns, and Bir Hacheim was evacuated.

Several Honours were granted for this phase of the Gazala battles. **PT 171** was awarded to an Indian armoured regiment, Gardner's Horse, and an Indian Field Artillery regiment was granted this as an Honour Title. **Retma** was awarded to one rifle regiment, **Bir el Igela** uniquely to the 8th Hussars, **Bir el Aslagh** to three armoured and one Yeomanry regiment and **Bir Hacheim** to one British and one Indian armoured regiments and to two British rifle regiments. **The Cauldron** was gained by two armoured and two Yeomanry regiments, and by three Infantry regiments and a Gurkha regiment.

Two South African Honours were awarded. **Alem Hamza 1942** was gained by three regiments and **PT 204** by a single regiment, the Royal Natal Carbineers. Two other Honours were unsuccessfully claimed, *Commonwealth Keep* by detachments only of three regiments and *Bir Temrad* by eight regiments but each only in company strength.

Rommel's capture of Bir Hacheim had turned the British flank and the 50th Division and 1st South African Division were in danger of being cut off until they were withdrawn. Fierce battles were fought on the ridges around 'Knightsbridge', El Adem and Acroma, the outer defences of Tobruk; these were largely armoured battles, with Infantry support, the Armageddon of the Desert War, and the British armour was severely mauled and its strength dangerously depleted. The battles were now definitely going in the enemy's favour and the situation was extremely critical. At this point Auchinleck himself took over direct command of the desert battle.

Another series of Honours were granted for this phase; it will be noted that so many of these have been won by very small groups of units, which points up the fragmented and individualistic nature of the battles, so unlike the battles of the Great War. **Knightsbridge** was awarded to three armoured regiments, two regiments of Guards and two rifle regiments and the Honourable Artillery Company, **Hagiag er Raml** to one Yeomanry regiment, The Sharpshooters, **Gabr el Fachri** and **Zt el Mrasses** both uniquely to the Durham Light Infantry (68th Foot), and **Via Balbia** to one armoured and one Infantry regiment. Two South African Honours were awarded, **Acroma Keep** to one regiment, the Transvaal Scottish, and **Best Post** to two regiments, and claimed by two more.

Tobruk was now the key to the defences. Rommel had already outflanked the port and reached Sidi Rezegh once more, decimating an armoured brigade in the process. Tobruk had been held in siege for eight months the previous year and hopes were high of the same thing happening again, but although it was not known at the time Auchinleck apparently had other ideas and had ordered its evacuation before investment became effective while still requiring it to be defended as long as possible. The defences had not been maintained or improved to the proper condition for siege, and it was only intended to be part of the defence line between the coast and El Adem.

The commander of 2nd South African Division, General Klopper, responsible for its defence, was now put into an equivocal and impossible position, in spite of the considerable forces at his disposal, which were nevertheless not really sufficient to hold the very long perimeter around the town. The defenders included, as well as his own division, a Guards Brigade and an Indian Infantry brigade.

Rommel now directly attacked the defences, supported by dive bombers and almost all his armour, which he could now afford to do having virtually destroyed all the British armour, and cut off the port. A South African counterattack, mounted piecemeal, failed and most of the few available British tanks in the perimeter were destroyed. Confusion reigned everywhere. The garrison fought with great gallantry, but the situation rapidly became hopeless. Food and ammunition was running out, there could be no resupply in the circumstances, and only terrible casualties could result from continued fighting. General Klopper therefore surrendered on 21 June. His action, and the adverse effect on morale which arose from it, was a blow to all the desert hopes, because Tobruk had become synonymous with 'backs to the wall' defence. Even to this day, forty years later, it is a very sensitive issue with South Africans, who feel that it was a slur on their fighting prowess. But Klopper was in fact the scapegoat for the Commander-in-Chief's decision not to hold the port, which appears to have been known only to his most senior staff and was never communicated to Churchill in London. It was one of the saddest and most unnecessary actions of the war, and one which, with the ineffective and indeterminate action of the armour during the retreat from Agheila five months earlier, almost lost Britain the Desert War.

Three individual Battle Honours were awarded. **Sidi Rezegh 1942** was gained by one armoured regiment, the 9th Lancers, **Tobruk 1942** by the Coldstream Guards, the Cameron Highlanders, an Indian and a Gurkha regiment, and **The Kennels** by an Indian armoured regiment. A Campaign Honour was also awarded for the period between the first attack on the Gazala Line and the fall of Tobruk. **Gazala** was gained by eight British armoured and two Yeomanry regiments, by the Scots Guards and by fourteen Infantry regiments, and by eleven South African regiments. An Indian Field Artillery regiment was granted it as an Honour Title, and it was claimed unsuccessfully by two South African armoured car regiments.

The loss of Tobruk meant that the frontier position to which the main army had been falling back was now untenable, and it was decided to withdraw still further to a better position around Mersa Matruh. Rommel followed up closely, using the impetus of his recent victories, with a force of about ten divisions, against which were some complete, but also some *ad hoc* formations, which did not amount in all to more than half this total, most of them battle-weary after a long retreat and hard fighting. A fallback position, if Mersa Matruh could not be held, was being constructed at El Alamein between the sea and the Quattara Depression.

Rommel's attack on the Mersa Matruh position was a facsimile of the one on the Gazala Line, except that this time he first broke through the centre of the line and then fanned out north and south to encircle the defenders.

Minqar Qaim, taking the place of Bir Hacheim at the southern end of the position, was held by the 2nd New Zealand Division; it was surrounded and the New Zealanders were attacked furiously and unceasingly all day, beating off all assaults. After dark they broke out eastwards, charging with bayonets fixed, and reached the Alamein positions. The Indian brigade in the centre, which had borne the brunt of the initial assault, also broke out with great gallantry. The divisions on the coast retreated, until the whole force took up new positions at El Alamein.

Several Honours were granted for this phase. Two were uniquely awarded, **PT 174** to the Durham Light Infantry (68th Foot) and **Fuka** to the Highland Light Infantry (71st Foot). **Minqar Qaim** was awarded to the Sharpshooters (Yeomanry) and to fifteen New Zealand Infantry battalions. The overall Honour, **Mersa Matruh**, was gained by two British armoured, one Yeomanry and five Infantry regiments, by fifteen New Zealand Infantry regiments, and by the Madras Engineers and two Indian Infantry regiments. Two South African armoured car regiments claimed the Honour unsuccessfully.

The retreat to El Alamein was pursued by Rommel, who was seeking a chance to attack the 8th Army while it was still off balance and before it could properly fortify the new, and final possible, position before Cairo, the Nile and the Suez Canal. The South Africans were heavily attacked and in the south a fierce battle raged all day around the Indian position at Deir el Shein and a gap in the line was opened. Rommel threw everything he could into the battle against the South Africans and 1st Armoured Division to enlarge the gap, and although he broke through he was strongly counterattacked in the flank by two British armoured brigades and the New Zealand division, and withdrew again leaving the British position intact. Further attacks in the area were also thrown back, and it is strange, as will be seen later, that none of the South African or New Zealand troops were awarded any Honours for these actions. Everywhere that Rommel attacked the 8th Army, bloodied but unbroken in spite of all the casualties it had suffered since the attack at Gazala only six weeks earlier, he was repulsed, and this was really the moment at which his hopes of the capture of Egypt must have started to fade.

The British now went over to the attack, and a British/New Zealand column carried out a successful raid on Fuka airfield. The 9th Australian Division had now arrived at the front and immediately attacked and captured the Tel el Eisa ridge. This ridge, and the Ruweisat ridge, was the scene of furious battles over the next few days and changed hands several times. A few days later still a larger attack was mounted in this area and towards El Mreir and the Miteirya ridge by the 2nd New Zealand and 5th Indian Divisions; but support from the armour did not materialise and the New Zealanders were driven back with heavy casualties. Another attack by the Australians on the Makh Khad and Miteirya ridges was initially successful but they had to withdraw in the face of counterattacks, the same thing happened when they were supported by the New Zealanders on the Ruweisat Ridge. The positions were now finely balanced and it was unlikely that either side could have achieved much without some rest and reorganisation.

During this period Honours for a number of actions were awarded. **Deir el Shein** was gained by one Yeomanry and two British Infantry regiments, and one Indian and one Gurkha regiment. **Ruweisat** was gained by two armoured, one Yeomanry and four Infantry and rifle regiments and **Fuka Airfield** by two rifle regiments, all of them British. **Tel el Eisa** was awarded to three Australian regiments, one armoured and two Infantry, and **Point 93** to one Yeomanry regiment, the ubiquituous Sharpshooters. **Ruweisat Ridge** was a larger affair and was awarded to one British armoured, one Yeomanry and two Infantry regiments, to an Australian machine gun battalion, to one Indian Infantry regiment and to sixteen New Zealand regiments. **Tell el Makh Khad** and **Sanyet el Miteirya** were each awarded to four regiments, all Australian, **El Mreir** to sixteen New Zealand Infantry regiments and **Qattara Track** uniquely to an Australian regiment, although it was claimed by four South African regiments as well.

There was one South African Honour awarded and claimed, which coincided with the British one for the Ruweisat ridge, **Alamein Box**, which was gained by two regiments and claimed by a third. *Springbok Road* was claimed by three regiments but in each case only in company strength. Finally there was an overall Honour for the period, **Defence of the Alamein Line**, known to the South Africans as **Alamein Defence**. This was awarded to six British armoured, one Yeomanry, two Guards and nine Infantry regiments, by one Australian armoured, seven Infantry and one machine gun regiment, by sixteen New Zealand regiments, by one Indian Infantry regiment and by eleven South African regiments. It was claimed by two South African armoured car regiments.

During August, while both sides were licking their wounds and reorganising, the most significant changes took place in the British High Command during a visit to the front by Winston Churchill, the CIGS and other very senior personnel. First, General Auchinleck was replaced by General Alexander, whom we last saw commanding the Burma retreat, as Commander-in-Chief; secondly, General Gott was appointed to command the 8th Army, but two days later, before he could take up the post, he was killed in an air crash and the command devolved on General Montgomery. Once more Alexander and Montgomery were together, once more in a very tense and difficult situation, but one which happily would have a very different outcome from that in France two years earlier. In fact the whole team at the top was reorganised and now fitted in well with the senior Navy and Air commanders.

Reinforcements, awaited since the start of the last phase of the Desert War, were getting into the battle, the 44th Home Counties Division and 51st Highland Division, the latter now brought up to strength since the debacle at St Valery, in addition to the 9th Australian Division already mentioned. The destroyed tanks had been replaced and many extra ones were available, and other supplies were beginning to pour in. Rommel had also been reinforced but he was having difficulty with his supplies. He was clearly planning an assault and this was confirmed by prisoners, but Montgomery had issued his orders that there would be absolutely no withdrawals for any reason.

On 30 August Rommel made his last play for Egypt, his tactics again being those used at Gazala. It was a very heavy attack, intended to break the British line in the south and attack northwards towards the coast. Montgomery had anticipated this and the British armour had been ordered to delay the Germans but to let their armour through and then destroy the transport which followed. The main British positions, strongly entrenched at Alem el Halfa, would then be in a position to hit the advancing armour in the flank and bear the brunt of the attack. After breaking through with difficulty, and being suspicious, Rommel halted to encourage a counterattack, but nothing happened and he moved on again. But now he was heavily attacked from the air, but, unlike at Gazala, had no room to manoeuvre; his massed forces formed perfect artillery targets and he was now in great trouble. Tanks stuck in soft sand and he was very short of petrol, since his transport had been destroyed, which added to his general immobility. The battle was not yet over and went on for a week; the British did not escape without serious losses, but eventually Rommel withdrew.

The role of this battle in finally ending Rommel's bid for Alexandria, and the brilliant way in which it was fought by the British commander, made it one of the key battles of the whole war, probably even more significant and vital than the breakthrough at El Alamein which was to follow. Only two Battle Honours were awarded, one for an action and the other for the battle as a whole. **West Point 23** was gained by one Yeomanry regiment, the Royal Gloucestershire Hussars this time, and by one Australian armoured and one Infantry regiment. **Alam el Halfa** was gained by eight armoured, five Yeomanry and six Infantry regiments of the British army, and by two Australian and sixteen New Zealand regiments. For some obscure reason no Honours were awarded to South African regiments, although the 1st South African Division and two other armoured car regiments participated in the battle.

During the next month and a half the Desert Army built up its strength and its resources while Rommel built up his defences. The date for the next great attack had to be delayed because Montgomery refused to start before he had all the resources in troops, munitions and supplies that he considered were necessary. The period was not without incident, and a new idea was tried out with little success — seaborne raids on enemy rear areas. Three were carried out on the night of 13/14 September, one on Tobruk, another on Benghazi and the third on Barce, and a few days later one on Gialo. They did not achieve anything because in several cases no troops could be landed, although they undoubtedly caused alarm. Only one, probably because of the small numbers involved, was claimed as an Honour and awarded, **Benghazi Raid** by the SAS. On 30 September there was a sharp attack by two battalions on **Deir el Munassib** which was awarded as an Honour to the Queen's Royal Regiment (2nd Foot).

In August a very large convoy sailed for Malta, which was again suffering near-starvation. The enemy mounted a major air and sea attack against it and the losses were such that, apart from warships sunk or damaged, only five out of 14 merchant ships reached Grand Harbour, but even that small number was vital.

On the night of 23 October the decisive British attack at

El Alamein opened with the supporting fire of 1,000 guns. As there was no open flank, progress could only be made by a breakthrough, and to this end four divisions, supported by two armoured divisions to exploit any successes, attacked in the north. At the same time other divisions made diversionary attacks in the south, sufficiently strongly to hold the German armour. Rommel had expected to be attacked in the centre near the Ruweisat ridge, because of false plans which had been planted, and this was where he had his main troop concentrations, but the deception meant that he now had to reorganise quickly. Fierce fighting continued all along the front for ten days. Counterattacks were launched and repulsed, and slowly the German and Italian strength was worn down. The direction and location of the British attacks was changed to keep the defences off-balance. The Australians attacked northwards towards the coast from the bulge created by the initial attacks, which put the Germans holding the north of their line in danger of being cut off. And now a major force of four divisions was withdrawn from the immediate battle as a new reserve for the breakthrough which was imminent.

On 2 November this force assaulted under a massive artillery barrage. But the German defences had been strengthened and a bitter engagement followed. The armour then moved in but also met heavy resistance. On 4 November an Indian brigade attacked south of Tel el Aqqaqir and was successful. A hole had been punched in the defences, and was soon widened, and the way was open for the tanks to pursue the retreating Germans and Italians across the open desert. A single Honour, **El Alamein,** was awarded and was won by thirteen British armoured, seven Yeomanry, twenty-one Infantry regiments and the Honourable Artillery Company, by one Australian armoured, nine Infantry, one machine gun and one pioneer regiments, by the New Zealand Scottish armoured cars and fifteen New Zealand, two Indian Infantry and one Gurkha regiments, and by eleven South African regiments, although two South African armoured car regiments were again not rewarded.

After the battle the Australians were pulled out and ended their tour in the Middle East with a fine record of achievement. They were returned to Australia and then to New Guinea.

The pursuit began, against initial scattered resistance, and thousands of prisoners were taken including General von Thoma, commander of the Afrika Korps. Rommel's objective was to extricate as much as possible of his armour, and now at last he had some luck as heavy rainfall bogged down the pursuers, restricting them largely to the roads. On 11 November a small force captured Halfaya and the Honour for this, **Capture of Halfaya Pass 1942**, was awarded to the King's Royal Rifle Corps and four New Zealand regiments. But the main force had already bypassed it.

Places famous or notorious in the past for their battles—Bardia, Sollum, Sidi Rezegh, Tobruk (entered appropriately by South African armoured cars), Derna, Benghazi—were passed with virtually no resistance and at high speed, and will be heard of no more in the narrative of the war. On 12 December El Agheila was occupied and five days

later the advance guard reached Nofilia. By the end of the year Buerat had been taken and a halt was called for reorganisation; unfortunately bad weather had again intervened, and much of Rommel's armour had managed to escape the net.

El Agheila was awarded as an Honour to three British armoured, two Yeomanry and one Infantry regiments and to fourteen New Zealand regiments. **Nofilia** was awarded to the Royal Scots Greys (2nd Dragoons) and to the King's Royal Rifle Corps (60th Foot), and to fifteen New Zealand Infantry regiments.

So ended 1942 in the desert, a year which saw many changes as the battle ebbed and flowed, but which concluded with a magnificent victory which changed the whole history of the war and with the defeat, if not the final destruction, of the German and Italian Desert Armies.

After the victory at El Alamein and Rommel's retreat the siege of Malta was virtually lifted and supplies were now able to get through to the island. The siege was officially deemed to have ended on 20 November after almost two and a half years. Although much of the defence had been carried out actively by the Royal Air Force and the Royal Navy, neither of these could have existed there without the holding of the island which was carried out by the Army. The Honour **Malta 1940–42** was awarded to eleven British Infantry regiments and to the Malta Regiment.

North Africa, 1942

Whilst the 8th Army was still retreating to El Alamein, and there was still every possibility of Rommel reaching the Nile delta, plans for a major extension of the war were being laid in London. Not only was there a need to draw off some of the German strength from both the Commonwealth armies in the desert and also from the Russian front, but only a small proportion of the American forces could be used in the Pacific and there was a need to employ others of their very large forces in an active theatre.

It was therefore decided in July to invade the western end of the North African coast with a joint British/American Army, under the American command of General Eisenhower, who had risen to this high position straight from a relatively junior Pentagon staff position without ever having been in action. This territory was French, and officially part of the unoccupied zone of France, but an invasion there would allow an advance to be made on Tunis, hopefully in concert with the 8th Army from the east, to drive the Axis forces finally from the African continent.

Planning went on during the late summer and early autumn, and it was hoped that the French in Algeria, Tunisia and Morocco would accept the invasion as a benefit to them and offer no, or only a nominal show of, resistance. It was decided to land at three points at which the surface ships could be provided with air protection, which could only come from Gibraltar. There were four possibilities where major facilities existed, excluding Tunis itself which was too far away from Gibraltar, and too near to Malta, still under heavy air attack, to be practicable.

Oran and Algiers had to be two of these ports but the

question was whether Casablanca or Bone should be the third. The former was eventually chosen, largely because there was a rail link, even though a tortuous one, to it from Oran and Algiers, which could be of value if things went wrong and an evacuation became necessary to save troops from being bottled up in the Mediterranean, although this meant that the Army would have to cover a longer distance eastwards to Tunis.

On good advice it was also decided that the French General Giraud, who was reputed to be very popular in North Africa, should be taken from captivity in southern France to raise the banner in support of the Allies. His extraction from prison was carried out successfully, but the plan failed because Giraud considered that his honour and that of France could only be salved if he had overall command of the operation, which was clearly impossible because of his lack of recent military knowledge and strategy.

The three landings took place on 8 November. 11 Infantry Brigade landed west of Algiers without opposition and advanced inland, but at Algiers itself the attack was carried out against stiff opposition from the harbour batteries and two destroyers carrying troops were crippled. But as soon as the American follow-up troops were landed the port and area around was quickly captured. At Oran the French forces, particularly the Navy, resisted very strongly for two days until they were subdued. At Casablanca there was also trouble, partly from the French Navy but mainly from the weather which turned bad and inhibited the landing of reinforcements.

The next problem was Giraud again, who turned out after all to be unpopular in North Africa and to have little influence on the course of events. The final problem was that Admiral Darlan turned up unexpectedly, and accidently, in Algiers at the time of the landing. He was very anti-British and the danger was that he would bring out the French fleet against the Allies. It was hoped that he could be persuaded to change his allegiance rather than be imprisoned, but these hopes faded until the Germans started to occupy southern France in violation of the 1940 armistice and then Darlan co-operated. Unfortunately the French army had sworn allegiance to Marshall Petain in Vichy, and he refused to release them from their vow; when Darlan ordered them to cease fighting, Petain dismissed him from his command, a rather academic action in the circumstances, and ordered the troops to resist. Just over a month later Admiral Darlan was assassinated by a young man who seemed to think that he was saving France from a wicked leader and dishonour.

Before the allied force could make any real progress eastwards the Germans began to reinforce the Tunis area, although only moving their screens towards the border. This, with the lack of French co-operation at this stage, was making the situation very different from that which had been envisaged in the planning stages. But the fighting in Casablanca, a wholly American operation, had soon stopped and Dakar was captured, which secured the line of retreat should it become necessary.

The British 1st Army under General Anderson quickly started to move towards Tunisia, now hampered by a new problem when the weather turned very wet long before it was expected to do and inhibited adequate air support. Nevertheless it progressed very rapidly. Commandos landed and parachutists dropped at Bone, the first operational drop by the Parachute Regiment, and were soon joined by 6 Royal West Kent Regiment, and 36 Infantry Brigade landed at Bougie. During the next fortnight the force pressed on into Tunisia at Tebouka, where it first came into contact with German ground forces, which were brushed aside, although not without some fighting. On 16 November advanced troops reached Djebel Abiod, where the Royal West Kents were for the first time attacked by German tanks, and the Parachute Regiment captured Beja and joined forces with the French troops who were now fighting with the Allies. The advance became two-pronged, the inland arm moving through Souk-Ahras and Souk-el-Arba towards Medjez-el-Bab, where there was a sharp battle until the Northamptonshire Regiment entered the town. Finally by 28 November the northern prong had reached Meteur and the southern Djedeida from where the Army could look down on Tunis itself.

A number of Honours were awarded for this first phase, mostly uniquely. **Jebel Abiod** was gained by the Royal West Kent Regiment (50th Foot), **Soudia** by the Parachute Regiment, and **Medjez-el-Bab** by one Yeomanry and two Infantry regiments. **Tebourba** was gained by the East Surrey Regiment (31st Foot) and **Djedeida** by the Northamptonshire Regiment (48th Foot).

The advance so far had been easy, but now that resistance was building up the force was too weak to reach Tunis, and German counterattacks made it prudent for the advance guard brigade of Anderson's army to make a tactical withdrawal to a line from just forward of Medjez-el-Bab to the coast. The Parachute Regiment now attacked Oudna airfield to support a raid on Tunis; the raid was cancelled without the information getting to them, but although surrounded they fought their way out and back to Medjez. The Argyll and Sutherland Highlanders reached Sedjenane, but now the Army was being repulsed all along the line.

A small detachment of Americans had meanwhile made a parachute landing at Youks and had advanced through Tebessa and Kasserine to Gafsa, which could form a base for a major force to protect the flank of the 8th Army's advance when they had reached that far, or perhaps save it the trouble of advancing the whole way to Tunis. German armour attacked the Tebourba Gap and caused a British withdrawal to Longstop Hill, and now heavy rain intervened for three days. Longstop Hill, Tebourba and Bou Aoukaz were given up. The Coldstream Guards attacked and captured Longstop again and were relieved there by the Americans. The Americans were driven off and the Coldstream Guards again captured it, but this time were themselves driven off. 6 Armoured Division entered the battle and occupied Bou Arada, south of Medjez.

Several more Honours were awarded for the withdrawal phase up to the end of the year. **Djebel Azzag 1942** was won by two Infantry regiments, **Oudna** by the Parachute Regiment, **Tebourba Gap** by one armoured, one Yeomanry and one Infantry regiment, and **Longstop Hill 1942** by the Coldstream Guards.

At the end of the year the American and British armies

were poised for an attack, but the cold, wet weather in the mountains, which soon bogged down all transport movement, meant that this would have to be delayed.

Madagascar

The very large island of Madagascar, off the East African coast, was a French colony, administered by Vichy but inadequately defended, and could be occupied by the Japanese at any time, thus endangering the British sea routes to the Middle and Far East. It was decided therefore that a British expedition must occupy the island first, which should not have been too difficult unless there was a leak of the plan which could make the Vichy French reinforce the garrison and perhaps attempt to interfere with a landing.

This was to be a seaborne amphibious landing, the first of the war and the first since the landing at Gallipoli in 1915. The assault force, British and South African, with a massive escort, assembled at Durban and reached the island on 5 May; it landed on the virtually undefended west coast, with support from the Royal Navy and a Fleet Air Arm attack on Diego Suarez bay. At the end of the day, with two brigades ashore, marines were landed with great daring at Antisirane and captured the naval depot. The following day the French surrendered the northern area of the island.

The French were not prepared to change their pro-Vichy attitude, however, and further operations were planned. In September British Infantry captured Majunga on the west coast, where an East African brigade landed a few days later and set out for Tananariva, the capital. A British brigade re-embarked and landed at Tamatave without much opposition, then moved to join the South and East Africans at Tananariva, which immediately fell. The French Governor was still resisting, but was soon captured and at the beginning of November accepted surrender terms.

The whole amphibious operation was brilliantly planned and executed, at a time when affairs elsewhere were not going very well. An Honour, **Madagascar**, was awarded to six British and three South African Infantry regiments and to the King's African Rifles, and the Commandos and was claimed by a South African armoured car squadron.

North West Europe, 1942

After a gap of nearly two years North West Europe again came into the picture, not with the 'Second Front' which was being demanded by the Russians, but with episodes which prepared and gave experience for it.

It had been discovered from aerial reconnaissance that the Germans had erected a chain of radar stations on the French and Belgian coasts, one of which was on top of a 400-foot cliff at Bruneval near Le Havre. During the night of 27 February, in snow, a paratroop detachment, accompaned by radar experts, landed on the cliffs behind the radar station. In a very short time the station had been captured, vital equipment photographed and destroyed or removed to the beach where the Navy took the party off. Casualties were very light. The Honour, **Bruneval**, was awarded to the Parachute Regiment.

A month later another raid was carried out, this time by a naval force with a Commando, on the harbour at St Nazaire. Although casualties were heavy it was a success and blocked the use of the port by U-boats for a period. The Honour **St Nazaire** was awarded to the Commandos.

A much bigger landing operation took place in August. It had originally been planned for July, but bad weather had inhibited it and at first it was abandoned; but the need for a large-scale operation to gain experience for planning a cross-Channel assault over-ruled caution. Therefore a raid on Dieppe was planned in great secrecy and very quickly, using an all-Canadian force. Although nothing leaked out to the Germans of the plan they were taking precautions against such a possibility whenever moon and tides were favourable, and a full-scale German division was on alert when the raid took place.

The greatest gallantry was shown by the troops taking part, and although the results were not at all what were hoped for a great deal of experience was gained of landings against a defended enemy coast, and the raid was by no means the failure it has sometimes been made out to be. Nevertheless the casualties were very high, well over 3,000 of all categories of which nearly 1,000 were captured, in all over 60 per cent of the force employed. **Dieppe** was awarded as an Honour to the Commandos and to eight Canadian Infantry regiments.

South West Pacific, 1942

By the spring of 1942 the Japanese had captured a large number of the Pacific islands, and although the Americans were still holding out in the Philippines their resistance could not last much longer. There was thus a considerable threat to the Australian continent, and Australian troops, which had been sent to New Guinea soon after the attack on Malaya and Singapore, were now virtually the only ground-based forces in contact with the enemy in the South West Pacific theatre.

Even before Singapore finally fell the Japanese had attacked Rabaul in New Britain on 23 January, and after brief but bitter fighting the small Australian garrison retired and most of them were made prisoner, after which 150 were massacred. A small force, mostly from the Papua New Guinea Volunteer Rifles, marched into the mountains, continued guerilla warfare and helped the coast watchers, who had first been installed in the early 1920s for this very eventuality. They were subsequently evacuated to New Guinea and finally to Australia. The Honour of **Rabaul** was awarded to the 22nd Australian Regiment and to the Papua New Guinea Volunteer Rifles.

Elsewhere in the islands an Australian brigade had been split up into single battalions, and distributed to various unrelated places, although none of them was strong enough by itself to stem the overwhelming Japanese onslaught. The Japanese, advancing through the East Indies, first attacked Amboina at the end of January and on 3 February the single Australian battalion surrendered, although one company at Laha resisted determinedly for a while longer, the survivors being taken prisoner and many executed. **Ambon** and **Laha** were awarded to the 21st Australian Regiment.

The attack on Timor followed on 19 February by the Japanese brigade which had captured Amboina, and although the battalion there, supported by a British Light Anti-aircraft battery, defended desperately, the garrison of Koepang was surrounded four days later and forced to surrender. An Independent Company garrisoning Dili escaped to the centre of the island, was later reinforced by another company, and waged guerilla warfare for almost a year until it was evacuated. **Koepang** was awarded as an Honour to the 40th Regiment, but Dili could not be awarded as the unit participating was not a recognisable unit for the purpose.

A fourth small Australian force, consisting of a machine gun battalion and a Pioneer battalion, supported by a Field Company, a British squadron of tanks of 3 Hussars and some anti-aircraft artillery, with some Dutch colonial troops, was attacked in Java. When the Japanese convoys approached naval battles developed, but the allied warships were outnumbered and most of them were sunk. It was decided that no reinforcements would be sent and that the garrison should be left to fight to the last against three Japanese divisions which landed at the end of February. Dutch resistance was negligible and the Australians were isolated and split up. Although the Australian/British force defended strongly for several days it was forced to fall back on Bandoeng and surrendered eight days after the attack. **Java 1942** was awarded to the two Australian regiments, but again the 3rd Hussars squadron was not of sufficient size to be recognised for it.

Two Australian divisions were returning from the Middle East, the troops that Churchill had wanted to divert to Burma (see page 158), and they were now sent straight on to Australia instead of going to Java and Sumatra as originally planned, but now obviously pointless. The only allied bases left in the islands were now in the south-eastern part of New Guinea and Papua. The Japanese were planning to invade and capture Port Moresby with a force from Rabaul, but the Battle of the Coral Sea, fought by the American fleet and the first sea battle in history in which the opposing surface forces never got within sight of each other, prevented this to a large extent, although the Japanese probably threw away their advantage by not pursuing the invasion. The garrison of Port Moresby was reinforced, although only minimally, and a base was established at Milne Bay on the south-eastern tip of Papua.

In July it became clear that the Japanese now intended to attack the northern coast of New Guinea at Buna, and it was decided to take action to defend it from the garrison at Port Moresby by occupying the Kokoda Trail in case they were planning an overland assault. This was an incredibly difficult route which switchbacked over the Owen Stanley range between the two ports. The Japanese landed in the Buna area on 22 July with a comparatively small force which was subsequently greatly increased. The weak Australian force was forced to withdraw and a week later the Japanese occupied Kokoda, from which they intended to mount an attack along the Trail towards Port Moresby. The American landing on Guadalcanal surprised them and threw them off balance, and the attack was postponed, and instead a subsidiary attack was planned on Milne Bay to support the land attack on Port Moresby.

The Japanese landed near Milne Bay on 26 August and at first confused fighting took place in torrential rain. Their armour soon bogged down in the mud and an Australian counterattack supported by close air-to-ground attack drove them back. The Japanese made a number of resolute attacks, but every time they were repulsed with very heavy casualties. The Australians, mostly young militiamen, counterattacked again and the enemy was on the run in the mud. Eventually in early September the Japanese forces were evacuated. Australian casualties were light compared with the Japanese who lost nearly five times as many killed and a far higher percentage of wounded.

The Australian commander, General Clowes, was severely criticised by General MacArthur, now Commander-in-Chief South West Pacific, for not attacking strongly enough and not keeping him supplied with information, although it was very difficult to do this and such information as was supplied to him by MacArthur's staff was wildly confusing and inaccurate in the first place. None of his HQ staff, which did not include a single Australian officer, had any experience of fighting in the prevailing conditions. This, and many other similar subsequent criticisms, inevitably caused a lot of resentment from the Australians and did not help the allied cause. **Milne Bay** was awarded as an Honour to five Australian regiments.

The day after the landing at Milne Bay the Japanese started their attack over the Kokoda Trail and during the next seven weeks advanced on and captured Deniki, Isurava, Eora Creek, Templetons Crossing and Efogi. During the following week the Australians further withdrew through Menari to Ioribaiwa only 30 miles as the crow flies from Port Moresby itself. The defenders fought gallantly in appalling conditions and inflicted heavy casualties on the Japanese. There were many sharp engagements, often by quite small bodies of troops. From one such action Lieutenant-Colonel Owen was posthumously awarded the Distinguished Service Cross by the Americans, the first American award to an Australian during the war. The Australians counterattacked at Deniki and Isurava but were overwhelmed. Reinforcements arrived at Port Moresby and were immediately committed. Supply was very difficult, as was the evacuation of wounded, and the natives volunteered to help, becoming known as 'Fuzzy Wuzzy Angels'. The Australians had to give ground against heavy attacks, although they inflicted enormous losses on the enemy in the process, and a number of VCs were awarded. The withdrawal to Ioribaiwa now began.

General MacArthur, an American hero after his defence of Corregidor in the Philippines, again severely and unjustly criticised the Australian troops as lacking in aggressiveness and efficiency. But he was sitting back in Australia, never set foot in New Guinea, and had no idea of the conditions under which they were fighting, and even detailed reports failed to change his mind. His staff entirely misinterpreted the situation on the Kokoda Trail and did not appreciate the strength of the Japanese, preferring their own estimates to those of people on the spot, and also had no conception of the extraordinary difficulties of the Trail, the steps of the 'Golden Staircase', the fact that in part it could only be climbed on hands and knees, and that distances were measured in hours rather than miles and rates in hours per mile. The weather did not help either, being hot and humid by day and freezing at night, with continuous heavy rain. Some supplies were carried by native bearers and some dropped by air, but without parachutes and very inaccurately. One big cause of conflict between the Australians and the Americans at this time was probably the great superiority of the former in jungle fighting, which the latter never seemed to be able to assimilate, and the Australian offer to teach them which was flatly refused.

Honours were awarded for **Kokoda-Deniki** to the Pacific Islands Regiment and to the 39th Regiment, for **Isurava**, **Eora Creek-Templetons Crossing I** and **Efogi-Menari** each to three regiments, of which two were the same in each case, 14th and 16th Regiments, and **Ioribaiwa** to six regiments.

Late in September more reinforcements arrived, including American troops, and there were now three divisions in Papua-New Guinea. Moreover the Japanese now had the problem of supply over the Trail and they were starving, and they started to withdraw again to the Buna-Gona area. A counterattack at Ioribaiwa met with little resistance to the surprise of the attackers and a counteroffensive began. The Japanese retreated rapidly and Nauro, Menari, Efogi and Myola were entered without opposition. But at the great ravine through which flowed the turbulent Eora Creek at Templetons Crossing strong rearguards were encountered and in the Oivi-Goravi area the Japanese defended fanatically until they were driven out with suicidal losses. This latter battle the Australian troops called the 'Death Valley Massacre', because they were forced to kill wounded Japanese who continued fighting with their bare hands, and to shoot corpses because of the Japanese habit of shamming dead and then attacking when bypassed.

The cost to the Australians of driving the Japanese back into Buna had been high, but the Japanese losses outnumbered the Australian ones many times over. Honours were awarded for **Eora Creek-Templetons Crossing II** and **Oivi-Gorari** to the identical six Australian regiments, and for the whole operation, **Kokoda Trail**, to the Pacific Islands Regiment and to ten Australian regiments. The battle became as famous, legendary and emotional a part of Australian history as Gallipoli and Tobruk.

An Australian advance now started from Milne Bay directed on the Buna-Gona area. It was a very difficult task and involved a lot of ferrying by small boats over the frequent rivers and inlets. It was accomplished, but the Japanese strength had not been correctly assessed and they had fortified the Buna-Gona area very strongly. American troops joined in and in November they and the Australians closed in on the beachhead, but were rapidly halted with heavy losses. MacArthur still thought that it was lack of enterprise by the troops which caused delays rather than the fanaticism of the Japanese defenders, although he should have known better, and it was in fact the Americans who were inefficient, largely owing to their previous soft living and the lack of understanding of what was required to defeat the Japanese, and eventually some of them were put under Australian command.

In the attack on Cape Endaiadere the Australians suffered severely. The Japanese defensive position astride the Sanananda road was very strong and the Australians had reached the end of their endurance after desperate battles. They were relieved by fresh American troops who stated that now that they had come it was just a matter of mopping up and the Australians could go home. But after a week they were broken without having achieved anything and had to be relieved themselves by the Australians. The capture of the Sanananda position marked the end of the battle, and also the first defeat of Japanese land forces during the war, with a known loss of 65 per cent of their forces and a probable loss of as much as 90 per cent. It was an enormous achievement by the Allies, particularly by the Australians who had borne the brunt of the fighting for six months. The victory also destroyed any Japanese hopes of invading Australia, and had probably more effect on the outcome of the war in the Pacific than the Coral Sea battle and Solomon Island victories.

It was a cruel campaign and although the Japanese were eventually forced back into the sea they had defended their positions with counterattacks and suicidal conduct until starvation overcame them. The Battle for Papua did not end there until January 1943.

Honours were awarded for **Gona** to eight regiments, for **Sanananda Road** to nine regiments including the 7th Cavalry, of which only two regiments gained both Honours, for **Amboga River** to two regiments, for **Cape Endaiadere-Sinemi Creek** to four and for **Sanananda-Cape Killerton** to three regiments. The overall Honour for the battle, **Buna-Gona,** was awarded to eighteen regiments.

Thus 1942 ended on a high note with the Japanese invasion of Papua New Guinea having been defeated, and the realisation that in spite of their fanaticism the Japanese could be beaten.

The Western Desert, 1943

At the turn of the year the enemy was presumed to have withdrawn to his next defensive position covering Buerat. The British forces were nearing the effective end of their supply line from Benghazi and it became imperative to capture Tripoli and open the port as soon as possible. The German position at Buerat had no southern defensive flank and there was a danger, note a 'danger', that a further withdrawal would be made which could not be followed up quickly enough because of supply problems, and might thus enable Rommel to have time to prepare another defensive position before Tripoli. The strategy, therefore, was not to alert the enemy and the main attacking forces were held well back.

The weather now intervened again with a gale which wrecked Benghazi harbour, sinking one ship in the entrance, damaging others badly and reducing the flow of supplies. This followed a gale just before Christmas which had, among other damage, sunk the NAAFI supply ship with the troops' supply of drink on board, which was not as serious militarily but certainly affected morale! Once more the army was forced to rely on resupply from Tobruk, with a very long road haul, which was only achieved by immobilizing 10 Corps at Agheila, instead of it being moved forward, and using all its transport, as well as that of supporting formations, for the ferry.

The assault on Buerat opened with 51 Division moving forward on the coast, while 7 Armoured Division and 2 New Zealand Division carried out an outflanking movement; the coastal attack was commanded directly by Montgomery as there was only one Corps HQ available and the distance between the thrusts was too wide for one commander to direct both.

The flanking formations soon reached and crossed the Wadi Zem Zem, the German armour showing little fighting spirit, and were then dispatched on another wide outflanking movement towards Tripoli. Progress continued along the coast, Homs was captured and the advance on Tripoli was now mounted in earnest. A week after the capture of Buerat 22 Armoured Brigade, supported by 51 Division, captured Tripoli on 23 January; the goal for so long was in British hands at last and in exactly three months the Desert Army had advanced 1,400 miles, destroying the Afrika Korps in the process. There had been extensive demolitions in the harbour but they were quickly repaired and the first supply ships entered the port ten days later. Before the next advance the Prime Minister, Winston Churchill, visited the victorious 8th Army and a major parade was held in the city.

A single Honour was awarded to cover this period of activity, **Advance on Tripoli**, which was gained by five British armoured, two Yeomanry and seven Infantry regiments, and by a single New Zealand regiment, which seems small enough reward, particularly for a whole New Zealand division, but in the context of desert warfare in a quick advance against failing opposition probably fairly reflected the actual battle engagement of the troops taking part.

The next obvious enemy defensive position beyond Tripoli was at Mareth, a very strong position guarded on the south by the Matmata hills and with an advanced position at Medenine. The advance continued initially from Tripoli with only 7 Armoured Division, while the other formations were reorganising, and at the beginning of February it crossed the frontier into Tunisia, which meant that the whole of Italian North Africa was in British hands at last. But the weather turned wet again and the advance was necessarily delayed, because even the desert can become an impassable bog in such weather conditions.

Ben Gardane was entered and 51 Division was brought forward for the attack on Medenine. This key point soon fell despite spirited resistance against heavy attack. At this point a Free French force under General Leclerc, which had crossed the Sahara from Lake Chad, now joined the 8th Army and from then on operated on its left flank, always threatening the enemy's open desert flank. Considerable pressure was now brought to bear on the main Mareth position, mainly to draw off enemy troops from their attack on the Americans at Gafsa and Tebessa, and although this achieved its objective it made the task of the 8th Army that much more difficult.

The British force was increased in strength and although Rommel made probes against the leading formations he was too late now to breach the Army's positions. Nevertheless he did attempt a strong counterattack at Medenine

with a large force of armour, but everywhere it was contained and was defeated. **Medenine** was awarded as an Honour to six British and nine New Zealand Infantry regiments and the New Zealand Scottish, and for the same day's fighting two unique Honours were awarded also, **Zemlet el Lebene** to the Black Watch (42nd Foot) and **Tadjera Khir** to the Scots Guards.

The Mareth Line had originally been constructed by the French, based on the Wadi Zigzaou, to guard against any Italian attack on Tunisia from Libya, and had been further fortified by the Germans. It was therefore very strong and the desert flank on the Matmata hills was considered virtually impregnable. But it could be outflanked by a very wide movement through very bad going in waterless desert, which had also been pronounced by the French as impassable. In spite of the difficulties such an outflanking movement was mounted by the New Zealand Division which was strongly reinforced with armour for the purpose, ordered to move only by night until discovered by the enemy, and accompanied by a remarkable regiment of 'medium' Artillery, which consisted of batteries of captured German 88 mm and Italian 90 mm antiaircraft guns manned by volunteers, which if all had been taken could have manned several regiments, drawn from British AA regiments stationed for the defence of Tripoli. It rendered very positive assistance to the delighted New Zealanders. The force was already behind the German defences, such was its progress, when the main attack took place, and it inevitably caused the defences to be reduced to cover the threat when it was discovered.

The assault on Mareth was made initially by 50 Division on the coast, supported inland by 51 and 7 Armoured Divisions, with 4 Indian Division in reserve; in other words the whole of the regular and long-standing 8th Army formations were employed. Against desperate opposition the Northumbrians crossed the Wadi Zigzaou and gained a tenuous foothold in the defences. German counterattacks in heavy rain regained much of the captured ground, so that it became impracticable to continue the frontal assault, and Montgomery decided to maintain a holding position there and depend on the outflanking movement, to which 1 Armoured Division was now committed. 4 Indian Division was dispatched to get behind the enemy lines closer to the main battle by advancing through the theoretically impregnable Matmata hills, which it succeeded in doing, although not without trouble and casualties.

The New Zealanders were held up at the Tebaga Gap, almost overlooking their objective, and a quick attack was now necessary on the whole position to resolve the situation. An attack was mounted at Tebaga and despite stiff opposition and fierce fighting the New Zealand division and 1 Armoured Division broke through to El Hamma. The 'left hook', as it was called, was accomplished, and the whole German position was caught in a neat pincer movement, and Rommel had once again to retire, towards Gabes. The breaching of the Mareth Line was one of the great desert battles, and the hardest that the 8th Army had fought since Alamein itself. Close controlled air support played a very important part in the victory.

A number of Honours were granted for the period of

the battle, some of them gained uniquely. **Mareth** was awarded to the Royal Tank Regiment and to eleven British Infantry regiments and 2nd Gurkha Rifles, and **Wadi Zeuss East** to the Cheshire Regiment (22 Foot). **Wadi Zigzaou** was gained by four British Infantry regiments and **Point 201 (Roman Wall)** by one British armoured and two Yeomanry regiments and by ten New Zealand regiments. **Tebaga Gap** was awarded to four British armoured, three Yeomanry and four Infantry regiments and to sixteen New Zealand regiments, and **El Hamma** to five British armoured, three Yeomanry and one Infantry regiment and the Honourable Artillery Company, and to the same sixteen New Zealand regiments. Finally **Matmata Hills** was gained by the Essex Regiment (44 Foot) and the 4/6 Rajputana Rifles, both of 4 Indian Division.

Just north of El Hamma lies the marshy region of the Shott el Fejadj and between this and the sea is the Wadi Akarit, naturally defended on its northern side by two groups of broken hills. This was Rommel's next defensive position. The position was soon reached, with the New Zealanders, who had captured Gabes, on the seaward flank and 1 Armoured Division on its left. The attack on the Wadi began on 6 April with 51 Division, 4 Indian Division and 50 Division passing through the New Zealanders.

The 4th Indian Division attack was made on the Fatnassa massif on the left of the front, ahead of the others and at night without any preliminary bombardment. By dawn they had captured most of the massif and the main attack began. The fighting was very fierce with counterattacks being made on every British gain. Both sides were holding grimly to the ground which they had and strongly contesting any effort to dislodge them. But a breakthrough was forced, during a night attack, in spite of the resistance and Rommel pulled back in full retreat, with fewer and fewer places left in which he could stand before he reached the sea. This was one of the toughest battles of the whole campaign, and in one day three Infantry divisions, employing only sixteen battalions, had dislodged three armoured and six Infantry divisions of the German–Italian Armies from a very strong position.

Several Honours were awarded. **Akarit**, for the main battle, was gained by three British armoured, two Yeomanry and eleven Infantry regiments, and by three Indian regiments, the 4/6th Rajputana again and their machine gun battalion and 2nd Gurkha Rifles, **Djebel el Meida** was gained by the Royal Sussex Regiment (35 Foot) and the 1/2nd and 1/9th Gurkha Rifles, and **Wadi Akarit East** by the Cheshire Regiment and the Black Watch. **Djebel Roumana**, the group of hills nearest the coast, was awarded to one Yeomanry and four British Infantry regiments.

The day after the Battle of Wadi Akarit contact was made with the American Army. During the next few days contact was also made with the British 1st Army, and Sfax and Sousse were captured, the former being important because it was another port through which the army could be supplied and Tripoli was now 300 miles away. The actions as the advance continued up the coast towards Sfax and Enfidaville produced three more unique Honours, each awarded to a Yeomanry regiment, **Sebkret en Noual**, **Chebket en Nouiges** and **Djebel el Telil**.

It was now clear that the enemy intended to try and make his last stand in a curve around Tunis, from Enfidaville in the south-east to Sedjenane in the north-west. 8th Army's role was to put pressure on Rommel at Enfidaville while the final attack was mounted by 1st Army, and to help this 1 Armoured Division and the King's Dragoon Guards armoured cars were transferred to this army. An attack was mounted on the Enfidaville position but was abandoned as being too expensive in casualties in the circumstances. Consequently a minimum holding force was left there and more 8th Army formations, 7 Armoured and 4 Indian Divisions and a Guards Brigade, were also transferred to 1st Army. This was a remarkable move as when darkness fell they were in a defensive position at Enfidaville and the following morning they were attacking in a different direction with another army. In the event, bearing in mind the fighting which 8th Army had incurred in the past few months, not to mention the past few years, the 11th Hussars of 7 Armoured Division, which still considered themselves as part of 8th Army really, were the first troops to enter Tunis.

After mopping-up operations, and taking a very large number of prisoners, the last enemy resistance ended on 12 May. The desert war was over at last and in the short span of under six months the 8th Army had advanced almost 1,900 miles against a very determined and efficient enemy and had destroyed him, a stupendous achievement, which was soon to be increased even further in Sicily and on the mainland of Europe in Italy.

The Battle Honours awarded for the final phase of the campaign were numerous. **Enfidaville** was gained by one British armoured, two Yeomanry and three Infantry regiments, by one Gurkha regiment and by the New Zealand Scottish and fifteen New Zealand Infantry regiments, **Takrouna** was gained by two British Yeomanry regiments and fifteen New Zealand regiments, **Djebel Garci** was awarded to the Essex Regiment, 4/6 Rajputs and 1/9 Gurkhas, all of 5 Indian Brigade, **Djebel Terhouna** and **Djebel es Srafi** were each awarded to the same four New Zealand Infantry regiments, **Djebibina** was awarded to ten New Zealand regiments and finally **Djebel Tebaga** was awarded uniquely to the Royal Fusiliers (7 Foot).

Altogether thirty Honours were awarded for the campaign since El Alamein, but this was only three quarters of the number of battles, actions, etc, listed by the Battles Nomenclature Committee, the remainder being fought by limited detachments which could not qualify for the Honour for their regiments, or were considered unworthy of Honour by the participants.

The Honour **North Africa 1940–43** was also awarded, but since it was gained by all regiments of both Armies, according to date, it will be noted after the account of the North African (1st Army) battles.

North Africa, 1943

At the end of 1942 the 1st Army advance had petered out and there was strong German resistance all along the front. At the beginning of January an attack was mounted on two hills, called Green Hill and Bald Hill, and on Djebel Azzag at the north of the front, but failed, and further south the Derbyshire Yeomanry lost an observation post on Two Tree Hill and decided to recover it. The first attack on Two Tree Hill was repulsed, a second attack gained it but it was lost once more to a counterattack. Honours were awarded for **Djebel Azzag 1943** to the Buffs (3 Foot) and the Parachute Regiment, and for **Two Tree Hill** to the Royal Inniskilling Fusiliers (27 Foot).

A German armoured thrust south of Bou Arada was repulsed by a heavy Artillery concentration and considerable damage was inflicted. But the armoured forces reformed and then attacked the French troops in the Robaa Valley; the Infantry of 6 Armoured Division captured a strong defensive position but were counterattacked and driven off. 36 Brigade having been relieved in the north, 46 Division now entered the fray and repulsed several attacks by the rampant German tanks. Supported by the Parachute Brigade they attacked a number of hill positions including the formidable Djebel Alliliga, but the defences were too strong and they had to withdraw. No gains had been made but at least the armoured counterattack had been repulsed. Honours were awarded for **Bou Arada** to one armoured, two Yeomanry and three Infantry regiments, for **Robba Valley** uniquely to the Buffs and for **Djebel Alliliga** also uniquely to the Parachute Regiment.

Meanwhile American formations had been dispatched far to the south to protect the flank of 8th Army advancing up the coast of Tunisia, in co-operation with the French. German armour, attempting to remove the threat to their flank, attacked through passes in the Dorsal Mountains in the area of Sbeitla and Sbiba and drove back the Americans who retreated somewhat precipitately towards the Kasserine Pass. British troops were sent to support them and help to prevent a fiasco, including the Guards Brigade which moved to defend the Sbiba Pass, and a battalion which was sent to establish a defensive zone at Thala. The Americans were attacked again in the Kasserine Pass, broke and were driven back, and another small detachment of British troops was sent there also to try to relieve a dangerous situation which was now developing. The positions were held and the German effort to break through was broken, thanks to the great fighting spirit and defensive capabilities of the British Army in spite of the American shortcomings through lack of experience and, partly, through lack of decisive direction from the Commander-in-Chief. Several Battle Honours were awarded. **Kasserine** was gained by two armoured, two Yeomanry and two Infantry regiments, **Sbiba** by the Coldstream Guards and the Honourable Artillery Company and **Thala** by one armoured, one Yeomanry and two Infantry regiments, and again the HAC.

German counterattacks now switched to the northern sector, where the defences were thinly spread because the situation at Kasserine had necessitated the withdrawal of a number of battalions, and as a result were entrusted largely to *ad hoc* formations. 46 Division was still there but was raw and untried at that time, and 1 Division would not be able to reinforce them until mid-March. The problem was to hold out until then with very limited resources because the German threat in the south prevented the withdrawal of troops from returning northwards. For the time being the Germans had turned the tables.

The first attacks came on 26 February on Fort MacGregor and Djebel Djaffa, and the fighting was furious. The latter was held by the French who were driven off, but a counterattack recaptured the hill. The former position was also captured by the enemy, but very heavy gunfire was laid on it, and, the defenders having suffered heavy casualties and being dazed by the bombardment, it was recaptured by a British patrol. Heavy German armoured attacks were also mounted on El Hadjeba and Stuka Farm, and large Infantry forces assaulted Steamroller Farm via El Aroussa and Sidi Nsir. Although tactical withdrawals were made initially all the losses were retaken during extremely fierce fighting. The Honour of **El Hadjeba** was awarded to the London Irish Rifles and the Parachute Regiment, **Djebel Djaffa** uniquely to the Northamptonshire Regiment (48 Foot) and **Sidi Nsir** similarly to the Royal Hampshire Regiment (37 Foot). **Fort Macgregor** was awarded to the East Surrey Regiment (31 Foot), **Stuka Farm** to the London Irish Rifles and the Royal Irish Fusiliers (87 Foot) and **Steamroller Farm** to the Coldstream Guards, to the Derbyshire Yeomanry, and to the Commandos.

On the following day a valley named Hunt's Gap was attacked by tanks and infantry, as were Montagne Farm, the Kef-Ouiba Pass and the area around Sedjenane. Fierce fighting resulted in limited withdrawals but the front as a whole still held. The small village of Tamera was assaulted in early March and the enemy was repulsed. Intense fighting continued for several days, and eventually the Germans gave up trying to reach their objectives of Beja, Medjez-el-Bab and Djebel Abiod, and the crisis was over. The three weeks of hectic fighting had further weakened the enemy and his ability to hold out in North Africa.

A number of Honours were awarded. **Hunt's Gap** was gained by the North Irish Horse and the Royal Hampshire Regiment, **Montagne Farm** by two Infantry regiments, **Kef-Ouiba Pass** and **Djebel Guerba** uniquely and respectively were gained by the Argyll and Sutherland Highlanders (91 Foot) and the Sherwood Foresters (45 Foot), **Sedjenane I** by one Yeomanry and two Infantry regiments, and the Commandos and **Tamera** by one armoured and one infantry regiment and the Parachute Regiment.

The link between the 1st and 8th Armies already referred to was achieved at this time, and during the period another Battle Honour, **Maknassy,** was awarded uniquely to the Derbyshire Yeomanry.

Another major allied assault was now planned for the breakthrough while the enemy was still tired, retiring and off balance. This was to be in the area of Fondouck and through the Pass towards Kairouan, a major and ancient Muslim religious centre, in order to allow 6 Armoured Division to break out on to the coastal plain. This division was to attack on the left of the Americans, who were destined to attack the scene of a previous disaster, Fondouck itself. The village of Pichon was captured, but the American attack again failed and to their great chagrin 26 Armoured Brigade was put in on their front. A further assault was made under intense fire and this time the objectives were eventually captured, and for the first time in the campaign the armour was able to advance as a brigade in open formation.

A number of Honours were awarded for this phase.

Fondouck was gained by three armoured, two Yeomanry and four Infantry regiments, **Pichon** and **Djebel el Rhorab** were gained uniquely and respectively by the Royal Hampshire Regiment (37 Foot) and the Welsh Guards, **Fondouck Pass** was won by one Yeomanry and one Infantry regiment, **Sidi Ali** by the Lothians and Border Horse and **Kairouan** and **Bordj** each by the 16/5th Lancers with a different yeomanry regiment, the Derbyshire Yeomanry and Lothians and Border Horse respectively.

After a brief halt the battle had again opened in the north. The initial attack was made on the left flank where the Parachute Brigade captured two wooded heights in pouring rain and 138 Brigade broke through and occupied the area of the ore mine at Sedjenane. Four Battle Honours were awarded. The first two, **Djebel Dahra** and **Kef el Debna,** were gained by the Parachute Regiment, **Mine de Sedjenane** by four Infantry regiments, and **Djebel Choucha** by the Commandos.

The next objective was the recapture of the mountain range in front of Medjez, including Longstop Hill, but it would be a long and difficult operation through rough and broken country against stiff opposition. The opening attack east of Oued Zarga succeeded without undue problem, and Djebel el Mahdi, Mergueb Chaouach, the village of Toukabeur, followed by Djebel Bech Chekaoui and Djebel Rmel were all taken. Fierce fighting, with repeated counterattacks from a German Mountain division, resulted in the capture of a hill for long a thorn in 1st Army side, Djebel Ang. A bid was now made for Djebel Tanngoucha and a key village on its forward slope, Heidous, but these were very strongly defended and the attacks failed initially although both fell in due course.

Battle Honours were awarded for **Oued Zarga,** to cover the whole operation, to six Infantry regiments, for **Djebel bel Mahdi** to two Infantry regiments, for **Mergueb Chaouach** to a single Yeomanry regiment, the North Irish Horse, **Djebel Bech Chekaoui** uniquely to the Buffs, for **Djebel Rmel** also to the North Irish Horse, and for **Djebel Ang** to three Infantry regiments. For some obscure reason the East Surrey Regiment was not awarded, or perhaps did not claim, an Honour for their capture of Toukabeur, although it is listed by the Battle Nomenclature Committee as worthy of Honour.

The two armies in North Africa were now poised for their final assault on Tunis, and while the 8th Army's task was to draw off and contain as much as possible of the enemy armour on its own front, to its chagrin, as it had set its sights on capturing Tunis as the culmination of its advance from Egypt, the 1st Armoured Division was transferred to 1st Army. The differences in style and appearance of the battle-hardened troops of 8th Army from the 1st Army was truly remarkable and excited comment from both sides, but the troops soon settled their differences and were ready to advance together.

But at this moment, with both Armies straining at the leash and the enemy thought to be virtually defeated, the Germans launched an unexpected counterattack towards Medjez el Bab, scene of so many battles already. It arrived at a time when changes of responsibility were being made and troops were relieving each other, and confusion soon reigned in 1st Army. A bloody and blazing battle developed, but the British line held, although with some withdrawals, and the crack Hermann Goering Division, which had made the counterattack, eventually withdrew with heavy losses. The Honours of **Banana Ridge** and **Djebel Kesskiss** were each awarded to two Infantry regiments, and **Djebel Djaffa Pass** was awarded uniquely to the East Surrey Regiment.

The British forces now went back on the attack against some rocky features near Selchet el Kourzia, or the Sugar Lake, and in spite of significant casualties and the weariness of the troops the objectives were captured, including Two Tree Hill. **El Kourzia** was awarded as an Honour to six armoured, two Yeomanry and four Infantry regiments, **Ber Rabal** uniquely to the Royal Hampshire Regiment (37 Foot) and **Argoub Sellah**, the final objective of the attack, to two Infantry regiments.

The attacks were then resumed on Djebel Tanngoucha and Heidous, but they were still strongly defended and caused heavy casualties. Nevertheless the attack was pressed and eventually, on Easter Sunday, the objectives were taken after prolonged and tough fighting. Longstop Hill was also taken, an emotional moment. The Battle Honours of **Djebel Tanngoucha** and **Heidous** were awarded respectively to three and two Infantry regiments, and **Longstop Hill 1943** to the North Irish Horse and to four Infantry regiments.

The focus of the attacks now shifted slightly further south to the Medjez front, while the Battle for Longstop Hill was still going on. Of the initial objectives, Grich el Oued and Gueriat el Atach, the former was taken by the Guards Brigade of 1 Infantry Division, but the latter, after furious fighting, remained untaken that day although it fell on the following day. Attacks on Peters Corner, and its surrounding hills, and Sidi Abdallah were also repulsed. Objectives were taken and counterattacks threw off the captors, and the battle raged to and fro, the Germans defending in desperation the last bastions before the plain could be reached, with Tunis in sight.

The Guards now moved forward towards Djebel Bou Aoukaz, and finding little initial opposition the assault on the Djebel was launched. But it was strongly defended and was only captured after fierce fighting. There now occurred one of the unfortunate ironies of war, when the Battalion HQ of the Scots Guards, believing in the confusion that the attack had been repulsed, ordered the battalion to reassemble at the foot of the mountain. With communications poor, and as good guardsmen obeying orders, they did so, abandoning the summit which they had gained so dearly. They made another attack to recover the ground once the situation became known, but this was bloodily repulsed and a German armoured counterattack drove the Guards off the part of the ridge which they were still holding. But the Panzers withdrew during the darkness, and another attack the following day once more captured this key feature, during the fighting for which two Victoria Crosses were won.

A number of Honours were awarded for this phase of the attacks. **Grich el Oued** was won by the Scots Guards, **Gueriat el Atach Ridge** by four Infantry regiments and **Peters Corner** and **Si Mediene** uniquely by the Royal Fusiliers (7 Foot) and the Black Watch (42 Foot) respectively.

Djebel Bou Aoukaz, 1943, I was gained by two Guards and one Infantry regiment and **Si Abdallah** by two more. **Gab Gab Gap** was awarded to two Infantry regiments, **Sidi Ahmed** to the Northamptonshire Regiment (48 Foot), **Argoub el Megas** to the 60th Rifles and **Djebel Kournine** to four armoured, one Yeomanry and two Infantry regiments. Finally for the week-long battle, **Medjez Plain** was awarded to the Royal Tank Regiment, three Guards and eleven Infantry regiments, although surprisingly not to six Infantry regiments and to none of the armour or Yeomanry, mostly the ones engaged at Djebel Kournine.

In the south the American 9th Corps offensive had failed, although in the far north their 2nd Corps gained limited objectives after learning some sharp lessons in warfare from the defenders. The 8th Army on the east coast had come up against the massif of Zaghouan and a short pause was called. To resolve the impasse three of the best 8th Army formations, 4 Indian and 7 Armoured Divisions and 201 Guards Brigade, were now also transferred to 1st Army, and after a night move went into action within twenty-four hours of having left their defensive positions, which caused considerable surprise to the enemy who thought that they were safely out of the way, held up by Zaghouan. General Horrocks also moved across to take over command of 9th British Corps.

A massive assault was now mounted on 5 May by four divisions and the two Guards brigades, together at last. At the same time 5th Corps gave flank support and 1 Armoured Division created diversions around Djebel Kournine. The assault opened with a huge bombardment from over 650 guns, the biggest concentration of artillery fire since the Battle of Alamein, and was answered with heavy counterbombardment and counterbattery fire. Initially the notorious Djebel Bou Aoukaz was captured, with some of its surrounding hills, as a preliminary to the main attack, and held in spite of heavy counterattacks.

The main attack began, Montarnaud and Ragoubet Souissi were soon taken and the divisions advanced through cornfields and over the rough hills. Wadi Chafron and St Cyprien were taken, which allowed the armour to gain the ridge overlooking Tunis and to advance across the flat ground into the suburbs of the city and soon into the city itself, led by the 11th Hussars and the Derbyshire Yeomanry, for whom it was a fitting honour. Tunis had been captured at last, but the battle was not yet over. On the same day the American 9th Division entered Bizerta in the north. **Djebel Bou Aoukaz, 1943, II** was awarded to two Infantry regiments, the Duke of Wellington's (33 Foot) and the Kings Shropshire Light Infantry (53 Foot), **Montarnaud** was awarded uniquely to the East Surrey Regiment (31 Foot) and **Ragoubet Souissi** to the Essex Regiment (44 Foot) and the 1/9th Gurkha Rifles, both of 4 Indian Division. The capture of Tunis was a reward for the gallant fighting of the 1st Army, although half the formations taking part in the final battle were 8th Army units which had fought their way through the desert for two years or more.

An attempt was made to cut the neck of the Cape Bon peninsula to prevent the Germans from escaping into it and perhaps doing a 'Dunkirk', although the Royal Navy was on the watch for this. After a furious battle, when all

seemed to be over, Hammam Lif and its defile were captured and the armour raced across the peninsula to reach the coast at Hammamet, taking the Creteville Pass and Gromballa on the way. Then they turned south to take Bou Ficha in the rear of Zaghouan which was still obstructing a much reduced 8th Army; not only had formations been transferred but some divisions required for the next battle for Sicily had already been withdrawn for refitting and training in the amphibious role.

Battle Honours were awarded for **Hammam Lif** to one armoured, one Yeomanry, two Guards and two Rifle regiments, for **Creteville Pass** to three armoured regiments and for **Gromballa** to the 16/5th Lancers, who also gained **Bou Ficha** together with the Lothians and Border Horse. The overall award for the final week of battle was **Tunis**, and it was gained as an Honour by nine armoured, five Yeomanry, two Guards and fourteen Infantry regiments, the Honourable Artillery Company and 1/2 Gurkha Rifles.

The whole of North Africa had now been captured and enemy resistance had ceased after so many successes, so many disasters and so many anxious moments, and after so many casualties. The Campaign Honour, **North Africa 1940-43**, was awarded to cover the whole period on both fronts from 12 June 1940 to 12 May 1943, only a month less than three years. It was won and proudly borne by the two Household Cavalry regiments, by fifteen armoured and eleven Yeomanry regiments, by all five Guards regiments, by forty-eight Infantry regiments, by the Honourable Artillery Company, by the Parachute and the Special Air Services Regiments and the Commandos of the British Army. It was also won with great honour by three Australian armoured, twenty-six Infantry, one machine gun and two pioneer regiments, by the New Zealand Scottish, fourteen Infantry and one machine gun regiments, and by five Indian Cavalry regiments, the three regiments of Sappers and Miners, by the Indian Guards and Parachute regiments and by fourteen Infantry and six Gurkha Rifle regiments. Just to be different an Indian regiment (now the 13th Lancers of the Pakistan Army) was awarded the Honour of **Libya and Egypt 1942**, and the South Africans awarded their own Honour, **Western Desert 1941-43** to thirteen regiments although six regiments were excluded. An overall complement of 183 gallant regiments, but more actual battalions than that as several of some regiments shared in the Honours.

Sicily, 1943

The decision to invade Sicily once the North African campaign was successfully completed had been taken at the Casablanca Conference in January 1943, and, like the North African landings before it, long before it was to become a practicality. The assault would involve new concepts; seaborne landings against strong defences, the Italians now fighting on their own territory and homeland, and probably supported by heavy German concentrations. Although two previous seaborne landings had been successfully carried out, on Madagascar and at the western end of the North African coast, neither had been strongly contested and this next one undoubtedly would be. General Eisenhower was not in favour of the operation, preferring an attack on Sardinia, but he was eventually persuaded by Churchill and by General Alexander, who as deputy to Eisenhower in North West Africa had held the operational command. For the Sicilian invasion Eisenhower was again Supreme Commander, but each of the three services arms was commanded by a Briton.

The largest force of its kind so far was assembled for the operation, including over 150,000 men and 3,000 ships of all kinds. Since the main objective was to capture ports and airfields as soon as possible, as well as to secure a bridgehead for development, it was decided to employ airborne troops on a large scale for the first time, to land ahead of the seaborne landings. The British 8th Army consisted of six Infantry divisions, plus one Infantry brigade and two armoured brigades, an airborne division and three Commandos, while the American 7th Army comprised four Infantry and one armoured divisions, an airborne division and a Commando, although not all of these would be used in the initial assault. Some of the troops were seasoned desert warriors, but others were to come from Britain, the USA, the Middle East and Malta. Both armies were to land on the south of the island, the British on the south-east corner with their objective the eastern part of the island, and the Americans on their left to capture the western part of Sicily.

Before the assault could begin the small island of Pantelleria, which was being used as an air base by the enemy and lay on the sea route to Sicily, had to be captured. Supported by an initial bombardment this turned out not to be a difficult task and there were no casualties except, according to legend, a soldier who was bitten by a mule!

The assault on the island was made on 10 July, in the face of adverse weather conditions, which not only made seaborne landings hazardous but created problems for the airborne forces. Many of the gliders in the latter, towed by American aircraft with inexperienced pilots, were cast off too far out to sea and failed to reach land at all, whilst those that did were widely scattered. In the event this had some advantage as the Italian coastal forces now had no idea where the main landings would be. The 8th Army landing was entirely successful, took its initial objectives, quickly captured the ports of Augusta and Syracuse, with airborne support and against heavy German counter-attacks in the case of the former, and then pressed on northwards towards the airfields on the Catania plain.

A major attack was mounted in the area of Lentini, where the airfields were, supported by parachutists and Commandos who were to capture the key Primasole bridge and remove any destructive charges from it. The bridge was captured intact but enemy resistance was stubborn and it took two days of hard fighting, perhaps the hardest during the campaign, to establish a bridgehead over the River Simeto. The country was now more mountainous, but the Canadians captured Vizzini and Piazza Armerina and laid the foundations for an attack to force the narrow bottleneck between Mount Etna and the sea, with Catania at its base, by attacking the south western side of the volcano. Thus after six days the 8th Army was in position at the base of Mount Etna on the coast, and reserves were called forward.

A number of Battle Honours were awarded during this first phase. The assault itself, **Landing in Sicily**, was gained by one Yeomanry and eighteen British Infantry regiments, the Special Air Service Regiment, the Glider Pilot Regiment and the Commandos, and by eleven Canadian regiments. **Solarino** was gained by three British Infantry regiments, and **Vizzini** and **Augusta** uniquely by the Black Watch (42 Foot) and the Seaforth Highlanders respectively. **Francofonte** was awarded to three British Infantry regiments, **Lentini** to one Yeomanry and two Infantry regiments and **Primasole Bridge** to the Royal Tank Regiment, four Infantry regiments and the Parachute Regiment. **Grammichele** ænd **Piazza Armerina** were each awarded to two Canadian regiments.

The Canadians now attacked towards Leonforte, Agira and Adrano, 78 Division, initially in reserve in North Africa, was directed on Centuripe and 51 Division on Sferro and Paterno. Fierce fighting was encountered, since now that the Americans had cleared most of the west of the island the remaining enemy were concentrated in the north-east corner, where they could organise strong defensive positions in the hilly country. At Agira the Canadians met very heavy opposition and the British brigade had to withdraw five times after successful attacks to conform to the Canadians. An all-out attack was planned for 1 August.

During the second phase several more Battle Honours were awarded. **Sferro** was gained by three British Infantry regiments, **Simeto Bridgehead** by one Yeomanry and six Infantry regiments and **Gerbini** by the Royal Tank Regiment and two Infantry regiments. **Valguarnera** was awarded to eight Canadian regiments, **Assoro** and **Leonforte** each to two Canadian regiments and **Agira** to one British and eight Canadian regiments.

The main attack on Adrano was successful after several days of heavy fighting and resulted in the award of more Honours. **Adrano** was gained by the Royal Tank Regiment and eleven British Infantry regiments and by two Canadian armoured and eight Infantry regiments, and **Catenanuova** by two Canadian regiments. **Regalbuto** was awarded to three British and three Canadian regiments, **Sferro Hills** to four British Infantry regiments, **Centuripe**, the storming of which place was a brilliant achievement, to eight British and one Canadian regiments and **Troina Valley** to two Canadian armoured and two Infantry regiments.

With the main German position at Adrano captured the defensive line had been broken and the way was now clear for thrusts to be made on both sides of Mount Etna which would meet near Taormina. Catania was captured after a strong rearguard action, and the upper reaches of the Salso and Simeto Rivers were crossed, but in difficult terrain the advance was slow, although it made steady progress. The final phase was a chase for Messina to try to prevent too many enemy from escaping across the Straits to the mainland and thus interfering with the next campaign, for which the initial assault force had already been withdrawn from 8th Army's line of battle. Eventually Messina was reached by American forces, just in front of the British, but by this time most of the Germans had flown and only the broken and destroyed Italians remained in the island. On 17 August, after thirty-eight days' fighting since the landings, the whole of Sicily was in allied hands. The 8th

Army, having been created and having done most of its fighting in the desert, had managed to adapt itself to very different conditions with great success and this boded well for the next stage of the war, the invasion of Italy itself.

More Battle Honours were awarded for the final phase. **Salso Crossing** was gained by two and **Simeto Crossing** by three British Infantry regiments, **Monte Rivoglia** and **Malleto** each by two British regiments, and **Pursuit to Messina** by four British infantry, the Commandos and one Canadian armoured regiment. The Campaign Honour, **Sicily 1943**, was awarded to two British armoured, one Yeomanry and thirty-two Infantry regiments, the Honourable Artillery Company, the Parachute Regiment, the Special Air Service Regiment, the Glider Pilot Regiment and the Commandos and to four Canadian armoured and thirteen Infantry regiments.

Italy, 1943

Following the capture of Sicily it was decided to invade the mainland as rapidly as possible, before the Germans had an opportunity to build up strong defensive positions in the 'toe' of Italy. A two-pronged attack was planned, initially an assault across the Straits of Messina followed about a week later by a seaborne assault near Salerno. It was hoped that by the time of the second phase of the attack the initial landing force would have advanced sufficiently far northwards to be able to render support to the seaborne landing, or at least would have drawn off and contained enough enemy formations to make the landing easier.

While the planning was going on, secret negotiations were taking place for an armistice with the Italians, and an instruction to all Italian troops to lay down their arms, to be announced just before the second landing. It was hoped that this would undermine the German defensive plans, and might cause them to withdraw to the north of Italy or even from the country altogether. This was to prove false optimism.

The assault across the straits was made on 3 September, the fourth anniversary of the outbreak of war by two divisions, 5 British and 1 Canadian, landing north of Reggio and supported by the fire from the massed guns of 30 Corps behind Messina and by a bombardment from Naval vessels. Italian coastal troops immediately surrendered and soon after the landing Reggio was captured. The two divisions were initially advancing rapidly up each coast of the 'toe', 5 British on the west and 1 Canadian on the east, supported by Commando landings planned to take place ahead of them to cut off the defenders.

The terrain was very mountainous and gave ample opportunity to the Germans to delay the advance by carrying out demolitions of road and rail bridges, and as the demolitions were well sited they were almost impossible to go around. The sappers were therefore kept extremely busy building Bailey bridges so that the advance could continue. The advance was inevitably slowing down, and an independent Infantry brigade was landed at Pizzo four days after the assault. Nevertheless the narrow 'neck' running through Catanzaro, the first objective, was reached in a week, after an advance of 100 miles, and it was clear by

now that the main German defences had evacuated the 'toe'.

On 8 September the Italian armistice was announced and on the following day the US 5th Army, including 10 British Corps, landed at Salerno. Also on 9 September 1st Airborne Division landed by sea at Taranto, well ahead of the ground troops, and established a bridgehead there. 8th Army continued to advance and on 14 September had reached the next 'neck' of land between Belvedere and Spezzano, attempting to pin down the German formations and prevent them reinforcing at Salerno.

The situation at Salerno was serious, as will be narrated later, but on 16 September patrols of 5 Division made contact with the Americans south of Salerno and patrols of the Canadian division made contact with patrols from the Taranto bridgehead. Three days later 5 Division captured Auletta and 1 Canadian Division captured Potenza, both on a line east of Salerno. At the end of the first phase, therefore, an advanced line, albeit thinly held, existed across Italy from Salerno to Taranto, and 8th Army had advanced 300 miles in seventeen days.

Four Battle Honours only were awarded in this first phase. **Landing at Reggio** was gained by six Canadian regiments, **Landing at Porto San Venere** by three British Infantry regiments of the independent brigade and the Commandos, **Taranto** by the Parachute Regiment and **Potenza** by two Canadian regiments. It appears strange that no Honours at all were awarded to regiments of 5 British Division, which took part in the landing at Reggio and also took an equivalent part with the Canadians in the advance northwards, but the amount of actual fighting that they did was small.

At Salerno it was unfortunate that the Italian armistice had been announced just before the landing, because the Germans disarmed the Italians, rapidly brought up reinforcements and took over all the defences, causing the landing troops to suffer heavier casualties than would have otherwise occurred. The British troops met stronger opposition than the Americans, who rapidly advanced nearly 10 miles inland on the south of the bridgehead, mainly because they were on the northern side where it was easier for the Germans to reinforce and more vital to defend, but nevertheless succeeded in capturing Battipaglia, Montecorvo airfield, which could not, however, be used immediately as it was under enemy fire, and Salerno itself.

The Germans continued to reinforce the defences of the bridgehead, withdrawing some troops opposing the 8th Army advance, and held positions dominating the bridgehead and the beach. For several days the situation was critical and the Germans retook Battipaglia, but allied reinforcements started to arrive and after bitter fighting for eleven days the battle was over.

Several Honours were awarded, all to British regiments, for the period of the battle. **Salerno** was awarded to two armoured, three Guards and twelve Infantry regiments and the Commandos, **St Lucia** to three Infantry regiments, **Vietri Pass** to two Infantry regiments, **Salerno Hills** to three Infantry regiments and **Battipaglia** to one armoured, two Guards and three Infantry regiments.

On 8th Army front light forces and patrols were pushing

forward ahead of the main body, and reinforcements, in the shape of 78 Division, had arrived. The airfields on the Foggia plain had been abandoned by the enemy, and the advance continued through and beyond them. The Gargano peninsula was cleared, and Termoli, on the coast, was captured by a Commando landing followed by the landing of a brigade of 78 Division. Termoli was counterattacked but the bridgehead over the river Biferno held and the enemy fell back a few miles to the river Trigno. Meanwhile in the centre, among the mountains, the Canadians were advancing steadily against strong opposition and captured Vinchiaturo, and by 14 October 8th Army held a line from there through Campobasso to Termoli.

Battle Honours were awarded for **Motta Montecorvino** to four Canadian regiments, for **Termoli** to one Yeomanry and eight British Infantry regiments, the Commandos and the Special Air Service Regiment and to one Canadian regiment, **Monte San Marco** uniquely to one, **Gambatesa** to two and **Campobasso** to three Canadian regiments.

On 5th Army front 10 British Corps now drove on from the Salerno bridgehead and in a few days Naples was in allied hands. This was a major achievement as, although the harbour had been heavily damaged, within a fortnight it had been repaired sufficiently to handle a considerable weight of supplies, and there were airfields available. An unusual, and probably unique, event occurred during this phase when on 27 September 169 Brigade was relieved by 131 Lorried Brigade. Both of these brigades were composed of three battalions of the Queen's Royal Regiment, so that in fact the 10 Corps advance was then being led by six battalions of the same Regiment.

The advance continued until the River Volturno, a major obstacle which was strongly defended, was reached. It was now clear that the Germans did not mean to withdraw from Italy but to defend the long 'leg' all the way. It was now autumn, winter was approaching quickly, and the mountainous terrain away from the coastal littoral would make the task of the two armies immeasurably harder than the first six weeks had been. Although their help would be only limited, on 13 October the Italian government declared war on Germany.

Several more Honours, all to British regiments, were awarded for operations on the west coast during the period up to the halt on the Volturno. **Capture of Naples** was gained by two armoured and two Infantry regiments, **Cava di Tirreni** by four Infantry regiments, **Scafati Bridge** by one armoured and one Infantry regiment, and three Honours uniquely—**Cappezano** by the Coldstream Guards, **Monte Stella** by the Queen's Regiment (2 Foot) and **Cardito** by the Rifle Brigade.

After a brief pause to allow the administrative tail to catch up, 10 British and 6 US Corps began their attacks on the River Volturno defences and after ten days of very hard fighting established themselves in a bridgehead across it. They now advanced again, albeit against desperate rearguard actions, until they reached the River Garigliano, the next major obstacle. This formed part, with the River Sangro on the east coast, of the German main defences for the winter, the *Winterstellung* ('Winter Line'). The weather was bad, the troops had been fighting hard for two months

without a break, divisions now had to be withdrawn to go into training in England for the Second Front, the invasion of Normandy, and a sort of stalemate set in. It became clear that the next stage of the advance to capture Rome, and the next major objective, the defensive line on the road from Rome through Avezzano to Pescara, would be a hard slogging match now that the enemy had been massively reinforced.

Battle Honours to British regiments awarded for this period were **Volturno Crossing**, gained by three armoured, one Yeomanry, three Guards and nine Infantry regiments, **Monte Maro** and **Rocchetta e Croce**, gained uniquely and respectively by the Cheshire Regiment (22 Foot) and the Scots Guards, and **Teano** gained by six Infantry regiments.

Meanwhile 8th Army had been on the move again. The Army had now been reinforced by 8 Indian Division with 2 New Zealand Division in reserve around Foggia. Heavy and continuous rain hampered operations, but at the end of October the River Trigno was crossed in appalling conditions, of which the enemy took every advantage, and the San Salvo ridge was attacked, whilst inland Cantalupo was taken on the way to Isernia. After severe fighting the San Salvo position was captured, Vasto was cleared and 13 Corps took Isernia after delays owing to immense demolitions. At the end of the first week in November 78th British and 8th Indian divisions were on the ridge overlooking the main winter position on this front, the River Sangro.

Battle Honours were awarded for **Baranello** to a single regiment, the Seaforths of Canada, **Colle d'Anchise** to two Canadian regiments and **The Trigno** to seven British Infantry regiments. **Torella** was awarded to three Canadian regiments, **San Salvo** to two British Infantry regiments and **Perano** to a New Zealand armoured regiment, although now borne by three regiments which it represented.

On the western side of the peninsula, but inland from the coast, 5th Army was attacking the main German positions in front of the River Garigliano, itself defended by the formidable heights of Monte Cassino. Roads were scarce and the enemy defended every height overlooking them. The mighty massif of Monte Camino was assaulted, but it took the 5th Army a month to capture it, a month of desperate and fierce fighting during which innumerable actions took place of which only some were awarded as Honours. Eventually the task was completed but the army, having closed up to the river, had to stop to regroup and regain its strength, pausing until the beginning of the next year, a momentous one not only in Italy but in North West Europe as well.

Several Honours were awarded for this phase. **Monte Camino** was won by one armoured, three Guards and eleven Infantry regiments of the British Army and one Canadian regiment, **Calabritto** was gained by six British Infantry regiments, and **Monte la Difensa–Monte la Remetanea** uniquely by a Canadian regiment, the Special Service Regiment.

8th Army in the east was now faced with the difficult task of breaking through the 'Winter Line' over the River Sangro before the worst of the winter weather set in. An advance in the central area in the mountains offered little hope at this time of year, although it could outflank the main defences, because of poor communications and the likelihood of the few road axes being blocked by snow. Therefore the main assault had to be made on the coastal plain and in the mountains bordering it, themselves formidable in winter. The river itself was by now a torrent, guarded by an escarpment on the attacking side and by a narrow plain with a high range of hills, the Sangro ridge, on the enemy side, but there was no alternative to frontal attack, which could only be offset by surprise.

Heavy rain continued, with snow in the mountains, but in early November 78 Division managed to cross the river near the coast and establish a bridgehead from which patrols could operate up to the Sangro ridge. Towards the end of the month 2 New Zealand Division also crossed the river further inland in the direction of Castel Frentano, and in the centre 8 Indian Division, supported by 4 Armoured Brigade, captured Mozzagrogna, where in very heavy fighting they beat off repeated counterattacks. Heavy air support assisted the attacks, and progress, although slow and strongly contested, continued with the capture of Fossacessia and Lanciano, followed by San Vito on the coast. By the beginning of December 8th Army was established on the Sangro ridge and the 'Winter Line' had been broken.

For the sake of perspective it must not be forgotten that the fighting on the Sangro took place just a year after the Battle of El Alamein, and for an army to have advanced such an enormous distance in that time, including seaborne assaults, and embracing every sort of terrain and climate, from the heat and dust of the desert to the mountains in snow, must always remain an incredible achievement.

1 Canadian Division was now in the line in the coastal sector and gained a bridgehead over the River Moro. Further inland this river was also crossed by a battalion of the Royal West Kent Regiment (50 Foot) in an almost unbelievable operation in which in the face of intense fire, a bridge over the river was built from the enemy side, since there was no room on the British side to assemble it, so precipitous was the approach to the river, and no progress could be made by Infantry or armour until it was built.

Guardiagrele was attacked by the New Zealanders, but the bastion of Orsogna, perched on a high cliff, was considered too difficult for frontal assault and was eventually attacked from the flank. Nearer the coast 5 Division captured Arielli, 8 Indian Division captured Villa Grande and advanced towards Tollo, and the Canadians, in the face of tenacious German paratroops, eventually captured Ortona. Thus at the end of the year 8th Army was through the Winter Line and threatening Chieti and the next major objective, the road from Pescara through Avezzano to Rome.

Numerous Battle Honours were awarded for the six-week period of hard fighting from the crossing of the Sangro to the end of the year. **The Sangro** was awarded to one British armoured, one Yeomanry and fifteen Infantry regiments, to seven New Zealand armoured and fifteen Infantry regiments, to three Canadian regiments, and to one Indian armoured regiment (now in the Pakistan army) and to two Infantry and one Gurkha regiment. **Castel di Sangro** and **Mozzagrogna** were gained uniquely and respectively by one Canadian and one British regiment, **Fossa-**

cesia was gained by one Yeomanry and two Infantry regiments, all British, and **Castel Frentano** by seven armoured and fifteen Infantry regiments, all from New Zealand. **Romagnoli** was won uniquely by the Royal West Kent Regiment and **Orsogna** by the Parachute Regiment and by the same New Zealand regiments which had gained Castel Frentano. **The Moro** was awarded to three Canadian regiments and **Moro Bridge**, or **Impossible Bridge** as it was alternatively named, to the Royal West Kent Regiment. **San Leonardo** was gained by five regiments, **The Gully** by three armoured and nine Infantry regiments and **Casa Berardi** by two regiments, all Canadian. **Caldari** was awarded to one British and one Gurkha regiment, **Ortona** to eight Canadian regiments, **Villa Grande** to two British Infantry regiments, **San Nicola–San Tommaso** uniquely to the 48th Highlanders of Canada, and finally **Point 59** or **Torre Mucchia** to three Canadian regiments.

Middle East, 1943

At the time of their armistice the Italians still maintained garrisons in the Dodecanese Islands in the southern part of the Aegean Sea near the coast of Turkey. It seemed possible and was therefore hoped that with a little encouragement they might be persuaded to overcome the Germans, whom they greatly outnumbered, which would give the Allies access to the Aegean Sea, and thence to the Black Sea and Russia and the bases from which to neutralise the Germans in the Balkans area. Three islands had been picked which would most give this encouragement— Rhodes, Cos and Leros. This had for a long time been a consequential plan for an Italian surrender.

Not that there were many troops available to carry out the plan, nor shipping to transport them, at this stage, but success might be obtained by *ad hoc* means if landings could be carried out quickly and if they were supported locally. The first attempt was an unarmed one on Rhodes, where Major Lord Jellicoe of the SAS, the son of the First War admiral, parachuted in single-handed immediately after the armistice. But the Italians, suffering from low morale and in spite of their numbers, were not prepared to overthrow their masters, and Jellicoe had to leave precipitately without any success.

A full seaborne assault was out of the question as 8th Indian Division, which had been trained for and assigned the task, had now to be sent to Italy, and the only other formation of sufficient size in the Middle East was 10th Indian Division, newly arrived in the theatre and still acclimatising and training. Nevertheless detachments of troops and aircraft were sent to some of the islands which were then undefended—Castelrosso, Cos, Leros and Samos—but without Rhodes in allied hands the position of these detachments was hazardous. The undertaking was doomed to failure before it had started.

Strong air support could have helped but General Eisenhower did not appear to appreciate the value of the operation; and in any case the Americans did not welcome British 'interference' in the Balkans, and this was denied. Cos became the first objective of enemy counterattack and a German airborne assault there was developed. The single battalion in defence was rapidly cut off and overwhelmed after a fortnight of fighting. The Honour of **Cos** was awarded uniquely to the Durham Light Infantry (68 Foot).

Leros was now reinforced by an Infantry brigade which had been in the garrison of Malta throughout the siege of that island, but the enemy started bombing attacks and virtually sealed off the island and its fate. The island was much too large to be defended adequately by three battalions against concentrated attacks, and German seaborne and airborne attacks on 12 November cut the island into three areas, in each of which was one battalion which could be eliminated piecemeal. Another battalion was sent from Samos to the island, but this was but a drop in the ocean of need. The brigade fought desperately for four days until it was exhausted and had to surrender against overwhelming odds. **Leros** was awarded as an Honour to three British Infantry regiments, and why it was not awarded to the fourth battalion involved, the King's Own (4th Foot), is not apparent.

Most of the detachments on the other islands and the survivors from Cos and Leros were evacuated by small ships, but the plan as a whole had been a failure. Thus the attempt to drive the Germans from the Aegean, and possibly to bring Turkey into the war on the side of the Allies was thwarted by lack of American imagination and their rigidity of thought.

Burma, 1943

During the retreat in 1942 the coastal province of Arakan, with Akyab Island in its midst, was evacuated like the rest of Burma, and the Army now stood just across the Indian border near Chittagong. It was considered that some offensive action was necessary, to improve morale and before the Japanese built up their strength in Burma, and the Arakan seemed the most obvious place as the troops in the area had not been involved in the retreat to the frontier.

The offensive which was planned had only limited objectives, clearing the Mayu peninsula, which ran from just south of the frontier to a point near Akyab, and the capture of the island itself. The terrain was difficult as the precipitous Mayu range runs down the centre of the peninsula, forested and with very limited flat ground on each side between the mountains and the sea on the west and the Mayu River on the east. This was not the most attractive country for an orthodox advance and would favour the enemy in innumerable defensive positions, but nevertheless this was the plan decided upon, as opposed to a seaborne landing near the tip of the peninsula for which sufficient landing craft could not be made available.

The advance actually began in the middle of December 1942, and the Mayu range, which was considered impracticable, if not impassable, for movement, divided the advance into two unsupported prongs. At the start all went well and Maungdaw and Buthidaung, and the lateral road between them above the Mayu tunnels, were captured without opposition, and by the end of the year the army was approaching Donbaik and Rathedaung only about 15 miles from the tip of the peninsula. But by now the Japanese had brought up reinforcements and had built bunkers in strategic positions, and deliberate attacks on the two towns both failed.

Reinforcements from India were sent forward until 14 Indian Division consisted of nine brigades, as large as an average corps and impossible to handle and command adequately from its small HQ. More frontal assaults were made and each time they foundered on the Japanese bunkers and the extremely heavy fire which was brought down on any attack. The final attack on Donbaik was made in the middle of March, still by frontal assault although General Slim had proposed that the town should be outflanked by sending a force along the supposedly impassable Mayu ridge. But the bunkers remained impervious to normal methods of attack and all hope of capturing the town was abandoned. Two Battle Honours were awarded. **Rathedaung** was gained by one British regiment, the Lancashire Fusiliers (20 Foot) and one Indian regiment, and **Donbaik** by six British and two Indian regiments.

The Japanese now counterattacked and cut off the brigade at Rathedaung, which only escaped after fierce fighting and retired up the Mayu River. A catastrophe was imminent and Slim was sent with his Corps HQ to stand by to take over operational command when required, although the administrative responsibilities were to be retained by Army HQ. But before he had had time even to review the situation the Japanese struck again, destroyed another brigade on the Mayu river, crossed the 'impassable' Mayu range and destroyed yet another brigade retiring from Donbaik, ending up by infiltrating among the defenders on the coast. All was now confusion. **Htizwe** and **Point 201 (Arakan)** were each awarded as unique Honours, to the Lancashire Fusiliers again and to the Royal Lincolnshire Regiment (10 Foot) respectively.

An attempt to trap the Japanese south of the Mayu tunnels failed when the regiments at the base of the 'box' broke, the Japanese captured Point 551 and a further retreat was necessary. Maungdaw was abandoned. New defensive positions near the frontier were occupied and only the outbreak of the monsoon discouraged the Japanese from any further attacks, and probably averted a complete disaster. One final Honour was awarded, **The Stockades**, to 2/5 Gurkha Rifles.

So ended a most unfortunate incident, which might have been even more serious if the rain had not prevented the Japanese from advancing across the frontier towards Cox's Bazaar and Chittagong. More serious than the casualties and the loss of equipment was a further deterioration in morale, and it was clear that every effort would have to be taken to build it up again before any advance into Burma could be anticipated, and in particular a further offensive into the Arakan.

But by October planning was well advanced for a new offensive in the Arakan, this time with an extra division, 81 West African, scheduled to move down the Kaladan valley to protect the left flank of the advance. This division, because of the nature of the country, would have to be supplied and maintained entirely by air, the first example of this in operations; not only that, but it would have to, and did, create its own track into the valley through the jungle and mountains. The advance began at the beginning of December, and, against limited resistance but nevertheless with some fierce local fights, had almost reached the line of the Maungdaw–Buthidaung road once more by late in the month.

But before the real assault began it was this time decided that lateral communications had to be established, and a supply route had to be found across the Mayu range. This was achieved by first improving a track and then building a road over the Ngakyedauk Pass, Okey-Doke Pass to the British soldier. It was a vital, successful and incredible task. The first attack, following its completion, was at Razabil, and on the last day of the year Maungdaw was entered. The Burma Army, now known as the 14th Army under command of General Slim, and later christened by its members 'the Forgotten Army', was poised to emulate in 1944 its sister armies in Europe.

In between the two attacks on the Arakan another event had occurred in the Burma theatre which, although not particularly successful in itself, had caught the imagination of the world, helped to boost morale and laid the foundations for future operations. This was the first long-range penetration expedition by Wingate's Chindits, the name 'Chindit' being derived from the mythological Burmese beast, the Chinthe.

Brigadier Orde Wingate was a strange man, moody, fanatical, but with the power to generate enthusiasm. He had previously carried out irregular operations with partisans in Abyssinia and now suggested a similar operation in Burma against the Japanese lines of communication. His brigade pushed eastwards into Burma, on foot but supplied by air. The troops managed to destroy a number of bridges and railway lines, but in fact the damage was slight and quickly repaired, and the Japanese division that they had hoped to inconvenience had been moved. About a third of his force were lost as casualties or as prisoners, which made it an expensive failure, but it had been planned to take place in conjunction with a Chinese advance which did not materialise.

Nevertheless it was a success on psychological and morale-building grounds, and helped to take attention away from the Arakan failure, and thus was worth all the hardships that the men of the column had had to endure. A Battle Honour, **Chindits 1943,** was awarded to the only full regiments employed, the King's Regiment (8 Foot) and 2 Gurkha Rifles.

South West Pacific, 1943

The Australians had been holding Wau since the beginning of hostilities with little interference apart from air raids, but in January 1943 the Japanese launched an attack on Wau from Mubo on Nassau Bay. Although the defenders knew about the move bad weather initially delayed the arrival of reinforcements to the small garrison. However the Japanese made heavy weather of their advance and by the time they made their assault reinforcements had been delivered, the attack was repulsed with heavy casualties, and the Australians drove the attackers back to Mubo. The Honour of **Wau** was awarded to three Australian regiments and to the Papua and New Guinea Volunteer Rifles.

In April the Australians attacked Mubo themselves and

isolated it from the Japanese bases at Salamaua and Lae, and during the next two months carried out a number of attacks and patrol activities in the mountainous jungle areas between Wau and Salamaua, including bloody clashes on the Bobdubi and Lababia ridges to contain the Japanese, while an assault was being planned by the Americans in the Nassau Bay area. The Honours of **Mubo I** and **Lababia Ridge** were each awarded to a single regiment.

On 30 June an American force landed in Nassau Bay in order to draw the Japanese defenders from Lae, which was the primary objective now, and to support an Australian advance on Salamaua. On a dark and stormy night the beaches were not easy to locate, in spite of Australian pathfinders, few troops got ashore and the landing was not a success. The small bridgehead was harried by a handful of Japanese troops but held on and was eventually reinforced, but problems now arose in co-operation since an American force refused to serve under Australian command, although the Australians were experienced in warfare in the prevailing terrain and conditions whereas the Americans had no experience of warfare, let alone in the jungle.

The Japanese were strongly entrenched and frontal attacks were costly, the only sure way to success being to surround their positions and to cut off their tenuous supply lines. The Americans had to, and did, learn some bitter lessons. The Japanese reinforced Salamaua from Lae, as it had been hoped that they would, and strongly defended the area around Mount Tambu, which dominated the area and was most bitterly defended. Fresh troops were landed at Tambu Bay, were strongly opposed but joined the fray against the apparently impregnable Mount Tambu. But the mountain was eventually taken by surrounding it. In early September the Australians entered Salamaua and prepared for the next advance up the coast to Lae.

Honours were awarded for **Bobdubi II** to six regiments, for **Nassau Bay** to the Pacific Islands Regiment, for **Mubo II** and for **Mount Tambu** each to two regiments; **Tambu Bay** was gained by three Australian regiments and the Pacific Islands Regiment and **Komiatum** by six regiments of which five were the same that had won Bobdubi.

On 4 September a major land, sea and air attack was mounted. The 9th Australian Division landed from the sea in the area of the Busu and Bulu Rivers, the first Australian seaborne assault against a defended coast since Gallipoli. They were supported by an American Parachute brigade to which was attached an Australian field artillery regiment, most of whose members had had some quick instruction but had never jumped before, in an airborne landing. Both these landings were unopposed and took the Japanese completely by surprise. The 7th Australian Division was flown into Nadzab, and advanced up the coast, being delayed by defences at the Busu River and in front of Lae, but entered the latter town on 16 September. A lot of the Japanese garrison escaped into the mountains although some were overtaken and cut down by Australian patrols. Australian casualties were significant, but were still only a small proportion of the Japanese losses.

Busu River was awarded as an Honour to four regiments, **Lae Road** to four Infantry regiments and a pioneer regiment, and **Lae-Nadzab** to thirteen Infantry regiments and to one machine gun and one pioneer regiment. The advance did not halt and moved into the Markham and Ramu River valleys, where there was strong opposition and captured Kaiapit.

The operation to gain Finschhaven and the Huon peninsula now began, and this coincided with the start of the major campaign for the liberation of Australian New Guinea which lasted until the end of the war. On 22 September an Australian brigade of 9th Division was landed by American amphibious forces north of Finschhaven on what was known by the code name of Scarlet Beach. They actually landed at the wrong place, which was in fact an advantage since the planned landing beach was more strongly defended, and their initial objectives were quickly captured.

The advance on Finschhaven met heavy resistance at the Bumi River, but the troops forded the torrent and established a bridgehead. Although the American command objected, believing that the Japanese were in little strength in the area, another battalion was now landed on Scarlet Beach to protect it for the landing of supplies. Ten days later the brigade captured Finschhaven and met a battalion advancing up the coast from Lae. **Scarlet Beach** was awarded as an Honour to three Australian regiments and the Pacific Islands Regiment and **Bumi River** to two regiments.

But the Australians, in spite of their successes, were very isolated and Japanese reinforcements were now assembling and had occupied the peak of the Sattelberg, which dominated the beachhead through which the Australians were being supplied. The Japanese mounted a counterattack on the beachhead, and also attacked from the Sattelberg on the Australian positions at Jivenaneng and Kumawa but were bloodily repulsed. Australian reinforcements continued to arrive and in the middle of November they launched an attack on the Sattelberg. They captured the hill of Pabu on the Gusika–Wareo road and held it in the face of heavy counterattacks and casualties. After a week of these desperate counterattacks they surrounded the Sattelberg, and when they put in an assault on the mountain they found that it had been abandoned. In early December they attacked and captured Gusika, Nongora and Wareo, against strong opposition in each case, and the battle for the Huon peninsula was virtually over.

Honours were awarded for **Defence of Scarlet Beach** to six Infantry and one pioneer regiment, for **Jivenaneng-Kumawa** to two regiments and for **Siki Cove,** to one Infantry and one pioneer regiment. **Pabu** was awarded to two regiments and **Sattelberg** to five, including one dismounted armoured regiment and one machine gun battalion, **Gusika** and **Nongora** were uniquely awarded, and **Wareo** was awarded to two Infantry regiments and to the dismounted 1 Lancers. The overall Honour for the operation, **Finschhaven** was gained by 1 Lancers, the Pacific Islands Regiment, ten Infantry regiments, a machine gun regiment and a pioneer regiment. Honours were also awarded for **Kalueng River** uniquely to the 22nd Regiment, for **Wareo-Lakona** to 1 Lancers and to two Infantry regiments and for **Gusika-Fortification Point** to 1 Lancers and four Infantry regiments.

Inland, in December, the Australians had prevented the Japanese from infiltrating back into the Ramu valley and had established themselves in the Finisterre mountains. At the end of the year they gained a foothold on the dominant Shaggy Ridge. **Finisterres I** was awarded to six regiments, **Ramu Valley** to a further six Infantry regiments and a pioneer regiment and **Shaggy Ridge** to nine Infantry and one pioneer regiment.

Meanwhile in September and October had occurred one of the unsung and incredible operations of the war, known as Operation Jaywick, when an old Japanese fishing boat, renamed the *Krait*, sailed from Australia to Singapore, the operation being devised by and under the command of Major Lyon of the Gordon Highlanders who had escaped capture by the Japanese when Singapore fell and had helped many people to escape from there before finally escaping himself. The little ship reached Pandjang Island 30 miles from Singapore where the raiding party embarked in canoes and paddled into Singapore harbour. There were no defences against this sort of attack and the raiders were able to fix limpet mines to a number of ships and escape unscathed. After the mines exploded and the damage was done, and a number of ships including an oiltanker had been sunk, the Japanese mounted a massive search operation, but the canoeists were not discovered and rejoined the *Krait*. Apart from minor alarms she returned to Australia in the middle of October. A further raid was attempted the following year but it was a tragic failure and the whole party, including Lyon, was either killed or executed after capture by the Japanese only a month before the end of the war. What actually happened cannot ever be known as there were no survivors, but the members of the expedition were all decorated posthumously.

South Pacific, 1942–3

At the outbreak of the war with Japan a small New Zealand force was in Fiji, where it remained, slightly augmented, until July 1942. It returned to New Zealand, was reinforced to become 3 Division, although that was not its official title, with a larger than normal artillery element, and at the end of the year moved to New Caledonia for training in island warfare. In August 1943 the Division moved to Guadalcanal in the Solomon Islands; when the earlier battles were over the Japanese had retreated 200 miles north to the New Georgia Islands group, and the attack on these islands was to become 3 Division's first task, although in fact it never operated complete but only in brigade groups during the Pacific war.

The first operation was against Vella Lavella island, while the Americans were driving the Japanese from the other islands in the group, and had already landed on the southern tip of Vella Lavella. The landing took place in September 1943 and there were plenty of sharp clashes with the enemy, mostly in small combat groups, until the main Japanese force was encountered. The island was densely forested and therefore impractical for much movement inland, and the New Zealanders mostly moved round the coast from bay to bay. One party which did penetrate the jungle was surrounded by a small Japanese force and had to fight its way with difficulty back to the beach. But in early October the enemy evacuated the island and the first New Zealand action in the Solomons was a success.

The Battle Honour **Vella Lavella** was awarded to five Infantry regiments.

Very soon the second operation took place with an attack on the Treasury Islands, 8 Brigade group carrying out an opposed landing on Mono Island, where the Japanese were in greater strength than at Vella Lavella, a few days before the American landing on Bougainville Island. There were remarkably few casualties during the landing and a number of enemy strongpoints were soon over-run, although in some cases, in their fashion, the Japanese went to ground, shamming dead, only to 're-cover' and take the attackers in the rear. The enemy quickly recovered from his initial surprise and resistance became stronger, the landing beaches being heavily shelled. Gradually the Japanese were driven back when patrols operated into the jungle and along the coast, but they still defended strongly although their casualties were heavy. All resistance was overcome and the capture was completed a week after the landing, although there were still fierce clashes with refugee groups of Japanese for some time afterwards. The Honour **Treasury Island** was awarded to nine Infantry regiments.

Above: The Bombing of Cassino. This picture was taken on 15 March 1944, as 2,500 tons of bombs rained down on Cassino. When the barrage lifted the fight for the ruins began. *IWM*

19 World War 2: Part 3, 1944-5

Italy, 1944

At the beginning of 1944 the 8th Army, having already broken through the Winter Line and made contact with the Gustav Line, consisted of 1st Canadian Division on the coast, now supported by the newly-arrived 5th Canadian Armoured Division and forming together 1st Canadian Corps, 8th Indian, 2nd New Zealand, and 78th Divisions and 2nd Parachute Brigade, left behind when the rest of 1st Parachute Division returned to Britain for the Second Front. The 5th Army, although under American command with American divisions, also included 5th, 4th Indian, 46th and 56th Divisions. 6th Armoured Division was still in the wings in Tunisia, as were the armoured brigades, but the mountainous terrain made the use of armour very limited at present. General Alexander, as Commander-in-Chief, also had under his command a French/French Colonial division and two Polish divisions.

Most of the early action in the year was to be on the 5th Army front, while the 8th Army maintained its pressure on the Gustav Line, the first time that the Army had been static for a very long time. The objective of 5th Army was to break through into the Liri valley, the route to Rome, which involved crossing the River Garigliano and circumventing or capturing Monte Cairo and the massif of Monte Cassino, crowned with its centuries-old monastery, which dominated the main road to the political objective. It was hoped that the breach of the valley would be helped by a landing on the coast 60 miles further north at Anzio.

The first task was to close up to the River Rapido, which with the Liri became the Garigliano. An American attack on Monte Porchia was repulsed and left 46 Division in a very difficult situation on Colle Cedro. But eventually the attacks gained ground supported by the French Colonial troops.

Colle Cedro was awarded as an Honour to the York and Lancaster Regiment (65 Foot).

But now the formations nearer the coast made a crossing of the Garigliano so that an outflanking movement could be made on the Liri valley. A bridgehead was established, and after very heavy fighting, in which the battle flowed to and fro, the villages of Minturno, Damiano and Castelforte were captured, although further up the river the Americans again suffered heavy casualties. Honours were awarded for the **Garigliano Crossing** to two armoured and nineteen Infantry regiments, for **Minturno** to seven Infantry regiments, for **Damiano** to eight Infantry regiments and for **Monte Tuga** to four regiments. **Monte Ornito** was awarded to the Coldstream and Welsh Guards, the Royal Hampshire Regiment and the Commandos, and **Cerasola** uniquely to the Royal Hampshire Regiment.

While these attacks were being made and tying down the German defenders, a seaborne landing was made initially by one American and one British division at Anzio. At first there was no opposition and the advance could probably have gone through to the main highway to Rome, although it would have been largely unsupported. But the Americans, who were in command of the landing, saw danger in this, and restrained the advance to the limited bridgehead, which had been planned against expected opposition, for several days during which the Germans were able to reinforce the sector, which they did in great strength with formations rushed down from the north. The initial surprise and initiative had been lost by too much caution and by rigid adherence to a plan which had been made with limited intelligence, and which did not allow for the typically British attribute of opportunism, the results of which tardiness and bureaucracy would soon be apparent.

The Germans tried to cut off the advanced troops, and only a spirited and gallant defence by the Grenadier Guards, during which Major Sidney, a descendant of Sir Philip of Zutphen fame and later to become Lord de Lisle, won the Victoria Cross for extreme heroism, as had his father-in-law before him, General Lord Gort. The Scots Guards were caught in similar danger and eventually the whole division had to withdraw. The Germans now mounted a strong counterattack to drive the bridgehead into the sea, but it was repulsed with appalling casualties, which, with those being sustained at Cassino during roughly the same period, were perhaps the most concentrated in the whole of the war. But by now the German casualties had also become a cause for concern and the attacks were called off.

Although the battle known as Anzio continued for a further three months it was for the remainder of that time largely a holding action and stalemate while the main attack was centred on the main highway northwards to the capital. **Anzio** was awarded as an Honour to the Royal Tank Regiment, the Yorkshire Dragoons, three Guards and twenty-four Infantry regiments and the Commandos, **Aprilia** to the Irish Guards, **Campoleone** to the Scots Guards and three Infantry regiments and **Carroceto** to two Guards and six Infantry regiments.

And now, instead of Anzio being used to draw off the

defenders from the area of Cassino, Cassino had to be attacked to prevent stagnation and to relieve the pressure on the Anzio bridgehead. Although the Americans had made gains inland in the mountains, no movement was possible forward of Cassino until the monastery and its mountain had itself been captured. With the target of Cassino, the New Zealand Corps had been formed as at Mareth, consisting of the two old and probably best desert divisions, 2 New Zealand and 4 Indian. The plan was for a pincer movement between them, but only two brigades could be deployed initially on a task which had bloodied the equivalent of six American brigades with heavy losses. The future looked grim.

The monastery had been declared sacrosanct on the basis that it would not be defended, although it was now clear that it was being used at least as an observation post, and probably as a fortress. It was therefore decided to reduce its effectiveness by bombing, which activity was entrusted to the American Air Force, with which decision the British troops were not enamoured owing to their lack of faith in its accuracy as had been evidenced in the desert. The raid was carried out by heavy bombers from England and had two adverse effects; first it destroyed the monastery but also made it open to full defence, and secondly it destroyed the town of Cassino which as a result became quite impossible for movement by anything but Infantry. In fact the Germans were the only real beneficiaries of the attack since the British Infantry could not exploit the effects of the raid due to lack of warning of its time of arrival.

The 4th Indian Division attack opened with an assault by the Royal Sussex Regiment on Point 593 which dominated the approaches to the monastery from the north, but was not a success although it partially gained its objectives and a counterattack was driven off. Two Gurkha battalions now joined the fray, advancing on Monastery Hill itself where they suffered greatly. A small detachment of Gurkhas actually entered the monastery but were rapidly thrown out again on to the open slopes of the hills. In conjunction with the Indians the New Zealanders attacked over the River Rapido to outflank Cassino town. A Maori battalion crossed but was strongly counterattacked and had to retire across the river. The Honour of **Monastery Hill** was awarded to the Royal Sussex Regiment, to one New Zealand, one Indian and a Gurkha regiment.

78 Division was now transferred from its sojourn in the mountain fastnesses of the centre of the country to join the New Zealanders, but was not used immediately due to the problems being encountered from mountain and river and the decision to have another go at bombing the monastery and town into submission. On 15 March the New Zealanders and Indians were withdrawn, hopefully out of harms way, and a huge force of bombers went in. The devastation of the monastery and town was completed, and several other unplanned locations also became targets, anything which looked vaguely like Monte Cassino in fact, with or without a monastery on top, with some allied casualties including the destruction of a British medium gun position at least 5 miles back from the front. Faith in close-support bombing, particularly by Americans, was hardly improved by this episode. The aircraft bombardment was followed up with a heavy artillery bombardment, and then the attack began. But the German 1 Parachute Division was in the ruins of the town and the New Zealanders attacking there were not only amazed to see them but soon suffered heavy casualties, being without the support of their tanks which could not move in the streets strewn and blocked by rubble.

Meanwhile the Indian division attacked Castle Hill, but the attack was delayed until after dark and by then the enemy had somewhat recovered from the shock of the bombardment and defended strongly. The fighting was severe and progress was slow, but some of the 1/9th Gurkhas crossed a most hazardous and steep slope to reach Hangman's Hill, named for a battered and twisted pylon which stood there looking like a gibbet, and were joined there the following day by the rest of the battalion. The positions on both Castle Hill and Hangman's Hill were desperate and were continuously counterattacked. The troops were covered with smoke, considerable damage being done by the falling base-plates of the smoke-shells, and hung on although the task of supplying them was extremely difficult; during this episode the gunner OP officer was recommended for a Victoria Cross which was not granted. In spite of a battalion of 78 Division, 6 Royal West Kent Regiment, going to their assistance, no advance was possible, and after ten days of hell the Indian and British troops of the division were withdrawn under cover of night.

This was a classic battle between outstandingly brave men on both sides and was an epic of World War II, deservedly; the Germans allowed immunity to stretcher-bearers recovering the wounded, and even some prisoners helped with this task. It showed that the chivalry of war was not entirely dead. It was one of the greatest battles, out of many glorious achievements, of this famous Indian division.

But the New Zealanders had not been idle and continued to attack the town, of which the Continental Hotel was their greatest problem as it overlooked them, against impossible odds. They hung on but suffered terrible casualties until they too had to withdraw. All in all the first few months of 1944 in Italy, at Anzio and Cassino, provided some of the hardest fighting of the whole war, if not the hardest of all, and certainly some of the most gallant. Honours were awarded for **Castle Hill** to two British and two Indian regiments, for **Hangman's Hill** to the Essex Regiment and the 1/9th Gurkha Rifles, for **Cassino Railway Station** to four New Zealand regiments, and finally for **Cassino I** to seven New Zealand armoured regiments, to the Madras Sappers and Miners, and to six British and fourteen New Zealand Infantry regiments, to one Indian machine gun and three Gurkha regiments.

Although the attack on the Gustav Line had not been a tactical success it proved to have been a strategic one as the Germans had had to throw in a lot of their reserves and had made the retention of Rome a major political requirement, as much as its capture was an allied one. The Germans were now committed to the defence of Cassino and Anzio at all costs, as only success there could save Rome, and they had already suffered heavy casualties. Alexander had the potential for attacking either place or both, and of possibly destroying or severely mauling a large number of enemy formations. Unfortunately, so many experienced formations having been returned to England to train for the invasion of Normandy, which was now imminent, reinforcements were scarce, but had to be obtained from somewhere. And some were found from the largely moribund Middle East theatre which was now virtually safe from attack, and 4th British, 6th Armoured and 10th Indian Divisions were dispatched to Italy, followed by an unexpected bonus from the newly formed 6th South African Armoured Division, composed of troops who had agreed to fight for the allied cause outside the African continent. Two more French Colonial divisions had also arrived.

The allied objective was still the same as before, to break through into the Liri valley and to exploit up the main highway to the capture of Rome. The hard-hit Indian and New Zealand divisions which had mounted the initial attacks were relieved, the former going to the 8th Army front on the Sangro and the New Zealanders into the central mountains. The whole of the front including Cassino and the Liri villey was now entrusted to 8th Army, with 5th Army, to their chagrin, operating only on the coastal strip and Anzio, 13 Corps taking responsibility for the Cassino front, with the Canadian Corps of 1st Infantry and 5 Armoured Divisions, behind it ready to be used for exploitation.

The plan was for two British divisions to attack across the Rapido while the Polish divisions attacked Monastery Hill, while a further attack was to be made at Anzio to cut the highway to Rome, and a major change of divisional responsibilities took place. The Germans became increasingly nervous from false information indicating that another seaborne assault was to be made north of Rome at Civitavecchia, and reinforced that area, thus dissipating their resources.

The second great assault on Cassino and the Liri valley began on the night of 10/11 May with the support of 700 guns. The plan called for the two Polish divisions on the right to assault the mountain which would give them a base from which to attack the monastery, while on the left 4th British and 8th Indian Divisions crossed the Rapido, scene of the earlier American disaster and the failure of the New Zealanders. On the coast 5th Army were to keep as many enemy as possible in front of them by limited activity, although General Clark had grander ideas than this, which he did not disclose to the Commander-in-Chief, and planned his own advance, making full use of the French colonial divisions.

4 Division, on the right, crossed the Rapido just below Cassino town in boats, combating a strong current, and, in spite of heavy mortar and machine gun fire and minefields, established a precarious bridgehead. In daylight their position became desperate. 8 Indian Division, on the left, attacked Sant' Angelo and had an even harder time to establish and maintain the bridgehead, particularly since the Germans had created an artificial fog with smoke mines and they were invisible for support. But eventually a bridge was built and the tanks of the Canadians crossed to their assistance. Further to the right the Poles had also run into trouble, having failed to capture their objectives

in the dark, and being exposed to heavy and punishing fire in daylight, and had to withdraw to their start line.

A bridge was built on 4 Division's front and 26 Armoured Brigade was able to cross and to advance, and at last the bridgehead could be expanded. Sant' Angelo was captured by the Indians, as was Panaccioni. On the coast the French, after furious fighting, had captured Monte Fanto and Monte Majo and were exploiting. 5 Royal West Kent Regiment of the 8th Indian Division created a deep salient towards Pignataro, which was captured the following day by the Frontier Force Rifles. 78 Division, in reserve until now, was launched to exploit the expanded bridgehead and to cut the highway beyond Monte Cassino. The village of Sinagogga was taken. The Poles began their second assault, and after hard battling for two days captured the monastery at long last, and the Germans withdrew to their next defensive position, the Hitler Line covering Rome.

The Battle Honours awarded for the capture of Cassino and the breakout, a much harder battle than perhaps the limited narrative indicates, were **Sant Angelo in Teodice** to the Ontario Regiment and the 1/5th Gurka Rifles, **Massa Vertechi** uniquely to the Royal Hampshire Regiment, **Pignataro** to the Calgary Regiment, also uniquely, **Massa Tambourini** to the Royal Inniskilling Fusiliers and **Casa Sinagogga** to the London Irish Rifles. The overall Honours for the battle were **Cassino II** awarded to two British, three New Zealand, and three Canadian armoured regiments, to the Derbyshire Yeomanry and the Lothian and Border Horse, to the Bengal Sappers and Miners, and to nineteen British, seven Canadian, one Gurkha and eight South African regiments and the Honourable Artillery Company, and **Gustav Line** awarded to three New Zealand and three Canadian armoured regiments and to seven Canadian Infantry regiments. The Essex Regiment and the Royal West Kent Regiment emblazoned the Honours for **Cassino I** and **Cassino II** as a single combined Honour, **Cassino,** as they were the only two regiments engaged in both battles. **Cassino II** was also awarded as an Honour Title to an Indian anti-tank regiment.

An attempt was now made to break through the Hitler Line before it could be properly manned. There were now three Corps of 8th Army, the Polish, 13th British and 1 Canadian, and one of 5th Army, the French, operating in a very narrow area which limited the amount to which each could be committed. At the same time it was planned to break out of the Anzio bridgehead towards the highway at Valmontone. From the bridgehead the British and Americans advanced, but within sight of Valmontone General Clark changed the axis of advance, as he was determined to reach Rome before the British, even if his intended route, against Alexander's express orders and without any thought for the support and mutual co-operation of the armies, was more heavily defended.

The assault on the Hitler Line began. Aquino was reached but could not be captured. Then the Canadians broke through the Line and reached Pontecorvo. Piedmonte Hill was captured and the River Melfa crossed. The German defences were in confusion and they were withdrawing all along the line, although not without strong rearguard actions. After heavy fighting and many casualties Monte Orio and Monte Piccolo were captured. The Gurkhas attacked Arce and took it after hard fighting, and the Canadians entered Ceprano and Torrice. The Army was now poised for its final advance on Rome.

A number of Honours were awarded for this phase. **Hitler Line** was gained by the North Irish Horse and two Canadian armoured and ten Infantry regiments, **Aquino** by the Derbyshire Yeomanry, two Canadian armoured and two British Infantry regiments, **Piedmonte Hill** by the Royal West Kent Regiment, **Melfa Crossing** by five Canadian armoured and two British and seven Canadian Infantry regiments, **Monte Piccolo** by two British armoured, one Yeomanry and two Guards regiments, **Ceprano** by one Canadian armoured and two Infantry regiments, **Rocca D'Arce** by 1/5 Gurkha Rifles and **Torrice Crossroads** by the Lord Strathcona's Horse of Canada. The Honour for the whole phase of the breakthrough, **Liri Valley,** was awarded to one British and nine Canadian armoured regiments, four Yeomanry regiments, to the Welsh Guards and ten British and fifteen Canadian Infantry regiments.

In the centre of the country in the mountains the New Zealand division now made a rapid advance and reached Sora, and ten days later entered the old 8th Army objective of six months earlier, Avezzano. But by then Rome had fallen. No time had been wasted after the breaking of the Hitler Line and the advance on the capital continued without a break. Frosinone was captured after a fierce battle by the Canadians, followed by Ferentino and Anagni.

Meanwhile the Americans were struggling around the Alban Hills, until resistance flagged and only rearguards had to be overcome, although the British divisions on the coast were still meeting strong opposition. On 5 June the Americans entered Rome, having won the race as Clark had intended, rather than co-operate with 8th Army, working their way up Route 6, in helping to cut off a large number of German troops who had now been allowed to escape, presumably to satisfy his personal vanity.

Two British Battle Honours only were awarded for this period. They were **Rome**, gained by the Yorkshire Dragoons and eight British Infantry regiments, and **Advance to the Tiber**, awarded to the Royal Wiltshire Yeomanry and seven British Infantry regiments. **The Tiber** was awarded as a South African Honour to the Natal Mounted Rifles, and another South African Honour, *Paliano*, was claimed by single squadrons of each of five regiments.

The pursuit continued through most difficult country centred on the valleys of the Tiber and then the Arno Rivers, the major objective being Florence. It was a strange advance, in very hot weather, slogging up mountains, running into strongpoints and heavy resistance which after a day or two suddenly disappeared in the darkness. The Germans were withdrawing to their major defensive position before the mountains gave way to the Po valley, the Gothic Line, and delaying the opposition as long as possible in the process to enable them to man it fully and to strengthen it into what they fondly hoped was impregnability. Apart from the annoyances caused by the enemy, the troops of the 8th Army, having been used to adulation and to being the cynosure of all eyes, suddenly found themselves unnoticed and unsung, to their great frustration. The

landing in Normandy had taken place under their old boss the day after the capture of Rome, which was barely noticed in England, and now Italy had become a backwater and a sideshow and all eyes were turned on North West Europe. But at least the countryside had not been fought over, villages were still intact, as were their wine vats, and the inhabitants were friendly and the land was beautiful for those who had time to look at it.

6th South African Armoured Division had entered the battle just south of Rome; it was an unusual formation, consisting of South African armoured and motorised Infantry brigades and a British Guards brigade. To each the other was an enigma, so totally different was their approach to life, soldiering and warfare, but they had great respect for each other and worked extremely well together. They captured Civita Castellano, and a few days later the Guards captured Bagnoregio, a typical Italian village of the area perched on top of a precipitous hill. Two days later the South Africans entered Orvieto. Other divisions now joined the chase pioneered by the South Africans, 6th British Armoured, 78th, 4th British and 8th Indian Divisions, and the latter captured Terni on the same day that Orvieto was entered.

The Rifle Brigade of 6th Armoured Division advanced quickly and seized Monte Malbe, and the Guards entered Perugia, which was expected to be strongly defended but was abandoned. Assisi was entered without opposition and the Gurkhas suffered heavy casualties capturing the Ripa ridge. Meanwhile units of 78 Division had entered Citta della Pieve and were thrown out again after a fire fight, but after a fierce battle captured Monte Gabbione. The army was now up against a temporary defensive position based on and around Lake Trasimene.

A number of Honours were awarded for the advance from Rome to Trasimene which had taken just a fortnight. **Monte Rotondo** was won by the Lothian and Border Horse and by the Rifle Brigade and the Tower Hamlets Rifles, **Celleno** by five South African regiments, **Bagnoregio** by a single South African regiment, the Pretoria Regiment, **Allerona** by two South African regiments, **Ficulle** by the Warwickshire Yeomanry, **Monte Gabbione** by the Northamptonshire Regiment, **Citta Della Pieve** by the 3rd Hussars, the Royal Wiltshire Yeomanry and the Royal West Kent Regiment, and claimed by five South African regiments, **Capture of Perugia** by three armoured, one Yeomanry, two Guards and two Infantry regiments, all British, **Ripa Ridge** by the Royal Fusiliers and 1/5 Gurkha Rifles and **Monte Malbe** by the Rifle Brigade and by a territorial regiment, the London Rifle Brigade.

The attack on the Trasimene Line began with an assault on Santafucchio which was heavily repulsed, and reserves were brought forward. But before they could arrive another assault with fierce fighting gained this village and other villages nearby and Monte Pilonica. The South Africans found that Chiusi had been abandoned and the lake was transversed from both sides. A few days later Gabbiano was entered. Battle Honours gained were for **Santafucchio** awarded to the Warwickshire Yeomanry, the London Irish Rifles and the Ontario Regiment, **Gabbiano** to the Royal Fusiliers, and the overall Honour **Trasimene Line** to two Yeomanry regiments, the Scots Guards, twelve

British Infantry and three Canadian armoured regiments. Four South African Honours were awarded or claimed. **Chiusi** was awarded to two regiments, and claimed by two regiments and by two others who were only represented by one squadron, **Sarteano** and **La Foce** were both awarded uniquely to the Pretoria Regiment, and *Sinalunga* was claimed by the Imperial Light Horse and the Kimberley Regiment.

The next objective was Arezzo. Cortona and Castiglione Fiorentini were entered, but the New Zealanders had now to be recalled to the battle and with the Grenadier Guards fought their way over the mountainous country to capture Monte Lignano overlooking Arezzo, and three days later that city fell. Meanwhile the Poles had advanced up the east coast north of Ancona, and the Americans, who had been advancing steadily up the west coast, entered Leghorn. **Ancona**, on the east coast, was awarded as an Honour to the 7th Hussars. Honours were also awarded for **Arezzo,** gained by four British and three Canadian armoured regiments, two Yeomanry and two Guards regiments, and by six British and thirteen New Zealand Infantry regiments, **Tuori** gained by the Kings Regiment and **Monte Lignano** gained by a single New Zealand regiment, although such was their system that The Honour is now borne on the Colours of five regiments.

The advance on Florence now became two-pronged, one advance being made through the wooded country in the area between Arezzo and Siena to its west, and the other through the mountains east of Arezzo and the River Arno. Strangely when Battle Honours came to be awarded, only the left-hand thrust was regarded as the advance to Florence, perhaps because the other eventually passed by to the east of the city, although it undoubtedly contributed to its capture. It was ever thus, and Honours will always be granted enigmatically.

The left-hand thrust was multinational, consisting of the New Zealand, South African and 8th Indian Divisions, of which the latter contained a large number of British troops, and a Canadian armoured brigade. The right prong was only binational, consisting of 4th and 10 Indian Divisions, probably the best mountain warfare team that has existed in any army in the world, and a British armoured brigade. In training for this phase the 4th Indian Division gunners had practised hauling their guns up mountain sides until the gun-towers could go no further, and then winching them up the rest of the way on ground anchors assisted by drag ropes; only on a few occasions was this necessary during the battle but the guns certainly got into some incredible positions, which would have been believed to be totally impossible by the boffins of Larkhill.

With Florence only 30 miles away it seemed that the objective was within easy reach in a few days. But, as often, it did not quite work out like that, although the left hand had a much easier time then the right if only because of the more benign terrain. On the right 10 Indian Division had entered Umbertide and advanced up the Tiber valley in pace with the advance on Arezzo on its left, reaching Citta di Castello, but only capturing it after some sharp fighting and counterattacks which lasted for a week. On their left 4 Indian Division, with its decimated Indian battalions replaced although the British and Gurkha contin-

gents soldiered on, covered the trackless mountains between their sister division and the northward line through Arezzo in great style, and having taken the Alpe di Poti held the peaks against repeated counterattacks. Pressing forward again they attacked the key village of Campriano, during which assault they were thrilled to discover that they were being watched by King George VI.

It was grim fighting, and every mountain crest attained revealed even more mountains ahead, each defended desperately by the enemy to gain more time for manning the Gothic Line. It was often quite impossible to tell which peak was held by friends and which by foes, because they mostly looked alike and map reading became more a matter of luck and magic than logic. The troops in the valleys usually only distinguished one peak from the other by the ones which fired on them and were therefore presumably enemy held. A notorious case in point was Monte Cedrone which changed hands several times with few but the participants knowing it, although an artillery battery position suddenly came under machine gun fire from the heights, and against all the evidence to the contrary divisional headquarters still maintained that the Royal Sussex Regiment had captured the peaks! They had—twice—although they were not awarded an Honour for this, but this was not one of the times that they were holding it!

A number of Honours were gained. **Montone** was awarded to the Kings Own Regiment, **Trestina** to 2/4 Gurkha Rifles and **Monte Della Gorgace** to two Indian and one Gurkha regiments, **Monte Cedrone** was won by the Royal Wiltshire Yeomanry and 2/4 Gurkha Rifles, **Citta di Castello** by 3 Hussars, the Royal Wiltshire Yeomanry and one British and one Indian regiments, **Pian di Maggio** by the 1/2nd Gurkha Rifles. **Campriano** by the Warwickshire Yeomanry and the 2/7th Gurkha Rifles, **Citerna** by 12 Lancers, **Poggio del Grillo** by the Cameron Highlanders and 2/7 Gurkha Rifles, and **Cerrone** by the Calgary Regiment of Canada.

On the left flank the 8th Indian Division, the South Africans and New Zealanders attacked through the Chianti Hills, entered San Casciano, and had to fight hard to gain the range of hills in front of Florence which the Germans called the Paula Line, having used an alphabetical series of girls' names for their defensive positions for some time since the more noble and important sounding names did not appear to bear any magical defensive properties. But eventually Paula succumbed to the wiles of the New Zealanders, and the outskirts of Florence were entered on 4 August. They and the South Africans got as far as the River Arno, over which all the bridges except the Ponte Vecchio had been blown, and there stuck with the enemy on the other bank. Florence had been declared an open city but the German Parachute Corps had defied Kesselring's order and were defending inside the city itself. But at last they had to withdraw, from pressure on their flanks which threatened to surround them, and the centre of the city was occupied on 1 August by the Buffs. The 'easy bit of warfare' had been a very hard struggle all the way and up to the last.

Honours awarded for this phase were **Monte san Michele** to the Scots Guards, **Cerbaia** to four New Zealand armoured and fourteen Infantry regiments, **Monte Fili** to two

South African regiments and claimed by another, **Monte Domini** to the Coldstream Guards and also claimed by a South African regiment, **Monte Scalari** to three British Infantry regiments, **San Michele** to ten New Zealand armoured and fifteen Infantry regiments, the **Paula Line** to the same twenty-five New Zealand regiments, **Il Castello** to two Indian and one Gurkha regiments and **Incontro** to the Duke of Cornwall's Light Infantry. Overall the Honour of **Advance to Florence** was awarded to five British, ten New Zealand and three Canadian armoured regiments, to five Yeomanry regiments, to three Guards regiments, and to eight British, fifteen New Zealand and two battalions of one Indian regiment. There were also a number of purely South African Honours. *Monte Majone* was claimed by a squadron of the Pretoria Regiment, **Monte Querciabella** was awarded to the Witwatersrand Rifles and the Regiment de la Rey, **Florence** was awarded to ten regiments of the 6th South African Armoured Division and **The Greve** to eight regiments and claimed by two others.

The Gothic Line was now being approached rapidly and a major reorganisation took place for the assault, after the plan had been altered several times, again more to satisfy personal vanities than for purely tactical reasons. The main attack was to be made on the mountains near the east coast by 46th, 56th and 1st Canadian Divisions supported by 4th Indian Division, with 1st Armoured, 4th British and 2nd New Zealand Divisions initially held in reserve, with the idea of breaching on to the plain and rolling up the German defensive line from east to west where the going was easier. The Polish divisions were on the coastal strip itself, and 10 Indian Division was in the mountains on the left with a mixed collection of armoured units in support.

To their great annoyance 13th Corps, consisting of 6 British and 6th South African Armoured Divisions, 1st British and 8th Indian Divisions, were placed under American command in 5th Army to advance north of Florence towards Bologna. It was not the task but the command which bothered them, as they would have preferred to remain under command of the Army with which they had formed a part since before Alamein. But they started in good heart and soon had made two captures which resulted in unique Honours. **Fiesole** was awarded to the Loyal Regiment (47 Foot) and **Montorsoli** to the Hertfordshire Regiment.

The old original Desert Rats, 7 Armoured Brigade, also joined the 8th Army again, including two regiments, 2 Royal Tank Regiment and 7 Hussars, who had been to Burma to help to stem the Japanese advance there since serving in the desert. Only another 30 miles, the magical figure again, lay between the positions being taken up for the Gothic Line assault and the Romagna Plain of the southern Po valley, but it was 30 miles of jagged mountains and rough terrain, in which was sited the last major German defensive position in Italy, which could therefore be expected to be defended desperately and ferociously.

But before the main assault on the Gothic Line itself could take place final positions had to be assumed and this involved further fighting to reach and secure the start line. The first move forward was made through some Italian divisions which were holding the area just in from the coast, kept well back from the enemy positions just in case,

although they did not realise this; not having been let into the secret of the impending attack, they were greatly surprised when the 8th Army vanguard moved through their positions without encountering the enemy and disappeared into the distance. On the night of 25/26 August forces crossed the River Vanco and advanced quickly with little opposition owing to local withdrawals. In the next two days they advanced about 8 miles until the Canadians attacked the hill town of Monteciccardo, which they entered, were thrown out of by counterattack and only finally captured after a day of hard fighting. The River Foglia, the start of the Gothic Line proper, had been reached.

Bitter fighting now ensued and casualties were considerable, but the advance continued. Monte Luro and Monte Peloso were captured by the Canadians and on the coast the Household Cavalry and 7 Hussars, supporting the Poles, mopped up around Pessaro, and the River Metauro was crossed. On the left of the Canadians 46 Division also had success after grim fighting, storming Monte Gridolfo, and capturing Monte Vecchio and Mondaino. Further left still the Indians, who had had further to advance than the other formations before the Gothic Line, entered Urbino, the birthplace of the painter Rafael, and stormed the stronghold of Montecalvo.

Honours awarded up to this point were **Monteciccardo** gained by the Edmonton Regiment of Canada, **Montecalvo** gained by the 4/11th Sikh Regiment, **Montecchio** gained by four Canadian regiments, **Point 204**, with its alternative name of **Pozzo Alto Ridge**, which was gained by four more Canadian regiments, **Borgo Santa Maria** won by the Canadian Royal 22nd Regiment, **Monteluro** won by the Edmonton Regiment, **Tomba di Pessaro** won by two Canadian armoured regiments and **Monte Gridolfo** awarded to four British Infantry regiments.

By now there was no shortage of ammunition or guns to fire it and even minor attacks were supported by divisional bombardments; in terms of artillery support the Infantry had never had it so good. 4 Indian Division now had a hard fight to capture their next objective, Tavoleto, and 56 Division was committed. 46 Division captured their next objective and the Gothic Line had now been breached and penetrated all along the front, with the plain just a step away. But it was a major step even now, and first two ridges, Coriano and Gemmano, had to be captured. The river Conca was crossed but the attack was repulsed and the battle reached a temporary stalemate. The enemy was not retiring as had been hoped and anticipated. Honours were awarded for **Tavoleto** to the Cameron Highlanders and the 2/7th and 1/9th Gurkha Rifles.

The British part of 5th Army advanced towards the Il Giogo Pass north of Florence. 8th Indian Division captured Monte Citerna and Monte Veruca and breached their part of the Gothic Line thereby. A number of Honours were awarded. **Montegaudio** was gained by the Royal Hampshire Regiment, **Pratelle Pass** by the Indian Parachute Regiment, **Alpe di Vitigliano** by 1/5th Gurkha Rifles, **Femmina Morte** also uniquely by 1/5th Gurkha Rifles and **Monte Porro Del Bagno** (which should properly be Pozzo Del Bagno although a spelling mistake appears to have got into the Honours title) by two South African regiments and claimed by a third. The overall Honour for this phase of breaking through the enemy defences, **Gothic Line,** was gained by six British, six Canadian and one Indian armoured regiments, by the North Irish Horse, by two Guards regiments, by twenty-one British, fifteenth Canadian, four Indian and two Gurkha Infantry regiments and by eleven South African regiments.

Meanwhile 8th Army had not been idle and on 5 September the Gemmano-Coriano-San Savino feature was assaulted again. A furious battle raged. 4 Indian Division gained Pian di Castello and 56 Division reached the village of Gemmano but were repulsed from the massive ridge itself. The village of Croce was a major stumbling block and casualties were heavy on both sides. But the ridge held out. On 12 September another assault was made further to the right and the Canadians captured Coriano village and the ridge around it. Another attack was mounted on Croce, but although the Fabbri spur was taken the village could not be. Now 4 Indian Division was directed at the obstinate ridge, and this time, with many further casualties, the village of Croce was captured, and a base was established for exploitation on Gemmano ridge. On the right Ospedaletto was entered by 4 British Division against stiff opposition, Montescudo was taken by the Indians, as was the massif of San Marino, an independent republic within Italy, where the Cameron Highlanders scaled the heights during the night as they had done at Keren. At the same time the Canadians had attacked the San Fortunato ridge. The plain had been reached at last for some formations, but now it was raining hard again and the dream of flat ground had become a nightmare of mud.

Honours for this period were **San Clemente,** gained by 4 Hussars and two British infantry regiments, **Poggio San Giovanni,** gained by the 2/11th Sikh Regiment and 1/2 Gurkha Rifles, **Pian di Castello,** gained by two British Infantry regiments, **Croce** won by four British Infantry regiments, **Gemmano Ridge** won by eight British Infantry regiments and the overall Honour **Coriano** gained by five British and two Canadian armoured regiments and the Yorkshire Dragoons, and by thirteen British, six Canadian, one Indian and four Gurkha Infantry regiments, and the Honourable Artillery Company. In addition **Montebello-Scorticata Ridge** was awarded to the Cameron Highlanders and 2/7 Gurkha Rifles, **Sant Arcangelo** to the 10th Hussars and three Gurkha Rifles regiments, **Monte Reggiano** to two British infantry regiments and 1/2 Gurkha Rifles, **Savignano** to the Cheshire Regiment uniquely and **Misano Ridge** to four armoured and six Infantry regiments, all Canadian.

Further Honours were awarded for the breaking of the Rimini Line on the coast. The overall Honour **Rimini Line** was awarded to four British armoured regiments and the Yorkshire Dragoons, and to twelve British and ten Canadian Infantry regiments, **Monte Colombo** to the Leicestershire Regiment, **Casa Fabbri Ridge** and **Montescudo** each to two British Infantry regiments, **San Martino–San Lorenzo** to five Canadian Infantry regiments, **San Marino** to three British, one Indian and one Gurkha regiments, **Frisoni** to the Royal Hampshire Regiment, **Ceriano Ridge** to the Bays (2 Dragoon Guards), the Yorkshire Dragoons and four British Infantry regiments, **San Fortunato** to seven Canadian Infantry regiments, **Casale** to two Canadian ar-

moured and two Infantry regiments and **Rio Fontanaccia** to three New Zealand armoured and thirteen Infantry regiments. On the 13th Corps front north of Florence Honours were awarded for **Marradi** to two British Infantry regiments, for **Catarelto Ridge** to the Coldstream and Scots Guards, and to one South African regiment, and claimed by another, and for **Monte Vigese** to three South African regiments.

At this point the command of 8th Army changed again and General McCreery took over from Leese. The attack continued unabated and the Rubicon was crossed, in the opposite direction to Caesar, a small stream 5 miles north-west of the Marecchio, and the crossing was no walk-over. 10 Indian Division captured Sogliano and Monte Farneto but the weather conditions made all movement difficult. In the middle of October 4 Indian Division was relieved and pulled out of the battle as being no longer a fighting formation; since coming to Italy at the beginning of the year and being committed at Cassino they had had over 12,000 casualties and there was no longer any means of replacing them, any available Britons being needed in North West Europe and Indians in Burma. Monte Spaccato, Carpinetta and Monte Chicco were taken, the latter by the Gurkhas who were only held there by massive artillery concentrations which continued for 36 hours, and now the Army could overlook the River Senio, one of the major ones in the area, which would not be crossed for some months yet.

On the 13th Corps front Monte Battaglia had been won and counterattacked with heavy German losses. Monte Gamberaldi was stormed several times before it was captured, as was Monte Ceco. 78 Division now relieved an American division and continued the advance beyond Santerno. Monte La Pieve and Monte Spaduro were assaulted but the attacks failed. The South African division attacked and captured Monte Stanco and Monte Salvaro, but the Americans were still having great difficulty in advancing although Bologna was almost in sight. Cesena was entered and the advance on the right reached the River Savio. Troops of 8 Indian Division now captured Monte Pianoereno against intense enemy fire and 78 Division captured Monte La Pieve and Monte Spaduro, although with heavy casualties and held it against furious counterattacks. Still it poured with rain and still the weary troops slogged on.

A large number of Honours were awarded, for **San Martino Sogliano** to the King's Own Regiment and to the Indian Parachute Regiment, for **Monte Farneto** to the North Irish Horse, one Indian and one Gurkha regiment, for **Montilgallo** to two British Infantry regiments and for **Carpineta** to the Bays and two British Infantry regiments and **Monte Chicco** to the 2/6 Gurkhas. **Sant Angelo in Salute** was gained by seven New Zealand and two Canadian armoured regiments and by ten New Zealand Infantry regiments, **Bulgaria Village** by the Hastings and Prince Edward Regiment of Canada, **Cesena** by two British armoured and two British and two Canadian Infantry regiments, **Pisciatello** by ten New Zealand armoured and fourteen New Zealand and two Canadian Infantry regiments, **Savio Bridgehead** by 27 Lancers and three British and five Canadian Infantry regiments, **Monte Gamberaldi** by three British Infantry regiments, **Battaglia** by the Grenadier and Welsh Guards, **Monte Casalino** by the Argyll and Sutherland Highlanders, **Monte Ceco** by six British Infantry regiments, **Monte la Pieve** by the Northamptonshire Regiment and the Three Rivers Regiment of Canada, **Monte Pianoereno** by the Royal West Kent Regiment, **Monte Spaduro** by eight British Infantry regiments and the Three Rivers Regiment, **Orsara** by the Rifle Brigade and the London Rifle Brigade territorials, **Monte Stanco** by six South African regiments and **Monte Salvaro** by four South African regiments and claimed by one more. A South African Honour, **Monte Pezza,** was gained by four regiments and claimed by one other.

Unfortunately, in spite of advancing over 40 miles through difficult mountain terrain, with most of the brunt of the attacks falling on the Infantry, and against desperate defence by the German troops, the Armies were just not strong enough to break out on to the plain of the Po valley before winter started. But for all the wet weather the attacks had to be pursued, if for no other reason than to contain the Germans and prevent them from thinning out the defences and sending reinforcements to North West Europe, where they were becoming badly needed.

The 8th Army's objectives were Ravenna with exploitation across the Rivers Lamone and Senio. The 5th Army's were still to take Bologna, and then to advance towards Ferrara including a pincer movement with 8th Army. But at the same time the Armies' resources had been reduced by the need to send troops, 4th Indian Division, 23rd Armoured and 2nd Parachute Brigades, to Greece to combat the communist rising and the possibility of civil war, unleashed in the wake of the withdrawing German forces.

Forli was the first 8th Army objective, and 10 Indian Division captured Monte Cavallo. 4 Division crossed the River Ronco, only to find that the heavy rain which followed had made the river impassable and stranded the troops which had crossed it on the far bank without support, to their mortification. The Indian division attacked again through Meldola to Grisignano, and the outskirts of Forli. 46 Division took over the advance as the Germans withdrew from the town and were followed up by a crossing of the River Montoni, with a momentary setback on the River Ronco with the inevitable casualties. 4 Division reached the River Lamone near Faenza, having *en route* carried out an assault crossing of the canalised River Cosina. By the end of November 8th Army was set to cross the River Lamone, although by this time it had suffered another loss of resources when 4 British Division also had to be sent to Greece.

Honours were awarded for **Monte Cavallo** to the North Irish Horse, the Indian Parachute Regiment and the 2/3rd Gurkha Rifles, for **Capture of Forli** to two armoured and five Infantry regiments, all British, for **Casa Fortis** to the North Irish Horse and three British Infantry regiments, for the **Cosina Canal Crossing** to 10 Hussars and four British Infantry regiments and for **Casa Bettini** to the North Irish Horse and one Indian regiment.

On 13 Corps front, in 5th Army area, at first only 8 Indian Division was active and it stormed and captured Monte San Bartolo. On the left flank Monte Grande was still creating a formidable and costly obstacle. 1 Division captured Monte Castellazzo, but was counterattacked and

had to withdraw again. **Monte san Bartolo** was awarded as an Honour to 1/5 Gurkha Rifles.

Nearer the coast the Canadians now came into action again, and early in December they entered Ravenna and turned towards the Lamone. Their first attempt to cross the river was a ghastly failure with very heavy losses. Near Faenza 46 Division supported by the New Zealanders was more successful, but only managed to hold a limited bridgehead, which was ferociously counterattacked and held out. The Canadians and 1 Division now attacked again and this time managed to cross the river, and although they pressed on and crossed the Naviglio Canal they too were heavily counterattacked and only just managed to hang on. Honours were gained for **Lamone Crossing** by three British and five Canadian armoured regiments, the North Irish Horse, and by five British and twelve Canadian Infantry regiments and 2/6 Gurkha Rifles, for **Pideura** by the 9th Lancers and the Royal Hampshire Regiment, for **Defence of Lamone Bridgehead** by two British armoured and four Infantry regiments, for **Capture of Ravenna** by the 27 Lancers and the Princess Louise's Dragoon Guards of Canada and for **Naviglio Canal** by three armoured and eight Infantry regiments, all Canadian.

13 Corps attacked again and gained an entry into Tossignano with much difficulty, but had little success in exploiting this capture. But the Poles captured Brisighella, having been transferred to this front, and the Germans, in danger of being surrounded, evacuated Faenza; then they advanced to the River Senio but were unable to establish a bridgehead over it. During this period Monte Grande had at last been captured. **Monte Grande** was awarded as an Honour to seven British Infantry regiments, **Tossignano** to two British regiments, **Fosso Vecchio** to five Canadian regiments and **Fosso Munio** to three Canadian armoured and seven Infantry regiments. **Celle** was awarded to three New Zealand armoured and eleven Infantry regiments, **Pergola Ridge** to the Durham Light Infantry and **Faenza Pocket** to three armoured and fourteen Infantry regiments of the New Zealand forces.

The year 1944 had shown enormous advances in Italy, starting with the storming of Cassino and followed by the capture of Rome, the advance to Florence and the breaking of the Gothic Line. But the war in Italy was by no means over yet, although, but for isolated incidents, the final denouement had to wait for some months because of the weather. At the end of the year Alexander became Supreme Commander Mediterranean as a Field Marshal, three months after a similar promotion had been granted to Montgomery, although the award was backdated to the fall of Rome which re-established his seniority.

South West Pacific, 1944

At the end of 1943 the Australians had cleared most of the Huon peninsula and were advancing westwards along the coast. The Japanese were in retreat, although by no means defeated, and it was by now clear that they were not impregnable on land as had at one time been imagined after their advance in Burma and through the islands. On 15 January the Australians entered Sio and the 5th Australian Division took over the pursuit from the 9th. Just prior to this an American regimental combat team had landed at Saidor, well ahead of the Australian advance, to cut off the withdrawing Japanese. In the middle of February patrols linked up with the Australians advancing along the coast. Inland the Australians broke through strong defensive positions in the Finisterres range, captured Barum in March and shortly afterwards also linked up with the Americans patrolling southwards. They continued to advance, captured Bogajim on Austrolabe Bay in the middle of April and on 24 April entered Madang.

Battle Honours were awarded for **Sio** to three regiments, for **Finisterres II** to six regiments, for **Barum** to two regiments and for **Bogadjim** and **Madang** uniquely to the 60th and 30th Regiments respectively.

Apart from the advance from Sio to the Sepik River in the first half of the year, for which the Honour **Sio–Sepik River** was awarded to the Pacific Islands Regiment and to two Infantry regiments, the Australians carried out no further major actions until the very end of the year. It was MacArthur's plan that the Australian advance should be halted, so that they could relieve the Americans in the islands and allow the latter to continue the advance into the Philippines and the Pacific islands. The reason behind this can be well imagined. The Americans meanwhile had leapfrogged and landed at Hollandia and Aitape, and were containing a large Japanese force which could only be supplied by submarine due to the American control of the surrounding seas and were slowly starving to death, too weak to launch a breakout.

At the end of 1944 the Australians relieved American formations in a number of areas in the South West Pacific, mainly to mop up Japanese garrisons which had been bypassed and to allow the Americans to reorganise to invade the Philippines. This caused a great deal of discord between the two nations. Most of the fighting in the islands took place in the following year.

Burma, 1944

The new advance into the Arakan in 1944 began as before with attacks on Buthidaung, Maungdaw and Razabil. At Razabil the attack was initially against a heavily-defended hill called the 'Tortoise', and it took a week to reduce the outpost positions, so strong were they. Other troops bypassed the Tortoise and entered Maungdaw, and the little port was cleared and became a major supply line for 15 Corps. 5 Indian Division continued the assault on Razabil, and were supported by a tank formation, the first time that they had been used in Burma other than almost individually.

Attacks slowly ate into the defences of the Tortoise, although casualties were heavy. The main attack was switched by 7 Indian Division to Buthidaung, and the division, supported by a brigade of 5 Indian Division with artillery and tanks, crossed the Ngakyedauk Pass. The Japanese had meanwhile been reinforced and it was expected that they were about to launch a series of counterattacks; these came at the beginning of February as part of an outflanking operation, and 26th Indian and 36th British Divisions were committed. The Japanese captured Taung Bazar and attacked the rear of 7 Indian Division,

but this time the beleagured troops dug in and resisted instead of trying to break out of the encirclement, and their positions were held in spite of strong attacks, during one of which the defences were breached and the Japanese captured a field dressing station, massacred the wounded and executed the doctors treating them. Counterattacks were made, and the fighting was desperate against the usual fanatical Japanese defenders.

During this operation 81 West African Division was still advancing down the Kaladan valley, thus threatening Kyauktaw and the Japanese flank and rear. 26th Indian and 36 British Divisions started to advance each side of the Mayu range and the Japanese were being squeezed between them and the beleaguered 5th and 7th Indian Divisions, the tactic which had been attempted in 1943 and failed. This time the manoeuvre did not fail, and by the middle of February the Japanese were pulling out, and 5th and 7th Indian Divisions were relieved and able to resume their role in the attack.

In March Buthidaung fell, followed by Razabil and the Mayu Tunnel forts, and to the east 81 West African Division captured Kyauktaw and Apaukwa but was counterattacked and forced to withdraw. Buthidaung was voluntarily abandoned to form a stronger defensive line, but the rest of the captured territory was held, and to all intents and purposes the battle for the Arakan was over, although there was still some fighting to come before the district was finally cleared of the enemy.

Maungdaw was awarded to two British regiments, **Mowdok** to the Gambia Regiment and **Ngakyedauk Pass** to the 25th Dragoons, the Madras Sappers and Miners, and to four British and three Indian regiments. **Buthidaung** was added to the Colours of 25 Dragoons, three British, two Indian and one Gurkha regiments, and **Razabil** to the same armoured regiment, two British and two Indian Infantry regiments, **Kaladan** was gained by the Sierra Leone, Nigeria, Gold Coast and Gambia Regiments, **Point 551** by one British, one Gurkha and two Indian regiments and **Mayu Tunnels** by five British Infantry regiments. **The Yu** was awarded uniquely to the Northamptonshire Regiment (48 Foot), **Defence of Sinzweya,** known at the time as the 'Battle of the Boxes', to the Bombay Sappers and Miners and one British regiment, and the overall Honour, **North Arakan,** to 25th Dragoons, seventeen British regiments, to one Indian regiment, one Gurkha regiment and to the four West African regiments previously named. A unique Honour, **Alethangyaw,** was awarded to the Commandos for a raid on the Arakan coast to pin down the enemy forces while the battle for the Mayu position was in progress.

While the Battle for the Arakan was being fought a second Chindit expedition under Brigadier Wingate was launched. This was a much more ambitious operation than the previous one and involved six brigades. 16 Brigade was to march in and set off in February, and three of the others were to be flown in in early March. There was an early setback to the fly-in when air photographs showed one of the landing grounds, nicknamed 'Piccadilly', to be obstructed by tree trunks and it was suspected that news of the operation had leaked, although this was subsequently found to be not the case. Nevertheless it was decided to continue the operation, leaving out this particular strip.

The fly-in was not a success, partly because the Dakotas were each towing two gliders, which, with the steep climb which was necessitated to cross the mountains, was beyond their capability, and only 35 out of 61 gliders reached 'Broadway', another of the landing strips. Even then a number of them crashed on landing, but the landing strips were quickly cleared of wreckage and repaired and Dakotas started flying in. The Japanese had been taken completely by surprise and were slow to react, but even when they knew the situation did not divert any of the troops from their impending attack on the frontier defences of India, which it had been hoped that they would.

The British troops advanced, destroying a Japanese detachment at Mawlu and achieving their primary objective, the cutting of the road and rail communications supplying the Japanese opposing General Stillwell in the northern area of Burma. There is a doubt, however, whether that objective should not have been changed in the circumstances to the interdiction of the Japanese troops now attacking at Imphal and Kohima. A block was established at 'White City', Henu, and an attack which almost succeeded was made on the airfield at Indaw. Another block was established at 'Blackpool', Hopin, and Mogaung was captured, and further heavy fighting occurred around 'Broadway' and at the Kyusanlai Pass, Point 2171-Hill 60 and at Myitkyina. Reinforcements were flown in, but the expedition suffered a serious loss when Wingate himself was killed in an air crash. He was replaced in command by Brigadier Lentaigne, and the operation continued. The Japanese had by now discovered the locations of the Special Force and made a number of attacks on it which were bloodily repulsed. On Stillwell's front a hazardous advance by a mixed Chinese/American force captured Myitkyina, and only held it after it had changed hands several times. Eventually the Chindits were withdrawn, short of food and supplies and exhausted by hardship. The Honour, **Chindits 1944**, was awarded to thirteen British and five Gurkha regiments and to the Nigeria Regiment. *Mogaung* was unsuccessfully claimed by 5 Gurkha Rifles.

The main battle of 1944, however, was fought on the central Assam front from March to July in the area of Imphal and Kohima, and was the first of the decisive battles of the Burma campaign. A breakthrough into India was essential for the Japanese, who were now suffering heavy losses of shipping in the Pacific which in turn caused their troops, strung out across the islands, to be in danger of being cut off and starved out, for morale reasons and to outflank China. From the British point of view India must be defended to the utmost, and only the wearing down and destruction of the Japanese forces in Burma would allow an advance to be made to recapture the country. Because a British advance was being planned both these areas were full of stores and administrative establishments, with very little in the way of defences against ground attack. Both areas were supplied from the railhead at Dimapur and were therefore very vulnerable to any Japanese attacks which could cut the road which had been built to join them both to the railhead.

4th Corps had 17th and 20th Indian Divisions forward around Tiddim and Tamu respectively, with about 80 miles of jungle-covered and almost impassable mountains be-

tween them, with 23 Indian Division in reserve at Imphal. General Slim decided to withdraw the two forward divisions slowly to Imphal, impeding Japanese progress where they could and giving the enemy, instead of himself, the disadvantage of difficult communications, hoping that he could destroy the Japanese on the Imphal plain. Small blocking forces were left to stem the Japanese advance. It was to be a battle planned to destroy the Japanese and render them incapable of defending Burma.

Early in March the Japanese attacked a detachment defending the bridge over the Manipur River at Tonzang, north of Tiddim, and a brigade of 17 Indian Division was sent to its aid. The Japanese then crossed the river south of Tiddim and advanced northwards to isolate 17 Division. The division withdrew and the Japanese cut the road behind it and established a defensive position on the Tuitum Saddle. The Gurkhas attacked Tuitum and drove off the Japanese, but the road was still cut further north. At the same time another larger enemy force crossed the River Chindwin further north and advanced towards Litan and Ukhrul with the intention of cutting off Imphal, and also advanced towards Kohima.

In the mountainous jungle terrain it was difficult to find out just what was happening, or who was where, but the original plan for concentrating at Imphal, and keeping the road open, was adhered to. The Indian Parachute Brigade and a battalion of 23 Indian Division defended Ukhrul desperately but were eventually forced to fall back. There was fierce hand-to-hand fighting a few miles south at Sangshak and the brigade there had to break out and try to reach Imphal.

Another fierce battle was going on at Litan as the Japanese attempted to encircle the Imphal position, until the defenders were also withdrawn to Imphal. Another brigade of 23 Indian Division was fighting down the Tiddim road to relieve 17 Indian Division fighting up it, but the Japanese infiltrated both divisions and again the situation became obscure. The detachment on the Tuitum Saddle, which had held on in spite of fanatical counterattacks was now withdrawn, blowing up the bridge over the Manipur river after them, and meanwhile 17 Division continued to fight back northwards and reached the comparative safety of Imphal early in April. 20 Indian Division, which all this while had been at Tamu in the Kabaw valley, also withdrew to Imphal, assisted by a brigade of 23 Division which held a strong rearguard position at Sittaung during this part of the withdrawal towards Shenam and Tengnoupal.

Honours were awarded for this phase of the battle to 1/3 and 1/10 Gurkha Rifles for **Tuitum,** to one British and three Gurkha regiments for **Sakawng,** and to 3 Dragoon Guards, the Madras Sappers and Miners and three British and two Gurkha regiments for **Tamu Road. Sangshak** was gained by one Indian regiment, and, although the actual battles extended beyond the period so far narrated, **Shenam Pass** was gained by three British, one Indian and four Gurkha regiments and **Litan** by one British, one Indian and one Gurkha regiment. **Tiddim Road** was awarded to an Indian regiment, the 4/7th Rajputs.

While the opening battle for Imphal raged, another Japanese advance was building up strength and momentum towards Kohima and Dimapur, and with only small garrisons they were in considerable peril, as was India. 5 Indian Division was rapidly flown in from the Arakan, being replaced there by the newly formed 25 Indian Division, and 7 Indian Division and 2 British Division were put on alert to follow it. Non-combatants were evacuated from Assam to allow the limited supply of rations to be allocated to the fighting troops. The Assam Regiment was out in front covering the approaches to Kohima and it took the brunt of the Japanese attack. The only defence of Kohima itself was a battalion of the Royal West Kent Regiment and some miscellaneous troops. Luckily the Japanese orders were to take Kohima rather than to by-pass it and capture Dimapur if this proved more practical, and they made constant frontal assaults on Kohima, whose garrison desperately managed to hold out during its investment, short of rations and particularly of water, and the Japanese suffered very heavy casualties.

2 British Division had now arrived in the area and two brigades were sent to relieve the garrison, which was able to march out with great honour for a truly gallant defence. **Defence of Kohima** was awarded as an Honour to the Royal West Kent Regiment (50 Foot) and to the Assam Regiment, **Jessami** to the Assam Regiment and **Relief of Kohima** to three British and one Indian regiment.

The British forces now started to attack but the Japanese resistance was strong and progress was inevitably slow. A number of strong positions, including Naga Village and Jail Hill, around Kohima were attacked and some were won, but with heavy casualties, and held against heavy counterattacks, and eventually the Japanese started to fall back. **Jail Hill** was awarded to the Bengal Sappers and Miners, **Naga Village** to three British and one Indian regiment and **Aradura** to three British regiments and the Assam Regiment.

Meanwhile a bitter battle had also been going on at Imphal. The areas of Litan and Ukhrul were still being held and grim fighting went on for the twin peaks of Nungshigum until the Japanese counterattackers could stomach no more casualties. Some of the heaviest fighting was at Tengnoupal in the Shenam Pass, where attacks and counterattacks followed each other with regularity, and at Bishenpur, where the battle raged for two months; although the Japanese gained some positions they were thrown out again and generally their assaults were repulsed. At Kanglatongbi, which was a major supply depot on the Imphal–Kohima road, the Japanese also made strong attacks, and although they initially won the position they were gradually pushed back again, the Infantry now being supported by the tanks of the Carbineers.

After several weeks of hard fighting the Japanese attack was halted all along the Assam front in late June and 14th Army could itself now go over to the offensive. Mao Songsang was captured when the Japanese withdrew and the attack was carried towards Ukhrul. The Imphal–Kohima Battle could now be seen to have been won, desperate and grim as it had been, the first major allied victory in Burma. As during the American Civil War the battle of Pickett's Post was said to have been the 'high water mark of the Confederacy', so was the Japanese attack on Imphal and Kohima, although this may not have been obvious to the fighting soldier at the time.

Nungshigum was gained by 3 Dragoon Guards and two Indian regiments and **Mao Songsang** by two British regiments. **Bishenpur** was added as an Honour to the Colours of 3 Dragoon Guards, the Madras Sappers and Miners, two British, one Indian and seven Gurkha regiments, and **Kanglatongbi** was awarded to the 3rd Dragoon Guards again and to two British, three Indian and one Gurkha regiment. For the overall battle **Imphal** was awarded to 3 Dragoon Guards, the Indian 7th Cavalry, and to seven British and one Indian Infantry regiments, and to eight Gurkha battalions representing five regiments, and **Kohima** was awarded to the Indian 11th Cavalry and to fifteen British and three Indian regiments.

In view of his heavy losses in manpower and material it was possible that the Japanese commander would now want to reorganise and feed in reinforcements. General Slim was determined to make this as difficult as possible by attempting to establish bridgeheads over the River Chindwin during the monsoon period, keeping up pressure all the time, so that the British forces were poised to attack southwards as soon as the weather improved again.

The first objective was Ukhrul, which was encircled by 7th and 20th Indian Divisions at the beginning of July, and by the end of the month it had been captured and the Japanese positions around it had been destroyed. The weather during this and other attacks at the time was appalling, typical monsoon weather with heavy continuous rain, which made the tracks into seas of mud and impassable to all but the most determined troops, which was very descriptive of the 14th Army. The advance continued, found stiff resistance at Lokchao, eventually encircling the position so that the Japanese had to withdraw again, and 2 British Division passed through to Tamu which was reoccupied without opposition. As the advance progressed the number of Japanese dead and the litter of discarded equipment made it clear that the Japanese defeat in front of Imphal and Kohima had been even more complete than had been realised at the time. Changes were made in the British formations because most of them had fought now for over four months in the most difficult conditions of terrain and weather and against a fanatical enemy, and were in need of rest and recuperation. Obviously this could not be achieved at once, but 4 Corps was relieved and 11 East African Division took over from 23 Indian Division.

The East African Division was soon in action, advancing eastwards towards Sittaung and southwards to Kalemyo in the Kabaw valley, their main objective. The southerly advance was held up at Mawlaik and it took more than a month to dislodge the Japanese and to establish a bridgehead over the Chindwin. Soon the advance was only a few miles from Kalemyo when it met the heaviest resistance; 11 Division linked up with 5 Indian Division advancing down the Tiddim Road, and Kalemyo was entered.

5 Indian Division had been advancing steadily but against stubborn resistance and therefore slowly. Tangnoupal had been taken, followed by Tongzang on the Manipur River, and the river was crossed, which in itself was an achievement, even without Japanese interference, while it was in spate through the monsoon. Progress had continued up to the notorious Chocolate Staircase, where the road climbed 3,000 feet in 7 miles with 38 hairpin bends, and the

consistency of the ground and sauce-like appearance gave rise to its name, and occupied Tiddim.

The next heavy Japanese resistance was at the highest point on the road, Kennedy Peak. But this position was outflanked and after a week of grim fighting the peak was captured, and with the assistance of the RAF, created havoc and enormous casualties among the retreating Japanese. The Lushai Brigade of irregulars had been supporting 5 Indian Division, which was now pulled out to refit in India, and the Brigade was now set to advance by itself through the Chin Hills southward to Gangaw. In spite of the enormous front which it was covering and the conditions the Brigade reached the Myittha area in the middle of November and pushed on towards Gangaw which was heavily defended.

The main objective of 11 East African Division, Kalewa, now had to be tackled and against stubborn opposition the town was entered at the beginning of December. One brigade advancing from Mawlaik had managed to cross the Chindwin and now advanced down the east bank of the river and attacked the Japanese forces holding the bank opposite Kalewa. The rest of the division crossed the river south of the town and joined up with the brigade, and together they attacked the enemy position, and with the stiff opposition encountered it was a week before the Japanese gave way and withdrew towards Shwegyin. A bridge was built over the river, supplies were brought up and in spite of clashes with rearguards Shwegyin was entered in the middle of December. This was the real end of the Imphal-Kohima Battle, as the threat to India was now removed once and for all and the Japanese had suffered another major defeat with the British crossing of the Chindwin.

Battle Honours awarded for this phase were **Ukhrul** to three British, one Indian and one Gurkha regiment, **Tengnoupal** to one British, four Indian and two Gurkha regiments, **Tongzang** to a single Indian regiment, **Kennedy Peak** to 3 Dragoon Guards and three Indian regiments, **Mawlaik** to the King's African Rifles and the Northern Rhodesia Regiment and to the Assam Regiment, **Pinwe** to six British regiments, and **Kalewa** to the same two East African regiments and to one Indian regiment.

The campaign in 1944 had ended on a very high note in Burma, with 14th Army recapturing a large slice of the country and now being poised for its next advance towards the River Irrawaddy, and on to Mandalay and Rangoon.

North West Europe, 1944

Considerable pressure had been exerted on the British and Americans as early as 1942 to open a so-called Second Front to assist the Russians, but this had not been possible with the limited forces and facilities available, and particularly with a large British force tied down in the Western Desert. The assault on North Africa had been planned to draw off German troops from the Eastern Front and to help the situation in the Middle East, but this meant that no forces would be available for North West Europe in 1943 either. Thus the Italian campaign was planned and implemented in 1943 and the invasion of Europe postponed to 1944. A landing in North West Europe would be

a major operation, needing maximum ground, air and sea forces culled from the various existing theatres throughout the world, together with a vast supply of landing craft, and in addition technical forces and formations to capture and open up ports or to create artificial ones on the beaches.

At the end of 1943 Eisenhower was made Supreme Commander for the venture, with Montgomery as his Deputy and Commander of 21 Army Group, which would be responsible for the landing. Montgomery was thus responsible for planning the assault and for operational command until enough American forces could be deployed to form an American Army Group. A plan was finally agreed, although subsequently changed somewhat in detail, to make a seaborne landing between the Carentan estuary, at the base of the Cotentin peninsula, and the River Orne east of Caen, with five divisions, building up to eight divisions and fourteen tank regiments on D Day, with a follow-up of a further five divisions and up to ten armoured brigades by six days after D Day.

Montgomery's overall strategic plan, which was never really understood by the Americans then and is probably not even today, was to produce the threat of a breakout at Caen, which was a vital communications centre for the Germans. This would draw the major enemy forces, particularly armour, to that area, where they would be fought and committed, while the weakening of the western portion of the front would allow the Americans to break through to the River Loire, and drive eastwards towards Paris and the Seine, the whole of the armies using Caen as a pivot for the purpose. This would be aided by a massive air interdiction programme to destroy the bridges over the Seine and Loire and so make German reinforcement difficult. In addition the Americans were to capture Cherbourg and then the Brittany peninsula in order to provide port facilities for their supply and reinforcement. It was a masterly and brilliant concept, which could have only been thought out by one of the most remarkable military men of this or any age.

To meet the requirements of this strategy 1st US Army was directed to land on two beaches in the western sector with three Infantry divisions, supporting armour and two airborne divisions, and 2nd British Army to land on three beaches in the eastern sector with four Infantry divisions, supporting armour and one airborne division. British Commandos and American Ranger Groups were also to be employed in the landings.

The world was now to see the greatest amphibious landing operation against a defended enemy coast that had ever been mounted in the history of warfare. It had been long awaited with bated breath since no such landing, even of very much more limited size, had ever achieved real success. The assault was scheduled for 5 June, one of three days only during the month when the required conjunction of tide and moonlight occurred. In the event the weather and sea were so bad that day that the assault was postponed for one day; the weather forecast was not much better even then, but with so many preparations made, and a massive bombardment force, whose time could be limited by fuel usage, already at sea it was decided to take a chance.

At 0200 hours on 6 June a number of parties of 6 Airborne Division were dropped, the first objectives being the capture of bridges over the Canal de Caen and River Odon between the beaches and Caen itself. Shortly afterwards two airborne brigades were landed east of the River Orne, secured bridgeheads, over-ran the coastal battery at Merville and subsequently blew a number of bridges over the River Dives. The landings were more scattered than had been planned, but this had the effect of confusing the enemy as to their exact intentions. Nevertheless the left flank of the seaborne landings was now secured. In the west American airborne landings had been made on the base of the Cotentin (Cherbourg) peninsula to protect the right flank, and also hopefully to clear the defences of the causeways across the inundations which had been created inland of the American beaches.

In spite of the high seas running, the seaborne armada approached the coast, unmolested by any enemy activity and supported by heavy bombing attacks and bombardment from the sea of the coastal defences. Because of the times of high tide the Americans in the west landed first on Omaha and Utah Beaches and had considerable opposition, particularly at Ste Mere Eglise, although eventually a bridgehead was established. The British 2nd Army assault was made on three beaches between Ouistreham and Arromanches, 50 Division of 30 Corps on the right on Gold Beach, 3 Canadian Division of 1 Corps on Juno Beach in the centre and 3 British Division, also of 1 Corps, on the left on Sword Beach.

50 Division, supported by two armoured regiments and a Royal Marine Commando, landed and moved inland to its objectives on the Bayeux–Caen road, latterly against stiff resistance, and the Marines set off towards Port-en-Bessin and the American landing beaches. In the centre the Canadian landings were late owing to rough seas and they encountered heavy opposition, but, again supported by tanks, they moved steadily towards their objectives. 3 Division also met with stiff opposition and fire on their beach and were unable to link up with 6 Airborne Division on the Orne as planned, but still made steady progress. The initial landings had achieved surprise and had gained a toehold in Europe, and the losses suffered were much less than anticipated. The results so far were encouraging.

A single Battle Honour was awarded for the landings on D Day, **Normandy Landing**, which was gained by three British and three Canadian armoured regiments, five Yeomanry regiments and nineteen British and eleven Canadian Infantry regiments, together with both British and Canadian Parachute Regiments, the Glider Pilot Regiment and the Commandos, although at least one other regiment took part but did not at the time claim the Honour. Two other Honours were awarded for the day's events, **Pegasus Bridge** and **Merville Battery,** both to the Parachute Regiment and the Glider Pilot Regiment, the former also being awarded to the Oxfordshire and Buckinghamshire Light Infantry (43 Foot).

Montgomery's three priorities were to link up the British and American bridgeheads, covering a front of 50 miles, to maintain the initiative and to guard against any setbacks. On 7 June British troops captured Port-en-Bessin, and on the following day 50 Division linked up with the Americans near Bayeux. Caen itself was strongly defended and was clearly going to be a major obstacle, but the attack was pressed towards the city. Also on 7 June 3 Canadian Division captured Putot en Bessin, Bretteville l'Orgueilleuse and Authie, although the latter was evacuated again under heavy counterattack, whilst on the following day 3 British Division captured Sully and Cambes after desperate fighting. These successes were followed by the capture of Le Mesnil Patry by the Canadians and Breville by 3 British Infantry and 6 Airborne Divisions. At this point logistic support and maintenance was helped by the positioning of floating docks, known as Mulberry, adjacent to the beaches, although much equipment still had to be landed across the beaches themselves.

Honours were awarded for **Port en Bessin** to the Devonshire Regiment (11 Foot), for **Authie** to three Canadian regiments, for **Sully** to the South Wales Borderers (24 Foot), for **Cambes** to one Yeomanry and four British Infantry regiments, for **Putot en Bessin** to the 24th Lancers and three Canadian regiments, for **Bretteville l'Orgueilleuse** to the Regina Rifle Regiment of Canada, for **Le Mesnil Patry** to two Canadian regiments and for **Breville** to one armoured and two Infantry regiments and the Parachute Regiment, all British.

During the next week, whilst the Americans were developing operations to cut off the Cotentin peninsula and capture Cherbourg, British attacks continued towards Villers Bocage and Tilly sur Seules to create a pincer movement on Caen. 7 Armoured Division entered Villers Bocage but was heavily counterattacked in an exposed position and withdrew. 49 Division had now been landed and joined 50 Division in its advance on Tilly, but everywhere along the line German reinforcements had been brought forward and resistance had stiffened considerably. Tilly was captured, nevertheless, on 19 June and one half of the pincer was established. Two Honours were awarded for this phase, **Villers Bocage** to three armoured, three Yeomanry and five Infantry regiments and **Tilly sur Seulles** to the 24 Lancers and nine Infantry regiments, all of these being British.

In the next period of the expansion of the bridgehead Caen and Cherbourg became the main targets, the latter being captured on 25 June. One half of the pincers on Caen having been established, the next objective for the other half was to gain a crossing of the River Odon, but this advance was delayed by bad weather, both on land and, more importantly, at sea which delayed the build-up of reinforcements. As a diversion 51 Division entered St Honorine, on the left of the front and north east of Caen, and held it against determined counterattacks. On the right of the main thrust 49 Division captured Fontenay against stiff opposition and reached the high ground around Tessel-Bretteville, and there was heavy fighting around Rauray. In a major attack the following day 15 Division took Cheux after hard fighting and reached the line of the railway at Grainville and Colleville, while 11 Armoured Division reached Mouen. The next day, after more heavy and confused fighting the Odon was crossed and a bridgehead was established south of Caen. Strong counterattacks were launched by the enemy using five Panzer divisions, but in spite of some withdrawals the main positions were held and the Germans suffered heavy losses. British casualties had also been considerable but the initiative had been maintained.

Honours awarded for this period, all to British regiments, were **Fontenay le Pesnil** gained by one armoured, one Yeomanry and six Infantry regiments, **Cheux** gained by two Yeomanry and seven Infantry regiments, **Tourmauville Bridge** gained uniquely by the Argyll and Sutherland Highlanders (91 Foot) and **Defence of Rauray** gained by one armoured, three Yeomanry and seven Infantry regiments. In addition the overall Honour, **The Odon**, was awarded to five armoured, three Yeomanry and twenty-five Infantry regiments.

The most sensitive point on the front to the Germans was still undoubtedly Caen, which was not only the lynch-pin of Montgomery's strategy but the plan included its capture to contain even more enemy troops. A direct assault was now mounted on the city by the three divisions of 1 Corps. 3 Canadian Division began the attack against the village of Carpiquet and its airfield which resisted for several days. Bomber Command was now for the first time engaged in a purely tactical role and bombed the defensive positions north of the city as a prelude to the main assault, and this type of employment proved very successful although problems arose, as at Cassino, from heavy cratering which restricted vehicle and tank movement.

3rd and 59th British and 3rd Canadian Divisions entered the city from three directions on 10 July and reached the river, over which all bridges had been destroyed. The attack was now switched to the area west of the town between the Rivers Odon and Orne. 43 Division captured Hill 112, and although it also entered Maltot it was driven out by a counterattack. A few days later 59 Division surrounded Noyers with the intention of exploiting towards Villers Bocage, and 15 Division, operating at night and for the first time using 'movement light', searchlights reflecting light from the clouds, entered Bougy and Esquay against heavy opposition, repelling frequent counterattacks. The fighting had been severe and very little ground had been gained, but the attack had succeeded in its main purpose of sucking the German armour, which had started to move westwards to oppose the Americans, back into the battle. To further contain it 2nd British Army was now poised for a breakout to the south.

Honours awarded for the battle of Caen were **Carpiquet**, gained by six Canadian regiments, **The Orne**, gained by three British Infantry regiments, with its alternative Canadian title **The Orne (Buron)** gained by two armoured and eight Infantry regiments, **Hill 112**, awarded to six British regiments, **Esquay** to seven Infantry regiments and **Noyers** to three regiments. The overall Honour, **Caen**, was awarded to four armoured, five Yeomanry and twenty-eight Infantry regiments of the British Army and to five armoured and eleven Infantry regiments of the Canadian Army.

The major breakout was made east of Caen in a southerly direction on 18 July by 8 Corps with its three armoured divisions, the objective being to fight, contain and destroy the German armour, the operation being known as 'Goodwood', whilst 3 Canadian Division supported by 2 Canadian Division attacked on its right through the southern suburbs of the city and 3 British Division

attacked on its left. The attack was supported by over 2,000 bombers, including heavies, in direct support. It was at this point that news broke of a bomb attack on Hitler's life by disaffected German officers which had failed.

Resistance to this advance was very strong and stubborn, but the front was nevertheless pushed forward several miles towards the Bourguebus ridge. Cagny and Faubourg de Vaucelles were taken and two days later St André sur Orne was captured and 3 Division entered the outskirts of Troarn. Maltot was entered at last and an attack was launched in the area of Verrieres and Tilly la Campagne, which was initially successful although a strong counter-attack recaptured Tilly. British armoured casualties had been heavy, as had been expected in a battle of this sort, and the divisions, having achieved their main objective of engaging and destroying German armour and preventing it from moving into the American front, were withdrawn into reserve.

Honours were awarded for **Cagny** to seven British regiments, mainly of the Brigade of Guards, **Troarn** to nine British regiments, **Faubourg de Vaucelles** to two Canadian armoured and thirteen Infantry regiments and **St Andre sur Orne** to seven Canadian regiments, one of which was armoured. **Maltot** was gained by two British and one Canadian Infantry regiment and **Verrières Ridge-Tilly la Campagne** by ten Canadian regiments. The Battle Honour of **Bourguebus Ridge** was awarded to a large number of regiments, to four British armoured and five Yeomanry regiments, to the Welsh Guards, twelve Infantry regiments and the Honourable Artillery Company, and to twenty-one Canadian regiments.

On 25 July the Americans in the west began their breakout from St Lo and captured Coutances and Avranches. The enemy was now in retreat, and over the next ten days the American forces made rapid progress southwards, fanning out into the Brittany peninsula and reaching the outskirts of Vire and Mortain. The advance was supported on its left flank by a British armoured attack, which crossed the River Souleuvre, captured Le Beny Bocage and also reached the outskirts of Vire.

Meanwhile a British thrust was being made, mainly by 30 Corps, which met extremely heavy resistance. Jurques was captured and a few days later Villers Bocage was at last entered by 50 Division. 2nd British Army was converging on the Mont Pincon area and on 6 August 43 Division gained a foothold on Mont Pincon itself.

Honours for this first phase of the main breakout from the bridgehead, all to British regiments, were awarded for **Quarry Hill** to five regiments, for **Jurques** to one armoured, one Yeomanry and two Infantry regiments, for **La Varinière** to two Infantry regiments, for **The Souleuvre** to the two armoured regiments of the Household Brigade and three Infantry regiments, for **Catheolles** uniquely to the Inns of Court Regiment, for **Le Perier Ridge** to one armoured, one Yeomanry and five Infantry regiments and for **Brieux Bridgehead** to two Infantry regiments. **Mont Pincon,** the overall Honour, was awarded to eight armoured and two Yeomanry regiments, to all five regiments of the Brigade of Guards, and to twenty-seven Infantry regiments.

8 Corps continued its advance over the next few days whilst the Americans cut off the Brittany peninsula and

executed a massive left wheel around the south of the British advance. A German attack on the Americans at Mortain on 7 August was thrown back in confusion after heavy fighting, and the way was open for a further advance during which Le Mans was captured on 9 August and Argentan on 13 August. Honours were gained by British regiments for **St Pierre La Vielle** by two armoured and seven Infantry regiments, for **Estry** by two Guards and five Infantry regiments and for **Noireau Crossing** by the Life Guards, the Royal Horse Guards, the Sherwood Rangers Yeomanry and by three Infantry regiments.

The American advance had now created a deep pocket in which it was hoped that a large part of the German army might be trapped between Falaise and Argentan. British and Canadian troops started southward thrusts from Caen to try to close the pocket. The Canadians advanced down the Caen–Falaise road and bitter fighting developed, particularly on the River Laison. But it was overcome, not without heavy casualties, and Falaise was reached on 17 August. To the west 30 Corps captured Conde and 8 Corps took Flers.

On 19 August the pocket was closed when the Polish Armoured Division linked up with the Americans at Chambois and 4 Canadian Armoured Division entered St Lambert sur Dives, both in the face of desperate fighting. When 11 Armoured Division captured Bailleul the pocket started shrinking rapidly and the plight of the enemy was hopeless, with the remains of eight divisions, including three Panzer divisions, being caught in the trap.

A number of Honours were awarded for the battles resulting in the closing of the Falaise pocket. **Falaise Road** was gained by two Yeomanry and three British Infantry regiments and by ten Canadian armoured and fourteen Infantry regiments, **Quesnay Road** was gained by four and **Claire Tizon** by nine Canadian regiments, **The Laison** was awarded to one British Yeomanry and ten Canadian armoured and seventeen Infantry regiments, **Chambois** to five armoured and eight Infantry regiments, all Canadian, and **St Lambert sur Dives** to two Canadian regiments. Finally **Falaise** was added to the Colours of three British armoured, three Yeomanry and twenty-four Infantry regiments and of eleven Canadian armoured and twenty-four Infantry regiments.

Now that an appreciable amount of the German Army had been destroyed in the Normandy battles and in the Falaise pocket, it was essential to advance with maximum speed towards and over the River Seine and into the Low Countries before the enemy had time to recover from the shock. It was also becoming essential to open the Channel ports as the supply situation was becoming difficult with only Cherbourg and the beaches, now far away and getting farther, still to cover all maintenance. Such an advance necessitated a formidable manoeuvre in switching the front of the British Army and its axis through 90 degrees, from facing south to facing east, without relaxing the pressure on the enemy, complicated by the fact that two American Corps were actually crossing the front from the south.

The pursuit began with 1 Corps and 2 Canadian Corps on the coast, which would enable divisions in each, by accident or design, to repay old scores, and 12th and 30th Corps further south. 8 Corps had been grounded to pro-

vide transport for the other Corps. The advance was rapid, notwithstanding a number of fierce battles. The Rivers Touques and Risle were crossed, Lisieux and Pont l'Evêque were captured and more heavy fighting took place in the Forêt de Bretonne and the Forêt de la Londe near Rouen, but in ten days the Seine was reached, although the Germans managed to evacuate more troops than it was hoped would be possible.

A number more Honours were awarded. **Dives Crossing** was gained by two British armoured, two Yeomanry and two Infantry regiments and by the British and Canadian Parachute Regiments and the Commondos, **La Vie Crossing** was gained by one British armoured, two Yeomanry and six Infantry regiments and **Lisieux** was won by two armoured and three Yeomanry regiments and by a single Infantry regiment, the Seaforth Highlanders (72 Foot). **La Touques Crossing** was awarded to one armoured and two Infantry regiments and the Parachute Regiment, **Risle Crossing** was awarded to two British armoured and two Infantry regiments, **Foret de Bretonne** to the East Riding Yeomanry and the York and Lancaster Regiment and **Foret de la Londe** to nine Canadian regiments. Finally **The Seine 1944** was won by two British armoured, one Yeomanry and five Infantry regiments and by one Canadian armoured and six Infantry regiments.

On 17 August the Americans had reached Orléans, Chartres and Dreux, and three days later General Patten's army crossed the Seine near Mantes and his right flank reached Fontainebleau. It was agreed that the French should be the first to enter Paris, and on 24 August their 2nd Division entered the city and the German garrison capitulated.

Meanwhile an assault had been launched on the south of France, between Toulon and Cannes, and around Marseilles, on 15 August. There had been a strong difference of opinion about such a landing between the Allies. The Americans favoured it at the expense of the Italian campaign, with which they had never really agreed, whilst the British considered the Italian campaign strategically of great importance and believed that if there were to be any diversion it should be at the north of the Adriatic Sea in order to mount a thrust towards central Europe which was of course totally against the Russian plan for the domination of central and eastern Europe. Roosevelt, therefore, led as always by the Russians whom for some reason he always believed to be honest in their approach, supported Stalin against Churchill, who could see the pitfalls of which the Americans in their isolationism were entirely blind.

It was unlikely that any landing in the south would in any way influence the situation in North West Europe, but the American lack of any understanding of the strategy, coupled with their position of strength of numbers, overrode all objections. In hindsight it is now abundantly clear that the British view was the right one, and that without the losses of forces for their South of France landing Alexander would probably have broken through and ended the Italian campaign by the end of 1944. He could then have gone on to Vienna, which would not have suited the Russians or the Americans, neither of whom wanted a British presence or influence in central Europe.

There was very little opposition to the landing and the

British part in it was very slight, being only part of an airborne division. Two lines of advance were made, one through Avignon-Lyons-Dijon and the other through Grenoble-Bourg-Besançon, and on 11 September the southern and northern forces met at Sombernon. Since the Germans had had virtually no defences in the south and did not see this advance as a threat to Germany, as indeed it was not, no withdrawals of any consequence took place from where it mattered, in the north east. The Honour **Southern France** was gained by the Parachute Regiment and the Glider Pilot Regiment.

The first stage of the pursuit was over and the second about to begin without a break. But first a decision had to be made on the development of the allied offensive beyond the Seine, and again a bitter argument arose which was basically between pragmatic and sound strategy and American prestige. Montgomery, the most experienced of the Army commanders and the only one to have seen more than a few weeks of action, favoured a single thrust through Belgium and a burst across the Rhine north of the Ruhr, the capture of the Ruhr cities then taking place concurrently with a breakout on to the north German plain where the allied armour could be used to greater advantage. This of course would have created a vast salient, but the Rhine would have been as big a barrier to the Germans in retreat as it was to the British in attack, and would have utilised one of the main maxims of military success, concentration of force.

But Eisenhower, Supreme Commander but the least experienced commander in the field, favoured a broad front up to the line of the Rhine and a set-piece crossing, which would of course bring more American troops into prominence. It could be said, of course, that Montgomery's approach, while good stretegically, would equally have favoured the British and Canadian armies under his own command. Be all this as it may, fact and conjecture both, Eisenhower's plan was adopted by *force majeure*.

The British part in the plan was for 1st Canadian Army, which had now been formed including 1 Corps, comprising 49th and 51st Divisions, under command, to operate in the coastal belt and capture the Channel ports as rapidly as possible to ease the supply situation, whilst 2nd British Army operated inland on the axis of Brussels and Antwerp.

The Seine crossing started on 25 August, and on the right, after three days, 43rd Division and 8th Armoured Brigade had crossed the river near Vernon and 11 Armoured Division and the Guards Armoured Division were following them across. 15 Division, on the left of 2nd Army, also crossed without major difficulty except at one point where severe casualties were caused, and were followed by 53 Division and 7 Armoured Division. On the Canadian Army front crossings were also successful, albeit against strong opposition in some places, and by 1 September all their troops were across and moving forward. Meanwhile on 31 August 11 Armoured Division captured Amiens together with an intact bridge over the River Somme. The Seine was now crossed everywhere, and one priority was to capture the sites of the V 1 flying bombs, the Doodlebugs, which had been launched heavily against London and the Home Counties since June.

The speed of the advance now increased and passed through areas made famous, or perhaps notorious, during the First World War without any hold-ups. Arras was taken and on 2 September 11 Armoured Division reached the outskirts of Lille and bypassed the city. On 3 September, five years after the outbreak of the war, the Belgian frontier was crossed and by that night the Guards Armoured Division was in Brussels, to scenes of wild excitement probably not seen there since the victory of Waterloo 129 years before. Stronger resistance was encountered on the left but 7 Armoured Division brushed it aside and pressed on to Ghent, and on 4 September 11 Armoured Division entered Antwerp, where enemy elements hung on for some days although the port installations were undamaged. 2nd British Army had advanced 250 miles in six days. The Guards reached the Meuse-Scheldt Canal on 10 September, by which time the Americans in the south had reached the line of Epinal-Nancy-Metz-Luxemburg and Aachen.

Honours were awarded for **Amiens 1944** to the Household Cavalry regiments, 23rd Hussars and the Inns of Court Yeomanry, for **Brussels** to the Household Cavalry again and to the Welsh Guards, and for **Antwerp** to one armoured, one Yeomanry and five Infantry regiments, and to the Honourable Artillery Company.

Meanwhile 1st Canadian Army had been advancing up the coast. 49 Division swung into the Le Havre peninsula, while 51 Division repaid old scores by capturing St Valéry on 2 September, just over four years after its tragedy there. The attack on Le Havre itself was strongly resisted and needed a set-piece attack, but it finally surrendered on 12 September, by which time the Canadians had isolated Boulogne and Calais and occupied Nieuport and Ostend on 9 September. After prolonged battles and heavy fighting Boulogne was entered on 22 September and Calais was captured on 28 September. The Channel ports were free. Battle Honours were awarded for **Dunkirk 1944** to eight Canadian regiments, for **Le Havre** to one British armoured, two Yeomanry and eleven Infantry regiments and the Honourable Artillery Company supported by a Canadian APC regiment, for **Moerbrugge** to four Canadian regiments, for **Boulogne 1944** to the Lothians and Border Horse and to nine Canadian regiments including the armoured Fort Garry Horse and for **Calais 1944** to the Lothian and Border Horse again and to the 1st Canadian Hussars and nine Infantry regiments.

The 2nd British Army advance continued without delay, the objective being to reach and cross the Rhine, although this was a tall order after a long advance and, in some places, heavy fighting, and with limited administrative support as the port of Antwerp could not be used until the Scheldt estuary was cleared. In addition autumn was approaching and weather conditions might reduce air support. Nevertheless advances were made across the Albert Canal and bridgeheads were established over the Escaut Canal against spirited German counterattacks and resistance. A number of Honours were awarded, all to British regiments for this phase. **Hechtel** was gained by 15/19 Hussars, Inns of Court Yeomanry, Welsh Guards and three Infantry regiments, **Gheel** by the Sherwood Rangers and four Infantry regiments, **Heppen** uniquely by the Coldstream Guards, **Neerpelt** by the Household Cavalry regiments and the Irish Guards and **Aart** by five Infantry regiments.

During the second part of September 1st Canadian Army had started on their task of clearing the area between the Ghent-Bruges line and the Scheldt estuary and advancing north of Antwerp to clear the area up to the River Maas, including the isolation and reduction of Beveland and Walcheren and the capture of the port of Flushing. Progress was slower than anticipated but the first objective was achieved up to the Leopold Canal by the end of the month, and a bridgehead had been established over the Antwerp-Turnhout Canal. Three Battle Honours were awarded, for **Moerkerke** to two Canadian regiments, for **Wyneghem** uniquely to the Calgary Highlanders and **Antwerp-Turnhout Canal** was added to the Colours of eight British and ten Canadian regiments.

The objectives of 2nd British Army in closing up to the Rhine included three river and two major canal crossings. Individually each of these could be a major obstacle and Montgomery therefore decided to try to reduce the time factor and the difficulties by securing bridges and bridge-heads over these by massive airborne operations, followed closely by ground attack. The line of advance ran through Eindhoven, Uden, Grave, Nijmegen to Arnhem. For this operation there were available one British and two American airborne divisions and the Polish Parachute Brigade. The ultimate aim was a bridgehead at Arnhem for which 1st British Airborne Division was detailed, supported by the Poles, whilst 101st US Airborne Division was to capture the area between Eindhoven and Grave and 82nd US Airborne Division was to capture the area between Grave and Nijmegen and the bridges over the Rhine at the latter. 30 Corps, with the Guards Armoured Division as the spearhead and 43rd and 50th Infantry Divisions as follow-up, constituted the ground forces.

The landings began on 17 September and 101st US Division quickly secured the area between Eindhoven and Veghel including an intact bridge at the latter place, and 82nd US Division captured the bridge over the Maas at Grave and bridges over the Maas-Waal Canal, all against light opposition, but could not immediately reach Nijmegen where the bridge was so far still intact. The ground forces pushed forward against strong opposition but made a good advance. On the following day Eindhoven was captured. On the flank 8 Corps crossed the Escaut Canal but the resistance there was increasing.

Meanwhile, at Arnhem, 1 British Airborne Division was meeting extremely difficult problems, and these and the whole story of Arnhem are too well documented to make anything but a brief reference necessary in this narrative. The drop had been made some distance from the town, too far as it turned out, and the Germans, in spite of intelligence to the contrary, were holding Arnhem in strength. The division had become very split up and while it was trying to concentrate west of the town some airborne forces had reached and were holding the western end of the bridge and part of the town. The weather turned bad and both supplies and reinforcements were badly hampered, as was any close air support. To make matters worse communications had failed and the force was unable

to warn anybody that the dropping zone for those supply planes which could get through was in enemy hands.

On 20 September Guards Armoured Division, with American support, launched an attack on Nijmegen to capture the bridge, the Americans making a hazardous river crossing to seize the northern end. Fighting was desperate but the Guards won through and eventually managed to cross the bridge before it could be destroyed. But at Arnhem the situation of 1 Airborne Division was critical and enemy counterattacks were increasing, and every effort was made to rush the ground forces towards their relief.

During the next few days the attacks were pressed and the salient was gradually deepened and widened. Veghel had been taken after a counterattack had cut the axis of the advance for a short time, and Best had also been captured after extremely fierce fighting. But the ground forces could not reach Arnhem and it was decided to evacuate the parachutists from their now untenable position. Altogether 2,400 men of 1 Airborne Division and the Polish Parachute Brigade, which had eventually managed to land part of its strength, only about 25 per cent of the total, were evacuated, but the division had suffered very heavy losses in killed and captured.

The Battle of Arnhem had failed, but only just, largely through the weather conditions and the very limited resources available for a most imaginative and strategically brilliant operation. 1 Airborne Division had fought magnificently against overwhelming odds, some due to the enemy and some owing to technical failings beyond their control, and without the planned reinforcements. But at the same time crossings had beeen established over four of the major water obstacles including the Maas and the Waal.

Battle Honours for the operation were richly deserved, and were awarded for **Arnhem 1944** to four Infantry regiments, the Parachute and Glider Pilot Regiments, all British, and to the Ontario Regiment of Canada, for **Nijmegen** to the Life Guards, the Royal Horse Guards, the Grenadier and Irish Guards, for **Veghel** to 1 Royal Dragoons and for **Best** to 8 Hussars and six British Infantry regiments. The overall Honour, **The Nederrijn,** was gained by seven British armoured regiments, the Sherwood Rangers, the Coldstream and Welsh Guards and by twenty-five British Infantry regiments.

Since the battle for the Rhineland could clearly not now be fought immediately, it was decided, in view of the onset of winter and the likelihood of difficult beach working for the maintenance of supplies, to concentrate on clearing the Scheldt estuary and opening the port of Antwerp. This operation would include the sealing off and then then clearance of South Beveland and the capture of Walcheren, and was to be carried out mainly by the Canadians.

On 1 October the Canadians opened their advance over the Antwerp-Turnhout Canal and round the north of Antwerp, and initially made good progress, but resistance stiffened and it was not until a fortnight later that they captured the village of Woensdrecht at the mouth of the Beveland isthmus. On their right 49 Division advanced towards Tilburg, in spite of heavy counterattacks, and on 27 October reached Roosendaal whilst the Canadian 4 Armoured Division reached Bergen-op-Zoom. In the Leopold

Canal area, where the enemy positions were very strong, progress was slow at the beginning of the month but advances were made gradually. 52 British Division now joined the Canadians and on 22 October captured Breskens.

The advance along the Beveland isthmus now began, but the waterlogged nature of the country made progress here slow also. The advance was supported by a landing on the south of Beveland by a brigade of 52 Division and the clearance of the island continued more rapidly, reaching the Walcheren causeway by the end of the month. Meanwhile the clearance of the area beyond Breskens continued, and by early November Zeebrugge was reached by an advance westwards along the coast. The attack on Walcheren began with a heavy bombing attack which breached the sea dykes and flooded the island. Seaborne Commando landings were made at Westkapelle and another seaborne landing was made by 52 Division, which captured Flushing. Only mopping-up remained, in the circumstances a very appropriate title for the operation, and by 4 November the Scheldt estuary was in allied hands, and the first convoy reached Antwerp three weeks later.

A number of Honours were awarded for this phase of the operation. **Leopold Canal** was won by four Canadian regiments, **Woensdrecht** by thirteen regiments, **Savojaards Plaat** by three regiments and **Breskens Pocket** by fourteen regiments, all of these being Canadian. **South Beveland** was awarded to three British and eleven Canadian regiments, **Walcheren Causeway** to three British and three Canadian regiments, **Flushing** to three British regiments and the Commandos and **Westkapelle** to the Lothian and Border Horse and also to the Commandos. The overall Battle Honour for the period, **The Scheldt,** was added to the Colours of one armoured, two Yeomanry and ten British Infantry regiments and of ten Canadian armoured and twenty-four Infantry regiments.

At the same time as the Scheldt estuary was being cleared by the Canadians, British forces were clearing the area further east up to the River Maas. During the second half of October and early November Buxtel was captured, as were Breda and s'Hertogenbosch, and Tilburg was entered. **Aam** was awarded as an Honour to the Irish Guards and three Infantry regiments and **Opheusden** uniquely to the Duke of Cornwall's Light Infantry (32 Foot).

The fighting now turned to the region west of the River Meuse, or Maas in Holland, still held by the enemy. Attacks began against the northern part of the German salient, captured Overloon and after some hard-fought battles reached Venraij and occupied the town. Meijel was also taken, but through a heavy counterattack the enemy recaptured the town on 27 October and this area was not finally cleared until mid-November. Honours were awarded for **Venraij** to two armoured regiments, the Westminster Dragoons, the Coldstream Guards and ten Infantry regiments, for **Meijel** again to the Westminster Dragoons and the Coldstream Guards and also to six Infantry regiments and for its alternative title **Asten** to two more Infantry regiments, and the overall Honour for the operation, **The Lower Maas,** was won by three British armoured, four Yeomanry and eighteen Infantry regiments, and by six Canadian armoured, six Infantry regiments and an Armoured Personnel Carrier (APC) Regiment. The Royal Artillery gained a further Honour title, **Asten Battery**.

Two enemy pockets now remained west of the Rivers Roer and Maas, around Geilenkirchen and Venlo. 43 Division with an American division in support attacked the former and captured it on 23 November, although further progress towards the river was made impossible by heavy rain which made the ground impassable. Venlo was also assaulted but only succumbed after three weeks of hard fighting. **Geilenkirchen** was awarded to two armoured, two Yeomanry and five Infantry regiments, **Venlo Pocket** was added to the Colours of four armoured and three Yeomanry regiments, the Scots Guards and sixteen Infantry regiments. The scene was now set, at the end of the year, for the Battle of the Rhineland, but most unexpectedly the enemy struck first, in the Ardennes.

The Germans were very sensitive to the threat of an allied invasion of the German homeland, and with the close approach of the armies to the Rhine they made a last desperate throw to prevent the British and the Americans reaching the river and crossing it by trying to break their line, and almost succeeded. On 16 December the enemy attacked in the classic area through northern Luxemburg and the Ardennes, achieved complete surprise and rapidly over-ran the American divisions. As the German advance continued 30 Corps was transferred to the area between the Meuse and Brussels and concentrated there, while other detachments were sent to the line of the Meuse between Liège and Namur and southwards to Givet. Apart from around Bastogne, where the Americans resisted strongly, the Germans continued their advance towards the Meuse until they were finally stopped on 23 December when one of their thrusts was only a few miles from Dinant, although heavy fighting carried on for some days.

An allied counterattack was launched at the beginning of January 1945. 30 Corps entered the battle and secured Bure and Grimbiermont after fierce fighting by 6 Airborne Division, brought from UK as a reinforcement, and 53 Division. The Americans were thrusting towards Houffalize, and 30 Corps towards Laroche on the River Ourthe, which was captured on 10 January, with 51 Division coming into the line on their right on the Ourthe. By 16 January the Americans had reached Houffalize and the Allies were able to join up and reduce the salient to a small bulge. The British troops were then withdrawn to re-equip and regroup for the Rhineland battle in the north. One Honour was awarded to British troops, **The Ourthe,** which was gained by one armoured, four Yeomanry and nine Infantry regiments and by the Parachute Regiment.

And so ended the year 1944, with a small overlap into 1945, which had started, in terms of the campaign, seven months before on the Normandy beaches, had cleared France and Belgium and most of Holland, and was reaching the Rhine and Germany itself, and ended with a massive defeat of the enemy in which they had very heavy losses in men and equipment which was shortly to cost them dearly.

Greece, 1944–5

It had been decided in August 1944 to send a British force to Greece as soon as the Germans began to withdraw, to prevent a political and power vacuum in the country. In September this withdrawal began and at the beginning of October the force, consisting of 2 Parachute Brigade and 23 Armoured Brigade, moved in to liberate and to begin to restore the country. Patras was occupied on 4 October, and on 13 October paratroops landed near Athens and on the following day occupied the city on the heels of the German retreat.

But communist-controlled ELAS (Peoples National Army of Liberation) bands were at large in the country and, although they had agreed to support the legitimate Greek government, soon began to seize their opportunity and try to take over the country, to a large extent by terrorism of the population among whom they had very limited support. Full-scale rebellion was imminent and the Greeks asked Britain to control the situation, as they had done in 1941. 4 Indian Division was sent from Italy in November and occupied Salonika, Athens and Patras.

On 3 December civil war broke out, the ELAS were ordered by the British commander, General Scobie, to evacuate Athens and the Piraeus, but instead they attempted to seize the capital. British troops were ordered only to fire on the rebels if absolutely necessary to maintain order, but with British hands so tied the ELAS forces quickly gained control of Athens, except for the area occupied by troops in the centre and on the Acropolis. A counterattack began, troops clearing the city street by street. In mid-December 4 British Division was also sent to Greece, in spite of condemnation by the American press of British action there, and the extra forces tipped the scales in favour of the British, who were by now fighting desperately in the city.

Progress was made slowly in Athens and the Piraeus with some fierce street fighting, the troops being continually sniped from roof-tops and bombed, mostly by ELAS members or supporters in civilian clothes, often girls, and were thus unrecognisable as enemy until too late. Eventually the order to use only rifle fire was rescinded and the use of guns and tanks was sanctioned. This rapidly accomplished the objective of driving the ELAS forces out of the city, causing only very little damage to property, and forcing them to capitulate, which they did on 11 January. British troops then occupied the whole country.

The Honour **Athens** was awarded to the King's Dragoon Guards and eleven Infantry regiments, all British, and the Parachute Regiment, and **Greece 1944–45** was awarded to the King's Dragoon Guards, thirteen British Infantry regiments, the Parachute Regiment, the Special Air Service Regiment and the Commandos, and to the Central Indian Horse, the Bombay Sappers and Miners, four Indian Infantry regiments and two Gurkha regiments.

Middle East, 1944

The only operations in the Middle East in 1944 were in the Adriatic Sea area, eight raids in support of guerillas in Jugoslavia, and an Honour **Adriatic** was awarded to the Highland Light Infantry (71 Foot), the Special Air Service Regiment and the Commandos.

A campaign Honour **Middle East 1941–44** was also awarded to cover the campaigns in Crete in 1941, Madgascar in 1942, the Aegean in 1943 and the Adriatic in 1944. This Honour was gained by seventeen British Infantry regiments and the Special Air Service Regiment, by the King's African Rifles and the Northern Rhodesia Regiment, by six Australian and by sixteen New Zealand regiments. Unaccountably it was not awarded to six other British and three South African regiments which were also engaged and awarded individual Honours during the various campaigns.

North West Europe, 1945

Following the successful outcome of the Ardennes battle, Eisenhower's plan was to close up to the Rhine, destroying the enemy west of the river in the process, to cross the Rhine on a broad front and then to drive into Germany in a north easterly direction on two main axes, the first or northern one directed through the Ruhr towards Bremen, Hamburg and the Baltic and the second through Karlsruhe to Kassel.

The year opened, as soon as the British Army had regrouped, with an assault to clear the enemy out of the Roermond triangle between Heinsberg and Roermond itself, with the eventual object of destroying all opposition between the Meuse and the Rhine. Operations began on 16 January and a week later Heinsberg was captured. Enemy resistance lessened and a few days afterwards the task was completed. **The Roer** was awarded as an Honour to five armoured and three Yeomanry regiments, to the Coldstream Guards and to fifteen Infantry regiments, and to the Canadian APC Regiment, and **Zetten** to five Infantry regiments, all British. Meanwhile, further west, **Kapelshe Veer** was awarded to four Canadian regiments.

The battle for the Rhineland began on 8 February with an assault by 1st Canadian Army, with 30 Corps under command, on the area of the Reichswald Forest, supported by a heavy artillery bombardment. The ground was waterlogged and extensive minefields were encountered, but in most places the opposition was at first only moderate. Further north 15 Division was heading for Cleve and reached the outskirts the following day whilst the forest was being rapidly cleared, and 3 Canadian Division was operating in the floods of the Waal. The Germans reinforced the front and resistance became fiercer, the terrible nature of the ground also materially helping the defence. Nevertheless, within a week the forest and the Waal Flats had been cleared and Cleve captured after some very sharp fighting.

Honours were awarded for **The Reichswald** to one British armoured, two Yeomanry, three Guards and seventeen Infantry regiments, and to three Canadian regiments and the APC Regiment. **Waal Flats** was awarded to 13/18 Hussars and to ten Canadian Regiments, and **Cleve** to 4/7 Dragoon Guards, the Sherwood Rangers, the Coldstream and Scots Guards, and to eight British Infantry regiments, as well as to the ubiquitous Canadian APC Regiment.

The attacks continued in a south-easterly direction towards Goch, Calcar and the Hochwald. Goch was soon captured and the Canadians crossed the Goch-Calcar road and captured Moyland, although Calcar itself held out for several days. The advance went on and by early March the Hochwald Forest and Weeze had been cleared. The Honour of **Goch** was gained by 13/18 Hussars, the Sherwood Rangers, the Coldstream Guards and nineteen Infantry regiments, all British, **Moyland**, also known by its alternative title of **Moyland Wood**, was gained by two Guards and three British Infantry regiments and four Canadian regiments, and **Goch-Calcar Road** by five Canadian and the APC regiments. **Weeze** was awarded to the Sherwood Rangers and five British Infantry regiments, **The Hochwald** to two armoured, one Yeomanry, three Guards and eight British Infantry regiments and to eight Canadian armoured and twenty Infantry regiments and the APC Regiment and **Schaddenhof** uniquely to the East Yorkshire Regiment.

Finally on 8 March the Canadians captured Xanten and Veen, and enemy rearguards blew the bridge and retreated to Wesel. The battle of the Rhineland, with the Americans operating to the south towards Dusselfdorf, Uerdingen and Homberg, had been won and the River Rhine had been reached along a great deal of its northern length. Two individual Battle Honours were awarded. **Xanten** was gained by two British Infantry regiments and by two Canadian armoured, ten Infantry regiments and the APC Regiment, and **Veen** by eight Canadian regiments. The overall Honour for the battle, **The Rhineland,** was awarded to five British armoured, four Yeomanry, four Guards and thirty-one Infantry regiments, and to eleven Canadian armoured and twenty-four Infantry regiments and to the APC Regiment. The Germans had suffered another crippling defeat.

Now that the allied armies had closed up to the Rhine, and the Americans had captured the bridge at Remagen intact and established a bridgehead there and had also captured Mainz and Worms, and since the battle in Italy was drawing to a successful conclusion, in March 1st, 5th and 46th British Divisions and 1st Canadian and 5 Canadian Armoured Divisions were transferred from Italy to North West Europe to strengthen the forces there. The force for the crossing of the Rhine was composed of 2nd British Army, which included 8th, 12th, 30th and 2nd Canadian Corps, and 18th Airborne Corps consisting of 6th British and 17th US Airborne Divisions, the area of its attack being from north of the River Lippe at Wesel to Rees. The primary objective was to enable a breakout to be made into central Germany and the North German Plain by the armour.

The assault began with river crossings by Infantry and armour on the night of 23/24 March, a number of divisions being involved. As they moved forward and established bridgeheads the combined airborne forces dropped 5 to 10 miles ahead of the ground assault forces, suffered remarkably few casualties and 6 Airborne Division made several crossings of the River Issel. The airborne drop coming after the assault crossing confused the enemy and excellent progress was made, even though resistance was desperate particularly around Rees where there was fierce fighting and a number of counterattacks were launched.

The Canadians in the north of the British sector turned towards Emmerich and the high ground at Hoch Elten, and in spite of heavy resistance captured the area at the beginning of April. Only two Battle Honours were awarded for the Rhine crossing, in themselves and with the numbers of regiments which gained them sufficient to exemplarise the great assault. **Emmerich-Hoch Elten** was awarded to nine Canadian regiments and **The Rhine** to eight British armoured, seven Yeomanry, four Guards and twenty-seven Infantry regiments, together with the Parachute and Glider Pilot Regiments, the Commandos and the Honourable Artillery Company, and to two Canadian armoured and sixteen Infantry regiments, together with the Canadian Parachute and APC Regiments.

In the south the Americans had captured Frankfurt and Kassel, and surrounded the Ruhr, and all was now ready for the breakout to the River Elbe and the capture of the whole of Germany, which would end the war in the west.

2nd British Army began its advance with, from right to left, 8th, 12th and 30th Corps, their objective being the line of the Elbe and the reduction of Bremen and Hamburg, and on the Army's left 1st Canadian Army had as its objective the clearance of western and northern Holland and the adjacent parts of north west Germany. The resistance was very variable and, although some delays were caused, particularly on the Dortmund-Ems Canal, and most bridges over the numerous rivers and canals had been destroyed, requiring a great deal of bridging, the advance was rapid, and by the end of April the line of the west bank of the Elbe had been reached and cleared of enemy.

8 Corps crossed the Dortmund-Ems Canal, captured Osnabrück and Minden, crossed the River Aller and took Celle. Resistance stiffened at Uelzen but after a few days the town was entered, as was Lüneburg, and the Elbe was reached at Artlenberg and opposite Lauenburg. Honours were awarded for **Ibbenburen** to three armoured and eleven Infantry regiments, for **Dreirwalde** to six Infantry regiments, for **Leese** to the Inns of Court Yeomanry, two Infantry regiments and the Commandos, for **The Aller** to three armoured, two Yeomanry and eleven Infantry regiments and again the Commandos, for **Uelzen** to two Guards and six Infantry regiments and for **Artlenberg** to seven Infantry regiments.

12 Corps in the centre also met little resistance until it reached the Rheine area on the Dortmund-Ems Canal where there was some stiff fighting. But after this delay they captured Soltau and the advance was continued to Harberg, on the Elbe opposite Hamburg. 30 Corps met bitter resistance at Lingen on the Dortmund-Ems Canal, but overcame it and only encountered the next determined resistance at Bremen, which needed a set-piece attack to capture it. The Corps then advanced to the Elbe estuary and Cuxhaven at the mouth of the great river. Honours were awarded for **Lingen** to the Household Cavalry regiments, the Staffordshire Yeomanry, three Guards regiments and six Infantry regiments, for **Bentheim** to the Household Cavalry and the Irish Guards, for **Brinkum** to five Infantry regiments and for **Bremen** to four armoured and fifteen Infantry regiments. These were the last individual Battle Honours awarded to British regiments of 2nd Army during the war, although 8th and 12th Corps crossed

the Elbe and reached the Baltic, Hamburg itself being surrendered. On 2 May 11th Armoured Division reached Lübeck on the Baltic and liberated Denmark, and 6th Airborne Division, now fighting as Infantry, linked up with the Russians at Wismar.

By the end of April the Americans in the far south had entered Munich and Innsbruck and forces had progressed through the Brenner Pass to link up with the victorious armies in Italy. The three fronts had now joined forces.

Meanwhile 2 Canadian Corps had struck northwards to Zutphen, crossed the Twente Canal against stiff opposition and then steadily advanced towards Oldenburg, where it met strong counterattacks. It eventually reached the coast between Groningen and Wilhelmshaven. 1 Canadian Corps on the left, with 49 British Division under command, captured Arnhem by encirclement, seven months after the great battle there, and continued to Apeldoorn and the mouth of the River Ijssel. It eventually cleared the whole of northern Holland east of the Zuider Zee, but was stopped there by inundations and the threat of complete destruction of the water defences by the Germans, which would have caused needless damage to the Dutch with the war so nearly over.

Numerous Honours were awarded, all to Canadian regiments unless specifically stated otherwise. **Twente Canal** was gained by the Dorset Regiment (39 Foot), and by five armoured and five Infantry regiments, **Zutphen** by two armoured and seven Infantry regiments, **Deventer** by two armoured and six Infantry regiments and **Arnhem 1945**, appropriately, by five British Infantry regiments. **Groningen** was awarded to four armoured, nine Infantry and the APC regiments, **Friesoythe** to three Infantry regiments and **Apeldoorn** to two armoured and ten Infantry regiments. **Ijsselmeer** was won by four armoured and four Infantry regiments, **Küsten Canal** by five Infantry regiments, **Leer** by four Infantry regiments, **Delfzijl Pocket** by two armoured and five Infantry regiments, **Bad Zwischenahm** by seven armoured and four Infantry regiments and **Oldenburg** by three armoured and eight Infantry regiments. No overall Battle Honour was awarded for the final advance from the Rhine to the Baltic or for the final submission of Germany.

In the last few days the enemy forces had disintegrated and virtually ceased to exist or resist. By now the Russians had encircled Berlin, and on 30 April Hitler committed suicide in the bunker in the city and Admiral Doenitz was appointed his successor. In the south the Americans had joined up with the Russians advancing from the east and to all intents and purposes the war in North West Europe was over everywhere. It appeared that the German leaders were ready to surrender, and particularly to surrender to the British and Americans, anticipating that they would receive little mercy from the Russians. Unconditional surrender was demanded and this was accepted by Admiral Doenitz and by Field Marshal Keitel. Capitulation became effective and the 'cease fire' was ordered on 5 May, unconditional surrender was accepted by Montgomery, again appropriately, on 7 May and hostilities ceased at midnight on 8 May, the actual signing of the surrender document being carried out on 9 May.

The landing in Europe and the advance from Normandy to the Baltic, including the destruction of the German Army, had taken just eleven months.

The Campaign Honour, **North West Europe 1944-45**, was added to the Colours of the Household Cavalry, twelve armoured and ten Yeomanry regiments, the five Regiments of Foot Guards, which had largely been fighting as armoured regiments, of fifty-eight Infantry regiments and the Honourable Artillery Company, and the Parachute, Glider Pilot and Special Air Service Regiments and the Commandos of the British Army, and of twenty-four armoured and thirty-eight Infantry regiments, the Parachute and Armoured Personnel Carrier Regiments of the Canadian Army.

It is perhaps interesting to compare the number of regiments which gained this Honour with those which gained the Honour for the battles in North Africa. Thirteen fewer regiments were involved in North West Europe, although again a number of Infantry regiments fielded more than one battalion, slightly fewer British regiments but three quarters as many Canadian regiments as the combined forces of Australia, New Zealand, India and South Africa. It must also be remembered that the Desert War lasted three times as long and that the numbers of regiments destroyed or captured there was very considerable, requiring replacements over the long period.

Italy, 1945

The year opened much as 1944 had finished, in mud and filthy weather. But there had to be some offensive action, and the Canadians advanced on the coastal plain, now frost-hardened, to the coastal lake of Comacchio. They were joined by 56 Division and continued their advance to the River Senio, capturing the jumping-off area for the assault on the river and Granarolo *en route*; in the face of stiff opposition and of the weather there was, however, no hope of crossing the river until the spring. Honours were awarded for **Senio Pocket** to two British armoured and two Infantry regiments and for **Senio Floodbank** to three British Infantry regiments, Skinners Horse and two Gurkha regiments, for **Conventello-Comacchio** to two British and two Canadian armoured regiments and three Canadian Infantry regiments and for **Granarolo** to two Canadian Infantry regiments. The scene was set for the final operation of the campaign.

The final offensive opened on 1 April, Easter Sunday, with the intention of spreading the enemy resources, which had already been thinned by moving a division north of Venice in case of another seaborne assault, and thereby reducing the defences of the main objective. The subsidiary attack was made by SAS and Commandos along the spit of land separating Lake Comacchio from the sea and was entirely successful, the enemy having apparently been taken completely by surprise. **Valli di Comacchio** was awarded as an Honour to the 10th Hussars, the North Irish Horse, four British Infantry regiments, the Special Air Service Regiment and the Commandos.

The next attack was made along the south side of the lake to cross the Senio and then the River Santerno, but the very defendable high floodbanks made this a daunting endeavour. It was made by 8th Indian and 2nd New Zealand Divisions, supported by massive air and artillery bombardment and flamethrowing tanks. The defence was desperate but the attack was pressed home. Both the Senio and the Santerno were crossed, and Menate and Filo were captured, and great deeds of gallantry were accomplished and in several cases rewarded by Victoria Crosses. The army was now ready to attack Argenta, the main objective and the key to the defences of northern Italy.

The Fossa Marina was assaulted and considerable casualties were incurred. The second attack was repulsed, and on the left flank an advance was made on Bastia but that too failed at first. Honours were awarded for **The Senio** to one British and six New Zealand armoured regiments, the North Irish Horse, five British and fourteen New Zealand, one Indian and one Gurkha regiments and the Honourable Artillery Company, for the **Santerno Crossing** to one British and six New Zealand armoured regiments and to one British and fourteen New Zealand Infantry regiments, and for **Menate** and **Filo** identically to the 27th Lancers and the Queens Regiment (2 Foot). The attacks had been held and it was now the turn of 13 Corps to attack towards Bologna, which had defied all American attempts to reach it throughout the winter. Monte Pigno was captured and the South African Division was again brought into the battle.

But 8th Army was still attacking at Argenta with 56th and 78th Divisions. The Fossa Marina was taken at last, although not without further significant casualties, and Argenta was occupied. Consandolo was captured and the attackers raced towards San Nicolo. The San Nicolo Canal was crossed, the Fossa Cembalina was cleared after stiff opposition, and Galbo on the Bologna-Ferrara road was entered. **Argenta Gap** was awarded as an Honour to eight armoured and two Yeomanry regiments and to two Guards and sixteen Infantry regiments and the Commandos, all British. **Fossa Cembalina** was gained by one armoured, one Yeomanry and two Infantry regiments, **San Nicolo Canal** by the Royal Irish Fusiliers (87 Foot) and **Traghetto** by the 16/5 Lancers. It is surprising that the Fossa Marina was not considered worthy of Honour.

Meanwhile on the 5th Army front the River Sillaro had been crossed and Medecina entered in an outflanking movement to cut off Bologna. The River Gaiana was crossed, after an initial repulse, by 10 Indian Division, and the New Zealanders captured Budrio and after furious fighting crossed the River Idice, which destroyed the German defences of Bologna, and captured Mezzolara. Now that it was almost surrounded the Germans began to evacuate Bologna and the city was entered by the Poles. The advance was rapidly becoming a rout, and the first troops of 8th Army to reach the River Po were 8 Indian Division, which had advanced around Ferrara.

A number of Honours were awarded for what was to prove the last battle of the campaign. **Bologna** was awarded to three British and ten New Zealand armoured regiments, to fifteen New Zealand Infantry regiments and to the 2/10th Gurkhas. **Sillaro Crossing** was won by one British and seven New Zealand armoured regiments, one British and fourteen New Zealand Infantry regiments and again the 2/10th Gurkha Rifles, a South African Honour of **Caprara** was won by five regiments, **Medecina** by the

14/20th Hussars and 2/6th Gurkha Rifles, **Gaiano Crossing** by the 27th Lancers, four New Zealand armoured and six Infantry regiments and three regiments of Gurkha Rifles, **Idice Bridgehead** by 12th Lancers, six New Zealand armoured and fourteen Infantry regiments, the Indian Parachute Regiment and one Infantry regiment and finally **Camposanto Bridge** by two South African regiments and claimed by another one.

Although the German situation was now hopeless they had been ordered to continue fighting and did so as long as they could. The River Po was crossed and the advance continued at great speed with minimal resistance. The River Adige was reached, and although it might have been a strong defensive position it was crossed with negligible opposition and on 29 April Padua was entered, just four weeks after the final offensive had begun. One final South African Honour was awarded for this last battle and another one unsuccessfully claimed. **Po Valley** was awarded to twelve regiments, and *Finale* was claimed by six regiments and a squadron of Prince Alfred's Guard.

By now the enemy had had enough and emissaries of the German command signed surrender terms on 29 April. On 2 May hostilities ceased in Italy. But meanwhile the advance had gone on without ceasing, Venice was entered by the New Zealanders, the Rivers Piave and Isonzo of First World War fame were passed, and Trieste and Udine were reached by the time of the cease fire.

The long Italian campaign was over, and the Battle Honour for it, **Italy 1943–45,** was awarded to eighteen British, ten New Zealand, nine Canadian and two Indian armoured regiments, to seven Yeomanry regiments, to the five Regiments of Foot Guards, to fifty-eight British Infantry regiments, the Honourable Artillery Company, the Parachute Regiment, the Special Air Service Regiment and the Commandos, to fifteen New Zealand, twenty Canadian, eleven Indian and nine Gurkha Infantry regiments, to the Canadian Special Service Regiment, to the three regiments of Indian Sappers and Miners and to the Indian Guards and Parachute Regiments, and to twelve South African regiments.

South West Pacific, 1945

The 3rd Australian Division and two independent brigades had landed in Bougainville in the Solomon Islands in October 1944, and having established themselves started to drive the Japanese back both northwards and southwards along the coast, between the central mountain range and the sea. They encountered a number of strong Japanese rearguard positions and some furious fighting occurred with fanatical Japanese defenders, including a particularly desperate action to cross the Puriata River and another fierce battle at Slater's Knoll. Apart from these actions only small-scale battles took place, but nevertheless they qualified for a number of Battle Honours to be awarded which in itself proves that the fighting was of more than a little significance.

Artillery Hill, Pearl Ridge and **Adele River,** all actually fought in 1944, were uniquely awarded, to the 9th, 25th and 15th Regiments respectively, **Mawaraka** was gained by four regiments and **Mosigetta** and **Puriata River** each by three regiments, **Darara** was uniquely gained, again by the 25th Regiment, **Slater's Knoll** was gained by 4 Motor Regiment and 25th Regiment, and **Hongorai River, Egan's Ridge-Hongorai Ford** and **Hari River** were all gained by 4 Motor Regiment with in addition five, three and four Infantry regiments respectively. **Commando Road** was another unique Honour, this time to 60th Regiment, **Ogorata River** was gained by four regiments, **Mobiai River** by three, **Mivo River** by the 4th Motor Regiment and five Infantry regiments and finally **Mivo Ford** by two regiments.

Advancing northwards the Australians had also encountered strong and fanatical resistance as they attacked through the swamps of the coastal littoral towards the Bonis peninsula. But by the end of the war they had achieved their objects and the remaining Japanese were trapped in a small area on the peninsula in the north of the island. **Tsimba Ridge** was awarded to two regiments and **Bonis-Porton** to four regiments.

The 5th Australian Division relieved the Americans in New Britain, landing on the south coast at Jacquinot Bay, and with a two-pronged advance drove the Japanese into the Gazelle peninsula on which lay Rabaul. Actions were limited and casualties were relatively light, and the Australians strove to regain the first place at which they had had to surrender three years earlier. One Honour was awarded, **Waitavolo,** to four regiments.

But all the while fighting had still been continuing in New Guinea, where the process of driving the Japanese westwards was slow but steady, and where the Americans had been on the defensive the Australians immediately assumed the offensive. Advancing from Aitape, where they had relieved the American landing force, they captured Wewak in May, after a series of bitter battles in the jungle and around native villages in which the Japanese had settled and were farming to feed themselves, and the Japanese retreated again supported by strong rearguards. Australian casualties in battle were light, but from malaria and other diseases were very high.

A number of Honours were awarded for this final phase in New Guinea. **Matapau, Perembil** and **Balif** were gained uniquely, the first by the 11th Regiment and the other two by the 5th Regiment. **Abau-Malin** was gained by 6th Cavalry and two Infantry regiments, **Nambut Ridge** by two Infantry and the 3rd Machine Gun Regiment and **Anumb River** by 6th Cavalry and the machine gun regiment. But **Dagua** was gained by three Infantry regiments and the machine gun regiment, **Maprik** by 6th Cavalry and two Infantry regiments and **Hawain River** by 4 Motor Regiment and three Infantry regiments. **Wewak** and **Wirui Mission** were both gained by 6th Cavalry, 4 Motor Regiment and two Infantry regiments, **Mount Shirubangu–Mount Tazaki** was won by two regiments, **Yamil-Ulupu** by three and finally **Kaboibus-Kiarivu** by the same three Infantry regiments and the Pacific Islands Regiment.

The overall Honour for the period from September 1943 to August 1945 **Liberation of Australian New Guinea** was awarded to one Cavalry, two Light Horse and forty-one Infantry regiments, and to one machine gun and one pioneer regiment, all of course Australian.

The major Australian operation in 1945 was carried out in Borneo. It began with the invasion of Tarakan Island.

The landing on 13 April was unopposed but the troops encountered stiff resistance once they started to advance inland, and it took them three weeks to capture the high ground overlooking the beachhead and the eponymous capital of the island. The fighting went on for some time, but was eventually over by mid-June. Unfortunately the airfield could not be seized in time for it to be used as a base against Borneo itself.

9th Australian Division was put ashore in Brunei Bay on 10 June, followed a fortnight later by 24 Brigade on Labuan Island and 25 Brigade on the south side of Brunei Bay. Although there was determined resistance all these assaults were successful and captured their objectives. Meanwhile 7th Australian Division assaulted at Balikpapan and also pressed inland against increasing resistance. But by the middle of August all was over and Japanese hostilities had ceased. Honours were awarded for **Tarakan** to 9th Cavalry fighting dismounted, and to three Infantry regiments and a pioneer regiment, for **Brunei** to three Infantry regiments and a machine gun regiment, for **Labuan** to 9th Cavalry, two Infantry and a machine gun regiment, for **Beaufort** and **Miri** each to three regiments, for **Balikpapan** to eleven regiments and for **Milford Highway** to six regiments. Overall **Borneo** was awarded to three Cavalry regiments, eighteen Infantry regiments, and two machine gun and three pioneer regiments.

With hindsight the whole of the Australian effort in the islands in 1945 was a waste of time, and the same result could have been obtained by bypassing the islands and leaving the Japanese to starve quietly to death. The Australian divisions could have been used to much greater advantage in attacking the more important islands, but that would have reduced the impact of the Pacific War as an entirely American affair, as it was normally reported as being, and this would not have suited MacArthur's fiercely nationalistic pride. It would of course have created a lot more Australian casualties, so in spite of the damage to, and slight on, national pride it may have been a blessing in disguise.

So ended the Pacific War, which had gone on in very hard conditions for three and a half years, as far as the Australians were concerned, and other than in their homeland largely unnoticed and unsung, although like so many unsung heroes they had carried out a difficult task magnificently and deserve to be lauded highly for it. The Campaign Honour, **South West Pacific 1942–45,** was awarded to seven armoured or motor regiments, to forty-nine Infantry, four machine gun and four pioneer regiments, to the Pacific Islands Regiment and to the Papua and New Guinea Volunteer Rifles—a large total from a comparatively small and low-populated country.

Burma, 1945

During the final stages of the battle for Imphal and Kohima a directive for the campaign after the crossing of the Chindwin was issued. This included, for 14th Army, an advance across the Shwebo plain to the River Irrawaddy and the capture of Mandalay, followed by a turn southwards to capture Rangoon, with the possibility of an airborne and seaborne assault on Rangoon, which seemed rather unlikely to be achieved at this stage, while the land forces were approaching the capital. The most propitious place for the first main battle appeared to be the Shwebo plain, which it was expected that the Japanese would defend, albeit with their backs to the Irrawaddy loop north west of Mandalay, since they would have a large preponderance of numbers.

The problem for 14th Army was the maintenance of the forward troops, across the Chindwin and over 400 miles from the railhead, which would require a massive airlift to make the advance possible. 15th Corps, in the Arakan, would still be containing as many troops of the enemy as possible and making a limited advance. In addition some of the Indian divisions were now having to have Indian battalions drafted in to replace British ones, as reinforcements from Europe were in short supply, but others were kept going by drafting in anti-aircraft artillerymen, now no longer needed in Indian rear areas.

Tactics would have to change with the changing conditions, as the fighting would be, for a time, in open country where armoured forces could be deployed, instead of in jungle. 5th and 17th Indian Divisions were now reorganised on to a mechanised basis, in place of an animal transport, and 19 Indian Division joined the Army. The offensive had actually begun in December 1944 with the crossing of the Chindwin at Mawlaik and the extension of the Kalewa bridgehead, as already narrated. 2 British Division advanced towards Pyingaing and 19 Indian Division moved forward from the Sittaung bridgehead towards Pinlebu.

The first obstacle was the ridge of Zibyu Taungdau, but in spite of Japanese rearguards this was quickly passed. Late in December Pinlebu was entered and the advance concentrated on Shwebo. It soon became clear that the enemy did not intend to fight on the Shwebo plain, but beyond the Irrawaddy, and to counter this the advance down the Gangaw valley was restarted, its objective being to cross the Irrawaddy and capture Meiktila, which would outflank the Japanese defence of the Irrawaddy further north at Mandalay. The Gangaw-Meiktila operation was to be a clandestine one with the enemy still being made to believe that Shwebo was the major, and only, objective. In early January both Shwebo and Gangaw, after hard battles, were entered. **Shwebo** was awarded as an Honour to 3rd Dragoon Guards, five British and two Gurkha regiments, and **Gangaw** to the Bihar Regiment.

14th Army was now rapidly approaching the River Irrawaddy which was a most formidable obstacle, being the main waterway in Burma and one of the world's major rivers. True it was low in water at this time of the year, but would still require a major assault crossing task even without Japanese opposition; at its junction with the Chindwin near Myingyan it is about 2½ miles wide. Patrols of 19 Indian Division on the north of the front reached the river first, while 2 British Division was advancing southwards from Shwebo towards Myinmu and 20 Indian Division was approaching Monywa. 4 Corps was nearly up to the river at Pakokku, with 7 Indian Division behind it, and 17 Indian Division was preparing to re-enter the battle. In the far north 36 British Division had crossed the Irrawaddy in its upper reaches at Katha and was advancing in a south

easterly direction towards Myitson and Kyaukme. The airforces, both British and American, supporting 14th Army were giving invaluable service and making the life of the enemy very uncomfortable, even as far away as Rangoon.

The plan was now for 19 Indian Division to cross the river well north of Mandalay, to give the impression of being about to link with 36 British Division, and so draw Japanese troops to its front. 2nd British and 20th Indian Divisions were to attempt to cross the river opposite Mandalay and in any case to draw off more enemy, while the main thrust would be made at Meiktila, in the south, which it was hoped would take the enemy by surprise. But the main problem for all the crossings was to assemble enough boats and equipment to make them possible. Boats particularly were in short supply and the divisions had to make do with what was available and what they could find, which would mean many ferry crossings, which against the strong opposition anticipated would not be easy.

After a patrol crossing at Thabeikkyin 19 Indian Division made its main crossing on 14/15 January at Kyaukmyaung. It met little opposition at first, as the Japanese had not expected a crossing there, and as more troops got across it was able to expand its bridgehead to a good defensive position, by which time the resistance was growing and soon fierce counterattacks were made. As had been hoped the Japanese moved strong forces against the division and it had to beat off some very heavy assaults.

While the battle of the bridgehead was going on 20 Indian Division attacked the very strong position at Monywa, and, in spite of considerable casualties, captured the town and could now cross the Chindwin about 40 miles above its confluence with the Irrawaddy. Shortly afterwards other 20 Division troops, which had already crossed the Chindwin, reached the Irrawaddy at Myinmu and also met stubborn resistance from the retreating Japanese. Further east they had a bitter battle with the last Japanese position west of the river at Sagaing.

In the middle of February the main battle for Mandalay opened when 20 Indian Division crossed the river at Myinmu. The Japanese launched a series of counterattacks, but suffered very heavy losses and gradually became exhausted and discouraged. Further north 36 British Division had crossed the River Shweli and established a small bridgehead, which it had to defend desperately.

Battle Honours during this period were awarded for **Monywa 1945** to the Northamptonshire Regiment (48 Foot) and to an Indian Cavalry regiment, for **The Shweli** to five British regiments and the Indian Parachute Regiment, for the **Kyaukmyaung Bridgehead** to an Indian armoured regiment and to two British, two Indian and one Gurkha Infantry regiments, for **Sagaing** to 3 Dragoon Guards, for **Myinmu** to an Indian Cavalry regiment and for **Myinmu Bridgehead** to four British Infantry regiments, the Bombay Sappers and Miners and three Gurkha regiments.

In the south 4 Corps captured Pauk and 7 Indian Division took over the advance to the river, an advance which was completely unknown to the Japanese who were now without any practical air reconnaissance potential. Strong resistance, however, was met on the west bank of the Irrawaddy at Kankla, and a first attack failed, but a second attack drove out the enemy. A crossing was attempted at Pagan and Nyaungu on 13 February, but because of the difficulties with finding channels through the sand banks in the very low water and opposition on the banks of the landing zone at Nyaungu the assault failed. However at Pagan the Japanese had moved out to oppose the other landing and the river was crossed and the town entered without opposition. Further south still an East African brigade had entered Seikpyu with little opposition, and Singu had been captured. On the following night another assault was launched at Nyaungu and it was found that the enemy had withdrawn, and a bridgehead was established; the Japanese returned and mounted counterattacks, which were repulsed, and the bridgehead held out. But there were still some Japanese on the west bank and they now launched a counterattack at Letse, south of the road from Pauk to Chauk where another feint crossing was made. The counterattack was repulsed with heavy casualties to the enemy, but the battle there, threatening the lines of communication, continued for some weeks.

17th Indian Division now crossed into the Nyaungu bridgehead, ready to make the thrust towards Meiktila. Opposite Mandalay 20th Indian and 2 British Divisions now prepared to cross the river. 2 Division crossed west of the 20 Division Sagaing bridgehead at Ngazun, encountered far less resistance than had been expected and established a strong bridgehead. In the 36th British Division area a desperate battle was raging at Myitson on the Shweli River, but the town was eventually captured.

For this phase Honours were gained for the **Nyaungu Bridgehead** and **Letse**, both by the East Lancashire Regiment (40 Foot), together with a Sikh regiment for the former and with the King's African Rifles for the latter, for **Seikpu** by the King's African Rifles, for **Singu** by 8 Gurkha Rifles, and for **Myitson** by three British regiments. **Letse** was also granted as an Honour Title to an Indian Field Artillery Regiment.

At this point it seemed to the Japanese that the main threat was to Mandalay, and they therefore reinforced this area most strongly for what they called the Battle of the Irrawaddy Shore, by withdrawing divisions from other areas. This was what it was intended that they should do, and 5 Indian Division was now committed to the battle.

In the latter part of February the advance on Meiktila began with 17 Indian Division and 255 Tank Brigade. Rearguards were encountered and largely brushed aside without too much trouble. Taungtha was taken against strong resistance, and the following day Mahlaing was entered. The strongest position was met about 8 miles from Meiktila, but after an encircling movement a strong armoured attack over-ran the position, and soon the outskirts of Meiktila were reached. The town itself was very strongly defended. The battle was hard, and the defence as fanatical as only the Japanese knew how, protected by numerous bunkers, and the fighting raged for four days. Once the outskirts had been passed the fighting became largely short-range and hand-to-hand, and the Japanese died in droves where they stood. Finally on 2 March Meiktila fell. The town was badly damaged and the Japanese casualties were huge, but it was at last in British hands and threatened cutting-off the Japanese army in Burma.

The Honour of **Taungtha** was awarded to the Royal West Kent Regiment and to two Indian regiments, and **Capture of Meiktila** was awarded to the West Yorkshire Regiment (14 Foot) and to two armoured, two Infantry and two Gurkha regiments of the Indian army. An Indian Field Artillery Regiment was granted the Honour Title of **Meiktila.**

The Japanese reacted quickly to their dangerous situation and the troops being sent to reinforce Mandalay were redirected to Meiktila to attempt to recapture it. The defence of the town was carried out by offensive rather than defensive action, with Infantry and armoured hunting parties ambushing and attacking the Japanese formations which were arriving piecemeal on the battlefield, and preventing them building up or consolidating any large formations. As the numbers of Japanese troops built up, even without being in formations, the fighting was fierce in the extreme, and it was not until the end of the month that the enemy gave up and fell back. **Defence of Meiktila** was awarded to the West Yorkshire Regiment and to two armoured regiments, the Bombay Engineers, five Infantry and three Gurkha regiments of the Indian Army. The overall Honour for the period, **Meiktila**, was awarded to three Indian Cavalry regiments, the Madras and Bengal Sappers and Miners, and to five British, one Indian and three Gurkha Infantry regiments. The Royal Artillery gained another Honour title **Meiktila Battery**.

The area in the south around Taungtha was cleared and Myingyau entered, against desperate opposition, which provided the first usable port on the Irrawaddy. A Japanese counterattack had little success. But the area around Mount Popa was also heavily defended and until 4 Corps had reorganised it could go no further.

But meanwhile two other attacks had developed, one against Mandalay and the other in the Arakan. In addition 36 British Division had cleared Myitson, was advancing southwards towards Mandalay, and by the end of March had captured Mogok and Kyaukwe. Three divisions, 2 British and 19 and 20 Indian, were poised to attack the area of Mandalay, each with a bridgehead over the river.

The advance was rapid and the Japanese defences were quickly over-run, and the only significant resistance in Mandalay was on Mandalay Hill and at Fort Dufferin. Both attracted bitter fighting and the Japanese once again fought fanatically, literally to the last man. British and Indian troops fought through the city with much hand-to-hand fighting. The Fort and the city were at last captured. 19 Indian Division made a rapid advance south eastwards to Maymyo and burst on to a totally unprepared Japanese defence, which was soon over-run in its turn, and 2 British Division attacked and captured Ava.

A mobile force of 20 Indian Division had struck south from Myittha, reached the Rangood–Mandalay railway at Wundwin, having overcome stiff opposition *en route*, and then turned northwards towards Mandalay up the railway. They attacked and captured Kyaukse, a major Japanese supply centre, and with this as well as the capture of Meiktila they virtually sealed the fate of the Japanese in Burma.

Honours were added to the Colours of a number of regiments. **Fort Dufferin** was gained by the Royal Berkshire Regiment (49 Foot) and two Indian and one Gurkha regiments, **Maymyo** by the Welch Regiment (41 Foot) and 6 Gurkhas and **Ava** by 3 Dragoon Guards, two British and one Indian Infantry regiment and **Kyaukse 1945** by the Devonshire Regiment (11 Foot) and two Gurkha regiments. The overall Honour for this phase, **Mandalay**, was awarded to 3 Dragoon Guards and 7 Indian Cavalry, and to ten British, one Indian and four Gurkha regiments.

In the Arakan at the end of 1944 15th Corps, comprising 25th and 26th Indian Divisions, 81st and 82nd West African Divisions, a Commando and an Indian Tank Brigade, were on the approximate line of Buthidaung, from which a tactical withdrawal had been made, to just north of Kyauktaw in the Kaladan valley. At the beginning of 1945 Buthidaung was retaken. An advance down the Mayu valley had begun in September 1944 and an Indian brigade had captured a key feature, Point 1433, after bitter hand to hand fighting. Towards the end of the year the Japanese had launched a fierce counterattack against the West African Division's base at Tinma which was defeated with heavy losses to the enemy. The advance continued in 1945 and by the middle of January had reached the tip of the peninsula opposite Akyab island, and 81 West African Division advancing down the Kaladan had taken Myohaung after heavy fighting. Akyab island was captured single-handed by an AOP (Air Observation Post) artillery officer, flying an Auster aircraft, who saw friendly waves from the populace and decided to land on the airstrip, to find to his relief that the Japanese had pulled out. **Point 1433** was awarded as an Honour to 3/2 Gurkha Rifles, **Tinma** to the Gold Coast Regiment, **Mayu Valley** to the Nigeria and Gold Coast Regiments and **Myohaung** to the Sierra Leone, Nigeria, Gold Coast and Gambia Regiments.

It was now planned to carry out seaborne landings to try and entrap the retreating Japanese, although the coast was anything but inviting for this purpose. The first landing was made at Myebon, with little resistance, followed by landings at Ramree and Kangaw, the latter being strongly defended. Nevertheless a brigade of 25 Indian Division was landed on the beachhead held by the Commandos, and captured the village of Kangaw. A Japanese counterattack was decisively defeated. Kyaukpu, at the north of Ramree island, was assaulted and proved a more exacting task, and the small island of Cheduba in the south was occupied without opposition. **Myebon** was awarded to 2 Gurkha Rifles and the Commandos, **Ramree** to the Royal Lincolnshire Regiment (10 Foot) and an Indian regiment, and **Kangaw** to the Nigeria and Gold Coast Regiments and the Commandos, and to two Indian regiments.

It was essential to try to open up the An Pass to provide a route to the Irrawaddy and Minbu. To this end a landing was made at Ru-ywa, which was held against furious counterattacks, and the bridgehead was slowly developed for the attack on An at the same time as the battles for Meiktila and Mandalay were raging. A breakthrough to the river via the An Pass would further outflank the Japanese and threaten Prome, but air supply needed for the latter battles reduced that available to 15 Corps, which was now reduced to two active divisions only.

Nevertheless an advance was made from Ru-ywa on Tamandu and Dalet, both of which places fell early in March,

and another landing was made at Letpau, from which a brigade of 26 Indian Division and an East African brigade advanced southwards towards Taungup, although the attacks on the An Pass and on Taungup itself, which would also open the road to Prome, had to be postponed. **Ru-Wya** was gained as an Honour by the Indian Madras Regiment, **Dalet** by the Nigeria Regiment and **Tamandu** again by the Nigeria Regiment and by one British regiment and 2 Gurkha Rifles.

Eventually Taungup was taken, but by then the race for Rangoon had started, and its capture was of little real importance to the final outcome of the war. **Taungup** was awarded to the King's African Rifles, the Northern Rhodesia Regiment, the Rhodesian African Rifles and the Gold Coast Regiment, and to one Indian regiment, and the overall Honour for this period in the Arakan, the last, **Arakan Beaches**, was awarded to three British regiments, 2nd Gurkha Rifles, the Nigeria, Gold Coast and Northern Rhodesia Regiments and the King's African Rifles and the Rhodesian African Rifles.

Now that the battle for central Burma was over, 14th Army had Rangoon in its sights as the ultimate objective. The Japanese Armies were disintegrating, and, although formidable still, could cause little more than delaying actions, but the real race for Rangoon was against the onset of the monsoon, as it had been during the retreat three years earlier, which gave the Army about two months' grace. In addition the race depended on whether the British armour and transport, which had been now committed for months in largely impossible conditions with only local maintenance and repair facilities, which nevertheless had done wonders to keep it going, would hold out for the final 400-mile advance down the River Irrawaddy and the Sittang river/railway routes.

General Slim decided to put the more mechanised and air-transportable divisions of 4th Corps, 5th and 17th Indian Divisions with 255th Tank Brigade on the railway route, and 33rd Corps, with 7th and 20th Indian Divisions, on the Irrawaddy, 2nd British Division being returned to India as it had been weakened by the lack of the ability to replace casualties and 19th Indian Division being left initially to clean up the Mandalay–Meiktila area and subsequently the left flank of 4th Corps. The Japanese were blocking both routes.

The area between Mandalay and Meiktila was cleared of most of the Japanese rearguards, and the only strong opposition was encountered at Mount Popa, an extinct volcano. Some fierce fighting developed but soon after the middle of April the Japanese withdrew and **Mount Popa** was awarded to three British and one Indian regiment. Meanwhile Kyaukpadaung, Gwegyo and Chauk were entered, and after another crossing of the Irrawaddy Yenangyaung was taken after brisk fighting with rearguards, as was Magwe. The Honour of **Yenangyaung 1945** was gained by 3 Dragoon Guards and the Queen's Regiment (2 Foot), and **Magwe** by two Indian regiments and 2 Gurkha Rifles.

On the other front 4 Corps had closed up on Pyawbwe, where the Japanese were clearly determined to make a strong stand. The fighting here was grim, much of it hand-to-hand, but by the middle of April Pyawbwe and the surrounding villages were in British hands, and the surviving Japanese had departed, although many were later destroyed by hunting patrols. The advance continued, and although it seemed as if the Shwemyo Bluff might be an obstacle it was outflanked and the defenders ousted from their entrenched positions. Pyinmana was also found to be strongly held, but it was also outflanked and subsequently cleared. **Pyawbwe** was added to the Colours of two British, three Indian and two Gurkha regiments, and **Pyinmana** of one Indian regiment.

The advance was now nearing Toungoo, the last likely major obstacle on the route apart from Pegu, and 5 Indian Division reached the town in late April after some very rapid movement. They erupted into the town, to the complete surprise of the Japanese who had not believed them to be anywhere near it and fled, after a much easier battle than had been expected. **Toungoo** was awarded to two British regiments and two Indian, the Assam Regiment and 6 Gurkha Rifles and **Rangoon Road** was awarded to six British, four Indian and four Gurkha regiments. The race was on for Pegu. The Japanese were strongly entrenched there, but again the Indians, with their tails well up, burst in and although the fighting was hard, and the terrain did not allow for the use of tank support, a major attack launched on the town found that the Japanese had again withdrawn after the initial fighting. **Pegu 1945** was awarded to two Indian and two Gurkha regiments.

As this point, at the beginning of May, the monsoon burst and immediately the countryside became waterlogged and very difficult for all movement, when Rangoon was only 40 miles away and could have been reached in a couple of days. However, on the same day 26 Indian Division had landed from the sea just north of Rangoon, in support of the final stage of the advance, after a heavy bombardment of the city and in spite of the weather and dangerous seas, and on 3 May they entered the city with little or no opposition.

Way back north, while 4 Corps had been pressing on with all speed, and Japanese garrisons had been bypassed for future attention, 33 Corps had been trying to prevent the Japanese west of their route interfering with or cutting it. At Shandatgyi 7 Indian Division destroyed a Japanese rearguard, the survivors of which and the main body then travelled downstream to Kama. The division, together with troops of 20 Indian Division, surrounded them there and when the Japanese tried to break out they repulsed most of their attacks, causing appalling casualties after heavy fighting. Some managed to escape into the hills, but were no longer a force which could in any way hinder 4 Corps' advance. The Honour of **Shandatgyi** was awarded to one Indian and one Gurkha regiment, and **Kama** to one British and three Indian regiments. The Honour **The Irrawaddy** was awarded to 3 Dragoon Guards and six British Infantry regiments and to one Indian and three Gurkha regiments.

With the capture of Rangoon the battle was virtually over and Burma had been regained during a magnificent campaign. But fighting was still going on, because many of the Japanese forces had been bypassed and many who had escaped from the various battles were still holding out in the jungle and the hills, and they still had to be rounded up, destroyed or pushed out of Burma. Most armies in

their situation would have surrendered, there being little hope for their survival, but being fanatical Japanese they did not do so. They tried to break out, which meant crossing the Sittang River, scene of a British disaster in 1942 and now to be the scene of a Japanese one. The ground was under water from the monsoon and operations were difficult.

The end of the war was almost in sight, but nobody knew that then and the destruction of the rest of the Japanese armies in Burma was paramount to prevent them escaping to Malaya, which had to be the next phase of the war for the British. The Indian positions were strongly counterattacked and the battle continued in what was virtually an enormous swamp. There were few possible tracks and these were blocked by the Indians, and the Japanese trying to use them were annihilated. Even those who survived had to cross the Sittang in flood without any equipment and few succeeded. By early August it was all over. A few Japanese had escaped but many more than usual had surrendered, an unheard-of thing in the past, and to all intents and purposes the campaign in Burma had come to an end. **Sittang 1945** was awarded as an Honour to six British, six Indian and seven Gurkha regiments.

A few days later the first atomic bomb was dropped on Hiroshima, followed by one on Nagasaki, and shortly afterwards the Japanese surrendered. The recapture of Burma had been a remarkable effort, and few Honours were more deserved than the Honour for the campaign as a whole, both the retreat and the return, **Burma 1942-45**. It was awarded to four British and six Indian armoured regiments, to the three regiments of Indian Sappers and Miners, to forty-six British, thirty-five Indian and over twenty Gurkha battalions relating respectively to eighteen Indian and all ten Gurkha regiments, to four West African and three East African regiments.

South Pacific, 1944

The next task for the New Zealanders, who were still in the Solomon Islands, was to attack and capture the Green Islands group at the northern end of the island chain, beyond Bougainville and only 100 miles from Rabaul. One problem was that so little was known about the islands, until a very successful reconnaissance raid by 30 Battalion at the end of January obtained information about them and about Japanese positions on them.

The landing on Nissan Island was made by 14 Brigade in the middle of February and met very little resistance initially. Patrols moved steadily forward into the light jungle which covered the atoll, supported by a few tanks. A fierce action took place on the small island of Sirot in the north, but the Japanese were finally cornered in a small area in the south of Nissan Island, and in spite of spirited resistance the battle was over by the end of the month, and the Solomon Islands campaign was over.

The Honour **Green Islands** was gained by five Infantry regiments, and the overall Honour **Solomons** was awarded to the fourteen Infantry regiments which were represented in the three island battles.

Although for a time the Division was held in readiness for further operations it in fact took no further part in the war. It returned to New Zealand and was disbanded in late October. The Battle Honour **South Pacific 1942–44** was awarded to three Armoured Regiments, the NZ Scottish and to fifteen Infantry regiments, all of the New Zealand Army.

Conclusions

Many books have been written which go into great detail about the conclusions to be gained from World War II, but this is not the place for such a treatise.

Suffice to say that in terms of Battle Honours, the main sphere of interest here, the war was served royally with more than ever before. Perhaps they were almost too multitudinous and every small action appears to have been considered worthy by the Nomenclature Committee, although the regiments themselves seem to have had other ideas and there are a remarkable number of possible Honours which have not been awarded. But all this shows clearly how so many battles were fought in small groups, often far removed from each other, rather than in the mass attacks of the Great War with its far fewer Honours awarded, although these too would have been far more if all the actions and other engagements listed had also been awarded.

Although the main enemy, Germany and Japan, were totally defeated, it was now to be the allied countries, Russia and some of the British colonies and Dominions which had supported the mother country loyally throughout the long struggle that were to cause the problems over the next several decades.

Above: The Caen Canal bridge known as Pegasus Bridge, captured by the Parachute and Glider Pilots Regiments on D-Day, 6 June 1944. One of the crashed gliders is just beyond the bridge. *IWM*

20 The Cold War and 'Bush Fires', 1945-70

World War II was over, but there was little relaxation in hostilities in various parts of the world. The USSR had survived Hitler's attacks almost entirely due to the supply of equipment by Britain and the USA without which her vast reserves of manpower would have counted for little. But as a result one monster had been exchanged for another, for a new menace which also had considerable territorial and imperialist ambitions whilst publicly forswearing them and condemning imperialism.

In Europe the partition of occupied Germany had favoured the USSR, because only Churchill saw, or perhaps wanted to see, the inherent danger in giving in to Russian demands, and the countries on the Russian side of the demarcation line, contiguous with her own frontiers, soon found themselves captive and being treated as Russian colonies, although with a far greater ruthlessness and totalitarianism than those colonies which formed part of the British Empire. Since most of these countries had been previously occupied and over-run by Germany, stripped and ravaged, there was little that they could do to preserve their sovereignty, and what little their patriots were capable of was soon put down with a ruthlessness and disregard of human values which at least matched that of Hitlerism and the Gestapo.

Now what became known as the 'Cold War' began, the fight against Russian ideology without, hopefully, getting into actual war with the USSR, although nevertheless with numerous countries into which she had introduced or instilled communist ideals, often supported by people too illiterate or unintelligent to realise why they were fighting or what for.

Pressure was put on Britain, more from without by the USA and the USSR than from any internal desire at this stage, to relinquish her colonies and Empire; and such a line of action was accepted with gusto by a socialist government, much further to the left than those of the electorate who had voted for it fully understood, which dismantled with indecent haste and little thought beyond ideology what had been so painfully built up over the years with thousands of British lives. Thus many of the British Army's 'Bush Fire' engagements have been as a result of this dismemberment—Malaya, Kenya, Cyprus, South Arabia to name but some of the more obvious—and most of its activities have been involved with keeping the peace in the other and less known ones.

The year 1970 was originally chosen as the end of the era and in fact the end of the present narrative, because apart from the advent of another major war and the running sore of Northern Ireland, which is purely a policing operation, no other Honours seemed to be likely to be awarded in the foreseeable future, although the recent exception of the Falkland Islands war has changed this to some extent. Although most of the actions over these twenty-five years were in former colonies, and thus the same argument can be applied as for the American War of Independence that they were civil wars, a war is a war whether civil or not and weapons have the same effect whether fired by enemies or ex-colonists who are, for some peculiar reason, not supposed to be enemies.

Although no battles in the sense of full-scale warfare have taken place in these campaigns, campaign medals, mostly as clasps to the General Service medals, have been awarded to individuals, and it seems indefensible, therefore, as in the 2nd Boer War, that the campaigns and battles in which the regiments to which these soldiers belonged took part should not be recognised on the Colours of the regiments. During both world wars Campaign Honours were awarded to all those regiments at any time in the theatre during particular time limits; many of the regiments who carry Campaign Honours from these wars have done far less to deserve them than the regiments, often the same ones, which have taken part in the campaigns of the recent past.

But then the award of Honours, in spite of the rules and criteria brought in in 1920, has always been a matter of whimsy rather than logic, and one wonders how much self-interest has played a part as it certainly did 300 years ago and less.

There are of course two exceptions to the above. The first is the Korean War of 1950 to 1953, where battles were fought and Honours were awarded. The second has required a further short chapter, because it occurred twelve years after the era of this book was over, and is of course the Falkland Islands war, for which Honours have now been awarded, although in one case not according to the rules. That at least cannot be called a civil war, but in the circumstances one cannot but wonder just how much politics has been involved in the decision to award them.

Palestine, 1945-8

Apart from a lack of sympathy with Zionist leanings in Palestine, the need for Britain to maintain a cordial relationship with the Arab states, in whose countries the war was being fought and through whose countries the lifeline to the Far East still led, caused the British government in the early 1940s to halt Jewish immigration to Palestine. But Jews were still being evacuated from Europe and there was nowhere for them to go. The Americans advocated more evacuation and the lifting of immigration restrictions to a country already overcrowded, although it would have been more sensible and more humane if they had opened their own country to immigration, if only temporary. As a result of all this the Zionists mounted an intense propaganda campaign against Britain, and as early as 1942 terrorist activities were begun against British troops in Palestine by the Irgun Zwei Leumi and the Stern Gang, one of whose most militant leaders, Begin, was until recently Prime Minister of Israel.

Britain continued to maintain her peace-keeping role in accordance with her Mandate during the war and afterwards. But the Jews wanted Palestine entirely for their own and this meant the elimination or eviction of the Arabs, which inevitably meant war between them. The rest of the world, particularly the USA and the USSR, took great delight in sniping at Britain in a situation which certainly the former could in no way understand, apparently knowing little about geography but having a big chip on her shoulder about reducing British influence in the world.

A United Nations commission sat, and again as in the 1930s recommended partition, but this time, totally illogically and almost as if to provoke war rather than peace, allotted the vast area of the Neqeb, totally Arab settled, as well as the Arab portions of Gallilee, to the Jews. The United States strongly supported Jewish aspirations, but then Jewish votes and money are important in American elections and one was due in 1948, unlike the situation in 1941 when an election was just over. Fighting had begun between Jews and Arabs in December 1947, but prior to that bitter attacks had been made on British troops by both sides indiscriminately. One of the more cowardly was the blowing up of the King David Hotel in Jerusalem, used as British headquarters, by the Stern Gang.

Britain now opted to give up her Mandate, having had more than enough from all concerned—USA, USSR, Arabs and Jews—in May 1948, as it was obvious what was going to happen. She was accused of behaving callously in deserting the country in its hour of need when she might have acted as a buffer, with all the casualties and discomforts that this would have inevitably meant, but it was basically the total irresponsibility of the United Nations—not for the first nor the last time—in enforcing partition without ensuring any provision for peace-keeping, which was to blame, aided and abetted by the USA who above all wanted to see Britain ousted from the Middle East.

In 1948 an attack was made on the Jews by an undisciplined, untrained, unorganised and unsupplied force of Arabs, backed by Egypt, but with no chance against them. The Jews had had a Jewish Brigade, trained on western lines, during the war and hundreds of officers and men who had served in the allied armies now formed an effective force, armed by weapons largely stolen from British depots during the war and hidden for 'the day'. They quickly defeated the Arabs and occupied the whole of Palestine.

After the British withdrawal various Arab states' armies entered Palestine and drove the Jews back. A truce was arranged by the UN, and had the Arabs then sued for terms they would have probably improved their share in the partition plan. But Egypt, although careful not to become involved herself, decided that hostilities should be reopened as a political manoeuvre. The Jews had recovered their strength and poise and the Arabs were once again driven back.

The account of British participation in Palestine finishes with the withdrawal of all troops after over 30 years. In this latest phase nine armoured, four Guards, twenty-eight Infantry and the Parachute Regiments had taken part.

Malaya, 1948-60

At the end of the Burma campaign and the war against Japan there were still a number of Japanese troops in Malaya which had to be rounded up. This task was given to the guerilla army which had been raised in Malaya during the war by Colonel Spencer Chapman, 'Elephant Bill' as he had been nicknamed, and others and which had already proved itself highly effective against the Japanese, but had a strong communist element within it. Most of the guerillas were Chinese Malays, who hated the Japanese, but who were also unpopular with the Malays who saw them as wanting to take over the country on behalf of China.

The guerillas completed their task, but by then there was little outside control over them and they began to engage in terrorism on a large scale based on their old jungle hideouts. By 1948 they had been persuaded by their communist mentors to turn against the British as well, although their leaders had had this idea in mind even before the Japanese invasion.

British troops were sent in to destroy the power of the insurgents, and succeeded with remarkable speed in subduing them, particularly successfully when compared with the situation in Vietnam 20 years later, very similar in many respects, which the Americans totally failed to control. Most of the fighting was in comparatively small detachments, commanded by young officers, or even NCOs, and was totally different from normal forms of warfare. The troops there became extremely good at it, even though it was not very pleasant.

The Emergency, as it was known, was not elevated to the title of war although that was what it really was, certainly during the periods of heavy fighting. It lasted until 1960, long after the majority of the communists had been eliminated, although by this time Britain had lost most of her power in the Far East and Malaya itself had become independent in 1957. No Campaign Honour was awarded although a clasp to the General Service Medal was granted to troops who took part. Nevertheless, overall during the period seven armoured, three Guards and twenty-six Infantry regiments, and the Special Air Service Regiment, were involved in the fighting.

Korea, 1950-3

Until the war started there Korea was a little known country and most people had never even heard of it. Physically it is about twice the length and about the same width as Scotland, with a mountain range near the east coast and the highest mountains in the north, although the centre is also mountainous, each hill appearing to come out of the plain as distinct from growing out of each other. The northern border is with China, which had had the dominating influence in the country for nearly 2,000 years although it is only 120 miles from the Japanese mainland. However, in 1894 there occurred a Chinese/Japanese war which the Chinese lost, and in 1904 Korea figured in the Russo-Japanese war. The result was that with waning Chinese influence Korea was annexed by Japan in 1910. It was of little value to her, partly on account of very poor communications and little industry.

Before the end of World War II summit conferences had promised Korea its independence after the defeat of Japan. However, in 1945 it was arbitrarily divided on the 38th Parallel by the Americans without reference to the Allies, so that the Russians could accept the Japanese surrender in the north, where most troops were, while the Americans accepted it in the south. Russia had only declared war on Japan six days earlier, when she knew that she would not have to fight but could gain her share of the spoils. The Americans were too busy accepting the ceremonial handover of Japan, and therefore only arrived a month after the surrender. By this time the Russians had moved into the north, and very soon had established communism, made North Korea a separate country, developed its Army and closed the border.

There was now no chance of realising a united Korea, except under Russian domination, and the Americans, who had created the situation, did not want that to happen. However, the United Nations undertook the totally impractical task of uniting the country in 1947, and in 1948 recognised the Republic of Korea, which had come into existence in the south, as the lawful authority for the whole country, although it had no validity in fact. In 1949 the Americans decided to wash their hands of the whole affair and withdrew, leaving behind a hostile and explosive situation. The North Korean Army was equipped with Soviet equipment, aircraft and weapons and was an effective force, whilst the South Korean Army had been established very slowly and hardly armed at all by the Americans—no tanks, medium guns or transport—who regarded it as a constabulary border control force. There were communist cells in South Korea, and clashes were frequent in the country as well as on the border. It should be noted that the American withdrawal took place only a year after the Americans had vilified the British for withdrawing from Palestine in similar circumstances.

On 25 June 1950 the North Korean Army crossed the border with the object of taking over the south and the Korean War began. Kaesong was soon captured and the advance was directed at Seoul, the capital, and down the east coast. The United Nations Security Council recommended that help be given to South Korea, and although the Americans were reluctant to become involved in any affair in the Far East while the 'Cold War' in Europe was at its height, General MacArthur, who was then still in Japan, was authorised to intervene as a representative of the United Nations, although his primary interest was in evacuating US nationals from Seoul.

On 28 June Seoul was occupied by the North and the South Korean Army was broken and in full retreat. Still the US hesitated, but on 30 June they agreed to take action and the first troops arrived on 1 July. They took up positions near Taejon, but were soon forced to retreat and were only saved from a serious reverse by a pause in the North Korean advance which allowed more US troops to arrive in time. Britain had sent warships on 28 June, and these were soon joined by others from Australia, Canada, New Zealand and Holland.

Air attacks were mounted and by early July the North Korean Navy and Air Force had ceased to exist. Their Army was still full of fight however; Taejon fell on 20 July and Chinju nine days later, and in early August the Pusan perimeter defence was established. At the end of August the North Koreans attacked the perimeter defences and on 5 September 27 British Commonwealth Brigade, consisting of 1 Middlesex Regiment and 1 Argyll and Sutherland Highlanders, was committed near Waegwon on the Naktong River. On 22 September the Middlesex crossed the Naktong River and attacked some hill positions overlooking Songju and captured them. Meanwhile the Argylls attacked and captured two hills south west of the Middlesex but were heavily counterattacked. Air support was called up but unfortunately the American pilots mistook the positions and bombed the Argylls, and a fighting withdrawal was made. Ten days later a major attack on the Middlesex Regiment was repulsed, for which the Honour **Naktong Bridgehead** was awarded to them. Shortly afterwards 3rd Royal Australian Regiment joined the brigade and the Pusan perimeter was strengthened.

General MacArthur now produced an ambitious plan for an amphibious landing to try to cut off the North Koreans, but the American powers that be were reluctant to sanction it as MacArthur was thought to be too provocative! Nevertheless a landing was made on 15 September at Inchon by 1st Marine Division and 7th Infantry Division, supported by British warships and aircraft carriers, from whose Royal Marine detachments came the landing and lane-marking parties, and which gave air support. In spite of the portents against such a landing and the difficulties of making it against largely unreconnoitred defences, it succeeded and great credit must go to the American troops, particularly the Marines. The airfield was occupied two days later and Seoul was captured on 26 September after heavy street fighting.

An offensive was launched from the Pusan bridgehead in conjunction with the landings and the North Korean Army withdrew to avoid being trapped. The advance in which the British Commonwealth Brigade participated was rapid and joined up with 7 Infantry Division on the day Seoul was recaptured. Thousands of prisoners were taken and the North Korean Army gave little resistance, was broken and virtually ceased to exist. By the end of the month the whole of South Korea had been recaptured and the 38th Parallel was crossed in order to destroy the remaining North Koreans.

In three weeks the advance, and the change from weakness to complete control, had been spectacular and it looked as of the war would now be short-lived. British troops led the US divisions towards Sariwon, which was captured, and the advance continued now led by the Australians. In ten days the line of Pyongyang (the North Korean capital) to Wonsan was reached, and Pyongyang was taken on 19 October by the South Koreans, and the Middlesex Regiment entered the city a few hours later. The United Nations, sitting in their ivory tower among the flesh pots, again decreed that the country would be unified. Next Yongyu was taken by the Australians in a hard battle, and the Middlesex, having entered Sinanyu, crossed the Chongchon River by assault and the brigade encountered fierce opposition at Chongju, which was overcome. Honours were awarded for **Sariwon** and **Yongyu** uniquely to the Royal Australian Regiment and for **Chongju** to the Middlesex Regiment and to the Royal Australian Regiment. The advance continued into the north of the country with the objective of closing up to the Yalu River, approximately the border between North Korea and China.

At the end of September China had warned that she would not stand idly by while a communist country was invaded, although this situation was clearly anything but true, and started to concentrate troops on the Yalu River, the limit laid down for the United Nations advance. Little notice was taken of this at the time, until a South Korean division reached the Yalu near Chosan, and was then ambushed and wiped out, and a few days later in early November a US Combat Team was decimated in the Unsan Valley. Now the Chinese warning was believed, especially when it was found that the Chinese had crossed the border unnoticed a fortnight earlier, so appalling was the US-based UN intelligence. A fierce defensive action was fought by 27 Commonwealth Brigade in early November and the Honour **Pakchon** was awarded to the Argyll and Sutherland Highlanders and to the Royal Australian Regiment.

By now winter was setting in and the UN forces were without heavy clothing, it not having occurred to the commissariat that Korea had almost arctic winters, and morale slumped again. Intelligence of what was happening was still poor. 29 British Infantry Brigade, consisting of the Royal Northumberland Fusiliers, the Royal Gloucestershire Regiment and the Royal Ulster Rifles, had now arrived and joined 27 Commonwealth Brigade, and the latter, moving forward, ran into major Chinese formations. A South Korean attack failed and they and the Americans started to withdraw, 27 Brigade following them across the Chongchon River after heavy fighting. The Honour **Chongchon II** was awarded to the Middlesex Regiment. The Chinese were becoming more aggressive and the retreat from the Yalu River, which had never actually been reached by the United Nations forces, began and soon became in some places almost a rout. It is perhaps significant that the only order for the retreat given to the British Brigade by the American Commander-in-Chief was 'General, we're gonna pull'; and it says much for British organisation, endurance and warlike spirit that 'pull' they did with a fraction of the American casualties, although they frequently formed the rearguard.

Pyongyang was evacuated in early December and the retreat reached the lower reaches of the Imjin River by 13 December. The withdrawal had now covered 120 miles in ten days through difficult country, with few supplies, with

the hardship of winter weather, and largely out of touch with the enemy. Ten days later the 38th Parallel was crossed again, and General Ridgway took over command of the armies from General Walker, who had been killed in a car accident.

Early in January 1951 the Chinese offensive recommenced, 27 Brigade providing the rearguard for the withdrawal of the UN forces. At Uijongbu the Chinese cut the road behind them, but the Royal Australian Regiment broke through and allowed the other battalions to escape. They formed the next defensive position around Seoul, and after heavy fighting in extremely cold weather were again forced to withdraw to prepared positions, and Seoul and Inchon were evacuated. During the retreat some British Battle Honours were awarded. **Uijongbou** was gained by the Royal Australian Regiment, and **Seoul** was gained by 8 Hussars, the Royal Northumberland Fusiliers (5 Foot) and the Royal Ulster Rifles (83 Foot) for an action in defence of the city. The Chinese were unable to exploit further through lack of transport and supplies, and the defensive line was stabilised through Ansong-the Imjin River-Samchok. The idea of an early end to the war had gone again.

Luckily for all concerned General Matthew Ridgway was made of sterner and more pragmatic fibre than some of his predecessors in command, and believed in the well-tried military dictum that offence is the best form of defence. A month later, having achieved a degree of organisation previously lacking, he began on 17 February a counter-offensive against the now grounded Chinese and gradually moved northwards again occupying successive lines of objectives, until in April he reached the mystic line of the 38th Parallel north of Seoul, through Chorwon, and the Hwachon reservoir to Taepo-ri on the east coast.

There was much heavy and tough fighting during the offensive and several Battle Honours were awarded to the British brigades. **Chuam-ni** was gained by the Middlesex Regiment and the Royal Australian Regiment during an advance on the road from Yongsu-Ri to Chipyong-Ni. 29 Brigade attacked a series of hills and the Gloucestershire Regiment, in the lead, captured one of them in the area of Kyongan-Ni, named **Hill 327**, after a fierce battle for which they were awarded the Honour together with 8 Hussars who supported them. **Maehwa-San** was won by the Royal Australian Regiment and **Kapyong-Chon** by the Middlesex Regiment. By this time nearly a million men of both sides were involved in the war, the North Korean/Chinese having roughly a four to three advantage in manpower, and the fighting in general was very heavy and frequently ferocious, particularly as the Chinese had little regard for the level of their casualties.

Early in the month the Gloucestershire Regiment had occupied a defensive area near the village of Solma-ri, three miles south of the Imjin River, which at this point runs through a deep gorge, the main defensive position being on Hill 235 with the rest of the brigade nearby. Initially all was quiet, but in this war of seesaw motion the Chinese, having been resupplied, began another offensive on 22 April. The outlying positions were overrun and most of the brigade was ordered to withdraw, which they did in the face of strong opposition. But the Gloucesters on Hill

235, supported by 170 Mortar Battery, Royal Artillery, could not do so as they were by now surrounded, and although some managed to get away under cover of darkness, the majority fought on. They suffered heavy casualties and inflicted heavier ones on the Chinese but eventually fought themselves to a standstill and were forced to surrender. Over 600 men were made prisoners of war and two Victoria Crosses were won during this most courageous action. A Battle Honour, perhaps one of the most prestigious of all Honours, **The Imjin,** was awarded to 8 Hussars, the Royal Northumberland Fusiliers (5 Foot), the Royal Gloucestershire Regiment and the Royal Ulster Rifles. But in addition to the Battle Honour both the Gloucestershire Regiment and 170 Mortar Battery were awarded the American Presidential Citation for their epic defence and 170 Battery was also granted the Honour Title of **Imjin Battery.** The Gloucesters also added 'The Glorious Gloucesters' to their nicknames.

As a sideline to the battle it is perhaps worthy of note that the vast majority of the prisoners survived and were eventually released, although not entirely unscathed in mind or body. But that this should have been so is one of the strongest recommendations for the old British regimental organisation and tradition, now so sadly lost by the amalgamations and disbandments forced upon the Army by the nameless inconoclasts in the name of progress, without which, as happened to other non-British nationals, so many might have given up through malnutrition and the lack of the will to live. Being part of a family which cares for its members is as important today as it was and has ever been, in spite of modern dogma. Let us pray that one day the powers that be may recognise again this strongest of all facets of the British Army, disband the conglomerates and return to the regimental system which has withstood over 300 years of fighting and adversity, and would still if it were allowed to do so. Perhaps a pious hope in a computer age in which we are all cyphers.

At the same time as the Gloucester's heroic action, 27 Commonwealth Brigade was also fighting a fierce delaying action near Kapyong. Although it was unable to prevent the Kapyong–Chunchon road being cut it nevertheless held the Chinese offensive on the northern bank on the Han River. The Honour **Kapyong** was awarded to the Middlesex Regiment, the Royal Australian Regiment and to Princess Patricia's Canadian Light Infantry, who had now joined the brigade.

All along the front the Chinese offensive had been held and a strong defensive line had been established. Further attacks were made, but the line held. And now yet another counter-offensive was launched, which carried the United Nations forces back across the 38th Parallel once more. It could have progressed further into North Korea, since the Chinese were now unable to stand up to western firepower, but for reasons neither understood nor explained the order was given to halt.

And now, a year after the war had started and after several offensives on both sides, stalemate had been reached which lasted for another two years while peace negotiations were being carried out. There were no further major offensives and only limited actions which did not change the position of the front very much. Nevertheless

there was still some heavy fighting to come and in the east the Americans were engaged in bitter combat in July. On 1 July the British Commonwealth Division was formed.

Although the war had become static it was still necessary for both sides to carry out raids and some minor offensives to take prisoners from whom information might be gained and to anticipate any major operations. One United Nations offensive began in October 1951, when for the first time the Commonwealth Division went into action as a complete formation. It captured the railway line to Chorwon and pushed back the enemy several miles, and was altogether a successful baptism. Honours were awarded for an engagement where the division attacked near Changdan at **Kowang-San** to the 8th Hussars and three British Infantry regiments and to the Royal Australian Regiment, for **Maryang-San,** a defensive action in which there was very heavy fighting, to two British regiments and for **Hill 227 I**, again a fierce defensive battle, uniquely to the King's Shropshire Light Infantry (53 Foot).

Patrol clashes and larger actions continued into and throughout 1952 with little visible result for the hardships suffered during the winter months in the extreme cold. The Chinese had been building up their strength under cover of the peace negotiations which continued in a desultory fashion. In November 1952 they launched an attack, primarily to improve their bargaining position at the peace talks, on a strong position known as The Hook which stood in what was to become the Demilitarised Zone. The Commonwealth troops defended gallantly and inflicted heavy casualties on the enemy, and eventually the attack petered out. The Honour **The Hook 1952** was awarded to the 5th Dragoon Guards, fighting largely dismounted, and to the Black Watch (42 Foot).

In May 1953, when the war seemed to be virtually over, President Sigmun Rhee stated that he would not accept the armistice terms agreed by the United Nations and communist negotiators, and the enemy reaction was strong, inevitable and immediate. A new offensive was launched and again the Hook position astride the Samichon River was attacked and at one stage over-run, although sharp counterattacks recovered it and again the Chinese lost very heavy casualties. The Honour **The Hook 1953** was awarded to the King's Regiment and the Duke of Wellington's Regiment (8 and 33 Foot). The last days of the war gave another Honour, **The Samichon,** to the Royal Australian Regiment, although this was more in respect of the long, hard and gallant fighting that they had endured throughout the war than for any particular notable action.

The war officially came to an end on 27 July 1953 after protracted negotiations with very few benefits having accrued to either side, in spite of the United Nations forces having suffered some 400,000 casualties and the communist forces having suffered an estimated one and a half million. The country was still divided and the economies of both North and South had been devastated. If the United Nations had continued strong pressure instead of resting on their laurels the western democracies might have gained more, but such is modern government. However, the war had proved that the United Nations would defend against communist aggression and oppression in the Far East, and it undoubtedly prevented, for a few years at any rate, a number of the smaller Asian countries being swallowed up. The Battle Honour **Korea 1950-53** was awarded to eighteen British, one Australian and four Canadian regiments.

Kenya, 1952-6

For a number of years, even before World War II, there had been a militant faction of the Kikuyu tribe in Kenya which was dedicated to getting rid of white rule in the country. The leader of this faction, although initially somewhat reluctantly, was Johnstone 'Jomo' Kenyatta, who after a limited education had for a while studied the phonetics of the Kikuyu language in India and had become a left-wing politicist. In 1952 it was discovered that there was within the Kikuyu a secret society called the Mau Mau, the origin of which name nor its precise meaning having never been determined. The society was proscribed and Kenyatta, who was now found to be its leader, was imprisoned. A State of Emergency was declared by the Governor.

The State of Emergency had the effect of goading the Kikuyu into open defiance of colonial rule, and the Mau Mau had already made a number of attacks on isolated farms and had committed various murders and other atrocities. The battalions of the King's African Rifles, who always remained loyal to the Crown, were placed upon a war footing and the Kenya Regiment was raised from among the settlers. Initially the settlers were not unduly worried by the situation, but when the atrocities became more widespread their representatives demanded action from the government, British troops were brought in and determined action was taken to root out the Mau Mau. The security forces gradually gained the initiative, although not without some unpleasant fighting.

In 1954 a massive operation was launched to clear the Mau Mau strongholds in the mountains and by the end of the year the movement was no longer a threat, although the Emergency actually lasted for another six years. In fact, in spite of the publicity given to Mau Mau atrocities, only 32 European civilians were killed during the Emergency, although the settlers lived in constant fear of attack and most of their Kikuyu servants and their families had been driven off the farms whether they were loyal to their employers or not. Many more natives died at the hands of the Mau Mau than whites.

On the political front the Kikuyu were included in the Governor's Executive Council in 1957, and in 1959 elections were held which ensured an African-dominated legislature, so keen did the British government appear to be to get rid of its embarrassing colonies whether they were capable of governing themselves or not. Kenyatta was released from prison and in 1961 was nominated as the President-elect of an independent Kenya, independence being granted at the end of 1963.

As in all the 'bush fire wars' the troops taking part had a very hard and unpleasant duty to perform but no Honour was awarded for the fighting in the campaign. Between 1952 and 1956, however, eleven British regiments participated as well, of course, as the King's African Rifles and the Kenya Regiment, the latter ceasing to exist at the end of the Emergency.

Cyprus, 1955-9

In the late 19th century any threat to British routes to India and the Far East, particularly those through the Mediterranean and the Suez Canal, was unacceptable. In 1878 Turkey offered Britain the lease of the island of Cyprus as a base to defend Turkey's Asian possessions against possible Russian incursions, and this was gladly accepted as it would also be a base from which to defend the sea routes. Britain had actually had a previous short interest in Cyprus in 1191, when King Richard I had governed the island on the way to one of the Crusades, and had married Berengaria of Navarre at Limassol, the only time in British history that the Monarch has been married, and his Consort crowned, outside Britain.

Britain annexed Cyprus in 1914 on the day that war was declared on Turkey, and in 1925 the island became a Crown Colony, a move that was of considerable benefit to the island. After World War II Britain's main reason for retaining Cyprus had gone with the withdrawal from India, but it was still important as a base to defend Middle East oil supplies and to guard against any Russian entry into the Mediterranean. In 1955 the Greek Cypriots demanded union with Greece, Enosis, and the USSR championed the two Cypriot leaders, Archbishop Makarios and Colonel George Grivas, who led the Cypriot communists; at the same time the Turkish Cypriots demanded union with Turkey, neither of which was acceptable to Britain. A clash was inevitable and the island was garrisoned by an Indian regiment from Malta.

Guerilla warfare erupted in the island with a wave of armed insurgence and bombing attacks, and in 1956 Makarios and the other leaders were arrested and exiled. British troops were brought in to restore order, which they did with much difficulty, and comparative peace descended. But the Emergency continued and early in 1958 rioting and fighting broke out again, the British troops being heavily attacked by both Greeks and Turks, particularly the former. At the end of the year a cease fire was called for, largely as a result of diplomatic intervention by the USSR and the United States, both of whom had their own, but quite different, reasons for wanting Britain out of Cyprus. In 1959 the London Agreement was signed and Cyprus became an independent republic, although Britain was allowed to retain very limited Sovereign Base Areas at Akrotiri and Dhekeilia.

The fighting and conditions for the troops on the island had been arduous and dangerous and casualties had been heavy, but the actions were regarded as a civil war or a disobedience campaign and therefore no Honours were awarded. During the Emergency a large number of British regiments were involved at one time or another, including the Household Cavalry, the Grenadier and Irish Guards, thirty-one Infantry regiments and the Parachute Regiment.

Suez, 1956

After the battle of Tel el Kebir in 1882 Britain maintained a military presence in Egypt, which was virtually ruled as a Dominion. During the Great War Britain saved Egypt from again becoming a Turkish province, and the country declared its independence in 1922 when Sultan Fuad be-

213

came King Fuad I. By treaty rights a British military garrison was, however, still maintained to control the Suez Canal and the lifeline of the Empire through it to India and Australia. Fascist ambitions in Africa in the 1930s made the British garrison, although initially unpopular, again acceptable to the Egyptians, and of course during World War II their presence was again necessary to prevent the capture of the country by the Germans, and once again Egypt became virtually under British rule.

After the war the King, by now Farouk, was overthrown by the nationalist Gamal Abdel Nasser, and the pressure was exerted for the withdrawal of British troops. The garrison was maintained, however, until 1954 when a treaty was signed allowing the Suez Canal Zone military base to be held for a further two years, when the last British troops pulled out after seventy-four years of beneficial occupation under one name or another. But in 1956 Nasser nationalised the Suez Canal in spite of its international ownership. He offered 'full compensation' to the shareholders, but this did not satisfy Britain who thereby lost control of its operation, now mainly a commercial undertaking as the independence of India and Pakistan and the virtual autonomy of Australia made the Canal no longer a life line.

Britain brought strong diplomatic pressure on Egypt at first to accept international control and, when this failed to have any effect, military pressure. Although many countries agreed with Britain, particularly France who was another major shareholder, most of the world, including the USA who was not a shareholder and certainly not a supporter of the British Commonwealth ideal, opposed it. Nevertheless planning for military action continued during the autumn months jointly with France, and supported by Israel who had her own reasons for wanting to attack Egypt, since the Arab nations, led by Egypt, had virtually been at war with her since the inception of the country in 1948.

At the end of October Israel invaded Sinai, and Britain and France issued an ultimatum to Israel and Egypt to stop fighting and withdraw their forces to 10 miles on each side of the Canal. Israel, being nowhere near the Canal, accepted the ultimatum, and on the basis of its terms moved her forces up to the 10-mile line. Egypt, who would have had to withdraw from territory not yet attacked, did not accept.

On 4 November, therefore, paratroops landed near Port Said, followed by seaborne landings the following day by the Anglo-French force, which captured the city and advanced along the Canal to ensure that the ultimatum was obeyed. In retaliation Egypt sank a number of ships in the Canal to block it, a blockage which remained for several years, and her Syrian allies blew up oil pipelines which threatened the Western countries with an oil shortage. The world turned against Britain, France and Israel. The Americans, under President Eisenhower, from whom Britain had expected support, and the Russians motivated a United Nations vote for a cease fire and Britain, faced with the withdrawal of international credit, had no choice but to accept and to withdraw her forces when a UN peace-keeping force moved in.

Naturally no Honour was awarded, although some fighting had been fierce, but the Royal Tank Regiment,

two Guards and six Infantry regiments and the Parachute Regiment participated in the abortive invasion.

Arabian Peninsula, 1957–60
Aden and the area of the Aden peninsula was ceded to Britain in January 1839 as compensation for a passenger ship which had been wrecked two years earlier and the passengers maltreated. Initially a Dependency of the Government of India it was used as a coaling port, and Aden became a Crown Colony in 1937. The hinterland was not occupied, although treaties were made with tribal leaders for their protection and thus a Protectorate was created. The Yemen had always been a thorn in the side of Aden, and after it became independent in 1919 its ruler had claimed the Protectorate because the Yemen had occupied it between 1630 and 1750.

In 1956, after the Suez campaign, Egypt became hostile towards the Colony and supported the Yemen and all other states in attempts at Arab nationalisation. There were troubles in all the states of the southern part of the Arabian peninsula after the Federation of Arab Emirates was formed in 1959. British regiments were used to keep order between 1957 and 1960; local actions took place, but their role was mainly peace-keeping and no Honour was awarded, although the Life Guards, two Cavalry and ten Infantry regiments were employed at various times.

Brunei and Borneo, 1962–6
When the Federation of Malaya was created it included the old British protectorates in North Borneo and the surrounding areas. This resulted in protests from President Sukarno of Indonesia who claimed these territories and would have liked to annexe the whole of Malaya. In 1962 he became involved in military confrontation in Borneo, Brunei and Sarawak, and British troops were called in to help the Malayans. They spent three years in an unpleasant war in difficult terrain rooting out Indonesian infiltrators from these areas, until Sukarno was deposed in 1966 and the new Indonesian government ordered a cease fire. Singapore had meanwhile become an independent republic in 1965, and there had been disturbances in the Malay peninsula.

No Campaign Honour was awarded, but three Infantry regiments distinguished themselves in Brunei, two armoured regiments, the Scots Guards and six Infantry regiments participated in Borneo, and the Life Guards, Scots Guards and three Infantry regiments had been involved in the Malay peninsula.

The Radfan, 1964
In 1962 a revolution took place in the Yemen, inspired by Egypt, and there was much propaganda against Britain. The Federation of Arab Emirates demanded action from Britain to protect them from incursions into their territories, and in June 1963 Aden joined the Federation. The hostility of Yemen and other Arab entities increased and at the end of 1963, when a bomb attack was made on the

High Commissioner, the frontier with Yemen was closed and a State of Emergency was declared.

Insurgency by local tribesmen, who were excellent guerillas, increased in the hinterland, particularly in the Radfan area which included the caravan route to the Yemen, the *Doub el Haj* or Sacred Road used also as a pilgrim route to Mecca. The country was wild and mountainous, and divided by deep ravines, and the only roads were camel tracks. At the beginning of 1964 it was decided to take military action, largely as a demonstration in force, initially mainly by units of the Federation Regular Army. But they soon felt the strain of the campaign and withdrew.

A British force was now introduced into the area to take over the show of force, and it was decided to capture the main features. Fierce fighting took place and the objectives were taken only in the face of strong opposition. The first phase being completed 39 Infantry Brigade took over as the attacking force. Fighting continued until August as British troops moved forward, and the dissidents were reduced to small groups of guerillas while the initiative remained in the hands of the security forces.

The campaign proved to the Arab states, particularly Egypt and the Yemen, that insurgency in British-protected areas would be dealt with firmly and efficiently, provided that politics did not interfere. No Honour was awarded for the short campaign, with its considerable hardships, but two armoured regiments, two Guards and four Infantry regiments, the Royal Marine Commandos, the Parachute Regiment and the Special Air Service Regiment all participated.

South Arabia, 1964–7

Although swift counteraction had taken care of the guerilla warfare in the mountains of the hinterland during the campaign in the Radfan, terrorism was increasing in Aden State, the old colony, in 1964, especially in the urban areas. The situation was not improved by a Government Defence White Paper which stated that although Britain intended to maintain her military base in Aden, South Arabia would be granted independence in 1968.

This was an open invitation to the Egyptian-backed nationalists to try and gain power by then to prevent the Federation being able to control the area, and to achieve this the Federal and British governments had to be discredited and Britain forced to withdraw from the base altogether. The local Arabs, knowing that British troops would not be around to protect them from the nationalists, saw no point in remaining loyal to Britain or the Federation, and a major terrorist campaign began at the end of 1964 and lasted for three years, growing all the time in intensity. A number of separate Arabist organisations existed and carried on their campaigns, sometimes allied and sometimes at enmity, as each had differing objectives and therefore formed alliances for limited periods to help their own ends.

Methods, as in most guerilla campaigns, involved intimidation of the population, neutralisation of intelligence by intimidation of the police forces, trade union troubles and propaganda. One problem for the authorities was that

Aden State opposed strongly the security measures of the British government and would not co-operate, and another was that the area was a warren of urban alleyways and open on all sides to insurgents from other states.

Initially two brigades defended Aden. One was in Little Aden, across the harbour from the town where the oil refineries were situated, and the other in the town and the surrounding areas. Although the organisation of terrorism was at first poor, it improved with time which accounted for the increase in incidents and casualties. The British and Federal troops had a very difficult time, in a situation which might have been bearable and have been subdued if it had been purely a military matter; but every action was overshadowed by political and civil factors, and the role of the army in the twilight zone between peace and war was frustrating and unenviable. Further the enemy was indistinguishable from civilians unless caught in the act. The situation was very similar to that in Northern Ireland today.

During 1965 and 1966 action continued in the Radfan area, with some fierce encounters, and in Aden itself direct rule from Britain was imposed and State power curtailed as it was no longer viable or trustworthy. But strong enough action was limited because, as so often had happened and was to happen again shortly in Northern Ireland, the British government contained members who sympathised with the socialist ideals of the terrorists and would not sanction the ultimate deterrent. The security forces were only allowed to use their weapons in self-defence, even when an obvious act of terrorism was being committed and they were themselves being shot at, such is the absurd theory of minimum force, the direct legacy of Dwyer and the Amritsar riots nearly 50 years earlier, so frustrating the troops engaged in internal security operations who are never free from the possible consequences of their actions although acting in good faith. This is asking a great deal of young soldiers who see their comrades shot, killed and maimed without being able to reply, especially when they know that those countries which will make the most noise about it are those who themselves are quite prepared to murder in cold blood.

At the beginning of 1966 another typical Defence White Paper, which could only have been socialist-inspired, announced that Britain would abdicate her responsibilities in the area and withdraw from the base when independence was granted. It is doubtful if a more stupid, irresponsible or treacherous announcement has ever been made by so-called responsible politicians, and this obviously had disastrous consequences, making the task of the security forces even harder, as perhaps had been intended, as there was now and henceforth no co-operation at all from the local inhabitants, governmental or otherwise, and the terrorist activities were even more increased. During 1966 and 1967 military activity and direct confrontation were stepped up but this did not decrease the terrorism, the terrorists intelligence being so complete that they could anticipate every move. A major battle was fought at the notorious trouble spot of Skeikh Othman north of the town, but although a number of terrorists were killed it did not really solve any problems and the incidents continued.

Hostility further increased when the Arabs believed that

Britain had helped the Israelis during the Israeli–Egyptian war of 1967, with its crushing defeat for Egypt. But even if they had wanted to do so Britain's forces had by now been reduced to such a low ebb that it is doubtful if they could have done anything useful.

Finally a pusillanimous government took the decision to withdraw British troops at the end of 1967 in advance of the grant of independence. The garrison withdrew into a small area on the peninsula north of Aden town whence the evacuation by helicopter to waiting aircraft carriers proceeded smoothly; the final withdrawal took place on 29 November 1967. No Honours were awarded for this very difficult three years because it was an internal security operation throughout. But during this time six armoured, three Guards and fifteen Infantry regiments were involved as well as the Parachute Regiment and the Special Air Service Regiment.

It may be thought that the narrative of this particular campaign has gone into undue length, but there is a good reason. It indicates the almost impossible task of troops engaged in internal security operations for which no recognition is ever given by a grateful (*sic!*) government, and which has subsequently been experienced to an even greater extent for fifteen desperate years in Northern Ireland. The terrorists there are largely able to continue without much British Army activity except in a purely passive sense, which is all that the Army is allowed to do, the terrorists being supported by overt action by the Irish in other countries, particularly in the United States, many of them apparently in influential positions.

Above: Suez—Men of A Company 3 Para at the airfield of El Gamil, Port Said on the morning of 5 November 1956. *IWM*

21 The Falkland Islands, 1982

The Falkland Islands consist of two large islands and a huge number of small or very small islands, lying 300 miles off the coast of the Argentine and over 8,000 miles from Britain. They were discovered in 1592 and have been a Crown Colony for 150 years. The islands are basically a crofting community and the capital, Stanley, is the most southern city in the world.

The ownership of the islands has been in dispute between the Argentine and Britain for most of the past 150 years since they became a colony, although there is little enough there for them to be of any great value to anybody. Nevertheless they have always been available to Britain as a naval base in the South Atlantic and have been used as such during both World Wars. But during the last twenty years the dispute has become passionate politics to the Argentinians and early in 1982 there were debates in the United Nations and considerable international diplomacy to try and solve the dispute, although with notable lack of success.

Then, without any warning and whilst the debate was still going on, Argentina invaded the islands and troops landed at Stanley on 2 April, taking the tiny Royal Marine garrison by surprise and overwhelming them. At the same time an incident occurred on South Georgia, one of the smaller islands, where some Argentinian scrap metal dealers had illegally landed and were attacked by a small Royal Marine detachment from a naval ice-patrol ship to round them up. Unfortunately the dealers had been a decoy, although they swore that this was not so and subsequently demanded huge sums in repreparation, and had been reinforced by Argentinian troops and the detachment was soon surrounded, outnumbered and forced to surrender.

It subsequently became clear that Argentina believed that Britain would take no action beyond words at the United Nations. In fact Britain reacted rapidly, more rapidly in fact than most of the world believed possible, although nobody realised that she had had early intelligence of the possible situation. Only three days after the landing two aircraft carriers and an assault ship sailed from Portsmouth, followed during the next few days by requisitioned liners full of troops of 3 Commando Brigade and a task force of naval vessels. But it was a long way for the armada to go and while it was on the way more diplomacy was tried, and many hoped and believed that there would be no fighting.

Such hopes were pious, and at the beginning of May Stanley airfield was bombed, an Argentinian cruiser, the *Belgrano*, was sunk, and the British ship *Sheffield* was destroyed by an Exocet missile. The war had started with a vengeance. By the middle of the month the troops and fleet were in the war zone, but so far no landing site had been selected and the fleet was kept hanging around in dangerous waters. Meanwhile a party of Marines and SAS had landed in mid-April on South Georgia during a blizzard, crossed the island and rounded up the Argentinian force there.

The landing area for 3rd Commando Brigade, consisting of 2nd and 3rd Parachute battalions and 40th, 42nd and 45th Commandos, had now been selected in San Carlos Water, which gave sheltered sites but was about the furthest point on the island from Stanley. The landing was not without incident nor did it go smoothly, but at least it succeeded and the British force was ashore and ready for action, the Argentinian defenders initially remaining silent and inconspicuous. Not that they remained silent for very long and air attacks on shipping were heavy and caused casualties; but the Argentinians attacked the warships rather than the troop and supply ships and thereby made a big mistake which possibly deprived them of victory, so vulnerable was the attacking force.

The first major battle occurred a week after the landing. 2 Parachute Battalion advanced south from San Carlos Water along the east side of Brenton Loch towards, and then down, the narrow isthmus joining the two halves of East Falkland, their objective being the townships of Darwin and Goose Green. The Argentinians had established a strong defensive line across the isthmus from Darwin and a desperate battle developed on each coast. Casualties were heavy in the open terrain, including the Battalion Commander, Colonel 'H' Jones, who was killed during an incredibly brave two-man attack on a fire trench for which he was posthumously awarded the Victoria Cross. But the attack was pressed with great gallantry and drove back the enemy, and although Goose Green was held by a crack Argentine strategic reserve regiment, 1,000 men strong, this regiment surrendered rather than wait for the final attack by the parachutists when issued with an ultimatum to do so. The victory was a remarkable feat for an Infantry attack with limited small arms and practically no other support. The Battle Honour **Goose Green** was awarded to the Parachute Regiment. On the following day 42 Commando assaulted and seized Mount Kent in the centre of the island.

One of the reguisitioned liners which left Portsmouth on 12 May was the *Queen Elizabeth II* carrying the Scots and Welsh Guards and 1/7 Gurkha Rifles of 5 Brigade, sailing alone at 29 knots nonstop. QE 2 rendezvoused with *Canberra* in South Georgia, transferred 5 Brigade and picked up survivors from naval sinkings and other casualties and returned to England, covering 16,000 miles in a month in the process. 5 Brigade was landed at San Carlos on the day after the victory at Goose Green, its objective being to advance on Stanley in company with 2 Parachute Battalion. In fact the parachute battalion moved first, making a quick and ingenious dash by helicopter to occupy Fitzroy and Bluff Cove three quarters of the way to Stanley, their position at Goose Green being taken over by 1/7 Gurkha Rifles.

As part of the two-pronged attack planned on Stanley, the western prong consisting of 3 Parachute Battalion and 45 Commando moved on foot from San Carlos to Estancia House, about 12 miles from Stanley, by a long and very arduous march over the mountains of the northern part of the island. The next and difficult task was to get the Scots and Welsh Guards, who were to form the eastern prong of the attack, to Bluff Cove. There was no helicopters available and there was not time for them to march, so the only way was by sea.

Then occurred one of the major disasters of the war when two Logistical Landing Ships, *Sir Galahad* and *Sir Tristram*, which were carrying two companies of the Welsh Guards, were destroyed by Argentinian air attack. Many reasons have been given for the catastrophe in which over 50 men were killed and many more wounded, and no doubt many more theories and stories will emerge in due time, but basically it was a combination of the eternal military problem of order, counterorder and disorder, lack of proper liaison or radio command nets, and the unwillingness of the government in London to expose either of the assault ships, *Intrepid* and *Fearless*, to possible air attack and loss. Whatever the reason, it is clear that the disaster should not have happened and could have been avoided.

In spite of the problems all the troops were eventually in position for the final assault on Stanley which began on 12 June. The assault was planned in two phases—Phase I with attacks by 3 Parachute Battalion on Mount Longdon, by 42 Commando on Mount Harriet and by 45 Commando on the Two Sisters, and Phase 2 the following night with attacks by 2 Parachute Battalion on Wireless Ridge overlooking Stanley itself, and on Tumbledown Mountain and Mount William by the Scots Guards and 1/7 Gurkha Rifles respectively. The Welsh Guards had been largely destroyed as a fighting force at Bluff Cove, but secured the start line for the 42nd Commando assault. Part of the reason for this peak to peak advance was the hope that the Argentinian commander would have time the see the hopelessness of his position and surrender, before a pitched battle had to be fought in Stanley which could have destroyed the town.

3 Parachute Battalion's attack on Longdon Hill was not entirely silent as intended as a landmine was detonated before the Argentinian position was reached and the de-

fenders opened heavy fire. There was very fierce fighting as the Argentinians had the advantage of infra-red night glasses, but after several hours the position was taken in hand-to-hand fighting with the bayonet, and there were considerable casualties. The attacks on Mount Harriet and the Two Sisters were much more easily successful and the two Commandos captured their objectives after heavy fighting, but with remarkably few casualties and a large number of prisoners. **Mount Longdon** was awarded as an Honour to the Parachute Regiment.

The second phase was delayed by 24 hours, during which the attackers were constantly shelled. 2 Parachute Battalion assaulted Wireless Ridge and had a hard battle, as difficult a task as their sister battalion on Mount Longdon. The Parachute Regiment was awarded **Wireless Ridge** as an Honour. On Tumbledown Mountain the Scots Guards also had a desperate battle assaulting in the dark under heavy artillery fire. The hill was steep but eventually captured with the help of the bayonet at close quarters. It was a bloody battle and in fact the last of the war. **Tumbledown Mountain** was awarded as an Honour to the Scots Guards.

The Argentinians were now in full retreat towards Stanley. The British troops were similarly striving to get there as soon as possible and, although the entry routes were thickly and dangerously strewn with mines, they wasted no time in penetrating the outskirts of the town. Some of the Marines who entered Stanley had been those who fought the original invasion. At 9.00 pm on 15 June, in a snowstorm, the Argentinians surrendered and the war was over just ten weeks after the first ships of the armada had sailed from England. There were so many prisoners, many more than had been believed to be in Stanley, that the comparatively small British force was quite incapable of looking after them, and they were left to their own devices, some of them for a time still armed, until they could be shipped back home.

Little mention has been made of the Gurkhas during the battles. Their role initially was mostly reconnaissance duties and rounding up of enemy patrols, there being some political considerations involved, and the only set piece attack which they were allotted was on Mount William where, after strong resistance during the night, the enemy broke and ran rather than face their reputation. No mention either has been made of the two Royal Artillery regiments which participated, or of the detachment of light tanks of the Blues and Royals, and too little about the naval air support. But all these troops were vital to the final victory.

The first real war for thirty years was over, and hopefully the expertise and expedition with which it was won, in spite of the mistakes and the acknowledged lucky breaks, will prevent any further real, or unreal, wars in which British troops are involved for a similar or longer time.

The Battle Honour **Falkland Islands 1982** was awarded to the Blues and Royals, the Scots and Welsh Guards, the 7th Gurkha Rifles, the Parachute and the Special Air Service Regiments. The Royal Marines, like the Royal Artillery, are of course never awarded individual Honours.

PART III
Chronology of Battles and Battle Honours

Above: 'The Devil's Own.' The 88th Foot (later 1st Battalion The Connaught Rangers) at the siege of Badajoz, 1812. Wash drawing by R. Caton Woodville, 1908. *NAM*

Introduction

Part III lists Honoured and unhonoured battles in chronological order, grouped by the campaigns of which they formed a part. Details of the regiments Honoured for each battle are shown, and of those regiments that participated both in Honoured battles, to the extent that they would today have merited the award of the Honour, and in unhonoured battles. Claims made by individual regiments for the Honour are also shown, as are Honours borne as badges or in some form other than as straightforward titles of battles, and where the battle or campaign has been awarded as an Honour Title to Batteries of the Royal Artillery.

This chronology of battles with their Honoured regiments and participants includes both British and Commonwealth regiments. Although British regiments were involved in the majority of battles, in some only Commonwealth regiments participated. In other cases, battles have been given by the Commonwealth countries different titles to those devised by the War Department or, more recently, by the Battle Nomenclature Committee, and some countries, in particular South Africa, have also added to the list battles not included by the British.

An indicator system has been used to name the regiments, since to include their full titles on every occasion would take up far too much space and produce an unmanageable book. The Indicator List that precedes the chronology translates the codes used in the chronology and gives the title or titles of each regiment, sometimes abbreviated to familiar titles, with major changes at specific dates. The method followed in the chronology is described below.

British Regiments

In the earliest days of the Standing Army regiments were known by the names of their Colonels. Eventually they were numbered and in some cases given titles, and were thus referred to in the records prior to 1881, somewhat indiscriminately, either by number or by title. Since 1881, and the allotment of recognised territorial titles, these titles have normally been used. In most cases where Militia, and later Territorial Army, Battalions were involved in battles, the Honours are borne by their parent regular regiments; but some of the Territorial Army Battalions had no parents and therefore are listed separately. In the case only of the South African War, 2nd Boer War, Honours were awarded to individual militia battalions and where the parent regular battalions were not involved they did not inherit the Honours.

In the lists and indexes there are inevitably a number of irregularities, but basically:

(a) Cavalry in the period up to 1914 are shown by the number and either DG (Dragoon Guards), D (Dragoons) or LD (Light Dragoons). Subsequent to that the Dragoons and Light Dragoons are designated H (Hussars) or L (Lancers). After the 1922 amalamations these regiments are shown by their amalgamated numbers.

(b) Yeomanry regiments are shown by the letters YEO followed by the number allotted in 1908, or in a few cases by the initial letters of their titles.

(c) Infantry, extant or perpetuated until recently, are shown by the regimental number of Foot before amalgamations in 1881.

(d) Infantry which were amalgamated in 1881, and also in 1957 and in subsequent amalgamations where applicable, are shown by the number of the senior partner only.

(e) Regiments which were disbanded before 1881 are shown by the number or name which they bore at the time of the battle.

Australian Regiments

Virtually all regiments have always been referred to in wars by number rather than title, and this method has been perpetuated in the lists. Nevertheless the actual titles have also been shown in the index for comprehensiveness. In the lists

(a) Regular or unnumbered Infantry regiments are shown by the initial letters of their titles.

(b) Militia Cavalry (LH = Light Horse) and infantry regiments are indicated by the numbers allotted in about 1921, and their title then, as well as the numbers and titles used in World Wars I and II, are also shown.

Canadian Regiments

During World War I, although all Canadian Militia regiments had titles, these were not used in battle. For obscure reasons, mainly thought to be political, Canadian Expeditionary Force (CEF) numbered battalions were formed, which included part or all of the personnel of existing Militia regiments together with volunteer personnel, and these numbers were used in the records. After the war the CEF Battalions were perpetuated by the relevant Militia regiments and the Honours which the CEF Battalions had gained were awarded to these regiments. During World War II militia regiments served as units in their own right, and the titles themselves were used in the records. In the lists

(a) Regular Cavalry and Infantry regiments are shown by the initials of the title.
(b) Militia Cavalry and Infantry regiments are shown by the numbers allotted in the late 1880s or on subsequent raising, or by their title when they were actually raised after World War II and therefore had no numbers; although they were awarded participating Honours.
(c) A number of Militia Infantry regiments were converted to Armour during World War II. These have still been listed under Infantry to avoid confusion. They are GGFG 1, 6, 21, 25, 34, 54, 58, 86, and Calgary.

Indian Regiments

The Indian Army regiments are probably the most difficult to identify accurately and comprehensively. There have been many changes of number and title over the years, and many regiments raised in the early days of British involvement in India, largely by the East India Company and for the three Presidency Armies of Bengal, Madras and Bombay, were soon disbanded. A further complication is the number of regiments, mainly from Bengal, which mutinied in 1857 and whose records were expunged as punishment. Most of these regiments had already given good service to Britain, participated in many campaigns and won Honours, and these chronological lists now create the only current availability of this information. The major renumbering and retitling occurred in 1903 and again in the 1920s, and these parts of the indicator list are easily comprehensible; an earlier title has been included as these are sometimes used in narratives and it enables these regiments to be related to the earlier ones which ceased to exist. It is hoped that details of the regiments which did not figure in the 1903/1922 changes have been made reasonably comprehensible. In the lists and indexes

(a) Regular Cavalry, Artillery, Engineer and Infantry which existed from 1903 until after World War II (until partition) are shown by successive titles.
(b) A separate identification has had to be used for Cavalry and Infantry regiments during World War II. It would be totally confusing to use the earlier numbers and titles.
(c) Native Cavalry and Infantry regiments, all of which had British officers, are shown by the most meaningful titles used between 1824 and 1903. 'Native' is used as the terminology to show that these regiments had Indian personnel.
(d) Details of the Bengal native Cavalry and Infantry regiments which mutinied in 1857 are shown with their locations at the time.

New Zealand Regiments

As for the Australian regiments, numbers rather than titles have been used in the records. In the lists both Mounted Rifle (MR) and Infantry regiments are shown by number, except in one or two early cases, and the Indicator List indicates their actual titles.

South African Regiments

Because of the nature of the wars that have been fought in South Africa, and the vast size of the country and the limited population, an enormous number of volunteer or militia units, often very small and in no way able to be called regiments, were raised for short periods and then disbanded. Few of these have participated in sufficient numbers for them to be recognised for Honours or for participation. Some militia units, however, have been perpetuated in the existing Citizen Force regiments, although frequently with different titles and sometimes in a different arm. The chronological lists show all regiments by the relevant arm (MR—Mounted Rifles, SAMR—South African Mounted Rifles or Infantry) and by the numbers allotted in 1913. The Indicator List shows both the titles of the regiments prior to 1913, sometimes several, and the titles subsequently awarded or used. It does not show the titles allotted in the 1960 reorganisation. It will be appreciated that in some cases prior to 1913 more than one original regiment participated in a battle and that only one number is shown to represent the later title of which these regiments formed a part; but the text of Part II indicates these participants

African Regiments

These have not been shown in the Indicator Lists as they are included in the Chronological Tables without abbreviation. Although they originated as regiments of the British Army, they were subsequently administered by the Colonies from which they were raised, and are shown in the Tables after the letters 'AF' for clarity.

The Regiments included, the titles being those by which they were known at the time of the award of Honours, are

The Gambia Regiment
The Gold Coast Regiment
The King's African Rifles (recruited in various East African countries)
The Queen's Own Nigeria Regiment
The Northern Rhodesia Regiment
The Rhodesian African Rifles
The Sierra Leone Regiment
The West African Regiment

In each entry no national prefix is deemed necessary for British regiments, but Commonwealth regiments are prefixed appropriately. Additionally each list of regiments is also prefixed by the arm, e.g. Inf-, except for an initial entry of British Cavalry regiments. Although 'Cavalry' is now an outdated term it has been used for consistency, as have such identities as LH (Light Horse) or MR (Mounted Rifles), as these are still frequently used in the titles of the regiments.

Indicator Lists

Abbreviations (excluding those of regiments listed as Indicators)

AF	African Regiments	**IC**	Irregular Cavalry (Indian)
APC	Armoured Personnel Carrier	**IND**	India
App	Applied for Honour	**Inf**	Infantry
Arty	Artillery	**L**	Lancers
AUS	Australia	**LC**	Light Cavalry
Ben	Bengal	**LD**	Light Dragoons
Bn	Battalion	**LH**	Light Horse
Bom	Bombay	**LI**	Light Infantry
Bty	Battery	**LR**	London Regiment (TF/TA)
Cav	Cavalry	**(m)**	Mutinied
CDN	Canada	**Mad**	Madras
CLR	City of London Regiment (TF/TA)	**MG**	Machine Gun
Comp	Composite	**MR**	Mounted Rifles
Coy	Company	**Mtn**	Mountain
D	Dragoons	**NC**	Native Cavalry
DG	Dragoon Guards	**NI**	Native Infantry
FF	Frontier Force	**NWF**	North West Frontier
Fus	Fusiliers	**NZ**	New Zealand
Gds	Guards	**Regt**	Regiment
Gren	Grenadier	**SA**	South Africa
GR	Gurkha Rifles	**SAMR**	South African Mounted Rifles
H	Hussars (British) or Horse	**S&M**	Sappers and Miners
Hldrs	Highlanders	**Yeo**	Yeomanry

Above: The 16th Lancers breaking the square of Sikh infantry at the Battle of Aliwal, 28 January 1846, during the 1st Sikh War. Watercolour by Michael Angelo Hayes, c1850. *NAM*

British Regiments—Cavalry/Armour

Indicator	Title in Great War or earlier	Indicator	Title after 1922 and in World War II
LG	Life Guards	LG	Life Guards
RHG	Royal Horse Guards	RHG	Royal Horse Guards
1DG	1st King's Dragoon Guards	1DG	1st King's Dragoon Guards
2DG	2nd Queen's Dragoon Guards	2DG	The Queen's Bays (2nd Dragoon Guards)
3DG	3rd Prince of Wales's Dragoon Guards	3DG	3rd Carabiniers (Prince of Wales's Dragoon Guards)
4DG	4th Royal Irish Dragoon Guards	4/7DG	4th/7th Royal Dragoon Guards
5DG	5th Princess Charlotte of Wales's Dragoon Guards	5DG	5th Royal Inniskilling Dragoon Guards
6DG	6th Dragoon Guards (Carabiniers)	3DG	3rd Carabiniers (Prince of Wales's Dragoon Guards
7DG	7th Princess Royal's Dragoon Guards	4/7DG	4th/7th Royal Dragoon Guards
1D	1st Royal Dragoons	1D	1st Royal Dragoons
2D	2nd Dragoons (Royal Scots Greys)	2D	Royal Scots Greys (2nd Dragoons)
3D	3rd King's Own Hussars	3H	3rd King's Own Hussars
4D	4th Queen's Own Hussars	4H	4th Queen's Own Hussars
5D	5th Royal Irish Lancers	16/5L	16th/5th Lancers
6D	6th Inniskilling Dragoons	5DG	5th Royal Inniskilling Dragoon Guards
7D	7th Queen's Own Hussars	7H	7th Queen's Own Hussars
8D	8th King's Royal Irish Hussars	8H	8th King's Royal Irish Hussars
9D	9th Queen's Royal Lancers	9L	9th Queen's Royal Lancers
10D	10th Prince of Wales's Own Royal Hussars	10H	10th Prince of Wales's Own Royal Hussars
11D	11th Prince Albert's Own Hussars	11H	11th Prince Albert's Own Hussars
12D	12th Prince of Wales's Royal Lancers	12L	12th Prince of Wales's Royal Lancers
13D	13th Hussars	13/18H	13th/18th Royal Hussars (Queen Mary's Own)
14D	14th King's Hussars	14/20H	14th/20th King's Hussars
15LD	15th King's Hussars	15/19H	15th/19th King's Royal Hussars
16LD	16th Queen's Lancers	16/5L	16th/5th Lancers
17LD	17th Duke of Cambridge's Own Lancers	17/21L	17th/21st Lancers
18LD	18th King's Irish Hussars	13/18H	13th/18th Royal Hussars
19LD	(1st Bengal European Light Cavalry) 19th Hussars	15/19H	15/19th King's Royal Hussars
20LD	(2nd Bengal European Light Cavalry) 20th Hussars	14/20H	14th/20th King's Hussars
21LD	(3rd Bengal European Light Cavalry) 21st Empress of India's Lancers	17/21L	17th/21st Lancers
22LD	22nd Light Dragoons	22D	22nd Dragoons
23LD	23rd Lancers	23H	23rd Hussars
24LD	24th Light Dragoons	24L	24th Lancers
25LD	25th Light Dragoons	25D	25th Dragoons
26LD	26th Light Dragoons	26L	26th Lancers
27LD	27th Light Dragoons	27L	27th Lancers
RTR	Royal Tank Corps	RTR	Royal Tank Regiment

British Regiments—Yeomanry

Indicator	Title after 1908	Indicator	Title after 1908
Yeo		Yeo	
1	Royal Wiltshire	11	North Somerset
2	Warwickshire	12	Duke of Lancaster's
3	Yorkshire Hussars	13	Lanarkshire
4	Sherwood Rangers	14	Northumberland Hussars
5	Staffordshire	15	South Nottinghamshire Hussars
6	Shropshire	16	Denbighshire
7	Ayrshire	17	Westmoreland and Cumberland
8	Cheshire	18	Pembrokeshire
9	Yorkshire Dragoons	19	Royal East Kent
10	Leicestershire	20	Hampshire

British Regiments—Yeomanry (cont)

Indicator Yeo	Title after 1908	Indicator Yeo	Title after 1908
21	Royal Bucks Hussars	41	Norfolk
22	Derbyshire	42	Sussex
23	Dorset	43	Glamorgan
24	Royal Gloucestershire Hussars	44	Lincolnshire
25	Hertfordshire	45	City of London (Rough Riders)
26	Berkshire	46	2nd County of London, Westminster Dragoons
27	1st County of London, Middlesex Hussars	47	3rd/4th County of London (Sharpshooters)
28	Royal 1st Devon	48	Bedfordshire
29	Suffolk	49	Essex
30	Royal North Devon	50	King Edward's Horse
31	Worcestershire Hussars	51	Northamptonshire
32	West Kent	52	East Riding
33	West Somerset	53	Lovats Scouts
34	Oxfordshire Hussars	54	Scottish Horse
35	Montgomeryshire	WH	Welsh Horse
36	Lothian and Border Horse	Inns	Inns of Court
37	Glasgow	NIH	North Irish Horse
38	Lancashire Hussars	SIH	South Irish Horse
39	Surrey		
40	Fife and Forfar		

British Regiments—Guards

Indicator Guards	Title
GG	Grenadier Guards
CG	Coldstream Guards
SG	Scots Guards
IG	Irish Guards
WG	Welsh Guards

British Regiments—Infantry

Indicator Inf	Abbreviated Title prior to 1881	Indicator Inf	Commonest Title after 1881
1	Royal Scots	1	Royal Scots
2	Queen's Own Regiment	2	Queen's (Royal West Surrey) Regiment
3	East Kent Regiment (The Buffs)	3	Buffs (Royal East Kent Regiment)
4	King's Own Royal Regiment	4	King's Own (Lancaster) Regiment
5	Northumberland Fusiliers	5	Northumberland Fusiliers
6	Royal (First) Warwickshire Regiment	6	Royal Warwickshire Regiment
7	Royal Fusiliers	7	Royal Fusiliers (City of London Regiment)
8	King's Regiment	8	King's (Liverpool) Regiment
9	East Norfolk Regiment	9	Royal Norfolk Regiment
10	North Lincolnshire Regiment	10	Royal Lincolnshire Regiment
11	North Devonshire Regiment	11	Devonshire Regiment
12	East Suffolk Regiment	12	Suffolk Regiment
13	First Somersetshire Regiment	13	Somerset Light Infantry (Prince Albert's)
14	Buckinghamshire Regiment	14	The Prince of Wales's Own (West Yorkshire Regiment)
15	Yorkshire East Riding Regiment	15	East Yorkshire Regiment
16	Bedfordshire Regiment	16	Bedfordshire Regiment/Bedfordshire and Hertfordshire Regiment
17	Leicestershire Regiment	17	Leicestershire Regiment

British Regiments—Infantry (cont)

Indicator	Abbreviated Title prior to 1881	Indicator	Commonest Title after 1881
18	Royal Irish Regiment	18	Royal Irish Regiment (Disbanded 1922)
19	Yorkshire North Riding Regiment	19	Green Howards
20	East Devonshire Regiment	20	Lancashire Fusiliers
21	Royal North British Fusiliers	21	Royal Scots Fusiliers
22	Cheshire Regiment	22	Cheshire Regiment
23	Royal Welsh Fusiliers	23	Royal Welsh Fusiliers
24	Second Warwickshire Regiment	24	South Wales Borderers
25	King's Own Borderers	25	King's Own Scottish Borderers
26	Cameronians	26	1 Battalion Cameronians (Scottish Rifles)
27	Inniskilling Regiment	27	1 Battalion Inniskilling Fusiliers
28	North Gloucestershire Regiment	28	1 Battalion Gloucestershire Regiment
29	Worcestershire Regiment	29	1 Battalion Worcestershire Regiment
30	Cambridgeshire Regiment	30	1 Battalion East Lancashire Regiment
31	Huntingdonshire Regiment	31	1 Battalion East Surrey Regiment
32	Cornwall Light Infantry	32	1 Battalion Duke of Cornwall's Light Infantry
33	First Yorkshire West Riding Regiment	33	1 Battalion Duke of Wellington's Regiment
34	Cumberland Regiment	34	1 Battalion Border Regiment
35	Dorsetshire/Sussex Regiment	35	1 Battalion Royal Sussex Regiment
36	Hertfordshire Regiment	36	2 Battalion Worcestershire Regiment
37	North Hampshire Regiment	37	1 Battalion Hampshire Regiment
38	First Staffordshire Regiment	38	1 Battalion South Staffordshire Regiment
39	East Middlesex/Dorsetshire Regiment	39	1 Battalion Dorsetshire Regiment
40	Second Somersetshire Regiment	40	1 Battalion South Lancashire Regiment
41	Welch Regiment	41	1 Battalion Welch Regiment
42	Royal Highland Regiment	42	1 Battalion Black Watch (Royal Highlanders)
43	Monmouthshire Light Infantry	43	1 Battalion Oxfordshire Light Infantry/1 Battalion Oxfordshire and Buckinghamshire Light Infantry
44	East Sussex Regiment	44	1 Battalion Essex Regiment
45	First Nottinghamshire Regiment	45	1 Battalion Sherwood Foresters
46	South Devonshire Regiment	46	2 Battalion Duke of Cornwall's Light Infantry
47	Lancashire Regiment	47	1 Battalion Loyal (North Lancashire) Regiment
48	Northamptonshire Regiment	48	1 Battalion Northamptonshire Regiment
49	Hertfordshire Regiment	49	1 Battalion Royal Berkshire Regiment
50	The Queen's Own Regiment	50	1 Battalion Queen's Own Royal West Kent Regiment
51	Second Yorkshire West Riding Regiment	51	1 Battalion King's Own Yorkshire Light Infantry
52	Oxfordshire Regiment	52	2 Battalion Oxfordshire Light Infantry/2 Battalion Oxfordshire and Buckinghamshire Light Infantry
53	Shropshire Regiment	53	1 Battalion King's Shropshire Light Infantry
54	West Norfolk Regiment	54	2 Battalion Dorsetshire Regiment
55	Westmoreland Regiment	55	2 Battalion Border Regiment
56	West Essex Regiment	56	2 Battalion Essex Regiment
57	West Middlesex Regiment	57	1 Battalion Middlesex Regiment
58	Rutlandshire Regiment	58	2 Battalion Northamptonshire Regiment
59	Second Nottinghamshire Regiment	59	2 Battalion East Lancashire Regiment
60	60th Royal Americans	60	King's Royal Rifle Corps
61	South Gloucestershire Regiment	61	2 Battalion Gloucestershire Regiment
62	Wiltshire Regiment	62	1 Battalion Wiltshire Regiment (Duke of Edinburgh's)
63	West Suffolk Regiment	63	1 Battalion Manchester Regiment
64	Second Staffordshire Regiment	64	1 Battalion North Staffordshire Regiment (Prince of Wales's)
65	Second Yorkshire North Riding Regiment	65	1 Battalion York and Lancaster Regiment
66	Berkshire Regiment	66	2 Battalion Royal Berkshire Regiment

British Regiments—Infantry (cont)

Indicator	Abbreviated Title prior to 1881	Indicator	Commonest Title after 1881
67	South Hampshire Regiment	67	2 Battalion Hampshire Regiment
68	Durham Regiment	68	1 Battalion Durham Light Infantry
69	South Lincolnshire Regiment	69	2 Battalion Welch Regiment
70	Glasgow Lowland Regiment	70	2 Battalion East Surrey Regiment
71	Glasgow Highland Regiment	71	1 Battalion Highland Light Infantry
72	Seaforth (Duke of Albany's) Regiment	72	1 Battalion Seaforth Highlanders (Ross-shire Buffs)
73	Perthshire Regiment	73	2 Battalion Black Watch (Royal Highlanders)
74	74th Highlanders Regiment	74	2 Battalion Highland Light Infantry
75	Stirlingshire Regiment	75	1 Battalion Gordon Highlanders
76	Hindoostan Regiment	76	2 Battalion Duke of Wellington's Regiment
77	East Middlesex Regiment	77	2 Battalion Middlesex Regiment
78	Rosshire Buffs	78	2 Battalion Seaforth Highlanders (Ross-shire Buffs)
79	Cameron Highlanders	79	Queen's Own Cameron Highlanders
80	Staffordshire Volunteers	80	2 Battalion South Staffordshire Regiment
81	Loyal Lincoln Volunteers	81	2 Battalion Loyal (North Lancashire) Regiment
82	Prince of Wales's Volunteers	82	2 Battalion South Lancashire Regiment
83	Royal Glasgow Volunteers/ County of Dublin Regiment	83	1 Battalion Royal Irish Rifles/1 Battalion Royal Ulster Rifles
84	York and Lancaster Regiment	84	2 Battalion York and Lancaster Regiment
85	Bucks Volunteers	85	2 Battalion King's Shropshire Light Infantry
86	Shropshire Volunteers/Royal County Down Regiment	86	2 Battalion Royal Irish Rifles/2 Battalion Royal Ulster Rifles
87	Prince of Wales's Irish Regiment	87	1 Battalion Royal Irish Fusiliers
88	Connaught Rangers	88	1 Battalion Connaught Rangers (Disbanded 1922)
89	Princess Victoria's Regiment	89	2 Battalion Royal Irish Fusiliers
90	Perthshire Light Infantry	90	2 Battalion Cameronians (Scottish Rifles)
91	Argyllshire Regiment	91	1 Battalion Argyll and Sutherland Highlanders
92	92nd Highland Regiment	92	2 Battalion Gordon Highlanders
93	Sutherland Fencibles	93	2 Battalion Argyll and Sutherland Highlanders
94	Scotch Brigade	94	2 Battalion Connaught Rangers (disbanded 1922)
95	Derbyshire Regiment	95	2 Battalion Sherwood Foresters
96	96th Regiment	96	2 Battalion Manchester Regiment
97	Earl of Ulster's Regiment	97	2 Battalion Queen's Own Royal West Kent Regiment
98	Prince of Wales's Regiment	98	2 Battalion North Staffordshire Regiment
99	Lanarkshire Regiment	99	2 Battalion Wiltshire Regiment (Duke of Edinburgh's)
100	Royal Canadians	100	1 Battalion Prince of Wales's Leinster Regiment (disbanded 1922)
101	1st Bengal European Fusiliers	101	1 Battalion Royal Munster Fusiliers (disbanded 1922)
102	1st Madras European Fuisiliers	102	1 Battalion Royal Dublin Fusiliers (disbanded 1922)
103	1st Bombay Fusiliers	103	2 Battalion Royal Dublin Fusiliers (disbanded 1922)
104	2nd Bengal European Fusiliers	104	2 Battalion Royal Munster Fusiliers (disbanded 1922)
105	2nd Madras European Fusiliers	105	2 Battalion King's Own Yorkshire Light Infantry
106	2nd Bombay European Light Infantry	106	2 Battalion Durham Light Infantry
107	3rd Bengal Light Infantry	107	2 Battalion Royal Sussex Regiment
108	3rd Madras European Fusiliers	108	2 Battalion Inniskilling Fusiliers

British Regiments—Infantry (cont)

Indicator	Abbreviated Title prior to 1881	Indicator	Commonest Title after 1881
109	3rd Bombay European Light Infantry	109	2 Battalion Prince of Wales's Leinster Regiment (disbanded 1922)
RB	Rifle Brigade	RB	Rifle Brigade

Specialist Units

Indicator		Indicator	
Para		Para	Parachute Regiment
SAS		SAS	Special Air Service Regiment
GPR		GPR	Glider Pilot Regiment
Cdos		Cdos	Commando Association

British Army—Territorial Infantry

Indicator	Title after 1908	Indicator	Title after 1908
1CLR	1st City of London (Royal Fusiliers)	18LR	18th London (London Irish Rifles)
2CLR	2nd City of London (Royal Fusiliers)	19LR	19th London (St Pancras)
3CLR	3rd City of London (Royal Fusiliers)	20LR	20th London (The Queen's Own)
4CLR	4th City of London (Royal Fusiliers)	21LR	21st London (First Surrey Rifles)
5CLR	5th City of London (London Rifle Brigade)	22LR	22nd London (The Queen's)
6CLR	6th City of London (City of London Rifles)	23LR	23rd London (East Surrey)
7CLR	7th City of London (Post Office Rifles)	24LR	24th London (The Queen's)
8LR	8th London (Post Office Rifles)	25LR	25th London (County of London Cyclists)
9LR	9th London (Queen Victoria's Rifles)	28LR	28th London (Artist's Rifles)
10LR	10th London (Hackney)	Bucks	The Buckinghamshire Battalion
11LR	11th London (Finsbury Rifles)	Cambs	Cambridgeshire Regiment
12LR	12th London (The Rangers)	Hereford	Herefordshire Light Infantry
13LR	13th London (Kensington)	Herts	Hertfordshire Regiment
14LR	14th London (London Scottish)	Mon	Monmouthshire Regiment
15LR	15th London (Civil Service Rifles)	HAC	Honourable Artillery Company
16LR	16th London (Queen's Westminsters)	Cam U	Cambridge University OTC
17LR	17th London (Poplar & Stepney Rifles/Tower Hamlets Rifles)		

Australian Regiments—Light Horse/Armour

Indicator AUS-LH	Great War Title	Indicator AUS-LH	1921 Title	Indicator AUS-LH	World War II Title
1	7 (New South Wales Lancers)	1	1 (New South Wales Lancers)	1	1 Tank Battalion (Royal NSW Lancers)
2	2 (Queensland Mounted Infantry)	2	2 (Moreton) (Queensland Mounted Infantry)	2	2 Cavalry (Moreton Light Horse)
3	22 (South Australian Mounted Rifles)	3	3 (South Australian Mounted Rifles)	3	3 Recce Regiment (South Australian Mounted Rifles)
4	20 (Corangamite Light Horse)	4	4 (Corangamite Light Horse)	4	4 Motor Regiment (Corangamite Light Horse)
5	1 (Central Queensland Light Horse)	5	5 (Central Queensland Light Horse)	5	5 Motor Regiment (Wide Bay & Burnett Light Horse)
6	9 (New South Wales Mounted Rifles)	6	6 (New South Wales Mounted Rifles)	6	6 Cavalry (NSW Mounted Rifles)
7	11 (Australian Horse)	7	7 (Australian Horse)	7	7 Cavalry (Australian Horse)
8	16 (Indi)	8	8 (Indi)	8	8 Cavalry (Indi Light Horse)
9	24 (Flinders)	9	9 (Flinders)	9	9 Cavalry (Flinders Light Horse)

Australian Regiments—Light Horse/Armour (cont)

Indicator AUS-LH	Great War Title	Indicator AUS-LH	1921 Title	Indicator AUS-LH	World War II Title
10	25 (Western Australian Mounted Infantry)	10	10 (Western Australian Mounted Infantry)	10	10 Light Horse
11	3 (Darling Downs)	11	11 (Darling Downs)	11	11 Motor Regiment (Darling Downs)
12	5 (New England)	12	12 (New England)	12	12 Motor Regiment (New England Light Horse)
13	13 (Gippsland)	13	13 (Gippsland)	13	13 Motor Regiment (Gippsland Light Horse)
14	27 (North Queensland Light Horse)	14	14 (North Queensland)	14	14 Motor Regiment (West Moreton)
15	4 (Northern River Lancers)	15	15 (Northern River Lancers)	15	15 Motor Regiment (Northern River Lancers)
16	6 (Hunter River Lancers)	16	16 (Hunter River Lancers)	16	16 Motor Regiment (Hunter River Lancers)
17	17 (Campaspie Light Horse)	17	17 (Bendigo)	17	17 Motor Regiment (Prince of Wales's Light Horse)
18	18 (Light Horse)	18	18 (Adelaide Lancers)	18	18 Armoured Regiment (Adelaide Lancers)
19	19 { 19 (Yarrowee) / 29 (Port Phillip Horse) }	19	19 (Yarrowee)	19	{ 101 Motor Regiment (Wimmera Regiment) / 19 Machine Gun Regiment (Yarrowee Light Horse) }
20	15 (Victoria Mounted Rifles)	20	20 (Victoria Mounted Rifles)	20	20 Motor Regiment (Victoria Mounted Rifles)
21	28 (Illawarra)	21	21 (Illawarra)	21	21 Cavalry (Riverina Horse)
22	26 (Tasmanian Mounted Infantry)	22	22 (Tasmanian Mounted Infantry)	22	22 Motor Regiment (Tasmanian Mounted Infantry)
23	23 (Barossa)	23	23 (Barossa)	23	23 Recce Coy (Barossa Light Horse)
24	—	24	—	24	24 Motor Regiment (Gwydir Regiment)
25	—	25	—	25	25 Cavalry
26	—	26	—	26	26 Motor Regiment
2 A T Bn	—	2 A T Bn	—	2 A T Bn	2 Army Tank Battalion

Australian Regiments—Infantry

Indicator AUS-Inf	Great War Title	Indicator AUS-Inf	1921 Title	Indicator AUS-Inf	World War II Title
1	21 (Woollahra)	1	1 (East Sydney)	1	1/45 Infantry
2	16 (Newcastle)	2	2 (City of Newcastle)	2	41/2 Infantry
3	43 (Werriwa)	3	3 (Werriwa)	3	3/22 Infantry
4	—	4	4 (Australian Rifles)	4	4 Infantry
5	{ 51 (Albert Park) / 52 Infantry }	5	5 (Victorian Scottish)	5	5 Infantry
6	{ 62 (Carlton Rifles) / 64 (City of Melbourne) }	6	6 (Royal Melbourne)	6	6 Infantry
7	66 (Mount Alexander)	7	7 (North West Murray Borderers)	7	{ 8/7 Infantry }
8	{ 70 (Ballarat) / 71 (City of Ballarat) }	8	8 (City of Ballarat)	8	

Australian Regiments—Infantry (cont)

Indicator AUS-Inf	Great War Title	Indicator AUS-Inf	1921 Title	Indicator AUS-Inf	World War II Title
9	7 (Moreton)	9	9 (Moreton)	9	9 Infantry
10	78 (Adelaide Rifles) / 79 (Torrens) 80 (Gawler)	10	10 Adelaide Rifles	10	10 Infantry
11	87 Infantry / 88 (Perth)	11	11 (City of Perth)	11	11 Infantry
12	91 (Tasmanian Rangers)	12	12 (Launceston)	12	12/40 Infantry – 12/50 Infantry
13	14 (Hunter River)	13	13 (Maitland)	13	13/33 Infantry
14	49 (Prahran) / 50 (St Kilda)	14	14 (Prahran)	14	14/32 Infantry
15	8 (Oxley)	15	15 (Oxley)	15	15 Infantry
16	84 (Goldfields)	16	16 (Cameron Highlanders of Western Australia)	16	16 Infantry
17	17 Infantry / 18 (North Sydney)	17	17 (North Sydney)	17	17 Infantry
18	19 (Kuring-Gai)	18	18 (Kuring-Gai)	18	18 Infantry
19	22 Infantry	19	19 (South Sydney)	19	19 Infantry
20	20 (Parramatta) / 41 (Blue Mountains)	20	20 (Parramatta and Blue Mountains)	20	20/34 Infantry
21	73 Infantry	21	21 (Victorian Rangers)	21	23/21 Infantry
22	56 (Yarra Borderers)	22	22 (Richmond)	22	22 Infantry
23	69 Infantry / 72 Infantry	23	23 (City of Geelong)	23	23/21 Infantry
24	48 (Kooyong)	24	24 (Kooyong)	24	24 Infantry
25	11 (Darling Downs)	25	25 (Darling Downs)	25	25 Infantry
26	9 (Logan and Albert)	26	26 (Logan and Albert)	26	26 Infantry
27	74 (Boothby)	27	27 (South Australian Scottish)	27	27 Infantry
28	85 Infantry	28	28 (Swan)	28	28 Infantry
29	55 (Collingwood)	29	29 (East Melbourne)	29	29/46 Infantry
30	25 (City of Sydney)	30	(New South Wales Scottish)	30	30 Infantry
31	2 (Kennedy)	31	31 (Kennedy)	31	31/51 Infantry
32	65 (City of Footscray)	32	32 (Footscray)	32	14/32 Infantry
33	13 Infantry	33	33 (New England)	33	13/33 Infantry
34	37 (Illawarra)	34	34 (Illawarra)	34	20/34 Infantry
35	15 Infantry	35	35 (Newcastle's own)	35	35 Infantry
36	29 Infantry / 31 (Leichardt)	36	36 (St George's English Rifles)	36	36 Infantry
37	—	37	37 (Henty)	37	37/52 Infantry
38	67 (Bendigo)	38	38 (Bendigo)	38	38 Infantry
39	53 (Glenferrie)	39	39 (Hawthorn-Kew)	39	39 Infantry
40	93 (Derwent)	40	40 (Derwent)	40	40 Infantry – 12/40 Infantry
41	12 (Byron)	41	41 (Byron)	41	41 Infantry – 41/2 Infantry
42	3 (Port Curtis)	42	42 (Capricornia)	42	42 Infantry
43	76 (Hindmarsh) / 77 Infantry	43	43 (Hindmarsh)	43	43 Infantry
44	86 (West Australian Rifles)	44	44 (West Australian Rifles)	44	44 Infantry
45	38 Infantry / 39 Infantry	45	45 (St George's)	45	1/45 Infantry
46	46 (Brighton Rifles)	46	46 (Brighton Rifles)	46	29/46 Infantry
47	4 (Wide Bay)	47	47 (Wide Bay)	47	47 Infantry
48	—	48	48 (Torrens)	48	48 Infantry

Australian Regiments—Infantry (cont)

Indicator AUS-Inf	Great War Title	Indicator AUS-Inf	1921 Title	Indicator AUS-Inf	World War II Title
49	5 Infantry	49	49 (Stanley)	49	49 Infantry
50	81 (Wakefield) 82 (Barrier)	50	50 (Tasmanian Rangers)	50	50 Infantry – 12/50 Infantry
51	92 (Launceston)	51	51 (Far North Queensland)	51	31/51 Infantry
52	45 (Gippsland)	52	52 (Gippsland)	52	37/52 Infantry
53	35 Infantry	53	53 (West Sydney)	53	55/53 Infantry
54	42 (Lachlan-MacQuarie)	54	54 (Lachlan-MacQuarie)	54	54 Infantry
55	34 Infantry	55	55 (New South Wales Rifles)	55	55/53 Infantry
56	44 (Riverina)	56	56 (Riverina)	56	56 Infantry
57	57 Infantry	57	57 (Merri)	57	57/60 Infantry
58	58 (Essendon Rifles)	58	58 (Essendon-Cobourg-Brunswick Rifles)	59	58/59 Infantry
59	59 (Moreland Rifles) 63 (East Melbourne)	59	59 (Hume)		
60	54 (Merri) 60 (Brunswick-Carlton)	60	60 (Heidelburg)	60	57/60 Infantry
61	—	61	61 (Queensland and Cameron Highlanders)	61	61 Infantry
62	—	62	62 (Merauke)	62	62 Infantry
PIR	—	PIR	—	PIR	New Guinea Infantry (Pacific Islands Regiment)
PNG	—	PNG	—	PNG	Papua and New Guinea Volunteer Rifles
RAR	—	RAR	—	RAR	Royal Australian Regiment (formed in 1946 from 65, 66 and 67 Infantry Battalions of World War II)

Canadian Regiments—Cavalry

Indicator CDN-cav	1914–18 Title	Indicator	1940–46 Title
RCD	Royal Canadian Dragoons	RCD	1st Armd Car Regt (Royal Canadian Dragoons)
Strathcona	Lord Strathcona's Horse	Strathcona	2nd Armd Regt (Lord Strathcona's Horse)
FGH	Fort Garry Horse	FGH	10th Armd Regt (Fort Garry Horse)
GGBG	Governor General's Body Guard	GGBG	3rd Armd Recce Regt (Governor General's Horse Guards)
1	1st Hussars	1	6th Armd Regt (1st Hussars)
4	4th Hussars	4	4th Recce Regt (4th Princess Louise Dragoon Guards)
5	5th Princess Louise Dragoon Guards		
7	7th Hussars	7	16th Armd Regt (7th/11th Hussars) (see 11)
8	8th (Princess Louise's) New Brunswick Hussars	8	5th Armd Regt (Princess Louise's New Brunswick Hussars)
9	9th Mississauga Horse	9	3rd Armd Recce Regt (Governor General's Horse Guards)
11	11th Hussars	11	16th Armd Regt (7th/11th Hussars) (see 7)
12	12th Manitoba Dragoons	12	18th Armd Regt (12th Manitoba Dragoons) (Converted to Artillery)
14	14th Kings Canadian Hussars 27th Light Horse	14	8th Recce Regt (14th Canadian Hussars)
15	15th Light Horse	15	31st Recce Regt (Alberta Light Horse) (see 21)

Canadian Regiments—Cavalry (cont)

Indicator	1914–18 Title	Indicator	1940–46 Title
CDN-Cav			
16	16th Light Horse	16	Battleford Light Infantry (16th/22nd Saskatchewan Light Horse) (see 22 & Inf-Battleford)
17	17th Duke of York's Royal Canadian Hussars	17	7th Recce Regt (17th Royal Canadian Hussars)
18	18th Mounted Rifles	18	Manitoba Mounted Rifles
19	19th Alberta Dragoons	19	19th Alberta Dragoons (see Alta MR)
21	21st Alberta Hussars	21	31st Recce Regt (Alberta Light Horse) (see 15)
22	22nd Saskatchewan Light Horse	22	Battleford Light Infantry (see 16)
30	30th British Columbia Horse	30	9th Armd Regt (British Columbia Dragoons)
36	36th Prince Edward Island Light Horse	36	17th Armd Regt (Prince Edward Island Light Horse)
Alta MR	Alberta Mounted Rifles	**Alta MR**	19th Alberta Dragoons (see 19) See also Inf-GGFG. 1. 6. 21. 25. 34. 54. 58. 86. Calgary

Canadian Regiments—Infantry

Indicator	1914–18 Title	Indicator	1940–46 Title
CDN-Inf			
RCR	Royal Canadian Regiment	RCR	Royal Canadian Regiment
PPCLI	Princess Patricia's Canadian Light Infantry	PPCLI	Princess Patricia's Canadian Light Infantry
R22R	22nd (Canadien Francais) Battalion	R22R	Royal 22ieme Regiment
GGFG	Governor General's Foot Guards	GGFG	21st Armd Regt (Governor General's Foot Guards)
1	Canadian Grenadier Guards	1	22nd Armd Regt (Canadian Grenadier Guards)
2	Queen's Own Rifles of Canada	2	Queen's Own Rifles of Canada
3	Victoria Rifles of Canada	3	Victoria Rifles of Canada
5	Royal Highlanders of Canada	5	Black Watch (Royal Highland Regiment) Canada
6	Duke of Connaught's Own Rifles	6	13th Armd Regt (British Columbia Regiment)
7	7th Fusiliers	7	Canadian Fusiliers
8	Royal Rifles	8	Royal Rifles of Canada
9	Voltigeurs de Quebec	9	Voltigeurs de Quebec
10	Royal Grenadiers	10	Royal Regiment of Canada (Converted to Artillery)
11	Irish Fusiliers of Canada	—	
12	York Rangers	—	25th Armd Regt (Queen's York Rangers) (see Queen's)
13	Hamilton Regiment	13	Royal Hamilton Light Infantry (Wentworth Regiment) (see 77)
14	Princess of Wales's Own Rifles	—	Kingston Regiment (The Princess of Wales's Own) (converted to Artillery)
15	Argyll Light Infantry	—	
19	Lincoln Regiment	—	Lincoln and Welland Regiment (see 44)
20	Halton Rifles	20	Lorne Scots (Peel, Dufferin and Halton Regiment) (see 36)
21	Essex Fusiliers	21	Essex Scottish
22	Oxford Rifles	—	Oxford Rifles
23	Northern Fusiliers	—	Algonquin Regiment (see 97)
24	Kent Regiment	—	Kent Regiment
25	Elgin Regiment	25	25th Armd Delivery Regt (The Elgin Regiment)
28	Perth Regiment	28	Perth Regiment
29	Waterloo Regiment	29	Highland Light Infantry of Canada
31	Grey Regiment	—	26th Army Tank Bn (Grey and Simcoe Foresters) (see 35)
34	Ontario Regiment	34	11th Armd Regt (The Ontario Regiment)
35	Simcoe Foresters	—	26th Army Tank Bn (Grey and Simcoe Foresters) (see 31)
36	Peel Regiment	—	Lorne Scots (Peel, Dufferin and Halton Regiment) (see 20)

Canadian Regiments—Infantry (cont)

Indicator	1914–18 Title	Indicator	1940–46 Title
CDN-Inf			
37	Haldimand Rifles	— }	(Converted to Artillery)
38	Dufferin Rifles of Canada	— }	
40	Northumberland (Ontario) Regiment	—	Midland Regiment (see 46)
41	Brockville Rifles	—	(Converted to Artillery)
42	Lanark and Renfrew Regiment	42	Lanark and Renfrew Scottish
43	Duke of Cornwall's Own Rifles	43	Cameron Highlanders of Ottawa
44	Lincoln and Welland Regiment	44	Lincoln and Welland Regiment (see 19)
46	Durham Regiment	—	Midland Regiment (see 40)
48	48th Regiment Highlanders	48	48th Highlanders of Canada
49	Hastings Regiment	49	Hastings and Prince Edward Regiment
50	Gordon Highlanders of Canada	50	Canadian Scottish Regiment
51	Soo Rifles	—	Sault Ste Marie and Sudbury Regiment
52	Prince Albert Volunteers	—	Prince Albert Volunteers
53	Sherbrooke Regiment	53	Sherbrooke Regiment
54	Carabiniers de Sherbrooke	54	27th Armd Regt (Fusiliers de Sherbrooke)
57	Peterborough Rangers	—	Prince of Wales's Rangers (Peterborough Regiment)
58	Westmount Rifles	58	32nd Recce Regiment (Royal Montreal Regiment)
59	Stormont and Glengarry Regiment	59	Dundas, Stormont and Glengarry Highlanders
60	60th Rifles	—	20th Army Tank Bn (South Saskatchewan Regiment)
62	St John Fusiliers	—	South New Brunswick Regiment (see 74)
63	Halifax Rifles	—	23rd Armd Regt (Halifax Rifles)
65	Carbiniers Mont-Royal	65	Fusiliers Mont-Royal
66	Princess Louise Fusiliers	66	Princess Louise Fusiliers
67	Carleton Light Infantry	67	Carleton and York Regiment
69	Annapolis Regiment	69	West Nova Scotia Regiment (see 75)
72	Seaforth Highlanders	72	Seaforth Highlanders of Canada
73	Northumberland Regiment	73	North Shore (New Brunswick) Regiment)
74	New Brunswick Rangers	—	South New Brunswick Regiment (see 62)
75	Lunenburg Regiment	—	West Nova Scotia Regiment (see 69)
76	Colchester and Hants Rifles	76	North Nova Scotia Highlanders (see 93)
77	Wentworth Regiment	—	Royal Hamilton Light Infantry (Wentworth Regiment (see 13)
78	Pictou Highlanders	—	Pictou Highlanders
79	Cameron Highlanders of Canada	79	Queen's Own Cameron Highlanders of Canada
85	Regiment de Maisonneuve	85	Regiment de Maisonneuve
86	Three Rivers Regiment	86	12th Armd Regt (The Three Rivers Regiment)
90	Winnipeg Rifles	90	Royal Winnipeg Rifles
91	Canadian Highlanders	91	Argyll and Sutherland Highlanders of Canada
92	Dorchester Regiment	92	Regiment de la Chaudiere
93	Cumberland Regiment	—	North Nova Scotia Highlanders (see 76)
94	Victoria Regiment (Argyll Highlanders)	94	Cape Breton Highlanders
95	95th Rifles Saskatchewan	95	Regina Rifle Regiment
96	Lake Superior Regiment	96	Lake Superior Regiment
97	Algonquin Rifles	97	Algonquin Regiment (see 23)
99	Manitoba Rangers	—	(Converted to Artillery)
100	Winnipeg Grenadiers	100	Winnipeg Grenadiers
101	Edmonton Fusiliers	—	Edmonton Fusiliers
102	Rocky Mountain Rangers	—	Rocky Mountain Rangers
103	Calgary Rifles	103	Calgary Highlanders
104	Westminster Fusiliers	104	Westminster Regiment
105	Saskatoon Fusiliers	105	Saskatoon Light Infantry
106	Winnipeg Light Infantry	106	Winnipeg Light Infantry
110	Irish Regiment	110	Irish Regiment
Calgary	Calgary Regiment (1920)	**Calgary**	14th Armd Regt (Calgary Regiment)
Edmonton	Edmonton Regiment (1920)	**Edmonton**	Loyal Edmonton Regiment

Canadian Regiments—Infantry (cont)

Indicator	1914–18 Title	Indicator	1940–46 Title
CDN-Inf			
Vancouver	Vancouver Regiment (1920)	—	(Converted to Artillery)
Battleford	Battleford Light Infantry (1922)	—	Battleford Light Infantry (16th/22nd Saskatchewan Horse)
Queens	Queen's Rangers (1922)	—	25th Armd Regt (Queen's York Rangers) (see 12)
SAR	South Alberta Regiment (1922)	—	South Alberta Regiment
Sask	Saskatchewan Border Regiment (1922)	**Sask**	South Saskatchewan Regiment
Weyburn	Weyburn Regiment (1922)		
TS	Toronto Scottish	**TS**	Toronto Scottish
McGill	McGill University Contingent	—	—
Newfoundland	Newfoundland Regiment	—	Royal Newfoundland Regiment
	—	**Para**	Canadian Parachute Regiment
	—	**1 SS**	1st Special Services Regiment
	—	**1 APC**	1st Armoured Personnel Carrier Regiment

Indian Regiments—Cavalry/Armour

Indicator	Title in 1861 or before	Indicator	1903 Title	Subsequent title
IND-Cav		**IND-Cav**		
1	1 Skinners Horse	**1**	1 Lancers (Skinner's)	1 Lancers
2	2 Gardners Horse	**2**	2 Lancers (Gardner's)	2 Lancers
3	4 Baddeleys Horse	**3**	3 Skinner's Horse	1 Lancers
4	Oude Auxiliary Cavalry	**4**	4 Cavalry	2 Lancers
5	7 Irregular Cavalry	**5**	5 Cavalry	3 Cavalry
6	8 Irregular Cavalry	**6**	6 Cavalry	18 King Edward's Own Lancers
7	17 Irregular Cavalry	**7**	7 Hariana Lancers	
8	18 Irregular Cavalry	**8**	8 Cavalry	3 Cavalry
9	1 Hodson's Horse	**9**	9 Hodsons Horse	4 Hodson's Horse
10	2 Hodson's Horse	**10**	10 Lancers (Hodson's)	
11	1 Sikh Irregular Horse	**11**	11 Lancers (Probyn's)	5 King Edward's Own Lancers
12	2 Sikh Irregular Horse	**12**	12 Cavalry	
13	4 Sikh Irregular Horse	**13**	13 Lancers (Watson's)	6 Lancers (Watson's Horse)
14	Jat Horse	**14**	14 Murrays Jat Lancers	20 Lancers
15	Cureton's Multani Cavalry	**15**	15 Lancers (Cureton's Multanis)	
16	Rohilkand Horse	**16**	16 Cavalry	6 Lancers (Watson's Horse)
17	Robart's Horse	**17**	17 Cavalry	15 Lancers
18	2 Mahratta Horse	**18**	18 Lancers	19 King George's Own Lancers
19	Fane's Horse	**19**	19 Lancers (Fane's)	
20	1 Nizams Cavalry (Hyderabad)	**20**	20 Deccan Horse	9 Royal Deccan Horse
21	1 Punjab Cavalry	**21**	21 Cavalry (Daly's)	11 Prince Albert Victor's Own Cavalry
22	2 Punjab Cavalry	**22**	22 Sam Browne's Cavalry	12 Sam Browne's Cavalry
23	3 Punjab Cavalry	**23**	23 Cavalry (Frontier Force)	11 Prince Albert Victor's Own Cavalry
25	5 Punjab Cavalry	**25**	25 Cavalry (Frontier Force)	12 Sam Browne's Cavalry
26	1 Madras Native Cavalry	**26**	26 Light Cavalry	8 King George's Own Light Cavalry
27	2 Madras Native Cavalry	**27**	27 Light Cavalry	16 Light Cavalry
28	3 Madras Native Cavalry	**28**	28 Light Cavalry	7 Light Cavalry
29	2 Nizams Cavalry (Hyderabad)	**29**	29 Lancers (Deccan)	9 Royal Deccan Horse

Indian Regiments—Cavalry/Armour (cont)

Indicator IND-Cav	Title in 1861 or before	Indicator IND-Cav	1903 Title	Subsequent title
30	4 Nizams Cavalry (Hyderabad)	30	30 Lancers (Gordon's)	8 King George's Own Light Cavalry
31	1 Bombay Native Cavalry	31	31 Lancers ⎫	13 Duke of Connaught's
32	2 Bombay Native Cavalry	32	32 Lancers ⎬	Own Lancers
33	3 Bombay Native Cavalry	33	33 Light Cavalry ⎫	17 Queen Victoria's Own
34	Poona Horse	34	34 Poona Horse ⎬	Poona Horse
35	1 Scinde Horse	35	35 Scinde Horse ⎫	14 Cavalry (Scinde
36	2 Scinde Horse	36	36 Jacob's Horse ⎬	Horse)
37	—	37	37 Lancers (Baluch)	15 Lancers
38	1 Central India Horse	38	38 Central India Horse ⎫	
39	2 Central India Horse	39	39 Central India Horse ⎬	21 Central India Horse
Guides	Corps of Guides	Guides	Guides (Lumsden's)	10 Guides Cavalry
Aden	Aden Troop	Aden	Aden Troop	Aden Troop (disbanded 1929)

Indian Cavalry Regiments in World War II

Indicator IND-Cav	Title	Previous Indicator(s)	Indicator IND-Cav	Title	Previous Indicator(s)
1	1 Lancers (Skinner's)	1 & 3	13	13 Duke of Connaught's Own Lancers	31 & 32
2	2 Lancers (Gardner's)	2 & 4	14	14 Cavalry (Scinde Horse)	35 & 36
3	3 Cavalry	5 & 8	15	15 Lancers	17 & 37
4	4 Hodson's Horse	9 & 10	16	16 Light Cavalry	27
5	5 King Edward's Own Lancers	11 & 12	17	17 Queen Victoria's Own Poona Horse	33 & 34
6	6 Lancers (Watson's Horse)	13 & 16	18	18 King Edward's Own Cavalry	6 & 7
7	7 Light Cavalry	28	19	19 King George's Own Lancers	18 & 19
8	8 King George's Own Light Cavalry	26 & 30	20	20 Lancers	14 & 15
9	9 Royal Deccan Horse	20 & 29	21	21 Central India Horse	38 & 39
10	10 Guides Cavalry	Guides	40	40 Cavalry	—
11	11 Prince Albert Victor's Own ¿ Cavalry	21 & 23	41	41 Cavalry	—
12	12 Sam Browne's Cavalry	22 & 25	42	42 Cavalry	—

Indian Regiments—Cavalry (Disbanded)

Indicator IND-Ben NC (m)	Title before 1861	Indicator IND-Ben NC (m)	Title before 1861
1	1 Bengal Light Cavalry, mutinied 1857 Lucknow	8	8 Bengal Native Cavalry, mutinied 1857 Mian Mir
2	2 Bengal Light Cavalry, disbanded 1841	9	9 Bengal Light Cavalry, mutinied 1857 Sialkote
3	3 Bengal Native Cavalry, mutinied 1857 Meerut	10	10 Bengal Light Cavalry, mutinied 1857 Ferozepore
4	4 Bengal Native Cavalry, mutinied 1857 Umballa	11	11 Bengal Light Cavalry, mutinied 1857 Cawnpore
5	5 Bengal Native Cavalry, mutinied 1857 Peshawar		
6	6 Bengal Native Cavalry, mutinied 1857 Jullundur	1 Roh H	1 Rohilla Horse, mutinied 1857 Saugor
7	7 Bengal Native Cavalry, mutinied 1857 Lucknow	2 Roh H	2 Rohilla Horse, disbanded 1819
		3 Roh H	3 Rohilla Horse, transferred to Oude

Cavalry (Disbanded) (cont)

Indicator IND-Ben IC(m)	Title before 1861	Indicator IND-Ben IC (m)	Title before 1861
9	9 Bengal Irregular Cavalry, mutinied 1857 Hoshiarpore and Bunnu	15	15 Bengal Irregular Cavalry, mutinied 1857 Rawalpindi
10	10 Bengal Irregular Cavalry, mutinied 1857 Berhampore	4 Pun Cav	4 Punjab Cavalry, disbanded 1882
11	11 Bengal Irregular Cavalry, mutinied 1857 Sewgowlie	3 Sikh Cav	3 Sikh Irregular Cavalry, disbanded 1861
12	12 Bengal Irregular Cavalry, mutinied 1857 Benares	Oude Cav	Oude Irregular Cavalry, disbanded 1861
		Linds H	Linds Pathan Cavalry, disbanded 1861
13	13 Bengal Irregular Cavalry, mutinied 1857 Jhansi and Nowgong	1 Gwal Cav	1 Gwalior Cavalry, mutinied 1857
14	14 Bengal Irregular Cavalry, mutinied 1857 Sultanpore	2 Gwal Cav	2 Gwalior Cavalry, mutinied 1857
		Lahore	Lahore Light Horse, disbanded 1862

Indicator IND-Mad NC (1780)		Indicator IND-Mad NC (1780)	
1	1 Madras Native Cavalry (1780 raising), mutinied 1784	4	4 Madras Native Cavalry (1780 raising), mutinied 1784
2	2 Madras Native Cavalry (1780 raising), mutinied 1784		

Indicator IND-Mad NC (1785)		Indicator IND-Mad NC (1785)	
3	2 Madras Native Cavalry (1785 raising), disbanded 1796	4	3 Madras Native Cavalry (1785 raising), disbanded 1892

Indicator IND-Mad NC		Indicator IND-Mad NC (1785)	
5	5 Madras Native Cavalry, disbanded 1860	7	7 Madras Native Cavalry, disbanded 1860
6	6 Madras Native Cavalry, disbanded 1860	8	8 Madras Native Cavalry, mutinied 1857
		3 Scinde H	3 Scinde Horse, disbanded 1882
		2 S Mah H	2 Southern Mahratta Horse, disbanded 1862
		3 Hyd Cav	3 Hyderabad Cavalry, disbanded 1901

Indian Regiments—Infantry

Indicator IND-Inf	Title in 1824 or before	Indicator IND-Inf	1903 Title	Subsequent title
1	21 Bengal Native Infantry	1	1 Brahmans	disbanded 1932
2	31 Bengal Native Infantry	2	2 Rajput Light Infantry	1 (Queen Victoria's Own Light Infantry)/7 Rajput
3	32 Bengal Native Infantry	3	3 Brahmans	disbanded 1922
4	33 Bengal Native Infantry	4	4 Rajputs	2 (Prince Albert Victor's)/ 7 Rajput
5	42 Bengal Native Infantry	5	5 Light Infantry	disbanded 1922
6	43 Bengal Native Infantry	6	6 Jat Light Infantry	1 Royal (Light Infantry)/ 9 Jat
7	47 Bengal Native Infantry	7	7 Rajputs	3 (Duke of Connaught's Own)/7 Rajput
8	59 Bengal Native Infantry	8	8 Rajputs	4/7 Rajput
9	Bhopal Levy	9	9 Bhopal	4 (Bhopal)/16 Punjab
10	65 Bengal Native Infantry	10	10 Jats	3/9 Jat
11	70 Bengal Native Infantry	11	11 Rajputs	5/7 Rajput
12	3 Shah Shujas Infantry	12	12 (Khelat-i-Ghilzie) Pioneers	disbanded 1933
13	Shekhawati Battalion	13	13 Rajputs	10 (Shekhawati)/6 Rajputana Rifles

Indian Regiments—Infantry (cont)

Indicator IND-Inf	Title in 1861 or before	Indicator IND-Inf	1903 Title	Subsequent title
14	Ferozepore Battalion	14	14 Sikhs	1 (Ferozepore)/11 Sikh
15	Ludhiana Regiment	15	15 Sikhs	2 (Ludhiana)/11 Sikh
16	Lucknow Regiment	16	16 Rajputs	10 (Lucknow)/7 Rajput
17	Loyal Purbiah Regiment	17	17 Infantry (Loyal)	disbanded 1921
18	Alipore Regiment	18	18 Infantry	10/9 Jat
19	7 Punjab Infantry	19	19 Punjabis	1/14 Punjab
20	8 Punjab Infantry	20	20 Infantry (Brownlow's)	2 (Brownlow's)/14 Punjab
21	9 Punjab Infantry	21	21 Punjabis	10/14 Punjab
22	11 Punjab Infantry	22	22 Punjabis	3/14 Punjab
23	15 (Pioneer) Punjab Infantry	23	23 Sikh Pioneers	1 Sikh Light Infantry
24	16 Punjab Infantry	24	24 Punjabis	4/14 Punjab
25	17 Punjab Infantry	25	25 Punjabis	1/15 Punjab
26	18 Punjab Infantry	26	26 Punjabis	2/15 Punjab
27	19 Punjab Infantry	27	27 Punjabis	3/15 Punjab
28	20 Punjab Infantry	28	28 Punjabis	4/15 Punjab
29	21 Punjab Infantry	29	29 Punjabis	10/15 Punjab
30	22 Punjab Infantry	30	30 Punjabis	1/16 Punjab
31	23 Punjab Infantry	31	31 Punjabis	2/16 Punjab
32	24 (Pioneer) Punjab Infantry	32	32 Sikh Pioneers	2 Sikh Light Infantry
33	Allahabad Levy	33	33 Punjabis	3/16 Punjab
34	Futtehgurh Levy	34	34 Sikh Pioneers	3 (Royal) Sikh Light Infantry
35	Mynpoorie Levy	35	35 Sikhs	10/11 Sikh
36	Bareilly Levy	36	36 Sikhs	4/11 Sikh
37	Meerut Levy	37	37 Dogras	1 (Prince of Wales's Own)/17 Dogra
38	Agra Levy	38	38 Dogras	2/17 Dogra
39	Allygurh Levy	39	39 Garhwal Rifles	18 Royal Garhwal Rifles
40	Shahjehanpore Levy	40	40 Pathans	5/14 Punjab
41	1 Gwalior Infantry	41	41 Dogras	3/17 Dogra
42	Meena Battalion	42	42 Deoli	disbanded 1921
43	Erinpura Infantry	43	43 Erinpura	disbanded 1921
44	Mhairwara Battalion	44	44 Merwara	disbanded 1922
45	1 Bengal Military Police Battalion	45	45 Sikhs	3 (Rattray's)/11 Sikh
46	—	46	46 Punjabis	10/16 Punjab
47	—	47	47 Sikhs	5 (Duke of Connaught's Own)/11 Sikh
48	—	48	48 Pioneers	disbanded 1926
50	—	50	50 Kumaon Rifles	disbanded 1923
51	1 Sikh Infantry	51	51 Sikhs (Frontier Force)	1 (Sikhs/12 Frontier Force Regiment
52	2 Sikh Infantry	52	52 Sikhs (Frontier Force)	2 (Sikhs)/12 Frontier Force Regiment
53	3 Sikh Infantry	53	53 Sikhs (Frontier Force)	3 (Sikhs)/12 Frontier Force Regiment
54	4 Sikh Infantry	54	54 Sikhs (Frontier Force)	4 (Sikhs)/12 Frontier Force Regiment
55	1 Punjab Infantry	55	55 Coke's Rifles	1 (Coke's)/13 Frontier Force Rifles
56	2 Punjab Infantry	56	56 Punjabi Rifles	2/13 Frontier Force Rifles
57	4 Punjab Infantry	57	57 Wilde's Rifles	4 (Wilde's)/13 Frontier Force Rifles
58	5 Punjab Infantry	58	58 Vaughan's Rifles	5/13 Frontier Force Rifles
59	6 Punjab Infantry	59	59 Scinde Rifles	6 Royal Scinde/13 Frontier Force Rifles

Indian Regiments—Infantry (cont)

Indicator IND-Inf	Title in 1861 or before	Indicator IND-Inf	1903 Title	Subsequent title
61	1 Madras Native Infantry	61	61 Pioneers	disbanded 1938
62	2 Madras Native Infantry	62	62 Punjabis	1/1 Punjab
63	3 Madras Native Infantry	63	63 Palamcottah Light Infantry	disbanded 1922
64	4 Madras Native Infantry	64	64 Pioneers	disbanded 1933
65	5 Madras Native Infantry	65	65 Carnatic Light Infantry	absorbed by 2/6 Gurkha Rifles
66	6 Madras Native Infantry	66	66 Punjabis	2/1 Punjab
67	7 Madras Native Infantry	67	67 Punjabis	1/2 Punjab
8 GR	8 Madras Native Infantry	8 GR	8 Gurkha Rifles	absorbed by 8 Gurkha Rifles
69	9 Madras Native Infantry	69	69 Punjabis	2/2 Punjab
10 GR	10 Madras Native Infantry	10 GR	70 Burma Rifles	20 Burma Rifles
71	11 Madras Native Infantry	71	71 Coorg Rifles	absorbed by 2/9 Gurkha Rifles
72	12 Madras Native Infantry	72	72 Punjabis	3/2 Punjab
73	13 Madras Native Infantry	73	73 Carnatic	disbanded 1928
74	14 Madras Native Infantry	74	74 Punjabis	disbanded 1939
75	15 Madras Native Infantry	75	75 Carnatic	disbanded 1926
76	16 Madras Native Infantry	76	76 Punjabis	3/1 Punjab
77	17 Madras Native Infantry	77	77 Moplah Rifles	disbanded 1907
78	25 Madras Native Infantry	78	78 Moplah Rifles	absorbed by 2/7 Gurkha Rifles
79	19 Madras Native Infantry	79	79 Carnatic	disbanded 1923
80	20 Madras Native Infantry	80	80 Carnatic	disbanded 1921
81	21 Madras Native Infantry	81	81 Pioneers	disbanded 1933
82	22 Madras Native Infantry	82	82 Punjabis	5/1 Punjab
83	23 Madras Native Infantry	83	83 Wallajahbad Light Infantry	disbanded 1923
84	24 Madras Native Infantry	84	84 Punjabis	10/1 Punjab
85		85	85 Burma Rifles	3/20 Burma Rifles
86	26 Madras Native Infantry	86	86 Carnatic	disbanded 1926
87	27 Madras Native Infantry	87	87 Punjabis	5/2 Punjab
88	28 Madras Native Infantry	88	88 Carnatic	disbanded 1922
89	29 Madras Native Infantry	89	89 Punjabis	1/8 Punjab
90	30 Madras Native Infantry	90	90 Punjabis	2/8 Punjab
91	31 Madras Native Infantry	91	91 Punjabis (Light Infantry)	3/8 Punjab
92	32 Madras Native Infantry	92	92 Punjabis	4 (Prince of Wales's Own)/8 Punjab

Indian Regiments—Infantry (cont)

Indicator IND-Inf	Title in 1861 or before	Indicator IND-Inf	1903 Title	Subsequent title
93	33 Madras Native Infantry	93	93 Burma	5 (Burma)/8 Punjab
94	1 Nizams Infantry	94	94 Russell's	1 (Russell's)/19 Hyderabad
95	2 Nizams Infantry	95	95 Russell's	10 (Russell's)/19 Hyderabad
96	3 Nizams Infantry	96	96 Berar	2 (Berar)/19 Hyderabad
97	4 Nizams Infantry	97	97 Deccan	disbanded 1931
98	7 Nizams Infantry	98	98 Infantry	4/19 Hyderabad
99	8 Nizams Infantry	99	99 Deccan	disbanded 1924
101	1 Grenadier Bombay Native Infantry	101	101 Grenadiers	1/4 Bombay Grenadiers
102	2 Bombay Native Infantry	102	102 Grenadiers	2 (King Edward's Own)/4 Bombay Grenadiers
103	3 Bombay Native Light Infantry	103	103 Mahratta Light Infantry	1/5 Mahratta Light Infantry
104	4 Bombay Native Infantry	104	104 Wellesley's	1 (Wellesley's)/6 Rajputana Rifles
105	5 Bombay Native Infantry	105	105 Mahratta Light Infantry	2/5 Mahratta Light Infantry
106	6 Bombay Native Infantry	106	106 Hazara Pioneers	disbanded 1933
107	7 Bombay Native Infantry	107	107 Pioneers	disbanded 1933
108	8 Bombay Native Infantry	108	108 Infantry	disbanded 1930
109	9 Bombay Native Infantry	109	109 Infantry	disbanded 1930
110	10 Bombay Native Infantry	110	110 Mahratta Light Infantry	3/5 Mahratta Light Infantry
111	11 Bombay Native Infantry	111	111 Mahars	disbanded 1922
112	12 Bombay Native Infantry	112	112 Infantry	disbanded 1923
113	13 Bombay Native Infantry	113	113 Infantry	10/4 Bombay Grenadiers
114	14 Bombay Native Infantry	114	114 Mahrattas	10/5 Mahratta Light Infantry
115	15 Bombay Native Infantry, disbanded 1882			
116	16 Bombay Native Infantry	116	116 Mahrattas	4/5 Mahratta Light Infantry
117	17 Bombay Native Infantry	117	117 Mahrattas	5 (Royal)/5 Mahratta Light Infantry
118	18 Bombay Native Infantry, disbanded 1882			
119	19 Bombay Native Infantry	119	119 Infantry (Mooltan)	2 (Mooltan)/9 Jat
120	20 Bombay Native Infantry	120	120 Rajputana	2/6 Rajputana Rifles
121	21 Marine Bombay Native Infantry	121	121 Pioneers	disbanded 1926
122	22 Bombay Native Infantry	122	122 Rajputana	3/6 Rajputana Rifles
123	23 Bombay Native Infantry	123	123 Outram's Rifles	4 (Outram's)/6 Rajputana Rifles
124	24 Bombay Native Infantry	124	124 Baluchistan	1 (Duke of Connaught's Own)/10 Baluch)
125	25 Bombay Native Infantry	125	125 Napier's Rifles	5 (Napier's)/6 Rajputana Rifles
126	26 Bombay Native Infantry	126	126 Baluchistan	2/10 Baluch

Indian Regiments—Infantry (cont)

Indicator IND-Inf	Title in 1861 or before	Indicator IND-Inf	1903 Title	Subsequent title
127	1 Baluch Battalion	127	127 Baluch Light Infantry	3 (Queen Mary's Own)/ Baluch
128	28 Bombay Native Infantry	128	128 Pioneers	disbanded 1933
129	2 Baluch Battalion	129	129 Baluchis	4 (Duke of Connaught's Own)/10 Baluch
130	1 Jacob's Rifles	130	130 Baluchis (Jacob's Rifles)	5 (Jacobs Rifles)/ Baluch
Guides	Corps of Guides Infantry	Guides	Queen's Own Corps of Guides (Lumsden's)	5 (Corps of Guides)/ Frontier Force
150	—	150	150 Infantry	
151	—	151	151 Sikh Infantry	
152	—	152	152 Punjabis	disbanded 1922
153	—	153	153 Punjabis	
154	—	154	154 Infantry	
1 GR	4 Nasiri Rifle Battalion	1 GR	1 Gurkha Rifles (Malaun)	1 King George V's Own Gurkha Rifles
2 GR	Sirmoor Battalion	2 GR	2 Gurkha Rifles (Sirmoor)	2 King Edward VII's Own Gurkha Rifles
3 GR	Kamaon Battalion	3 GR	3 Gurkha Rifles	3 Queen Alexandra's Own Gurkha Rifles
4 GR	Extra Gurkha Regiment	4 GR	4 Gurkha Rifles	4 Prince of Wales's Own Gurkha Rifles
5 GR	25 Punjab (Hazara)	5 GR	5 Gurkha Rifles (Frontier Force)	5 Royal Gurkha Rifles (Frontier Force)
1/6 GR	1 Assam Light Infantry	1/6 GR	6 Gurkha Rifles	6 Gurkha Rifles
2/7 GR	—	2/7 GR	7 Gurkha Rifles	7 Gurkha Rifles
1/8 GR	16 Sylhet Local Battalion	1/8 GR	1/8 Gurkha Rifles	8 Gurkha Rifles
2/8 GR	2 Assam Light Infantry	2/8 GR	2/8 Gurkha Rifles	
1/9 GR	69 Bengal Native Infantry	1/9 GR	9 Gurkha Rifles	9 Gurkha Rifles
10 GR	—	10 GR	10 Gurkha Rifles	10 Gurkha Rifles
11 GR	—	11 GR	11 Gurkha Rifles	11 Gurkha Rifles

Indian Regiments—Infantry (disbanded)

Indicator IND-Ben Sepoys (1764)	Title before 1861	Indicator IND-Ben Sepoys (1764)	Title before 1861
2	2 Bengal Sepoys, destroyed at Patna 1763	5	5 Bengal Sepoys, destroyed at Patna 1763
3	3 Bengal Sepoys, destroyed at Patna 1763	7	7 Bengal Sepoys, mutinied 1784

Indicator IND-Ben Sepoys (1784)		Indicator IND-Ben Sepoys (1784)	
18	18 Bengal Battalion, absorbed 1796	26	26 Bengal Battalion, absorbed 1796
21	21 Bengal Battalion, absorbed 1796	28	28 Bengal Battalion, disbanded 1785
24	24 Bengal Battalion, absorbed 1796	32	32 Bengal Battalion, disbanded 1785

Indicator IND-Ben NI (m)			
1	1 Bengal Native Infantry, mutinied 1857 Cawnpore	5	5 Bengal Native Infantry, mutinied 1857 Umballa
2	2 Bengal Native Infantry, mutinied 1857 Barrackpore	6	6 Bengal Native Infantry, mutinied 1857 Allahabad
3	3 Bengal Native Infantry, mutinied 1857 Phillour	7	7 Bengal Native Infantry, mutinied 1857 Dinapore
4	4 Bengal Native Infantry, disbanded 1861	8	8 Bengal Native Infantry, mutinied 1857 Dinapore

Indian Regiments—Infantry (Disbanded) (contd)

Indicator IND-Ben NI (m)	Title before 1861	Indicator IND-Ben NI (m)	Title before 1861
9	9 Bengal Native Infantry, mutinied 1857 Aligarh	40	40 Bengal Native Infantry, mutinied 1857 Dinapore
10	10 Bengal Native Infantry, mutinied 1857 Fatehgarh	41	41 Bengal Native Infantry, mutinied 1857 Sitapore
11	11 Bengal Native Infantry, mutinied 1857 Meerut	44	44 Bengal Native Infantry, mutinied 1857 Agra
12	12 Bengal Native Infantry, mutinied 1857 Nowgong and Jhansi	45	45 Bengal Native Infantry, mutinied 1857 Ferozepore
13	13 Bengal Native Infantry, mutinied 1857 Lucknow	46	46 Bengal Native Infantry, mutinied 1857 Sialkote
14	14 Bengal Native Infantry, mutinied 1857 Jhelum	47	47 Bengal Native Infantry, mutinied 1824
15	15 Bengal Native Infantry, mutinied 1857 Nasirabad	48	48 Bengal Native Infantry, mutinied 1857 Lucknow
16	16 Bengal Native Infantry, mutinied 1857 Mian Mir	49	49 Bengal Native Infantry, mutinied 1857 Mian Mir
17	17 Bengal Native Infantry, mutinied 1857 Azamgarh	50	50 Bengal Native Infantry, mutinied 1857 Nagode
18	18 Bengal Native Infantry, mutinied 1857 Bareilly	51	51 Bengal Native Infantry, mutinied 1857 Peshawar
19	19 Bengal Native Infantry, mutinied 1857 Barrackpore	52	52 Bengal Native Infantry, mutinied 1857 Jubbulpore
20	20 Bengal Native Infantry, mutinied 1857 Meerut	53	53 Bengal Native Infantry, mutinied 1857 Cawnpore
22	22 Bengal Native Infantry, mutinied 1857 Fyzabad	54	54 Bengal Native Infantry, mutinied 1857 Delhi
23	23 Bengal Native Infantry, mutinied 1857 Mhow	55	55 Bengal Native Infantry, mutinied 1857 Nowshera
24	24 Bengal Native Infantry, mutinied 1857 Peshawar	56	56 Bengal Native Infantry, mutinied 1857 Cawnpore
25	25 Bengal Native Infantry, mutinied 1857	57	57 Bengal Native Infantry, mutinied 1857 Ferozepore
26	26 Bengal Native Infantry, mutinied 1857 Mian Mir	58	58 Bengal Native Infantry, mutinied 1857 Rawalpindi
27	27 Bengal Native Infantry, mutinied 1857 Peshawar	60	60 Bengal Native Infantry, mutinied 1857 Umballa
28	28 Bengal Native Infantry, mutinied 1857 Shahjehanpore	61	61 Bengal Native Infantry, mutinied 1857 Jullundur
29	29 Bengal Native Infantry, mutinied 1857 Moradabad	62	62 Bengal Native Infantry, mutinied 1858 Multan
30	30 Bengal Native Infantry, mutinied 1857 Nasirabad	64	64 Bengal Native Infantry, mutinied 1857 Peshawar
34	34 Bengal Native Infantry, mutinied 1844 Barrackpore	67	67 Bengal Native Infantry, mutinied 1857 Agra
35	35 Bengal Native Infantry, mutinied 1857 Amritsar	68	68 Bengal Native Infantry, mutinied 1857 Bareilly
36	36 Bengal Native Infantry, mutinied 1857 Jullundur	69	69 Bengal Native Infantry, mutinied 1857 Multan
37	37 Bengal Native Infantry, mutinied 1857 Benares	71	71 Bengal Native Infantry, mutinied 1857 Lucknow
38	38 Bengal Native Infantry, mutinied 1857 Delhi	72	72 Bengal Native Infantry, mutinied 1857 Neemuch
39	39 Bengal Native Infantry, mutinied 1857 Dera Ismail Khan	73	73 Bengal Native Infantry, mutinied 1857 Jalpaigori & Dacca

Indian Regiments—Infantry (cont)

Indicator	Title before 1861
IND-Ben NI (m)	
3 Pun	3 Punjab, disbanded 1882
12 Pun	12 Punjab, disbanded 1861
14 Pun	14 Punjab, disbanded 1861
1 Gwal	1 Gwalior Regiment, disbanded 1882
2 Gwal	2 Gwalior Regiment, disbanded 1861
Ramgarh	Ramgarh Local Battalion, disbanded 1826
IND-Mad Sepoys	
2	2 Madras Coast Sepoys, disbanded 1785
11	11 Madras Coast Sepoys, disbanded 1769
IND-Mad NI (1777)	
18	18 Madras Native Infantry, disbanded 1796
IND-Mad NI (1786)	
22	22 Madras Native Infantry, disbanded 1785
23	23 Madras Native Infantry, disbanded 1785
24	24 Madras Native Infantry, disbanded 1785
IND-Mad NI	
18	18 Madras Native Infantry, disbanded 1864
34	34 Madras Native Infantry, disbanded 1882
35	35 Madras Native Infantry, disbanded 1882
36	36 Madras Native Infantry, disbanded 1882
37	37 Madras Native Infantry, disbanded 1882
38	38 Madras Native Infantry, disbanded 1882
39	39 Madras Native Infantry, disbanded 1882
IND-Bom Sepoy	
3	3 Bombay Sepoys, disbanded 1796
4	4 Bombay Sepoys, disbanded 1796
6	6 Bombay Sepoys, absorbed 1784
10	10 Bombay Sepoys, disbanded 1785
11	11 Bombay Sepoys, destroyed at Bednor 1784
IND-Bom NI	
6	6 Bombay Native Infantry, disbanded 1882
11	11 Bombay Native Infantry, disbanded 1882
15	15 Bombay Native Infantry, disbanded 1882
IND-Ben NI (m)	
Dinajpur	Dinajpur Local Battalion, disbanded 1826
Champaran	Champaran Light Infantry, disbanded 1826
Gwalior Contingent	2, 3, 4, 5, 6, 7 Battalions, mutinied 1857
IND-Mad Sepoys	
13	13 Madras Coast Sepoys, disbanded 1785
IND-Mad NI (1786)	
25	25 Madras Native Infantry, disbanded 1785
27	27 Madras Native Infantry, disbanded 1785
IND-Mad NI	
41	41 Madras Native Infantry, disbanded 1882
43	43 Madras Native Infantry, disbanded 1864
45	45 Madras Native Infantry, disbanded 1862
49	49 Madras Native Infantry, disbanded 1862
Mad Rif	Madras Rifle Corps, disbanded 1830
Mad Bdgd	Madras Bodyguard
IND-Bom Sepoy	
12	12 Bombay Sepoys, absorbed 1784
13	13 Bombay Sepoys, absorbed 1784
14	14 Bombay Sepoys, absorbed 1784
15	15 Bombay Sepoys, destroyed at Bednor 1784
IND-Bom NI	
18	18 Bombay Native Infantry, disbanded 1882
21	21 Bombay Native Infantry, disbanded 1857
Kandesh	Kandesh Bhil Battalion, became Police Corps 1850

Indian Infantry Regiments in World War II

Indicator	Title	Previous Indicator	Indicator	Title	Previous Indicator
1/1	1 Punjab Regiment	62	5/9	9 Jat Regiment	—
2/1		66	6/9		—
3/1		76	MG/9		
5/1		82	1/10	10 Baluch Regiment	124
10/1		84	2/10		126
1/2	2 Punjab Regiment	67	3/10		127
2/2		69	4/10		129
3/2		72	5/10		130
5/2		87	1/11	11 Sikh Regiment	14
7/2		—	2/11		15
13/2		—	3/11		45
1/4	4 Bombay Grenadiers	102	4/11		36
2/4		108	5/11		47
3/4		—	7/11		—
4/4		—	10/11		35
5/4		—	1/12	12 Frontier Force Regiment	51
9/4		—	2/12		52
10/4		113	3/12		53
1/5	5 Mahratta Light Infantry	103	4/12		54
2/5		105	5/12		Guides
3/5		110	1/13	13 Frontier Force Regiment	55
4/5		116	2/13		56
5/5		117	4/13		57
6/5		—	5/13		58
10/5		114	6/13		59
17/5		—	1/14	14 Punjab Regiment	19
1/6	6 Rajputana Rifles	104	2/14		20
2/6		120	3/14		22
3/6		122	4/14		24
4/6		123	5/14		40
5/6		125	10/14		21
6/6		—	1/15	15 Punjab Regiment	25
7/6		—	2/15		26
8/6		—	3/15		27
10/6		13	4/15		28
17/6		—	10/15		29
MG/6		—	1/16	16 Punjab Regiment	30
1/7	7 Rajput Regiment	2	2/16		31
2/7		4	3/16		33
3/7		7	4/16		9
4/7		8	10/16		46
5/7		11	1/17	17 Dogra Regiment	37
6/7		—	2/17		38
10/7		16	3/17		41
17/7		—	4/17		—
20/7		—	1/18	18 Royal Garhwal Regiment	39
1/8	8 Punjab Regiment	89	2/18		
2/8		90	3/18		
3/8		91	10/18		—
4/8		92	1/19	19 Hyderabad Regiment	94
5/8		93	2/19		96
14/8		—	4/19		98
15/8		—	6/19		—
1/9	9 Jat Regiment	6	10/19		95
2/9		119	1/20	20 Burma Rifles	
3/9		10	2/20		70
4/9		10	4/20		
			10/20		85
			3/20		

Indian Infantry Regiments in World War II (cont)

Indicator	Title	Previous Indicator	Indicator	Title	Previous Indicator
1 Sikh LI		23	3GR	3 Queen Alexandra's Own Gurkha Rifles	3GR
2 Sikh LI	Sikh Light Infantry	32	4GR	4 Prince of Wales's Own Gurkha Rifles	4GR
3 Sikh LI		34	5GR	5 Royal Gurkha Rifles	5GR
Gds	Brigade of Guards	—	6GR	6 Gurkha Rifles	6GR
Para	Parachute Regiment	—	7GR	7 Gurkha Rifles	7GR
Bihar	Bihar Regiment	—	8GR	8 Gurkha Rifles	8GR
Assam	Assam Regiment	—	9GR	9 Gurkha Rifles	9GR
Jammu & Kashmir	Jammu and Kashmir Regiment	—	10GR	10 Gurkha Rifles	10GR
1GR	1 King George V's Own Gurkha Rifles	1GR	11GR	11 Gurkha Rifles	—
2GR	2 King Edward VII's Own Gurkha Rifles	2GR			

Indian Regiments—Artillery

Indicator IND-Mtn Bty	Title in 1861 or before	Indicator IND-Mtn Bty	1903 Title	Subsequent Title
1	2 Horse Light Field Battery Punjab Frontier Force	1	21 Kohat Mountain Battery Frontier Force	1 Royal (Kohat) Mountain Battery
2	3 Horse Light Field Battery Punjab Frontier Force	2	22 Derajat Mountain Battery Frontier Force	2 (Derajat) Mountain Battery
3	Peshawar Mountain Train Punjab Frontier Force	3	23 Peshawar Mountain Battery Frontier Force	3 (Peshawar) Mountain Battery
4	Hazara Mountain Battery Punjab Frontier Force	4	24 Hazara Mountain Battery Frontier Force	4 (Hazara) Mountain Battery
5	1 Company Bombay Golandas Battalion Native Artillery	5	25 Quetta Mountain Battery Frontier Force	5 (Bombay) Mountain Battery
6	3 Company Bombay Golandas Battalion Native Artillery	6	26 Jacob's Mountain Battery Frontier Force	6 (Jacob's) Mountain Battery
7	—	7	27 Gujrat Mountain Battery Frontier Force	7 (Bengal) Mountain Battery
8	—	8	28 Lahore Mountain Battery Frontier Force	8 (Lahore) Mountain Battery
9	—	9	29 Murree Mountain Battery Frontier Force	9 (Murree) Mountain Battery
10	—	10	30 Abbottabad Mountain Battery Frontier Force	10 (Abbottabad Mountain Battery
11	—	11	—	11 (Dehra Dun) Mountain Battery
12	—	12	—	12 (Poonch) Mountain Battery
13	—	13	—	13 (Dardoni) Mountain Battery
14	—	14	—	14 (Rajputana) Mountain Battery
15	—	15	—	15 (Jhelum) Mountain Battery

Indian Regiments—Artillery (cont)

Indicator	Title in 1861 or before	Indicator	1903 Title	Subsequent Title
16	—	16	—	16 (Zhob) Mountain Battery
17	—	17	—	17 (Nowshera) Mountain Battery
18	—	18	—	18 (Sohan) Mountain Battery
19	—	19	—	19 (Maymyo) Mountain Battery

Indicator	Title before 1861
IND-Hyd Bty	
1	1 Field Battery Hyderabad Contingent, disbanded *c.* 1850
2	2 Field Battery Hyderabad Contingent, disbanded *c.* 1850
4	4 Mountain Battery Hyderabad Contingent, disbanded *c.* 1850

Indian Regiments—Engineers

Indicator	Title in 1861 or before	Indicator	1903 Title	Subsequent Title
IND-S&M		**IND-S&M**		
Ben S&M	Bengal Sappers & Miners	**Ben S&M**	1st Sappers and Miners	King George V's Own Bengal Sappers and Miners
Mad S&M	Madras Sappers & Miners	**Mad S&M**	2nd Queen's Own Sappers and Miners	Queen Victoria's Own Madras Sappers and Miners
Bom S&M	Bombay Sappers & Miners	**Bom S&M**	3rd Sappers and Miners	Royal Bombay Sappers and Miners
—		**Bur S&M**	Burma Company, Madras Sappers and Miners	Burma Sappers and Miners

New Zealand Regiments—Mounted Rifles/Armour

Indicator	Great War title	Indicator	Subsequent title	World War II formation
NZ-MR		**NZ-MR**		
1	Canterbury Yeomanry Cavalry	1	Canterbury Yeomanry Cavalry	C
2	Queen Alexandra's Wellington West Coast	2	Queen Alexandra's Wellington West Coast	B
3	Auckland	3	Auckland East Coast	A
4	Waikato	4	Waikato	A
5	Otago Hussars	5	Otago	C
6	Manawatu	6	Manawatu	B
7	Southland	7	(amalgamated with 5)	
8	South Canterbury	8	(amalgamated with 1)	
9	Wellington East Coast	9	Wellington East Coast	B
10	Nelson	10	Nelson-Marlborough	C
11	North Auckland	11	North Auckland	A
12	Otago	12	(amalgamated with 5)	
NZ Scot	—	**NZ Scot**	New Zealand Scottish Armoured Car Regiment	Division Cavalry, 2nd New Zealand Division

New Zealand Regiments—Infantry

Indicator NZ-Inf	Great War title	Indicator NZ-Inf	Subsequent title	World War II formation
1	Canterbury	1	Canterbury	F
2	South Canterbury	2	(amalgamated with 1)	
3	Auckland (Countess of Ranfurly's Own)		Auckland (Countess of Ranfurly's Own	D
4	Otago	4	Otago	F
5	Wellington Rifles	5	Wellington	E
6	Hauraki	6	Hauraki	D
7	Wellington West Coast	7	Wellington West Coast	E
8	Southland Rifles	8	Southland	F
9	Hawkes Bay	9	Hawkes Bay	E
10	North Otago Rifles	10	(amalgamated with 4)	
11	Taranaki Rifles	11	Taranaki	E
12	Nelson			
13	North Canterbury & Westland	12	Nelson, Marlborough & West Coast	F
14	South Otago Rifles	14	(amalgamated with 8)	
15	North Auckland	15	North Auckland	D
16	Waikato	16	Waikato	D
17	Ruahine	17	Ruahine	E
27	—	27	27 Machine Gun Battalion	—
28	—	28	28 (Maori) Battalion	—
34	—	34	34 Infantry Battalion	—
35	—	35	35 Infantry Battalion	—

Notes on World War II formations

A   18 Armoured Regiment
B   19 Armoured Regiment, 3 Division Tank Squadron   } from 6 October 1942
C   20 Armoured Regiment
D   18, 21, 24 Infantry Battalions (2 New Zealand Division), 29 Infantry Battalion (3 New Zealand Division)
E   19, 22, 25 Infantry Battalions (2 New Zealand Division), 36 & 1 Ruahine Battalions (3 New Zealand Division)
F   20, 23, 26 Infantry Battalions (2 New Zealand Division), 30, 37 Infantry Battalions (3 New Zealand Division)

18, 19, 20 only until 5 October 1942

South African Regiments—Mounted Rifles/Armour

Indicator (1913 number) SA-MR	Some previous titles	Indicator (1913 number)	Subsequent titles (World War II or later)
	Frontier Light Horse		Disbanded 1902
1	Weenen Yeomanry Cavalry	1 }	Royal Natal Carbineers
2	Weenen Yeomanry Cavalry	2	
3	Victoria Mounted Rifles / Alexandra Mounted Rifles / Border Mounted Rifles	3	Natal Mounted Rifles
4	Greytown Mounted Rifles / Zululand Mounted Rifles / Natal Hussars	4	Umvoti Mounted Rifles

South African Regiments—Mounted Rifles/Armour (cont)

Indicator (1913 number)	Some previous titles	Indicator (1913 number)	Subsequent titles (World War II or later)
SA-MR			
5	Imperial Light Horse / Eastern Rifles	5	Imperial Light Horse/ Light Horse Regiment
6	Border Light Horse / Cape Light Horse		—
SA-SAMR			
1	Cape Mounted Riflemen		—
SAP (2, 3, 4, 5,)	—	SAP (2, 3, 4, 5)	South African Police Battalions
SA-Dismounted Rifles			
9	Bechuanaland Rifles	9	—

South African Regiments—Infantry

Indicator (1913 number) SA-Inf	Some previous titles	Indicator (1913 number)	Subsequent titles (World War II or later)
1	Royal Durban Rifles / Maritzburg Rifles / Natal Royal Rifles	1	Royal Durban Light Infantry
2	Cape Town Irish / Cape Royal Rifles	2	Duke of Edinburgh's Own Rifles/ Cape Town Rifles
3	Oudtshoorn Volunteer Rifles / Uitenhage Volunteer Rifles / Port Elizabeth Volunteer Rifle Corps	3	Prince Alfred's Guard
4	First City Volunteers of Grahamstown / Queenstown Rifle Volunteers	4	First City Regiment
5	1st Cape Mounted Yeomanry / Buffalo Rifle Volunteers	5	Kaffrarian Rifles
6	Cape Town Highlanders	6	Cape Town Highlanders
7	Kimberley Light Horse / Kimberley Rifles / Kimberley Scots	7	Kimberley Regiment
8	Transvaal Scottish	8	Transvaal Scottish
9	Cape Peninsular Rifles	9	—
10	Railway Pioneer Regiment / Transvaal Light Infantry	10	Witwatersrand Rifles
11	Transvaal Cycle Corps	11	Rand Light Infantry
12	Northern Rifles / Central SA Railway Volunteers	12	Pretoria Regiment
13	Dutoitspan Hussars / Diamond Fields Horse	13	Kimberley Regiment
RB	—	RB	Regiment Botha/Regiment Pongola
RPS	—	RPS	Regiment President Steyn/Regiment Bloemfontein
Irish	—	Irish	South African Irish Regiment
MR	—	MR	Middellandse Regiment/Groot Karoo
DLR	—	DLR	Regiment de la Rey
WR	—	WR	Regiment de Wet
PH	—	PH	Pretoria Highlanders
SSB	—	SSB	Special Service Battalion

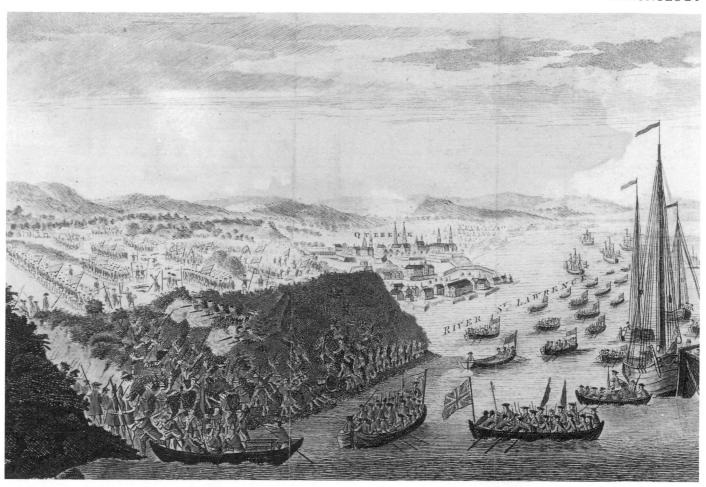

Above: 'The Taking of Quebeck by the English Forces commanded by General Wolfe, 13 September 1759.' This coloured engraving published c1759, shows the storming of the Heights by the Louisberg Grenadiers. *NAM*

Left: 'The left wing of the British Army in action at the Battle of Waterloo, 18 June 1815.' Coloured aquatint by T. Sutherland after W. Heath. *NAM*

Chronology

Dates	**Honoured** or *Non-Honoured* Battle	**Honour awarded** to or *Participants in* Battle	Remarks
TANGIER			
1662–1680	**Tangier 1662–80**	**1D.** Inf-**GG. CG. 1. 2.**	
DUNDEE'S INSURRECTION			
27 Jul 1689	*Killiecrankie*	Inf-*13. 25.*	
21 Aug 1689	*Dunkeld*	Inf-*26.*	
IRELAND			
1 Jul 1690	*The Boyne*	*LG, RHG. 1 DG, 2 DG, 5 DG, 6 DG, 7 DG, 1 D. 3 D. 5 D. 6 D.* Inf-*4. 5. 6. 8. 12. 13. 18. 19. 20. 22. 23. 27.* Foot-*Disney's. Guise's. La Caillemotte's. Lisburne's.*	App by 22. 27.
1689 12 Jul 1691	*Ireland 1689–91*	Inf-*2. 9. 11. 20.*	
WAR OF THE LEAGUE OF AUGSBURG (Treaty of Ryswyck)			
27 Aug 1689	*Walcourt*	*LG. RHG.* Inf-*CG. 1. 3. 7. 16.*	App by CG. 1. 7. 16.
1691	*Leuse*	*LG.*	
3 Aug 1692	*Steenkirk*	*LG. 3 DG. 4 DG. 6 DG. 4 D.* Horse-*Princess Anne of Denmark's. The Princess's.* Inf-*GG. CG. SG. 1. 3. 4. 6. 7. 10. 16. 19. 21. 25. 26.* Foot-*Disney's. MacKay's. Balfour's. Wauchope's. Skelton's.*	App by 4 DG. 4 D. CG. 1. 7. 10. 16. 26. 94.
18 Jul 1693	*Dottignies*	Inf-*10.*	App by 7 DG. 10.
29 Jul 1693	*Landen*	*LG. 1 DG. 3 DG. 4 DG. 6 DG. 4 D.* Inf-*GG. CG. SG. 1. 2. 3. 4. 7. 14. 16. 19. 21. 25. 26.* Foot-*Balfour's.*	App by 4 DG. GG. CG. SG. 1. 2. 7. 14. 16. 19. 94.
3–15 Jul 1695	**Namur 1695**	Inf-**GG. CG. SG. 1. 2. 4. 6. 7. 14. 16. 17. 18. 23. 25.** *5 D. 7 D.* Inf-*19. 27. 30.* Foot-*Cunningham's.*	App by 4 DG. 1 D. 19. 27. 30. 94. as part of the covering force.
Aug 1689–1697	*Flanders 1689–97*	*LG. RHG. 1 DG. 2 DG. 3 DG. 4 DG. 5 DG. 6 DG. 7 DG. 1 D. 2 D. 3 D. 4 D. 5 D. 7 D.* Horse-*Princess Anne of Denmark's; The Princess's.* Inf-*GG. CG. SG. 1. 2. 3. 4. 6. 7. 10. 14. 15. 16. 17. 18. 19. 21. 22. 23. 25. 26. 27.* Foot-*Disney's. MacKay's. Balfour's. Wauchope's. Skelton's. Hale's. Cunningham's. Hamilton's. Castleton's.*	App by 2 DG. 4 DG. 1 D. 2 D. 5 D. 1. 2. 5. 27. 94. under various titles.

Dates	**Honoured** or *Non-Honoured* Battle	**Honour awarded** to or *Participants in* Battle	Remarks

WAR OF THE SPANISH SUCCESSION*
(F = Flanders, P = Peninsula, WI = West Indies)

Dates	Battle	Honour / Participants	Remarks
Sep 1702	*Venloo* (F)	*1 DG.* Inf-*8. 9. 13. 17. 18.*	App by 17.
3 Oct 1702	*Liege* (F)	*1 DG. 2 D.* Inf-*8. 9. 15. 17. 18. 23.*	App by 9. 17.
12 Oct 1702	*Vigo 1702* (P)	*Shannon's Marines.*	App by 2. 4. 7. 31. 34.
9–10 May 1703	*Tongres* (F)	Inf-*2.*	App by 94.
May 1703	*Guadaloupe 1703* (WI)	Inf-*19. 20. 22. 27. 29. 35. 36.*	App by 19. 22. 27. 29.
1704–5	**Gibraltar 1704–5** (P)*	Inf-**GG. CG. 4. 13. 30. 31. 32. 35.**	
2 Jul 1704	*Schellenberg* (F)	*1 DG. 3 DG. 5 DG. 6 DG. 7 DG. 2 D. 5 D.* Inf-*GG. 1. 3. 8. 10. 15. 16. 18. 21. 23. 24. 26. 27. 37.*	App by 7 DG. 2 D. 5 D. GG. 1. 10. 15. 16. 23. 24. 37.
13 Aug 1704	**Blenheim** (F)	**1 DG. 3 DG. 5 DG. 6 DG. 7 DG. 2 D. 5 D.** Inf-**GG. 1. 3. 8. 10. 15. 16. 18. 21. 23. 24. 26. 37.**	
18 Jul 1705	*Elixheim* (F)	*5 DG. 5 D.* Inf-*GG. 1. 3. 8. 10. 21. 29.*	App by 2 D. 5 D. but for previous day.
8 May 1705	*Valenza* (P)	*2 DG.* Inf-*2. 9. 17. 33.*	Also known as Valencia de Alcantara.
1705	*Albuquerque* (P)	*2 DG.* Inf-*2. 9. 17. 33.*	
1705	*Badajoz 1705* (P)	*2 DG.* Inf-*2. 9. 17. 33.*	
Sep–Oct 1705	*Barcelona 1705* (P)	*1 D. 8 D.* Inf-*GG. CG. 4. 6. 13. 30. 31. 32. 34. 35. 36.*	App by 1 D. 8 D. GG. CG. 4. 6. 30. 34. 36.
8 Jan 1706	*San Mateo* (P)	*1 D.* Inf-*13. 35.*	
26 Jan 1706	*San Estevan* (P)		App by 8 D. 31.
3 Apr 1706	*Barcelona 1706* (P)	*8 D.* Inf-*GG. 7. 34.*	App by 8 D. GG. 34.
Apr 1706	*Alcantara* (P)	*2 DG.* Inf-*2. 9. 17. 33.*	App by 17.
23 May 1706	**Ramillies** (F)	**1 DG. 3 DG. 5 DG. 6 DG. 7 DG. 2 D. 5 D.** Inf-**GG. 1. 3. 8. 10. 15. 16. 18. 21. 23. 24. 26. 28. 29. 37.**	App by 94 as descendent of regiment in Dutch pay.
27 Jun 1706	*Madrid* (P)	*2 DG.* Inf-*2. 9. 17. 33.*	
Jun–Jul 1706	*Ostend* (F)		App by 29.
22 Aug 1706	*(Siege of) Menin* (F)	*3 DG. 6 DG. 2 D.* Inf-*8. 10. 18. 21. 23.*	App by 10.
21 Sep 1706	*Aeth* (F)		App by 1.
1706	*Valencia* (P)	*1 D.* Inf-*CG.*	App by 1 D. 8 D. for general service in campaign of 1706.
25 Apr 1707	*Almanza* (P)	*2 DG. 3 D. 4 D. 7 D. 8 D.* Horse-*La Fabreque's Dragoons. Pearce's Dragoons.* Inf-*GG. CG. 2. 4. 6. 9. 11. 13. 17. 28. 32. 33. 35. 36. 39.* Foot *Pearce's. Breton's. Orrery's. Kerr's. MacCartney's. Mountjoy's. Nassau's.*	App by 4 D. 8 D. CG. 9. 11. 17. 28. Badge of 9th Foot dates from this battle.
11 Jul 1708	**Oudenarde** (F)	**1 DG. 3 DG. 5 DG. 6 DG. 7 DG. 2 D. 5 D.** Inf-**GG. CG. 1. 3. 8. 10. 15. 16. 18. 21. 23. 24. 26. 37.**	App by 94.
Aug–Sep 1708	*(Siege of) Lille* (F)	*2 D.* Inf-*GG. 1. 16. 18. 21. 23. 24.*	App by 1. 16. 24.

Dates	**Honoured** or *Non-Honoured* Battle	**Honour awarded** to or *Participants in* Battle	Remarks
8 Sep 1708	*Ennevelin* (F)		App by 15.
24 Sep 1708	*Minorca 1708* (P)	8 D. Inf-4. 6.	
28 Sep 1708	*Wynendaele* (F)	Inf-1. 23. 26.	App by 1. 12. 26.
7 May 1709	*Caya* (P)	Inf-5. 13. 20. 39. Foot-*Stanwix's. Paston's.*	App by 5. 39.
11 May 1709	**Malplaquet** (F)	**1 DG. 3 DG. 5 DG. 6 DG. 7 DG. 2 D. 5 D. Inf-GG. CG. 1. 3. 8. 10. 15. 16. 18. 19. 21. 23. 24. 26. 37.** Foot-*Evan's. Orrery's.*	App by 94.
Jul–Sep 1709	*Siege of Tournay* (F)	1 DG. 3 DG. 2 D. Inf-GG. 1. 3. 8. 10. 15. 16. 18. 37.	App by 1. 10. 15. 16.
1709	*Siege of Mons* (F)		App by 11.
Apr–Jun 1710	*Douai* (F)	1 DG. 6 DG. Inf-15. 19. 21. 23. 24. 26. 34. Foot-*MacCartney's. Wynne's.*	App by 19. 24. 34.
27 Jul 1710	*Almenara* (P)	2 DG. 1 D. 8 D.	App by 2 DG. 8 D.
18 Aug 1710	*Saragossa* (P)	2 DG. 1 D. 8 D. Inf-6. 33. Foot-*Pearce's. Tunbridge's. Lepell's.*	App by 2 DG. 1 D. 8 D. Represented in badge of 6th Foot.
9 Nov 1710	*Aire* (F)		App by 1. 10.
9 Dec 1710	*Brihuega* (P)	2 DG. 1 D. 8 D. Inf-6. 33. Foot-*Pearce's. Dalzell's. Mohun's. Tunbridge's.*	
Aug-Sep 1711	*Bouchain* (F)	1 DG. 3 DG. 5 DG. 2 D. 5 D. Inf-GG. CG. 10. 15. 16. 18. 19. 21. 23. 24. 26. 34.	App by 19. 24.
1703–10	*Malaga 1703–10* (P)		App by 30. with Naval Crown.
1702–13	*Naval Service 1702–13*		App by 31. 32. as Naval Crown with dates.
1702–13	*Flanders 1702–13* (F)	1 DG. 3 DG. 5 DG. 6 DG. 7 DG. 2 D. 5 D. Inf-GG. CG. 1. 3. 8. 9. 10. 11. 12. 15. 16. 17. 18. 19. 21. 23. 24. 26. 28. 29. 34. 36. 37. Foot-*Evans's. Orrery's. MacCartney's. Wynne's. Mar's. Strathnaver's. Mordaunt's. Townshend's.*	App by 1 D. 2 D. 5 D. 1. 9. 11. 13. 17. 24. 28. 29. 34. 94. for various dates and titles.
1702–13	*Peninsula 1702–13* (P)	2 DG. 1 D. 3 D. 4 D. 7 D. 8 D. Dragoons-*La Fabrequet's. Pearce's. Trappard's. De Magny's.* Inf-GG. CG. SG. 2. 4. 5. 6. 7. 9. 11. 13. 17. 20. 28. 29. 30. 31. 32. 33. 34. 35. 36. 39. Foot-*Pearce's. Breton's. Orrery's. Kerr's. MacCartney's. Mountjoy's. Nassau's. Stanwix's. Paston's. Lepell's. Tunbridge's. Dalzell's. Mohun's. Trappard's. De Magny's. Elliot's. Brudenell's. Ikerrin's. Sybourg's. Hotham's. Jones's. Gorges's. Dungannon's. Slane's. Lovelace's. Inchiquin's. Carles's. Rooke's. Soames's.*	App by 2 DG. 1 D. 8 D. CG. 2. 5. 7. 9. 11. 13. 17. 28. 30. 33. 34. 36. 39. for various dates and titles.

OLD PRETENDER'S REBELLION

| 13 Nov 1715 | *Sheriffmuir* | 2 D. 3 D. 4 D. 6 D. 7 D. Inf-11. 16. 17. 21. 25. 36. | |
| 1715 | *Preston* | 2 DG. 9 D. 11 D. 13 D. 14 D. Inf-23. 26. | |

WAR WITH SPAIN

10 Jun 1719	*Glenshiel*	Inf-11. 14. 15.	
21 Sep 1719	*Vigo 1719*	Inf-GG. CG. SG. 3. 19. 24. 28. 33. 34. 37.	
22 Feb–23 Jun 1727	*Gibraltar 1727*	Inf-GG. 5. 13. 14. 18. 20. 22. 25. 26. 29. 30. 34. 39.	App by 5. 14. 20. 29. 30. 34. 39.

Dates	Honoured or Non-Honoured Battle	Honour awarded to or Participants in Battle	Remarks

WAR OF JENKINS'S EAR

| 9 Apr 1741 | *Fort St Lazar (Cartagena)* | Inf-*15. 16. 24. 36. Wynyard's Marines.* | |

WAR OF THE AUSTRIAN SUCCESSION (Treaty of Aix La Chappelle)

27 Jun 1743	**Dettingen**	**LG. RHG. 1 DG. 7 DG. 1 D. 2 D. 3 D. 4 D. 6 D. 7 D. Inf-GG. CG. SG. 3. 8. 11. 12. 13. 20. 21. 23. 31. 32. 33. 37.**	
11 May 1745	*Fontenoy*	*LG. RHG. 1 DG. 7 DG. 1 D. 2 D. 6 D. 7 D. Inf-GG. CG. SG. 1. 3. 8. 11. 12. 13. 19. 20. 21. 23. 25. 28. 31. 32. 33. 34. 42.*	App by LG. RHG. 1 DG. 7 DG. 1 D. 2 D. GG. CG. SG. 1. 11. 12. 19. 20. 28. 31. 33. 42. App by 34 refused.
30 Jun 1745	*Ghent*	Inf-*1. 23.*	
9 Jul 1745	*Melle*	*4 D.* Inf-*1. 16. 20. 31.*	App by 4 D. 16.
1 Oct 1746	*Port l'Orient*	Inf-*1. 15. 28. 30. 39. 42.*	
11 Oct 1746	*Roucoux*	*6 DG. 2 D. 6 D. 7 D.* Inf-*8. 11. 13. 19. 26. 33. 43.*	App by 2 D. 11. 19.
5 May 1747	*Sandberg (Hulst)*	Inf-*1. 28. 42.*	App by 1.
3 May–14 Oct 1747	*Finnisterre*		App by 30 for 3 May, and by 39 for 14 Oct.
2 Jul 1747	*Lauffeld (Val)*	*2 D. 4 D. 6 D. 7 D. Duke of Cumberland's LD.* Inf-*GG. SG. 3. 4. 8. 13. 19. 21. 23. 25. 32. 33. 36. 37. 48.*	App by 2 D. 4 D. 4. 19. 36. 48.
1742–8	*Flanders 1742–48*	*LG. RHG. 1 DG. 6 DG. 7 DG. 1 D. 2 D. 3 D. 4 D. 6 D. 7 D. Duke of Cumberland's LD.* Inf-*GG. CG. SG. 1. 3. 4. 8. 11. 12. 13. 16. 19. 20. 21. 23. 25. 26. 28. 31. 32. 33. 34. 36. 37. 42. 48. 64.*	App by 2 D. 1. 11. 31. 36. 48.

YOUNG PRETENDER'S REBELLION

| 17 Jan 1746 | *Falkirk* | *10 D. 13 D. 14 D.* Inf-*1. 3. 4. 14. 48.* | App by 48. |
| 16 Apr 1746 | *Culloden* | *10 D. 11 D. Duke of Kingston's LH.* Inf-*1. 3. 4. 8. 13. 14. 20. 21. 25. 27. 34. 36. 37. 48. Wolfe's Marines.* | App by 48. |

SEVEN YEARS WAR: CONQUEST OF INDIA

23 Sep–14 Nov 1751	**Arcot**	Inf-**102.**	
12 Jan 1757	*Hooghly*	Inf-*39.*	
4 Feb 1757	*Mahratta Ditch*	Inf-*39.*	
23 Jun 1757	**Plassey**	Inf-**39. 101. 102. 103.** IND-**Bengal NI (m)-1.**	Also **Plassey Battery.** Borne as embellishment by 102. 103.
9 Dec 1758	**Condore**	Inf-**101. 102.** IND-*Ben NI (m)-1. Ben Sepoys (1764)-2.*	
14 Dec 1758–16 Feb 1759	*Fort St George*	Inf-*79.* 102. IND-Inf-*61. Coast Sepoys-2.*	
8 Apr 1759	**Masulipatam**	Inf-**101.** IND-*Ben NI (m)-1.*	
25 Nov 1759	**Badara**	Inf-**101.** IND-*Ben NI (m)-5. Ben Sepoys (1764)-3.*	
22 Jan 1760	**Wandewash**	Inf-**102.** Inf-*79. 84.*	App by 84 on behalf of previous regiment of that number.

Dates	**Honoured** or *Non-Honoured* Battle	**Honour awarded** to or *Participants in* Battle	Remarks
Sep 1760–5 Apr 1761	**Pondicherry**	Inf-**102.** Inf-*79. 84. 89. 96.*	Honour awarded to cover participation in sieges of 1778 & 1793 as well.

SEVEN YEARS WAR: CONQUEST OF CANADA

16 Jun 1755	*Fort Beausejour*	Inf-*40.*	
8 Jul 1755	*Monongahela*	Inf-*44. 48.*	
4–9 Aug 1757	*Fort William Henry*	Inf-*35.*	
8 Jun–27 Jul 1758	**Louisburg**	Inf-**1. 15. 17. 22. 28. 35. 40. 45. 47. 48. 58. 60. 62.** Inf-*Fraser's Highlanders.*	Also **Louisburg Battery.**
8 Jul 1758	*Ticonderoga 1758*	Inf-*27. 42. 44. 46. 55. 60.* *Gage's LI (80).*	App by 42. 55.
25 Nov 1758	*Fort Duquesne*	Inf-*Montgomery's Highlanders.*	
1758	*Martinique 1758*	Inf-*4*	App by 4.
24 Jan–1 May 1759	**Guadeloupe 1759**	Inf-**3. 4. 38. 42. 61. 63. 64. 65.**	
3–24 Jul 1759	*Niagara 1759*	Inf-*44. 46. 60.*	App by 46.
26 Jul 1759	*Ticonderoga 1759*	Inf-*1. 17. 27. 42. 55. Montgomery's Highlanders.* *Gage's LI (80)*	
13 Sep 1759	**Quebec 1759**	Inf-**15. 28. 35. 43. 47. 58. 60.** Inf-*22. 40. 48. Fraser's Hldrs.*	App by 22. 40. 45. in respect of Gren Coys forming Louisburg Grenadiers and by 34. Also **Quebec 1759 Battery.**
28 Apr 1760	*Sainte Foy*	Inf-*15. 28. 35. 43. 47. 48. 58. 60. Fraser's Hldrs.*	
Apr 1760	*Cherokee Rising*	Inf-*1. Montgomery's Hldrs.*	
1749–62	*North America 1749–62*	Inf-*1. 15. 17. 22. 27. 28. 35. 40. 42. 43. 44. 45. 46. 47. 48. 55. 58. 60. 62. 71. Montgomery's Hldrs. Fraser's Hldrs.*	App by 1. 17. 22. 27. 28. 43. 45. 47. 55. under various dates and titles.

SEVEN YEARS WAR: EUROPE AND WEST INDIES (TREATY OF PARIS)

19 Apr–28 Jun 1756	*Minorca*	Inf-*4. 23. 24. 34.*	App by 4. 24. 34.
8 Aug–11 Sep 1758	*Cherburg – St Cast*	Inf-*GG. 5. 24. 30. 33. 34. 36. 67. 68. 72.*	
1 Aug 1759	**Minden**	Inf-**12. 20. 23. 25. 37. 51.**	Also **Minden Batteries** (2).
10 Jul 1760	*Corbach (Sachsenhausen)*	*1 DG. 2 DG. 3 DG.* Inf-*5. 8. 24. 50. 51.*	App by 50. 51.
16 Jul 1760	**Emsdorf**	**15 D.**	
31 Jul 1760	**Warburg**	**RHG. 1 DG. 2 DG. 3 DG. 6 DG. 7 DG. 1 D. 2 D. 6 D. 7 D. 10 D. 11 D.** Inf-*87. 88. Gren Coys of 12. 20. 23. 25. 37. 51. Flank Coys of 5. 8. 11. 24. 33. 50.*	App by 87. 88. as successor regiments. App by 5. 11. 20. 24. 50. 51. on behalf of Gren or Flank Coys.
16 Oct 1760	*Kloster Kampen*	*1 D. 6 D. 10 D. 15 D.* Inf-*11. 20. 23. 25. 33. 51. 87. 88.*	
8 Apr–7 Jun 1761	**Belleisle**	Inf-**3. 9. 19. 21. 30. 36. 67. 69.** Inf-*75. 85. 90. 94. 97. 98.*	App by 16 D.

Dates	Honoured or Non-Honoured Battle	Honour awarded to or Participants in Battle	Remarks
6 Jun 1761	*Dominica 1761*	Inf-*1. 4. 22. 94. Montgomery's Hldrs.*	App by 22 and 4 (Gren Coy only).
15–16 Jul 1761	*Vellinghausen (Kirsh Denkern)*	*1 DG. 3 DG. 7 DG. 1 D. 2 D. 6 D. 7 D. 10 D. 11 D. Inf-GG. CG. SG. 5. 8. 11. 12. 20. 23. 24. 25. 37. 50. 51. 87. 88.*	App by 7 DG. GG. CG. 5. 11. 24. 50.
16 Jan–12 Feb 1762	**Martinique 1762**	Inf-**15. 17. 22. 27. 28. 35. 38. 40. 42. 43. 48. 60. 69.** Inf-*1. 4. 46. 65. 75. 90. 91. 94. 97. 98. 100. Montgomery's Hldrs.*	App by 4.
11 Jun 1762	*Dominica 1762*	Inf-*4. 22. 42.*	App by 22 as 'West Indies 1761–65'.
24 Jun 1762	**Wilhelmsthal**	Inf-**5.** *RHG. 1 DG. 2 DG. 3 DG. 1 D. 2 D. 6 D. 10 D. Inf-GG. CG. SG. 8. 87. 88. Gren Coys of 11. 24. 33. 50. Flank Coys of 12. 20. 23. 25. 37. 51.*	App by 2 D. CG. SG. 11.
30 Jul 1762	**The Moro**	Inf-**56.** Inf-*1. 22. 90.*	App by 1. 22 but less than 50% present. App by 15 refused in 1829.
7 Jun–14 Aug 1762	**Havannah**	Inf-**1. 9. 15. 17. 22. 27. 28. 34. 35. 40. 42. 43. 56. 58. 60.** Inf-*4. 46. 48. 72. 90. 98. Montgomery's Hldrs.*	App by 4.
26 Jul–26 Aug 1762	*Peninsula 1762*	*16 D.* Inf-*3. 67. 75. 83. 85. 91. 92. 115.*	App by 16 D. as 'Portugal 1762'. 16 D. authorised to wear Cap Plate.
21–22 Sep 1762	*Amöneberg*	*RHG. 1 DG. 15 D. Inf-GG. CG. SG. 87. 88.*	App by GG. CG.
6 Oct 1762	*Manila*	Inf-*79.*	
1758–63	*Westphalia 1758–63*	*RHG. 1 DG. 2 DG. 3 DG. 6 DG. 7 DG. 1 D. 2 D. 6 D. 7 D. 10 D. 11 D. 15 D. Inf-GG. CG. SG. 5. 8. 11. 12. 20. 23. 24. 25. 33. 37. 50. 51. 87. 88.*	App by 2 DG. 1 D. 2 D. CG. 5. 11. 24. 37. 50. 51.

HINDOOSTAN CAMPAIGN AGAINST SURAJAH DOOLAH OF OUDE

Dates	Honoured or Non-Honoured Battle	Honour awarded to or Participants in Battle	Remarks
22 Feb 1760	*Seerpore*	Inf-*101.*	Against Emperor Shah Alum.
28 Apr 1760	*Patna 1760*	Inf-*101.* IND-*Ben NI (m)-1.*	
16 Jun 1760	*Beerpore*	Inf-*101.* IND-*Ben NI (m)-1.*	
19 Jul 1763	*Kutwah*	Inf-*84. 101.*	
2 Aug 1763	*Gheriah*	Inf-*84. 101.* IND-*Ben Sepoys (1764)-7.*	Against Meer Cassim, Nawab of Oude.
5 Sep 1763	*Oondwa Nullah*	Inf-*84. 101.*	App by 84. as successor regiment.
6 Nov 1763	*Patna 1763*	Inf-*84. 101.* IND-*Ben Sepoys (1764)-2. 3. 5.*	Bengal Sepoy regiments destroyed in the battle.
23 Oct 1764	**Buxar**	Inf-**101. 102. 103.** IND-**Ben NI (m)-2. 3. 5. 8. 9. 10.** Inf-*84. 89. 96.* IND-Inf-*Ben Sepoys (1764)-7. Ben Sepoys(1784)-18.*	Against Meer Cassim and Shah Alum combined.

PONTIAC'S CONSPIRACY

Dates	Honoured or Non-Honoured Battle	Honour awarded to or Participants in Battle	Remarks
5–6 Aug 1763	*Bushy Run*	Inf-*42. 60. Montgomery's Hldrs.*	
May 1763–1764	**North America 1763–64**	Inf-**42. 60.** Inf-*Montgomery's Hldrs.*	App by 55 but less than 50% present.

Dates	Honoured or Non-Honoured Battle	Honour awarded to or Participants in Battle	Remarks
CAMPAIGN AGAINST HYDER ALI			
2 Sep 1767	*Chengamah*	Inf-*102.* IND-Inf-*61. 62. 64. 67. 2/6 GR. Mad Sepoys-13.*	
26 Sep 1767	*Trinomally*	Inf-*102.* IND-Inf-*61. 62. 64. 66. 67. GR-2/6. 10. Mad Sepoys-11.*	
10 Nov–6 Dec 1767	**Amboor**	IND-Inf-**10 Madras.** Inf-*1. 102.*	
22 Sep–28 Oct 1771	**Tanjore**	Inf-**102.** IND-**Inf-62. 64. 66. 69. GR-2/6. 1/7. Mad Sepoys-11.**	
1st ROHILLA WAR			
1774	**Rohilcund 1774**	Inf-**101.** IND-*Ben NI (m)-8. 9. 11. 14. 15. 16. Ben Sepoys (1764)-7.*	Battle of Miranpur Katra on 23 Apr 1774.
CARIB WAR			
1772–3	*West Indies 1772–73*		App by 14 for Carib War.
AMERICAN WAR OF INDEPENDENCE			
19 Apr 1775	*Lexington*	Inf-*4. 5. 10. 18. 23. 38. 43. 47. 52. 59.*	
17 Jun 1775	*Bunker Hill*	*17 LD.* Inf-*4. 5. 10. 18. 22. 23. 35. 38. 42. 43. 47. 52. 59. 63. 65.*	App by 5. 10. 52. App by 49 refused 1833.
12 Sep–3 Nov 1775	*Quebec 1775*	Inf-*7.*	App by 7.
27 Aug 1776	*Brooklyn*	*17 D.* Inf-*GG. Comp Regt of Foot Gds. 4. 5. 10. 15. 17. 22. 23. 27. 28. 33. 35. 37. 38. 40. 42. 43. 44. 45. 46. 49. 52. 54. 55. 57. 63. 64. 71.*	App by 49.
28 Oct 1776	*White Plains*	*16 LD. 17 LD.* Inf-*GG. CG. 5. 27. 28. 35. 49.*	App by 28. 49.
16 Nov 1776	*Fort Washington*	*17 LD.* Inf-*GG. CG. 4. 10. 15. 22. 23. 27. 28. 33. 38. 42. 52. 71.*	App by 49.
1776	*Long Island*		App by 22.
3 Jan 1777	*Princeton*	Inf-*17. 40. 55.*	App by 17.
25 Apr 1777	*Danbury*	Inf-*4. 15. 23. 27. 44. 64.*	
11 Sep 1777	*Brandywine*	*16 LD.* Inf-*Comp Regt of Ft Gds. 4. 5. 10. 15. 17. 23. 27. 28. 33. 37. 40. 42. 44. 46. 49. 52. 55. 64. 71.*	App by CG. 5. 17. 27. 28. 49. 55. App by 49 refused in 1833.
11 Sep–4 Oct 1777	*Philadelphia*		App by 43. 52.
19 Sep 1777	*Bemis Heights*	Inf-*9. 20. 21. 24. 62.*	App by 9. Also known as Freemans Farm or Stillwater.
18–24 Sep 1777	*Lake George*	Inf-*47. 53.*	
20 Sep 1777	*Paoli*		App by 49.
4 Oct 1777	*Germantown (Saratoga)*	*16 LD.* Inf-*Composite Regt of Foot Gds. 4. 5. 10. 15. 27. 28. 33. 37. 40. 42. 44. 55.*	App by 5. 17. 27. 40. 49.
6 Oct 1777	*Fort Montgomery*	Inf-*52. 57.*	
6 Oct 1777	*Fort Clinton*	*17 LD.* Inf-*17. 26. 63.*	
9 Aug 1778	*Rhode Island*	Inf-*23.*	App by 22. 39. 43. 52. Naval battle.

The bracket spanning White Plains, Brooklyn, Fort Washington reads: App by 5. 17. 27. 39. 43. 52. 63 jointly as New York.

Dates	**Honoured** or *Non-Honoured* Battle	**Honour awarded** to or *Participants in* Battle	Remarks
29 Dec 1778	*Savannah 1778*	Inf-*71. 82.*	App by 16.
28 Jul 1779	*Penobscot*	Inf-*74. 82.*	
9 Oct 1779	*Savannah 1779*	Inf-*16. 60. 71.*	
12 Apr–9 May 1780	*Charleston*	*17 LD.* Inf-*GG. 7. 16. 23. 33. 42. 63. 64.*	App by 16. 63.
16 Aug 1780	*Camden*	*17 LD.* Inf-*23. 33. 71. 105.*	
17 Jan 1781	*Cowpens*	*17 LD.* Inf-*7. 16. 71.*	
15 Mar 1781	*Guildford*	Inf-*Composite Regt of Foot Gds. 16. 23. 33. 60. 71*	App by GG. CG. SG.
25 Apr 1781	*Hobkirks Hill*	Inf-*60. 63. 105.*	App by 63 as 'Carolina 1781'.
May 1781	*Pensacola*		App by 16.
8 Sep 1781	*Eutaw Springs*	Inf-*3. 19. 63. 64.*	
28 Sep–19 Oct 1781	*Yorktown*	Inf-*GG. CG. SG. 17. 23. 33. 42. 43. 60. 71. 76. 82.*	
19 Apr 1775–82	*North America 1775–82*	*16 LD. 17 LD.* Inf-*GG. CG. SG. 3. 4. 5. 7. 9. 10. 15. 16. 17. 18. 19. 20. 21. 22. 23. 24. 26. 27. 28. 29. 30. 31. 33. 35. 37. 38. 40. 42. 43. 44. 45. 46. 47. 49. 52. 53. 54. 55. 57. 59. 60. 62. 63. 64. 65. 71. 74. 76. 82. 105.*	App by 16 LD. CG. 4. 5. 9. 16. 17. 22. 24. 27. 28. 29. 30. 31. 37. 40. 42. 43. 47. 49. 52. 54. 55. 57. 63. by various titles and dates.

KORAH

Dates	**Honoured** or *Non-Honoured* Battle	**Honour awarded** to or *Participants in* Battle	Remarks
10 Jun 1776	**Korah**	IND-**Ben NI (m)-1. 10.**	

WAR AGAINST FRANCE AND SPAIN

Dates	**Honoured** or *Non-Honoured* Battle	**Honour awarded** to or *Participants in* Battle	Remarks
13–18 Dec 1778	**St Lucia 1778**	Inf-**4. 5. 15. 27. 28. 35. 40. 46. 49. 55.**	
6 Jul 1779	*Grenada 1779*	Inf-*5. 40.*	App by 5 as Naval Crown with dates '1779–80'
Jun 1779–6 Feb 1783	**Defence of Gibraltar 1779–83**	Inf-**12. 39. 56. 58. 71.** Inf-*25. 59. 65. 72. 73. 97.*	App by 14. Borne as an embellishment although originally the name **Gibraltar** was granted in 1784. Also **Gibraltar Batteries** (5).
16 Jan 1780	*St Vincent 1780*		App by 71.
6 Jan 1781	**Jersey 1781**	Inf-**Royal Jersey Light Infantry (Militia).** Inf-*71. 72. 95.*	Included 1st West Bn, 2nd East Bn and 3rd South Bn R Jersey LI.
20 Aug 1781–5 Feb 1782	*Minorca 1781–82*	Inf-*51. 61.*	App by 51. 61.
11 Jan 12 Feb 1782	*St Kitts*	Inf-*1. 15. 69.*	App by 1. App by 28 as Naval Crown with date '1782'.
12 Apr 1782	**The Saints**	Inf-**69.**	Borne as an embellishment as a Naval Crown and date.

Dates	**Honoured** or *Non-Honoured* Battle	**Honour awarded** to or *Participants in* Battle	Remarks
PONDICHERRY AND GUZERAT			
Oct 1778	*Pondicherry 1778*	Inf-*102*.IND-Inf-*61. 62. 69. 72. 73. 76. 80. GR-1/7. 10. Mad NI (1777)-18.*	
19 May 1778–17 May 1782	**Guzerat**	Inf-**101. 102. 103.** IND-Inf-**Ben NI (m)-2. 3. 5. 7. 11. 13.** IND-Inf-*101. 107. 108. 1/7 GR. Ben NC (m)-2.*	Also covers campaign of 1804-05.
1st MYSORE WAR (against HYDER ALI and TIPPOO SAHIB)			
10 Sep 1780	*(Pollilore 1780) Conjeveram 1780*	Inf-*102.* IND-Inf-*61. 62. 67. 71.*	
Apr 1781–8 Feb 1782	*Tellicherry*	IND-Inf-*101. 103. Mad Sepoys-10. 11.*	
1 Jul 1781	*Porto Novo*	Inf-*71. 101. 102.* IND-Cav-*27. Inf-61. 62. 64. 69. 74. 75. 76. 79. 80. Mad NC (1780)-1. 2. 4. Mad NI (1777)-18.*	
27 Aug 1781	*Pollilore 1781 (Conjeveram 1781)*	Inf-*71. 101. 102.* IND-Cav-*27. Inf-61. 64. 69. 74. 75. 76. 79. 80. 1/7 GR. Ben NI (m)-4. 12. 22. Ben Sepoys (1784)-24. 26. Mad NC (1780)-1. 2. 4. Mad NI (1777)-18.*	
27 Sep 1781	**Sholinghur**	Inf-**71. 101. 102.** IND-Cav-**27.** Inf-**61. 62. 63. 64. 66. 69. 72. 73. 74. 75. 76. 79. 80. GR-2/6. 1/7. Mad S&M.** IND-*Ben NI (m)-4. 12. 22. Ben Sepoys (1784)-24. 26. Mad NC (1780)-1. 2. 4. Mad NI (1777)-18.*	
2nd MYSORE WAR (against HYDER ALI and TIPPOO SAHIB)			
2 Jun 1782	*Arnee*	Inf-*71. 72. 101. 102.*	
27 Nov 1782	*Panianee*	Inf-*73. 98. 100.* IND-Inf-*101. 103. Bom Sepoys-11.*	
26–27 Jan 1783	*Hyderghur*	Inf-*73.*	
13 Jun 1783	*Cuddalore*	Inf-*71. 72. 101. Sandford's (101). 102.* IND-Inf-*64. 75. 76. 80. GR-2/6. 1/7. Ben NI (m)-4. 12. 22. Ben Sepoys (1784)-24. 26. Mad NC (1780)-2. Mad NI (1777)-18.*	
23 May 1783–30 Jan 1784	**Mangalore**	Inf-**73.** IND-Inf-**101.** Inf-*42.* IND-Inf-*108.*	
14 Dec 1783	*Cananore*	Inf-*52.* IND-Inf-*105. Bom Sepoys-13. 14.*	App by 52.
3rd MYSORE WAR (against TIPPOO SAHIB)			
29 Dec 1789	*Lines of Travancore*	Inf-*75.*	
14 Sep 1790	*Cheyoor*	*19 LD.* Inf-*36.* IND-Inf-*61. 2/6 GR. Mad NI (1786)-25.*	
7–21 Mar 1791	*Bangalore*	*19 LD.* Inf-*36. 52. 71. 72. 74. 76. 102.* IND-Cav-*26. 27. 28.* Inf-*73. Ben NI (m)-6. 13. Ben Sepoys (1784)-26. Mad NC (1785)-4. Mad NC-4. Mad NI (1786)-27.*	App by 36. 52.
15 May 1791	*Arikera*	*19 LD.* Inf-*36. 52. 71. 72. 74. 76. 102.* IND-Cav-*26. 28. S&M-Ben. Mad. Inf-61. 64. 66. 69. Ben NC (m)-1. Ben NI (m)-4. 13. 16. Ben Sepoys (1784)-26. 28. Mad NC (1785)-4. Mad NC-4. Mad NI (1786)-22. 23.*	App by 76. Could be called Seringapatam 1791.

Dates	Honoured or Non-Honoured Battle	Honour awarded to or Participants in Battle	Remarks
18 oct 1791	**Nundy Droog**	Inf-**102**. Inf-*36. 71*. IND-*63. 75. 10 GR. Ben NI (m)-4*.	App by 36. 71. Honour awarded by Madras Government.
6–7 Feb 1792	*Seringapatam 1792*	*19 LD*. Inf-*36. 52. 71. 72. 73. 74. 75. 76. 102, 103*. IND-*Madras Bodyguard. Cav-28. Mad S&M. Inf-61. 62. 66. 80. 101. 103. 107. 108. Ben NI (m)-4. 6. 13. 16. Ben Sepoys (1784)-26. 28. Mad NC (1785)-4. Mad NI (1786)-22. 23. Bom NI-6. Bom Sepoys-3. 4*.	App by 36. 52. 75. 76.
1747–92	**Carnatic**	Inf-**71. 72. 101. 102. 103**. IND-Cav-**27 LC. Mad S&M Inf.-61. 62. 63. 64. 66. 67. 69. 72. 73. 74. 75. 76. 79. 80. GR-2/6. 1/7. 10. Ben NI (m)-4. 5. 12. 22. Ben Sepoys (1784)-24. 26**. Inf-*79. 84*. IND-Inf-*71. 101. 103. 104. 105. 107. 108. 121. Mad NC (1780)-1. 2. 4. Mad NI (1777)-18. Bom Sepoys-3. 4. 11. 12. 14. 15*.	
1747–92	**Mysore**	**19 LD**. Inf-**36. 52. 71. 72. 73. 74. 75. 76. 77. 102. 103**. IND-Cav-**26. 27. 28. Mad S&M. Inf-61. 62. 63. 64. 66. 67. 73. 74. 75. 76. 79. 80. 81. 82. 101. 103. 104. 105. 107. 108. 109. GR-2/6, 1/7. 10. Ben NI (m)-4. 6. 13. 16. Ben Sepoys (1784)-26. 28. Mad NC (1780)-4**. IND-*Ben NC (m)-1. Mad NI (1786)-25. 27. Bom NI-6. Bom Sepoys-3. 4*.	

PONDICHERRY

Dates	Honoured or Non-Honoured Battle	Honour awarded to or Participants in Battle	Remarks
10–22 Aug 1793	**Pondicherry 1793**	Inf-**102**. *19 D*. Inf-*36. 52. 71. 72. 73*. IND-*Mad S&M. Inf-61. 62. 63. 66. 67. 68. 69. Mad NC (1780)-4. Mad NI-18. Mad NI (1786)-23. 24. 25*.	Honour covered by Siege of 1761. App by 52.

2nd ROHILLA WAR

Dates	Honoured or Non-Honoured Battle	Honour awarded to or Participants in Battle	Remarks
1794	**Rohilcund 1794**	Inf-**101**. IND-*Ben NI (m)-2. 3. 4. 12. 14. 16. 18. Ben Sepoys (1784)-18. 32*.	Honour for Rising in Rampur.

FRENCH REVOLUTION: CAMPAIGN IN THE AUSTRIAN NETHERLANDS
Medals Awarded: Naval GSM 1793–1840 for **Glorious 1st of June** with Clasp.

Dates	Honoured or Non-Honoured Battle	Honour awarded to or Participants in Battle	Remarks
8 May 1793	*St Amand*	Inf-*CG*.	App by CG.
23 May 1793	*Famars*	*11 D. 16 LD*. Inf-*GG. CG. SG. 14. 37. 53*.	App by 14. 37.
18 Aug 1793	**Lincelles**	Inf-**GG. CG. SG**.	
24 Aug 1793	*Rosendahl*	*2 DG. 3 DG. 6 D. 16 LD*. Inf-*GG. CG. SG. 14. 37. 53*.	App by 14 as 'Dunkirk'.
2–30 Oct 1793	**Nieupore**	Inf-**53**.	Honour awarded for a siege.
28 Oct 1793	*Lannoy*	*7 D. 15 D*. Inf-*CG. SG*.	
24 Apr 1794	**Villers en Cauchies**	**15 D**. *RHG. 3 DG. 1 D. 11 D*.	
26 Apr 1794	**Beaumont**	**RHG. 1 DG. 3 DG. 5 DG. 1 D. 7 D. 11 D. 16 D**.	
10 May 1794	**Willems**	**RHG. 2 DG. 3 DG. 6 DG. 1 D. 2 D. 6 D. 7 D. 11 D. 15 D. 16 D**.	
17–18 May 1794	*Turcoing*	*7 D. 15 D. 16 D*. Inf-*GG. CG. SG. 14. 37. 53*.	

Dates	**Honoured** or *Non-Honoured* Battle	**Honour awarded** to or *Participants in* Battle	Remarks
22 May 1794	**Tournay**	Inf-**14. 37. 53.**	Should have been called 'Pont a Chin'.
1 Jun 1794	**Glorious 1st of June**	Inf-**2. 29.** *Inf-69.*	Borne on badge as embellishment as Naval Crown and date. App by 69.
15 Sep 1794	*Boxtel*	*Inf-12. 33. 44. 89.*	App by 33.
19 Oct 1794	*Druten*	*Inf-37.*	App by 37.
4 Nov 1794	*Nimeguen*	*15 D. Inf-3. 8. 27. 28. 42. 55. 59. 63. 78.*	
30 Dec 1794–5 Jan 1795	*Geldermalsen*	*11 D. 15 D. Inf-14. 19. 27. 28. 33. 42. 78. 80.*	42 Foot gained the right to wear the Red Hackle.
8 Jan 1795	*Buurmalsen*	*Inf-14. 27. 28.*	
10 Jan 1795	*Tiel*	*Inf-40. 50. 79.*	

FRENCH REVOLUTION: CAMPAIGN AROUND THE MEDITERRANEAN

Dates	Battle	Honour	Remarks
1 Oct–15 Dec 1793	*Toulon 1793*	*Inf-1. 11. 18. 30. 69.*	App by 1. 11. 30. 69.
1 Oct 1793	*Mont Faron*	*Inf-11. 30. 69.*	
15 Nov 1793	*Fort Mulgrave*	*Inf-1. 18.*	
29 Nov 1793	*Aresnes*	*Inf-1. 11. 18. 30. 69.*	
7 Feb–10 Aug 1794	*Corsica 1794*	*Inf-1. 11. 18. 30. 50. 51. 69.*	App by 1. 11. 30. 51. 69.
17 Feb 1794	*Convention Redoubt*	*Inf-1. 50. 51.*	
19–31 Jul 1794	*Calvi*	*Inf-18. 50. 51.*	
14 Mar 1795	*Genoa 1795*		App by 11.
1 Oct 1793–1796	*Mediterranean 1793–96*	*Inf-1. 11. 18. 30. 50. 51. 69.*	App by 30.

FRENCH REVOLUTION: CAMPAIGN IN THE WEST INDIES

Dates	Battle	Honour	Remarks	
2 Feb–16 Apr 1794	*Tiburon*	*Inf-13. 20. 49.*		⎫
18 Feb 1794	*L'Acul*	*Inf-1. 13. 20. 49. 62.*		⎬ St Domingo.
31 May 1794	*Port au Prince*	*Inf-41.*		
2 Feb–31 May 1794	*St Domingo*	*Inf-1. 13. 20. 22. 41. 49. 62.*	App by 41. ⎭	
5 Feb–25 Mar 1794	**Martinique 1794**	Inf-**6. 9. 15. 21. 31. 39. 43. 58. 64. 65. 70.** *Inf-8. 12. 17. 22. 23. 33. 34. 35. 38. 40. 41. 44. 55. 56. 60. 66. 68.*	App by 40.	
1 Apr 1794	*St Lucia 1794*	*Inf-6. 9. 12. 31. 35. 43. 44. 56.*		
12 Apr 1794	*Guadeloupe 1794*	*Inf-8. 9. 12. 15. 17. 21. 22. 23. 31. 33. 34. 35. 38. 39. 40. 41. 43. 44. 55. 56. 60. 65. 66. 68.*	App by 40.	⎫
5–6 Jun 1794	*Fort Fleur D'Epee*	*Inf-43.*		⎬ Guadeloupe.
26 Sep–6 Oct 1794	*Berville*	*Inf-6. 8. 12. 17. 22. 23. 31. 39. 43. 56. 65.*	App by 22 as Fort Bizothon. ⎭	
2 Apr–15 Oct 1795	*Grenada 1795*	*Inf-25. 29. 68.*	App by 29.	

Dates	Honoured or Non-Honoured Battle	Honour awarded to or Participants in Battle	Remarks
10 Apr 1795–Jan 1796	*St Vincent 1795*	*Inf-40. 46. 54. 59. 60. 2 WI.*	⎫
5 Aug 1795	*Chateau Belair*	*Inf-46. 60.*	⎬ St Vincent.
8 Jan 1796	*Mount William*	*Inf-40. 54. 59. 2 WI.*	⎪
16 Apr–18 Jun 1795	*St Lucia 1795*	*Inf-9. 61. 68.*	⎭
9 Aug–18 Dec 1795	*Jamaica 1795*	*17 D. 18 D.*	App by 17 D. The Maroon War
25 Mar 1796	*Marquis Bay*	*17 D. Inf-3. 8. 9. 29. 63.*	Grenada
26 Apr–25 May 1796	**St Lucia 1796**	**Inf-27. 53.** *Inf-14. 28. 31. 34. 42. 44. 48. 55. 57. 61. 2 WI.*	App by 55. 57 but 55 refused. ⎫
28 Apr 1796	*Morne Chabot*	*Inf-53. 57. 2 WI.*	⎪
2 May 1796	*Cul de Sac River*	*Inf-14. 27. 28. 42. 44. 2 WI.*	⎬ St Lucia.
17 May 1796	*La Vigie*	*Inf-31.*	⎪
24 May 1796	*Morne Fortune*	*Inf-27.*	⎭
9 Jun 1796	*St Vincent 1796*	*Inf-3. 14. 34. 40. 42. 46. 55. 59. 2 WI.*	App by 14. 34. 42.
8–12 Aug 1796	*Jeremie*	*Inf-17.*	St Domingo.
17–30 Apr 1797	*Porto Rico*	*23 D. Inf-14. 42. 53. 60. 87.*	
1793–1798	*West Indies 1793–98*	*17 D. 18 D. 21 LD. 23 LD. Inf-1. 3. 6. 8. 9. 12. 13. 14. 15. 17. 20. 21. 22. 23. 25. 27. 28. 29. 31. 33. 34. 35. 38. 39. 40. 41. 42. 43. 44. 46. 48. 49. 53. 54. 55. 56. 57. 58. 59. 60. 61. 62. 63. 64. 65. 66. 68. 70. 87. 2 WI.*	App by 2. 9. 11. 14. 16. 17. 22. 28. 30. 31. 39. 49. 54. 59. 61. 63. 66. 70. 83.

FRENCH REVOLUTION: CAMPAIGN IN THE EAST

Dates	Honoured or Non-Honoured Battle	Honour awarded to or Participants in Battle	Remarks
11 Jul–15 Sep 1795	*Cape of Good Hope 1795*	*Inf-78. 84. 91. 95.*	App by 91 refused.
18 Aug 1795–15 Feb 1796	*Ceylon*	*Inf-52. 71. 72. 73. 77. IND-Mad S&M. Inf-61. 67. 69. 78. 101. 105. Mad NI (1786)-23.*	App by 73.

FRENCH REVOLUTION: CAMPAIGN AROUND EUROPE
Medals awarded: Naval GSM 1793–1840 for **St Vincent 1797** with clasp.

Dates	Honoured or Non-Honoured Battle	Honour awarded to or Participants in Battle	Remarks
14 Feb 1797	**St Vincent 1797**	**Inf-69.** *Inf-11.*	App by 11. Naval Battle of Cape St Vincent.
23 Feb 1797	**Fishguard**	**Pembroke Yeomanry (then Cardigan Militia)**	French landing in South Wales.
19–20 May 1798	*Ostend*	*Inf-CG. SG. 11. 23. 49.*	App by 11.
27 Aug 1798	*Castlebar*	*Inf-6.*	App by 17, and by 29 for restoration of Irish Harp badge awarded to the Militia later incorporated in the Regiment.
7–15 Nov 1798	*Minorca 1798*	*Inf-28. 42. 58. 90.*	

FRENCH REVOLUTION: HELDER CAMPAIGN

Dates	Honoured or Non-Honoured Battle	Honour awarded to or Participants in Battle	Remarks
27 Aug 1799	*Landing at the Helder*		App by GG. 27. 85.
27 Aug 1799	*Groete Keten*	*Inf-23. 55.*	
10 Sep 1799	*Zype Canal*	*Inf-20. 40.*	

Dates	**Honoured** or *Non-Honoured* Battle	**Honour awarded** to or *Participants in* Battle	Remarks
19 Sep 1799	*Schoorl-Oudkarspel*	*7 D. 11 D.* Inf-*GG. CG. SG. 5. 9. 17. 29. 35. 40. 56.*	App by 40 as 'Alkmaar'.
2 Oct 1799	**Egmont op Zee**	**15 D.** Inf-**GG. 1. 20. 25. 49. 63. 79. 92.** *7 D.* Inf-*CG. 2. 4. 5. 17. 23. 27. 29. 31. 35. 40. 55. 56.*	App by CG. 2. 4. 27. 29. 55.
2 Oct 1799	*Bergen*	Inf-*GG. CG. 2. 23. 27. 29. 31. 35. 55. 56. 85.*	App by 85. App by 29 refused.
2 Oct 1799	*Schoorldam*	Inf-*CG. SG.*	During this campaign the Royal Artillery was for the first time under separate command and had its own drivers. First action for the new Royal Horse Artillery – A troop, later Chestnut Troop.
6 Oct 1799	*Akersloot* ⎫	Inf-*GG. CG. SG.*	
6 Oct 1799	*Kastrikum* ⎬ *Alkmaar*	*7 D.* Inf-*4. 20. 31. 63.*	
10 Oct 1799	*Winckel* ⎭	Inf-*5.*	App by 5.
27 Aug–6 Oct 1799	*North Holland/Helder*	*7 D. 11 D.* Inf-*GG. CG. SG. 2. 4. 5. 9. 17. 20. 23. 27. 29. 31. 35. 40. 55. 56. 63. 85.*	App by CG. 2. 5. 9. 17. 29. 31. 49. 55. 63.
May 1793–Oct 1799	*Flanders 1793–99*	*RHG. 1 DG. 2 DG. 3 DG. 5 DG. 6 DG. 1 D, 2 D. 6 D. 7 D. 8 D. 11 D. 15 LD. 16 LD.* Inf-*GG. CG. SG. 1. 2. 3. 4. 5. 8. 9. 12. 14. 17. 19. 20. 23. 25. 27. 28. 29. 31. 33. 35. 37. 40. 42. 44. 49. 50. 53. 54. 55. 56. 57. 59. 63. 78. 79. 80. 85. 87. 88. 89. 92.*	App by 1 D. 2 D. 8 D. 16 LD. CG. 27. 28. 30. 37. 39. 42. 57. 63.

4th MYSORE WAR

Dates	**Honoured** or *Non-Honoured* Battle	**Honour awarded** to or *Participants in* Battle	Remarks
8 Mar 1799	**Seedaseer**	IND-Inf-**103. 105. 107.** Inf-*75. 77. 103.* IND-Inf-*109. Ben NI (m)-5. 6. 7. 11. 19. 22.*	App by 77.
27 Mar 1799	*Mallavelli*	*19 LD. 22 LD.* Inf-*12. 33. 74. Scotch Bde.* IND-Cav-*27. 28.* Inf-*61. 66. 73. 82. 83. 84. 1/7 GR. Ben NI (m)-14. 16.*	
5 Apr–4 May 1799	**Seringapatam (1799)**	**19 LD. 22 LD.** Inf-**12. 33. 73. 74. 75. 77. 94. 102. 103.** IND-Cav-**26. 27. 28. Mad Arty. Bom Arty. Mad S&M.** Inf-**61. 66. 71. 73. 76. 79. 80. 81. 82. 83. 84. 103. 104. 105. 107. 109. 1/7 GR. Mad NC-4. Ben NI (m)-14. 16. 36. 37. 38. 39. Bom NI-6.** IND-*Ben S&M. Bom S&M.* Inf- *Ben NI (m)-5. 6. 7. 11. 19. 22.*	Also **Seringapatam Batteries** (2).

FRENCH REVOLUTION: INDIA

Dates	**Honoured** or *Non-Honoured* Battle	**Honour awarded** to or *Participants in* Battle	Remarks
30 Apr 1800	*Arrakaira*	Inf-*73. 77.* IND-Inf-*73. 75. 83.*	
24 Jun–16 Sep 1800	*Bednore-Conagul*	*19 LD. 22 LD.* Inf-*73. 77.* IND-Cav-*26. 27.* Inf-*61. 75. 83. 104. 107. 109. 1/7 GR. Mad NC-4.*	In Mysore against Dhoondiah Singh.
31 Mar–23 May 1801	*Panjalamcoorchy*	Inf-*74. 77.* IND-Cav-*26.* Inf-*63. 64. 69. 85. 87.*	In Tinnevelly against the Polygars.
1 Oct 1801	*Caliarcoil*	Inf-*77.* IND-Inf-*63. 67. 74.*	
14–20 Dec 1801	*Ternakul Fort*	*22 LD.* Inf-*73.* IND-Inf-*75. 83. 90. Mad NC-4. 6.*	In Ceded Territories against the Polygars.
1800–2	*Southern India 1800–02*		App by 77.

Dates	**Honoured** or *Non-Honoured* Battle	**Honour awarded** to or *Participants in* Battle	Remarks

MALTA

Oct 1799–5 Sep 1800	**Malta 1800**	Inf-**35. Royal Malta Regiment.** Inf-*30. 89.*	Date borne on badge by 35.

EGYPT
Medals awarded: GSM 1793–1814 with clasp for campaign.

8 Mar 1801	*Aboukir*	Inf-*CG. SG. 1. 23. 27. 28. 40. 42. 54. 58. 90. 92.*	App by 1. 40. 58.
13 Mar 1801	*Roman camp*	*12 D.* Inf-*8. 13. 18. 23. 28. 40. 42. 58. 90. 92.*	
13 Mar 1801	**Mandora**	Inf.-**90. 92.** *11 D.* Inf-*CG. SG. 1. 2. 13. 28. 30. 44. 50. 79. 89.*	
13 Mar 1801	*Mareotis Bridge*	Inf-*44.*	
21 Mar 1801	*Alexandria*	Inf-*CG. SG. 1. 18. 23. 27. 28. 30. 40. 42. 44. 50.* *54. 58. 79. 89. 92.*	App by 27. 28. 30. 58. 28 gained right to 'Back Badge'.
26 Apr 1801	*Rahmanieh*	*11 D. 12 D.* Inf-*1. 2. 8. 18. 30. 40. 58. 79. 90.*	
21 Aug 1801	**Marabout**	Inf-**54.**	
8 Mar–26 Aug 1801	**Egypt**	**11 D. 12 D.** Inf-**CG. SG. 1. 2. 8. 10. 13. 18. 20. 23. 24. 25. 26. 27. 28. 30. 40. 42. 44. 50. 54. 58. 61. 79. 80. 86. 88. 89. 90. 92. 96. IND-Mad Arty. Bom Arty. Mad S&M.** Inf-**102. 113.** *8 D. 23 D.* Inf-*19.*	App by 8 D refused in 1827. Borne as badge and/or date on accoutrements. Also **Sphinx Batteries** (5).

DENMARK
Medals awarded: Naval GSM 1793–1840 with clasp for **Copenhagen.**

2 Apr 1801	**Copenhagen**	Inf-**49. RB.**	Also borne as Naval Crown with date on accoutrements.

FRENCH REVOLUTION: WEST INDIES 1803–5

22 Jun 1803	**St Lucia 1803**	Inf-**1. 64.** Inf-*68. WI.*	
26 Apr–5 May 1804	**Surinam**	Inf-**16. 64.** Inf-*60. WI.*	
22 Feb 1805	**Dominica**	Inf-**46. WI.**	
1803–1805	*West Indies 1803–05*		App by 11 for General Service Honour with dates 1801–06.

KANDIAN WAR

24–26 Jun 1803	*Kandy*	Inf-*19.*	App by 19, and also for 'Ceylon 1796–1818'.

1st MAHRATTA WAR
Medals awarded: India GSM 1799–1826 with clasps as shown.

8 Aug 1803	*Ahmednuggur*	*19 LD.* Inf-*74. 78.* IND-*Mad S&M.* Inf-*62. 63. 84. Mad NC-5. Mad NI-36.*	
29 Aug 1803	*Broach*	Inf-*61. 86.* IND-Inf-*101.*	
4 Sep 1803	**Ally Ghur** (clasp)	Inf-**76.** IND-**Ben NI (m)-7. 23. 35.** *24 LD.*	Should properly be called Aligarh.

Dates	**Honoured** or *Non-Honoured* Battle	**Honour awarded** to or *Participants in* Battle	Remarks
11 Sep 1803	**Delhi 1803** (clasp)	Inf-**76**. IND-Inf-**2. Ben NC (m)-2. 3. Ben NI (m)-1. 5. 22. 23. 28. 29. 30. 35.** *24 LD.*	
23 Sep 1803	**Assaye** (clasp)	**19 LD.** Inf-**74. 78.** IND-**Mad Arty. Bom Arty. Mad S&M.** Inf-**62. 64. 84. GR–1/7. 10. Mad NC-4. 5. 7.**	Borne by British regiments on badge. Also **Assaye Battery.**

2nd MAHRATTA WAR
Medals awarded: India GSM 1799–1826 with clasps as shown.

Dates	Honoured or Non-Honoured Battle	Honour awarded / Participants	Remarks
14 Oct 1803	*Barrabatta*	Inf-*22. 102.* IND- Inf-*69. Ben NI (m)-10. Mad NI-37.*	
18 Oct 1803	*Agra*	*8 LD. 25 LD.* IND-Inf-*2. 4. Ben NI (m)–12. 21. 28. 30.*	
18–20 Oct 1803	*Asirghar 1803 (Aseerghur) (clasp)*	Inf-*94.* IND-Inf-*66. 71. 79. 80. 81. 82.*	App by 94.
1 Nov 1803	**Leswaree** (clasp)	**8 D. 25 LD.** Inf-**76.** IND-Inf-**1. 2. 4. Ben NC (m)-1. 2. 3. 4. 6. Ben NI (m)-1. 12. 24. 30.** *24 LD.*	
28 Nov 1803	*Argaum (clasp)*	*19 LD.* Inf-*74. 78. 94.* IND-Cav-*28.* Inf-*62. 63. 64. 66. 71. 79. 80. 81. 82. 84. GR-1/7. 10. Mad NC-4. 5. 6. 7.*	*App by 74. 94.*
14 Dec 1803	*Gawilghur (clasp)*	Inf-*74. 78. 94.* IND-Inf-*62. 66. 79. 80. 81. 82. GR-1/7. 10.*	App by 74. 94.
13 Nov–24 Dec 1804	**Deig** (clasp)	Inf-**76. 101.** IND-Inf-**2. Ben NC (m)-2. 3. Ben NI (m)-5. 7. 9. 30. 44.** *8 D.* Inf-*22.* IND-*Ben NI (m)-12.*	App by 22. Siege began 13 Nov and fort captured 24 Dec.
17 Nov 1804	*Farakhabad*	*8 D. 24 LD. 25 LD.* Inf-*22.* IND-*Ben NC (m)-1. 4. 6. Ben NI (m)-1. 12.*	App by 8 D.
9 Jan–23 Feb 1805	*Bhurtpore 1805*	*8 D.* Inf-*22. 65. 75. 76. 86. 101.* IND-Inf-*2. 101. 104. 105. 117. Ben NI (m)-1. 5. 9. 12. Bom NI-18.*	App by 22. 73. 76.
23 Jan 1805	*Combir*	*24 LD.* IND-*Ben NC (m)-1. 2. Ben NI (m)-30.*	
2 Mar 1805	*Afzalghar*	*8 D. 24 LD. 25 LD.* IND-Cav-*1.*	App by 8 D.
Jul 1803–7 Jan 1806	*India 1803–06*		App by 80.

CAPE OF GOOD HOPE

Dates	Honoured or Non-Honoured Battle	Honour awarded / Participants	Remarks
8 Jan 1806	**Cape of Good Hope 1806**	Inf-**24. 59. 71. 72. 83. 93.** *20 LD.* Inf-*38.*	App by 38.

FRENCH REVOLUTION: ITALY AND EGYPT
Medals awarded: GSM 1793–1814 with clasp for **Maida**.

Dates	Honoured or Non-Honoured Battle	Honour awarded / Participants	Remarks
4 Jul 1806	**Maida**	Inf-**20. 27. 35. 58. 61. 78. 81.** *20 LD.*	Grenadier coy only of 61. Light coy of 56 also engaged.
31 Mar–21 Apr 1807	*Rosetta*	*20 LD.* Inf-*31. 35. 78.*	
1 Jan–17 Feb 1808	*Siege of Scilla*	Inf-*27. 58. 62.*	
1806–1812	*Sicily 1806-12*		App by 27 as General Service Honour.

Dates	**Honoured** or *Non-Honoured* Battle	**Honour awarded** to or *Participants in* Battle	Remarks
SOUTH AMERICA			
3 Feb 1807	**Monte Video**	Inf-**38. 40. 87. RB.**	App by 47 for detachment.
7 Jun 1807	*San Pedro*	Inf-*40. RB.*	App by 40.
5 Jul 1807	*Buenos Aires*	*6 DG. 9 D. 17 LD. Inf-5. 36. 38. 40. 45. 87. 88. RB.*	
DENMARK			
15 Aug–5 Sep 1807	*Copenhagen 1807*	*Inf-CG. SG. 4. 7. 8. 23. 28. 32. 43. 50. 52. 79. 82. 92.*	App by 4. 7. 28. 43. 50. 52. 82. RB.
INDIA			
12 Oct–18 Nov 1807	*Chumar (Komona)*	*Inf-17. IND-Ben S&M. Ben NC (m)-3. 6. Ben NI (m)-8. 26. 45. 53. 54.*	

FRENCH REVOLUTION: 1st PENINSULA CAMPAIGN (Sir John Moore)
Medals awarded: GSM 1793–1814 with clasps as shown (jointly for **Sahagun** and *Benavente*)

Dates	Battle	Honour	Remarks
17 Aug 1808	**Rolica** (clasp)	Inf-**5. 6. 9. 29. 32. 36. 38. 45. 60. 71. 82. 91. RB.** *20 LD.*	App by 20 LD. 50.
21 Aug 1808	**Vimiera** (clasp)	**20 LD.** Inf-**2. 5. 6. 9. 20. 29. 32. 36. 38. 40. 43. 45. 50. 52. 60. 71. 82. 91. 96. RB.** Inf-*42.*	Properly Vimiero.
21 Dec 1808	**Sahagun** (joint clasp)	**15 LD.**	
29 Dec 1808	*Benavente (joint clasp)*	*7 D. 10 D. 18 LD.*	
16 Jan 1809	**Corunna** (clasp)	Inf-**GG. 1. 2. 4. 5. 6. 9. 14. 20. 23. 26. 28. 32. 36. 38. 42. 43. 50. 51. 52. 59. 71. 76. 79. 81. 82. 91. 92. 96. RB.** *7 D. 10 D. 15 LD.*	Also **Corunna Batteries** (2).

FRENCH REVOLUTION: WEST INDIES 1809
Medals awarded: GSM 1793–1814 with clasp for **Martinique 1809**.

Dates	Battle	Honour	Remarks
30 Jan–24 Feb 1809	**Martinique 1809**	Inf-**7. 8. 13. 15. 23. 25. 60. 63. 90. WI.** Inf-*46.*	Also **Martinique Battery** and **Battle-axe Company.**
1–2 Feb 1809	*Morne Bruneau*	Inf-*7. 8. 23. WI.*	
14–17 Apr 1809	*The Saints*	Inf-*60. WI.*	App by 15.

TRAVANCORE

Dates	Battle	Honour	Remarks
1809	**Cochin**	IND-Inf-**93.** Inf-*12.*	

WAR AGAINST ARAB PIRATES

Dates	Battle	Honour	Remarks
1809	*Arabia 1809*	Inf-*47. 65. IND-Inf-104. 121.*	Said to be covered by award of **Arabia** 1819.

FRENCH REVOLUTION: PENINSULA 1809
Medals awarded. Clasp to GSM 1793–1814 for **Talavera**.

Dates	Battle	Honour	Remarks
12 May 1809	**Douro**	**14 LD.** Inf-**3. 48. 66.** *20 LD. Inf-CG. SG. 29. 38. 43. 52. 60. RB.*	App by 16 LD. CG. 28. 29. App by 83 refused.
27–28 Jul 1809	**Talavera**	**3 DG. 4 D. 14 LD. 16 LD.** Inf-**CG. SG. 3. 7. 24. 28. 29. 31. 40. 45. 48. 53. 60. 61. 66. 83. 87. 88.** *23 LD. Inf-6. 38. 42. 92. 96. RB.*	App by 43. 52. RB. and by 96 as successors to 97. Also **Talavera Battery.**

FRENCH REVOLUTION: FLANDERS 1809

Dates	Battle	Honour	Remarks
30 Jul–16 Aug 1809	*Walcheren*	Inf-*GG. 1. 5. 14. 23. 26. 32. 35. 36. 51. 59. 63. 68. 71. 76. 77. 78. 79. 81. 82. 85. 95. RB.*	App by 4. App by 2 and 65/84 as Flushing 1809.

Dates	**Honoured** or *Non-Honoured* Battle	**Honour awarded** to or *Participants in* Battle	Remarks

FRENCH REVOLUTION: WEST INDIES 1810
Medals awarded: Clasp to GSM 1793–1814 for **Guadeloupe 1810**.

| 28 Jan–4 Feb 1810 | **Guadeloupe 1810** | Inf-**15. 63. 70. 90. WI.**
Inf-*1. 13. 25. 46. 60. 96.* | |

FRENCH REVOLUTION: MEDITERRANEAN 1810

| 22 Mar–16 Apr 1810 | *Santa Maura* | Inf-*35.* | Ionian Islands. |
| 18 Sep 1810 | *Mili* | Inf-*21.* | |

FRENCH REVOLUTION: FAR EAST 1810

17 Feb 1810	**Amboyna**	Inf-**102.**	
7–10 Jul 1810	**Bourbon**	Inf-**69. 86.** IND-**Mad Arty. Mad S&M.** Inf-**66. 84. 104.** Inf-*12. 33. 56.*	Now **Reunion**
9 Aug 1810	**Banda**	Inf-**102.**	
28 Aug 1810	**Ternate**	Inf-**102.**	
1 Dec 1810	*Mauritius*	Inf-*12. 14. 19. 22. 33. 56. 59. 65. 69. 72. 84. 86. 87. 89.* IND-Inf-*104. Ben NI (m)-1. 9. 24. 30. 39. 49. 50.*	App by 12. 22. 30. 89, and by 84 as 'Ile de France 1810'.

FRENCH REVOLUTION: PENINSULA 1810
Medals awarded: Clasp to GSM 1793–1814 for **Busaco**.

23 Jul 1810	*The Coa*	*16 LD.* Inf-*43. 52. RB.*	App by 43. 52. RB.
27 Sep 1810	**Busaco**	Inf-**1. 5. 7. 9. 24. 28. 38. 42. 43. 45. 52. 60. 61. 74. 79. 83. 88. RB.** Inf-*CG. SG. 11. 27. 40. 96.*	App by CG. SG. 27. 34.
1810	*Cadiz 1810*		App by GG. 94.
1810	*Torres Vedras*		App by 1 D. 16 LD. 97 as either 'Retreat' or 'Pursuit'.

4th KAFFIR WAR SOUTH AFRICA

| 1811–1812 | *South Africa 1811–12* | SA-*Cape Mounted Riflemen* | |

FRENCH REVOLUTION: PENINSULA 1811
Medals awarded: Clasp to GSM 1793–1814 as shown.

5 Mar 1811	**Barrosa** (clasp)	Inf-**GG. CG. SG. 28. 67. 87. RB.** Inf-*9. 47. 82.*	App by 9. 47. 82. but 82 refused.
6–25 Mar 1811	*Casal Novo*		App by 43. 52. RB.
25 Mar 1811	*Campo Maior*	*13 LD.*	
3 Apr 1811	*Sabugal*	Inf-*5. 43. 44. 52. 60. 94. RB.*	App by 16 LD. 5. 43. 52. RB.
3–5 May 1811	**Fuentes d'Onor** (clasp)	**1 D. 14 LD. 16 LD.** Inf-**CG. SG. 24. 42. 43. 45. 51. 52. 60. 71. 74. 79. 83. 85. 88. 92. RB.** Inf-*1. 4. 5. 9. 44. 50. 94.*	App by 1. 50. Also **Bull's Troop.**
16 May 1811	**Albuhera** (clasp)	**3 DG. 4 D. 13 LD.** Inf-**3. 7. 23. 28. 29. 31. 34. 39. 48. 57. 60. 66.** Inf-*27. 97.*	App by 27. 97.
25 May 1811	*Usagre*	*3 DG. 4 D. 13 LD.*	
30 May–10 Jun 1811	*Siege of Badajoz*	Inf-*27. 40. 51. 85. 96.*	

Dates	**Honoured** or *Non-Honoured* Battle	**Honour awarded** to or *Participants in* Battle	Remarks

FAR EAST 1811
Medals awarded: Clasp to GSM 1793–1814 for **Java**.

4 Aug–16 Sep 1811	**Java**	Inf-**14. 59. 69. 78. 89.** IND-**GGBG. Mad Arty. Mad S&M.** Inf-**Ben NI (m)-25.** *22 LD.*	Also **Java Battery.**

FRENCH REVOLUTION: PENINSULA 1811–12
Medals awarded: Clasp to GSM 1793–1814 as shown.

25 Sep 1811	*El Bodon*	*11 LD.* Inf-*5. 60. 74. 77. 83.*	App by 11 LD (refused 1838) and by 5. 77.
27 Sep 1811	*Aldea da Ponte*		App by 7.
28 Oct 1811	**Arroyo dos Molinos**	Inf-**34.** *9 D. 13 LD.* Inf-*28. 39. 50. 71. 92.*	App by 28. 39. 50. 71. 92 (92 refused).
Dec 1811–Jan 1812	**Tarifa**	Inf-**47. 87.** Inf-*82. RB.*	App by 11. RB.
9–19 Jan 1812	**Ciudad Rodrigo** (clasp)	Inf-**5. 43. 45. 52. 60. 74. 77. 83. 88. 94. RB.** Inf-*CG. SG. 7. 24. 40. 42.*	App by 4 DG. CG. SG. 7. 24. 40.
17 Mar–6 Apr 1812	**Badajoz** (clasp)	Inf-**4. 5. 7. 23. 27. 30. 38. 40. 43. 44. 45. 48. 52. 60. 74. 77. 83. 88. 94. RB.** *13 LD.* Inf-*92.*	App by 4 DG.
11 Apr 1812	*Llerena*	*5 DG. 4 D. 12 LD. 14 LD. 16 LD.*	App by 4 DG. 16 LD. as 'Villa Garcia'.
19 May 1812	**Almaraz**	Inf-**50. 71. 92.** *13 LD.* Inf-*28. 60.*	App by 28. 34.
22 Jul 1812	**Salamanca** (clasp)	**5 DG. 3 D. 4 D. 11 LD. 12 LD. 14 LD. 16 LD.** Inf-**CG. SG. 1. 2. 4. 5. 7. 9. 11. 23. 24. 27. 30. 32. 36. 38. 40. 42. 43. 44. 45. 48. 51. 52. 53. 58. 60. 61. 68. 74. 79. 83. 88. 94. RB.**	Several applications initially refused but subsequently approved.
19 Sep–22 Oct 1812	*Siege of Burgos*	Inf-*CG. SG. 23. 24. 28. 32. 36. 42. 58. 61. 74. 79.*	App by CG.
23 Oct 1812	*Torquemada*	*11 LD. 12 LD. 16 LD.*	

NORTH AMERICA 1812
Medals awarded: Clasp to GSM 1793–1814 for **Detroit**.

16 Aug 1812	**Detroit**	Inf-**41.**	
13 Oct 1812	**Queenstown**	Inf-**41. 49.** CDN-*Essex Militia. York Vols.*	Properly Queenston.
21 Jan 1813	**Miami**	Inf-**41.**	Properly Frenchtown or Maumee.

FRENCH REVOLUTION: PENINSULA 1813
Medals awarded: Clasps to GSM 1793–1814 as shown.

12–13 Apr 1813	*Castalla*	Inf-*27. 58.*	App by 27.
18 June 1813	*San Millan*	Inf-*52. RB.*	
21 June 1813	**Vittoria** (clasp)	**3 DG. 5 DG. 3 D. 4 D. 13 LD. 14 LD. 15 LD. 16 LD.** Inf-**1. 2. 3. 4. 5. 6. 7. 9. 20. 23. 24. 27. 28. 31. 34. 38. 39. 40. 43. 45. 47. 48. 50. 51. 52. 53. 57. 59. 60. 66. 68. 71. 74. 82. 83. 87. 88. 92. 94. RB.** *LG. RHG. 10 LD.* Inf-*CG. SG.*	App by 1 D. CG.
25 Jul–31 Aug 1813	**San Sebastian** (clasp)	Inf-**1. 4. 9. 38. 47. 59.** Inf-*GG. CG. SG. 2. 7. 27. 40. 68. 82. 85. RB.*	App by CG. SG. 43. 52. RB. Full dates – 9 Jun–8 Sep.

Dates	**Honoured** or *Non-Honoured* Battle	**Honour awarded** to or *Participants in* Battle	Remarks
25 Jul 1813	*Roncesvalles*		App by 20.
25 Jul 1813	*The Maya*	Inf-*39. 71. 74. 82. 92.*	App by 28. 92.
25 Jul–2 Aug 1813	**Pyrenees** (clasp)	**14 LD.** Inf-**2. 3. 6. 7. 11. 20. 23. 24. 27. 28. 31. 32. 34. 36. 39. 40. 42. 43. 45. 48. 50. 52. 53. 57. 58. 60. 61. 66. 68. 71. 74. 79. 82. 88. 91. 92. 94. RB.** *13 LD. 15 LD. 18 LD.* Inf-*51. 87.*	App by 83 refused.
31 Aug 1813	*San Marcial*	Inf-*51. 68. 82. 85. RB.*	App by 43. 52, and by 51 as 'Lesaca'.
13 Sep 1813	*Ordal*	Inf-*27.*	
7 Oct 1813	*Bidassoa*	Inf-*GG. CG. SG. 3. 4. 9. 27. 30. 38. 43. 44. 47. 51. 52. 59. 60. 84. RB.*	App by GG. I. 9. 29. 30, and by 43. 52. RB. as Vera.
10 Nov 1813	**Nivelle** (clasp)	Inf-**2. 3. 5. 6. 11. 23. 24. 27. 28. 31. 32. 34. 36. 39. 40. 42. 43. 45. 48. 51. 52. 53. 57. 58. 60. 61. 66. 68. 74. 79. 82. 83. 87. 88. 91. 94. RB.** *13 LD.* Inf-*1. 4. 9. 20. 38. 59. 62. 84. 85. 92.*	App by CG. SG. 4. 76.
9–13 Dec 1813	**Nive** (clasp)	**16 LD.** Inf-**GG. CG. SG. 1. 3. 4. 9. 11. 28. 31. 32. 34. 36. 38. 39. 42. 43. 47. 50. 52. 57. 59. 60. 61. 62. 66. 71. 76. 79. 84. 85. 91. 92. RB.** *12 LD. 13 LD.* Inf-*5. 23. 27. 45. 68. 87. 94.*	App by 45. 88. 94. App by 83 refused.
13 Dec 1813	*St Pierre*	Inf-*GG. 31. 57.*	App by 57.

FRENCH REVOLUTION: GERMANY 1813

Dates	Battle	Honour / Participants	Remarks
16 Sep 1813	*Göhrde*	Inf-*73.*	App by 73. Near Leipzig.
13 Oct 1813	*Leipzig*		Rocket Troop only British unit present.

NORTH AMERICA 1813
Medals awarded: Clasps to GSM 1793–1814 as shown.

Dates	Battle	Honour / Participants	Remarks
27 Apr 1813	*York*	Inf-*8.* CDN-*Glengarry LI Fencibles.*	
27 May 1813	*Fort George*	Inf-*8.* CDN-*Glengarry LI Fencibles.*	
28 May 1813	*Sackett's Harbour*	Inf-*1. 8. 100. 104.* CDN-*Glengarry LI Fencibles. Voltigeurs.*	
6 Jun 1813	*Stoney Creek*	Inf-*8. 49.*	
5 Oct 1813	*Moravian Town*	Inf-*41.*	
26 Oct 1813	*Chateaugai* (clasp)	CDN-*Voltigeurs*	
11 Nov 1813	*Chrysler's Farm* (clasp)	Inf-*49. 89.* CDN-*Voltigeurs. Stormont Militia.*	App by 49 (refused 1850) and by 89.
19 Dec 1813	*Fort Niagara*	Inf-*1. 41. 100.*	
29 Dec 1813	*Buffalo*	Inf-*1. 8. 41. 89. 100.*	

FRENCH REVOLUTION: PENINSULA AND EUROPE 1814
Medals awarded: GSM 1793–1814 for campaign and clasps as shown.

Dates	Battle	Honour / Participants	Remarks
30 Jan 1814	*Merxem*	Inf-*54. 56. 73. RB.*	*In Belgium.*
Feb 1814	*St Etienne (I)*	Inf-*GG. CG. SG.*	
15 Feb 1814	*Garris*	Inf-*39. 66.*	App by 39.
27 Feb 1814	**Orthez** (clasp)	**7 D. 13 LD. 14 LD.** Inf-**3. 5. 6. 7. 11. 20. 23. 24. 27. 28. 31. 32. 34. 36. 39. 40. 42. 45. 48. 50. 51. 52. 58. 60. 61. 66. 68. 71. 74. 82. 83. 87. 88. 92. 94.** *15 LD. 18 LD.* Inf-*2. 91. RB.*	

Dates	Honoured or Non-Honoured Battle	Honour awarded to or Participants in Battle	Remarks
2 Mar 1814	*Aire*	*13 LD.* Inf-*3. 50. 57. 71. 92.*	
8–9 Mar 1814	*Bergen op Zoom*	Inf-*GG. CG. SG. 1. 21. 33. 37. 44. 59. 69. 91.*	App by 55.
20 Mar 1814	*Tarbes*	Inf-*RB.*	App by 43. 52. RB.
17 Apr 1814	*Genoa 1814*		App by 31.
10 Apr 1814	**Toulouse** (clasp)	5 DG. 3 D. 4 D. 13 LD. Inf-**2. 3. 5. 7. 11. 20. 23. 27. 28. 36. 40. 42. 43. 45. 48. 52. 53. 60. 61. 71. 74. 79. 83. 87. 88. 91. 94. RB.** Inf-*31. 32. 39. 66. 92.*	App by 34. 50.
14 Apr 1814	*St Etienne* (II)	Inf-*GG. CG. 38.*	
17 Aug 1808–14 Apr 1814	**Peninsula**	**LG. RHG. 3 DG. 4 DG. 5 DG. 1 D. 3 D. 4 D. 7 D. 9 D. 10 LD. 11 LD. 12 LD. 13 LD. 14 LD. 15 LD. 16 LD. 18 LD. 20 LD. 23 LD. Inf-GG. CG. SG. 1. 2. 3. 4. 5. 6. 7. 9. 10. 11. 20. 23. 24. 27. 28. 29. 30. 31. 32. 34. 36. 37. 38. 39. 40. 42. 43. 44. 45. 47. 48. 50. 51. 52. 53. 56. 57. 58. 59. 60. 61. 62. 66. 67. 68. 71. 74. 75. 76. 77. 79. 81. 82. 83. 84. 85. 87. 88. 91. 92. 93. 94. 96. RB.** Inf-*14. 21. 89.*	App by 40. 45. 60 for dates 1808–14. Laurel wreath awarded to all regts which served in the Peninsula as an embellishment to their badge. Also **Chestnut Troop** and **Lawson's Company.**

NORTH AMERICA 1814–15

Dates	Honoured or Non-Honoured Battle	Honour awarded to or Participants in Battle	Remarks
5 Jul 1814	*Street's Creek*	Inf-*1. 8. 100.*	
25 Jul 1814	*Lundy's Lane*	*19 LD.* Inf-*1. 8. 41. 89. 103. 104.* CDN-*Glengarry LI Fencibles.*	App by 1.
15 Aug 1814	*Fort Erie*	Inf-*1. 8. 41. 89. 100. 103. 104.* CDN-*Glengarry LI Fencibles*	App by 1 as Erie.
5 Jul–15 Aug 1814	**Niagara**	**19 LD. Inf-1. 6. 8. 41. 82. 89. 100. 103 (Somerset's). 104 (NB Regt)** CDN-**Glengarry LI Fencibles**	Honour presumed to cover all operations in Niagara peninsula. Also **Niagara** Battery.
24 Aug 1814	**Bladensburg**	Inf-**4. 21. 44. 85.**	
1814	*Plattsburg*		App by 33.
8 Jan 1815	*New Orleans*		App by 93.
1812–14	*North America 1812–1814*	*19 LD.* Inf-*1. 4. 6. 8. 21. 33. 39. 41. 44. 49. 58. 82. 85. 89. 93. 100. 103 (Somerset's). 104 (NB Regt).* CDN-*Essex Militia. Voltigeurs. Glengarry LI.*	App by 1, and by 58 as 'America 1814' by 39 as 'Defence of Canada 1814', and by 49 as 'Defence of Canada 1812–14'.

FRENCH REVOLUTION: FLANDERS 1815
Medal awarded: Waterloo Medal for battle.

Dates	Honoured or Non-Honoured Battle	Honour awarded to or Participants in Battle	Remarks
16–18 Jun 1815	**Waterloo**	**LG. RHG. 1 DG. 1 D. 2 D. 6 D. 7 D. 10 LD. 11 LD. 12 LD. 13 LD. 15 LD. 16 LD. 18 LD. 23 LD. Inf-GG. CG. SG. 1. 4. 14. 23. 27. 28. 30. 32. 33. 40. 42. 44. 51. 52. 69. 71. 73. 79. 92. RB.**	App by 35. Also celebrated by **Mercer's Troop, Ramsay's Troop, Bull's Troop, Sandham's Company, Lloyd's Company, Rogers's Company,** and X Battery.
16 Jun 1815	*Quatre Bras*		App by CG. SG. 1. 28. 30. 79.

Dates	**Honoured** or *Non-Honoured* Battle	**Honour awarded** to or *Participants in* Battle	Remarks
1813–15	*Low Countries 1813–15*		App by 37.
1814	*Netherlands 1814*		App by 54.

FRENCH REVOLUTION: WEST INDIES 1815

1815	*Gaudaloupe 1815*		App by 15.
1815	*West Indies 1815*		App by 63.

NEPAL
Medals awarded: Clasp to India GSM 1799–1826.

6 Oct 1814– 4 Mar 1816	*Nepal 1814–16*	*8 LD.* Inf-*14. 17. 24. 53. 66. 87.* IND-*Cav-2. Ben S&M.* Inf-*1. 2. 8. Ben NC(m)-2. 6. 7. Ben NI(m)-1. 2. 3. 4. 7. 9. 13. 18. 19. 20. 23. 24. 28. 34. 35. 36. 37. 38. 39. 41. 42. 44. 50. Ramgarh Local Inf. Champaran Light Inf.*	App by 8 LD. 24. 53. 87.

CEYLON

10 Jan 1815– Nov 1818	*Ceylon 1815–1818*	Inf-*19. 73. 83.*	App by 19 as 'Ceylon 1796–1820'.

3rd MAHRATTA WAR (PINDARI WAR)
Medals awarded: Clasps to India GSM 1799–1826 as shown.

5 Nov 1817	**Kirkee** (clasp)	Inf-**103.** IND-**Bom Arty.** Inf-**102. 112. 113. 123.**	Also **Kirkee Battery.**
17 Nov 1817	*Poona* (clasp)	Inf-*65. 103.* IND-Inf-*102. 103. 105. 107. 112. 113. 123. Ben NI(m)-44.*	
26–27 Nov 1817	**Seetabuldee** (clasp)	IND-**Mad Arty. Mad Bodyguard.** Inf-**61. Ben NC(m)-6. Mad NI-39.**	
16–24 Dec 1817	**Nagpore** (clasp)	Inf-**1.** IND-**Mad Arty. Mad S&M.** Inf-**6. 61. 62. 77. 81. 83. 86. 88. 97. Ben NC(m)-6. Mad NC-6. Mad NI-39.**	
23 Dec 1817	**Maheidpore** (clasp)	Inf-**1. 102.** IND-**Mad Arty. Mad S&M.** Cav-**28.** Inf-**63. 74. 87. 88. 91. 94. 95. Mad NC-4. 8. Mad NI-Mad Rif. 1 Hyd Bty.** *22 LD.* IND-*Mysore Horse.*	
1 Jan 1818	**Corygaum** (clasp)	IND-**Mad Arty.** Cav-**34.** Inf-**102.**	
17–29 May 1818	*Mulligaum*	Inf-*1. 102.* IND-Inf-*62. 86. 88. 94. 95. Mad NI-34.*	
8–31 Jan 1818	**Nowah**	IND-Inf-**94. 95. 96. 1 Hyd Bty.** IND-Inf-*97.*	
18 Mar–9 Apr 1819	*Asirgarh 1819*	Inf-*1. 30. 67. 102.* IND-Cav-*27. 28. 34. S&M–Ben. Mad.* Inf-*2. 66. 67. 74. 82. 83. 87. 88. 101. Ben NC(m)-6. 7. Ben NI(m)-1. 4. 13. 15. 17. 29. 30. 58. Mad NC-7. Mad NI-34. Bom NI-15. 18.*	App by 30 as 'Asseerghur'.

Dates	**Honoured** or *Non-Honoured* Battle	**Honour awarded** to or *Participants in* Battle	Remarks
Nov 1817–9 Apr 1819	*Pindari*	*8 LD. 17 LD. 22 LD. Inf-1. 14. 30. 47. 53. 59. 65. 67. 84. 86. 102. 103. IND-Cav-GGBG. 1. 2. 27. 28. 34. Mad Bodyguard. Mad Arty. Bom Arty. S&M-Ben. Mad. Bom. Inf-2. 6. 61. 62. 63. 64. 66. 67. 71. 74. 75. 77. 81. 82. 83. 84. 86. 87. 88. 91. 94. 95. 96. 97. 101. 102. 103. 104. 105. 107. 108. 109. 110. 112. 113. 114. 117. 119. 121. 123. Ben NC(m)-1. 2. 3. 4. 6. 7. 8. 2 Roh H. 3 Roh H. Ben NI(m)-1. 2. 3. 4. 9. 10. 13. 15. 16. 17. 20. 24. 27. 28. 29. 30. 36. 39. 44. 45. 47. 49. 50. 51. 53. 55. 56. 57. 58. Mad NC-4. 6. 7. 8. Mad NI-34. 39. 43. Mad Rif. 1 Hyd Bty. Mysore H. Bom NI-6. 11. 15. 18.*	

GENERAL SERVICE HONOURS IN INDIA

Dates	**Honoured** or *Non-Honoured* Battle	**Honour awarded** to or *Participants in* Battle	Remarks
1787–1826	**India** **(India 1796–1819)**	Inf-**12**(1798–1809). **14**(1807–31). **65**(1802–22). **67**(1805–26). **69**(1805–25). **75**(1787–1813). **84**(1796–1819 **with date incl).** **86**(1799–1819).	App by 22. Awarded for general service in India over various periods. Borne on badge with 'Royal Tiger' by 14. 65. 67. 75.
1780–1823	**Hindoostan**	**8 D**(1802–22). **24 LD**(1803–08). Inf-**17**(1804–23). **36**(1790–93). **52**(1790–93). **71**(1780–1800). **72**(1782–93). **76**(1790–1805).	Awarded for general service in India over various periods. Borne on badge with 'Royal Tiger' by 17 and with 'Elephant and Howdah' by 76.
1807–29	*India 1807–1829*		App by 47 as General Service Honour.
1815–19	*India 1815–1819*		App by 1 as General Service Honour.

5th KAFFIR WAR

Dates	**Honoured** or *Non-Honoured* Battle	**Honour awarded** to or *Participants in* Battle	Remarks
22 Jul–14 Aug 1819	*South Africa 1819*	Inf-*38. 72.* SA-*Cape Mtd Riflemen*	App by 38.

WAR AGAINST ARAB PIRATES

Dates	**Honoured** or *Non-Honoured* Battle	**Honour awarded** to or *Participants in* Battle	Remarks
3–19 Dec 1819	**Arabia**	Inf-**65.** Inf-*47.* IND-Inf-*103. 105.*	App by 47.
3–19 Dec 1819	**Persian Gulf 1819**	IND-Inf-**121.**	Same honour as Arabia above.
2 Mar 1821	**Beni Boo Alli**	Inf-**103.** IND-**Bombay Arty.** Inf-**103. 104. 105. 107. 113. 121. Bombay NI-18.** Inf-*65.* IND-*Bom S&M.*	App by 65.

ASSAM

Dates	**Honoured** or *Non-Honoured* Battle	**Honour awarded** to or *Participants in* Battle	Remarks
17 Jan 1824–29 Jan 1825	**Assam**	IND-**Ben NI(m)-46. 57.** IND-Inf-*1/6GR.* Ben NI(m)-*14.*	

1st BURMA WAR

Medals awarded: Clasp to India GSM 1799–1826 for **Ava** campaign.

Dates	**Honoured** or *Non-Honoured* Battle	**Honour awarded** to or *Participants in* Battle	Remarks
1–9 Dec 1824	**Kemendine**	IND-Inf-**86.** Inf-*102.*	
7 Mar–2 Apr 1825	*Donobyu*	Inf-*38. 47. 89. 102.*	

Dates	Honoured or Non-Honoured Battle	Honour awarded to or Participants in Battle	Remarks
26 Mar–1 Apr 1825	**Arracan**	IND-Cav-**2**. Inf-**5**. **Ben NI(m) 26. 40. 49. 62.** Inf-*44. 54.* IND-Inf-*4. 6. 9. 76.* GR-*10.* Ben NI(m)-*2. 7. 14. 39. 42. 44. 45. 52. 59.*	App by 54. Also **Arracan Battery.**
2 Dec 1825	*Napadi*	Inf-*13. 38. 47. 89.* IND-*Mad NI-38.*	
17 Jan 1824–24 Feb 1826	**Ava**	Inf-**1. 13. 38. 41. 44. 45. 47. 54. 87. 89. 102.** IND-Cav-**26. Mad Arty. Mad S&M.** Inf-**61. 63. 67. 69. 72. 76. 82. 86. 88. 90. 92. 10 GR. Ben NI-40. Mad NI-18. 36. 38. 43.** IND-Inf-*4. 6. 9. 61.* GR-*1/6. 1/7. 1/8.* Ben NC(m)-*3. 1 Roh H.* Ben NI(m)-*2. 7. 14. 26. 27. 39. 42. 44. 45. 46. 49. 52. 59. 62. Dinajpur Bn. Champaran LI.*	
As above	**Burmah**	IND-Inf-**121.**	Awarded instead of Ava.

JAT WAR
Medals awarded: Clasp to India GSM 1799–1826.

Dates	Honoured or Non-Honoured Battle	Honour awarded to or Participants in Battle	Remarks
Dec 1825–18 Jan 1826	**Bhurtpore**	**11 LD. 16 LD.** Inf-**14. 59. 101.** IND-Cav -**1. Beng S&M.** Inf-**1. 2. 3. 4. 9. 1/1 GR. 1/2 GR.** Ben NC(m)-**3. 4. 6. 8. 9. 10.** Ben NI(m)-**6. 11. 15. 18. 23. 35. 36. 37. 41. 58. 60.**	Also **Bhurtpore Battery.**

COORG

Dates	Honoured or Non-Honoured Battle	Honour awarded to or Participants in Battle	Remarks
2 Apr 1834	*Coorg*	Inf-*39. 48. 55.*	App by 55.

6th KAFFIR WAR
Medals awarded: South African Medal 1834–53.

Dates	Honoured or Non-Honoured Battle	Honour awarded to or Participants in Battle	Remarks
21 Dec 1834–17 Sep 1835	**South Africa 1835**	Inf-**27. 72. 75.** SA-*Cape Mtd Riflemen. Cape Mtd Yeomanry.*	

ADEN

Dates	Honoured or Non-Honoured Battle	Honour awarded to or Participants in Battle	Remarks
19 Jan 1839	**Aden**	Inf-**103.** IND-**Bom Arty.** Inf-**121. 124.**	

1st AFGHAN WAR
Medals awarded: Individual medals for **Ghuznee** (1839, 1842), **Jellalabad**, **Candahar**, **Defence of Kelat**, and **Cabul**.

Dates	Honoured or Non-Honoured Battle	Honour awarded to or Participants in Battle	Remarks
23 Jul 1839	**Ghuznee 1839**	**4 D. 16 LD.** Inf-**2. 13. 17. 101.** IND-Cav-**1. 3. 31. 34. Bom Arty. Bom S&M.** Inf-**119.** Ben NI(m)-**16. 35. 48.**	101 carry date '1838'.
13 Nov 1839	**Khelat**	Inf-**2. 17.** IND-Cav-**3. Bom Arty. Bom S&M.** Inf-*2.* IND-Cav-*34.*	Skinners Horse carry date '1840'.
1839	**Afghanistan 1839**	**4 D. 16 LD.** Inf-**2. 13. 17. 101.** IND-Cav-**1. 3. 31. 34. Bom Arty. S&M-Ben. Bom.** Inf-**2. 5. 6. 119.** Ben NC(m)-**2. 3.** Ben NI(m)-**16. 35. 37. 48.** IND-Inf-*102. 122. 123. 126.* Ben NI–*30.*	Also **Shah Shuja's Troop.**
16 May–28 Sep 1840	**Kahun**	IND-Inf-**105.**	
2 Nov 1841–12 Jan 1842	*Retreat from Kabul*	Inf-*44.* IND-*Ben S&M.* Ben NC(m)-*5.* Ben NI(m)-*5. 37. 54.*	
13 Nov 1841–7 Apr 1842	**Jellalabad**	Inf-**13.** IND-**Ben S&M.** Ben NC(m)-**5.** Ben NI(m)-**35.**	Carried on Badge with Mural Crown.
10 Mar 1842	**Candahar 1842**	Inf-**40. 41.** IND-Cav-**1. 34. Bom Arty. Ben S&M.** Inf-**5. 6. 12.** Ben NI(m)-**2. 16. 38.** IND-Inf-*120.* Ben NC(M)-*3.* Ben IC(m)-*9.* Ben NI(m)-*28.*	

Dates	**Honoured** or *Non-Honoured* Battle	**Honour awarded** to or *Participants in* Battle	Remarks
7 Dec 1841– 6 Mar 1842	**Ghuznee 1842**	Inf-**40. 41.** IND-Cav-**33.** Inf-**5. 6. 12. Ben NC(m)-3. 11. Ben NI(m)-2. 38.** IND-*Ben NI(m)-16. 27.*	
21 May 1842	**Khelat-i-Ghilzai**	IND-Inf-**12.** IND-Inf-*6.*	Carried on Badge.
15 Sep 1842	**Cabul 1842**	**3 D.** Inf-**9. 13. 31. 40. 41.** IND-Cav-**33. Ben S&M.** Inf-**4. 5. 6. 12. Ben NC(m)-1. 5. 10. Ben IC(m)-3. Ben NI(m)-2. 6. 26. 30. 35. 38. 60. 64.** IND-Cav-*1. Ben NC(m)-3. Ben IC(m)-9. Ben NI(m)-16. 53.*	Also **Kabul Battery.**

OPERATIONS IN SCINDE

1839–42	**Cutchee**	IND-Cav-**35. 36.** IND-Cav-*1.* Inf-*101. 105.*	

1st CHINA WAR
Medals awarded: First China War Medal

4 Jul 1840– 17 Aug 1842	**China Coast**	Inf-**18. 26. 49. 55. 98.** IND-**Mad S&M.** Inf-**62. 66. 74. Mad NI-36. 37. 41.** IND-*Ben NI(m)-18. 26. 49. Mad NI-39.*	Carried on Badge by British regts. Also **Dragon Troop** and **Dragon Battery** (3). Also known as the Opium War.

SCINDE WAR
Medals awarded: Scinde Campaign Medals

17 Feb 1843	**Meeanee**	Inf-**22.** IND-Cav-**34. 35. 36. Bom Arty. Mad S&M.** Inf-**112. 125. Ben NC(m)-9.** IND-Inf-*101.*	
24 Mar 1843	**Hyderabad** (*Dabo*)	Inf-**22.** IND-Cav-**33. 34. 35. 36. Bom Arty. Mad S&M.** Inf-**101. 108. 112. 125. Ben NC(m)-9.** IND-Inf-*120. 121. 124. Bom NI-6. 15. 21.*	Also **Eagle Troop.**
6 Jan–24 Mar 1843	**Scinde**	Inf-**22.** IND-Cav-**4. 35. 36. Ben NC(m)-9.** IND-Cav-*33. 34. Bom Arty. Mad S&M.* Inf-*101. 108. 112. 120. 121. 124. 125. Bom NI-6. 15. 21.*	App by 28.

GWALIOR CAMPAIGN
Medals awarded: Gwalior Star with clasps for battles.

29 Dec 1843	**Maharajpore**	**16 LD.** Inf-**39. 40.** IND-Cav-**GGBG. 3. Ben S&M.** Inf-**2. 6. 12. Ben NC(m)-1. 4. 5. 8. 10. Ben NI(m)-2. 14. 16. 56.** IND-*Ben NI(m)-62.*	Skinners Horse carry date '1842'. Also **Maharajpore Battery.**
29 Dec 1843	**Punniar**	**9 LD.** Inf-**3. 50.** IND-Cav-**6. Ben S&M. Ben NC(m)-5. 8. 11. Ben NI(m)-39. 50. 51. 58. Gwalior Contingent-Cav-1. 2.** Inf(m)-1. 2. 3. 4. 5. 6. 7.	

1st MAORI WAR
Medals awarded: New Zealand medal.

3 May 1845–Jul 1847	**New Zealand**	Inf-**58. 96. 99.**	Honour awarded without date

Dates	Honoured or *Non-Honoured* Battle	Honour awarded to or *Participants in* Battle	Remarks

1st SIKH WAR (SUTLEJ CAMPAIGN)
Medals awarded: Sutlej campaign medal with clasps for battles.

Dates	Honoured or *Non-Honoured* Battle	Honour awarded to or *Participants in* Battle	Remarks
18 Dec 1845	**Moodkee**	**3 D.** Inf-**9. 31. 50. 80.** IND-Cav-**GGBG. 3. 6.** Inf-**5. 7. Ben NC(m)-4. 5.** Ben IC(m)-**9. Ben NI(m)-2. 16. 24. 26. 45. 48. 73.** IND-Cav-*2.* Inf-*9. 102. 116. Ben NC(m)-8. Ben IC(m)-3. Ben NI(m)-9. 27.*	
21–22 Dec 1845	**Ferozeshah**	**3 D.** Inf-**9. 29. 31. 50. 62. 80. 101.** IND-Cav-**GGBG. 3. 6. Ben S&M.** Inf-**4. 5. 7. Ben NC(m)-4. 5. 8. Ben IC(m)-3. 9. Ben NI(m)-2. 12. 14. 16. 24. 26. 44. 45. 48. 54. 73.** IND-Cav-*2.* Inf-*9. 102. 116. Ben NI(m)-27.*	
28 Jan 1846	**Aliwal**	**16 LD.** Inf-**31. 50. 53.** IND-Cav-**GGBG. 3.** Inf-**7. 13. GR-1/1.1/2. Ben NC(m)-1. 3. 5. Ben NI(m)-24. 30. 48.** IND-Inf-*5. Ben NI(m)-27.*	
10 Feb 1846	**Sobraon**	**3 D. 9 D. 16 LD.** Inf-**9. 10. 29. 31. 50. 53. 62. 80. 101.** IND-Cav-**GGBG. 2. 6. Ben S&M.** Inf-**4. 5. 6. 7. 8. 9. GR-1/1. 1/2. Ben NC(m)-3. 4. 5. Ben IC(m)-9. Ben NI(m)-16. 26. 41. 68.** IND-*Ben NC(m)-1. Ben NI(m)-2. 4. 5. 9. 12. 24. 38. 45. 48. 73.*	

7th KAFFIR WAR
Medals awarded: South Africa Medal 1834–53.

Dates	Honoured or *Non-Honoured* Battle	Honour awarded to or *Participants in* Battle	Remarks
16 Mar 1846–16 Dec 1847	**South Africa 1846–7**	**7 DG.** Inf-**6. 27. 45. 73. 90. 91. RB.** SA-*Cape Mtd Riflemen. Cape Mtd Yeomanry*	

2nd SIKH WAR (PUNJAB CAMPAIGN)
Medals awarded: Punjab Campaign Medal with clasps for honoured battles.

Dates	Honoured or *Non-Honoured* Battle	Honour awarded to or *Participants in* Battle	Remarks
7 Sep 1848–22 Jan 1849	**Mooltan**	Inf-**10. 32. 60. 103.** IND-Cav-**5. 31. 35. 36. Guides. Bom Arty. 25 Mtn Bty. S&M-Ben. Bom.** Inf-**103. 104. 109. 119. Ben NC(m)-11. Ben IC(m)-10. 14. Ben NI(m)-8. 49. 51. 52. 72.**	
22 Oct 1848	*Ramnagar*	*3 D. 14 LD.* Inf-*24. 61.* IND-INF-*11. Ben NC(m)-5. 8. Ben IC(m)-11. Ben NI(m)-36. 46. 70.*	
3 Dec 1848	*Sadulapur*	*3 D. 9 D. 14 LD.* Inf-*24. 61.* IND-Inf-*2. Ben NC(m)–1. 5. 6. 8. Ben IC(m)-3. 11. Ben NI(m)-25. 36. 46. 56.*	
13 Jan 1849	**Chillianwallah**	**3 D. 9 D. 14 LD.** Inf-**24. 29. 61. 104.** IND-**Ben S&M.** Inf-**2. 11. Ben NC(m)-1. 5. 6. 8. Ben IC(m)-3. 9. Ben NI(m)-15. 20. 25. 30. 36. 45. 46. 56. 69. 70.**	
21 Feb 1849	**Goojerat**	**3 D. 9 D. 14 LD.** Inf-**10. 24. 29. 32. 53. 60. 61. 103. 104.** IND-Cav-**35. 36. Guides. S&M-Ben. Bom.** Inf-**2. 11. 103. 119. Ben (NC)m-1. 5. 6. 8. Ben IC(m)-3. 9. 10. 11. 13. 14. Ben NI(m)-8. 13. 15. 20. 25. 30. 36. 45. 46. 51. 52. 56. 69. 70. 72.**	

Dates	**Honoured** or *Non-Honoured* Battle	**Honour awarded** to or *Participants in* Battle	Remarks
1848–9	**Punjaub**	**3 D. 9 D. 14 LD. Inf-10. 24. 29. 32. 53. 60. 61. 98. 103. 104.** **IND-Cav-2. 5. 7. 31. 35. 36. Guides. 25 Mtn Bty. S&M-Ben. Bom. Inf-2. 11. 51. 52. 103. 104. 109. 119. 121. Ben NC(m)-1. 5. 6. 7. 8. 11. Ben IC(m)-3. 9. 10. 11. 13. 14. 15. 16. Ben NI(m)-1. 3. 4. 8. 13. 15. 18. 20. 22. 25. 29. 30. 36. 37. 45. 46. 49. 50. 51. 52. 53. 56. 69. 70. 71. 72. 73.**	

8th KAFFIR WAR
Medals awarded: South Africa Medal 1834–53.

24 Dec 1850– Mar 1853	**South Africa 1851–52–53**	**12 D. Inf-2. 6. 12. 43. 60. 73. 74. 91. RB.** Inf-*45. 72.* SA-*Cape Mtd Riflemen. Armstrong's Horse. Cape Mtd Yeomanry.*	

2nd BURMA WAR
Medals awarded: Clasp to India GSM 1854–95.

2 Apr 1852–Jun 1853	**Pegu**	**Inf-18. 51. 80. 101. 102.** **IND-Mad S&M. Inf-54. 61. 65. 69. 79. 86. Ben NI(m)-10. 67. 68. Mad NI-35. 49.** IND-Inf-*15. 84. 90. 2/4GR. Ben NI(m)-37. Mad NI-46.*	Capture of Pegu on 21 Nov 1852. Generic name referring to province where campaign took place.

CRIMEAN WAR
Medals awarded: Crimean War Medal

20 Sep 1854	**Alma**	**4 D. 8 D. 11 D. 13D. 17 LD. Inf-GG. CG. SG. 1. 4. 19. 20. 21. 23. 28. 30. 33. 38. 41. 42. 44. 47. 49. 50. 55. 63. 68. 77. 79. 88. 90. 93. 95. RB.** Inf-*46 (part).*	Also **Alma Battery.**
25 Oct 1854	**Balaclava**	**4 DG. 5 DG. 1 D. 2 D. 4 D. 6 D. 8 D. 11 D. 13 D. 17 LD. Inf-93.**	Also celebrated by C Battery.
5 Nov 1854	**Inkerman**	**4 D. 8 D. 11 D. 13 D. 17 LD. Inf-GG. CG. SG. 1. 4. 7. 19. 20. 21. 23. 28. 30. 33. 38. 41. 44. 47. 49. 50. 55. 57. 63. 68. 77. 88. 95. RB.** Inf-*46 (part).*	Also **Inkerman Battery** (3). App by 46.
18 Jun–8 Sep 1855	*The Redan*	Inf-*GG. 3. 7. 9. 17. 18. 19. 23. 28. 30. 33. 38. 41. 44. 47. 49. 55. 57. 62. 77. 88. 95. 97. RB.*	
19 Sep 1854–8 Sep 1855	**Sevastapol**	**1 DG. 4 DG. 5 DG. 1 D. 2 D. 4 D. 6 D. 8 D. 10 D. 11 D. 12 D. 13 D. 17 LD. Inf-GG. CG. SG. 1. 3. 4. 7. 9. 13. 14. 17. 18. 19. 20. 21. 23. 28. 30. 31. 33. 34. 38. 39. 41. 42. 44. 46. 47. 48. 49. 50. 55. 56. 57. 62. 63. 68. 71. 72. 77. 79. 82. 88. 89. 90. 93. 95. 97. RB.** *6 DG.*	
1854–55	**Mediterranean**	**Militia Bns of-3. 4. 7. 14. 38. 43. 47. 48. 49. 62.**	Distinction awarded for Garrison duties on Mediterranean Islands.

PERSIAN WAR
Medals awarded: Indian GSM 1858–95 with clasps for Honoured battles.

7 Dec 1856	**Reshire**	**Inf-64. 106.** **IND-Cav-33. 34. Bom S&M. Inf-104. 120. 129.** IND-Inf-*126.*	
12 Dec 1856	**Bushire**	**Inf-64. 106.** **IND-Cav-33. 34. Bom S&M. Inf-104. 120. 129.** IND-Inf-*126.*	

Dates	**Honoured** or *Non-Honoured* Battle	**Honour awarded** to or *Participants in* Battle	Remarks
8 Feb 1857	**Koosh-Ab**	Inf-**64. 78. 106.** IND-Cav-**33. 34. Bom S&M.** Inf-**104. 120. 126. 129.** *14 LD.* IND-*Aden Troop.*	
29 Nov 1856– 4 Apr 1857	**Persia**	**14 LD.** Inf-**64. 78. 106.** IND-Cav-**33. 34. 35. S&M-Mad. Bom.** Inf-**102. 103. 104. 108. 120. 122. 123. 125. 126. 128. 129. Bom NI-11. 15.** IND-Inf-*105. 109. 119. 121. Aden Tp. Bom NI-6.*	

INDIAN MUTINY
Medals awarded: India Mutiny Medal 1857–8 with clasps as shown.

Dates			
30 May–20 Sep 1857	**Delhi 1857** (clasp)	**6 DG. 9 D.** Inf-**8. 52. 60. 61. 75. 101. 104.** IND-Cav-**9. 10. 11. 21. 22. 25. Guides. Ben S&M.** Inf-**32. 54. 55. 56. 57. 127. Guides. GR-2. 3.**	India Mutiny began 10 May 1857. Also **Tomb's Troop.**
8 Jun 1857–20 Sep 1858	**Central India** (clasp)	**8 D. 12 D. 14 LD. 17 LD.** Inf-**27. 38. 71. 72. 78. 83. 83. 86. 88. 95. 108. 109.** IND-Cav-**20. 30. 31. 32. 33. 35. S&M-Mad. Bom.** Inf-**2. 44. 61. 79. 96. 98. 104. 110. 112. 113. 124. 125. Hyderabad Contingent** Cav-**3** Fd Btys-**1. 2. 4. Bom NC-3 Scinde Horse.** Inf-*33. 80. 84. 106. RB.* IND-Cav-*6. 34.* Inf-*119. Ben NC-3 Sikh H. Bom NC-2 S Mah H. Kandesh . Aden Tp. Gujarat H.*	App by 43. RB.
7 Jun 1857	*Badli-Ki Serai*		App by 75.
1857	**Mooltan 1857–8**	IND-Cav-**4.**	
30 Jun 1857–21 Mar 1858	**Lucknow** (clasp)	**2 DG. 7 D. 9 D.** Inf-**5. 8. 10. 20. 23. 32. 34. 38. 42. 53. 64. 75. 78. 79. 82. 84. 90. 93. 97. 101. 102. RB.** IND-Cav-**9. 10. 11. 21. 22. 25. S&M-Ben. Mad.** Inf-**14. 16. 32. 56. 57. 87.**	Also **Middleton's Company,** and **Residency Battery.** Celebrated by 136 Battery.
30 Jun–17 Nov 1857	*Defence of Lucknow* (clasp)	Inf-*32.* IND-Inf-*16.*	App by 32 instead of Lucknow.
12 Jul–27 Sep 1857	*Reinforcement of Lucknow* (clasp)	Inf-*5. 64. 78. 84. 90. 102.* IND-Inf-*14.*	Also **Maude's Battery.**
Jul 1857–Jan 1858	*Defence of Saugor*	IND-Inf-*2.*	
30 Jul–2 Aug 1857	**Arrah**	IND-Inf-**45.** Inf-*5.*	App by 5. Also **Eyre's Battery.**
16 Aug 1857	**Behar (Bithur)**	IND-Inf-**45.** Inf-*64. 78. 84. 102.* IND-Inf-*14.*	
12–23 Nov 1857	*Relief of Lucknow* (clasp)	**9 D.** Inf-*8. 23. 53. 75. 82. 84. 90. 93.* IND-Cav-*9. 10. 21. 22. 25. Ben S&M.* Inf-*32. 56. 57.*	
26 Nov–6 Dec 1857	*Cawnpore*	**9 D.** Inf-*8. 23. 32. 34. 38. 42. 53. 64. 78. 82. 84. 93. 102. RB.* IND-Cav-*9. 10. 21. 22. 25.* Inf-*87.*	App by 82.
6–21 Mar 1858	*Capture of Lucknow* (clasp)	**2 DG. 9 D.** Inf-*5. 10. 20. 23. 34. 38. 42. 53. 78. 79. 84. 90. 93. 97. 101. 102. RB.* IND-Cav-*9. 10. 11. 21. 25. S&M-Ben. Mad.* Inf-*14. 27. 56. 57. Ben NC-Pathan H. Benares H.*	App by 10. 93.

Dates	**Honoured** or *Non-Honoured* Battle	**Honour awarded** to or *Participants in* Battle	Remarks
1–6 Apr 1858	*Jhansi*	*14 LD. Inf-86. 109.* *IND-Cav-33. Inf-96. 98. 124. 125.*	App by 86.
7 Apr–23 May 1858	*Rohilcund 1858*	*6 DG. 9 D. Inf-42. 60. 64. 78. 79. 82. 93.* *IND-Cav-7. 15. 21. 22. Inf-25. 30. 51. 55. 127. GR-2. 3. Ben NC-Pathan Horse. Lahore Lt H.*	App by 60 to include Oude.
6 May–20 Jun 1858	*Gwalior 1858*	*8 D. 14 LD. Inf-71. 86. 95.* *IND-Cav-13. Inf-98. 110. 125.*	
20 Oct 1858	*Doadpur*		**Strange's Company.**
10 May 1857–1858	*India 1857–58*	*IND-Cav-9. 10. 11. 14. 21. 22. Guides. Ben S&M. Inf-14. 16. 19. 28. 31. 32. 45. 53. 54. 55. 56. 57. 58. Guides. GR-1/1. 1/2. 1/3. 1/8. Ben IC-12. 3 Sikh H. Oude Irreg Cav.*	App by 27; by 13 and 61 as 'Indian mutiny; by 37/67 with date 1857–59'.

2nd CHINA WAR
Medals awarded: Second China War Medal with clasps as shown.

28 Dec 1857–5 Jan 1858	**Canton** (clasp	Inf-**59.**	
21 Aug 1860	**Taku Forts** (clasp)	**1 DG. Inf-1. 2. 3. 31. 44. 60. 67.** **IND-Cav-11. 19. Mad S&M. Inf-20. 23.**	
18 Sep–13 Oct 1860	**Pekin 1860** (clasp)	**1 DG. Inf-1. 2. 60. 67. 99.** **IND-Cav-11. 19. Mad S&M. Inf-20. 23.**	Indian regiments bear Honour without the date.
Jan 1858–1862	**China 1858–62**	IND-Inf-**10. 11. 15. 22. 27. 105.** IND-Inf-*81. 103.*	

2nd MAORI WAR
Medals awarded: New Zealand Medal.

6 Mar 1860–14 Mar 1861	**New Zealand** *(1860–61)*	Inf-**12. 14. 40. 65.**	Also **New Zealand Battery.**
4 May 1863–15 Feb 1866	**New Zealand** *(1863–66)*	Inf-**12. 14. 18. 40. 43. 50. 57. 65. 68. 70.** NZ-**Taranaki**. AUS-*Waikato Militia.*	

NORTH WEST FRONTIER INDIA 1863
Medals awarded: Clasp to India GSM 1854–95.

19 Oct–17 Dec 1863	*Umbeyla*	*Inf-7. 51. 71. 93. 97. 98. 101.* *IND-Cav-11. Guides. Ben S&M. Inf-14. 20. 23. 32. 53. 55. 58. 59. Guides. 1/4 GR. 1/5 GR. Ben NI-3 Pun*	App by 7. 71.

NORTH EAST FRONTIER INDIA 1864–6
Medals awarded: Clasp to India GSM 1854–95.

28 Nov 1864–23 Feb 1866	*Bhutan*	*Inf-55. 80.* *IND-Cav-5. 14. Inf-11. 12. 17. 18. 19. 29. 30. 31. GR-3. 1/8. 2/8.*	

NORTH WEST FRONTIER, INDIA 1849–68
Medals awarded: Clasp to India GSM 1854–95.

3 Dec 1849–22 Oct 1868	*North West Frontier, India 1849–68*	*Inf-6. 19. 22. 24. 32. 60. 61. 81. 98.* *IND-Cav-1. 2. 5. 8. 9. 15. 16. 21. 22. 23. 25. Guides. Ben S&M. Inf-1. 2. 3. 12. 20. 21. 24. 26. 32. 45. 51. 52. 53. 54. 55. 56. 57. 58. 59. 103. Guides. GR-1/1. 1/2. 1/4. 1/5. Ben NC-7. 10. 4Pun. Ben IC(m)-13. 15. 16. Ben NI(m)-1. 3. 4. 9. 20. 23. 28. 29. 71. 3Pun. 12Pun. 14Pun.*	For various intermediate dates. App by 61, for North West Frontier 1849–50.

Dates	Honoured or Non-Honoured Battle	Honour awarded to or Participants in Battle	Remarks

ABYSSINIA
Medals awarded: Abyssinian War Medal.

| 21 Oct 1867–
13 Apr 1868 | **Abyssinia** | **3 DG. Inf-4. 26. 33. 45.**
IND-Cav-10. 12. 33. 25Mtn Bty. S&M-Mad. Bom.
Inf-21. 23. 102. 103. 110. 121. 125. 127. Bom NC-
3 Scinde H. Bom NI-18.
IND-Inf-*104.* | |

FENIAN RAIDS
Medals awarded: Canada GSM 1867–70.

| 25 May 1870 | **Eccles Hill** | CDN-Inf-**3.** | |
| 1866–70 | *Canada 1866–70* | *Inf-7. 16. 17. 25. 30. 47. 60. 69. RB.*
CDN-Cav-17. Inf-1. 2. 5. 8. 13. 14. 22. 41. 43. 51.
81. Royal Canadian Rifles. Whitby Rifles.
Toronto Fencibles. | Clasps for Fenian Raids 1866 and 1870, and for Red River. |

SOUTH AFRICA 1873

| 1873 | *Langalibalele* | *SA-MR-1.* | |

WEST AFRICA
Medals awarded: Ashantee Medal.

| 9 Jun 1873–
6 Feb 1874 | **Ashantee 1873–4** | Inf-**23. 42. RB.**
AF-**Nigeria. Gold Coast. WI.** | |

MALAYA 1875

| Dec 1875 | **Perak** | IND-**Mad S&M.**
Inf-*80.*
IND-Inf-*1 GR.* | App by 80. |

ZULU WAR AND SOUTH AFRICA
Medals awarded: Zulu and Basuto War Medal with clasps as shown – by dates.

1877–9	**South Africa 1877–8–9** (clasp)	**1 DG. 1 7D. Inf-3. 4. 13. 21. 24. 57. 58. 60. 80. 88.** **90. 91. 94. 99.** SA-**MR-1.** Inf-**1.**	App by 58 for additional dates 1880–81, and by Durban LI. Honour awarded to cover all actions.
22 Jan 1879	*Isandlhwana*	Inf-*24.* SA-*MR-1.*	App by 24, who wear Wreath of Immortelles awarded for this action and action at Rorkes Drift.
29 Mar 1879	*Kambula*	Inf-*13. 90.* SA-*Border Horse.*	SA regiment thought to have been awarded the Honour.
4 Jul 1879	*Ulundi*	*17 D. Inf-13. 21. 58. 80. 90. 94.* SA-*Frontier L.H.*	
11 Jan–31 Aug 1879	*Zululand*	*1 DG. 17 D. Inf-3. 13. 21. 24. 57. 58. 60. 80. 88. 90.* *91. 94. 99.* SA-*Frontier LH.MR-1. 3. 4. SAMR-1. Inf-2.*	
Mar 1879	*Morosi's Mountain*	SA-*SAMR-1. Inf-4. 5.*	In Basutoland.
Nov 1879	*Sekukuni 1879*	SA-*Border Horse.*	Said to have been awarded as an Honour.
1879	*Inyezane*	SA-*MR-1. (Alexandra MR)*	
1879	*Hlobane*	SA-*Border Horse.*	Said to have been awarded as an Honour.

Dates	**Honoured** or *Non-Honoured* Battle	**Honour awarded** to or *Participants in* Battle	Remarks

9th KAFFIR WAR
Medals awarded: Zulu and Basuto War Medal with clasps as shown – by date.

Dates	Battle	Honour awarded	Remarks
1877–9	**Transkei 1877–9**	SA-Inf-**2.** SA-Inf-*3.*	9th Kaffir War on Eastern Cape Frontier.
1877	**Gaika Gaeleka 1877** (clasp)	SA-Inf-**2. 4. 5. 13.**	
1877	*Umzintzani*	SA-Inf-*3.*	
Sep 1877	*'Utaba-'Nadodo*	SA-Inf-*4.*	
1878	*Gaikaland 1878*	SA-Inf-*5.*	
1878	*Sekukuni 1878*	SA-Inf-*13.*	
1878	**Griqualand West**(clasp)	SA-Inf-**13.**	
1878–9	*Northern Border*	SA-*2 Bty Cape Arty.*	
1877–9	*South Africa 1877–79*	Inf-*3. 4. 13. 24. 80. 88. 90. 99.* SA-*2 Bty Cape Arty. SAMR-1. Inf-2. 3. 4. 5. 13.*	

2nd AFGHAN WAR
Medals awarded: Afghanistan Medal with clasps as shown. Kabul to Kandahar Star for **Kahdahar 1880**.

Dates	Battle	Honour awarded	Remarks
20–21 Nov 1878	**Ali Masjid** (clasp)	10 D. Inf-**17. 51. 81. RB.** IND-Cav-**11. Guides. 4Mtn Bty. Ben S&M. Inf-6. 14. 20. 27. 45. 51. Guides. 4 GR.** IND-Inf-*82.*	
2 Dec 1878	**Peiwar Kotal** (clasp)	Inf-**8. 72.** IND-Cav-**12. 1 Mtn Bty. Inf-23. 29. 56. 5 GR.**	
6 Oct 1879	**Charasiah** (clasp)	9 D. Inf-**67. 72. 92.** IND-Cav-**12. 14. 25. 2 Mtn Bty. Ben S&M. Inf-23. 28. 58. 5 GR.**	
11–23 Dec 1879	**Kabul 1879** (clasp)	9 D. Inf-**9. 67. 72. 92.** IND-Cav-**12. 14. 25. Guides. Mtn Btys-1. 2. 4. Ben S&M. Inf-23. 28. 53. 58. Guides. GR-2. 4. 5.**	
1 Jan–15 Aug 1880	*Khyber Pass*	6 DG. 8 D. Inf-*5. 12. 14. 25. 51.* IND-Cav-*4. 5. 17. Mad S&M. Inf-8. 27. 30. 31. 32. 61. 64. 75. 1 GR. 9 GR.*	
19 Apr 1880	**Ahmed Khel** (clasp)	Inf-**59. 60.** IND-Cav-**19. 21. 22. Ben S&M.** Inf-**15. 19. 25. 52. 3 GR.**	
27 Jul 1880	*Maiwand*	Inf-*66.* IND-Cav-*3. 33. Bom S&M. Inf-101. 130. Bom NC-3 Scinde H.*	Also **Maiwand Battery.**
5 Aug–1 Sep 1880	**Kandahar 1880** (clasp)	9 D. Inf-**7. 60. 66. 72. 92.** IND-Cav-**3. 23. 33. 34. 38. 39. 2 Mtn Bty. Bom S&M. Inf-15. 23. 24. 25. 52. 53. 101. 104. 119. 128. 129. GR-2. 4. 5. Bom NC-3 Scinde H.** IND-Inf-*130.*	

Dates	Honoured or *Non-Honoured* Battle	Honour awarded to or *Participants in* Battle	Remarks
20 Nov 1878– 27 Apr 1881	**Afghanistan 1878–80**	6 DG. 8 D. 9 D. 10 D. 15 LD. Inf-5. 7. 8. 9. 11. 12. 14. 15. 17. 18. 25. 51. 59. 60. 63. 66. 67. 70. 72. 78. 81. 85. 92. RB. IND-Cav-1. 3. 4. 5. 8. 10. 11. 12. 13. 14. 15. 17. 18. 19. 21. 22. 23. 25. 26. 32. 33. 34. 35. 36. 38. 39. Guides. Mtn Btys-1. 2. 3. 4. 6. S&M-Ben. Mad. Bom. Inf-2. 3. 4. 5. 6. 8. 9. 11. 12. 13. 14. 15. 16. 17. 19. 20. 21. 22. 23. 24. 25. 26. 27. 28. 29. 30. 31. 32. 39. 42. 44. 45. 51. 52. 53. 55. 56. 57. 58. 61. 64. 75. 81. 90. 101. 104. 105. 108. 109. 110. 113. 116. 119. 123. 124. 127. 128. 129. 130. Guides. GR-1. 2. 3. 4. 5. 9. Bom NC-3 Scinde H. Bom NI-15. Inf-*82*. IND-*Ben NI-41*.	

NATIVE WARS IN SOUTH AFRICA

Dates	Honoured or *Non-Honoured* Battle	Honour awarded to or *Participants in* Battle	Remarks
13 Sep 1880– 27 Apr 1881	**Basutoland 1880–81**	SA-Inf-**2. 4. 13.** SA-*SAMR-1. 2 Bty Cape Arty. 1&2 Btys Cape Hy Arty. Inf-3. 5.*	⎫ App by South African participating regiments.
31 Oct 1880	*Lerotholi's Kraal*	SA-Inf-*3. 4.*	
1880	*Ramabidikwe*	SA-Inf-*4.*	
13 Sep 1880– 15 May 1881	**Transkei 1880–81**	SA-Inf-**13.** SA-*SAMR-1.*	
1880	*Mafeteng*	SA-Inf-*4. 5.*	
1880	*Kalabani*	SA-Inf-*4.*	
22 Mar 1881	*Tweefontein & Boleka*	SA-Inf-*4.*	⎭

1st BOER WAR
Medals awarded: Cape of Good Hope GSM 1880–97.

Dates	Honoured or *Non-Honoured* Battle	Honour awarded to or *Participants in* Battle	Remarks
16 Dec 1880– 23 Mar 1881	*Natal 1880–81*	*15 LD.* Inf-*58. 60. 92. 94.*	
28 Jan 1881	*Laing's Nek*	Inf-*58.*	

EGYPT 1882
Medal awarded: Egypt 1882–9 Medal with clasp for **Tel el Kebir**, Khedive's stars.

Dates	Honoured or *Non-Honoured* Battle	Honour awarded to or *Participants in* Battle	Remarks
13 Sep 1882	**Tel el Kebir**	LG. RHG. 4 DG. 7 DG. 19 H. Inf-GG. CG. SG. 18. 42. 46. 60. 72. 74. 75. 79. 84. 87. IND-Cav-2. 6. 13. Mad S&M. Inf-7. 20. 129.	Also **Broken Wheel Battery.**
11 Jul–23 Sep 1882	**Egypt 1882**	LG. RHG. 4 DG. 7 DG. 19 H. Inf-GG. CG. SG. 18. 35. 38. 42. 46. 49. 50. 53. 60. 63. 72. 74. 75. 79. 84. 87. 95. 96. 8 LR. RMA. IND-Cav-2. 6. 13. Mad S&M. Inf-7. 20. 129.	

SUAKIN EXPEDITION
Medals awarded: Egypt 1882–9 Medal with clasps for El Teb and Tamaii

Dates	Honoured or *Non-Honoured* Battle	Honour awarded to or *Participants in* Battle	Remarks
Feb–Apr 1884	**Egypt 1884** *(El Teb/Tamaii)*	10 H. 19 H. Inf-42. 60. 65. 75. 89.	App by 65. Commemorates El Teb (24 Feb) and Tamaii (13 Nov)

Dates	Honoured or Non-Honoured Battle	Honour awarded to or Participants in Battle	Remarks

1st SUDAN WAR
Medals awarded: Egypt 1882–9 Medal with clasps as shown.

Dates	Honoured or Non-Honoured Battle	Honour awarded to or Participants in Battle	Remarks
17–18 Jan 1885	**Abu Klea** (clasp)	**19 H. Inf-35.** Inf-*GG. CG. SG.*	Also **Abu Klea Battery.**
9 Feb 1885	**Kirbokan** (clasp)	Inf-**38. 42.** *19 H.*	
1884–7 Mar 1885	**Nile 1884–85** (clasp)	19 H. Inf-**18. 35. 38. 42. 46. 50. 56. 75. 79.**	App by 19. Khartoum Relief Expedition.
1 Mar–14 May 1885	**Suakin 1885** (clasp)	**5 L. 20 H. Inf-GG. CG. SG. 49. 53. 70.** IND-Cav-**Mad S&M.** Inf-**15. 17. 128.** AUS-Inf-**1. 3. 17.**	
20 Mar 1885	*Hasheen*	*5 L.* Inf-*GG. CG. SG. 49. 70.* IND-*9 L. Mad S&M.* Inf-*15. 17. 128.*	
23 Mar 1885	**Tofrek** (clasp) *(McNeill's Zariba)*	Inf-**49.** IND-**Mad S&M.** Inf-**15. 17. 128.** Inf-*CG.*	Prefix 'Royal' gained by 49.
30 Dec 1885	*Ginnis*	Inf-*19. 49. 50. 79. 106.*	Last battle fought in Red Coats.
1885–6	*Nile 1885–86*		App by 19. 106.

NORTH WEST CANADA
Medals awarded: North West Canada Medal 1885.

Dates	Honoured or Non-Honoured Battle	Honour awarded to or Participants in Battle	Remarks
Mar 1885	**Saskatchewan**	CDN-Inf-**RCR.**	
24 Apr 1885	**Fish Creek**	CDN-Cav-**FGH.** Inf-**10. 90.**	
9–12 May 1885	**Batoche**	CDN-Cav-**FGH.** Inf-**10. 90.**	
26 Mar–23 May 1885	**North West Canada 1885**	CDN-Cav-**RCD. FGH. GGBG. 12. 16.** Inf-**RCR. GGFG. 2. 7. 9. 10. 12. 35. 46. 52. 63. 65. 66. 90. 106. Moose Mountain Scouts.**	

BURMA 1885–7
Medals awarded: India GSM 1854–95 with clasp.

Dates	Honoured or Non-Honoured Battle	Honour awarded to or Participants in Battle	Remarks
14 Nov 1885–30 Apr 1887	**Burma 1885–87**	Inf-**2. 8. 13. 21. 23. 24. 37. 51. 67. 104. RB.** IND-Cav-**7. 26. 27. 31. S&M-Ben. Mad. Bom. Mtn Btys-4. 5. 7. 8.** Inf-**1. 2. 4. 5. 10. 11. 12. 16. 18. 26. 27. 33. 61. 63. 65. 72. 73. 74. 75. 76. 81. 83. 86. 87. 90. 95. 96. 101. 105. 107. 123. 125. 127. GR.- 3. 6. 8. 10 Hyd. Cav-3.**	

WEST AFRICA 1887
Medals awarded: East and West Africa Medal with numerous clasps for engagements.

Dates	Honoured or Non-Honoured Battle	Honour awarded to or Participants in Battle	Remarks
1887	**West Africa 1887**	**West India.**	

NORTH WEST FRONTIER, INDIA 1888–91
Medals awarded: India GSM 1854–95 with clasps as shown.

Dates	Honoured or Non-Honoured Battle	Honour awarded to or Participants in Battle	Remarks
3 Oct–9 Nov 1888	*Hazara 1888* (clasp)	Inf-*5. 12. 18. 78. 107.* IND-Cav-*15.* Inf-*14. 24. 25. 29. 34. 40. 45. 53. 57. 5 GR.*	
26 Jan–16 May 1891	**Samana 1891** (clasp)	IND-Inf-**36.** Inf-*60. 96.* IND-Cav-*19. 25.* Ben S&M. Inf-*15. 19. 27. 29. 53. 55. 56. 59.1/5 GR.*	
1 Mar–Apr 1891	*Hazara 1891* (clasp)	Inf-*23. 78.* IND-Cav-*11.* Ben S&M. Inf-*11. 32. 37. 54. Guides. 2/5 GR.*	

Dates	**Honoured** or *Non-Honoured* Battle	**Honour awarded** to or *Participants in* Battle	Remarks

NORTH EAST FRONTIER, INDIA 1888–97
Medals awarded: India GSM 1854–95 with clasp.

Dates	Battle	Honour / Participants	Remarks
9 Mar–26 Sep 1888	*Sikkim 1888* (clasp)	Inf-*95*. IND-Inf-*13. 32. 2/1 GR.*	
15 Nov 1889–12 Sep 1897	*North East Frontier India 1889–1897*	Inf-*25. 60.* IND-Cav-*18. 21. 23. Mtn Btys-7. 8. Ben S&M.* Inf-*2. 3. 7. 9. 10. 11. 13. 17. 18. 26. 32. 37. 38. 39. 40. 42. 43. 44. 51. 52. 54. 56. 62. 65. 72. 79. 128. GR-1/2. 2/2. 3. 2/4. 6. 8. 9. 10.*	Includes Chin Lushai and Manipur.

WEST AFRICA 1892–94
Medals awarded: East and West Africa Medal with numerous clasps for engagement.

Dates	Battle	Honour / Participants	Remarks
1892–4	**West Africa 1892–3–4**	**West India.**	

NORTH WEST FRONTIER, INDIA 1895–8
Medals awarded: India Medal 1895–1902 with clasps as shown.

Dates	Battle	Honour / Participants	Remarks
3 Mar–21 Apr 1895	**Defence of Chitral** (clasp)	IND-Inf-**14.** IND-Inf-*4 Kashmir Rifles.*	Participants were local police.
3 Apr 1895	*Malakand Pass*	Inf-*16. 25. 60. 75.* IND-Inf-*15. 37. 54. Guides.*	
7 Mar–15 Aug 1895	**Chitral** (clasp)	Inf-**3. 16. 25. 30. 60. 75. 78.** IND-Cav-**9. 11. Guides. Mtn Btys-2. 4. S&M-Ben. Mad.** Inf-**13. 15. 23. 25. 29. 30. 32. 34. 37. 54. 71. Guides. 3 GR. 4 GR.**	
10 Jun 1897	*Maizar*	IND-Inf-*51. 55.*	
26 Jul–2 Aug 1897	**Malakand** (clasp)	IND-Cav.**11. Guides. 28 Mtn Bty. Mad S&M.** Inf-**24. 31. 35. 38. 45. Guides.** Inf-*2. 3. 50. 74.* IND-Inf-*21. 22. 25. 39.*	App by 74.
1–2 Aug 1897	*Chakdara*	IND-Cav-*11. Guides.* Inf-*24. 38. 45. Guides.*	
7 Aug–3 Oct 1897	*Mohmund*	Inf-*3. 13. 21. 52.* IND-Cav-*11. 13. 23.* Inf-*20. 22. 30. 35. 36. 37. 38. 56. 128. 1 GR. 9 GR.*	
Jun 1879–Apr 1898	**Tirah** (clasp)	Inf-**2. 11. 19. 21. 25. 39. 48. 75. 95.** IND-Cav-**18. Mtn Btys-1. 2. 5. S&M-Ben. Mad. Bom.** Inf-**15. 30. 36. 53. 56. 128. GR-1. 2. 3. 4.** Inf-*18. 27. 32. 52. 74. 105. 107.* IND-Cav-*3. 6. 9.* Inf-*34. 39. 45. 81. 9 GR.*	App by 4 DG. 27.
12 Sep 1897	**Samana** (clasp)	IND-Inf-**36.**	
18–20 Oct 1897	*Dargai*	Inf-*25. 39. 48. 75. 95.* IND-Inf-*15. 53. 2 GR. 3 GR.*	App by 75.
10 Jun 1897–4 Apr 1898	**Punjab Frontier** (clasp)	IND-Cav-**3. 6. 9. 11. 13. 18. 38. 39. Guides. Mtn Btys-1. 2. 5. 8. S&M-Ben. Mad. Bom.** Inf-**12. 15. 20. 22. 24. 30. 31. 35. 36. 37. 38. 39. 45. 53. 56. 81. 128. GR-1. 2. 3. 4. 5. 9.** *11 D.* Inf-*2. 3. 11. 13. 19. 21. 25. 27. 32. 39. 48. 50. 52. 74. 75. 91. 95. 105.* IND-Cav-*23.* Inf-*21. 34. 51. 55. 95. 127. Guides. Jodpur L. Nahba. Kapwathala.*	

Dates	**Honoured** or *Non-Honoured* Battle	**Honour awarded** to or *Participants in* Battle	Remarks

RHODESIA
Medals awarded: British South Africa Company Medal.

| 24 Mar–31 Dec 1896 | *Rhodesia 1896* | *7 D. Inf-76. 84.* | |

BECHUANALAND 1896–7
Medals awarded: Cape of Good Hope GSM with clasp.

| 1 Aug 1896 | *Langeberg* | SA-*Diamond Fds Arty.* SAMR-*1.* Inf-*3. 4. 5.* | |
| 1896–7 | **Bechuanaland 1896–97** | SA-Inf-**2. 4. 5. 6. 7.** | |

EAST AFRICA
Medals awarded: East and West Africa Medal with clasp.

| 1896–9 | **British East Africa 1896–99** | IND-Inf-**104. 124. 127.**
IND-Inf-*14. 15.*
AF-*Uganda Rifles. East Africa Rifles.* | |

2nd SUDAN WAR
Medals awarded: Queen's Sudan Medal 1896–7. Khedive's Sudan Medal 1896–1908.

19–26 Sep 1896	**Hafir**	Inf-**64.**	
8 Apr 1898	**Atbara**	Inf-**6. 10. 72. 79.**	
5 Sep 1898	**Khartoum** *(Omdurman)*	**21 L.** Inf-**GG. 5. 6. 10. 20. 72. 79. RB.**	Celebrated by 80 Battery.

WEST AFRICA
Medals awarded: East and West Africa Medal.

| 1898–9 | **Sierra Leone 1898–9** | **West India.**
AF-**West Africa.** | |

2nd BOER WAR (SOUTH AFRICAN WAR)
Medals awarded: Queen's South Africa Medal 1899–1902 with clasps as shown. King's South Africa Medal 1901–2 with clasps for South Africa 1901 and South Africa 1902.

12 Oct 1899– 16 Feb 1900	**Defence of Kimberley** (clasp)	Inf-**47.** SA-Inf-**13.** SA-Cav-*7.*	
20 Oct 1899	*Talana Hill* (clasp)	Inf-*17. 60. 87. 103.*	
21 Oct 1899	*Elandslaagte* (clasp)	*5 D.* Inf-*11. 63. 92.* SA-*MR-5.*	App by 5 D. 75. 92.
21 Oct 1899– 24 Jun 1900	*Cape Colony* (clasp)	*7 DG. Yeo-2. 5. 8. 13. 20. 22. 29. 38. City Imperial Vols.* Inf-*3. 12. 41.* SA-Inf-*2. 4.*	
30 Oct 1899	*Lombard's Kop*	*5 DG. 5 D. 18 H. 19 H.* Inf-*11. 17. 28. 60. 63. 87. 103.* SA-*MR-1.*	
29 Oct 1899– 27 Feb 1900	**Defence of Ladysmith** (clasp)	**5 DG. 5 D. 18 H. 19 H.** Inf-**8. 11. 17. 28. 60. 63. 92. RB.** SA-**MR-1. 3. 5.** Inf-*87.* SA-*MR-3.*	
23 Nov 1899	*Belmont* (clasp)	*9 D.* Inf-*GG. CG. SG. 5. 58. 101. 105.*	
25 Nov 1899	*Graspan*	Inf-*5. 47. 58. 105.*	
28 Nov 1899	**Modder River** (clasp)	**9 D.** Inf-**GG. CG. SG. 5. 58. 71. 91. 105.** Inf-*47.*	App by 47. Battle actually fought on the Riet River. Celebrated by 151 Battery.

Dates	Honoured or Non-Honoured Battle	Honour awarded to or Participants in Battle	Remarks
11 Dec 1899	*Magersfontein*	*9 D. 12 D. Inf-GG. CG. SG. 71. 73. 75. 78. 91. 105.*	
15 Dec 1899	*Colenso*	*1 D. 13 D. Inf-2. 7. 11. 14. 21. 23. 27. 34. 60. 68. 70. 88. 90. 102. 103. RB.* *SA-MR-5.*	Also **Colenso Battery.**
16 Dec 1899– 6 Feb 1900	*Colesberg*	*LG. RHG. 6 DG. 6 D. 10 D. Inf-12. 16. 18. 19. 36. 41. 44. 66. 99.*	Also **Coles Kop Battery.**
6 Jan 1900	*Wagon Hill (Caesar's Camp)*	*5 DG. 5 D. 18 H. 19 H. Inf-11. 60. 63. 92. RB.*	
16 Jan-8 Feb 1900	*Tugela Heights (clasp)*	*1 D. 13 D. 14 D. Inf-2. 4. 11. 13. 14. 20. 27. 34. 40. 60. 65. 68. 70. 77. 88. 90. 103. RB.* *SA-MR-1. 5.*	
15 Feb 1900	**Relief of Kimberley** (clasp)	**LG. RHG. 6 DG. 2 D. 9 D. 10 D. 12 D. 16 D. Inf-3. 19. 33. 41. 43. 44. 61.** *6 D. 14 D.*	App by SA-MR-5.
17–27 Feb 1900	**Paardeberg** (clasp)	**LG. RHG. 6 DG. 2 D. 9 D. 10 D. 16 D. 3. 9. 10. 19. 25. 33. 41. 43. 44. 46. 61. 67. 73. 75. 78. 85. 91. 92.** CDN-Inf-**RCR.**	
27 Feb 1900	**Relief of Ladysmith** (clasp)	**1 D. 13 D. 14 D.** Inf-**2. 4. 7. 11. 13. 14. 20. 21. 23. 27. 34. 40. 54. 60. 65. 68. 70. 77. 88. 89. 90. 103. RB.** SA-**MR-4. 5.** Inf-**1.** *SA-MR-1.*	
10 Mar 1900	*Driefontein* (clasp)	*6 DG. 2 D. 10 D. 12 D. Inf-3. 19. 41. 44. 61.* AUS-*LH-1.*	
31 Mar 1900	*Sannah's Post*		Only **Sannah's Post Battery.** No Cav or Inf in sufficient numbers.
9–25 Apr 1900	*Wepener* (clasp)	CDN-*Strathcona's.* SA-*SAMR-1.* Inf-*5.*	
17 May 1900	*Relief of Mafeking* (clasp)	SA-Inf-*7. (Kimberley LH)*	App by SA-MR-5. Inf-3.
29 May 1900	*Doornkop*	*8 D.* Inf-*35. 46. 75. 79. 85. 95.* CDN-Inf-*RCR.*	App by 75.
29 May 1900	*Biddulphs berg* (clasp)	*-GG. SG. 97.*	
31 May 1900	*Johannesberg* (clasp)	*9 D. 16 LD. 17 LD.* Inf-*GG. CG. SG. 6. 9. 10. 19. 22. 24. 25. 30. 41. 44. 45. 67. 98.*	App by 16 LD. and by SA-Inf-4.
11 Jun 1900	*Aleman's Nek*	Inf-*2. 14. 54. 70. 77. 102.* SA-*MR-5.*	App by 54.
11–12 Jun 1900	*Diamond Hill* (clasp)	*LG. RHG. 6 DG. 7 DG. 2 D. 6 D. 8 D. 9 D. 10 D. 12 D. 14 D. 16 LD. 17 LD.* Yeo-*53.* Inf-*GG. CG. SG. 6. 19. 35. 41. 44. 45. 79.* AUS-*LH-1.*	App by 16 LD and by SA-Inf-4.
15–29 Jul 1900	*Wittebergen* (clasp)	*9 D. 16 LD.* Yeo-*53.* Inf-*SG. 16. 18. 35. 73. 78. 79. 99. 100. 101.* SA-Inf-*3.*	
23 Aug 1900	*Geluk*	Inf-*8.*	
26 Aug 1900	*Belfast* (clasp)	*LG. RHG. 6 DG. 7 DG. 2 D. 6 D. 8 D. 9 D. 10 D. 12 D. 14 D. 16 LD. 17 LD.* Inf-*GG. CG. SG. 6. 19. 41. 44.*	

Dates	**Honoured** or *Non-Honoured* Battle	**Honour awarded** to or *Participants in* Battle	Remarks
27 Aug 1900	*Bergendal*	*5 D. 6 D. 18 H. 19 H.* Inf-*8. 11. 17. 27. 60. 63. 92. RB.*	App by RB.
6–7 Nov 1900	*Komati River*	*5 D.* Inf-*12. 85.* CDN-Cav-*RCD.*	
13 Dec 1900	*Nooitgedacht*	Inf-*5. 105.*	
6 Feb 1901	*Lake Chrissie*	*5 D.* Inf-*12.*	App by 14.
30 Sep 1901	*Moedwill*	Yeo-*53.* Inf-*45.*	App by Yeo-53.
30 Oct 1901	*Baakenlaagte*	Yeo-*53.* Inf-*3.*	App by Yeo-53. Celebrated by 166 Battery.
1900–2	**St Helena**	**Militia Bns of 28. 62.**	Awarded for guarding Boer POW on the island.
1901–2	**Mediterranean 1901–02**	**Militia Bns of – 5. 7. 14. 47. 50. 51. 72. 101.**	Awarded for garrison duty in various places around the Mediterrean.
12 Oct 1899–31 May 1902	**South Africa 1899–1902**	**LG. RHG. 1 DG. 2 DG. 3 DG. 5 DG. 6 DG. 7 DG. 1 D. 2 D. 3 D. 5 D. 6 D. 7 D. 8 D. 9 D. 10 D. 12 D. 13 D. 14 D. 16 LD. 17 LD. 18 H. 19 L. 20 H.** Yeo-**1. 2. 3. 4. 5. 6. 7. 8. 9. 10. 11. 12. 13. 14. 15. 16. 17. 18. 19. 20. 21. 22. 23. 24. 25. 26. 27. 28. 29. 30. 31. 32. 33. 34. 35. 36. 37. 38. 40. 45. 46. 47. 53. 54. Inns.** Inf-**GG. CG. SG. 1. 2. 3. 4. 5. 6. 7. 8. 9. 10. 11. 12. 13. 14. 15. 16. 17. 18. 19. 20. 21. 22. 23. 24. 25. 26. 27. 28. 29. 30. 33. 34. 35. 36. 38. 40. 41. 42. 43. 44. 45. 46. 47. 54. 56. 58. 60. 61. 63. 65. 66. 67. 68. 70. 71. 73. 74. 75. 77. 78. 79. 81. 85. 86. 87. 88. 89. 90. 91. 92. 95. 96. 97. 98. 99. 100. 101. 102. 103. 104. 105. 108. 109. RB. Volunteer Bns. of – 1. 2. 3. 4. 5. 6. 7. 8. 9. 10. 11. 12. 13. 14. 15. 16. 17. 19. 20. 21. 22. 23. 24. 25. 26. 28. 29. 30. 31. 32. 33. 34. 35. 37. 38. 39. 40. 41. 42. 43. 44. 45. 47. 48. 49. 50. 51. 53. 57. 62. 63. 64. 65. 68. 71. 72. 75. 79. 91. Volunteer Bns – Cambs. Mon. Hereford. HAC. Cambridge University. CLR. 4. 5. 6. 7. LR – 8. 9. 11. 12. 13. 14. 15. 16. 17. 18. 19. 20. 21. 22. 23. 24. 28. Highland Cyclist Bn.** CDN-Cav-**RCD. Strathcona. GGBG. 1. 5. 12. 17.** Inf-**RCR. GGFG. 1. 2. 3. 6. 7. 8. 13. 43. 63. 66. 67. 90. 93.** AUS-**LH**-**1. 2. 3. 4. 6. 8. 9. 10. 12. 13. 14. 15. 16. 17. 19. 20.** Inf-**1. 3. 4. 5. 6. 8. 9. 10. 11. 12. 13. 16. 17. 27. 30. 31. 32. 38. 40. 44. 51.** NZ-**MR**-**1. 2. 3. 4. 5. 6. 7. 8. 9. 10. 11.** Inf-**1. 2. 3. 4. 5. 6. 7. 8. 9. 10. 11. 12.** SA-**MR**-**1. 3. 4. 5. SAMR**-**1.** Inf-**1. 2. 3. 4. 5. 6. 7.**	See page 352 for complete list of Militia Battalions Honoured.

3rd CHINA WAR: BOXER REBELLION
Medals awarded: Third China War Medal.

4–16 Aug 1900	**Pekin 1900**	Inf-**23.** IND-Cav-**1.** Inf-**7. 24. 51.**	
13 Jun–20 Dec 1900	**China 1900**	IND-Cav-**16. 33. S&M-Ben. Mad. Bom.** Inf-**2. 6. 14. 20. 34. 57. 61. 63. 88. 91. 98. 122. 126. 130. 4 GR.** IND-*1 Jodpur L. Alwar. Bikaner.*	

Dates	Honoured or *Non-Honoured* Battle	Honour awarded to or *Participants in* Battle	Remarks

WEST AFRICA
Medals awarded: Ashanti Medal 1900.

31 Mar–25 Dec 1900	**Ashanti 1900**	AF-**West Africa. Nigeria. Gold Coast. KAR.**	

EAST AFRICA
Medals awarded: Africa GSM 1902–56 with clasps.

1901–4	**Somaliland 1901–04**	IND-**Bom S&M.** Inf-**27. 52. 101. 102. 107.** AF-**KAR.** Inf-*37. 60.* IND-Inf-*123.*	App by 37.
1901	**British East Africa 1901**	IND-Inf-**116.**	

THIBET
Medals awarded: Tibet Medal.

1904	*Thibet 1904*	Inf-*7.* IND-Inf-*8 GR.*	App by 7.

ZULU REBELLION
Medals awarded: Zulu Rebellion Medal.

1906	**Natal 1906**	SA-**MR-1. 3. 4. 5.** Inf-**1.** Inf-*6.* SA-*SAMR-1.* Inf-*8. 10.*	App by SA-MR-5. as 'Native Rebellion 1906'.

THE GREAT WAR
FRANCE AND FLANDERS
Medals awarded: British War Medal 1914–20. 1914 Star for service in Flanders between 5 Aug and 23 Nov 1914. 1914–15 Star for service in any theatre up to end of 1915.

23–24 Aug 1914	**Mons**	LG. RHG. 2 DG. 3 DG. 4 DG. 5 DG. 6 DG. 2 D. 3 H. 4 H. 5 L. 9 L. 11 H. 12 L. 15 H. 16 H. 18 H. 20 H. Inf-GG. CG. IG. 1. 2. 5. 7. 8. 9. 10. 12. 16. 18. 21. 22. 23. 24. 25. 26. 28. 29. 31. 32. 33. 35. 38. 39. 40. 41. 43. 47. 48. 49. 50. 51. 57. 60. 62. 63. 71. 75. 83. 88. 91.	Includes action of Elouges.
24 Aug 1914	*Audregnies*		App by 22.
26 Aug 1914	**Le Cateau**	LG. RHG. 2 DG. 3 DG. 4 DG. 5 DG. 6 DG. 3 H. 4 H. 5 L. 9 L. 11 H. 16 H. 18 H. 19 H. Inf-1. 4. 5. 6. 7. 9. 10. 12. 13. 16. 18. 20. 21. 22. 23. 25. 26. 27. 29. 30. 31. 32. 33. 37. 39. 40. 44. 50. 51. 57. 62. 63. 72. 75. 83. 87. 91. 102. RB.	Also **Le Cateau Battery.**
24 Aug–5 Sep 1914	**Retreat from Mons**	LG. RHG. 2 DG. 3 DG. 4 DG. 5 DG. 6 DG. 2 D. 3 H. 4 H. 5 L. 9 L. 11 H. 12 L. 15 H. 16 H. 18 H. 19 H. 20 H. Yeo-**NIH.** Inf-GG. CG. SG. IG. 1. 2. 4. 5. 6. 7. 8. 9. 10. 12. 13. 16. 18. 20. 21. 22. 23. 24. 25. 26. 27. 28. 29. 30. 31. 32. 35. 37. 38. 39. 40. 41. 42. 43. 44. 47. 48. 49. 50. 51. 57. 60. 62. 63. 71. 72. 75. 79. 83. 87. 88. 91. 101. 102. RB.	Includes Battles of Mons and Le Cateau (separately Honoured) and actions of Solesmes, Le Grand Fayt, Etreux, Crepy-en-Valois, Nery.
1 Sep 1914	*Nery*	2 DG. 5 DG. 11 H. Inf-6. 23. 26. 57. 91. 102.	App by 5 DG. 11 H. Only **Nery Battery.**

Dates	**Honoured** or *Non-Honoured* Battle	**Honour awarded** to or *Participants in* Battle	Remarks
7–10 Sep 1914	**Marne 1914**	LG. RHG. 2 DG. 3 DG. 4 DG. 5 DG. 6 DG. 2 D. 3 H. 4 H. 5 L. 9 L. 11 H. 12 L. 15 H. 16 L. 18 H. 19 H. 20 H. Yeo-NIH. Inf-GG. CG. SG. IG. 1. 2. 4. 5. 6. 7. 8. 9. 10. 12. 13. 16. 18. 20. 21. 22. 23. 24. 25. 26. 27. 28. 29. 30. 31. 32. 33. 35. 37. 38. 39. 40. 41. 42. 43. 44. 47. 48. 49. 50. 51. 57. 60. 62. 63. 71. 72. 75. 79. 83. 87. 88. 91. 101. 102. RB.	Includes Passages of the Petit Morin and the Marne.
12–15 Sep 1914	**Aisne 1914**	LG. RHG. 2 DG. 3 DG. 4 DG. 5 DG. 6 DG. 2 D. 3 H. 4 H. 5 L. 9 L. 11 H. 12 L. 15 H. 16 L. 18 H. 19 H. 20 H. Yeo-NIH. Inf-GG. CG. SG. IG. 1. 2. 3. 4. 5. 6. 7. 8. 9. 10. 11. 12. 13. 14. 15. 16. 17. 18. 20. 21. 22. 23. 24. 25. 26. 27. 28. 29. 30. 31. 32. 33. 35. 37. 38. 39. 40. 41. 42. 43. 44. 45. 47. 48. 49. 50. 51. 53. 57. 60. 62. 63. 64. 65. 68. 71. 72. 75. 79. 83. 87. 88. 91. 100. 101. 102. RB.	Includes Passage of the Aisne and capture of Aisne Heights and Chemin des Dames Ridge.
10 Oct–2 Nov 1914	**La Bassee 1914**	4 DG. 5 DG. 7 DG. 9 L. 18 H. Inf-1. 5. 7. 9. 10. 11. 12. 16. 17. 18. 21. 22. 23. 25. 26. 29. 31. 32. 33. 39. 40. 42. 50. 51. 57. 62. 63. 72. 75. 83. 91. IND-Cav-4. 34. S&M-Ben. Bom. Inf-6. 9. 15. 39. 41. 47. 57. 58. 59. GR-2. 3. 8. 9.	
12 Oct–2 Nov 1914	**Messines 1914**	LG. RHG. 2 DG. 3 DG. 4 DG. 5 DG. 6 DG. 2 D. 3 H. 4 H. 5 L. 9 L. 11 H. 12 L. 16 L. 18 H. 20 H. Yeo-34. Inf-5. 7. 10. 23. 25. 26. 27. 40. 44. 50. 51. 57. 62. 75. 83. 88. 91. 14 LR. IND-Inf-9. 57. 58. 59. 129.	
13 Oct–2 Nov 1914	**Armentieres 1914**	LG. RHG. 2 DG. 3 DG. 4 DG. 5 DG. 6 DG. 3 H. 4 H. 9 L. 11 H. 16 L. 18 H. 19 H. Yeo-34. NIH. Inf-3. 4. 5. 6. 7. 10. 11. 13. 14. 15. 17. 20. 22. 23. 26. 27. 29. 30. 31. 32. 37. 39. 40. 44. 45. 53. 57. 62. 63. 64. 65. 68. 72. 75. 83. 87. 88. 91. 100. 102. RB. IND-Cav-34. Bom S&M. Inf-9. 15. 39. 47. 57. 58. 59. 129. GR-3. 9.	Includes capture of Meteren.
19 Oct–22 Nov 1914	**Ypres 1914**	LG. RHG. 2 DG. 3 DG. 4 DG. 5 DG. 1 D. 2 D. 3 H. 4 H. 5 L. 9 L. 10 H. 11 H. 12 L. 15 H. 16 L. 18 H. 20 H. Yeo-10. 11. 14. Inf-GG. CG. SG. IG. 2. 5. 6. 7. 8. 9. 10. 16. 19. 21. 22. 23. 24. 25. 28. 29. 33. 34. 35. 38. 40. 41. 42. 43. 47. 48. 49. 50. 51. 60. 62. 71. 75. 79. 83. 88. 101. 14 LR. Herts. IND-INF-129.	Includes Battles of Langemarck, Gheluvelt and Nonne Boschen (all separately Honoured).
25–30 Oct 1914	*Hollebeke Chateau*		App by 1 D.
21–24 Oct 1914	**Langemarck 1914**	LG. RHG. 1 D. 4 H. 10 H. 15 H. Yeo-14. Inf-GG. CG. SG. IG. 2. 6. 8. 16. 19. 21. 23. 24. 28. 29. 34. 38. 41. 42. 43. 47. 48. 49. 60. 62. 71. 75. 79. 88. 101.	
29–31 Oct 1914	**Gheluvelt**	LG. RHG. 1 D. 2 D. 3 H. 4 H. 5 L. 10 H. 15 H. 16 L. Yeo-14. Inf-GG. CG. SG. IG. 2. 6. 8. 16. 19. 21. 23. 24. 28. 29. 34. 35. 38. 41. 42. 43. 47. 48. 49. 60. 71. 75. 79. 88. 101. 14 LR. IND-Inf-129.	
11 Nov 1914	**Nonne Boschen**	LG. RHG. 3 DG. 1 D. 10 H. 15 H. Inf-GG. CG. SG. IG. 5. 7. 8. 10. 16. 21. 22. 24. 25. 28. 29. 33. 35. 38. 40. 41. 42. 43. 47. 48. 49. 60. 62. 71. 75. 79. 83. 88. 101. 14 LR. Herts.	

Dates	Honoured or Non-Honoured Battle	Honour awarded to or Participants in Battle	Remarks
23–24 Nov 1914	**Festubert 1914**	**17 L. Inf-17. 72. 88.** **IND-S&M-Ben. Bom.** Inf-6. 9. 39. 41. 57. 58. 59. 129. GR-2. 3. 8. 9.	
14 Dec 1914	*Wytschaete*		App by Liverpool Scottish.
20–21 Dec 1914 and 25 Jan 1915	**Givenchy 1914**	**7 DG. 8 H.** Inf-**CG. SG.** 12. 23. 24. 28. 35. 41. 42. 47. 48. 60. 63. 71. 72. 79. 88. 101. **14 LR.** IND-Cav-4. 9. 20. 30. **S&M-Ben. Bom.** Inf-9. 15. 41. 47. 57. 58. 59. 125. 129. GR-1. 2. 3. 4. 8. 9.	
10–13 Mar 1915	**Neuve Chapelle**	**2 D. 12 L. 20 H.** Yeo-14. 51. Inf-**GG. CG. SG.** 1. 6. 8. 10. 11. 12. 14. 16. 17. 19. 21. 23. 26. 29. 30. 34. 38. 42. 45. 48. 49. 57. 62. 63. 71. 72. 75. 79. 83. 88. **RB. CLR-3. 4. LR-13.** IND-Cav-4. 15. 20. **S&M-Ben. Bom.** Inf-6. 15. 39. 41. 47. 57. 58. 59. 125. 129. GR-1. 2. 3. 4. 8. 9.	
17–22 Apr	**Hill 60**	Inf-11. 16. 25. 31. 33. 50. 51. 79. **9 LR.**	
22 Apr–25 May 1915	**Ypres 1915**	**LG. RHG. 2 DG. 3 DG. 4 DG. 5 DG. 6 DG. 1 D. 2 D. 3 H. 4 H. 5 L. 9 L. 10 H. 11 H. 12 L. 15 H. 16 L. 18 H. 19 H. 20 H.** Yeo-10. 11. 34. 39. 49. 51. Inf-1. 3. 4. 5. 6. 7. 8. 9. 10. 11. 12. 13. 15. 16. 18. 19. 20. 22. 25. 28. 29. 30. 31. 32. 33. 34. 37. 39. 40. 41. 44. 50. 51. 53. 57. 60. 63. 65. 68. 71. 72. 75. 79. 83. 87. 88. 91. 100. 102. **RB. CLR-4. 5. LR-9. 12. HAC. Mon. Cambs.** IND-**Bom S&M.** Inf-9. 15. 40. 47. 57. 58. 59. 129. GR-1. 4. CAN-Cav-12. 14. 16. 19. Inf-**RCR. PPCLI. GGFG.** 1. 2. 3. 5. 6. 7. 8. 10. 11. 12. 13. 21. 28. 36. 38. 44. 48. 50. 57. 58. 65. 67. 72. 78. 79. 90. 96. 97. 100. 101. 103. 105. 106. **Calgary.**	Participated – Liv Scot. App by 1 DG for later dates. Includes Battles of Gravenstafel, St Julien, Frezenberg, and Bellewarde (all separately Honoured).
22–23 Apr 1915	**Gravenstafel**	**9 L. 18 H.** Inf-1. 3. 4. 5. 7. 8. 9. 10. 11. 12. 15. 18. 22. 25. 28. 31. 32. 33. 39. 41. 50. 51. 53. 57. 60. 63. 65. 68. 79. 87. 91. 100. **RB. LR-9. 12. Mon. Cambs.** CAN-Cav-19. Inf-**RCR. GGFG.** 2. 5. 6. 7. 10. 13. 38. 48. 50. 57. 58. 90. 103. 105. 106.	Includes the Gas Attack.
24 Apr–4 May 1915	**St Julien**	**LG. RHG. 3 DG. 4 DG. 2 D. 3 H. 4 H. 5 L. 9 L. 12 L. 16 L. 18 H. 20 H.** Yeo-10. 34. 49. Inf-1. 3. 4. 5. 6. 7. 8. 9. 10. 11. 12. 13. 15. 16. 18. 19. 20. 22. 25. 28. 30. 31. 32. 33. 37. 39. 40. 41. 44. 50. 51. 53. 57. 60. 63. 65. 68. 71. 72. 79. 87. 88. 91. 100. 102. **RB. CLR-4. 5. LR-9. 12. Mon. Cambs.** IND-**Bom S&M.** Inf-9. 15. 40. 47. 57. 58. 59. 129. GR-1. 4. CAN-Cav-19. Inf-**RCR. GGFG.** 2. 5. 6. 7. 10. 13. 38. 48. 50. 57. 58. 90. 103. 105. 106.	
4 May 1915	*Hill 60 Counterattack*		App by 22.
8–13 May 1915	**Frezenberg**	**LG. RHG. 2 DG. 3 DG. 4 DG. 5 DG. 1 D. 9 L. 10 H. 11 H. 15 H. 18 H. 19 H.** Yeo-10. 11. 49. Inf-1. 3. 4. 5. 6. 7. 8. 9. 10. 11. 12. 13. 15. 16. 18. 19. 22. 25. 28. 30. 31. 32. 34. 37. 40. 41. 44. 50. 51. 53. 57. 60. 63. 65. 68. 72. 75. 79. 83. 87. 91. 100. 102. **RB. CLR-5. LR-9. 12. Mon. Cambs.** CAN-Inf-**PPCLI.**	

Dates	**Honoured** or *Non-Honoured* Battle	**Honour awarded** to or *Participants in* Battle	Remarks
24–25 May 1915	**Bellewarde**	2 DG. 3 DG. 4 DG. 5 DG. 2 D. 3 H. 4 H. 5 L. 9 L. 11 H. 12 L. 15 H. 16 L. 18 H. 19 H. 20 H. Yeo-34. Inf-1. 3. 4. 5. 6. 7. 8. 9. 10. 12. 13. 15. 16. 18. 19. 20. 22. 25. 28. 30. 31. 32. 34. 37. 39. 40. 41. 44. 51. 53. 57. 60. 63. 65. 68. 72. 75. 79. 87. 91. 102. RB. LR-9. Mon. Liv Scot. CAN-Inf-**PPCLI**.	App by 43 for later date.
9 May 1915	**Aubers**	Inf-**GG. CG. SG.** 1. 2. 6. 7. 8. 10. 11. 12. 14. 16. 17. 19. 21. 23. 24. 26. 27. 28. 29. 30. 33. 34. 35. 38. 41. 42. 43. 45. 47. 48. 49. 57. 60. 62. 63. 71. 72. 75. 79. 83. 88. 101. RB. CLR-3. 4. LR-13. 14. 17. 21. IND-**S&M-Ben. Bom.** Inf-9. 15. 39. 40. 41. 47. 57. 58. 59. 125. GR-2. 3. 4. 8. 9.	
15–25 May 1915	**Festubert 1915**	Inf-**GG. CG. SG. IG.** 1. 2. 4. 6. 8. 16. 17. 19. 21. 23. 27. 29. 34. 38. 42. 43. 47. 49. 60. 62. 71. 72. 75. 79. 91. **Herts.** CLR-3. 4. 6. 7. LR- 8. 9. 15. 16. 17. 18. 19. 20. 21. 22. 23. 24. IND-Cav-**4. S&M-Ben. Bom.** Inf-6. 15. 39. 41. 47. 57. 58. 59. 123. GR-1. 2. 3. 4. 8. 9. CDN-Cav-**RCD. Strathcona.** 12. 14. 16. Inf-**RCR. GGFG.** 1. 2. 3. 5. 6. 7. 8. 10. 11. 12. 13. 21. 28. 36. 38. 44. 48. 50. 57. 58. 65. 67. 72. 78. 79. 90. 96. 97. 100. 101. 103. 105. 106. **Calgary**.	
19 and 30 Jul, 9 Aug 1915	**Hooge 1915**	Inf-3. 7. 12. 13. 14. 15. 17. 32. 43. 45. 51. 53. 57. 60. 65. 68. 75. RB. LR-9. 16.	
25 Sep–8 Oct 1915	**Loos**	RHG. 3 DG. 1 D. 10 H. Yeo-11. 14. 37. 49. 50. SIH Inf-**GG. CG. SG. IG. WG.** 1. 2. 3. 4. 5. 6. 7. 8. 9. 10. 11. 12. 13. 14. 15. 16. 19. 21. 22. 23. 24. 25. 26. 28. 29. 31. 34. 35. 38. 41. 42. 43. 44. 45. 47. 48. 49. 50. 51. 57. 60. 62. 64. 65. 68. 71. 72. 75. 79. 91. 101. CLR-6. 7. LR- 8. 9. 14. 15. 16. 17. 18. 19. 20. 21. 22. 23. 24. **Herts.** IND-**Ben S&M.** Inf-27. 33. 57. 58. 59. 69. 89. 93. 129. GR-1. 2. 9.	Includes actions of Pietre, Bois Grenier and Bellewarde.
25 Sep 1915	*Bois Grenier*		App by RB.
25 Sep 1915	*Pietre*		App by RB.
27 Mar–16 Apr 1916	*St Eloi Craters*		App by numerous Canadian regiments.
2–13 Jun 1916	**Mount Sorrel**	Inf-**CG.** 13. 32. 43. 53. CDN-Cav-**GGBG.** 5. 6. 7. 8. 9. 11. 12. 15. 18. 22. 30. **AltaMR.** Inf-**RCR. PPCLI. R22 R. GGFG.** 1. 2. 3. 5. 6. 7. 8. 9. 10. 12. 13. 14. 15. 19. 20. 21. 29. 38. 40. 43. 44. 48. 49. 50. 52. 57. 58. 60. 62. 63. 67. 74. 76. 78. 79. 90. 91. 95. 96. 99. 100. 101. 103. 104. 105. 106. **SAR. Queens. Edmonton. Calgary. Vancouver.**	

Dates	**Honoured** or *Non-Honoured* Battle	**Honour awarded** to or *Participants in* Battle	Remarks
1 Jul–18 Nov 1916	**Somme 1916**	LG. 1 DG. 2 DG. 4 DG. 7 DG. 6 D. 8 H. 9 L. 11 H. 15 H. 17 L. 18 H. 19 H. RTR. Yeo-12. 38. 48. NIH SIH. Inf-GG. CG. SG. IG. WG. 1. 2. 3. 4. 5. 6. 7. 8. 9. 10. 11. 12. 13. 14. 15. 16. 17. 18. 19. 20. 21. 22. 23. 24. 25. 26. 27. 28. 29. 30. 31. 32. 33. 34. 35. 37. 38. 39. 40. 41. 42. 43. 44. 45. 47. 48. 49. 50. 51. 53. 57. 60. 62. 63. 64. 65. 68. 71. 72. 75. 79. 83. 87. 88. 91. 100. 101. 102. CLR-1. 2. 3. 4. 5. 6. 7. LR-8. 9. 12. 13. 14. 15. 16. 17. 18. 19. 20. 21. 22. 23. 24. Cambs. Herts. Mon. HAC. Liv Scot. Newfoundland. IND-Cav-2. 4. 6. 9. 18. 19. 34. 36. 38. CDN-Cav-RCD. Strathcona. FGH. GGBG. 1. 6. 7. 8. 9. 11. 12. 15. 16. 18. 19. 22. 30. Inf-RCR. PPCLI. R22R. GGFG. 1. 3. 5. 6. 7. 8. 9. 10. 11. 12. 13. 14. 20. 21. 22. 25. 29. 34. 36. 38. 40. 42. 43. 44. 48. 49. 50. 52. 57. 58. 60. 62. 63. 65. 66. 67. 72. 74. 76. 78. 79. 90. 91. 95. 96. 99. 100. 101. 103. 104. 105. 106. TS. SAR. Queens. Edmonton. Calgary. Vancouver. 1MG. AUS-LH-13. Inf-1. 2. 3. 4. 5. 6. 7. 8. 9. 10. 11. 12. 13. 14. 15. 16. 17. 18. 19. 20. 21. 22. 23. 24. 25. 26. 27. 28. 29. 30. 31. 32. 45. 46. 47. 48. 49. 50. 51. 52. 53. 54. 55. 56. 57. 58. 59. 60. NZ-MR-5. 7. 12. Inf-1. 2. 3. 4. 5. 6. 7. 8. 9. 10. 11. 12. 13. 14. 15. 16. 17. SA-Arty Btys-71. 72. 73. 74. 75. 125. Inf-1. 2. 3. 4. 1 Fd Amb.	Includes Battles of Albert 1916 to Ancre 1916 inclusive (all separately Honoured).
1–13 Jul 1916	**Albert 1916**	LG. Yeo-12. 38. NIH. SIH. Inf-1. 2. 3. 4. 5. 6. 7. 8. 9. 10. 11. 12. 13. 14. 15. 16. 18. 19. 20. 21. 22. 23. 24. 25. 26. 27. 28. 29. 30. 31. 33. 34. 35. 37. 38. 39. 40. 41. 42. 43. 44. 45. 47. 48. 49. 50. 51. 53. 57. 60. 62. 63. 64. 65. 68. 71. 72. 75. 79. 83. 87. 91. 101. 102. RB. CLR-1. 2. 3. 4. 5. LR-9. 12. 13. 14. 16. Mon. SA-Arty Btys-72. 74. 75.	Includes actions of Montauban, Mametz, Fricourt, Contalmaison and La Boiselle.
1 Jul 1916	*Beaumont Hamel*		App by 7.
1 Jul 1916	*Schwaben Redoubt*		App by 83.
14–17 Jul 1916	**Bazentin**	7 DG. 8 H. Inf-1. 2. 3. 4. 5. 6. 7. 8. 10. 11. 12. 14. 15. 16. 17. 18. 19. 20. 21. 22. 23. 24. 25. 26. 27. 28. 29. 30. 31. 33. 34. 35. 38. 40. 41. 42. 43. 44. 45. 47. 48. 49. 50. 51. 53. 57. 60. 62. 63. 64. 68. 71. 72. 75. 79. 83. 91. 101. RB. IND-Cav-9. 18. 19. 20. 34. CDN-Cav-RCD. Strathcona. FGH. 1 MG. SA-Arty Btys-71. 72. 73. 75.	Includes actions of Longueval, Trones Wood and Ovillers.
15 Jul–3 Sep 1916	**Delville Wood**	Inf-2. 3. 4. 5. 6. 7. 8. 9. 10. 11. 12. 13. 15. 16. 18. 20. 21. 22. 23. 25. 28. 29. 31. 32. 33. 34. 35. 38. 42. 43. 44. 45. 48. 49. 50. 51. 53. 57. 60. 63. 64. 68. 71. 72. 75. 79. 91. 100. RB. IND-Cav-20. SA-Inf-1. 2. 3. 4. 1 Fd Amb.	
19 Jul 1916	*Fromelles*		App by 43.

Dates	Honoured or *Non-Honoured* Battle	Honour awarded to or *Participants in* Battle	Remarks
23 Jul–3 Sep 1916	**Pozieres**	9 L. Inf-1. 2. 3. 4. 5. 6. 7. 9. 10. 12. 14. 15. 16. 19. 20. 21. 22. 23. 24. 25. 26. 28. 29. 30. 31. 33. 34. 35. 38. 40. 41. 42. 43. 44. 45. 47. 48. 49. 50. 51. 57. 60. 62. 64. 65. 68. 71. 72. 75. 79. 83. 91. 101. CDN-Cav-**RCD. Strathcona. FGH. Inf-RCR. GGFG. 2. 5. 7. 10. 13. 38. 48. 50. 57. 58. AUS-LH-13.** Inf-1. 2. 3. 4. 5. 6. 7. 8. 9. 10. 11. 12. 13. 14. 15. 16. 17. 18. 19. 20. 21. 22. 23. 24. 25. 26. 27. 28. 45. 46. 47. 48. 49. 50. 51. 52. SA-**Arty Btys-71. 72. 73. 74. 75.**	Includes action of Mouquet Farm.
3–6 Sep 1916	**Guillemont**	Inf-2. 4. 6. 8. 9. 11. 13. 16. 18. 22. 23. 25. 27. 28. 31. 32. 34. 37. 40. 43. 47. 50. 51. 53. 60. 63. 64. 68. 75. 83. 87. 88. 100. 101. 102. **RB. CLR-2. 4. 5. LR-9. 12. 13. 14. 16.** NZ-**MR-5. 7. 12.**	
9 Sep 1916	**Ginchy**	Inf-**GG. WG.** 4. 8. 18. 20. 27. 37. 40. 45. 47. 57. 83. 87. 88. 100. 101. 102. **CLR-2. 3. 4. 5. LR-9. 12. 13. 14. 16. Liv Scot.** NZ-**MR-5. 7. 12.**	
15–22 Sep 1916	**Flers Courcelette**	2 DG. 4 DG. 5 DG. 7 DG. 8 H. 9 L. 11 H. 15 H. 18 H. 19 H. Yeo-**48.** Inf-**GG. CG. SG. IG. WG.** 1. 2. 3. 4. 5. 6. 7. 8. 9. 10. 11. 12. 13. 14. 15. 16. 17. 19. 20. 21. 22. 23. 24. 25. 26. 28. 31. 32. 33. 34. 35. 37. 38. 39. 40. 41. 42. 43. 44. 45. 47. 48. 49. 50. 51. 53. 57. 60. 63. 65. 68. 71. 72. 75. 79. 91. 101. **RB. CLR-2. 3. 4. 5. 6. 7. LR-8. 9. 12. 13. 14. 15. 16. 17. 18. 19. 20. 21. 22. 23. 24.** IND-Cav-**9. 18. 19. 20. 34.** CDN-Cav-**RCD. Strathcona. FGH. GGBG. 1. 6. 7. 9. 11. 16. 18. 19. 22. 30. Inf-RCR. PPCLI. R22 R. GGFG. 2. 3. 5. 6. 7. 12. 13. 14. 21. 38. 50. 57. 62. 76. 79. 91. 95. 96. SAR. Queens. Edmonton. Vancouver. 1MG.** NZ-**MR-5. 7. 12.** Inf-1. 2. 3. 4. 5. 6. 7. 8. 9. 10. 11. 12. 13. 14. 15. 16. 17. SA-**Arty Btys-71. 72. 73. 74. 75. 125.**	Includes action of Martinpuich.
25–28 Sep 1916	**Morval**	1DG. 5DG. 6D. 17L. Inf-**GG. CG. SG. IG. WG.** 2. 3. 4. 5. 6. 8. 9. 10. 11. 12. 13. 14. 15. 16. 17. 19. 20. 22. 23. 24. 25. 28. 31. 32. 33. 34. 35. 38. 40. 41. 42. 43. 44. 45. 47. 48. 49. 50. 51. 53. 57. 60. 65. 68. 79. 91. 101. **RB. CLR-2. 3. 4. 5. LR-9. 12. 13. 14. 15. 16. 17. 18. 19. 20. Liv Scot.** IND-Cav-**2. 6. 18. 19. 36. 38.** NZ-**MR- 5. 7. 12.** Inf-1. 2. 3. 4. 5. 6. 7. 8. 9. 10. 11. 12. 13. 14. 15. 16. 17. SA-**125 Bty.**	Includes actions of Combles, Les Boeufs and Guedecourt.
2–28 Sep 1916	**Thiepval**	Inf-2. 3. 5. 7. 9. 10. 12. 14. 15. 16. 19. 20. 22. 31. 33. 34. 35. 37. 38. 39. 42. 44. 45. 48. 49. 50. 57. 63. 65. **Cambs. Herts.** CDN-Cav-**6. Inf-R22 R.** 3. 5. 6. 12. 14. 21. 48. 50. 58. 62. 76. 90. 91. 95. 103. 105. 106. **SAR. Queens. Vancouver.** SA-**Arty Btys-71. 72. 73. 74. 125.**	App by Yorks D. and 40 for earlier dates.

Dates	Honoured or Non-Honoured Battle	Honour awarded to or Participants in Battle	Remarks
1–18 Oct 1916	**Le Transloy**	Inf-1. 2. 3. 4. 5. 6. 7. 8. 9. 12. 13. 14. 16. 17. 19. 20. 21. 22. 23. 25. 26. 29. 30. 31. 32. 33. 34. 35. 37. 40. 42. 43. 44. 45. 48. 49. 50. 51. 53. 57. 60. 62. 63. 65. 68. 71. 72. 75. 79. 87. 91. 102. **RB. CLR**-2. 3. 4. 5. 6. 7. **LR**-9. 12. 13. 14. 15. 16. 17. 18. 19. 20. 21. 22. 23. 24. **Newfoundland.** NZ-**MR**-5. 7. 12. Inf-1. 2. 3. 4. 5. 6. 7. 8. 9. 10. 11. 12. 13. 14. 15. 16. 17. SA-**125 Bty.** Inf-1. 2. 3. 4.	Includes actions of Eaucourt L'Abbaye, Le Sars and Butte de Warlencourt.
1 Oct–11 Nov 1916	**Ancre Heights**	Inf-1. 2. 3. 4. 5. 6. 7. 9. 12. 14. 15. 16. 19. 20. 21. 22. 23. 24. 25. 26. 28. 29. 30. 31. 33. 34. 35. 37. 40. 41. 42. 43. 44. 45. 47. 48. 49. 50. 57. 60. 62. 63. 64. 65. 68. 71. 72. 79. 83. 91. **RB. HAC. Cambs. Herts.** CDN-Cav-**GGBG.** 1. 7. 9. 11. 16. 18. 19. 22. 30. Inf-**RCR. PPCLI. R22R. GGFG.** 1. 2. 3. 5. 6. 7. 10. 12. 13. 14. 21. 38. 43. 48. 50. 57. 58. 60. 62. 67. 72. 76. 79. 90. 95. 96. 100. 103. 104. 105. 106. **TS. SAR. Queens. Edmonton. Calgary. Vancouver.** SA-**Arty Btys**-71. 72. 73. 74. 75. 125.	App by Yeo-9. Includes actions of Schwaben and Stuff Reboubts and Regina Trench.
13–18 Nov 1916	**Ancre 1916**	Inf-1. 2. 3. 4. 5. 6. 7. 8. 9. 10. 12. 13. 14. 15. 16. 19. 20. 21. 22. 23. 24. 27. 28. 29. 30. 31. 32. 34. 35. 37. 38. 39. 40. 41. 42. 43. 44. 45. 47. 48. 49. 50. 51. 53. 57. 60. 62. 63. 64. 65. 71. 72. 75. 91. 102. **RB. Cambs. HAC.** CDN-Inf-1. 5. 43. 50. 60. 67. 72. 100. 103. 104. **TS. Calgary.** SA-**Arty Btys**-72. 73. 74. 75. 125.	App by Yeo-9. 36. Includes capture of Beaumont Hamel.
17 Mar 1917	**Bapaume 1917**	Inf-8. 32. 38. 43. 44. 48. 57. AUS-**LH**-13. Inf-17. 18. 19. 20. 21. 22. 23. 24. 29. 30. 31. 32. SA-**Arty Btys**-71. 75.	App by Yeo-9. 36.
19 Apr–4 May 1917	**Arras 1917**	**LG. RHG. 2DG. 3DG. 4DG. 5DG. 6DG. 1D. 2D. 3H. 4H. 5L. 9L. 10H. 11H. 12L. 16L. 18H. 20H. RTR.** Yeo-10. 11. 34. 49. 51. Inf-1. 2. 3. 4. 5. 6. 7. 8. 9. 10. 11. 12. 13. 14. 15. 16. 19. 20. 21. 22. 23. 24. 25. 26. 27. 28. 29. 30. 31. 32. 33. 34. 35. 37. 38. 39. 40. 42. 43. 44. 45. 47. 48. 49. 50. 51. 53. 57. 60. 62. 63. 64. 65. 68. 71. 72. 75. 79. 87. 91. 100. 102. **RB. CLR**-1. 2. 3. 4. 5. **LR**-9. 12. 13. 14. 16. **Mon. HAC. Newfoundland** CDN-Cav-**GGBG.** 1. 6. 7. 9. 11. 14. 16. 18. 19. 22. Inf-**RCR. PPCLI. R22R. GGFG.** 1. 2. 3. 5. 6. 7. 8. 9. 10. 11. 12. 13. 14. 15. 19. 20. 21. 22. 23. 25. 29. 34. 35. 36. 38. 40. 42. 43. 44. 46. 48. 49. 50. 51. 52. 53. 57. 58. 60. 62. 63. 65. 66. 67. 69. 72. 73. 74. 75. 76. 77. 79. 90. 91. 93. 95. 96. 99. 100. 101. 102. 103. 104. 105. 106. 110. **TS. SAR. Sask. Weyburn. Queens. Edmonton. Calgary. Vancouver. McGill.** AUS-**LH**–13. SA-**Arty Btys**-72. 73. 74. 125. Inf-1. 2. 3. 4. **1 Fd Amb.**	Includes battles of Vimy, Scarpe (three battles) and Arleux (all separately Honoured).

Dates	**Honoured** or *Non-Honoured* Battle	**Honour awarded** to or *Participants in* Battle	Remarks
9–14 Apr 1917	**Vimy 1917**	Inf-6. 7. 9. 11. 13. 16. 22. 25. 28. 30. 31. 32. 35. 37. 42. 43. 45. 48. 50. 57. 71. 72. 75. 100. RB. CDN-Cav-GGBG. 1. 6. 7. 9. 11. 16. 18. 19. 22. 30. Inf-RCR. PPCLI. R22R. GGFG. 1. 2. 3. 5. 6. 7. 10. 12. 13. 14. 15. 21. 34. 38. 43. 48. 50. 57. 58. 60. 62. 67. 72. 76. 79. 90. 91. 95. 96. 100. 103. 104. 105. 106. TS. SAR. Queens. Edmonton. Calgary. Vancouver.	
I – 9–14 Apr 1917 II – 23–24 Apr 1917 III – 3–4 May 1917	Scarpe 1917	LG. RHG. 2DG. 3DG. 4DG. 5DG. 6DG. 1D. 2D. 3H. 4H. 9L. 10H. 11H. 12L. 16L. 18H. 20H. Yeo-10. 11. 34. 49. 51. Inf-1. 2. 3. 4. 5. 6. 7. 8. 9. 10. 11. 12. 13. 14. 15. 16. 19. 20. 21. 22. 23. 24. 25. 26. 27. 28. 29. 30. 31. 32. 33. 34. 35. 37. 38. 39. 40. 42. 43. 44. 45. 47. 48. 49. 50. 51. 53. 57. 60. 62. 63. 64. 65. 68. 71. 72. 75. 79. 87. 91. 102. RB. CLR-1. 2. 3. 4. 5. LR-9. 12. 13. 14. 16. Mon. HAC. Newfoundland. CDN-Inf-RCR. R22R. GGFG. 2. 3. 5. 6. 7. 10. 13. 38. 48. 50. 57. 58. 62. 76. 95. SAR. Vancouver SA-Arty Btys–74. 125. Inf-1. 2. 3. 4. 1 Fd Amb.	App by 22 for new separate names – I – Monchy Le Preux II – Gavrelle-Guemappe III – Fresnoy. Includes actions included in separate names applied for. I includes capture of Wancourt Ridge.
28–29 Apr 1917	**Arleux**	Inf-1. 4. 5. 6. 7. 8. 9. 10. 12. 13. 15. 16. 20. 21. 23. 25. 26. 29. 30. 32. 33. 35. 38. 42. 43. 44. 47. 48. 49. 53. 57. 60. 64. 65. 68. 71. 72. 75. 79. 91. 102. RB. HAC. CDN-Inf-RCR. PPCLI. R22R. GGFG. 2. 3. 5. 6. 7. 10. 13. 38. 48. 50. 57. 58. 62. 76. 90. 103. 105. 106. SAR. SA-Arty Btys-72. 73.	
28 Jun 1917	**Oppy**	Inf-6. 9. 15. 16. 22. 30. 50. 65. SA-Arty Btys-72. 73. 74. 125.	
3–17 May 1917	**Bullecourt**	Inf-2. 6. 7. 11. 14. 23. 33. 34. 38. 63. 75. HAC. CLR-2. 3. 4. 5. 7. LR-11. AUS-Inf-1. 2. 3. 4. 5. 6. 7. 8. 9. 10. 11. 12. 13. 14. 15. 16. 17. 18. 19. 20. 21. 22. 23. 24. 25. 26. 27. 28. 29. 30. 31. 32. 45. 46. 47. 48. 49. 50. 51. 52. 53. 54. 55. 56. 57. 58. 59. 60. SA-71. Bty.	App by Yeo-36. and 40.
15–25 Aug 1917	**Hill 70**	Inf-14. 38. 53. 68. CDN-Cav-FGH. GGBG. 6. 7. 9. 11. 14. 18. 22. 30. Inf-RCR. PPCLI. R22R. GGFG. 1. 2. 3. 5. 6. 7. 8. 9. 10. 11. 12. 13. 14. 15. 19. 20. 21. 22. 23. 29. 31. 34. 35. 36. 37. 38. 40. 44. 48. 49. 50. 51. 52. 53. 57. 58. 59. 60. 62. 63. 65. 66. 67. 69. 73. 74. 76. 77. 79. 90. 95. 96. 100. 101. 102. 103. 104. 105. 106. 110. TS. SAR. Sask. Weyburn. Queens. Edmonton. Calgary. Vancouver. McGill. SA-Arty Btys-72. 125.	Captured by the Canadians on 15 Aug.

Dates	**Honoured** or *Non-Honoured* Battle	**Honour awarded** to or *Participants in* Battle	Remarks
7–14 Jun 1917	**Messines 1917**	**RTR.** Yeo-**20. NIH.** Inf-**2. 3. 4. 5. 6. 7. 10. 14. 15. 16. 18. 19. 20. 21. 22. 23. 24. 27. 28. 29. 30. 31. 33. 34. 35. 37. 38. 39. 40. 41. 45. 47. 48. 50. 51. 57. 60. 62. 63. 64. 65. 68. 83. 87. 88. 100. 101. 102. RB. CLR-6. 7. LR-9. 15. 16. 17. 18. 19. 20. 21. 22. 23. 24.** AUS-**LH-4.** Inf-**13. 14. 15. 16. 33. 34. 35. 36. 37. 38. 39. 40. 41. 42. 43. 44. 45. 46. 47. 48. 49. 50. 51. 52.** NZ-**MR-5. 7. 12.** Inf-**1. 2. 3. 4. 5. 6. 7. 8. 9. 10. 11. 12. 13. 14. 15. 16. 17** SA-**74. Bty.**	Includes action of Wytschaete.
31 Jul–10 Nov 1917	**Ypres 1917**	**LG. RHG. RTR.** Yeo-**1. 12. 17. 37. 38. 50. NIH.** Inf-**GG. CG. SG. IG. WG. 1. 2. 3. 4. 5. 6. 7. 8. 9. 10. 11. 12. 13. 14. 15. 16. 17. 18. 19. 20. 21. 22. 23. 24. 25. 26. 27. 28. 29. 30. 31. 32. 33. 34. 35. 37. 38. 39. 40. 41. 42. 43. 44. 45. 47. 48. 49. 50. 51. 53. 57. 60. 62. 63. 64. 65. 68. 71. 72. 75. 79. 83. 87. 88. 91. 100. 101. 102. RB. Cambs. Herts. Mon. HAC. CLR-1. 2. 3. 4. 5. 6. 7. LR-8. 9. 10. 11. 12. 13. 14. 15. 16. 17. 18. 19. 20. 21. 22. 24. 28. Newfoundland.** CDN-Cav-**FGH. GGBG. 6. 7. 9. 11. 14. 18. 22. 30.** Inf-**PPCLI. R22R. GGFG. 1. 2. 3. 5. 6. 7. 8. 9. 10. 11. 12. 13. 14. 19. 20. 21. 22. 23. 24. 25. 29. 31. 34. 36. 37. 38. 40. 42. 43. 44. 48. 49. 50. 51. 52. 53. 57. 58. 59. 60. 62. 63. 65. 66. 67. 69. 72. 73. 74. 75. 76. 77. 79. 90. 91. 93. 94. 95. 96. 100. 101. 102. 103. 104. 105. 106. 110. TS. SAR. Queens. Edmonton. Calgary. Vancouver. McGill.** AUS-**LH-4. 13.** Inf-**1. 2. 3. 4. 5. 6. 7. 8. 9. 10. 11. 12. 13. 14. 15. 16. 17. 18. 19. 20. 21. 22. 23. 24. 25. 26. 27. 28. 29. 30. 31. 32. 33. 34. 35. 36. 37. 38. 39. 40. 41. 42. 43. 44. 45. 46. 47. 48. 49. 50. 51. 52. 53. 54. 55. 56. 57. 58. 59. 60.** NZ-**MR-5. 7. 12.** Inf-**1. 2. 3. 4. 5. 6. 7. 8. 9. 10. 11. 12. 13. 14. 15. 16. 17.** SA-**Arty Btys-71. 72. 73. 74. 75. 125.** Inf-**1. 2. 3. 4. 1 Fd Amb.**	App by Yeo-9. and 23 LR. Includes all battles from Pilckem to Passchendaele (two battles), all separately Honoured.
31 Jul–2 Aug 1917	**Pilckem**	Yeo-**38. 50. NIH.** Inf-**GG. CG. SG. IG. WG. 1. 2. 3. 4. 5. 6. 7. 8. 9. 10. 11. 12. 14. 15. 16. 18. 19. 20. 21. 22. 23. 24. 25. 26. 27. 28. 29. 30. 31. 34. 35. 37. 40. 41. 42. 44. 45. 47. 48. 49. 50. 57. 60. 62. 63. 64. 68. 71. 72. 75. 79. 83. 91. 100. RB. Cambs. Mon. Herts. HAC.** CDN-Inf-**12.** SA-**75 Bty.**	App by Yeo-9.
10 Aug 1917	*Westhoek*		App by 22.
16–18 Aug 1917	**Langemarck 1917**	Inf-**1. 5. 6. 7. 8. 9. 10. 11. 12. 13. 14. 15. 16. 18. 19. 20. 22. 23. 24. 25. 26. 27. 28. 29. 30. 31. 32. 33. 34. 35. 37. 38. 39. 40. 41. 43. 44. 45. 48. 49. 50. 51. 53. 57. 60. 63. 64. 65. 68. 71. 83. 87. 88. 100. 101. 102. RB. Mon. CLR-2. 3. 4. 5. LR-9. 12. 13. 14. 15. 16. 17. 18. 19. 20. Newfoundland.** CDN-Inf-**12.** SA-**75 Bty.**	

Dates	**Honoured** or *Non-Honoured* Battle	**Honour awarded** to or *Participants in* Battle	Remarks
22–27 Aug 1917	*St Julien 1917*		App by 43.
20–25 Sep 1917	**Menin Road**	Inf-**GG. CG.** 1. 2. 4. 5. 6. 7. 8. 10. 12. 13. 14. 15. 16. 19. 20. 21. 22. 23. 24. 25. 26. 28. 29. 30. 31. 32. 33. 35. 37. 38. 40. 41. 42. 43. 44. 45. 47. 50. 51. 53. 57. 60. 62. 63. 64. 65. 68. 71. 72. 75. 79. 91. **RB. Cambs. Herts.** CLR-2. 3. 4. 5. 6. 7. LR-9. 10. 11. 12. **Liv Scot.** CAN-Inf-**12.** AUS-Inf-**1.** 2. 3. 4. 5. 6. 7. 8. 9. 10. 11. 12. 13. 14. 15. 16. 17. 18. 19. 20. 21. 22. 23. 24. 25. 26. 27. 28. 29. 30. 31. 32. 45. 46. 47. 48. 49. 50. 51. 52. 53. 54. 55. 56. 57. 58. 59. 60. NZ-Inf-**5.** SA-**Arty Btys**-71. 73. 74. Inf-1. 2. 3. 4. **1 Fd Amb.**	
26 Sep–3 Oct 1917	**Polygon Wood**	Yeo-1. Inf-1. 2. 4. 5. 6. 7. 8. 9. 10. 11. 12. 13. 14. 15. 16. 17. 19. 20. 21. 22. 23. 24. 25. 26. 27. 28. 29. 30. 31. 32. 33. 34. 35. 37. 38. 39. 40. 41. 42. 43. 45. 47. 49. 50. 51. 53. 57. 60. 62. 63. 64. 65. 68. 71. 72. 75. 79. 91. 102. **RB. Cambs. Herts. HAC.** CLR-2. 3. 4. 5. 6. 7. LR-9. 10. 11. 12. CDN-Inf-**12.** AUS-Inf-**1.** 2. 3. 4. 5. 6. 7. 8. 9. 10. 11. 12. 13. 14. 15. 16. 17. 18. 19. 20. 21. 22. 23. 24. 25. 26. 27. 28. 29. 30. 31. 32. 33. 34. 35. 36. 38. 39. 40. 41. 42. 43. 44. 45. 46. 47. 48. 49. 50. 51. 52. 53. 54. 55. 56. 57. 58. 59. 60. NZ-Inf-**1.** 2. 3. 4. 5. 6. 7. 8. 9. 10. 11. 12. 13. 14. 15. 16. 17. SA-**Arty Btys**-71. 73. 74.	
4 Oct 1917	**Broodseinde**	**LG. RHG.** Yeo-1. Inf-**2.** 4. 5. 6. 7. 9. 10. 11. 13. 15. 16. 19. 20. 22. 23. 24. 25. 27. 28. 29. 30. 31. 32. 33. 34. 35. 37. 38. 39. 41. 43. 44. 45. 49. 50. 51. 57. 60. 62. 63. 64. 65. 68. 72. 75. 91. **RB. Cambs. Herts. HAC.** CDN-Inf-**12.** AUS-**LH-4.** Inf-1. 2. 3. 4. 5. 6. 7. 8. 9. 10. 11. 12. 17. 18. 19. 20. 21. 22. 23. 24. 25. 26. 27. 28. 33. 34. 35. 36. 37. 38. 39. 40. 41. 42. 43. 44. NZ-**MR-5.** 7. 12. Inf-1. 2. 3. 4. 5. 6. 7. 8. 9. 10. 11. 12. 13. 14. 15. 16. 17. SA-**Arty Btys**–71. 73. 74.	
9 Oct 1917	**Poelcappelle**	**LG. RHG.** Yeo-1. 17. Inf-**GG. CG. SG. IG. WG.** 1. 4. 6. 7. 8. 9. 10. 11. 12. 13. 14. 15. 16. 19. 20. 22. 23. 24. 25. 27. 28. 29. 30. 31. 32. 33. 34. 35. 37. 38. 39. 41. 42. 43. 44. 45. 47. 49. 51. 57. 60. 62. 63. 64. 65. 72. 75. 79. 91. **RB. Cambs. Herts. Mon. HAC. Newfoundland.** CDN-Inf-**12.** AUS-Inf-**1.** 2. 3. 4. 5. 6. 7. 8. 9. 10. 11. 12. 17. 18. 19. 20. 21. 22. 23. 24. 25. 26. 27. 28. 29. 30. 31. 32. 33. 34. 35. 36. 38. 39. 40. 41. 42. 43. 44. 53. 54. 55. 56. 57. 58. 59. 60. SA-**75 Bty.**	

Dates	**Honoured** or *Non-Honoured* Battle	**Honour awarded** to or *Participants in* Battle	Remarks
I – 12 Oct 1917 II – 26 Oct– 10 Nov 1917	**Passchendaele**	LG. RHG. Yeo-1. 12. 17. 37. Inf-GG. CG. SG. IG. WG. 1. 2. 3. 4. 5. 6. 7. 8. 9. 10. 11. 12. 13. 14. 15. 16. 19. 20. 22. 23. 24. 25. 26. 28. 29. 30. 31. 32. 33. 34. 35. 37. 38. 39. 40. 41. 42. 43. 44. 45. 47. 48. 49. 50. 51. 53. 57. 60. 62. 63. 64. 65. 68. 71. 72. 75. 79. 91. 101. RB. Cambs. Herts. HAC. CLR-2. 3. 4. 5. 6. 7. LR-8. 9. 10. 11. 12. 28. CDN-Cav-GGBG. 6. 7. 9. 11. 18. 22. 30. Inf-RCR. PPCLI. R22R. GGFG. 1. 2. 3. 5. 6. 7. 10. 12. 13. 14. 21. 34. 38. 43. 48. 50. 57. 58. 60. 62. 67. 72. 76. 79. 90. 91. 94. 95. 96. 100. 103. 104. 105. 106. TS. SAR. Queens. Edmonton. Calgary. Vancouver. AUS-LH-4. Inf-1. 2. 3. 4. 5. 6. 7. 8. 9. 10. 11. 12. 13. 14. 15. 16. 17. 18. 19. 20. 21. 22. 23. 24. 25. 26. 27. 28. 29. 30. 31. 32. 33. 34. 35. 36. 37. 38. 39. 40. 41. 42. 43. 44. 45. 46. 47. 48. 49. 50. 51. 52. 53. 54. 55. 56. 57. 58. 59. 60. NZ-MR-5. 7. 12. Inf-1. 2. 3. 4. 5. 6. 7. 8. 9. 10. 11. 12. 13. 14. 15. 16. 17. SA-Arty Btys-71. 72. 73. 74. 75. Inf-3. 1 Fd Amb.	
20 Nov–3 Dec 1917	**Cambrai 1917**	2 DG. 3 DG. 4 DG. 5 DG. 6 DG. 7 DG. 2 D. 3 H. 4 H. 5 L. 6 D. 8 H. 9 L. 11 H. 12 L. 15 H. 16 L. 17 L. 18 H. 19 H. 20 H. RTR. Yeo-9. 14. 34. 48. 50. Inf-GG. CG. SG. IG. WG. 1. 2. 3. 4. 5. 6. 7. 8. 9. 10. 12. 13. 14. 15. 16. 17. 19. 20. 22. 23. 24. 25. 27. 28. 29. 31. 32. 33. 34. 35. 37. 38. 40. 41. 42. 43. 44. 45. 47. 48. 49. 50. 51. 53. 57. 60. 64. 65. 68. 71. 72. 75. 83. 87. 91. 102. RB. Herts. Mon. CLR-1. 2. 3. 4. 5. 6. 7. LR-8. 9. 12. 13. 14. 15. 16. 17. 18. 19. 20. 21. 22. 23. 24. Liv Scot. Newfoundland. IND-Cav-2. 6. 9. 18. 19. 20. 34. 36. 38. CDN-Cav-RCD. Strathcona. FGH. 12. 1 MG Sqn. SA-Arty Btys-71. 125.	Includes the Tank Attack and actions of Bourlon Wood and the German Counterattacks.
20–21 Nov 1917	*Gouzeacourt*		App by GG. CG. SG. IG. WG.
I – 21 March– 5 Apr 1918 II – 21 Aug– 3 Sep 1918	**Somme 1918**	LG. 2 DG. 3 DG. 4 DG. 5 DG. 6 DG. 7 DG. 1 D. 2 D. 3 H. 4 H. 5 L. 6 D. 8 H. 9 L. 10 H. 11 H. 12 L. 15 H. 16 L. 17 L. 18 H. 19 H. 20 H. RTR. Yeo-1. 6. 8. 12. 14. 17. 18. 19. 20. 28. 29. 30. 32. 33. 34. 35. 37. 38. 40. 42. 43. 48. 49. WH. NIH. SIH. Inf-GG. CG. SG. IG. WG. 1. 2. 3. 4. 5. 6. 7. 8. 9. 10. 11. 12. 13. 14. 15. 16. 17. 18. 19. 20. 21. 22. 23. 24. 25. 26. 27. 28. 29. 30. 31. 32. 33. 34. 35. 37. 38. 39. 40. 41. 42. 43. 44. 45. 47. 48. 49. 50. 51. 53. 57. 60. 62. 63. 64. 65. 68. 71. 72. 75. 79. 83. 87. 88. 91. 100. 101. 102. RB. Cambs. Herts. HAC. CLR-1. 2. 3. 4. 5. 6. LR-8. 9. 10. 12. 13. 14. 15. 16. 17. 18. 19. 20. 21. 22. 23. 24. 28. CDN-Cav-RCD. Strathcona. FGH. 6. 12. Inf-R22R. 3. 6. 10. 12. 14. 21. 62. 76. 91. 95. 97. SAR. Queens. Vancouver. 1 MG.	App by 22 for new separate names – I – Somme 1918 II – Picardy with dates as shown. Includes all battles from St Quentin to Ancre 1918 (separately Honoured) Picardy includes Albert 1918, 2nd Battle of Bapaume and capture of Mont St Quentin.

Dates	**Honoured** or *Non-Honoured* Battle	**Honour awarded** to or *Participants in* Battle	Remarks
I – 21 March– 5 Apr 1918 II – 21 Aug– 3 Sep 1918	**Somme 1918** (cont)	AUS-**LH-13.** Inf-1. 2. 3. 4. 5. 6. 7. 8. 9. 10. 11. 12. 13. 14. 15. 16. 17. 18. 19. 20. 21. 22. 23. 24. 25. 26. 27. 28. 29. 30. 31. 32. 33. 34. 35. 36. 37. 38. 39. 40. 41. 42. 43. 44. 45. 46. 47. 48. 49. 50. 51. 52. 53. 54. 55. 56. 57. 58. 59. 60. NZ-**MR-5.** 7. 12. Inf-1. 2. 3. 4. 5. 6. 7. 8. 9. 10. 11. 12. 13. 14. 15. 16. 17. SA-**Arty Btys-72.** 74. 75.	
21–23 Mar 1918	**St Quentin**	2 DG. 3 DG. 4 DG. 5 DG. 7 DG. 1 D. 3 H. 5 L. 6 D. 8 H. 9 L. 10 H. 11 H. 12 L. 15 H. 17 L. 18 H. 19 H. 20 H. RTR. Yeo-1. 12. 14. 17. 20. 34. 38. NIH. SIH. Inf-**GG. CG. SG. IG.** 1. 2. 3. 4. 5. 6. 7. 8. 9. 10. 12. 13. 14. 15. 16. 17. 18. 19. 20. 21. 22. 23. 24. 25. 26. 27. 28. 29. 30. 31. 32. 33. 34. 35. 37. 38. 39. 40. 41. 42. 43. 44. 45. 47. 48. 49. 50. 51. 53. 57. 60. 62. 63. 64. 65. 68. 71. 72. 75. 79. 83. 87. 88. 91. 100. 101. 102. RB. Cambs. CLR-2. 3. 4. 6. 7. LR-8. 9. 15. 16. 17. 18. 19. 20. 21. 22. 23. 24. 28. CDN-Cav-**RCD. Strathcona. FGH.** 12. Inf-**97.** I MG.	
21–22 Mar 1918	*Fontaine-les-Clercs*		App by 27.
23 Mar 1918	*Cugny*		App by 83.
I – 24–25 Mar 1918 II – 31 Aug– 3 Sep 1918	**Bapaume 1918**	LG. 2 DG. 3 DG. 6 DG. 1 D. 3 H. 8 H. 15 H. 19 H. 20 H. RTR. Yeo-1. 6. 8. 12. 17. 18. 19. 20. 28. 29. 30. 32. 33. 34. 35. 37. 40. 42. 43. WH. NIH. Inf-**GG. CG. SG. IG. WG.** 1. 2. 3. 4. 5. 6. 7. 8. 9. 10. 11. 12. 13. 14. 15. 16. 17. 19. 20. 21. 22. 23. 24. 25. 28. 29. 30. 31. 32. 33. 34. 35. 37. 38. 39. 40. 41. 42. 43. 44. 45. 47. 48. 49. 50. 51. 53. 57. 60. 62. 63. 64. 65. 68. 71. 72. 75. 79. 88. 91. 100. 101. 102. Cambs. Herts. HAC. CLR-2. 3. 4. 6. LR-8. 9. 10. 12. 15. 16. 17. 18. 19. 20. 21. 22. 23. 24. 28. CDN-Cav-**6.** Inf-**97.** NZ-**INF-1.** 2. 3. 4. 5. 6. 7. 8. 9. 10. 11. 12. 13. 14. 15. 16. 17.	App by 22 for new separate names – I – Bapaume 1918 II – Mont St Quentin (already borne by Australian regiments). Many regiments bear Honour for II after Amiens, including all NZ.
26–27 Mar 1918	**Rosieres**	2 DG. 5 DG. 7 DG. 8 H. 9 L. 11 H. 15 H. 18 H. 19 H. Yeo-38. SIH. Inf-1. 2. 5. 6. 7. 8. 11. 13. 14. 15. 16. 18. 19. 20. 21. 22. 26. 27. 28. 29. 30. 31. 32. 34. 35. 37. 40. 42. 43. 45. 48. 49. 50. 53. 57. 60. 63. 64. 68. 75. 83. 87. 88. 91. 100. 101. 102. RB. Cambs. Herts. CDN-Cav-**6.**	
I – 28 Mar 1918 II – 26 Aug– 3 Sep 1918	**Arras 1918**	10 H. RTR. Yeo-3. 20. 21. 26. Inf-**GG. CG. SG. IG. WG.** 1. 2. 4. 5. 6. 7. 8. 10. 12. 13. 14. 15. 16. 18. 19. 20. 21. 22. 24. 25. 26. 28. 30. 31. 33. 34. 35. 37. 38. 40. 41. 42. 44. 45. 47. 48. 49. 50. 51. 53. 57. 60. 63. 65. 68. 71. 72. 75. 79. 91. 101. RB. HAC. CLR-1. 2. 4. 5. LR-9. 12. 13. 14. 16. 28.	App by 22 for new separate names – I – Arras 1918 II – Queant. 2nd Battle of Arras includes Battles of Scarpe 1918 and Drocourt-Queant (both separately Honoured).

Dates	**Honoured** or *Non-Honoured* Battle	**Honour awarded** to or *Participants in* Battle	Remarks
I – 28 Mar 1918 II – 26 Aug– 3 Sep 1918	**Arras 1918** (cont)	CDN-Cav-**FGH. GGBG. 1. 6. 7. 9. 11. 14. 16. 18. 19. 22. 30.** Inf-**RCR. PPCLI. R22 R. GGFG. 1. 2. 3. 5. 6. 7. 10. 11. 12. 13. 14. 15. 19. 20. 21. 22. 29. 31. 34. 35. 36. 38. 40. 41. 42. 43. 48. 50. 51. 52. 53. 57. 58. 59. 60. 62. 63. 65. 67. 69. 72. 73. 74. 75. 76. 79. 90. 91. 93. 94. 95. 96. 100. 101. 102. 103. 104. 105. 106. 110. TS. SAR. Queens. Edmonton. Calgary. Vancouver. Battleford. McGill. MG-1. 2. 3.** AUS-Inf-**13. 14. 15. 16.** NZ-**MR-5. 7. 12.** Inf-**1. 2. 3. 4. 5. 6. 7. 8. 9. 10. 11. 12. 13. 14. 15. 16. 17.** SA-**Arty Btys-72. 74. 75.**	1918 and Drocourt-Queant (both separately Honoured).
4 Apr 1918	**Avre**	**3 DG. 5 DG. 7 DG. 1 D. 6 D. 9 L. 10 H. 17 L.** Yeo-**SIH.** Inf-**2. 3. 7. 8. 13. 16. 26. 28. 31. 35. 43. 44. 48. 49. 50. 57. 60. 64. 101. 102. RB. CLR-6. LR. 8.** CDN-Cav-**6.** AUS-Inf-**33. 34. 35. 57. 58. 59. 60.**	
5 Apr 1918	**Ancre 1918**	Yeo-**37.** Inf-**1. 2. 3. 7. 9. 10. 12. 13. 16. 20. 23. 30. 33. 35. 39. 41. 44. 48. 49. 50. 57. 60. 63. 71. RB. Herts. LR-9. 15. 16. 17. 18. 19. 20. 21. 22. 23. 24. 28.** AUS-Inf-**13. 15. 16. 29. 30. 31. 32. 38. 39. 40. 41. 42. 44. 45. 46. 47. 48. 49. 50. 51. 52. 53. 54. 55. 56.** NZ-Inf-**1. 2. 3. 4. 5. 6. 7. 8. 9. 10. 11. 12. 13. 14. 15. 16. 17.**	
24–25 Apr 1918	**Villers-Brettoneaux**	**RTR.** Inf-**2. 7. 11. 14. 16. 29. 30. 44. 45. 48. 49. 50. 57. RB. CLR-2. 3. 4. 7. LR-8. 9. 10. 12.** AUS-Inf-**49. 50. 51. 52. 53. 54. 55. 56. 57. 58. 59. 60.**	
9–29 Apr 1918	**Lys**	**3 DG. 5 DG. 6 DG. 7 DG. 2 D. 3 H. 12 L. 17 L. 20 H.** Yeo-**1. 34. 38. 50.** Inf-**GG. CG. IG. 1. 2. 4. 5. 6. 7. 8. 9. 10. 11. 12. 13. 14. 15. 16. 17. 19. 20. 21. 22. 23. 24. 25. 26. 28. 29. 30. 31. 32. 33. 34. 35. 37. 38. 40. 41. 42. 43. 44. 45. 47. 49. 50. 51. 53. 57. 60. 62. 63. 64. 65. 68. 71. 72. 75. 79. 83. 87. 91. RB. Cambs. Herts. Mon. Liv Scot. Newfoundland.** AUS-**LH-4.** Inf-**1. 2. 3. 4. 5. 6. 7. 8. 9. 10. 11. 12.** NZ-**MR-5. 7. 12.** SA-**Arty Btys-71. 73. 125.** Inf-**1. 2. 4.**	Includes all battles from Estaires to Scherpenberg (all separately Honoured).
9–11 Apr 1918	**Estaires**	Yeo-**50.** Inf-**1. 4. 5. 6. 7. 8. 10. 12. 15. 19. 20. 21. 22. 24. 25. 28. 29. 30. 31. 32. 33. 34. 37. 40. 41. 42. 47. 53. 57. 68. 71. 72. 75. 79. 91. Liv Scot.** SA-**Arty Btys-71. 73. 125.**	
10–11 Apr 1918	**Messines 1918**	Yeo-**1.** Inf-**1. 5. 6. 8. 10. 12. 14. 15. 19. 22. 23. 24. 28. 29. 33. 34. 38. 40. 41. 42. 51. 53. 57. 60. 62. 64. 65. 71. 72. 79. 83. 87. 91. Mon.** SA-Inf-**1. 2. 4.**	
12–15 Apr 1918	**Hazebrouck**	**3 DG. 5 DG. 6 DG. 7 DG. 2 D. 3 H. 12 L. 17 L. 20 H.** Yeo-**34. 50.** Inf-**GG. CG. IG. 1. 2. 4. 5. 6. 7. 11. 12. 13. 14. 15. 16. 19. 20. 21. 22. 24. 25. 26. 28. 29. 30. 31. 32. 33. 34. 37. 40. 41. 42. 43. 44. 49. 50. 51. 53. 57. 65. 68. 71. 72. 75. 91. RB.** AUS-Inf-**1. 2. 3. 4. 5. 6. 7. 8. 9. 10. 11. 12.**	Includes actions of Hinges Ridge and Nieppe Forest.

Dates	**Honoured** or *Non-Honoured* Battle	**Honour awarded** to or *Participants in* Battle	Remarks
13–15 Apr 1918	**Bailleul**	Yeo-1. Inf-1. 2. 5. 6. 8. 9. 10. 12. 14. 17. 20. 21. 22. 23. 24. 26. 28. 29. 30. 33. 34. 37. 38. 40. 41. 45. 47. 51. 53. 57. 60. 62. 64. 65. 68. 71. 72. 83. 87. 91. **Newfoundland.** NZ-**MR-5. 7. 12.**	Includes action of Neuve Eglise.
I – 17–19 Apr 1918 II – 25–26 Apr 1918	**Kemmel**	Yeo-1. 38. Inf-1. 2. 5. 6. 8. 9. 10. 12. 14. 15. 16. 17. 19. 20. 22. 23. 24. 25. 26. 28. 29. 30. 33. 34. 35. 37. 38. 40. 41. 42. 45. 47. 50. 51. 53. 57. 60. 62. 63. 64. 65. 68. 71. 72. 79. 83. 87. 91. **Cambs. Herts. Newfoundland.** AUS-**LH-4.** Inf-**9. 10.** NZ-**MR-5. 7. 12.** SA-Inf-**1. 2. 4.**	App by 22 for new separate names – I – Kemmel 1918 II – La Clytte. Celebrated by 166 Battery.
18 Apr 1918	**Bethune**	Inf-1. 4. 5. 6. 7. 8. 12. 13. 20. 21. 24. 28. 33. 37. 41. 42. 43. 44. 47. 49. 53. 60. 72. 75. 79. 91. **RB.** SA-**Arty Btys-71. 73. 125.**	
22 Apr 1918	*Pacaut Wood*		App by 37.
29 Apr 1918	**Scherpenberg**	Yeo-38. Inf-5. 8. 9. 12. 15. 16. 17. 19. 20. 21. 22. 23. 24. 26. 29. 33. 34. 35. 38. 40. 41. 42. 45. 47. 51. 57. 62. 65. 68. **Cambs.** NZ-**MR-5. 7. 12.**	App by Herts.
27 May–6 Jun 1918	**Aisne 1918**	Inf-5. 6. 10. 11. 14. 15. 17. 19. 20. 22. 23. 24. 28. 29. 30. 34. 38. 40. 41. 45. 47. 48. 49. 51. 53. 57. 62. 64. 68. **RB.**	
6 Jun 1918	**Bligny**	Inf-**53.**	App by 22. 64.
6 Jun 1918	**Bois des Buttes**	Inf-**11.**	
4 Jul 1918	**Hamel**	AUS-Inf-**13. 14. 15. 16. 17. 18. 19. 20. 21. 22. 23. 24. 41. 42. 43. 44. 45. 46. 48. 49. 50. 51.**	
20 Jul–2 Aug 1918	**Marne 1918**	Inf-1. 2. 11. 13. 14. 22. 25. 26. 33. 35. 37. 42. 47. 51. 65. 68. 72. 75. 79. 91. **Hereford.** AUS-**LH-4.** NZ-**MR-5. 7. 12.**	Includes Battles of Soissonais-Ourcq and Tardenois (separately Honoured).
23 Jul–2 Aug 1918	**Soissonais-Ourcq**	Inf-1. 2. 13. 22. 25. 26. 35. 42. 47. 72. 75. 79. 91. **Hereford.**	
20–31 Jul 1918	**Tardenois**	Inf-1. 11. 14. 33. 37. 42. 51. 65. 68. 72. 75. 91. AUS-**LH-4.** NZ-**MR-5. 7. 12.**	
8–11 Aug 1918	**Amiens**	**2 DG. 3 DG. 4 DG. 5 DG. 6 DG. 7 DG. 1 D. 2 D. 3 H. 4 H. 5 L. 6 D. 8 H. 9 L. 10 H. 11 H. 12 L. 15 H. 16 L. 17 L. 18 H. 19 H. 20 H. RTR.** Yeo-**10. 11. 12. 17. 48. 49.** Inf-1. 2. 3. 7. 9. 10. 12. 14. 15. 16. 20. 31. 33. 34. 35. 39. 44. 45. 48. 49. 50. 51. 63. 71. 91. **Cambs. HAC. CLR-2. 3. 4. 6. 7. LR-8. 9. 10. 12. 16. 21.** CDN-Cav-**RCD. Strathcona. FGH. GGBG. 1. 6. 7. 9. 11. 12. 14. 16. 18. 19. 22. 30.** Inf-**RCR. PPCLI. R22 R. GGFG. 1. 2. 3. 5. 6. 7. 8. 9. 10. 11. 12. 13. 14. 15. 19. 20. 21. 22. 25. 29. 31. 34. 35. 36. 38. 40. 41. 42. 43. 48. 49. 50. 51. 52. 53. 54. 57. 58. 59. 60. 62. 63. 65. 66. 67. 69. 72. 73. 74. 75. 76. 78. 79. 86. 90. 91. 93. 94. 95. 96. 99. 100. 101. 102. 103. 104. 105. 106. 110. TS. SAR. Queens. Edmonton. Calgary. Vancouver. Battleford. McGill. 2 MMG. MG-1. 2. 3.**	App by Yeo-41 for later date.

Dates	**Honoured** or *Non-Honoured* Battle	**Honour awarded** to or *Participants in* Battle	Remarks
8–11 Aug 1918	**Amiens** (cont)	AUS-**LH-13**. Inf-1. 2. 4. 5. 6. 7. 8. 9. 10. 11. 12. 13. 14. 15. 16. 17. 18. 19. 20. 21. 22. 23. 24. 25. 26. 27. 28. 29. 30. 31. 32. 33. 34. 35. 37. 38. 39. 40. 41. 43. 44. 45. 46. 48. 49. 50. 51. 53. 54. 55. 56. 57. 58. 59. 60.	
8 Aug 1918	*Harbonnieres*		App by 5 DG.
21–23 Aug 1918	**Albert 1918**	**2 DG. 4 DG. 5 DG. 2 D. 8 H. 9 L. 11 H. 12 L. 15 H. 18 H. 19 H. 20 H. Yeo-12. 14. 17. 48. 49. Inf-GG. CG. SG. IG. WG. 1. 2. 3. 4. 5. 6. 7. 8. 9. 10. 12. 13. 14. 15. 16. 17. 18. 20. 21. 22. 23. 24. 25. 28. 30. 31. 32. 33. 34. 35. 38. 39. 41. 43. 44. 45. 48. 49. 50. 51. 53. 57. 60. 62. 63. 64. 68. 71. 75. 91. RB. Cambs. Herts. HAC. CLR-1. 2. 3. 4. 6. 7. LR-9. 10. 12. 13. 14. 15. 16. 17. 18. 19. 20. 21. 22. 23. 24. 28.** AUS-**LH-13**. Inf-5. 6. 8. 9. 10. 11. 12. 13. 14. 15. 17. 18. 19. 20. 21. 22. 23. 24. 25. 26. 27. 28. 29. 30. 31. 32. 33. 34. 35. 38. 39. 40. 41. 42. 43. 44. 45. 46. 48. 49. 50. 51. 53. 54. 55. 56. 57. 58. 59. 60. NZ-Inf-1. 2. 3. 4. 5. 6. 7. 8. 9. 10. 11. 12. 13. 14. 15. 16. 17.	
21–23 Aug 1918	**Albert 1918 (Chuignes)**	AUS-Inf-**1. 2. 4. 7.**	
29 Aug 1918	*Mont Vidaigne*		*App by 40.*
31 Aug–3 Sep 1918	**Mont St Quentin**	AUS-Inf-**17. 18. 19. 20. 21. 22. 23. 24. 25. 26. 27. 28. 29. 30. 31. 32. 33. 34. 35. 37. 38. 39. 40. 41. 42. 43. 44. 53. 54. 55. 56. 57. 58. 59. 60.**	
26–30 Aug 1918	**Scarpe 1918**	**LG. 5 L. Yeo-3. 21. 26. Inf-GG. CG. IG. 1. 4. 5. 6. 8. 10. 12. 13. 14. 15. 19. 20. 21. 22. 25. 26. 30. 33. 37. 38. 40. 42. 44. 45. 48. 49. 57. 65. 71. 72. 75. 91. 101. RB. HAC. CLR-1. 2. 4. 5. LR-9. 13. 14. 16.** CDN-Cav-**GGBG. 1. 6. 7. 9. 11. 16. 18. 19. 22. 30.** Inf-**RCR. PPCLI. R22 R. GGFG. 1. 2. 3. 5. 6. 7. 10. 12. 13. 14. 21. 34. 38. 43. 48. 50. 57. 58. 60. 62. 67. 72. 76. 79. 90. 91. 94. 95. 96. 100. 103. 104. 105. 106. TS. SAR. Queens. Edmonton. Calgary. Vancouver. 2 MMG. MG-1. 2. 3.** SA-**Arty Btys-72. 74. 75.**	Includes capture of Monchy-le-Preux.
2–3 Sep 1918	**Drocourt-Queant**	**10 H. Yeo-3. Inf-CG. SG. IG. WG. 1. 4. 5. 6. 7. 8. 10. 13. 14. 16. 18. 19. 20. 21. 24. 25. 26. 28. 33. 35. 37. 38. 40. 41. 42. 44. 45. 47. 48. 60. 65. 71. 72. 79. 101. RB. HAC. LR-28.** CDN-Cav-**1. 6. 16. 19.** Inf-**RCR. GGFG. 1. 2. 5. 6. 7. 10. 12. 13. 14. 34. 38. 43. 48. 50. 57. 58. 60. 67. 72. 79. 90. 91. 94. 95. 96. 100. 103. 104. 105. 106. TS. SAR. Queens. Calgary. Vancouver. 2 MMG. MG-1. 2.** SA-**Arty-Btys-72. 74. 75.**	

Dates	**Honoured** or *Non-Honoured* Battle	**Honour awarded** to or *Participants in* Battle	Remarks
12 Sep–9 Oct 1918	**Hindenburg Line**	LG. RHG. 2 DG. 3 DG. 4 DG. 5 DG. 6 DG. 7 DG. 1 D. 2 D. 3 H. 4 H. 5 L. 6 D. 8 H. 9 L. 10 H. 11 H. 12 L. 15 H. 16 L. 17 L. 18 H. 19 H. 20 H. RTR. Yeo-2. 3. 6. 8. 10. 11. 12. 15. 17. 18. 19. 28. 29. 30. 32. 33. 34. 35. 38. 40. 42. 43. 48. 49. 54. WH. NIH. Inf-GG. CG. SG. IG. WG. 1. 2. 3. 4. 5. 6. 7. 8. 9. 10. 11. 12. 13. 14. 15. 16. 17. 18. 19. 20. 21. 22. 23. 24. 25. 26. 27. 28. 29. 30. 31. 32. 33. 34. 35. 37. 38. 39. 40. 41. 42. 43. 44. 45. 47. 48. 49. 50. 51. 53. 57. 60. 62. 63. 64. 65. 68. 71. 72. 75. 79. 88. 91. 101. 102. RB. Cambs. Herts. Mon. HAC. CLR-1. 2. 3. 4. 5. 6. LR-8. 9. 10. 12. 13. 14. 16. 20. 24. 28. CDN-Cav-**RCD. Strathcona. FGH. GGBG.** 1. 6. 7. 9. 11. 12. 14. 16. 18. 19. 22. 30. Inf-**RCR. PPCLI. R22R. GGFG.** 1. 2. 3. 5. 6. 7. 10. 11. 12. 13. 14. 19. 20. 21. 22. 29. 31. 34. 35. 36. 38. 40. 41. 42. 43. 48. 49. 50. 51. 52. 57. 58. 59. 60. 62. 63. 65. 67. 69. 72. 73. 74. 75. 76. 79. 90. 91. 93. 94. 95. 96. 97. 99. 100. 101. 102. 103. 104. 105. 106. 110. **TS. SAR. Queens. Edmonton. Calgary. Vancouver. McGill. 2MMG. MG-**1. 2. 3. AUS-Inf-1. 2. 3. 4. 5. 6. 7. 8. 9. 10. 11. 12. 13. 14. 15. 16. 17. 18. 19. 20. 21. 22. 23. 24. 25. 26. 27. 28. 29. 30. 31. 32. 33. 34. 35. 37. 38. 39. 40. 41. 42. 43. 44. 45. 46. 48. 49. 50. 51. 53. 54. 55. 56. 57. 58. 59. 60. NZ-Inf-1. 2. 3. 4. 5. 6. 7. 8. 9. 10. 11. 12. 13. 14. 15. 16. 17. SA-**Arty Btys-**72. 74. 75. Inf-1. 2. 4. **1 Fd Amb.**	Includes all battles from Havrincourt to Cambrai 1918 (all separately Honoured).
12 Sep 1918	**Havrincourt**	Inf-**GG. CG. SG. WG.** 7. 11. 13. 14. 16. 23. 24. 32. 33. 37. 38. 43. 44. 49. 51. 60. 64. 65. 68. 71. RB. Herts. LR–20. NZ-Inf-3. 5. 6. 7. 9. 11. 15. 16. 17.	
18 Sep 1918	**Epehy**	LG. RTR. Yeo-2. 6. 8. 12. 15. 17. 18. 19. 28. 29. 30. 32. 33. 35. 40. 41. 42. 43. WH. NIH. Inf-2. 3. 5. 6. 7. 8. 9. 10. 11. 12. 13. 14. 15. 16. 17. 20. 23. 24. 25. 26. 28. 31. 33. 34. 35. 39. 41. 42. 44. 45. 47. 48. 49. 50. 51. 53. 60. 62. 63. 65. 68. 79. 91. Cambs. HAC. CLR-2. 3. 6. 7. LR-8. 9. 10. 12. 24. CDN-Inf-97. AUS-Inf-1. 2. 3. 4. 5. 6. 7. 8. 9. 10. 11. 12. 13. 14. 15. 16. 45. 46. 48. 49. 50. 51.	
27 Sep–1 Oct 1918	**Canal du Nord**	3 DG. 3 H. 4 H. 5 L. 16 L. Yeo-3. 10. 34. Inf-**GG. CG. SG. IG. WG.** 1. 4. 5. 6. 7. 8. 9. 10. 11. 12. 13. 14. 15. 16. 18. 19. 20. 21. 22. 25. 26. 28. 29. 30. 31. 32. 33. 37. 38. 39. 40. 43. 45. 47. 49. 50. 51. 53. 57. 60. 62. 63. 64. 65. 68. 71. 75. 91. 101. RB. CLR-2. 4. 5. LR-9. 13. 14. 16. 20. 28. CDN-Cav-**GGBG.** 1. 6. 7. 9. 11. 16. 18. 19. 22. 30. Inf-**RCR. PPCLI. R22R. GGFG.** 1. 2. 3. 5. 6. 7. 10. 12. 13. 14. 21. 34. 38. 43. 48. 50. 57. 58. 60. 62. 67. 72. 76. 79. 90. 91. 94. 95. 96. 100. 103. 104. 105. 106. **TS. SAR. Queens. Edmonton. Calgary. Vancouver. 2 MMG. MG-**1. 2. 3. NZ-Inf-1. 2. 3. 4. 5. 6. 7. 8. 9. 10. 11. 12. 13. 14. 15. 16. 17.	

Dates	**Honoured** or *Non-Honoured* Battle	**Honour awarded** to or *Participants in* Battle	Remarks
29 Sep–2 Oct 1918	**St Quentin Canal**	LG. 2 DG. 5 DG. 7 DG. 2 D. 6 D. 8 H. 11 H. 12 L. 15 H. 17 L. 19 H. 20 H. Yeo-2. 15. 48. 49. 54. NIH. Inf-1. 2. 3. 5. 7. 8. 9. 10. 15. 16. 17. 18. 20. 23. 24. 26. 28. 29. 31. 34. 35. 38. 39. 41. 42. 44. 45. 47. 48. 49. 50. 51. 57. 60. 62. 63. 64. 68. 71. 79. 91. 101. 102. Cambs. Mon. HAC. CDN-Cav-**RCD. Strathcona. FGH.** Inf-97. 1 MG. AUS-Inf-29. 30. 31. 32. 33. 34. 35. 37. 38. 39. 40. 41. 42. 43. 44. 53. 54. 55. 56. 57. 58. 59. 60.	
3–6 Oct 1918	**Beaurevoir**	LG. 2 DG. 3 DG. 5 DG. 7 DG. 1 D. 2 D. 8 H. 10 H. 11 H. 12 L. 15 H. 17 L. 19 H. 20 H. Yeo-2. 11. 15. 48. 49. 54. Inf-1. 5. 6. 7. 9. 10. 11. 17. 18. 19. 23. 24. 27. 28. 29. 34. 35. 38. 39. 41. 42. 45. 51. 60. 62. 63. 64. 68. 71. 91. 101. 102. Mon. CDN-Cav-**RCD. Strathcona. FGH.** Inf-97. 1 MG. AUS-Inf-17. 18. 19. 20. 21. 22. 23. 24. 25. 26. 27. 28. SA-1 **Fd Amb.**	
8–9 Oct 1918	**Cambrai 1918**	LG. RHG. 2 DG. 3 DG. 4 DG. 5 DG. 7 DG. 1 D. 2 D. 3 H. 6 D. 8 H. 9 L. 10 H. 11 H. 12 L. 15 H. 17 L. 18 H. 19 H. 20 H. Yeo-3. 11. 12. 17. 34. 38. 48. 49. 54. NIH. Inf-**GG. CG. SG. IG. WG.** 2. 3. 4. 5. 6. 7. 8. 9. 10. 11. 12. 13. 14. 15. 16. 17. 18. 19. 20. 22. 23. 24. 25. 26. 27. 28. 29. 30. 31. 32. 33. 34. 35. 37. 38. 39. 40. 41. 42. 43. 44. 45. 47. 48. 49. 50. 51. 53. 57. 60. 62. 63. 64. 65. 68. 71. 72. 75. 88. 91. 101. 102. RB. Herts. Mon. HAC. CLR-4. LR-13. 14. 20. 28. CDN-Cav-**RCD. Strathcona. FGH. GGBG.** 1. 6. 7. 9. 11. 16. 18. 22. 30. Inf-**RCR. R22R.** 3. 6. 10. 12. 14. 21. 34. 62. 76. 79. 91. 95. 96. 97. **SAR. Queens. Vancouver. 2MMG.** MG-1. 2. 3. NZ-Inf-1. 2. 3. 4. 5. 6. 7. 8. 9. 10. 11. 12. 13. 14. 15. 16. 17. SA-**Arty Btys-72. 74. 75.** Inf-1. 2. 4.	Includes action of Villers-Outreaux and capture of Cambrai.
28 Sep–2 Oct 1918	**Ypres 1918**	Yeo-7. 13. 16. 20. 21. 26. 37. 41. SIH. Inf-1. 2. 5. 7. 9. 12. 13. 14. 15. 18. 20. 21. 22. 23. 24. 25. 26. 27. 29. 30. 31. 34. 35. 37. 40. 42. 45. 47. 50. 51. 57. 60. 63. 64. 65. 68. 71. 72. 79. 83. 87. 91. 100. 102. Mon. Hereford. LR-9. 14. 16. 17. 23. Newfoundland.	App by Yeo-9.
14–19 Oct 1918	**Courtrai**	Yeo-9. 20. 21. 26. 37. 46. SIH. Inf-1. 2. 5. 7. 12. 13. 18. 20. 21. 22. 24. 25. 26. 27. 29. 31. 34. 35. 37. 40. 42. 45. 47. 50. 57. 60. 63. 64. 68. 71. 72. 79. 83. 87. 91. 100. 102. Mon. Hereford. LR-9. 14. 16. 17. 23. Newfoundland.	
17–25 Oct 1918	**Selle**	LG. 3 DG. 3 H. 11 H. RTR. Yeo-2. 3. 12. 14. 15. 17. 34. 38. 44. 52. 54. NIH. Inf-**GG. CG. SG. IG. WG.** 1. 2. 3. 4. 5. 6. 7. 8. 9. 10. 11. 12. 13. 14. 15. 16. 17. 19. 20. 21. 22. 23. 24. 25. 26. 27. 28. 29. 30. 31. 32. 33. 34. 35. 37. 38. 39. 40. 41. 42. 43. 44. 45. 47. 48. 49. 50. 51. 53. 57. 60. 62. 63. 64. 65. 68. 71. 72. 75. 79. 88. 91. 101. 102. RB. Herts. HAC. LR-20. NZ-Inf-1. 2. 3. 4. 5. 6. 7. 8. 9. 10. 11. 12. 13. 14. 15. 16. 17. SA-Inf-1. 2. 1 **Fd Amb.**	

Dates	**Honoured** or *Non-Honoured* Battle	**Honour awarded** to or *Participants in* Battle	Remarks
17–18 Oct 1918	*Le Cateau 1918*		App by Yeo-54.
31 Oct 1918	*Tieghem*		App by Yeo-41.
1–2 Nov 1918	**Valenciennes**	Yeo-3. 44. 52. Inf-4. 5. 6. 12. 13. 14. 19. 22. 23. 24. 28. 29. 30. 33. 37. 41. 43. 49. 51. 53. 57. 64. 65. 72. RB. CLR-2. 4. 5. LR-9. 13. 14. 16. CND-Cav-**GGBG. 6. 7. 9. 11. 18. 22.** Inf-1. 11. 34. 43. 60. 67. 72. 94. 96. 100. 102. 103. 104. TS. **Calgary.**	Includes capture of Mont Houy.
4 Nov 1918	**Sambre**	RHG. 3 DG. 3 H. 12 L. 20 H. Yeo-2. 3. 12. 14. 15. 17. 34. 44. 52. 54. NIH. Inf-**GG. CG. SG. IG. WG.** 1. 2. 3. 4. 5. 6. 7. 8. 9. 10. 11. 12. 13. 14. 15. 16. 17. 19. 20. 22. 23. 24. 25. 26. 27. 28. 29. 30. 31. 32. 33. 34. 35. 37. 38. 39. 40. 41. 42. 44. 45. 47. 48. 49. 50. 51. 53. 57. 60. 62. 63. 64. 65. 68. 71. 75. 79. 91. 101. 102. RB. **Herts. Mon. HAC.** CLR-2. 4. 5. LR-9. 13. 14. 16. 20. CDN-Cav-**GGBG. 6. 7. 9. 11.** Inf-**43. 72. 94. 100. TS.** NZ-Inf-1. 2. 3. 4. 6. 7. 8. 9. 10. 11. 12. 13. 14. 15. 16. 17. SA-1 **Fd Amb.**	Includes actions of Sambre-Oise Canal and Le Quesnoy.
4 Nov 1918	**Sambre (Le Quesnoy)**	NZ-Inf-**5.**	
4–11 Nov 1918	**Pursuit to Mons**	2 DG. 3 DG. 4 DG. 5 DG. 7 DG. 1 D. 2 D. 4 H. 5 L. 6 D. 8 H. 9 L. 10 H. 15 H. 16 L. 17 L. 18 H. 19 H. Yeo-6. 8. 10. 11. 18. 19. 28. 29. 30. 32. 33. 35. 40. 42. 43. 45. 47. 48. 49. 50. WH. Inf-**CLR-3. 6. 7.** LR-8. 9. 10. 12. 18. 19. 21. 22. 24. 28. **Cambs.** CDN-Cav-1. 12. 14. 16. 19. 30. Inf-**RCR. PPCLI. R22R. GGFG.** 2. 3. 5. 6. 7. 10. 12. 13. 14. 19. 20. 21. 22. 29. 31. 35. 36. 38. 40. 41. 42. 48. 49. 50. 51. 52. 57. 58. 59. 62. 63. 65. 69. 73. 74. 75. 76. 79. 90. 91. 93. 95. 99. 101. 103. 104. 105. 106. 110. **SAR. Queens. Edmonton. Vancouver. McGill.** 2 MMG. MG-1. 2. 3. SA-**Arty Btys-71. 72. 73. 74. 75. 125.** Inf-4.	App by LR-23.
4 Aug 1914– Nov 1918	**France and Flanders 1914–1918**	LG. RHG. 1 DG. 2 DG. 3 DG. 4 DG. 5 DG. 6 DG. 7 DG. 1 D. 2 D. 3 H. 4 H. 5 L. 6 D. 8 H. 9 L. 10 H. 11 H. 12 L. 13 H. 15 H. 16 L. 17 L. 18 H. 19 H. 20 H. RTR. Yeo-1. 2. 3. 6. 7. 8. 9. 10. 11. 12. 13. 14. 15. 16. 17. 18. 19. 20. 21. 26. 28. 29. 30. 32. 33. 34. 35. 36. 37. 38. 39. 40. 41. 42. 43. 44. 45. 46. 47. 48. 49. 50. 51. 52. 53. 54. NIH. SIH. WH. Inf-**GG. CG. SG. IG. WG.** 1. 2. 3. 4. 5. 6. 7. 8. 9. 10. 11. 12. 13. 14. 15. 16. 17. 18. 19. 20. 21. 22. 23. 24. 25. 26. 27. 28. 29. 30. 31. 32. 33. 34. 35. 37. 38. 39. 40. 41. 42. 43. 44. 45. 47. 48. 49. 50. 51. 53. 57. 60. 62. 63. 64. 65. 68. 71. 72. 75. 79. 83. 87. 88. 91. 100. 101. 102. RB. **Cambs. Herts. Mon. Hereford. HAC.** CLR-1. 2. 3. 4. 5. 6. 7. LR-8. 9. 10. 11. 12. 13. 15. 14. 16. 17. 18. 19. 20. 21. 22. 23. 24. 28. **Liv. Scot. Newfoundland.**	Canadian regiments not Honoured with **France & Flanders 1914–1918,** but which bear individual Honours for battles during the campaign are: Cav-5. 12. 14. 15. Inf-8. 9. 11. 15. 19. 20. 22. 23. 24. 25. 28. 29. 31. 35. 36. 37. 38. 40. 41. 42. 44. 46. 49. 51. 52. 53. 54. 59. 63. 65. 66. 69. 73. 74. 75. 77. 78. 86. 93. 99. 101. 102. 110. Weyburn. Sask. Battleford. McGill.

Dates	Honoured or *Non-Honoured* Battle	Honour awarded to or *Participants in* Battle	Remarks
4 Aug 1914–11 Nov 1918	**France and Flanders 1914–1918** (cont)	CDN-Cav-**RCD. Strathcona. FGH. GGBG. 1. 7. 8. 9. 11. 16. 18. 19. 21. 22. 30. Alta Mr.** Inf-**RCR. PPCLI. R22R. GGFG. 1. 2. 3. 5. 6. 7. 10. 12. 13. 14. 21. 34. 38. 43. 48. 50. 57. 58. 60. 62. 67. 72. 76. 79. 90. 91. 94. 95. 96. 97. 100. 103. 104. 105. 106. TS. SAR. Queens. Edmonton. Calgary. Vancouver. MMG-1. 2. MG-1. 2. 3. 1 MG Sqn.** IND-Cav-**1. 2. 4. 6. 9. 14. 15. 18. 19. 20. 30. 34. 36. 38. S&M-Ben. Mad. Bom.** Inf-**6. 9. 15. 27. 33. 39. 40. 41. 47. 57. 58. 59. 69. 89. 93. 125. 129. GR-1. 2. 3. 4. 8. 9.** AUS-LH-**4. 13.** Inf-**1. 2. 3. 4. 5. 6. 7. 8. 9. 10. 11. 12. 13. 14. 15. 16. 17. 18. 19. 20. 21. 22. 23. 24. 25. 26. 27. 28. 29. 30. 31. 32. 33. 34. 35. 36. 37. 38. 39. 40. 41. 42. 43. 44. 45. 46. 47. 48. 49. 50. 51. 52. 53. 54. 55. 56. 57. 58. 59. 60.** NZ-MR-**5. 7. 12.** Inf-**1. 2. 3. 4. 5. 6. 7. 8. 9. 10. 11. 12. 13. 14. 15. 16. 17.** SA-**Arty Btys-71. 72. 73. 74. 75. 125.** Inf-**1. 2. 3. 4. 1 Fd Amb.**	

THE GREAT WAR: ITALY
Medals awarded: British War Medal 1914–20.

Dates	Honoured or *Non-Honoured* Battle	Honour awarded to or *Participants in* Battle	Remarks
15–24 Jun 1918	**Piave**	Inf-**2. 5. 6. 11. 14. 19. 23. 28. 29. 33. 34. 35. 38. 43. 45. 49. 51. 63. 65. 68. 75. HAC.**	
24 Oct–4 Nov 1918	**Vittorio Veneto**	Yeo-**51.** Inf-**2. 5. 6. 11. 14. 19. 23. 28. 29. 33. 34. 35. 38. 43. 49. 51. 63. 65. 68. 75. HAC.**	
12 May 1917–4 Nov 1918	**Italy 1917–18**	Yeo-**20. 50. 51.** Inf-**2. 5. 6. 7. 9. 11. 14. 16. 19. 22. 23. 25. 28. 29. 31. 32. 33. 34. 35. 37. 38. 43. 45. 49. 50. 51. 57. 60. 63. 65. 68. 75. 91. 101. HAC.**	

THE GREAT WAR: MACEDONIA
Medals awarded: British War Medal 1914–20.

Dates	Honoured or *Non-Honoured* Battle	Honour awarded to or *Participants in* Battle	Remarks
7–8 Dec 1915	**Kosturino**	Inf-**27. 30. 37. 83. 87. 88. 100. 101. 102.**	Includes actions during the retreat from Serbia to Salonika.
17–18 Aug 1916	*Horseshoe Hill*		App by 43.
30 Sep–31 Oct 1916	**Struma**	Yeo-**4. 15. 22. 39.** Inf-**1. 3. 4. 5. 7. 12. 15. 18. 22. 27. 28. 31. 32. 37. 41. 51. 57. 65. 79. 83. 87. 88. 91. 100. 101. 102.**	Includes actions of Karajaloi'a, Yenikoi and Barakli Zuna'a.
24–25 Apr and 8–9 May 1917	**Doiran 1917**	Inf-**2. 4. 8. 11. 15. 20. 21. 22. 23. 24. 26. 28. 29. 30. 32. 34. 37. 40. 41. 42. 43. 47. 49. 53. 62. 63. 65. 91. LR-13. 14. 15. 16. 17. 18. 19. 20. 21. 22. 23. 24.**	App by Yeo-36.
1–2 Sep 1918	*Roche Noir*		App by 28.
12 Sep 1918	*'P' Ridge*		App by 22.
18–19 Sep 1918	**Doiran 1918**	Yeo-**36.** Inf-**3. 4. 11. 12. 21. 22. 23. 24. 26. 29. 30. 31. 32. 34. 37. 40. 41. 43. 49. 53. 57. 91.**	App by 28. 79.
5 Oct 1915–30 Sep 1918	**Macedonia 1915–18**	Yeo-**4. 15. 22. 27. 36. 39. 45. 47. 53. 54.** Inf-**1. 2. 3. 4. 5. 7. 8. 11. 12. 15. 18. 20. 21. 22. 23. 24. 26. 27. 28. 29. 30. 31. 32. 34. 37. 40. 41. 42. 43. 47. 49. 51. 53. 57. 60. 62. 63. 65. 68. 72. 79. 83. 87. 88. 91. 100. 101. 102. RB. LR-13. 14. 15. 16. 17. 18. 19. 20. 21. 22. 23. 24.** IND-Inf-**2. 39. 69. 89.**	

Dates	**Honoured** or *Non-Honoured* Battle	**Honour awarded** to or *Participants in* Battle	Remarks

THE GREAT WAR: THE DARDANELLES
Medals awarded: British War Medal 1914–20.

25 Apr–6 Jun 1915	**Helles**	Inf-1. 7. 20. 21. 24. 25. 27. 29. 30. 34. 37. 44. 63. 101. 102. IND-Inf-14. 89. GR-5. 6. 10. AUS-Inf-5. 6. 7. 8. NZ-Inf-1. 2. 3. 4. 6. 7. 8. 9. 10. 11. 12. 13. 14. 15. 16. 17.	Includes Landing at Helles and Krithia (both separately Honoured).
25–26 Apr 1915	**Landing at Helles**	Inf-1. 7. 20. 24. 25. 27. 29. 34. 37. 44. 101. 102.	Includes action at Sedd el Bahr.
I – 28 Apr 1915 II – 6–8 May 1915 III – 4 Jun 1915	**Krithia**	Inf-1. 7. 20. 24. 25. 27. 29. 30. 34. 37. 44. 63. 101. 102. IND-Inf-14. 69. 89. GR-5. 6. 10. AUS-Inf-5. 6. 7. 8. NZ-Inf-1. 2. 3. 4. 6. 7. 8. 9. 10. 11. 12. 13. 14. 15. 16. 17.	Third battle includes two actions of Kereves Dere.
25 Apr–30 Jun 1915	**Anzac**	AUS-LH-1. 2. 3. 4. 5. 6. 7. 8. 9. 10. 16. 17. 18. 19. 20. 21. 22. 23. Inf-1. 2. 3. 4. 5. 6. 7. 8. 9. 10. 11. 12. 13. 14. 15. 16. NZ-MR-1. 2. 3. 4. 5. 6. 7. 8. 9. 10. 11. 12. Inf-1. 2. 3. 4. 6. 7. 8. 9. 10. 11. 12. 13. 14. 15. 16. 17.	Includes Landing at Anzac and Defence of Anzac (but separately Honoured)
25–26 Apr 1915	**Landing at Anzac**	AUS-Inf-1. 2. 3. 4. 5. 6. 7. 8. 9. 10. 11. 12. 13. 14. 15. 16. NZ-Inf-1. 2. 3. 4. 6. 7. 8. 9. 10. 11. 12. 13. 14. 15. 16. 17.	
8 May–30 Jun 1915	**Defence of Anzac**	AUS-LH-1. 2. 3. 4. 5. 6. 7. 8. 9. 10. 22. Inf-1. 2. 3. 4. 5. 6. 7. 8. 9. 10. 11. 12. 13. 14. 15. 16. NZ-MR-1. 2. 3. 4. 5. 6. 7. 8. 9. 10. 11. 12. Inf-1. 2. 3. 4. 6. 7. 8. 9. 10. 11. 12. 13. 14. 15. 16. 17.	
6–21 Aug 1915	**Suvla**	Yeo-2. 4. 15. 21. 22. 23. 24. 25. 26. 27. 31. 45. 46. 47. Inf-1. 2. 4. 5. 6. 7. 9. 10. 12. 14. 15. 16. 18. 19. 20. 22. 23. 24. 25. 27. 28. 29. 30. 33. 34. 35. 37. 38. 39. 40. 41. 44. 45. 47. 48. 50. 57. 62. 63. 64. 65. 83. 87. 88. 100. 101. 102. Hereford. LR-10. 11. IND-Inf-14. GR-5. 6. 10. AUS-LH-1. 2. 3. 4. 5. 6. 7. 8. 9. 10. 11. 12. 22. Inf-1. 2. 3. 4. 5. 6. 7. 8. 9. 10. 11. 12. 13. 14. 15. 16. 17. 18. 19. 20. NZ-Inf-1. 2. 3. 4. 6. 7. 8. 9. 10. 11. 12. 13. 14. 15. 16. 17.	Includes Battles at Sari Bair, Landing at Sulva and Scimitar Hill (all separately Honoured).
6–10 Aug 1915	**Sari Bair**	Inf-4. 6. 22. 23. 24. 28. 29. 30. 37. 40. 41. 47. 62. 64. 83. 88. 100. 102. IND-Inf-14. GR-5. 6. 10. AUS-LH-1. 2. 3. 4. 5. 6. 7. 8. 9. 10. 11. 12. 22. Inf-5. 6. 8. 9. 10. 11. 13. 14. 15. 16. NZ-MR-1. 2. 3. 4. 5. 6. 7. 8. 9. 10. 11. 12. Inf-1. 2. 3. 4. 6. 7. 8. 9. 10. 11. 12. 13. 14. 15. 16. 17.	Includes actions of Lone Pine and Russell's Top.
6–10 Aug 1915	**Sari Bair – Lone Pine**	AUS-Inf-1. 2. 3. 4. 7. 12.	
6–15 Aug 1915	**Landing at Suvla**	Inf-2. 5. 9. 10. 12. 14. 15. 16. 18. 19. 20. 22. 23. 27. 33. 34. 35. 37. 38. 39. 41. 44. 45. 48. 50. 57. 63. 65. 87. 101. 102. Hereford. LR-10. 11.	Includes actions of Kanakol Dagh and Chocolate Hill.
21 Aug 1915	**Scimitar Hill**	Yeo-2. 4. 15. 21. 22. 23. 24. 25. 26. 27. 31. 45. 46. 47. Inf-1. 2. 5. 7. 9. 10. 12. 14. 15. 16. 19. 20. 22. 23. 24. 25. 27. 28. 29. 33. 34. 35. 37. 38. 39. 41. 44. 45. 48. 50. 57. 63. 65. 87. 88. 101. 102. Hereford. LR-10. 11.	

303

Dates	Honoured or Non-Honoured Battle	Honour awarded to or Participants in Battle	Remarks
27 Aug 1915	**Hill 60 (ANZAC)**	NZ-**MR**-1. 2. 3. 4. 5. 6. 7. 8. 9. 10. 11. 12.	
25 Apr 1915– 7 Jan 1916	**Gallipoli 1915–16**	Yeo-2. 4. 7. 13. 15. 19. 21. 22. 23. 24. 25. 26. 27. 28. 29. 30. 31. 32. 33. 40. 41. 42. 45. 46. 47. 53. 54. **WH. Inf**-1. 2. 4. 5. 6. 7. 9. 10. 12. 14. 15. 16. 18. 19. 20. 21. 22. 23. 24. 25. 26. 27. 28. 29. 30. 33. 34. 35. 37. 38. 39. 40. 41. 44. 45. 47. 48. 50. 57. 62. 63. 64. 65. 71. 83. 87. 88. 91. 100. 101. 102. **Hereford. CLR**-1. 2. 3. 4. **LR**-10. 11. **Newfoundland.** IND-**Inf**-14. 69. 89. **GR**-4. 5. 6. 10. AUS-**L H**-1. 2. 3. 4. 5. 6. 7. 8. 9. 10. 11. 12. 13. 16. 17. 18. 19. 20. 21. 22. 23. **Inf**-1. 2. 3. 4. 5. 6. 7. 8. 9. 10. 11. 12. 13. 14. 15. 16. 17. 18. 19. 20. 21. 22. 23. 24. 25. 26. 27. 28. NZ-**MR**-1. 2. 3. 4. 5. 6. 7. 8. 9. 10. 11. 12. **Inf**-1. 2. 3. 4. 6. 7. 8. 9. 10. 11. 12. 13. 14. 15. 16. 17.	App by Yeo-37.

THE GREAT WAR: EGYPT
Medals awarded: British War Medal 1914–20.

Dates	Honoured or Non-Honoured Battle	Honour awarded to or Participants in Battle	Remarks
26 Jan 1915– 12 Aug 1916	**Suez Canal**	Yeo-**25. 46.** IND-**Cav**-14. **Mad S&M. Inf**-2. 14. 24. 27. 33. 51. 53. 56. 62. 69. 89. 93. 124. 126. **GR**-5. 6. 7. 10. AUS-**Inf**-7. 8. NZ-**Inf**-1. 2. 3. 4. 6. 7. 8. 9. 10. 11. 12. 13. 14. 15. 16. 17.	
3–4 Feb 1915	*Defence of Suez Canal*		App by Yeo-12.
25 Dec 1915	*Wadi Majid*		App by Yeo-12.
23 Jan 1916	*Halazin*		App by Yeo-12. SA-Natal and OFS Regiment participated.
26 Feb 1916	**Agagiya**	Yeo-**23.** SA-**Inf**-1. 3.	Operations against the Sennussi. SA-CoGH & TVL and Rhodesia Regiments participated.
4–5 Aug 1916	**Rumani**	Yeo-2. 7. 24. 31. 45. 54. **Inf**-1. 2. 20. 21. 23. 25. 26. 30. 35. 44. 50. 57. 63. 71. 91. **Hereford.** AUS-**LH**-1. 2. 3. 5. 6. 7. 8. 9. 10. 11. 12. 14. 15. 22. NZ-**MR**-1. 2. 3. 4. 6. 8. 9. 10. 11.	App by Yeo-12.
23 Dec 1916– 9 Jan 1917	**Magdhaba-Rafah**	AUS-**LH**-1. 2. 3. 8. 9. 10. 14. 15. 22. NZ-**MR**-1. 2. 3. 4. 6. 8. 9. 10. 11.	
9 Jan 1917	**Rafah**	Yeo-**2. 24. 31. HAC.**	
26 Jan 1915– 8 Feb 1917	**Egypt 1915–17**	Yeo-2. 4. 5. 6. 7. 8. 13. 15. 16. 18. 19. 21. 22. 23. 24. 25. 26. 27. 28. 29. 30. 31. 32. 33. 35. 39. 40. 41. 42. 43. 44. 45. 46. 47. 52. 53. 54. **WH. Inf**-1. 2. 4. 5. 7. 9. 10. 11. 12. 14. 15. 16. 19. 20. 21. 22. 23. 24. 25. 26. 27. 28. 29. 30. 31. 33. 34. 35. 37. 38. 39. 40. 41. 42. 44. 45. 47. 48. 50. 51. 57. 63. 64. 65. 68. 71. 91. 101. 102. **Hereford. HAC. CLR.**-1. 2. 3. 4. **LR**-10. 11. **Newfoundland.** IND-**Cav**-7. 14. **Inf**-2. 9. 13. 14. 15. 23. 24. 27. 33. 39. 41. 51. 53. 56. 57. 58. 62. 69. 76. 89. 92. 93. 101. 124. 126. **GR**-2. 3. 4. 5. 6. 7. 8. 10.	App by Yeo-12.

Dates	**Honoured** or *Non-Honoured* Battle	**Honour awarded** to or *Participants in* Battle	Remarks
26 Jan 1915– 8 Feb 1917	**Egypt 1915–17** (cont)	AUS-**LH-1. 2. 3. 4. 5. 6. 7. 8. 9. 10. 11. 12. 13. 14. 15. 16. 17. 18. 19. 20. 21. 22. 23.** Inf-**1. 2. 3. 4. 5. 6. 7. 8. 9. 10. 11. 12. 13. 14. 15. 16. 17. 18. 19. 20. 21. 22. 23. 24. 25. 26. 27. 28. 29. 30. 31. 32. 45. 46. 47. 48. 49. 50. 51. 52. 53. 54. 55. 56. 57. 58. 59. 60.** NZ-**MR-1. 2. 3. 4. 5. 6. 7. 8. 9. 10. 11. 12.** Inf-**1. 2. 3. 4. 5. 6. 7. 8. 9. 10. 11. 12. 13. 14. 15. 16. 17.** SA-Inf-**1. 2. 3. 4. 1 Fd Amb.**	

THE GREAT WAR: PALESTINE
Medals awarded: British War Medals 1914–20.

Dates	**Honoured** or *Non-Honoured* Battle	**Honour awarded** to or *Participants in* Battle	Remarks
I – 26–27 Mar 1917 II – 17–19 Apr 1917 III – 27 Oct– 7 Nov 1917	**Gaza**	RTR. Yeo-**2. 4. 5. 6. 7. 8. 13. 15. 16. 18. 19. 21. 23. 24. 26. 27. 28. 29. 30. 31. 32. 33. 35. 40. 41. 42. 43. 44. 45. 46. 47. 52.** WH. Inf-**1. 2. 3. 9. 11. 12. 13. 16. 18. 21. 22. 23. 25. 26. 27. 32. 35. 37. 39. 41. 42. 44. 47. 48. 50. 53. 57. 62. 71. 83. 87. 88. 91. 100. 101. 102. Hereford. HAC.** LR-**10. 11. 13. 14. 15. 16. 17. 18. 19. 20. 21. 22. 23. 24.** IND-Cav-**14. Mad S&M.** Inf-**23. 58. 101. 125. 124. 126. GR-3.** NZ-**10 MR.** SA-**Arty Btys-1. 2. 4.**	App by Yeo-12. App by 22 for new separate names – I – Gaza II – Mukhadem III – Beersheba with dates as shown. Third battle includes capture of Beersheba and action of Sheria.
27 Oct–7 Nov 1917	**Gaza-Beersheba**	AUS-**LH-1. 2. 3. 4. 5. 6. 7. 8. 9. 10. 11. 12. 14. 15. 22.** NZ-**MR-1. 2. 3. 4. 6. 8. 9. 11.**	
8 Nov 1917	*Huj*		App by Yeo-2.
13 Nov 1917	**El Mughar**	Yeo-**2. 4. 5. 15. 21. 23. 24. 26. 27. 31. 44. 45. 46. 47. 52.** Inf-**1. 2. 9. 12. 13. 16. 21. 22. 23. 25. 26. 35. 37. 39. 41. 48. 50. 57. 71. 91. Hereford. HAC.** LR-**10. 11. 13. 14. 15. 16. 17. 18. 19. 20. 21. 22. 23. 24.** IND. Inf-**58. 3 GR.** AUS-**LH-1. 2. 3. 4. 5. 6. 7. 8. 9. 10. 11. 12. 14. 15. 22.** SA-**Arty Btys-1. 2. 4.**	App by Yeo-12.
17–24 Nov 1917	**Nebi Samwil**	Yeo-**2. 4. 5. 15. 21. 23. 24. 26. 27. 31. 44. 45. 47. 52.** Inf-**1. 2. 9. 11. 12. 13. 16. 21. 25. 26. 32. 37. 39. 47. 48. 62. 71. 91.** LR-**10. 11. 13. 14. 15. 16. 17. 18. 19. 20. 21. 22. 23. 24.** IND-Inf-**58. 123. 3 GR.** AUS-**LH-1. 2. 3. 4. 5. 6. 7. 8. 9. 10. 11. 12. 14. 15. 22.** SA-**Arty Btys-1. 2. 4.**	App by Yeo-12.
Capture – 7–9 Dec 1917 Defence – 26–30 Dec 1917	**Jerusalem**	Yeo-**2. 6. 7. 8. 13. 16. 18. 19. 24. 28. 29. 30. 31. 32. 33. 35. 40. 41. 42. 43. 46.** WH. Inf-**2. 3. 9. 11. 12. 13. 16. 18. 21. 22. 23. 27. 32. 35. 37. 39. 41. 42. 47. 48. 50. 53. 57. 62. 83. 87. 88. 100. 101. 102. Hereford. HAC.** LR-**10. 11. 13. 14. 15. 16. 17. 18. 19. 20. 21. 22. 23. 24.** IND-Inf-**58. 123. 3 GR.** AUS-**LH-1. 2. 3. 4. 5. 6. 7. 8. 9. 10. 11. 12. 14. 15. 22.** NZ-**MR-1. 2. 3. 4. 6. 8. 9. 10. 11.**	
21–22 Dec 1917	**Jaffa**	Inf-**1. 9. 12. 16. 21. 25. 26. 37. 44. 47. 48. 71. 91.** LR-**10. 11.** AUS-**LH-1. 2. 3. 22.** NZ-**MR-1. 2. 3. 4. 6. 8. 9. 10. 11.**	App by Yeo-12.

Dates	**Honoured** or *Non-Honoured* Battle	**Honour awarded** to or *Participants in* Battle	Remarks
19–21 Feb 1918	**Jericho**	Yeo-**6. 8. 16. 18. 35. 43. WH.** Inf-**2. 22. 23. 35. 41. 50. 53. 57.** LR-**13. 14. 16. 18. 19. 20. 21. 22. 23. 24.** AUS-**LH-1. 2. 3. 22.** NZ-**MR-1. 2. 3. 4. 6. 8. 9. 10. 11.**	
21 Mar–11 Apr 1918	**Jordan**	Inf-**2. 57. HAC.** LR-**13. 14. 15. 16. 17. 18. 19. 20. 21. 22. 23. 24.**	
I – 24–25 Mar 1918 II – 30 Apr– 4 May 1918	**Jordan (Es Salt)**	AUS-**LH-1. 2. 3. 4. 5. 6. 7. 8. 9. 10. 11. 12. 14. 15. 22.**	I – First Trans Jordan Raid. II – Occupation of Es Salt.
27–30 Mar 1918	**Jordan (Amman)**	AUS-**LH-1. 2. 3. 5. 6. 7. 14. 15. 22.** NZ-**MR-1. 2. 3. 4. 6. 8. 9. 10. 11.**	
8–12 Mar 1918	**Tell 'Asur**	Yeo-**6. 7. 8. 13. 16. 18. 19. 28. 29. 30. 32. 33. 35. 40. 41. 42. 43. WH.** Inf-**2. 3. 9. 11. 12. 16. 18. 21. 22. 23. 27. 32. 35. 37. 39. 41. 42. 47. 48. 50. 53. 57. 83. 87. 88. 100. 101. 102. Hereford.** LR-**10. 11. 14. 16. 17. 21. 22. 23. 24.** IND-Inf-**123. 3 GR.** SA-**Arty Btys-1. 2. 3. 4. 5.**	
19–25 Sep 1918	**Megiddo**	Yeo-**4. 5. 23. 24. 25. 27. 31.** Inf-**2. 7. 9. 12. 13. 16. 17. 18. 23. 32. 37. 39. 41. 42. 44. 48. 62. 63. 72. 87. 88. 100. HAC.** LR-**10. 11. 13. 19.** IND-Cav-**2. 6. 9. 14. 18. 19. 20. 34. 36. 38. S&M-Ben. Mad. Bom.** Inf-**20. 23. 28. 29. 38. 46. 47. 50. 51. 53. 56. 58. 59. 72. 74. 91. 92. 93. 97. 101. 105. 123. 124. 125. 127. 129. Guides. GR-1. 3. 7. 8.** AUS.-**LH-1. 2. 3. 4. 5. 6. 7. 8. 9. 10. 11. 12. 14. 15. 22.** NZ-**MR-1. 2. 3. 4. 6. 8. 9. 10. 11.** SA-**Arty Btys-1. 2. 3. 4. 5. Inf-6.**	App by Yeo-12. Includes Battles of Sharon and Nablus (both separately Honoured).
19–25 Sep 1918	**Sharon**	Yeo-**4. 5. 23. 24. 25. 27.** Inf-**2. 9. 12. 13. 16. 17. 32. 37. 39. 42. 44. 48. 62. 63. 72. 88. HAC.** LR-**10. 11. 13. 19.** IND-Cav-**2. 6. 9. 14. 18. 19. 20. 34. 36. 38. S&M-Ben. Mad. Bom.** Inf-**20. 21. 27. 29. 47. 50. 51. 53. 56. 58. 59. 72. 74. 91. 92. 93. 97. 105. 123. 124. 125. 127. 129. Guides. GR-1. 3. 7. 8.** AUS-**LH-4. 8. 9. 10. 11. 12.** SA-**Arty Btys-1. 2. 3. 4. 5.**	App by Yeo-12.
19–25 Sep 1918	**Nablus**	Yeo-**31.** Inf-**7. 18. 23. 41. 87. 100.** IND-**Bom S&M.** Inf-**20. 21. 23. 38. 46. 51. 53. 72. 74. 101. 105. 124. Guides.** AUS-**LH-1. 2. 3. 5. 6. 7. 14. 15. 22.** NZ-**MR-1. 2. 3. 4. 6. 8. 9. 10. 11.** SA-Inf-**6.**	App by Yeo-12.
1–26 Oct 1918	*Syria*		App by Yeo-12.
1 Oct 1918	**Damascus**	Yeo-**4. 5. 23. 24. 25. 27. 31.** Inf-**17. 42. HAC.** IND-Cav-**2. 6. 9. 14. 18. 19. 20. 34. 36. 38. S&M-Ben. Bom.** AUS-**LH-4. 8. 9. 10. 11. 12. 14. 15.**	

Dates	**Honoured** or *Non-Honoured* Battle	**Honour awarded** to or *Participants in* Battle	Remarks
26 Mar 1917–31 Oct 1918	**Palestine 1917–18**	Yeo-**2. 4. 5. 6. 7. 8. 13. 15. 16. 18. 19. 21. 23. 24. 25. 26. 27. 28. 29. 30. 31. 32. 33. 35. 40. 41. 42. 43. 44. 45. 46. 47. 52. WH. Inf-1. 2. 3. 7. 9. 11. 12. 13. 16. 17. 18. 21. 22. 23. 25. 26. 27. 32. 35. 37. 39. 41. 42. 44. 47. 48. 50. 53. 57. 62. 63. 71. 72. 83. 87. 88. 91. 100. 101. 102. Hereford. HAC. LR-10. 11. 13. 14. 15. 16. 17. 18. 19. 20. 21. 22. 23. 24. IND-Cav-2. 6. 9. 14. 18. 19. 20. 34. 36. 38. S&M-Ben. Mad. Bom. Inf-20. 21. 23. 27. 28. 29. 38. 46. 47. 50. 51. 53. 56. 58. 59. 72. 74. 91. 92. 93. 97. 101. 105. 123. 124. 125. 127. 129. Guides. GR-1. 3. 7. 8. AUS-LH-1. 2. 3. 4. 5. 6. 7. 8. 9. 10. 11. 12. 14. 15. 16. 17. 18. 19. 20. 21. 22. 23. NZ-MR-1. 2. 3. 4. 6. 8. 9. 10. 11. SA-Arty Btys-1. 2. 3. 4. 5. Inf-6. West India.**	App by Yep-12.

THE GREAT WAR: SOUTHERN ARABIA
Medals awarded: British War Medal 1914–20.

Dates	Battle	Participants	Remarks
3 Jul 1915–31 Oct 1918	**Aden**	Inf-**3. 31. 32. 37. Mon. HAC.** IND-**Cav-26. S&M-Ben. Bom. Inf-4. 7. 23. 33. 38. 51. 53. 56. 59. 62. 69. 113. 126..**	Includes actions of Lahej, Sheikh Othman, Jabir and Imad.

THE GREAT WAR: MESOPOTAMIA
Medals awarded: British War Medal 1914–20.

Dates	Battle	Participants	Remarks
6 Nov 1914–14 Apr 1915	**Basra**	Inf-**39.** IND-**Bom S&M. Inf-4. 7. 20. 22. 103. 104. 110. 117.**	Includes actions of Saihan and Sahil.
12–14 Mar 1915	**Shaiba**	Inf-**9. 37. 39.** IND-**Cav-7. 16. 33. Bom S&M. Inf-20. 22. 76. 103. 104. 110. 117. 119. 120. 7 GR.**	
5–24 Jul 1915	*Nasiriya*		App by 50.
28 Sep 1915	**Kut al Amara 1915**	Inf-**9. 37. 39. 43.** IND-**Cav-7. 16. S&M-Ben. Bom. Inf-4. 7. 20. 62. 67. 89. 103. 104. 110. 117. 119. 120. 7 GR.**	
22–24 Nov 1915	**Ctesiphon**	Inf-**9. 39. 43.** IND-**Cav-7. 16. 33. S&M-Ben. Bom. Inf-4. 6. 7. 22. 24. 66. 76. 103. 104. 110. 117. 119. 120. 7 GR.**	
7 Dec 1915–28 Apr 1916	**Defence of Kut al Amara**	Inf-**9. 39. 43. 50.** IND-**S&M-Ben. Bom. Inf-7. 22. 24. 66. 76. 103. 104. 110. 117. 119. 120. 7 GR.**	App by 37.
14 Jan–24 Apr 1916	**Tigris 1916**	**14 H.** Inf-**3. 4. 6. 11. 13. 17. 22. 23. 24. 28. 29. 30. 37. 40. 41. 42. 43. 47. 62. 63. 64. 71. 72. 88.** IND-**Cav-4. 7. 16. 33. S&M-Ben. Mad. Bom.** Inf-**4. 6. 9. 26. 31. 36. 37. 41. 45. 50. 51. 53. 56. 59. 62. 82. 89. 90. 91. 96. 102. 119. 124. 125. GR-1. 2. 4. 8. 9.**	Awarded for the three attempts to relieve Kut al Amara.
16 Dec 1916–25 Feb 1917	**Kut al Amara 1917**	**13 H. 14 H.** Inf-**3. 4. 6. 9. 11. 17. 22. 23. 24. 28. 29. 30. 37. 39. 40. 41. 42. 47. 62. 63. 64. 71. 72. 88.** IND-**Cav-13. 14. 21. 22. 32. S&M-Ben. Mad. Bom. Burma.** Inf-**4. 7. 9. 24. 26. 27. 28. 31. 36. 37. 40. 41. 45. 51. 53. 56. 59. 62. 82. 84. 91. 102. 105. 114. 124. 125. 126. GR-1. 2. 4. 7. 8. 9.**	

Dates	**Honoured** or *Non-Honoured* Battle	**Honour awarded** to or *Participants in* Battle	Remarks
25 Feb–30 Apr 1917	**Baghdad**	13 H. 14 H. Inf-3. 4. 6. 17. 22. 23. 24. 28. 29. 30. 37. 39. 40. 41. 42. 47. 62. 63. 64. 72. 88. IND-Cav-21. 22. 32. S&M-Ben. Mad. Bom. Burma. Inf-9. 20. 26. 27. 28. 31. 37. 41. 45. 51. 53. 56. 59. 62. 82. 87. 90. 91. 102. 114. 124. 125. GR-1. 2. 4. 7. 8. 9.	
28–29 Sep 1917	*Ramadi*		App by 39.
1 Oct–6 Dec 1917	**Tigris 1917**	IND-Inf-20. 28. 51. 53. 56. 92.	
26–27 Mar 1918	**Khan Baghdadi**	7 H. Inf-2. 39. 43. IND-Cav-10. 21. Guides. Ben S&M. Inf-6. 20. 24. 39. 50. 90. 91. 97. 119. 124. GR-5. 6.	
28–30 Oct 1918	**Sharquat**	7 H. 13 H. Inf-13. 37. 50. 71. IND-Cav-13. 14. 21. 32. Guides. Ben S&M. Inf-39. 45. 52. 113. 114. GR-3. 7. 10.	Celebrated by W Battery.
6 Nov 1914–5 Nov 1918	**Mesopotamia 1914–18**	7 H. 13 H. 14 H. Inf-2. 3. 4. 6. 9. 11. 13. 17. 22. 23. 24. 28. 29. 30. 31. 37. 39. 40. 41. 42. 43. 47. 50. 57. 62. 63. 64. 71. 72. 88. IND-Cav-4. 5. 7. 10. 12. 13. 14. 16. 21. 22. 32. 33. Guides. S&M-Ben. Mad. Bom. Burma. Inf-4. 6. 7. 9. 10. 14. 20. 22. 24. 25. 26. 27. 28. 31. 36. 37. 39. 40. 41. 45. 47. 50. 51. 52. 53. 56. 59. 62. 82. 84. 87. 89. 90. 91. 96. 97. 102. 103. 104. 105. 110. 113. 114. 117. 119. 120. 124. 125. 126. GR-1. 2. 3. 4. 5. 6. 7. 8. 9. 10.	Awarded individual Honours but not the Campaign Honour – IND-Inf-66. 67. 76.

THE GREAT WAR: PERSIA
Medal awarded: British War Medal 1914–20. GSM (Army & RAF) 1918–64.

Dates	Honoured Battle	Honour awarded	Remarks
10 Jan–9 Sep 1915	**Persian Gulf**	IND-Inf-**124.**	
1 Nov 1918	**Merv**	IND-Cav-**28.** Inf-**19.** IND-Inf-7.	
26 Aug–15 Sep 1918	**Baku**	Inf-**6. 29. 64.**	
11 Apr 1916–8 Aug 1919	**Persia 1916–19**	14 H. Inf-**6. 28. 29. 37. 64.** IND-Cav-7. 28. **S&M-Ben. Mad. Bom. Burma.** Inf-8. 16. 19. 26. 36. 50. 53. 95. 96. 98. 117. 120. 124. GR-2. 6.	Includes operations in South Persia, Persian Gulf, East Persia, Trans-Caspia, NW Persia and the Caspian.

THE GREAT WAR: INDIA
Medal awarded: British War Medal 1914–20.

Dates	Honoured Battle	Honour awarded	Remarks
28 Nov 1914–10 Aug 1917	**North-West Frontier 1914–18**	21 L. Inf-**2. 8. 13. 34. 35. 64. 68. 25 LR. Cyclist Corps.** Inf-*19. 33. 40. 98.* IND-Cav-**1. 14. 23. 25. 31. 35. Guides. S&M-Ben. Mad. Bom.** Inf-8. 10. 15. 21. 25. 38. 46. 50. 52. 54. 55. 72. 74. 82. 87. 95. 116. 124. Guides. GR-1. 4. 5. 6.	Includes operations against the Tochi, Mohmunds, Bunerwals, Swatis and Mahsuds.
2 Mar–10 Aug 1917	**Waziristan 1917**	IND-Cav-**15.** IND-Inf-*6GR.*	
18 Feb–8 Apr 1918	**Baluchistan 1918**	Inf-**40. Cyclist Corps.** IND-Cav-**1. S&M-Ben. Bom.** Inf-55. GR-2. 4.	

Dates	**Honoured** or *Non-Honoured* Battle	**Honour awarded** to or *Participants in* Battle	Remarks

THE GREAT WAR: RUSSIA
Medal awarded: British War Medal 1914–20.

Dates	Battle	Honour awarded	Remarks
29 Jun 1918–12 Oct 1919	**Murman 1918–19**	Inf-31. 35. 57. 71.	Includes the seizure of the railway and disarmament of the Bolsheviks, and operations in Karelia and winter 1919.
1 Aug 1918–27 Sep 1919	**Archangel 1918–19**	Inf-1. 7. 8. 19. 37. 43. 68. 71.	Includes seizure of the White Sea ports and the Battle of Troitsa (qv).
10 Aug 1919	**Troitsa**	Inf-7.	
23–24 Aug 1918	**Dukhovskaya**	Inf-57.	
8 Aug 1918–Jun 1919	**Siberia 1918–19**	Inf-37. 57.	Includes the Ussuri and Ufa operations, and the Battle of Dukhovskaya (separately Honoured).

THE GREAT WAR: CHINA AND AUSTRALASIA
Medals awarded: British War Medal 1914–20

Dates	Battle	Honour awarded	Remarks
23 Sep–7 Nov 1914	**Tsingtao**	Inf-**24.** IND-Inf-**36.**	
12 Sep 1914	**Herbertshohe**	AUS-Inf-**1. 2.**	

THE GREAT WAR: EAST AFRICA
Medals awarded: British War medal 1914–20. Africa GSM 1902–56 with clasps.

Dates	Battle	Honour awarded	Remarks
5–21 Mar 1916	**Kilimanjaro**	Inf-**7. 47.** IND-**Bom S&M.** Inf-**29. 129.** SA-Horse-**3. 4. Arty Btys-1. 2. 3. 4. 5.** Inf-**5. 6. 7. 8. 9. 10. 11. 1 Cape Corps.** AF-**KAR.**	Includes actions of Latema Nek and Kahe.
3–4 Jan 1917	**Beho Beho**	Inf-**7.** IND-Inf-**30. 33. 127. 129.** SA-Inf-**6. 1 Cape Corps.** AF-**Nigeria.**	
19 Jul 1917	**Narungombe**	IND-Inf-**30. 33. 40.** SA-Inf-**7. 8.** AF-**KAR. Gold Coast.**	
16–19 Oct 1917	**Nyangao**	Inf-**7.** IND-Inf-**30. 33.** SA-Horse-**10.** Inf-**7. 8. 1 Cape Corps.** AF-**KAR. Nigeria. Gambia.**	
15 Aug 1914–25 Nov 1918	**East Africa 1914–18**	Inf-**7. 47.** IND-Cav-**25. S&M-Mad. Bom.** Inf-**13. 29. 30. 33. 40. 50. 55. 57. 98. 101. 127. 129.** SA-Horse-**3. 4. 8. 9. 10. Arty Btys-1. 2. 3. 4. 5. 5 Mtn.** Inf-**5. 6. 7. 8. 9. 10. 11. 12. 1 Cape Corps. 2 Cape Corps.** AF-**KAR. Nigeria. Gambia. Gold Coast. N Rhodesia. Nyasaland. WI Regt.**	

Dates	**Honoured** or *Non-Honoured* Battle	**Honour awarded** to or *Participants in* Battle	Remarks

THE GREAT WAR: SOUTH WEST AFRICA
Medals awarded: British War Medal 1914–20.

25–26 Apr 1915	**Gibeon**	SA-**MR-1. 3. 4. 5.**	
20 Aug 1914–9 Jul 1915	**South West Africa 1914–15**	SA-**MR-1. 3. 4. 5. 8. 9. 10. 11. 17. 18. 20. SAMR-1. 2. 3. 4. 5. 3/5 Mtd Bde. Hartigan's H. Hy Arty Btys-6. 7. 8. Inf-1. 2. 4. 5. 6. 7. 8. 10. 11. 12. Inf-2. 7. 11. SA Irish. Rand SA Rifles. Bechuanaland Rifles. DisMR-4. 6.** AF-**N Rhodesia.**	

THE GREAT WAR: WEST AFRICA
Medals awarded: British War Medal 1914–20.

8–26 Aug 1914	**Kamina**	AF-**Gold Coast.**	Togoland.
26–27 Sep 1914	**Duala**	AF-**Nigeria. Gold Coast. Sierra Leone. West Africa.**	Includes capture of Duala and actions of Nsana Kang, Yabasi, Edea, Kuyuka, Buea and the Cameroon Mountains.
31 May–10 Jun 1915	**Garua**	AF-**Nigeria.**	
4–6 Nov 1915	**Banyo**	AF-**Nigeria.**	Cameroons.
6 Aug 1914–17 Feb 1916	**Cameroons 1914–16**	West India. AF-**Nigeria. Gold Coast. Gambia. Sierra Leone. West Africa.**	

3rd AFGHAN WAR
Medal awarded: India GSM 1908–35 with clasp.

6 May–8 Aug 1919	**Afghanistan 1919**	**1 DG. Inf-2. 8. 13. 19. 33. 34. 35. 40. 50. 64. 68. 25 LR. Cyclist Corps.** IND-Cav-**1. 3. 4. 13. 14. 16. 17. 21. 23. 25. 27. 28. 30. 31. 33. 37. 40. 41. 42. S&M-Ben. Mad. Bom. Burma. Inf-2. 6. 10. 11. 14. 15. 16. 19. 22. 26. 27. 30. 33. 35. 37. 39. 40. 41. 50. 54. 55. 56. 57. 66. 67. 69. 72. 76. 82. 89. 90. 97. 98. 102. 103. 109. 110. 112. 113. 119. 120. 124. 126. 129. Guides. 150. 151. 152. 153. 154. GR-1. 2. 3. 4. 5. 6. 7. 8. 9. 10. 11.** Inf-*7. 37.* IND-Cav-*12.* Inf-*3. 5. 12. 23. 24. 61. 81. 107.*	

MESOPOTAMIA 1919–21
Medals awarded: GSM (Army and RAF) 1918–64 with clasps.

1919	**Haifa-Aleppo 1919**	IND-Cav-**15.**	
4 Jun 1920–Jan 1921	**Iraq 1920**	IND-Cav-**35.** Inf-*46. 51.* IND-Inf-*23. 45.* GR-*5. 8. 11.*	App by 83.
1920–1	*Mesopotamia 1920–21*		App by 15.

MOPLAR RISING
Medals awarded: India GSM 1908–35 with clasp.

Aug 1921	*Malabar*	*RTR.* Inf-*39. 100.* IND-Inf-*39. 70. 83.* GR-*8. 9.*	App by 39.

Dates	**Honoured** or *Non-Honoured* Battle	**Honour awarded** to or *Participants in* Battle	Remarks

WAZIRISTAN 1919–23
Medals awarded: India GSM 1908–35 with clasp.

| Jun 1919–Jan 1923 | *Waziristan 1921* | Inf-*2. 23. 34. 41. 45. 49.*
IND-Cav-*7. 16. 17. 21. 27. 28.* Inf-*1. 2. 3. 4. 5. 6. 7. 9. 10. 12. 13. 16. 17. 18. 19. 21. 25. 26. 28. 30. 32. 34. 36. 37. 39. 41. 48. 50. 61. 69. 73. 82. 101. 102. 104. 109. 113. 119.* GR-*1. 2. 3. 4. 5. 6. 8. 9. 11.* | App by 2. |

NORTH WEST FRONTIER, INDIA 1930–40
Medals awarded: India GSM 1908–35 with clasp. India GSM 1936–9 with clasps.

Jun–Sep 1930	**North West Frontier 1930**	IND-**5 GR.** *15/19 H.* Inf-*34. 35. 40. 44. 51. 53. 68. 72.* IND-Cav-*10. 17. 20.* Inf-*Punjab-1. 2. 8. Rajput. Sikh. Baluch. FFR. Dogra. GR-1. 3. 4.*	
1936–7	**North West Frontier 1936–37**	IND-**5 GR.** Inf-*9. 17. 19. 24. 33. 37. 48. 71. 91.* IND-Inf-*Punjab-2. 8. 16. Raj Rif. Rajput. FFR-12. 13. Dogra. GR-1. 3. 4. 6.*	
1937–40	**North West Frontier 1937–40**	IND-Cav-**13.** Inf-**5 GR.** Inf-*6. 9. 12. 17. 19. 24. 37. 83. 91.* IND-Cav-*1. 5. 8. 14.* Inf-*Punjab-1. 2. 8. 14. 15. 16. Ind Gren. Mahratta LI. Raj Rif. Rajput. Jat. Sikh. Baluch. FFR-12. 13. Dogra. Garhwal. GR-1. 2. 3. 4. 6. 8. 9.*	

BURMA 1930–2
Medals awarded: India GSM 1908–35 with clasp.

| 22 Dec 1930–6 Jan 1932 | *Burma 1930–32* | IND-Inf-*2/5. 3/6. 3/10. 2/15. 3/10. 1/17. 3/20.* | |

WORLD WAR II: NORWAY
Medals awarded: British War Medal 1939–45. 1939–45 Star.

21–22 Apr 1940	**Vist**	Inf-**10.**	
25–26 Apr 1940	**Kvam**	Inf-**51.**	
28 Apr 1940	**Otta**	Inf-**19.**	
17–18 May 1940	**Stien**	Inf-**SG.**	
25–26 May 1940	**Pothus**	Inf-**IG.**	
21 Apr 1940–26 May 1940	**Norway 1940**	Inf-**SG. IG. 10. 17. 19. 24. 45. 51. 65.**	
27 Dec 1941	**Vaagso**	**Cdos.**	

WORLD WAR II: NORTH WEST EUROPE 1940–42
Medals awarded: British War Medal 1939–45. 1939–45 Star.

10 16 May 1940	**The Dyle**	**4/7 DG. 12 L. 13/18 H.** Inf-**GG. CG. 1. 22. 23. 49. 57. 63. 64. 68. 83.**	
17–19 May 1940	**Withdrawal to the Escaut**	**5 DG. 13/18 H. 15/19 H.** Yeo-**50.** Inf-**15. 22. 63. 75. 87.**	
19–22 May 1940	**Defence of the Escaut**	Inf-**CG. 1. 2. 3. 5. 6. 9. 15. 20. 23. 28. 29. 30. 31. 32. 34. 35. 43. 48. 50. 53. 57. 63. 64. 79.**	
20 May 1940	**Amiens 1940**	Inf-**35.**	
19–24 May 1940	**Defence of Arras**	**12 L.** Inf-**WG. 15. 19. 21. 27. 42. 48. 62. 63.**	
21 May 1940	**Arras Counterattack**	**12 L. RTR.** Inf-**5. 68.**	

Dates	Honoured or *Non-Honoured* Battle	Honour awarded to or *Participants in* Battle	Remarks
22–25 May 1940	**Boulogne 1940**	Inf-**IG. WG.**	
22–26 May 1940	**Calais 1940**	**RTR.** Inf-**60. RB. LR-9.**	
23–27 May 1940	**French Frontier 1940**	Inf-**15.**	
23–29 May 1940	**St Omer–La Bassee**	**5 DG. RTR.** Yeo-**52.** Inf-**WG. 1. 3. 4. 5. 9. 20. 22. 23. 28. 29. 35. 39. 44. 45. 49. 63. 68. 79. 87.**	
28 May 1940	**Wormhoudt**	Inf-**6. 22. 28. 29.**	
27–29 May 1940	**Cassel**	Yeo-**52.** Inf-**22. 28. 43.**	
27–28 May 1940	**Foret de Nieppe**	Inf-**35. 50.**	
26–28 May 1940	**Ypres–Comines Canal**	**13/18 H.** Inf-**6. 15. 21. 26. 27. 42. 43. 45. 48. 57. 62. 63. 64. 72. 75.**	
26 May–3 Jun 1940	**Dunkirk 1940**	**4/7 DG. 5 DG. 12 L.** Yeo-**40.** Inf-**GG. CG. 4. 5. 7. 10. 12. 15. 16. 19. 22. 25. 30. 31. 33. 34. 37. 40. 42. 45. 47. 49. 53. 57. 68. 75. 83.**	Also **Hondeghem Battery.**
24 May–5 Jun 1940	**The Somme 1940**	**2 DG. 9 L. 10 H. RTR.** Yeo-**36.** Inf-**21. 34. 42. 72. 75. 79. 91.**	
6–10 Jun 1940	**Withdrawal to the Seine**	**2 DG. 9 L.** Yeo-**36.** Inf-**3. 21. 72.**	
9–18 Jun 1940	**Withdrawal to Cherbourg**	Inf-**71.**	
10–12 Jun 1940	**St Valery-en-Caux**	Yeo-**36.** Inf-**9. 33. 42. 72. 75. 79. LR-13.**	
13 May 1940	**Saar**	Inf-**42. LR-13.**	
27–28 Feb 1942	**Bruneval**	**Para.**	
27–28 Mar 1942	**St Nazaire**	**Cdos.**	
19 Aug 1942	**Dieppe**	**Cdos.** CDN-Inf-**8. 13. 21. 65. 79. TS. Sask. Calgary.**	
19 May 1940–19 Aug 1942	**North West Europe 1940–42**	**2 DG. 4/7 DG. 5 DG. 9 L. 10 H. 12 L. 13/18 H. 15/19 H. RTR.** Yeo-**36. 40. 52.** Inf-**GG. CG. WG. 1. 2. 3. 4. 5. 6. 7. 9. 10. 12. 14. 15. 16. 19. 20. 21. 22. 23. 25. 26. 27. 28. 29. 30. 31. 32. 33. 34. 35. 37. 38. 39. 40. 42. 43. 44. 45. 47. 48. 49. 50. 53. 57. 60. 62. 63. 64. 65. 68. 71. 72. 75. 79. 83. 91. RB. LR-9. 13. Para. Cdos.** CDN-Inf-**8. 13. 21. 65. 79. TS. Sask. Calgary.**	Not Honoured but awarded individual Honours – **IG. 87.**

WORLD WAR II: NORTH WEST EUROPE 1944–5
Medals awarded: British War Medal 1939–45. 1939–45 Star. France and Germany Star.

6 Jun 1944	**Normandy Landing**	**4/7 DG. 13/18 H. 22 D.** Yeo-**4. 5. 46. 52. Inns.** Inf-**6. 8. 9. 10. 11. 12. 15. 19. 22. 24. 37. 39. 40. 43. 49. 53. 57. 83. Herts. Para. GPR. Cdos.** Inf-*25.* CDN-Cav-**FGH. 1.** Inf-**2. 29. 43. 50. 53. 54. 59. 73. 76. 90. 92. 95. Para.**	App by Inf-*25.*
6 Jun 1944	**Pegasus Bridge**	Inf-**43. Para. GPR.**	
6 Jun 1944	**Merville Battery**	**Para. GPR.**	
7–8 Jun 1944	**Port en Bessin**	Inf-**11.**	
7 Jun 1944	**Authie**	CDN-Inf-**53. 54. 76.**	
8–9 Jun 1944	**Sully**	Inf-**24.**	
9 Jun 1944	**Cambes**	Yeo-**52.** Inf-**10. 25. 57. 83.**	

Dates	**Honoured** or *Non-Honoured* Battle	**Honour awarded** to or *Participants in* Battle	Remarks
8 Jun 1944	**Putot en bessin**	**24 L.** CDN-Cav-**1.** Inf-**50. 90.**	
8–9 Jun 1944	**Bretteville L'Orgueilleuse**	CDN-Inf-**95.**	
11 Jun 1944	**Le Mesnil Patry**	CDN-Cav-**1.** Inf-**2.**	
10–13 Jun 1944	**Breville**	**13/18 H.** Inf-**42. 57. Para.**	
8–15 Jun 1944	**Villers Bocage**	**8 H. 11 H. 24 L.** Yeo-**4. 46. 47.** Inf-**2. 28. 39. 68. RB.**	
14–19 Jun 1944	**Tilly sur Seulles**	**24 L.** Inf-**11. 15. 19. 33. 37. 39. 44. 68. LR-13.**	
25 Jun–2 Jul 1944	**The Odon**	**4/7 D. 22 D. 23 H. 24 L. RTR.** Yeo-**4. 47. 51.** Inf-**1. 5. 12. 13. 15. 21. 25. 26. 29. 33. 40. 42. 53. 57. 62. 65. 71. 72. 75. 91. RB. Hereford. Mon. CLR-5. LR-13.**	
25–27 Jun 1944	**Fontenay le Pesnil**	**24 L.** Yeo-**4.** Inf-**10. 21. 33. 42. 51. 65.**	
26–27 Jun 1944	**Cheux**	Yeo-**40. 51.** Inf-**1. 21. 25. 26. 32. 71. 72.**	
27 Jun 1944	**Tourmauville Bridge**	Inf-**91.**	
29 Jun–2 Jul 1944	**Defence of Rauray**	**24 L.** Yeo-**4. 47. 51.** Inf-**1. 10. 21. 25. 42. 68. Hereford.**	
4–18 Jul 1944	**Caen**	**2 D. 13/18 H. 22 D. RTR.** Yeo-**5. 47. 51. 52. Inns.** Inf-**1. 5. 6. 9. 10. 11. 13. 15. 21. 23. 24. 25. 26. 30. 37. 38. 39. 42. 43. 53. 57. 62. 63. 64. 65. 72. 83. 91.** CDN-Cav-**FGH. 1. 14. 17.** Inf-**2. 29. 43. 50. 53. 54. 59. 73. 76. 90. 92. 95.**	
4–5 Jul 1944	**Carpiquet**	CDN-Cav-**FGH.** Inf-**2. 43. 73. 90. 92.**	
8–9 Jul 1944	**The Orne (Buron)**	Inf-**10. 57. 64.** CDN-Cav-**1.** Inf-**29. 43. 50. 53. 54. 59. 76. 90. 95.**	
10–11 Jul 1944	**Hill 112**	**2 D.** Inf-**13. 32. 37. 57. 62.**	
15–17 Jul 1944	**Esquay**	Inf-**1. 23. 25. 43. 63. 71. 91.**	
15–18 Jul 1944	**Noyers**	Yeo-**51.** Inf-**38. 64.**	
18–19 Jul 1944	**Cagny**	Yeo-**Inns.** Inf-**GG. CG. IG. WG. 5. Hereford.**	
18–23 Jul 1944	**Bourguebus Ridge**	**11 H. 13/18 H. 23 H. RTR.** Yeo-**40. 47. 51. 52. Inns.** Inf-**WG. 6. 10. 15. 29. 40. 53. 57. 62. RB. Hereford. Mon. HAC. CLR-5.** CDN-Cav-**1.** Inf-**2. 5. 8. 21. 29. 43. 53. 54. 59. 65. 73. 76. 79. 85. 90. 92. 95. 103. TS. Sask.**	
18–21 Jul 1944	**Troarn**	Yeo-**5.** Inf-**10. 15. 25. 40. 53. 57. 72. 83.**	
18–19 Jul 1944	**Faubourg de Vaucelles**	CDN-Cav-**1.** Inf-**2. 5. 8. 29. 43. 53. 54. 59. 73. 76. 85. 92. 95. 103.**	
19–23 Jul 1944	**St Andre sur Orne**	CDN-Inf-**21. 53. 54. 65. 79. TS. S Sask.**	
22–23 Jul 1944	**Maltot**	Inf-**29. 62.** CDN-Inf-**85.**	

Dates	**Honoured** or *Non-Honoured* Battle	**Honour awarded** to or *Participants in* Battle	Remarks
25 Jul 1944	**Verrieres Ridge – Tilly la Campagne**	CDN-Cav-**1**. Inf-**5. 8. 13. 65. 76. 79. 85. 103. TS.**	
30 Jul–9 Aug 1944	**Mont Pincon**	**LG. RHG. 4/7 DG. 5 DG. 8 H. 11 H. 13/18 H. RTR.** Yeo-**4. 51.** Inf-**GG. CG. SG. IG. WG. 1. 2. 6. 13. 15. 21. 22. 25. 26. 28. 29. 32. 37. 39. 53. 57. 60. 62. 64. 71. 72. 91. RB. Hereford. Mon. CLR-5. LR-16.**	
30 Jul–2 Aug 1944	**Quarry Hill**	Inf-**CG. SG. 71. 72. 91.**	
30 Jul–4 Aug 1944	**Jurques**	**11 H.** Yeo-**4.** Inf. **29.37.**	
4–9 Aug 1944	**La Variniere**	Inf-**29. 62.**	
30 Jul–1 Aug 1944	**The Souleuvre**	**LG. RHG.** Inf-**53. Hereford. Mon.**	
2–5 Aug 1944	**Catheolles**	Yeo-**Inns.**	
2–8 Aug 1944	**Le Perier Ridge**	**23 H.** Yeo-**40.** Inf-**9. 53. RB. Mon. CLR-5.**	
6–8 Aug 1944	**Brieux Bridgehead**	Inf-**9. 64.**	
9–16 Aug 1944	**St Pierre la Vielle**	**5 DG. 13/18 H.** Inf-**11. 15. 19. 22. 37. 39. 68.**	
6–12 Aug 1944	**Estry**	Inf-**CG. SG. 21. 25. 26. 71. 91.**	
14–17 Aug 1944	**Noireau Crossing**	**LG. RHG.** Yeo-**4.** Inf-**13. 29. 32.**	
7–22 Aug 1944	**Falaise**	**2 D. 22 D. RTR.** Yeo-**36. 47. 51.** Inf-**5. 6. 12. 21. 23. 24. 28. 30. 38. 40. 41. 42. 53. 57. 60. 63. 71. 72. 79. 91. RB. Hereford. Mon. CLR-5.** CDN-Cav-**FGH. 1. 12. 14. 15. 17.** Inf-**GGFG. 1. 2. 5. 6. 8. 13. 21. 29. 43. 44. 50. 53. 54. 59. 65. 73. 76. 79. 85. 90. 91. 92. 95. 96. 97. 103. TS. Sask.**	
7–9 Aug 1944	**Falaise Road**	Yeo-**36. 51.** Inf-**42. 72. 79.** CDN-Cav-**FGH. 1. 12. 14. 15.** Inf-**GGFG. 1. 2. 6. 13. 21. 44. 53. 54. 65. 73. 79. 85. 91. 96. 97. 103. TS. Sask.**	
10–11 Aug 1944	**Quesnay Road**	CDN-Cav-**1.** Inf-**2. 43. 73.**	
11–13 Aug 1944	**Clair Tizon**	CDN-Cav-**14.** Inf-**5. 8. 13. 21. 53. 54. 103. TS.**	
14–17 Aug 1944	**The Laison**	Yeo-**36.** CDN-Cav-**FGH. 1. 12. 14. 15. 17.** Inf-**GGFG. 1. 2. 6. 29. 43. 44. 50. 53. 54. 59. 65. 73. 76. 79. 90. 92. 95. 96. 97. Sask.**	
18–22 Aug 1944	**Chambois**	CDN-Cav-**1. 12.** Inf-**GGFG. 1. 6. 29. 44. 59. 73. 76. 92. 96. 97.**	
19–22 Aug 1944	**St Lambert sur Dives**	CDN-Cav-**15.** Inf-**91.**	
15–28 Aug 1944	**Southern France**	**Para. GPR.**	
17–20 Aug 1944	**Dives Crossing**	**8 H. 11 H.** Yeo-**22. 51.** Inf-**72. 91. Para. Cdos.** CDN-**Para.**	
18–20 Aug 1944	**La Vie Crossing**	**11 H.** Yeo-**22. 52.** Inf-**21. 42. 65. 72. 75. 79.**	
21–23 Aug 1944	**Lisieux**	**5 DG. 11 H.** Yeo-**22. 51. 52.** Inf-**72.**	
22–23 Aug 1944	**La Touques Crossing**	**11 H.** Inf-**21. 65. Para.**	

Dates	Honoured or Non-Honoured Battle	Honour awarded to or Participants in Battle	Remarks
25–27 Aug 1944	**Risle Crossing**	**5 DG. 11 H.** Inf-**24. 28.**	
25–28 Aug 1944	**The Seine 1944**	**4/7 DG. 15/19 H.** Yeo-**4.** Inf-**13. 29. 57. 62. 71.** CDN-Cav-**14.** Inf-**44. 73. 90. 91. 95. 97.**	
28–30 Aug 1944	**Foret de Bretonne**	Yeo-**52.** Inf-**65.**	
27–29 Aug 1944	**Foret de la Londe**	CDN-Inf-**5. 8. 13. 21. 65. 79. 85. 103. Sask.**	
31 Aug 1944	**Amiens 1944**	**LG. RHG. 23 H.** Yeo-**Inns.**	
3 Sep 1944	**Brussels**	**LG. RHG.** Inf-**WG.**	
4–7 Sep 1944	**Antwerp**	**23 H.** Yeo-**Inns.** Inf-**53. RB. Hereford. Mon. HAC. CLR-5.**	
8–10 Sep 1944	**Moerbrugge**	CDN-Cav-**15.** Inf-**44. 73. 91.**	
7–12 Sep 1944	**Hechtel**	**15/19 H.** Yeo-**Inns.** Inf-**WG. RB. Hereford. CLR-5.**	
8–11 Sep 1944	**Gheel**	Yeo-**4.** Inf-**15. 19. 22. 68.**	
8–9 Sep 1944	**Heppen**	Inf-**CG.**	
10 Sep 1944	**Neerpelt**	**LG. RHG.** Inf-**IG.**	
14–20 Sep 1944	**Aart**	Inf-**1. 21. 25. 71. 91.**	
8–15 Sep 1944	**Dunkirk 1944**	CDN-Inf-**5. 8. 65. 79. 85. 103. TS. Sask.**	
10–12 Sep 1944	**Le Havre**	**22 D.** Yeo-**36. 51.** Inf-**10. 21. 24. 28. 42. 44. 51. 57. 65. 72. 79. HAC.** CDN-**1 APC.**	
17–22 Sep 1944	**Boulogne 1944**	Yeo-**36.** CDN-Cav-**FGH.** Inf-**2. 29. 43. 59. 73. 76. 92. 1 APC.**	
25 Sep–1 Oct 1944	**Calais 1944**	Yeo-**36.** CDN-Cav-**1.** Inf-**2. 29. 50. 58. 73. 76. 90. 92. 95.**	
13–14 Sep 1944	**Moerkerke**	CDN-Inf-**73. 97.**	
21–22 Sep 1944	**Wyneghem**	CDN-Inf-**103.**	
24–29 Sep 1944	**Antwerp–Turnhout Canal**	Inf-**10. 17. 21. 24. 44. 51. 65. LR-13.** CDN-Cav-**FGH. 14.** Inf-**5. 53. 54. 65. 85. 103. TS. Sask.**	
17–27 Sep 1944	**The Nederrijn**	**LG. RHG. 4/7 DG. 1 D. 8 H. 15/19 H. RTR.** Yeo-**4.** Inf-**CG. WG. 1. 5. 10. 11. 13. 15. 19. 21. 22. 23. 25. 26. 29. 30. 32. 37. 53. 57. 62. 63. 71. 72. RB. Mon. CLR-5.**	
17–26 Sep 1944	**Arnhem 1944**	Inf-**25. 34. 38. 39. Para. GPR.** CDN-Inf-**34.**	
19–20 Sep 1944	**Nijmegen**	**LG. RHG.** Inf-**GG. IG.**	
22–23 Sep 1944	**Veghel**	**1 D.**	
22–27 Sep 1944	**Best**	**8 H.** Inf-**1. 21. 25. 26. 71. 72.**	
1 Oct–8 Nov 1944	**The Scheldt**	**RTR.** Yeo-**36. 40.** Inf-**1. 17. 21. 24. 25. 26. 44. 63. 65. 71.** CDN-Cav-**FGH. 14. 15. 17.** Inf-**GGFG. 1. 2. 5. 6. 8. 13. 21. 29. 43. 44. 50. 53. 54. 58. 59. 65. 73. 76. 79. 85. 90. 91. 92. 95. 96. 97. 103. TS. Sask.**	
6–16 Oct 1944	**Leopold Canal**	CDN-Inf-**50. 58. 90. 95.**	
1–27 Oct 1944	**Woensdrecht**	CDN-Cav-**FGH. 14. 15.** Inf-**5. 8. 13. 21. 65. 79. 85. 103. TS. Sask.**	

Dates	Honoured or Non-Honoured Battle	Honour awarded to or Participants in Battle	Remarks
9–10 Oct 1944	**Savojaards Plaat**	CDN-Inf-**29. 59. 76.**	
11 Oct–3 Nov 1944	**Breskens Pocket**	CDN-Cav-**17.** Inf-**2. 29. 43. 44. 50. 59. 73. 76. 90. 91. 92. 95. 97.**	
24–31 Oct 1944	**South Beveland**	Inf-**21. 26. 71.** CDN-Cav-**14.** Inf-**5. 8. 13. 21. 65. 79. 85. 103. TS. Sask.**	
31 Oct–4 Nov 1944	**Walcheren Causeway**	Inf-**26. 63. 71.** CDN-Inf-**5. 85. 103.**	
1–4 Nov 1944	**Flushing**	Inf-**1. 25. 63. Cdos.**	
1–3 Nov 1944	**Westkapelle**	Yeo-**36. Cdos.**	
20 Oct–7 Nov 1944	**The Lower Maas**	**5 DG. 8 H. 22 D.** Yeo-**22. 47. 51. 52.** Inf-**2. 21. 23. 30. 41. 42. 43. 51. 57. 63. 65. 71. 72. 75. 79. 91. RB. Mon.** CDN-Cav-**1. 15.** Inf-**GGFG. 1. 6. 44. 53. 54. 73. 91. 96. 97. 1 APC.**	
1–4 Oct 1944	**Aam**	Inf-**IG. 15. 22. 39.**	
5–7 Oct 1944	**Opheusden**	Inf-**32.**	
12–18 Oct 1944	**Venraij**	**15/19 H. 23 H.** Yeo-**46.** Inf-**CG. 6. 9. 10. 12. 15. 25. 40. 53. 57. Hereford.**	
27 Oct–5 Nov 1944	**Asten/Meijel**	Yeo-**46.** Inf-**CG. 1. 21. 25. 26. 57. 71. 72. 91.**	Asten by 26 and 71, Meijel remainder. Also **Asten Battery.**
18-23 Nov 1944	**Geilenkirchen**	**4/7 DG. 13/18 H.** Yeo-**4. 36.** Inf-**13. 29. 32. 39. 57.**	
14 Nov–3 Dec 1944	**Venlo Pocket**	**2 D. 22 D. 23 H. RTR.** Yeo-**46. 51. 52.** Inf-**SG. 1. 10. 21. 23. 25. 42. 57. 63. 72. 75. 79. 83. 91. Hereford. Mon. LR–13.**	
31 Dec 1944–31 Jan 1945	**Kapelsche Veer**	CDN-Cav-**15.** Inf-**44. 73. 91.**	
16–31 Jan 1945	**The Roer**	**4/7 DG. 5 DG. 8 H. 11 H. 13/18 H.** Yeo-**4. 36. 46.** Inf-**CG. 1. 2. 11. 13. 21. 25. 26. 37. 60. 62. 63. 68. 71. RB. LR-16.** CDN-**1 APC.**	
18–21 Jan 1945	**Zetten**	Inf-**17. 24. 28. 44. LR-13.**	
3–14 Jan 1945	**The Ourthe**	**23 H.** Yeo-**22. 40. 51. 52.** Inf-**23. 30. 42. 43. 63. 71. 72. 91. Mon. Para.**	
8 Feb–10 Mar 1945	**The Rhineland**	**4/7 DG. 2 D. 13/18 H. 15/19 H. RTR.** Yeo-**4. 22. 40. 47.** Inf-**CG. SG. IG. WG. 1. 5. 6. 9. 10. 13. 15. 21. 23. 25. 26. 29. 30. 32. 37. 40. 42. 43. 53. 57. 60. 62. 63. 71. 72. 75. 79. 91. Hereford. Mon. LR-16.** CDN-Cav-**FGH. 1. 12. 14. 15. 17.** Inf-**GGFG. 1. 2. 5. 6. 8. 13. 21. 29. 43. 44. 50. 53. 54. 59. 65. 73. 76. 79. 85. 90. 91. 92. 95. 96. 97. 103. TS. Sask. 1 APC.**	
8–13 Feb 1945	**The Reichswald**	**22 D.** Yeo-**22. 36.** Inf-**GG. CG. SG. 1. 21. 23. 25. 26. 30. 41. 42. 43. 57. 63. 71. 72. 75. 79. 91. Mon.** CDN-Inf-**58. 103. TS. 1 APC.**	
8–15 Feb 1945	**Waal Flats**	**13/18 H.** CDN-Inf-**2. 29. 43. 50. 59. 73. 76. 90. 92. 96.**	

Dates	Honoured or *Non-Honoured* Battle	Honour awarded to or *Participants in* Battle	Remarks
9–11 Feb 1945	**Cleve**	**4/7 DG.** Yeo-**4.** Inf-**CG. SG. 1. 13. 21. 25. 60. 62. 75. LR-16.** CDN-**1 APC.**	
12–21 Feb 1945	**Goch**	**13/18 H.** Yeo-**4.** Inf-**CG. 1. 13. 21. 23. 25. 29. 32. 37. 39. 42. 57. 60. 62. 63. 71. 72. 75. 79. LR-16.**	
14–21 Feb 1945	**Moyland/Moyland Wood**	Inf-**CG. SG. 26. 71. 72.** CDN-Inf-**50. 90. 95. 1 APC.**	Moyland Wood by 71. Moyland by the remainder.
19–21 Feb 1945	**Goch–Calcar Road**	CDN-Cav-**FGH.** Inf-**8. 13. 21. TS. 1 APC.**	
24 Feb–2 Mar 1945	**Weeze**	Yeo-**4.** Inf-**23. 30. 63. 71. Mon.**	
24 Feb–4 Mar 1945	**The Hochwald**	**2 D. 15/19 H.** Yeo-**47.** Inf-**CG. SG. IG. 9. 10. 13. 40. 53. 60. Hereford. Mon.** CDN-Cav-**FGH. 1. 15.** Inf-**GGFG. 1. 2. 5. 6. 8. 13. 21. 43. 44. 53. 54. 59. 65. 73. 76. 79. 85. 91. 92. 96. 97. 103. TS. Sask. 1 APC.**	
27–28 Feb 1945	**Schaddenhof**	Inf-**15.**	
8–9 Mar 1945	**Xanten**	Inf-**13. 62.** CDN-Inf-**5. 8. 13. 21. 53. 54. 65. 79. 85. 103. TS. Sask. 1 APC.**	
6–10 Mar 1945	**Veen**	CDN-Cav-**15.** Inf-**GGFG. 1. 6. 44. 91. 96. 97.**	
25 Mar–1 Apr 1945	**The Rhine**	**4/7 DG. 1 D. 8 H. 11 H. 13/18 H. 15/19 H. 22 D. RTR.** Yeo-**4. 5. 40. 47. 51. 52. Inns.** Inf-**GG. CG. SG. IG. 1. 11. 13. 21. 23. 25. 26. 29. 30. 32. 37. 39. 42. 43. 49. 57. 60. 62. 63. 71. 72. 75. 79. 83. 91. Mon. HAC. LR-16. Para. GPR. Cdos.** CDN-Cav-**17.** Inf-**2. 5. 29. 43. 50. 53. 54. 59. 65. 73. 76. 79. 90. 92. 95. 103. Sask. Para. 1 APC.**	
28 Mar–1 Apr 1945	**Emerich – Hoch Elten**	CDN-Cav-**17.** Inf-**2. 50. 54. 53. 73. 90. 92. 95.**	
1–6 Apr 1945	**Ibbenburen**	**5 DG. 11 H. 15/19 H.** Inf-**11. 23. 25. 30. 43. 53. 63. 68. 71. Hereford. Mon.**	
2–5 Apr 1945	**Lingen**	**LG. RHG.** Yeo-**5.** Inf-**CG. SG. WG. 6. 9. 10. 25. 53. 57.**	
2–3 Apr 1945	**Bentheim**	**LG. RHG.** Inf-**IG.**	
2–4 Apr 1945	**Twente Canal**	Inf-**39.** CDN-Cav-**14. 15.** Inf-**1. 6. 8. 13. 21. 44. 96. TS.**	
4–8 Apr 1945	**Dreirwalde**	Inf-**21. 25. 26. 60. 63. 71.**	
5–8 Apr 1945	**Leese**	Yeo-**Inns.** Inf-**RB. CLR-5. Cdos.**	
6–8 Apr 1945	**Zutphen**	CDN-Cav-**17.** Inf-**29. 43. 53. 54. 59. 73. 76. 92.**	
8–11 Apr 1945	**Deventer**	CDN-Cav-**17.** Inf-**2. 43. 50. 53. 54. 90. 95.**	
10–17 Apr 1945	**The Aller**	**2 D. 11 H. 15/19 H.** Yeo-**47. Inns.** Inf-**22. 23. 30. 53. 60. 63. 71. RB. Hereford. Mon. CLR-5. Cdos.**	
11–17 Apr 1945	**Apeldoorn**	CDN-Cav-**1.** Inf-**RCR. PPCLI. R22R. 48. 49. 52. 69. 72. 73. 86. Edmonton.**	
12–14 Apr 1945	**Arnhem 1945**	Inf-**10. 24. 44. 65. LR-13.**	

Dates	Honoured or *Non-Honoured* Battle	Honour awarded to or *Participants in* Battle	Remarks
13–16 Apr 1945	Groningen	CDN-Cav-**RCD. FGH. 14.** Inf-**5. 8. 13. 21. 65. 79. 85. 103. TS. Sask. 1 APC.**	
13–16 Apr 1945	Brinkum	Inf-**6. 9. 12. 15. 57.**	
14 Apr 1945	Friesoythe	CDN-Inf-**44. 91. 96.**	
14–18 Apr 1945	Uelzen	Inf-**CG. SG. 1. 21. 25. 71. 72. 91.**	
15–18 Apr 1945	Ijsselmeer	CDN-Cav-**Strathcona. GGHG. 8. 30.** Inf-**28. 76. 104. 110.**	
17–24 Apr 1945	Küsten Canal	CDN-Inf-**6. 73. 91. 96. 97.**	
18–26 Apr 1945	Bremen	**4/7 DG. 2 D. 13/18 H. RTR.** Inf-**1. 6. 10. 13. 15. 21. 25. 26. 40. 53. 57. 62. 63. 71. 83.**	
23 Apr–2 May 1945	Delfzijl Pocket	CDN-Cav-**8. 30.** Inf-**28. 66. 76. 104. 110.**	
25 Apr–4 May 1945	Bad Zwischenahm	CDN-Cav-**RCD. 1. 12. 15.** Inf-**GGFG. 1. 6. 76. 91. 96. 97.**	
27 Apr–5 May 1945	Oldenburg	CDN-Cav-**FGH. 14.** Inf-**5. 8. 13. 21. 79. 85. 103. TS. Sask.**	
28–29 Apr 1945	Leer	CDN-Inf-**29. 43. 59. 76.**	
29–30 Apr 1945	Artlenberg	Inf-**1. 21. 25. 26. 71. 72. 91.**	
6 Jun 1944–5 May 1945	North West Europe 1944–45	**LG. RHG. 4/7 DG. 5 DG. 1 D. 2 D. 8 H. 11 H. 13/18 H. 15/19 H. 22 D. 23 H. 24 L. RTR.** Yeo-**4. 5. 22. 36. 40. 46. 47. 51. 52. Inns.** Inf-**GG. CG. SG. IG. WG. 1. 2. 5. 6. 8. 9. 10. 11. 12. 13. 15. 17. 19. 20. 21. 22. 23. 24. 25. 26. 28. 29. 30. 32. 33. 34. 37. 38. 39. 40. 41. 42. 43. 44. 48. 49. 51. 53. 57. 60. 62. 63. 64. 65. 68. 71. 72. 75. 79. 83. 91. RB. Hereford. Mon. Herts. HAC. CLR-5. LR-13. 16. Para. SAS. GPR. Cdos.** CDN-Cav-**RCD. FGH. Strathcona. GGHG. 1. 4. 8. 12. 14. 15. 17. 30. 36.** Inf-**RCR. PPCLI. R22R. GGFG. 1. 2. 5. 6. 8. 13. 20. 21. 25. 28. 29. 34. 43. 44. 48. 49. 50. 53. 54. 58. 59. 65. 66. 69. 72. 73. 76. 79. 85. 86. 90. 91. 92. 94. 95. 96. 97. 103. 104. 105. 110. TS. Sask. Calgary. 1 APC. Para.**	

WORLD WAR II: ABYSSINIA
Medals awarded: British War Medal 1939–45. 1939–45 Star.

1–15 Jul 1940	Moyale	AF-**KAR.**	SOUTHERN CAMPAIGN – KENYA BORDER
10–12 Sep 1940	Wal Garis	AF-**Gold Coast.**	
15–17 Dec 1940	El Wak	AF-**Gold Coast.** SA-**MR-1.** Inf-**2. 8. 3 Armd Car Coy.** SA-1 *Lt Tk Coy*	
6–7 Nov 1940	Gallabat	IND-Inf-**3/18.**	SUDAN BORDER
10 Jan 1941	Jebel Dafeis	Inf-**14.**	

Dates	Honoured or Non-Honoured Battle	Honour awarded to or Participants in Battle	Remarks
21–23 Jan 1941	Jebel Shiba	Inf-71. IND-Inf-4/10. 3/18.	Eritrea
26 Jan 1941	Gogni	Inf-29. IND-Inf- 3/8. Sudan Regiment.	
28 Jan–1 Feb 1941	Agordat	Inf-7. 79. IND-Cav-1. Inf-Guards. 4/11.	
27 Jan–2 Feb 1941	Barentu	Inf-29. 71. IND-Inf-3/18.	
9–10 Feb 1941	Karora-Marsa Taclai	Inf-35.	
23 Feb 1941	Cubcub	Inf-35.	
1 Mar 1941	Mescelit Pass	Inf-35.	
16–18 Jan 1941	El Yibo	SA-MR-2. Inf-2 SSB. 1 Armd Car Coy.	SOUTHERN CAMPAIGN - SOUTHERN ABYSSINIA
15–18 Feb 1941	Mega	SA-MR-3. Inf-8. Irish. SSB-1. 2. Armd Car Coys-1. 2.	
9 Feb 1941	Todenyang – Namaraputh	AF-KAR.	
31 Mar 1941	Soroppa	AF-KAR.	
4–26 Feb 1941	The Juba	AF-KAR. Nigeria. Gold Coast. SA-MR-2. Inf.2. 8. SA-1 Lt Tk Coy. 3 AC Coy.	
4 Feb 1941	Beles Gugani	AF.KAR.	
13 Feb 1941	Bullo Erillo	AF-Gold Coast	THE JUBA RIVER
18–19 Feb 1941	Yonte	SA-Inf-8. SA-One Coy RNC.	
21–22 Feb 1941	Gelib	AF-Gold Coast.	
22 Feb 1941	Alessandra	AF-Gold Coast.	
24 Feb 1941	Goluin	AF-Nigeria.	
3 Feb–31 Mar 1941	Keren	Inf-7. 14. 29. 35. 71. 79. IND-Cav-1. Inf-Guards. 2/5. 4/6. 3/8. 4/11. 3/18. Para.	ERITREA
12–15 Mar 1941	Mount Engiahat	Inf-35.	
28–29 Mar 1941	Keren-Asmara Road	IND-Cav-21.	
30–31 Mar 1941	Ad Teclesan	Inf-14. IND-RI Arty. Inf-3/8. Para.	IND-23 Mtn Regt (J&K Mountain Batteries) awarded as Honour Title.
8 Apr 1941	Massawa	Inf-35. 71. IND-Inf-3/18.	
16 Mar 1941	Berbera	IND-Para.	
21–22 Mar 1941	Marda Pass	AF-Nigeria.	ADVANCE TO ADDIS ABABA
23–25 Mar 1941	Babile Gap	AF-Nigeria.	
26 Mar 1941	The Bisidmo	AF-Nigeria.	
29 Mar 1941	Diredawa	SA-1 Inf-8.	
2–3 Apr 1941	The Awash	AF-KAR.	

Dates	**Honoured** or *Non-Honoured* Battle	**Honour awarded** to or *Participants in* Battle	Remarks
9 Mar 1941	**Afodu**	AF-**KAR.**	} WESTERN ABYSSINIA
22 Mar 1941	**Gambela**	AF-**KAR.**	
9 Apr 1941	**Giarso**	AF.-**N. Rhodesia.**	} SOUTHERN BATTLE OF LAKES
8 Apr–10 May 1941	**Wadara**	AF-**Gold Coast.**	
17–26 Apr 1941	**Combolcia**	SA-**MR-1.** Inf-**2. 8. 3 Armd Car Coy.**	NORTH EAST ABYSSINIA
20 Apr–16 May 1941	**Amba Alagi**	Inf-**29.** IND-Inf-**3/8. 3/18.** SA-**MR-1.** Inf-**2. 8.** SA-*3 Armd Car Coy.*	ERITREA
1 May 1941	**Fike**	AF-**KAR.**	} NORTHERN BATTLE OF LAKES
13 May 1941	**Dadaba**	SA-**MR-3. 1 Lt Tk Coy. 2 Armd Car Coy.**	
19 May 1941	**Colito**	AF-**KAR. Nigeria.**	
31 May–6 Jun 1941	**The Omo**	AF-**KAR. Nigeria.**	} GALLA SIDAMO.
15 Jun 1941	**Lechemti**	AF-**Nigeria.**	
15 Oct–27 Nov 1941	**Gondar**	AF-**KAR.**	} GONDAR
15 Oct–28 Nov 1941	**Ambazzo**	AF-**KAR.**	
13–21 Nov 1941	**Kulkaber**	AF-**KAR.**	
13 Jun 1940–28 Nov 1941	**Abyssinia 1940–41**	**RTR.** Inf-**14. 29. 35. 44. 71. 79. 91.** IND-Cav-**1. 21. RI Arty. S&M-Mad. Bom.** Inf-**Guards. 2/5. 4/6. 17/6. 3/8. 14/8. 4/11. 3/18. Para.** AF-**KAR. Nigeria. N Rhodesia. Gold Coast.**	
13 Jun 1940–28 Nov 1941	**East Africa 1940–41** (SA)*	SA-**MR-1. 3.** Inf-**2. 8. RB. RPS. Irish.**	

WORLD WAR II: BRITISH SOMALILAND
Medals awarded: British War Medal 1939–45. 1939–45 Star.

Dates	Honoured or Non-Honoured Battle	Honour awarded	Remarks
11–15 Aug 1940	**Tug Argan**	AF-**KAR. N Rhodesia.**	
17 Aug 1940	**Barkasan**	Inf-**42.** AF-*KAR.*	
4–17 Aug 1940	**British Somaliland 1940**	Inf-**42.** IND-**Para.** AF-**KAR. N Rhodesia.**	

WORLD WAR II: IRAQ 1941
Medals awarded: British War Medal 1939–45. 1939–45 Star.

Dates	Honoured or Non-Honoured Battle	Honour awarded	Remarks
2–6 May 1941	**Defence of Habbaniya**	Inf-**4.**	
19–22 May 1941	**Falluja**	Inf-**4. 44.**	
28–31 May 1941	**Baghdad 1941**	**LG. RHG.** Inf-**44.**	
2–31 May 1941	**Iraq 1941**	**LG. RHG.** Yeo-**1. 2.** Inf-**4. 44.** IND-**Mad S&M.** Inf-**3/11. GR-2/4. 2/8. 10.**	

* (SA) indicates a South African Army honour. While South Africa Army units often received the same honours as other British and Commonwealth armies, occasionally it awarded an honour to a battle that the British Army either did not honour or honoured by a different name.

Dates	**Honoured** or *Non-Honoured* Battle	**Honour awarded** to or *Participants in* Battle	Remarks

WORLD WAR II: SYRIA 1941
Medals awarded: British War Medal 1939–45. 1939–45. Star.

Dates	Battle	Participants	
7–8 Jun 1941	**Syrian Frontier**	AUS-Inf-**14. 16. 31. 33.**	
9–10 Jun 1941	**The Litani**	**Cdos,** AUS-Inf-**16. 27.**	
9–27 Jun 1941	**Merjayun**	**2 D.** Inf-**4.** AUS-**LH-6.** Inf-**5. 25. 31. 33. 2 Pnr.**	
10–12 Jun 1941	**Adlun**	AUS-**LH-6.** Inf-**14. 27.**	
13–15 Jun 1941	**Sidon**	AUS-**LH-6. 9.** Inf-**16. 27. 3 MG.**	
14–24 Jun 1941	**Jezzine**	AUS-Inf-**14. 31. 3 MG.**	
16–21 Jun 1941	**Damascus (1941)**	Aus-Inf-**3.** IND-Inf-**4/6.**	
19 Jun 1941	**Wadi Zeini**	AUS-**LH-9.** Inf-**16.**	
21 Jun–3 Jul 1941	**Palmyra**	**LG. RHG.** Yeo-1. Inf-**44.**	
22–28 Jun 1941	**Dimas**	AUS-Inf-**3.**	
26 Jun–3 Jul 1941	**Chehim & Rharife.**	AUS-Inf-**25.**	
1–3 Jul 1941	**Deir ez Zor**	IND-Cav-**13.** Inf-**10 GR.**	
6–12 Jul 1941	**Damour**	AUS-**LH-6.** Inf-**3. 5. 14. 16. 25. 27. 31. 3 MG. 2 Pnr.**	
7–8 Jul 1941	**Mazraat ech Chouf**	Aus-Inf-**25. 2 Pnr.**	
8 Jul 1941	**Hill 1069**	AUS-Inf-**31**	
9–10 Jul 1941	**Badarene**	AUS-Inf-**31.**	
9–10 Jul 1941	**Raqaa**	IND-Cav-**13.**	
10–12 Jul 1941	**Jebel Mazar**	Yeo-**11.** Inf-**4. 17.** AUS-**LH-6.** Inf-**3 MG.**	
12 Jul 1941	**Djerablous 1941**	IND-Cav-**13.**	
7 Jun–12 Jul 1941	**Syria 1941**	**LG. RHG. 1 D. 2 D.** Yeo-**1. 2. 5. 8. 9. 11.** Inf-**2. 4. 7. 17. 44. 68. Cdos.** IND-Cav-**13. S&M-Mad. Bom.** Inf-**4/6. GR-2/4. 10.** AUS-**LH-6. 9.** Inf-**3. 5. 14. 16. 25. 27. 31. 33. 3 MG. 2 Pnr.**	

WORLD WAR II: PERSIA
Medals awarded: British War Medal 1939–45. 1939–45. Star.

Dates	Battle	Participants	
26 Aug 1941	**Qasr Sheikh**	IND-Cav-**13.**	
25 Aug 1941	**Ahwaz 1941**	IND-Cav-**13.**	
25–28 Jul 1941	**Persia 1941**	IND-Cav-**13.**	

WORLD WAR II: NORTH AFRICA (WESTERN DESERT)
Medals awarded: British War Medal 1939–45. 1939–45 Star. Africa Star with clasps for 1st and 8th Army.

Dates	Battle	Participants	
12 Jun–12 Sep 1940	**Egyptian Frontier 1940**	**7 H. 8 H. 11 H.** Inf-**CG. 60. RB.**	
13–17 Sep 1940	**Withdrawal to Matruh**	**11 H.** Inf-*CG.*	
19 Nov 1940	**Bir Enba**	**11 H.**	

Dates	**Honoured** or *Non-Honoured* Battle	**Honour awarded** to or *Participants in* Battle	Remarks
8–11 Dec 1940	**Sidi Barrani**	**3 H. 8 H. 11 H. RTR.** Inf-**CG. 2. 5. 7. 17. 22. 38. 60. 79. 91.** IND-Inf-**4/6.**	
11 Dec 1940	**Buq Buq**	**3 H. 8 H. 11 H.**	
3–5 Jan 1941	**Bardia 1941**	**11 H.** AUS-**LH-6.** Inf-**1. 2. 3. 5. 6. 7. 8. 11.**	
21–22 Jan 1941	**Capture of Tobruk**	**11 H.** Inf-**22.** AUS.-**LH-6.** Inf-**1. 2. 3. 4. 5. 6. 7. 8. 11.**	
27–30 Jan 1941	**Derna**	AUS-**LH-6.** Inf-**4. 5. 8. 11.**	
5–8 Feb 1941	**Beda Fomm**	**1 DG. 3 H. 7 H. 11 H. RTR.** Inf-**RB.**	
19–21 Mar 1941	**Giarabub**	AUS-**LH-6.** Inf-**9.**	
31 Mar 1941	**Mersa el Brega**	Inf-**RB. LR-17.**	
2 Apr 1941	**Agedabia**	Inf-**RB. LR-17.**	
4 Apr 1941	**Er Regima**	AUS-Inf-**13.**	
6–8 Apr 1941	**El Mechili**	IND-Cav-**2. 11. 18.**	
7 Apr 1941	**Derna Aerodrome**	Inf-**60. RB. LR-17.**	
15–27 May 1941	**Halfaya 1941**	**11 H.** Inf-**CG. SG. 68.** IND-Cav-**11.**	Indian Award to 11 Cav as Halfaya Pass 1941.
15–17 Jun 1941	**Sidi Suleiman**	**3 H. 11 H. RTR.** Inf-**SG. 3.** Inf-*79.* IND-Inf-**Guards. 2/5.** IND-Inf-*1/6.*	
8 Apr–10 Dec 1941	**Defence of Tobruk**	**1 DG.** Inf-**5.** IND-Cav-**18.** AUS-Inf-**9. 10. 12. 13. 15. 17. 23. 24. 28. 32. 43. 48. 1 Pnr.**	
13–14 Apr 1941	**El Adem Road**	AUS-Inf-**13. 15. 17. 48.**	
30 Apr–4 May 1941	**The Salient 1941**	AUS-Inf-**9. 10. 12. 15. 23. 24. 48. 1 Pnr.**	
18 Nov–10 Dec 1941	**Tobruk 1941**	**1 DG. 11 H. RTR.** Yeo-**11. 24. 47.** Inf-**CG. SG. 2. 4. 5. 16. 17. 34. 42. 44. 60. 65. 68. 79. RB. LR-17. SAS.** IND-Inf-**2/5.** AUS-Inf-**13.** NZ-**NZ Scot.** Inf-**1. 3. 4. 5. 6. 7. 8. 9. 11. 12. 15. 16. 17. 27. 28 MG.**	
19 Nov 1941	**Gubi I**	**11 H.** Yeo-**24. 47.**	
19–21 Nov 1941	**Gabr Saleh**	**11 H.** Yeo-**47.**	
19–23 Nov 1941	**Sidi Rezegh 1941**	**7 H. 8 H. 11 H. RTR.** Yeo-**24. 47.** Inf-**60. RB.** NZ-Inf-**1. 3. 4. 5. 6. 7. 8. 9. 11. 12. 15. 16. 17.** SA-**MR-1.** Inf-**2. 8. RB. RPS. Irish.** SA-*4 AC Regt. 3 Recce Bn.*	Also **Sidi Rezegh 1941 Battery.**
21–23 Nov 1941	**Tobruk Sortie 1941**	**1 DG.** Inf-**2. 4. 16. 42. 65.**	
21–30 Nov 1941	**Sidi Aziez**	NZ-**NZ Scot.** Inf-**1. 4. 5. 7. 8. 9. 11. 12. 17. 27. 28.**	
22 Nov–2 Dec 1941	**Omars**	Inf-**35.** IND-Inf-**4/11.** NZ-Inf-**3. 6. 15. 16.**	

Dates	**Honoured** or *Non-Honoured* Battle	**Honour awarded** to or *Participants in* Battle	Remarks
24–25 Nov 1941	**Taieb el Essom**	**11 H.** SA-*MR-1.* Inf-*2. 8. 4 AC Regt.*	
25 Nov–1 Dec 1941	**Belhamed**	**RTR.** Inf-**5. 16. 44.** AUS-Inf-**13.** NZ-Inf-**1. 3. 4. 5. 6. 7. 8. 9. 11. 12. 15. 16. 17.**	
30 Nov 1941	*Bir Sciafsciuf* (SA)	SA-*MR-1.* Inf-*2.*	
3 Dec 1941	**Zemla**	NZ-**NZ Scot.** Inf-**5. 7. 9. 11. 17. 28.**	
4–6 Dec 1941	**Gubi II**	**11 H.** Inf-**79.** IND-Inf-**2/5.** SA-*MR-1.* Inf-*2. 8.* IND-Inf-*1/6.*	
7–10 Dec 1941	**Relief of Tobruk 1941**	**1 DG. 8 H. 11 H.** Inf-**68.** IND-Cav-**21.**	
9 Dec 1941	**Marsa Belafarit** (SA)	SA-**MR-5.**	
12–17 Dec 1941	*Halfaya* (SA)	SA-*MR-3. 4.* Inf-*1. 5. 6. 8. MR. SSB. 7 Recce Bn. SAP.*	
14–16 Dec 1941	**Alem Hamza**	Inf-**3.** IND-Inf-**4/6.** NZ-Inf-**1. 4. 5. 7. 8. 9. 11. 12. 17. 28.** IND-Inf-*3/1.*	
15 Dec 1941–1 Feb 1942	*Agedabia* (SA)	SA-*6 AC Regt. Recce Bns-3. 7.*	
27–30 Dec 1941	**Chor es Sufan**	**12 L.** Yeo-**24. 47.** Inf-**RB. LR-17.**	
31 Dec 1941–2 Jan 1942	**Bardia 1942**	NZ-**NZ Scot.** SA-**MR-5.** Inf-**1. 5. 11. MR.** SA-Inf-*SAP. 7 Recce.*	
11–12 Jan 1942	**Clayden's Trench (Salum)**	SA-Inf-**8.** SA-*SAP.*	This battle is known as *Sollum* by the South Africans.
23 Jan 1942	**Saunnu**	**9 L. 10 H. 11 H.** Inf-**RB.**	
25 Jan 1942	**Msus**	**2 DG. 1 D. 11 H.** Inf-**CG.**	
27–29 Jan 1942	**Benghazi**	Inf-**35. 41.**	
29 Jan–5 Feb 1942	**Carmusa**	Inf-**79.**	
26 May–21 Jun 1942	**Gazala**	**1 DG. 2 DG. 1 D. 4 H. 8 H. 9 L. 10 H. RTR.** Yeo-**24. 47.** Inf-**SG. 15. 19. 22. 24. 29. 32. 45. 60. 68. 71. 79. RB. LR-12. 17.** SA-**MR-1. 3. 5.** Inf-**1. 2. 6. 8. 11. RB. MR. RPS.** SA-*AC Regts-4. 6.*	7 Fd Regt RI Arty granted Honour Title.
27 May 1942	**Point 171**	IND-Cav-**2.**	2 Fd Regt RI Arty granted Honour Title.
27 May 1942	**Retma**	Inf-**12 LR.**	
27 May 1942	**Bir el Igela**	**8 H.**	
27–31 May 1942	**Bir el Aslagh**	**2 DG. 9 L. 10 H.** Yeo-**24.**	
27 May–11 Jun 1942	**Bir Hacheim**	**1 DG.** Inf-**60. LR-12.** IND-Cav-**11.**	
28 May 1942	**Alem Hamza 1942** (SA)	SA-Inf-**2. 6. 8.**	
28 May 1942	*Commonwealth Keep* (SA)	SA-*Detachments of* Inf-*1. MR. SAP.*	

Dates	**Honoured** or *Non-Honoured* Battle	**Honour awarded** to or *Participants in* Battle	Remarks
5–6 Jun 1942	**The Cauldron**	**2 DG. RTR. Yeo-24. 47. Inf-5. 14. 71.** **IND-Inf-2/4 GR.**	
5 Jun 1942	**Point 204** (SA)	**SA-MR-1.**	
6–7 & 11–13 Jun 1942	**Knightsbridge**	**2 DG. 1 D. RTR. Inf-CG. SG. 60. RB. HAC.**	
6–18 Jun 1942	**Acroma Keep** (SA)	**SA-Inf-8.**	
7 Jun 1942	*Bir Temrad* (SA)	SA-*Detachments of MR-3. 5. Inf-1. 2. 6. 8. 11. RB.*	
11–13 Jun 1942	**Hagiag er Raml**	**Yeo-47.**	
14 Jun 1942	**Gabr el Fachri**	**Inf-68.**	
14 Jun 1942	**Via Balbia**	**2 DG. Inf-29.**	
14 Jun 1942	**Best Post**	**SA-MR-2. Inf-6.** SA-Inf-*SSB. 3 Recce.*	
15 Jun 1942	**Zt el Mrasses**	**Inf-68.** SA-*MR-3. 5. Inf-1. 6. 11. SSB. 6 AC Regt.* *3 Recce Bn.*	
17 Jun 1942	**Sidi Rezegh 1942**	**9 L.**	
20–21 Jun 1942	**Tobruk 1942**	**Inf-CG. 79.** **IND-Inf-2/5. 7 GR.** SA-*2 SA Division. One coy each of MR-1. 5. Inf-* *1. 2. 8. 11.*	
24 Jun 1942	**The Kennels**	**IND-Cav-18.**	
26–30 Jun 1942	**Mersa Matruh**	**2 DG. 8 H. Yeo-47. Inf-15. 22. 44. 68. 71.** **IND-Mad S&M. Inf-2/11. Para.** **NZ-Inf-1. 3. 4. 5. 6. 7. 8. 9. 11. 12. 15. 16. 17. 27.** **28.** SA-*AC Regts-4. 6.*	
27 Jun 1942	**Point 174**	**Inf-68.**	
27–28 Jun 1942	**Minqar Qaim**	**Yeo-47.** **NZ-Inf-1. 3. 4. 5. 6. 7. 8. 9. 11. 12. 15. 16. 17. 27.** **28.**	
28 Jun 1942	**Fuka**	**Inf-71.**	
1–27 Jun 1942	**Defence of Alamein Line**	**1 DG. 1 D. 4 H. 9 L. 11 H. RTR. Yeo-47. Inf-CG.** **SG. 14. 15. 19. 22. 44. 60. RB. LR-12. 17.** **AUS-LH-9. Inf-13. 23. 24. 28. 32. 43. 48. 2 MG.** **NZ-NZ Scot. Inf-1. 3. 4. 5. 6. 7. 8. 9. 11. 12. 15.** **16. 17. 27. 28.** **IND-Inf-3/7.**	
1–27 Jul 1942	**Alamein Defence** (SA)	**SA-MR-1. 3. 5. Inf-1. 2. 6. 8. 11. RB. MR. RPS.** SA-*AC Regts-4. 6.*	
1 Jul 1942	**Deir el Shein**	**Yeo-47. Inf-22. 44.** **IND-Inf-4/11. 2/3 GR.**	
2–4 Jul 1942	**Ruweisat**	**4 H. 9 L. Yeo-47. Inf-44. 60. RB. LR-12.**	
7 Jul 1942	**Fuka Airfield**	**Inf-60. LR-12.**	
10–11 Jul 1942	**Tel el Eisa**	**AUS-LH-9. Inf-24. 48.**	
11 Jul 1942	**Point 93**	**Yeo-47.**	
13 Jul 1942	**Alamein Box** (SA)	**SA-MR-5. Inf-1.** SA-Inf-*11.*	

Dates	**Honoured** or *Non-Honoured* Battle	**Honour awarded** to or *Participants in* Battle	Remarks
14–16 Jul 1942	**Ruweisat Ridge**	**9 L.** Yeo-**47.** Inf-**5. 44.** IND-Inf-**4/6.** AUS-**2 MG.** NZ-**NZ Scot.** Inf-**1. 3. 4. 5. 6. 7. 8. 9. 11. 12. 15. 16. 17. 27. 28.**	
15 Jul 1942	*Springbok Road (SA)*	SA-*One coy each of MR-3.* Inf-*RB. SSB.*	
17–18 Jul 1942	**Tell el Makh Khad**	AUS-**LH-9.** Inf-**28. 32. 43.**	
21–22 Jul 1942	**El Mreir**	NZ-**NZ Scot.** Inf-**1. 3. 4. 5. 6. 7. 8. 9. 11. 12. 15. 16. 17. 27. 28.**	
21–23 Jul 1942	**Sanyet el Miteirya**	AUS-**LH-9.** Inf-**28. 32. 2 MG.**	
26–27 Jul 1942	**Qattara Track**	AUS-Inf-**28.** SA-*MR-1.* Inf-*8. 11. SSB.*	
30 Aug–7 Sep 1942	**Alam el Halfa**	**1 DG. 2 D. 4 H. 8 H. 10 H. 11 H. 12 L. RTR.** Yeo-**4. 5. 22. 24. 47.** Inf-**3. 35. 50. 60. RB. CLR-5.** AUS-Inf-**15. 17.** NZ-**NZ Scot.** Inf-**1. 3. 4. 5. 6. 7. 8. 9. 11. 12. 15. 16. 17. 27. 28.** SA-*1 SA Division. AC Regts-4. 6.*	
1 Sep 1942	**West Point 23**	Yeo-**24.** AUS-**LH-9.** Inf-**15.**	
13-14 Sep 1942	**Benghazi Raid**	**SAS.**	
30 Sep 1942	**Deir el Munassib**	Inf-**2.**	
23 Oct–4 Nov 1942	**El Alamein**	**LG. RHG. 2 DG. 1 D. 2 D. 3 H. 4 H. 8 H. 9 L. 10 H. 11 H. 12 L. RTR.** Yeo-**1. 2. 4. 5. 9. 22. 47.** Inf-**2. 3. 5. 15. 19. 22. 35. 42. 44. 45. 50. 57. 60. 68. 72. 75. 79. 91. RB. HAC. CLR-5. LR-16.** IND-Inf-**4/6. 4/7. 1/2 GR.** AUS-**LH-9.** Inf-**13. 15. 17. 23. 24. 28. 32. 43. 48. 2 MG. 3 Pnr.** NZ-**NZ Scot.** Inf-**1. 3. 4. 5. 6. 7. 8. 9. 11. 12. 15. 16. 17. 27. 28.** SA-**MR-1. 3. 5.** Inf.**1. 2. 6. 8. 11. RB. MR. RPS.** SA-*AC Regts-4. 6.*	
10–11 Nov 1942	**Capture of Halfaya Pass 1942**	Inf-**60.** NZ-Inf-**3. 6. 15. 16.**	
13–17 Nov 1942	**El Agheila**	**1 DG. 1 D. 2 D.** Yeo-**4. 5.** Inf-**3.** NZ-**NZ Scot.** Inf-**1. 3. 4. 5. 6. 7. 8. 9. 11. 12. 15. 16. 17.**	
17–18 Dec 1942	**Nofilia**	**2 D.** Inf-**60.** NZ-**NZ Scot.** Inf-**1. 3. 4. 5. 6. 7. 8. 9. 11. 12. 15. 16. 17. 28.**	
15–23 Jan 1943	**Advance on Tripoli**	**1 DG. 1 D. 2 D. 11 H. 12 L.** Yeo-**4. 5.** Inf-**2. 3. 5. 42. 57. 72. 75.** NZ-**NZ Scot.**	
6 Mar 1943	**Medenine**	Inf-**CG. SG. 2. 5. 42. 91.** NZ-**NZ Scot.** Inf.**1. 3. 4. 6. 8. 12. 15. 16. 28.**	
6 Mar 1943	**Zemlet el Lebene**	Inf-**42.**	
6 Mar 1943	**Tadjera Khir**	Inf-**SG.**	
16–23 Mar 1943	**Mareth**	**RTR.** Inf-**GG. CG. 15. 19. 22. 42. 57. 68. 72. 75. 79.** IND-Inf-**1/2 GR.**	

Dates	Honoured or *Non-Honoured* Battle	Honour awarded to or *Participants in* Battle	Remarks
16–17 Mar 1943	**Wadi Zeuss East**	Inf-**22.**	
20–23 Mar 1943	**Wadi Zigzaou**	Inf-**15. 22. 72. 79.**	
21–30 Mar 1943	**Tebaga Gap**	**1 DG. 2 DG. 9 L. 12 L.** Yeo-**4. 5. 9.** Inf-**3. 60. RB. CLR-5.** NZ-**NZ Scot.** Inf-**1. 3. 4. 5. 6. 7. 8. 9. 11. 12. 15. 16. 17. 27. 28.**	
21–22 Mar 1943	**Point 201 (Roman Wall)**	**1 DG.** Yeo-**4. 5.** NZ-**NZ Scot.** Inf-**1. 4. 5. 7. 8. 11. 12. 17.**	
27–29 Mar 1943	**El Hamma**	**1 DG. 2 DG. 9 L. 10 H. 12 L.** Yeo-**4. 5. 9.** Inf-**3. HAC.** NZ-**NZ Scot.** Inf-**1. 3. 4. 5. 6. 7. 8. 9. 11. 12. 15. 16. 17. 27. 28.**	
25–28 Mar 1943	**Matmata Hills**	Inf-**44.** IND-Inf-**4/6.**	
6–7 Apr 1943	**Akarit**	**1 DG. 12 L. RTR.** Yeo-**5. 47.** Inf-**3. 15. 19. 22. 35. 42. 44. 57. 72. 79. 91.** IND-Inf-**4/6. MG/6. 1/2 GR.**	
6 Apr 1943	**Djebel el Meida**	Inf-**35.** IND-Inf-**GR-1/2. 1/9.**	
6–7 Apr 1943	**Wadi Akarit East**	Inf-**22. 42.**	
6–7 Apr 1943	**Djebel Roumana**	Yeo-**47.** Inf-**42. 57. 72. 79.**	
7 Apr 1943	**Sebkret en Noual**	Yeo-**5.**	
8 Apr 1943	**Chebket en Nouiges**	Yeo-**4.**	
9 Apr 1943	**Djebel el Telil**	Yeo-**5.**	
19–29 Apr 1943	**Enfidaville**	**11 H.** Yeo-**4. 5.** Inf-**22. 43. 44.** IND-Inf-**1/2 GR.** NZ-**NZ Scot.** Inf-**1. 3. 4. 5. 6. 7. 8. 9. 11. 12. 15. 16. 17. 27. 28.**	
20–21 Apr 1943	**Takrouna**	Yeo-**4. 5.** NZ-Inf-**1. 3. 4. 5. 6. 7. 8. 9. 11. 12. 15. 16. 17. 27. 28.**	
20 Apr 1943	**Djebel Garci**	Inf-**44.** IND-Inf-**4/6. 1/9 GR.**	
25–29 Apr 1943	**Djebel Terhouna**	NZ-Inf-**1. 4. 8. 12.**	
25–29 Apr 1943	**Djebel es Srafi**	NZ-Inf-**1. 4. 8. 12.**	
6–9 May 1943	**Djebibina**	NZ-**NZ Scot.** Inf-**1. 3. 4. 6. 8. 12. 15. 16. 28.**	
8–9 May 1943	**Djebel Tebaga**	Inf-**7.**	

WORLD WAR II: NORTH AFRICA (1st ARMY OPERATIONS)

Dates	Honoured or *Non-Honoured* Battle	Honour awarded to or *Participants in* Battle	Remarks
17 Nov 1942	**Djebel Abiod**	Inf-**50.**	
24 Nov 1942	**Soudia**	**Para.**	
25–26 Nov 1942	**Medjez el Bab**	Yeo-**22.** Inf-**20. RB.**	
27 Nov 1942	**Tebourba**	Inf-**31.**	
28–29 Nov 1942	**Djedeida**	Inf-**48.**	
28–30 Nov 1942	**Djebel Azzag 1942**	Inf-**50. 91.**	
29 Nov–3 Dec 1942	**Oudna**	**Para.**	

Dates	**Honoured** or *Non-Honoured* Battle	**Honour awarded** to or *Participants in* Battle	Remarks
1–10 Dec 1942	**Tebourba Gap**	**17/21 L.** Yeo-**22.** Inf-**37.**	
23–25 Dec 1942	**Longstop Hill 1942**	Inf-**CG.**	
5–7 Jan 1943	**Djebel Azzag 1943**	Inf-**3. Para.**	
13 Jan 1943	**Two Tree Hill**	Inf-**27.**	
18–25 Jan 1943	**Bou Arada**	**17/21 L.** Yeo-**22. 36.** Inf-**27. 87. LR-18.**	
31 Jan 1943	**Robaa Valley**	Inf-**3.**	
3–4 Feb 1943	**Djebel Alliliga**	**Para.**	
14–25 Feb 1943	**Kasserine**	**16/5 L. 17/21 L.** Yeo-**22. 36.** Inf-**RB. LR-17.**	
19–22 Feb 1943	**Sbiba**	Inf-**CG. HAC.**	
20–22 Feb 1943	**Thala**	**17/21 L.** Yeo-**36.** Inf-**RB. HAC. LR-17.**	
26 Feb 1943	**El Hadjeba**	Inf-**LR-18. Para.**	
26 Feb 1943	**Djebel Djaffa**	Inf-**48.**	
26 Feb 1943	**Sidi Nsir**	Inf-**37.**	
26–27 Feb 1943	**Fort McGregor**	Inf-**31.**	
26–28 Feb 1943	**Stuka Farm**	Inf-**87. LR-18.**	
26 Feb–1 Mar 1943	**Steamroller Farm**	Yeo-**22.** Inf-**CG. Cdos.**	
27–28 Feb 1943	**Hunt's Gap**	Yeo-**NIH.** Inf-**37.**	
28 Feb–2 Mar 1943	**Montagne Farm**	Inf-**17. 37.**	
28 Feb–4 Mar 1943	**Kef Ouiba Pass**	Inf-**91.**	
2 Mar 1943	**Djebel Guerba**	Inf-**45.**	
4 Mar 1943	**Sedjenane I**	Yeo-**NIH.** Inf-**10. 68. Cdos.**	
5–15 Mar 1943	**Tamera**	Yeo-**NIH.** Inf-**45. Para.**	
12–31 Mar 1943	**Maknassy**	Yeo-**22.**	
20–24 Mar 1943	**Djebel Dahra**	**Para.**	
28 Mar 1943	**Djebel Choucha**	**Cdos.**	
28 Mar 1943	**Kef el Debna**	**Para.**	
30–31 Mar 1943	**Mine de Sedjenane**	Inf-**10. 51. 65. 91.**	
7–11 Apr 1943	**Fondouk**	**16/5 L. 17/21 L. RTR.** Yeo-**22. 36.** Inf-**WG. 37. RB. LR-17.**	
8 Apr 1943	**Pichon**	Inf-**37.**	
9 Apr 1943	**Djebel el Rhorab**	Inf-**WG.**	
9 Apr 1943	**Fondouk Pass**	Inf-**RB. LR-17.**	
10 Apr 1943	**Sidi Ali**	Yeo-**36.**	
10 Apr 1943	**Kairouan**	**16/5 L.** Yeo-**22.**	
11 Apr 1943	**Bordj**	**16/5 L.** Yeo-**36.**	
7–15 Apr 1943	**Oued Zarga**	Inf-**20. 27. 31. 48. 50. 87.**	
7 Apr 1943	**Mergueb Chaouach**	Yeo-**NIH.**	
7 Apr 1943	**Djebel bel Mahdi**	Inf-**27. 87.**	

Dates	**Honoured** or *Non-Honoured* Battle	**Honour awarded** to or *Participants in* Battle	Remarks
9 Apr 1943	**Djebel bech Chekaoui**	Inf-**3.**	
10 Apr 1943	**Djebel Rmel**	Yeo-**NIH.**	
14–15 Apr 1943	**Djebel Ang**	Inf-**31. 50. 87.**	
14–25 Apr 1943	**Djebel Tanngoucha**	Inf-**27. 48. 87.**	
15–25 Apr 1943	**Heidous**	Inf-**3. LR-17.**	
21 Apr 1943	**Banana Ridge**	Inf-**33. 47.**	
21 Apr 1943	**Djebel Kesskiss**	Inf-**47. 64.**	
21–22 Apr 1943	**Djebel Djaffa Pass**	Inf-**31.**	
22–26 Apr 1943	**El Kourzia**	**2 DG. 9 L. 10 H. 12 L. 17/21 L. RTR.** Yeo-**9. 22.** Inf-**37. 68. RB. LR-17.**	
22 Apr 1943	**Ber Rabal**	Inf-**37.**	
22 Apr 1943	**Argoub Sellah**	Inf-**10. 51**	
23–30 Apr 1943	**Medjez Plain**	**RTR.** Inf-**GG. SG. IG. 3. 31. 32. 33. 42. 45. 47. 50. 64. 75. 91.**	Participated and gained individual Honours – **2 D. 10 H. 12 L. 16/5 L.** Yeo-**36. NIH.** Inf-**7. 48. 53. 60. 65. RB.**
23 Apr 1943	**Grich el Oued**	Inf-**SG.**	
23–24 Apr 1943	**Gueriat el Atach Ridge**	Inf-**33. 47. 53. 64.**	
23–26 Apr 1943	**Longstop Hill 1943**	Yeo-**NIH.** Inf-**3. 31. 50. 91.**	
24 Apr 1943	**Peters Corner**	Inf-**7.**	
25–26 Apr 1943	**Si Mediene**	Inf-**42.**	
27–28 Apr 1943	**Djebel bou Aoukaz 1943, I**	Inf-**SG. IG. 47.**	
27–30 Apr 1943	**Si Abdallah**	Inf-**32. 50.**	
28–30 Apr 1943	**Gab Gab Gap**	Inf-**47. 64.**	
28–30 Apr 1943	**Sidi Ahmed**	Inf-**48.**	
25–30 Apr 1943	**Djebel Kournine**	**2 DG. 10 H. 12 L. 16/5 L.** Yeo-**36.** Inf-**65. RB.**	
30 Apr 1943	**Argoub el Megas**	Inf-**60.**	

WORLD WAR II: NORTH AFRICA (1st & 8th ARMY OPERATIONS)

Dates	**Honoured** or *Non-Honoured* Battle	**Honour awarded** to or *Participants in* Battle	Remarks
5–12 May 1943	**Tunis**	**1 DG. 2 DG. 9 L. 10 H. 11 H. 12 L. 16/5 L. 17/21 L. RTR.** Yeo-**9. 22. 36. 47. NIH.** Inf-**CG. WG. 2. 16. 31. 33. 35. 42. 44. 45. 50. 53. 60. RB. HAC. CLR-5. LR-17.** IND-Inf-**1/2 GR.**	
5–6 May 1943	**Djebel bou Aoukaz 1943, II**	Inf-**33. 53.**	
6 May 1943	**Montarnaud**	Inf-**31.**	
6 May 1943	**Ragoubet Souissi**	Inf-**44.** IND-Inf-**1/9 GR.**	
8–9 May 1943	**Hammam Lif**	**17/21 L.** Yeo-**36.** Inf-**CG. WG. RB. LR-17.**	
8–11 May 1943	**Creteville Pass**	**2 DG. 9 L. 12 L.**	

Dates	Honoured or Non-Honoured Battle	Honour awarded to or Participants in Battle	Remarks
10 May 1943	**Gromballa**	**16/5 L.**	
11 May 1943	**Bou Ficha**	**16/5 L.** Yeo-**36.**	
12 Jun 1940– 12 May 1943	**North Africa 1940–43**	**LG. RHG. 1 DG. 2 DG. 1 D. 2 D. 3 H. 4 H. 7 H. 8 H. 9 L. 10 H. 11 H. 12 L. 16/5 L. 17/21 L. RTR.** Yeo-**1. 2. 4. 5. 9. 11. 22. 24. 36. 47. NIH.** Inf-**GG. CG. SG. IG. WG. 2. 3. 4. 5. 7. 10. 14. 15. 16. 17. 19. 20. 22. 24. 27. 29. 31. 32. 33. 35. 37. 38. 41. 42. 43. 44. 45. 47. 48. 50. 51. 53. 57. 60. 64. 65. 68. 71. 72. 75. 79. 87. 91. RB. HAC. CLR-5. LR-16. 17. 18. Para. SAS. Cdos.** IND-Cav-**2. 11. 17. 18. 21. S&M-Ben. Mad. Bom.** Inf-**Gds. 9/4. 1/5. 2/5. 3/5. 4/6. 17/6. MG/6. 3/7. 4/7. 3/8. 3/9. 2/11. 4/11. 3/18. GR-1/2. 2/3. 2/4. 2/7. 2/8. 1/9. Para.** AUS-**LH-6. 7. 9.** Inf-**1. 2. 3. 4. 5. 6. 7. 8. 9. 10. 11. 12. 13. 14. 15. 16. 17. 23. 24. 25. 27. 28. 32. 33. 43. 48. 2 MG. 1 Pnr. 3 Pnr.** NZ-**NZ Scot.** Inf-**1. 3. 4. 5. 6. 7. 8. 9. 11. 12. 15. 16. 17. 27. 28.**	
1941–3	**Western Desert 1941–3**	SA-**MR-1. 3. 5.** Inf-**1. 2. 5. 6. 8. 11. RB. MR. RPS. Irish.** SA-Inf-*SSB. SAP. AC Regts-4. 6. Recce Bns-3. 7.*	
1942	**Libya & Egypt 1942**	IND-Cav-**13.**	Honour awarded by Pakistan.

WORLD WAR II: SICILY
Medals awarded: British War Medal 1939–45. 1939–45 Star. Italy Star.

Dates	Honoured or Non-Honoured Battle	Honour awarded to or Participants in Battle	Remarks
9–12 Jul 1943	**Landing in Sicily**	Yeo-**47.** Inf-**11. 19. 21. 22. 26. 27. 34. 37. 38. 39. 42. 48. 65. 68. 71. 72. 75. 91. GPR. SAS. Cdos.** CDN-Inf-**RCR. PPCLI. R22R. 48. 49. 69. 72. 73. 86. 105. Edmonton.**	
11–13 Jul 1943	**Solarino**	Inf-**27. 62. 68.**	
11–14 Jul 1943	**Vizzini**	Inf-**42.**	
12–13 Jul 1943	**Augusta**	Inf-**72.**	
13–15 Jul 1943	**Francofonte**	Inf-**57. 72. 79.**	
13–18 Jul 1943	**Lentini**	Yeo–**47.** Inf-**19. LR-18.**	
13–18 Jul 1943	**Primosole Bridge**	**RTR.** Inf-**15. 22. 68. LR-14. Para.**	
15 Jul 1943	**Grammichele**	CDN-Inf-**49. 86.**	
16–17 Jul 1943	**Piazza Arminera**	CDN-Inf-**86. Edmonton.**	
15–20 Jul 1943	**Sferro**	Inf-**42. 57. 75.**	
17–19 Jul 1943	**Valguarnera**	CDN-Inf-**RCR. PPCLI. 48. 49. 69. 73. 86. 105.**	
18–21 Jul 1943	**Simeto Bridgehead**	Yeo-**47.** Inf-**22. 26. 27. 62. 65. LR-18.**	
18–21 Jul 1943	**Gerbini**	**RTR.** Inf-**42. 91.**	
20–22 Jul 1943	**Assoro**	CDN-Inf-**48. 49.**	
21–22 Jul 1943	**Leonforte**	CDN-Inf-**PPCLI. Edmonton.**	
24–28 Jul 1943	**Agira**	Inf-**39.** CDN-Inf-**RCR. PPCLI. 48. 49. 72. 86. 105. Edmonton.**	

Dates	Honoured or *Non-Honoured* Battle	Honour **awarded** to or *Participants in* Battle	Remarks
29 Jul–7 Aug 1943	**Adrano**	**RTR.** Inf-**20. 27. 31. 42. 48. 50. 72. 79. 87. 91. LR-18.** CDN-Cav-**4.** Inf-**RCR. R22R. 48. 49. 69. 72. 101. 105. Edmonton.**	
29–30 Jul 1943	**Catenanuova**	CDN-Inf-**R22R. 69.**	
29 Jul–3 Aug 1943	**Regalbuto**	Inf-**11. 37. 39.** CDN-Inf-**RCR. 48. 49.**	
31 Jul–3 Aug 1943	**Sferro Hills**	Inf-**42. 57. 72. 79.**	
31 Jul–3 Aug 1943	**Centuripe**	Inf-**3. 27. 31. 50. 87. 91. LR-13. 18.** CDN-Inf-**69.**	
2–6 Aug 1943	**Troina Valley**	CDN-Cav-**4.** Inf-**72. 86. Edmonton.**	
4 Aug 1943	**Salso Crossing**	Inf-**87. LR-18.**	
5 Aug 1943	**Simeto Crossing**	Inf-**27. 87. LR-18.**	
9 Aug 1943	**Monte Rivoglia**	Inf-**3. 50.**	
12–13 Aug 1943	**Malleto**	Inf-**87. LR-18.**	
2–17 Aug 1943	**Pursuit to Messina**	Inf-**27. 49. 65. LR-18. Cdos.** CDN-Inf-**34.**	
9 Jul–17 Aug 1943	**Sicily 1943**	**1 D. RTR.** Yeo-**47.** Inf-**3. 11. 15. 19. 20. 21. 22. 26. 27. 31. 37. 38. 39. 41. 42. 48. 49. 50. 51. 57. 62. 65. 68. 71. 72. 75. 79. 91. HAC. LR-13. 14. 18. Para. GPR. SAS. Cdos.** CDN-Cav-**4.** Inf-**RCR. PPCLI. R22R. 20. 25. 34. 48. 49. 67. 69. 72. 73. 86. 105. Edmonton.**	

WORLD WAR II: ITALY
Medals awarded: British War Medal 1939–45. 1939–45 Star. Italy Star.

Dates	Honoured or *Non-Honoured* Battle	Honour **awarded** to or *Participants in* Battle	Remarks
3 Sep 1943	**Landing at Reggio**	CDN-Cav-**4.** Inf-**RCR. R22R. 48. 69. 73.**	
8 Sep 1943	**Landing at Porto San Venere**	Inf-**11. 37. 39. Cdos.**	
9–22 Sep 1943	**Taranto**	**Para.**	
9–18 Sep 1943	**Salerno**	**2 D. RTR.** Inf-**GG. CG. SG. 2. 5. 7. 10. 17. 22. 37. 43. 45. 51. 65. 68. Cdos.**	
9–16 Sep 1943	**St Lucia**	Inf-**7. 22. 43.**	
9–16 Sep 1943	**Vietri Pass**	Inf-**10. 65.**	
9–17 Sep 1943	**Salerno Hills**	Inf-**37. 43. 51.**	
10–18 Sep 1943	**Battipaglia**	**2 D.** Inf-**CG. SG. 7. 22. 37.**	
19–20 Sep 1943	**Potenza**	CDN-Inf-**RCR. 69.**	
22 Sep–1 Oct 1943	**Capture of Naples**	**1 DG. 11 H.** Inf-**10. 65.**	
22–28 Sep 1943	**Cava di Tirreni**	Inf-**10. 37. 51. 65.**	
24–25 Sep 1943	**Cappezano**	Inf-**CG.**	
24–26 Sep 1943	**Monte Stella**	Inf-**2.**	
28 Sep 1943	**Scafati Bridge**	**1 DG.** Inf-**2.**	

Dates	**Honoured** or *Non-Honoured* Battle	**Honour awarded** to or *Participants in* Battle	Remarks
1–3 Oct 1943	**Motta Montecorvino**	CDN-Cav-**4.** Inf-**RCR. 49. Calgary.**	
3 Oct 1943	**Cardito**	Inf-**RB.**	
3–6 Oct 1943	**Termoli**	Yeo-**47.** Inf-**3. 20. 27. 50. 87. 91. LR-13. 18. SAS. Cdos.** CDN-Inf-**86.**	
6–7 Oct 1943	**Monte San Marco**	CDN-Inf-**72.**	
7–8 Oct 1943	**Gambatesa**	CDN-Inf-**69. 73.**	
11–14 Oct 1943	**Campobasso**	CDN-Inf-**RCR. 48. 49.**	
17–18 Oct 1943	**Baranello**	CDN-Inf-**72.**	
22–24 Oct 1943	**Colle d'Anchise**	CDN-Inf-**34. Edmonton.**	
22 Oct–5 Nov 1943	**The Trigno**	Inf-**3. 20. 27. 31. 44. 87. LR-18.**	
24–27 Oct 1943	**Torella**	CDN-Inf-**RCR. 48. 49.**	
12–25 Oct 1943	**Volturno Crossing**	**2 D. 11 H. RTR.** Yeo-**47.** Inf-**GG. CG. SG. 2. 5. 10. 22. 37. 45. 51. 65. 68.**	
22–23 Oct 1943	**Monte Maro**	Inf-**22.**	
22–23 Oct 1943	**Rocchetta e Croce**	Inf-**SG.**	
28–31 Oct 1943	**Teano**	Inf-**7. 22. 43. 68. LR-14. 18.**	
2–3 Nov 1943	**San Salvo**	Inf-**27. 50.**	
17 Nov 1943	**Perano**	NZ-**MR-2. 6. 9.**	
5 Nov–9 Dec 1943	**Monte Camino**	**1 DG.** Inf-**GG. CG. SG. 2. 5. 7. 22. 43. 45. 49. 65. 68. LR-14. 18.** CDN-**1 SS.**	
5 Nov–6 Dec 1943	**Calabritto**	Inf-**CG. 17. 49. 65. LR-14. 18.**	
2–8 Dec 1943	**Monte la Difensa – Monte la Remetanea**	CDN-**1 SS.**	
19 Nov–3 Dec 1943	**The Sangro**	**RTR.** Yeo-**47.** Inf-**3. 7. 20. 21. 22. 27. 31. 44. 48. 50. 60. 87. 91. LR-13. 18.** IND-Cav-**6.** Inf-**1/5. 5/5. 1/5 GR.** CDN-Inf-**R22R. 67. 69.** NZ-**MR-2. 3. 4. 6. 9. 11. NZ Scot.** Inf-**1. 3. 4. 5. 6. 7. 8. 9. 11. 12. 15. 16. 17. 27. 28.**	
23–24 Nov 1943	**Castel di Sangro**	CDN-Inf-**69.**	
27–29 Nov 1943	**Mozzagrogna**	Inf-**7.**	
30 Nov 1943	**Fossacesia**	Yeo-**47.** Inf-**87. LR–18.**	
1–2 Dec 1943	**Castel Frentano**	NZ-**MR-2. 3. 4. 6. 9. 11. NZ Scot.** Inf-**1. 3. 4. 5. 6. 7. 8. 9. 11. 12. 15. 16. 17. 27. 28.**	
30 Nov–1 Dec 1943	**Romagnoli**	Inf-**50.**	
3–24 Dec 1943	**Orsogna**	**Para.** NZ-**MR-1. 2. 3. 4. 5. 6. 9. 10. 11. NZ Scot.** Inf-**1. 3. 4. 5. 6. 7. 8. 9. 11. 12. 15. 16. 17. 27. 28.**	
5–7 Dec 1943	**The Moro**	CDN-Inf-**PPCLI. 49. 72.**	

Dates	**Honoured** or *Non-Honoured* Battle	**Honour awarded** to or *Participants in* Battle	Remarks
5–13 Dec 1943	**Moro Bridge** or **Impossible Bridge**	Inf-**50.**	
8–9 Dec 1943	**San Leonardo**	CDN-Inf-**RCR. 48. 49. 72. Calgary.**	
10–19 Dec 1943	**The Gully**	CDN-Inf-**RCR. PPCLI. 34. 48. 49. 67. 69. 72. 86. 105. Calgary. Edmonton.**	
14–15 Dec 1943	**Casa Berardi**	CDN-Inf-**R22R. 34.**	
13–14 Dec 1943	**Caldari**	Inf-**7.** IND-Inf-**1/5 GR.**	
20–29 Dec 1943	**Ortona**	CDN-Inf-**RCR. 34. 48. 49. 72. 86. 105. Edmonton.**	
22–28 Dec 1943	**Villa Grande**	Inf-**44. 50.**	
31 Dec 1943	**S Nicola – S Tommaso**	CDN-Inf-**48.**	
29 Dec 1943–4 Jan 1944	**Point 59** or **Torre Mucchia**	CDN-Inf-**R22R. 34. 67.**	
4–9 Jan 1944	**Colle Cedro**	Inf-**65.**	
17–31 Jan 1944	**Garigliano Crossing**	**1 DG. RTR.** Inf-**CG. 2. 5. 7. 10. 21. 22. 26. 27. 37. 43. 48. 49. 51. 62. 65. 72. LR-14. 18.**	
17–25 Jan 1944	**Minturno**	Inf-**19. 21. 22. 27. 51. 62. 65.**	
18–30 Jan 1944	**Damiano**	Inf-**2. 7. 22. 37. 43. 49. LR-14. 18.**	
26–30 Jan 1944	**Monte Tuga**	Inf-**10. 51. 65. 68.**	
2–20 Feb 1944	**Monte Ornito**	Inf-**CG. WG. 37. Cdos.**	
7–9 Feb 1944	**Cerasola**	Inf-**37.**	
20 Jan–25 Mar 1944	**Cassino I**	Inf-**3. 31. 35. 44. 50. 79.** IND-**Mad S&M.** Inf-**MG/6. GR-1/2. 2/7. 1/9.** NZ-**MR-1. 2. 5. 6. 9. 10. NZ Scot.** Inf-**1. 3. 5. 6. 7. 8. 9. 11. 12. 15. 16. 17. 27. 28.**	
15–18 Feb 1944	**Monastery Hill**	Inf-**35.** IND-Inf-**4/6. 1/2 GR.** NZ-Inf-**28.**	
15–24 Mar 1944	**Castle Hill**	Inf-**44. 50.** IND-Inf-**3/Gds. 4/6.**	
15–25 Mar 1944	**Hangman's Hill**	Inf-**44.** IND-Inf-**1/9 GR.**	
17 Mar 1944	**Cassino Railway Station**	NZ-Inf-**1. 4. 8. 12.**	
22 Jan–22 May 1944	**Anzio**	**RTR. Yeo-9.** Inf-**GG. SG. IG. 2. 3. 7. 19. 21. 22. 26. 27. 33. 43. 45. 47. 48. 49. 51. 53. 57. 62. 64. 65. 72. 75. LR-14. 18. Cdos**	
24–26 Jan 1944	**Aprilia**	Inf-**IG.**	
24–31 Jan 1944	**Campoleone**	Inf-**SG. 33. 45. 53.**	
7–10 Feb 1944	**Carroceto**	Inf-**SG. IG. 49. 53. 57. 64. LR-14. 18.**	

Dates	**Honoured** or *Non-Honoured* Battle	**Honour awarded** to or *Participants in* Battle	Remarks
11–18 May 1944	**Cassino II**	**16/5 L. 17/21 L.** Yeo-**22. 36.** Inf-**5. 7. 8. 13. 16. 20. 27. 31. 32. 37. 42. 48. 50. 87. 91. RB. HAC.** LR-**13. 17. 18.** IND-**Ben S&M.** Inf-**1/5 GR.** CDN-Inf-**RCR. R22R. 34. 48. 49. 67. 69. 86. 105. Calgary.** NZ-**MR-2. 6. 9.** SA-**MR-1. 5.** Inf-**1. 4. 6. 13. DLR. WR.**	
11–18 May 1944	**Gustav Line**	CDN-Inf-**RCR. R22R. 34. 43. 47. 52. 67. 69. 86. 105. Calgary.** NZ-**MR-2. 6. 9.**	
13 May 1944	**St Angelo in Teodice**	IND-Inf-**1/5 GR.** CDN-Inf-**34.**	
14 May 1944	**Massa Vertechi**	Inf-**37.**	
13–15 May 1944	**Pignataro**	CDN-Inf-**Calgary.**	
15 May 1944	**Massa Tambourini**	Inf-**27.**	
16 May 1944	**Casa Sinagogga**	Inf-**LR-18.**	
18–30 May 1944	**Liri Valley**	**16/5 L.** Yeo-**1. 22. 36. NIH.** Inf-**WG. 3. 27. 42. 50. 87. 91. RB.** LR-**13. 17. 18.** CDN-Cav-**RCD. Strathcona. GGHG. 4. 8. 30.** Inf-**RCR. PPCLI. R22R. 28. 34. 48. 49. 66. 67. 69. 72. 76. 86. 104. 105. 110. Calgary. Edmonton.**	
18–24 May 1944	**Hitler Line**	Yeo-**NIH.** CDN-Cav-**4.** Inf-**RCR. PPCLI. R22R. 48. 49. 67. 72. 73. 86. 105. Edmonton.**	
18–24 May 1944	**Aquino**	Yeo-**22.** Inf-**3. 91.** CDN-Inf-**34. Calgary.**	
20–21 May 1944	**Piedimonte Hill.**	Inf-**50.**	
24–25 May 1944	**Melfa Crossing**	Inf-**RB.** LR-**17.** CDN-Cav-**Strathcona. GGHG. 4. 8. 30.** Inf-**28. 66. 67. 73. 76. 104. 110.**	
26–28 May 1944	**Monte Piccolo**	**16/5 L. 17/21 L.** Yeo-**36.** Inf-**CG. WG.**	
26–27 May 1944	**Ceprano**	CDN-Cav-**8.** Inf-**28. 76.**	
27–29 May 1944	**Rocca d'Arce**	IND-Inf-**1/5 GR.**	
30 May 1944	**Torrice Crossroads**	CDN-Cav-**Strathcona.**	
22 May–4 Jun 1944	**Rome**	Yeo-**9.** Inf-**3. 22. 27. 33. 47. 62. 64. 75.** **SA**-*6th Armd Division*	
22 May–4 Jun 1944	**Advance to the Tiber**	Yeo-**1.** Inf-**21. 26. 27. 45. 62. 64. 65.**	
22 May–4 Jun 1944	**The Tiber** (SA)	SA-**MR-3.** SA-*6 Armd Division.*	
3 Jun 1944	*Paliano* (SA)	SA-*Sqn each of MR-1. 3.* Inf-*3. 4. 6.*	
6–7 Jun 1944	**Monte Rotondo**	Yeo-**36.** Inf-**RB.** LR-**17.**	
9 Jun 1944	**Celleno**	SA-**MR-3. 5.** Inf-**3. 13. SSB.**	
11–13 Jun 1944	**Bagnoregio**	SA-Inf-**12.** SA-*MR-1.*	
15 Jun 1944	**Allerona**	SA-Inf-**WR. DLR.**	

Dates	**Honoured** or *Non-Honoured* Battle	**Honour awarded** to or *Participants in* Battle	Remarks
15 Jun 1944	**Ficulle**	Yeo-**2.**	
16–17 Jun 1944	**Monte Gabbione**	Inf-**48.**	
16–19 Jun 1944	**Citta Della Pieve**	**3 H.** Yeo-**1.** Inf-**50.** SA-*MR-1.* Inf-*4. 6. WR. DLR.*	
18–20 Jun 1944	**Capture of Perugia**	**1 DG. 16/5 L. 17/21 L.** Yeo-**36.** Inf-**CG. WG. RB. LR-17.**	
18–19 Jun 1944	**Ripa Ridge**	Inf-**7.** IND-Inf-**1/5 GR.**	
19–20 Jun 1944	**Monte Malbe**	Inf-**RB. CLR-5.**	
20–30 Jun 1944	**Trasimene Line**	Yeo-**1. 2.** Inf-**SG. 3. 8. 13. 16. 20. 27. 32. 37. 48. 50. 87. LR-18.** CDN-Inf-**34. 86. Calgary.**	
20–21 Jun 1944	**Sanfatucchio**	Yeo-**2.** Inf-**LR-18.** CDN-Inf-**34.**	
21–22 Jun 1944	**Chiusi** (SA)	SA-Inf-**4. 6.** SA-*MR-3. 5.* Inf-*3. 13.*	
23 Jun 1944	**Sarteano** (SA)	SA-Inf-**12.**	
26 Jun 1944	**La Foce** (SA)	SA-Inf-**12.**	
30 Jun 1944	*Sinalunga* (SA)	SA-*MR-5.* Inf-*13.*	
1 Jul 1944	**Gabbiano**	Inf-**7.**	
2–18 Jul 1944	**Ancona**	**7 H.**	
4–17 Jul 1944	**Arezzo**	**LG. RHG. 1 DG. 16/5 L.** Yeo-**22. 36.** Inf-**CG. WG. 13. 50. 60. RB. CLR-5. LR-17.** CDN-Inf-**34. 86. Calgary.** NZ-Inf-**1. 3. 4. 5. 6. 7. 8. 9. 11. 12. 15. 16. 17.**	
5 Jul 1944	**Tuori**	Inf-**8.**	
14 Jul 1944	**Monte Lignano**	NZ-Inf-**5. 7. 9. 11. 17.**	
5–7 Jul 1944	**Montone**	Inf-**4.**	
10 Jul 1944	**Trestina**	IND-Inf-**2/4 GR.**	
8–14 Jul 1944	**Monte della Gorgace**	IND-Inf-**3/5. 2/3 GR. Para.**	
13–18 Jul 1944	**Monte Cedrone**	Yeo-**1.** IND-Inf-**2/4 GR.**	
16–22 Jul 1944	**Citta di Castello**	**3 H.** Yeo-**1.** Inf-**4.** IND-Inf-**3/18.**	
19–20 Jul 1944	**Pian di Maggio**	IND-Inf-**1/2 GR.**	
17 Jul–10 Aug 1944	**Advance to Florence**	**LG. RHG. 16/5 L. 17/21 L. RTR.** Yeo-**1. 2. 22. 36. NIH.** Inf-**CG. SG. WG. 7. 13. 32. 37. 42. 50. RB. LR-17.** IND-Inf-**1/5. 5/5.** CDN-Inf-**34. 86. Calgary.** NZ-**MR-1. 2. 3. 4. 5. 6. 9. 10. 11. NZ Scot.** Inf-**1. 3. 4. 5. 6. 7. 8. 9. 11. 12. 15. 16. 17. 27. 28.**	
18–20 Jul 1944	**Monte San Michele**	Inf-**SG.**	
19 Jul 1944	*Monte Majone* (SA)	SA-Inf-*One Coy of 12.*	

Dates	Honoured or Non-Honoured Battle	Honour awarded to or Participants in Battle	Remarks
21–23 Jul 1944	Monte Fili	SA-Inf-WR. DLR. SA-Inf-One Coy of 12.	
20 Jul 1944	Monte Querciabella (SA)	SA-Inf-WR. DLR.	
21–23 Jul 1944	Florence (SA)	SA-MR-1. 3. 5. Inf-1. 3. 4. 6. 12. 13. SSB.	
21–24 Jul 1944	Monte Domini	Inf-CG.	
24 Jul–2 Aug 1944	The Greve (SA)	SA-MR-1. 5. Inf-4. 6. 10. 13. DLR. SSB. SA-MR-3. Inf-3.	
27–29 Jul 1944	Cerbaia	NZ-MR-2. 6. 9. NZ Scot. Inf-1. 3. 4. 5. 6. 7. 8. 9. 11. 12. 15. 16. 17. 27.	
27–30 Jul 1944	Monte Scalari	Inf-7. 42. 50.	
28–30 Jul 1944	San Michele	NZ-MR-1. 2. 3. 4. 5. 6. 9. 10. 11. NZ Scot. Inf-1. 3. 4. 5. 6. 7. 8. 9. 11. 12. 15. 16. 17. 27. 28.	
30 Jul–4 Aug 1944	Paula Line	NZ-MR-1. 2. 3. 4. 5. 6. 9. 10. 11. NZ Scot. Inf-1. 3. 4. 5. 6. 7. 8. 9. 11. 12. 15. 16. 17. 27. 28.	
3–8 Aug 1944	Il Castello	IND-Inf-3/5. 2/3 GR. Para.	
5–8 Aug 1944	Incontro	Inf-32.	
20–28 Jul 1944	Campriano	Yeo-2. IND-Inf-2/7 GR.	
25–26 Jul 1944	Citerna	12 L.	
4–8 Aug 1944	Poggio del Grillo	Inf-79. IND-Inf-2/7 GR.	
25 Aug 1944	Fiesole	Inf-47.	
25–31 Aug 1944	Cerrone	CDN-Inf-Calgary.	
1–5 Sep 1944	Montorsoli	Inf-Herts.	
3–5 Sep 1944	Misano Ridge	CDN-Cav-RCD. Strathcona. GGHG. 8. Inf-RCR. 42. 48. 49. 66. 104.	
25 Aug–22 Sep 1944	Gothic Line	LG. RHG. 1 DG. 12 L. 27 L. RTR. Yeo-NIH. Inf-GG. WG. 1. 2. 7. 10. 17. 22. 35. 37. 45. 47. 53. 57. 63. 64. 65. 68. 79. RB. Herts. CLR-5. LR-14. IND-Cav-21. Inf-1/5. 5/5. MG/6. 4/11. GR-1/2. 2/8. CDN-Cav-RCD. Strathcona. GGHG. 4. 8. 30. Inf-RCR. PPCLI. R22R. 28. 48. 49. 66. 67. 69. 72. 76. 104. 105. 110. Edmonton. SA-MR-1. 3. 5. Inf-1. 3. 6. 12. 13. WR. DLR. SSB.	
27–28 Aug 1944	Monteciccardo	CDN-Inf-Edmonton.	
29–31 Aug 1944	Monte Calvo	IND-Inf-4/11.	
30–31 Aug 1944	Montecchio	CND-Cav-8. Inf-28. 76. 110.	
31 Aug 1944	Point 204 or Pozzo Alto Ridge	CDN-Cav-Strathcona. 30. Inf-28. 72.	
1 Sep 1944	Monte Luro	CDN-Inf Edmonton.	
1 Sep 1944	Borgo Santa Maria	CDN-Inf-R22R.	
1–2 Sep 1944	Tomba di Pesaro	CDN-Cav-4. 8.	

Dates	Honoured or Non-Honoured Battle	Honour awarded to or Participants in Battle	Remarks
30 Aug–2 Sep 1944	**Monte Gridolfo**	Inf-**10. 17. 37. 63.**	
1–4 Sep 1944	**Tavoleto**	Inf-**79.** IND-Inf-**GR-2/7. 1/9.**	
28 Aug 1944	**Montegaudio**	Inf-**37.**	
6 Sep 1944	**Pratelle Pass**	IND-**Para.**	
12–15 Sep 1944	**Alpe di Vitigliano**	IND-Inf-**1/5.**	
17–18 Sep 1944	**Femmina Morta**	IND-Inf-**1/5 GR.**	
15–18 Sep 1944	**Monte Porro del Bagno**	SA-**MR-5.** Inf-**13.** SA-*One Sqn SSB.*	Should be called Monte Pozzo del Bagno.
3–15 Sep 1944	**Coriano**	**2 DG. 4 H. 9 L. 10 H. RTR.** Yeo-**9.** Inf-**3. 7. 22. 37. 41. 43. 45. 60. 63. 65. 79. HAC. LR-14. 18.** IND-Inf-**2/11. GR-1/2. 2/6. 2/8. 2/10.** CDN-Cav-**Strathcona. 8.** Inf-**28. 42. 66. 76. 104. 110.**	
3–4 Sep 1944	**San Clemente**	**4 H.** Inf-**63. 65.**	
3–5 Sep 1944	**Poggio San Giovanni**	IND-Inf-**2/11. 1/2 GR.**	
5–8 Sep 1944	**Pian di Castello**	Inf-**35. 79.**	
5–9 Sep 1944	**Croce**	Inf-**7. 41. LR-14. 18.**	
5–15 Sep 1944	**Gemmano Ridge**	Inf-**2. 10. 22. 43. 51. 63. 65. 68.**	
14–21 Sep 1944	**Rimini Line**	**2 DG. 4 H. 7 H. RTR.** Yeo-**9.** Inf-**8. 22. 32. 37. 41. 42. 50. 63. 65. 79. LR-14. 18.** CDN-Inf-**RCR. PPCLI. R22R. 48. 49. 67. 69. 72. 105. Edmonton.**	
14 Sep 1944	**Monte Colombo**	Inf-**17.**	
14 Sep 1944	**Casa Fabbri Ridge**	Inf-**2. 42.**	
14–17 Sep 1944	**Montescudo**	Inf-**37. 63.**	
14–18 Sep 1944	**San Martino – San Lorenzo**	CDN-Inf-**RCR. R22R. 48. 69. 72.**	
16–18 Sep 1944	**Frisoni**	Inf-**37.**	
17–20 Sep 1944	**San Marino**	Inf-**10. 65. 79.** IND-Inf-**4/11. 1/9 GR.**	
17–21 Sep 1944	**Ceriano Ridge**	**2 DG.** Yeo-**9.** Inf-**22. 41. LR-14. 18.**	
18–20 Sep 1944	**San Fortunato**	CDN-Inf-**PPCLI. R22R. 49. 67. 69. 72. Edmonton.**	
22–24 Sep 1944	**Montebello – Scorticata Ridge**	Inf-**79.** IND-Inf-**2/7 GR.** IND-Inf-*3/12.*	
22–24 Sep 1944	**Santarcangelo**	Inf-**10 H.** IND-Inf-**GR-2/6. 2/8. 2/10.**	
24 Sep–1 Oct 1944	**Monte Reggiano**	Inf-**35. 79.** IND-Inf-**1/2 GR.**	
27–30 Sep 1944	**Savignano**	Inf-**22.**	
23–25 Sep 1944	**Casale**	CDN-Cav-**Strathcona. 4.** Inf-**42. 104.**	

Dates	Honoured or Non-Honoured Battle	Honour awarded to or Participants in Battle	Remarks
24–25 Sep 1944	**Rio Fontanaccia**	NZ-**MR-1. 5. 10. Inf-1. 3. 4. 5. 6. 7. 8. 9. 11. 12. 15. 16. 17.**	
21–24 Sep 1944	**Marradi**	Inf-**1. 64.**	
25–29 Sep 1944	**Monte Gamberaldi**	Inf-**1. 47. Hereford.**	
28 Sep–3 Oct 1944	**Catarelto Ridge**	Inf-**CG. SG.** SA-Inf-**12.** SA-Inf-*1.*	
30 Sep–6 Oct 1944	**Monte Vigese**	SA-**MR-1. 5. Inf-13.**	
4–5 Oct 1944	**San Martino – Sogliano**	Inf-**4.** IND-**Para.**	
6–7 Oct 1944	**Monte Farneto**	Yeo-**NIH.** IND-Inf-**2/3 GR. Para.**	
7–8 Oct 1944	**Montilgallo**	Inf-**37. 63.**	
12–15 Oct 1944	**Carpineta**	**2 DG.** Inf-**51. 65.**	
13–14 Oct 1944	**Monte Chicco**	IND-Inf-**2/6 GR.**	
21–23 Oct 1944	**Monte Cavallo**	Yeo-**NIH.** IND-Inf-**2/3 GR. Para.**	
11–15 Oct 1944	**Sant'Angelo in Salute**	CDN-Cav-**RCD. 4.** NZ-**MR-1. 2. 5. 6. 9. 10. NZ Scot.** Inf-**1. 3. 4. 6. 8. 12. 15. 16. 27. 28.**	
13–14 Oct 1944	**Bulgaria Village**	CDN-Inf-**49.**	
15–20 Oct 1944	**Cesena**	**2 DG. 10 H.** Inf-**63. 68.** CDN-Inf-**R22R. 105.**	
16–19 Oct 1944	**Pisciatello**	CDN-Inf-**RCR. Edmonton.** NZ-**MR-1. 2. 3. 4. 5. 6. 9. 10. 11. NZ Scot.** Inf-**1. 3. 4. 5. 6. 7. 8. 9. 11. 12. 15. 16. 17. 27.**	
20–23 Oct 1944	**Savio Bridgehead**	**27 L.** Inf-**7. 42. 50.** CDN-Inf-**PPCLI. 69. 72. 105. Edmonton.**	
2–12 Oct 1944	**Battaglia**	Inf-**GG. WG.**	
2–23 Oct 1944	**Monte Casalino**	Inf-**91.**	
3–17 Oct 1944	**Monte Ceco**	Inf-**20. 33. 45. 47. 53. Herts.**	
13–19 Oct 1944	**Monte la Pieve**	Inf-**48.** CDN-Inf-**86.**	
17–23 Oct 1944	**Monte Pianoereno**	Inf-**50.**	
19–24 Oct 1944	**Monte Spaduro**	Inf-**3. 20. 27. 50. 87. 91. LR-13. 18.** CDN-Inf-**86.**	
25–26 Oct 1944	**Orsara**	Inf-**RB. CLR-5.**	
7–13 Oct 1944	**Monte Stanco**	SA-**MR-1.** Inf-**1. 4. 6. WR. DLR.**	
17 Oct 1944	**Monte Pezza** (SA)	SA-**MR-1.** Inf-**1. 4. 6.** SA-Inf-**3.**	
19–23 Oct 1944	**Monte Salvaro**	SA-**MR-5.** Inf-**13. WR. DLR.** SA-*MR-1.*	
7–9 Nov 1944	**Capture of Forli**	**9 L. 12 L.** Inf-**8. 13. 31. 37. 63.**	
9–11 Nov 1944	**Casa Fortis**	Yeo-**NIH.** Inf-**7. 42. 50.**	

Dates	**Honoured** or *Non-Honoured* Battle	**Honour awarded** to or *Participants in* Battle	Remarks
20–23 Nov 1944	**Cosina Canal Crossing**	**10 H.** Inf-**13. 37. 45. 68.**	
24 Nov–1 Dec 1944	**Casa Bettini**	Yeo-**NIH.** IND-Inf-**14/8.**	
11–14 Nov 1944	**Monte San Bartolo**	IND-Inf-**1/5 GR.**	
1 Nov–12 Dec 1944	**Monte Grande**	Inf-**47. 53. 57. 87. 91. Herts. LR-18.**	
2–13 Dec 1944	**Lamone Crossing**	**2 DG. 9 L. RTR.** Yeo-**NIH.** Inf-**10. 37. 60. 63. 65.** IND-Inf-**2/6 GR.** CDN-Cav-**RCD. Strathcona. GGHG. 8. 30.** Inf-**RCR. R22R. 28. 48. 49. 66. 67. 69. 76. 104. 105. 110.**	
4–7 Dec 1944	**Pideura**	**9 L.** Inf-**37.**	
9 Dec 1944	**Defence of Lamone Bridgehead**	**2 DG. 9 L.** Inf-**4. 51. 63. 65.**	
14–15 Dec 1944	**Celle**	NZ-**MR-3. 4. 11.** Inf-**1. 4. 5. 7. 8. 9. 11. 12. 17. 27. 28.**	
14–16 Dec 1944	**Pergola Ridge**	Inf-**68.**	
19–20 Dec 1944	**Faenza Pocket**	NZ-**MR-1. 5. 10.** Inf-**1. 3. 4. 5. 6. 7. 8. 9. 11. 12. 15. 16. 17. 27.**	
3–4 Dec 1944	**Capture of Ravenna**	**27 L.** CDN-Cav-**4.**	
12–15 Dec 1944	**Naviglio Canal**	CDN-Cav-**Strathcona. 4. 30.** Inf-**PPCLI. 42. 49. 67. 72. 104. 105. Edmonton.**	
16–18 Dec 1944	**Fosso Vecchio**	CDN-Cav-**RCD.** Inf-**RCR. 48. 49. 105.**	
19–21 Dec 1944	**Fosso Munio**	CDN-Cav-**Strathcona. GGHG. 30.** Inf-**PPCLI. 28. 72. 76. 105. 110. Edmonton.**	
12–16 Dec 1944	**Tossignano**	Inf-**RB. CLR-5.**	
2–6 Jan 1945	**Conventello – Comacchio**	**4 H. 12 L.** CDN-Cav-**8. 30.** Inf-**28. 76. 110.**	
3–5 Jan 1945	**Granarolo**	CDN-Inf-**PPCLI. 72.**	
4–5 Jan 1945	**Senio Pocket**	**4 H. 10 H.** Inf-**2. LR-14.**	
23 Feb–3 Mar 1945	**Senio Floodbank**	Inf-**2. 22. LR-18.** IND-Cav-**1.** Inf-**GR-2/6. 2/10.**	
1–8 Apr 1945	**Valli di Commacchio**	**10 H.** Yeo-**NIH.** Inf-**7. 22. LR-14. 18. SAS. Cdos.**	
9–12 Apr 1945	**The Senio**	**4 H.** Yeo-**NIH.** Inf-**3. 7. 20. 50. 91. HAC.** IND-Inf-**1/5. 1/5 GR.** NZ-**MR-1. 3. 4. 5. 10. 11.** Inf-**1. 3. 4. 5. 6. 7. 8. 9. 11. 12. 15. 16. 17. 28.**	
11–12 Apr 1945	**Santerno Crossing**	**4 H.** INF-**91.** NZ-**MR-1. 3. 4. 5. 10. 11.** Inf-**1. 3. 4. 5. 6. 7. 8. 9. 11. 12. 15. 16. 17. 28.**	
10–11 Apr 1945	**Menate**	**27 L.** Inf-**2.**	
12–14 Apr 1945	**Filo**	**27 L.** Inf-**2.**	

Dates	**Honoured** or *Non-Honoured* Battle	**Honour awarded** to or *Participants in* Battle	Remarks
13–31 Apr 1945	**Argenta Gap**	2 DG. 4 H. 9 L. 10 H. 16/5 L. 17/21 L. 27 L. RTR. Yeo-22. 36. Inf-CG. SG. 2. 3. 7. 20. 27. 31. 41. 48. 50. 60. 87. 91. RB. LR-13. 14. 18. Cdos.	
20–21 Apr 1945	**Fossa Cembalina**	17/21 L. Yeo-22. Inf-RB. CLR-5.	
21 Apr 1945	**San Nicolo Canal**	Inf-87.	
14–21 Apr 1945	**Bologna**	12 L. 14/20 H. 27 L. IND-Inf-2/10 GR. NZ-MR-1. 2. 3. 4. 5. 6. 9. 10. 11. NZ Scot. Inf-1. 3. 4. 5. 6. 7. 8. 9. 11. 12. 15. 16. 17. 27. 28.	
14–16 Apr 1945	**Sillaro Crossing**	12 L. Inf-68. IND-Inf-2/10 GR. NZ-MR-1. 2. 5. 6. 9. 10. NZ Scot. Inf-1. 3. 4. 5. 6. 7. 8. 9. 11. 12. 15. 16. 17. 27.	
15–18 Apr 1945	**Monte Sole Caprara** (SA)	SA-Inf-1. 4. 6. WR. DLR.	
16 Apr 1945	**Medecina**	14/20 H. IND-Inf-2/6 GR.	
17–19 Apr 1945	**Gaiana Crossing**	27 L. IND-Inf-GR-2/6. 2/8. 2/10. NZ-MR-2. 6. 9. NZ Scot. Inf-5. 7. 9. 11. 17. 27.	
20–21 Apr 1945	**Idice Bridgehead**	12 L. IND-Inf-3/5. Para. NZ-MR-1. 3. 4. 5. 10. 11. Inf-1. 3. 4. 5. 6. 7. 8. 9. 11. 12. 15. 16. 17. 28.	
19–20 Apr 1945	**Traghetto**	16/5 L.	
19–30 Apr 1945	**Po Valley** (SA)	SA-MR-1. 3. 5. Inf-1. 3. 4. 6. 12. 13. WR. DLR. SSB.	
21 Apr 1945	**Camposanto Bridge**	SA-Inf-WR. DLR. SA-Inf-3.	
22–23 Apr 1945	*Finale* (SA)	SA–MR–5. Inf-*1. 4. 6. 13. SSB.*	
3 Sep 1943–22 Apr 1945	**Italy 1943–45**	LG. RHG. 1 DG. 2 DG. 1 D. 2 D. 3 H. 4 H. 7 H. 9 L. 10 H. 11 H. 12 L. 14/20 H. 16/5 L. 17/21 L. 27 L. RTR. Yeo-1. 2. 9. 22. 36. 47. NIH. Inf-GG. CG. SG. IG. WG. 1. 2. 3. 4. 5. 7. 8. 10. 11. 13. 16. 17. 19. 20. 21. 22. 26. 27. 31. 32. 33. 35. 37. 38. 39. 41. 42. 43. 44. 45. 47. 48. 49. 50. 51. 53. 57. 60. 62. 63. 64. 65. 68. 71. 72. 75. 79. 91. RB. HAC. Herts. CLR-5. LR-12. 13. 14. 16. 17. 18. Para. SAS. Cdos. IND-Cav-1. 21. S&M-Ben. Mad. Bom. Inf-3/Gds. 1/5. 3/5. 5/5. 4/6. 17/6. MG/6. 20/7. 14/8. 2/11. 4/11. 3/18. GR-1/2. 2/3. 2/4. 1/5. 2/6. 2/7. 2/8. 1/9. 2/10. Para. CDN-Cav-RCD. Strathcona. GGHG. 4. 8. 30. Inf-RCR. PPCLI. R22R. 20. 25. 28. 34. 42. 48. 49. 66. 67. 69. 72. 73. 76. 86. 94. 104. 105. 110. Calgary. Edmonton. 1 SS. NZ-MR-1. 2. 3. 4. 5. 6. 9. 10. 11. NZ Scot. Inf-1. 3. 4. 5. 6. 7. 8. 9. 11. 12. 15. 16. 17. 27. 28. SA-MR-1. 3. 5. Inf-1. 3. 4. 6. 12. 13. WR. DLR. SSB.	

Dates	**Honoured** or *Non-Honoured* Battle	**Honour awarded** to or *Participants in* Battle	Remarks

WORLD WAR II: GREECE 1941
Medals awarded: British War Medal 1939–45. 1939–45 Star.

Dates	Battle	Honour awarded / Participants	Remarks
10–18 Apr 1941	**Mount Olympus**	AUS-Inf-**1. 2. 3. 8. 1 MG.** NZ-**NZ Scot.** Inf-**1. 3. 4. 5. 6. 7. 8. 9. 11. 12. 15. 16. 17. 28.**	
11–13 Apr 1941	**Aliakmon Bridge**	NZ-**NZ Scot.**	
13–18 Apr 1941	**Servia Pass**	AUS-**1 MG.** NZ-Inf-**1. 3. 4. 5. 6. 7. 8. 9. 11. 12. 15. 16. 17.**	
15–16 Apr 1941	**Platamon Tunnel**	NZ-Inf-**3. 6. 15. 16.**	
15–17 Apr 1941	**Olympus Pass**	NZ-Inf-**1. 4. 5. 7. 8. 9. 11. 12. 17. 28.**	
18 Apr 1941	**Tempe Gorge**	AUS-Inf-**2. 3.** NZ-**NZ Scot.** Inf-**3. 6. 15. 16.**	
10–12 Apr 1941	**Veve**	Inf-**60. LR-12.** AUS-Inf-**4. 8.** NZ-Inf-**27.**	
13 Apr 1941	**Soter**	AUS-Inf-**4.**	
13 Apr 1941	**Proasteion**	**4 H.** Inf-**LR-12.**	
18 Apr 1941	**Elasson**	NZ-**NZ Scot.** Inf-**3. 5. 6. 7. 9. 11. 15. 16. 17.**	
22–24 Apr 1941	**Brallos Pass**	AUS-Inf-**1. 4. 11.**	
22–25 Apr 1941	**Molos**	NZ-Inf-**1. 3. 4. 5. 6. 7. 8. 9. 11. 12. 15. 16. 17.**	
26 Apr 1941	**Corinth Canal**	**4 H.**	
10–29 Apr 1941	**Greece 1941**	**4 H. RTR.** Inf-**60. LR-12.** AUS-Inf-**1. 2. 3. 4. 5. 6. 7. 8. 11. 1 MG.** NZ-**NZ Scot.** Inf-**1. 3. 4. 5. 6. 7. 8. 9. 11. 12. 15. 16. 17. 27. 28.**	

WORLD WAR II: GREECE 1944–5
Medals awarded: British War Medal 1939–45. 1939–45 Star.

Dates	Battle	Honour awarded / Participants	Remarks
2 Dec 1944– 15 Jan 1945	**Athens**	**1 DG.** Inf-**7. 8. 13. 16. 37. 42. 44. 50. 68. 71. LR-16. Para.**	
16 Sep 1944– 15 Jan 1945	**Greece 1944–45**	**1 DG.** Inf-**7. 8. 13. 16. 31. 37. 42. 44. 50. 60. 68. 71. LR-16. Para. SAS. Cdos.** IND-Cav-**21. Bom S&M.** Inf-**9/4. 4/6. MG/6. 2/11. GR-1/2. 1/9.**	

WORLD WAR II: CRETE
Medals awarded: British War Medal 1939–45. 1939–45 Star.

Dates	Battle	Honour awarded / Participants	Remarks
20 May–1 Jun 1941	**Crete**	**3 H.** Inf-**17. 41. 42. 60. 65. 91. LR-12. Cdos.** AUS-Inf-**1. 4. 7. 8. 11. 1 MG.** NZ-**NZ Scot.** Inf-**1. 3. 4. 5. 6. 7. 8. 9. 11. 12. 15. 16. 17. 27. 28.**	
20–23 May 1941	**Maleme**	NZ-Inf-**1. 3. 4. 5. 6. 7. 8. 9. 11. 12. 15. 16. 17. 28.**	
20–25 May 1941	**Galatas**	NZ-**NZ Scot.** Inf-**1. 3. 4. 5. 6. 7. 8. 9. 11. 12. 15. 16. 17. 27.**	
20–27 May 1941	**Canea**	Inf-**41. LR-12.** AUS-Inf-**7. 8.** NZ-**NZ Scot.** Inf-**3. 5. 6. 7. 9. 11. 15. 16. 17. 28.**	
20–29 May 1941	**Heraklion**	Inf-**17. 42. 65. 91.** AUS-Inf-**4.**	
20–30 May 1941	**Retimo**	Inf-**LR-12.** AUS-Inf-**1. 11.**	

Dates	Honoured or Non-Honoured Battle	Honour awarded to or Participants in Battle	Remarks
27 May 1941	**42nd Street**	AUS-Inf-**7. 8.** NZ-**NZ Scot.** Inf-**1. 3. 4. 5. 6. 7. 8. 9. 11. 12. 15. 16. 17. 28.**	
28 May–1 Jun 1941	**Withdrawal to Sphakia**	Inf-**41.** AUS-Inf-**7. 8.** NZ-**NZ Scot.** Inf-**1. 3. 4. 5. 6. 7. 8. 9. 11. 12. 15. 16. 17. 28.**	

WORLD WAR II: MADAGASCAR
Medals awarded: British War Medal 1939–45. 1939–45 Star.

5 May–6 Nov 1942	**Madagascar**	Inf-**21. 23. 30. 40. 48. 72. Cdos.** AF-**KAR.** SA-Inf-**4. 12. PH.**	

WORLD WAR II: MIDDLE EAST 1943–4
Medals awarded: British War Medal 1939–45. 1939–45 Star.

3–16 Oct 1943	**Cos**	Inf-**68.**	
12–16 Nov 1943	**Leros**	Inf-**3. 50. 87.**	
18 Mar–21 Nov 1944	**Adriatic**	Inf-**71. SAS. Cdos.**	
20 May 1941–21 Nov 1944	**Middle East 1941–44**	Inf-**3. 21. 23. 27. 40. 41. 42. 50. 60. 62. 65. 68. 71. 72. 91. CLR-5. LR-12. SAS.** AUS-Inf-**1. 4. 7. 8. 11. 1 MG.** NZ-**NZ Scot.** Inf-**1. 3. 4. 5. 6. 7. 8. 9. 11. 12. 15. 16. 17. 27. 28.** AF-**KAR. N Rhodesia.**	Honour covers operations not falling within land campaigns in the area separately Honoured, i.e. North Africa, Greece, Syria, Iraq, British Somaliland and Abyssinia.

WORLD WAR II: MALTA
Medals awarded: British War Medal 1939–45. 1939—45 Star.

11 Jun 1940–20 Nov 1942	**Malta 1940–42**	Inf-**3. 4. 11. 20. 22. 37. 39. 50. 63. 68. 87. Malta Regiment.**	

WORLD WAR II: MALAYA 1941–2
Medals awarded: British War Medal 1939–45. 1939—45 Star. Burma Star.

8–23 Dec 1941	**North Malaya**	Inf-**91.** IND-Cav-**3.** Inf-**4/19. 2 GR.**	
8 Dec 1941	**Kota Bharu**	IND-Inf-**3/17.**	
10–13 Dec 1941	**Jitra**	IND-Inf-**2/7. GR-2/1. 2.**	4 Mtn Bty RI Arty awarded as Honour Title.
17–23 Dec 1941	**Grik Road**	Inf-**91.**	
26 Dec 1941–10 Jan 1942	**Central Malaya**	Inf-**91.** IND-Cav-**3.** Inf-**5/2. 2 GR.**	
26–29 Dec 1941	**Ipoh**	Inf-**91.** IND-Cav-**6.** Inf-**5/2.**	
27 Dec 1941–3 Jan 1942	**Kuantan**	IND-**Bom 9&M.** Inf-**5/11. 2/18.**	
30 Dec 1941–3 Jan 1942	**Kampar**	Inf-**17. 31.** IND-**Ben S&M.** Inf-**2/7. GR-2/1. 2.**	
7 Jan 1942	**Slim River**	Inf-**91.** IND-Inf-**4/19. 2 GR.**	

Dates	Honoured or Non-Honoured Battle	Honour awarded to or Participants in Battle	Remarks
14–31 Jan 1942	Johore	Inf-9. 47. Cambs. IND-Inf-2 GR. AUS-Inf-18. 19. 20. 26. 29. 30.	
14–15 Jan 1942	Gemas	AUS-Inf-30.	
16–23 Jan 1942	The Muar	Inf-9. IND-Inf-4/7. AUS-Inf-19. 29.	
21–26 Jan 1942	Batu Pahat	Inf-9. 47. Cambs.	
24–25 Jan 1942	Niyor	IND-Inf-5/11.	
26–27 Jan 1942	Jemaluang	AUS-Inf-18.	
8–15 Feb 1942	Singapore Island	Inf-5. 9. 12. 16. 45. 47. 63. 91. Cambs. IND-Inf-13/2. 2 GR. AUS-Inf-18. 19. 20. 26. 29. 30. 4 MG. Malay Regt. Singapore Vol Corps.	
8 Dec 1941– 15 Feb 1942	Malaya 1941–42	Inf-9. 12. 16. 17. 31. 45. 47. 63. 91. Cambs. IND-Cav-3. S&M-Ben. Mad. Bom. Inf-5/2. 13/2. 7/6. 2/7. 4/7. 5/11. 3/17. 2/18. 4/19. GR-2/1. 2. 2/9. AUS-Inf-18. 19. 20. 26. 29. 30. 4 MG. Malay Regt. Singapore Vol Corps.	

WORLD WAR II: SOUTH EAST ASIA 1941–2
Medal awarded: British War Medal 1939–45. 1939–45 Star.

Dates	Honoured or Non-Honoured Battle	Honour awarded to or Participants in Battle	Remarks
8–25 Dec 1941	Hong Kong	Inf-57. Hong Kong Vol Defence Corps. IND-Inf-5/7. CDN-Inf-8. 100.	
8 Dec 1941– 9 Mar 1942	South East Asia 1941–42	Inf-1. 57. IND-Inf-5/7. CDN-Inf-8. 100.	

WORLD WAR II: BURMA
Medal awarded: British War Medal 1939–45. 1939–45 Star. Burma Star.

Dates	Honoured or Non-Honoured Battle	Honour awarded to or Participants in Battle	Remarks
16–23 Feb 1942	Sittang 1942	Inf-33. 51. IND-Inf-GR-1/3. 2/5. 1/7.	5 Mtn Bty RI Arty awarded as Honour Title.
6–7 Mar 1942	Pegu 1942	7 H. Inf-14. 26. IND-Inf-GR-1/4. 1/7.	
7–8 Mar 1942	Taukyan	Inf-28.	
28–30 Mar 1942	Paungde	7 H. Inf-26. 28. 33.	
11–19 Apr 1942	Yenangyaung 1942	Inf-14. 26. 27. IND-Ben S&M. Inf-1/18. 2/5 GR.	5 Mtn Bty RI Arty awarded as Honour Title.
28–29 Apr 1942	Kyaukse 1942	IND-Inf-GR-1/3. 2/5. 7.	
30 Apr– 2 May 1942	Monywa 1942	Inf-28. IND-Inf-1/18. 10 GR.	
9–11 May 1942	Shwegyin	IND-Inf-7 GR.	
29 Dec 1942– 3 Feb 1943	Rathedaung	Inf-20. IND-Inf-8/6.	
8 Jan–18 Mar 1943	Donbaik	Inf-1. 10. 23. 27. 49. 68. IND-Inf-4/Gds. 1/17.	
6–16 Mar 1943	Htizwe	Inf-20.	
28–29 Mar 1943	Point 201 (Arakan)	Inf-10.	

Dates	Honoured or Non-Honoured Battle	Honour awarded to or Participants in Battle	Remarks
26–27 May 1943	**The Stockades**	IND-Inf-**2/5 GR.**	
Jan–Jun 1943	**Chindits 1943**	Inf-**8.** IND-Inf-**2 GR.**	
18–20 Jan 1944	**The Yu**	Inf-**48.**	
1 Jan–12 Jun 1944	**North Arakan**	25 D. Inf-**2. 10. 12. 13. 14. 21. 23. 24. 25. 28. 30. 35. 40. 50. 62. 63. 65.** IND-Inf-**1/18. 2 GR.** AF-**Nigeria. Sierra Leone. Gold Coast. Gambia.**	
16 Jan–3 Feb & 5 Mar–8 Apr 1944	**Buthidaung**	25 D. Inf-**10. 13. 25.** IND-Inf-**7/2. 1/11. 4/5 GR.**	
19–30 Jan & 10–17 Mar 1944	**Razabil**	25 D. Inf-**21. 50.** IND-Inf-**4/7. 3/9.**	
4 Feb–31 Mar 1944	**Kaladan**	AF-**Sierra Leone. Nigeria. Gold Coast. Gambia.**	
3 Apr–22 May 1944	**Point 551**	Inf-**62.** IND-Inf-**1/Guards. 2/7. 1/8 GR.**	
8 Mar–15 Apr 1944	**Alethangyaw**	**Cdos.**	
15 Mar–20 Apr 1944	**Mayu Tunnels**	Inf-**24. 28. 40. 50. 62.**	
1 Jan–31 May 1944	**Maungdaw**	Inf-**14. 65.**	
4 Feb–4 Mar 1944	**Ngakeydauk Pass**	25 D. Inf-**10. 13. 25. 62.** IND-**Mad S&M.** Inf-**7/2. 4/7. 1/18.**	
5–29 Feb 1944	**Defence of Sinzweya**	Inf-**14.** IND-**Bom S&M.**	
Feb–Aug 1944	**Chindits 1944**	Inf-**2. 4. 8. 16. 17. 20. 26. 33. 34. 38. 42. 44. 65.** IND-Inf-**GR-3/4. 5/5. 6. 3/9. 4/9.** AF-**Nigeria.**	
Jul 1944	*Mogaung*		App by IND-Inf-5/5GR.
12 Mar–22 Jun 1944	**Imphal**	3 DG. Inf-**11. 12. 14. 25. 34. 48. 72.** IND-Cav-**7.** Inf-**3/2.** GR-**1/3. 3/3. 2/5. 3/5. 1/7. 3/8. 4/8. 4/10.**	
16–24 Mar	**Tuitum**	IND-Inf-**GR-1/3. 1/10.**	
18–25 Mar 1944	**Sakawng**	Inf-**34.** IND-Inf-**GR-3/3. 2/5. 3/5.**	
Mar 1944	**Tiddim Road**	IND-Inf-**4/7.**	
12 Mar–4 Apr 1944	**Tamu Road**	3 DG. Inf-**11. 34. 48.** IND-**Mad S&M.** Inf-**GR-3/8. 4/10.**	
16–26 Mar 1944	**Sangshak**	IND-Inf-**4/5.**	
1 Apr–22 Jun 1944	**Shenam Pass**	Inf-**11. 34. 72.** IND-INF-**5/6.** GR-**3/1. 3/3. 3/5. 4/10.**	
5–13 Apr 1944	**Nungshigum**	3 DG. IND-Inf-**3/9. 1/17.**	
12 Apr–15 May 1944	**Litan**	Inf-**72.** IND-Inf-**15/8.** GR-**3/10.**	

Dates	Honoured or Non-Honoured Battle	Honour awarded to or Participants in Battle	Remarks
14 Apr–22 Jun 1944	Bishenpur	3 DG. Inf-14. 48. IND-Mad S&M. Inf-2/19. GR-3/1. 1/3. 1/4. 2/5. 1/7. 3/8. 4/10.	
21 Apr–22 Jun 1944	Kanglatongbi	3 DG. Inf-14. 25. IND-Inf-3/2. 3/9. 1/11. 4/8 GR.	
27 Mar–22 Jun 1944	Kohima	Inf-1. 2. 9. 20. 23. 29. 33. 34. 39. 40. 44. 49. 63. 68. 79. IND-Cav-11. Inf-2/4. 5/4. 4/7.	
4–18 Apr 1944	Defence of Kohima	Inf-50. IND-Inf-1 Assam.	
27 Mar–1 Apr 1944	Jessami	IND-Inf-1 Assam.	
5–20 Apr 1944	Relief of Kohima	Inf-1. 29. 79. IND-Inf-4/7.	
7–13 May 1944	Jail Hill	IND-Ben S&M.	
4 May–4 Jun 1944	Naga Village	Inf-20. 29. 79. IND-Inf-2/4.	
14 May–6 Jun 1944	Aradura	Inf-1. 9. 79. IND-Inf-1 Assam.	
15–19 Jun 1944	Mao Songsang	Inf-29. 49.	
3 May–12 Jun 1944	Mowdok	AF-Gambia.	
24 Jun–20 Jul 1944	Ukhrul	Inf-11. 25. 34. IND-Inf-4/3. 3/1 GR.	
21–28 Jul 1944	Tengnoupal	Inf-72. IND-Inf-4/5. 6/5. 5/6. 15/8. GR-3/3. 3/10.	
14–22 Sep 1944	Tongzang	IND-INF-3/2.	
3 Oct–7 Nov 1944	Kennedy Peak	3 DG. IND-Inf-3/2. 1/17. 4 Jammu Kashmir.	
28 Oct–10 Nov 1944	Mawlaik	IND-Inf-1 Assam. AF-KAR. N Rhodesia.	
8–12 Sep 1944	Point 1433	IND-Inf-3/2 GR. IND-Inf-17/5. 14/10.	
11–30 Nov 1944	Pinwe	Inf-21. 24. 28. 30. 35. 63.	
13 Nov–16 Dec 1944	Kalewa	IND-Inf-3/4. AF-KAR. N Rhodesia.	
19 Oct 1944	Haka	IND-Inf-1 Bihar.	
11 Nov 1944–10 Jan 1945	Gangaw	IND-Inf-1 Bihar.	
14–16 Dec 1944	Tinma	AF-Gold Coast.	
11–31 Dec 1944	Mayu Valley	AF-Nigeria. Gold Coast.	
6–9 Jan 1945	Shwebo	3 DG. Inf-1. 29. 49. 63. 79. IND-Inf-GR-4/4. 1/6.	
7–22 Jan 1945	Monywa 1945	Inf-48. IND-Cav-11.	
1 Jan–12 Feb 1945	The Shweli	Inf-3. 21. 24. 28. 35. IND-Para.	
9 Jan–12 Feb 1945	Kyaukmyaung Bridgehead	Inf-41. 49. IND-Cav-7. Inf-3/6. 1 Assam. GR-1/6.	

Dates	**Honoured** or *Non-Honoured* Battle	**Honour awarded** to or *Participants in* Battle	Remarks
23 Jan–12 Feb 1945	**Sagaing**	**3 DG.**	
15–25 Jan 1945	**Myohaung**	AF-**Sierra Leone. Nigeria. Gold Coast. Gambia.**	
12 Jan–29 Apr 1945	**Arakan Beaches**	Inf-**19. 43. 65.** IND-Inf-**2 GR.** AF-**KAR. Nigeria. N Rhodesia. Gold Coast. Rhodesian African Rifles.**	
12–21 Jan 1945	**Myebon**	**Cdos.** IND-Inf-**2 GR.**	
21 Jan–15 Feb 1945	**Ramree**	Inf-**10.** IND-Inf-**1/18.**	
23 Jan–17 Feb 1945	**Kangaw**	**Cdos.** IND-Inf-**1/Guards. 4/19.** AF-**Nigeria. Gold Coast.**	
17–23 Feb 1945	**Ru-Ywa**	IND-Inf-**17/3.**	
27 Feb–4 Mar 1945	**Dalet**	AF-**Nigeria.**	
27 Feb–11 Mar 1945	**Tamandu**	Inf-**43.** IND-Inf-**2 GR.** AF-**Nigeria.**	
3–29 Apr 1945	**Taungup**	IND-Inf-**1/18.** AF-**KAR. N Rhodesia. Gold Coast. Rhodesian African Rifles.**	
12 Feb–21 Mar 1945	**Mandalay**	**3 DG.** Inf-**1. 9. 21. 23. 29. 34. 39. 49. 68. 79.** IND-Cav-**7.** Inf-**3/6. GR-4/4. 1/6. 3/8. 1/10.**	
13 Feb–9 Mar 1945	**Myitson**	Inf-**3. 24. 28.**	
13 Feb–20 Mar 1945	**Ava**	**3 DG.** Inf-**23. 79.** IND-Inf-**4/3.**	
Feb–Mar 1945	**Myinmu**	IND-Cav-**11.**	
12 Feb–7 Mar 1945	**Myinmu Bridgehead**	Inf-**11. 34. 48. 63.** IND-**Bom S&M.** Inf-**GR-3/1. 3/8. 10.**	
9–20 Mar 1945	**Fort Dufferin**	Inf-**49.** IND-Inf-**3/4. 3/6. GR-1/6.**	
11–12 Mar 1945	**Maymyo**	Inf-**41.** IND-INF-**GR-4/6.**	
10–16 Feb 1945	**Seikpyu**	AF-**KAR.**	
8–21 Mar 1945	**Kyaukse 1945**	Inf-**11.** IND-Inf-**GR-3/1. 10.**	
12 Feb–30 Mar 1945	**Meiktila**	Inf-**14. 25. 34. 40. 50.** IND-Cav-**7. 11. 16. S&M-Ben. Mad.** Inf-**6/7. GR-1/3. 1/7. 1/10.**	Also **Meiktila Battery.**
12–21 Feb 1945	**Nyaungu Bridgehead**	Inf-**40.** IND-Inf-**1/11.**	
28 Feb–2 Mar 1945	**Capture of Meiktila**	Inf-**14.** IND-Cav-**9. 16.** Inf-**4/4. 6/7. GR-1/7. 1/10.**	Also awarded to 1 Fd Regt RI Arty as Honour Title.
3–29 Mar 1945	**Defence of Meiktila**	Inf-**14.** IND-Cav-**9. 16. Bom S&M.** Inf-**3/2. 4/4. 6/7. 1 Sikh LI. 4 Jammu Kashmir. GR-1/3. 1/7. 1/10.**	

Dates	**Honoured** or *Non-Honoured* Battle	**Honour awarded** to or *Participants in* Battle	Remarks
24 Feb 1945 & 14–28 Mar 1945	**Taungtha**	Inf-**50.** IND-Inf-**4/4. 4/7.**	
23 Feb–10 Apr 1945	**Letse**	Inf-**40.** AF-**KAR.**	Also awarded to 2 Fd Regt RI Arty as an Honour Title.
18 Feb–20 Mar 1945	**Singu**	IND-Inf-**4/8 GR.**	
29 Mar–30 May 1945	**The Irrawaddy**	**3 DG.** Inf-**25. 29. 40. 48. 63. 79.** IND-Inf-**1/11. GR-2. 4/5. 1/10.**	
2–20 Apr 1945	**Mount Popa**	Inf-**29. 39. 79.** IND-Inf-**1/3.**	
18–25 Apr 1945	**Yenangyaung 1945**	**3 DG.** Inf-**2.**	
11–23 Apr 1945	**Magwe**	IND-Inf-**4/17. 2 GR. Para.**	
6–13 May 1945	**Shandatgyi**	IND-Inf-**1/11. 4/8 GR.**	
20–30 May 1945	**Kama**	Inf-**25.** IND-Inf-**4/3. 1/11. Para.**	
1 Apr–6 May 1945	**Rangoon Road**	Inf-**14. 34. 41. 49. 50. 65.** IND-Cav-**7. 16.** Inf-**6/7. 1 Sikh LI. GR-1/3. 1/6. 1/7. 1/10.**	
1–10 Apr 1945	**Pyawbwe**	Inf-**14. 34.** IND-Cav-**9.** Inf-**4/4. 1 Sikh LI. GR-1/3. 1/7.**	
19–20 Apr 1945	**Pyinmana**	IND-Inf-**3/2.**	
22 Apr–6 May 1945	**Toungoo**	Inf-**49. 65.** IND-Inf-**1 Assam. GR-1/6.**	
27 Apr–2 May 1945	**Pegu 1945**	IND-Cav-**16.** Inf-**4/4. GR-1/3. 1/10.**	
10 May–15 Aug 1945	**Sittang 1945**	Inf-**2. 14. 15. 34. 41. 50.** IND-Cav-**8. 16.** Inf-**4/7. 1/11. 1 Sikh LI. GR-2. 4/5. 5/5. 6. 7. 4/8. 10. Para.**	
20 Jan 1942–15 Aug 1945	**Burma 1942–45**	**3 DG. 7 H. 25 D. RTR.** Inf-**1. 2. 3. 4. 6. 8. 9. 10. 11. 12. 13. 14. 15. 16. 19. 20. 21. 23. 24. 25. 26. 27. 28. 29. 30. 33. 34. 35. 38. 39. 40. 41. 42. 43. 44. 48. 49. 50. 51. 62. 63. 64. 65. 68. 72. 79. Cdos.** IND-Cav-**5. 7. 8. 9. 11. 16. S&M**-**Ben. Mad. Bom.** Inf-**1/Gds. 4/Gds. 3/2. 7/2. 1/3. 4/3. 2/4. 3/4. 4/4. 5/4. 4/5. 6/5. 17/5. 3/6. 5/6. 8/6. 2/7. 4/7. 6/7. 17/7. 15/8. 1/9. 3/9. 5/9. 6/9. MG/9. 1/11. 1/17. 4/17. 1/18. 2/19. 4/19. Assam. Bihar. Sikh LI. Jammu Kashmir. GR-3/1. 4/2. 1/3. 3/3. 1/4. 3/4. 4/4. 2/5. 3/5. 4/5. 5/5. 1/6. 4/6. 1/7. 1/8. 3/8. 4/8. 5/8. 3/9. 4/9. 1/10. 4/10. Para.** AF-**KAR. Sierra Leone. Nigeria. N Rhodesia. Gold Coast. Gambia. Rhodesian African Rifles.**	

WORLD WAR II: SOUTH WEST PACIFIC
Medals awarded: British War Medal 1939–45. 1939–45 Star. Pacific Star.

Dates	Honoured Battle	Honour awarded	Remarks
20–23 Feb 1942	**Koepang**	AUS-Inf-**40.**	
30 Jan–3 Feb 1942	**Ambon**	AUS-Inf-**21.**	
30 Jan–3 Feb 1942	**Laha**	AUS-Inf-**21.**	
23 Jan 1942	**Rabaul**	AUS-Inf-**22. PNG.**	

Dates	**Honoured** or *Non-Honoured* Battle	**Honour awarded** to or *Participants in* Battle	Remarks
22 Jul–13 Nov 1942	**Kokoda Trail**	AUS-Inf-**1. 2. 3. 14. 16. 25. 27. 31. 33. 39. PIR.**	
25 Jul–14 Aug 1942	**Kokoda Deniki**	AUS-Inf-**39. PIR.**	
15–30 Aug 1942	**Isurava**	AUS-Inf-**14. 16. 39.**	
31 Aug–5 Sep 1942	**Eora Creek – Templeton's Crossing I**	AUS-Inf-**14. 16. 39.**	
6–9 Sep 1942	**Efogi-Menari**	AUS-Inf-**14. 16. 27.**	
10–28 Sep 1942	**Ioribaiwa**	AUS-Inf-**3. 14. 16. 25. 31. 33.**	
8–30 Oct 1942	**Eora Creek – Templeton's Crossing II**	AUS-Inf-**1. 2. 3. 25. 31. 33.**	
4–13 Nov 1942	**Oivi–Gorari**	AUS-Inf-**1. 2. 3. 25. 31. 33.**	
16 Nov 1942– 22 Jan 1943	**Buna–Gona**	AUS-**LH-6. 7.** Inf-**1. 2. 3. 9. 10. 12. 14. 16. 25. 27. 31. 33. 36. 39. 49. 53.**	
19 Nov–9 Dec 1942	**Gona**	AUS-Inf-**3. 14. 16. 25. 27. 31. 33. 39.**	
19 Nov 1942– 14 Jan 1943	**Sanananda Road**	AUS-**LH-7.** Inf-**1. 2. 3. 12. 36. 39. 49. 53.**	
10–21 Dec 1942	**Amboga River**	AUS-Inf-**14. 39.**	
18 Dec 1942– 2 Jan 1943	**Cape Endaiadere – Sinemi Creek**	AUS-**LH-6.** Inf-**9. 10. 12.**	
15–22 Jan 1943	**Sanananda – Cape Killerton**	AUS-Inf-**9. 10. 12.**	
26 Aug–7 Sep 1942	**Milne Bay**	AUS-Inf-**9. 10. 12. 25. 61.**	
8 Mar 1942– 26 Feb 1943	**Wau**	AUS-Inf-**5. 6. 7. PNG.**	
22 Apr–29 May 1943	**Mubo I**	AUS-Inf-**7.**	
20–23 Jun 1943	**Lababia Ridge**	AUS-Inf-**6.**	
30 Jun–19 Aug 1943	**Bobdubi II**	AUS-Inf-**5. 6. 7. 24. 58. 59.**	
30 Jun–4 Jul 1943	**Nassau Bay**	AUS-Inf-**PIR.**	
7–14 Jul 1943	**Mubo II**	AUS-Inf-**5. 6.**	
16 Jul–19 Aug 1943	**Mount Tambu**	AUS-Inf-**5. 42.**	
17 Jul–29 Aug 1943	**Tambu Bay**	AUS-Inf-**15. 42. 47. PIR.**	
16–21 Aug 1943	**Komiatum**	AUS-Inf-**5. 6. 7. 42. 58. 59.**	
4–16 Sep 1943	**Lae–Nadzab**	AUS-Inf-**13. 14. 15. 17. 23. 24. 25. 28. 31. 32. 33. 43. 48. 2 MG. 2 Pnr.**	
8–12 Sep 1943	**Busu River**	AUS-Inf-**23. 24. 28. 43.**	
11–15 Sep 1943	**Lae Road**	AUS-Inf-**24. 25. 31. 33. 2 Pnr.**	
22 Sep–8 Dec 1943	**Finschhafen**	AUS-**LH-1.** Inf-**13. 15. 17. 22. 23. 24. 28. 32. 43. 48. PIR. 2 MG. 3 Pnr.**	

Dates	Honoured or Non-Honoured Battle	Honour awarded to or Participants in Battle	Remarks
22 Sep 1943	Scarlet Beach	AUS-Inf-13. 15. 17. PIR.	
23–24 Sep 1943	Bumi River	AUS-Inf-13. 15.	
16–28 Oct 1943	Defence of Scarlet Beach	AUS-Inf-13. 15. 17. 28. 32. 48. 3 Pnr.	
3 Oct–3 Nov 1943	Jivenaneng – Kumawa	AUS-Inf-13. 17.	
18–22 Oct 1943	Siki Cove	AUS-Inf-28. 3 Pnr.	
17–25 Nov 1943	Sattelberg	AUS-LH-1. Inf-23. 24. 48. 2 MG.	
19–26 Nov 1943	Pabu	AUS-Inf-32. 43.	
1943	Goodenough Island	AUS-Inf-12.	
29 Nov 1943	Gusika	AUS-Inf-28.	
1–8 Dec 1943	Wareo	AUS-LH-1. Inf-23. 24.	
2 Dec 1943	Nongora	AUS-Inf-15.	
18 Sep 1943– 8 Aug 1945	Liberation of Australian New Guinea	AUS-LH-1. 4. 6. Inf-1. 2. 3. 4. 5. 6. 7. 8. 9. 10. 11. 12. 13. 14. 15. 16. 17. 19. 22. 24. 25. 26. 27. 29. 30. 31. 32. 33. 35. 36. 42. 46. 47. 51. 52. 53. 58. 59. 60. 61. PIR. 3 MG. 2 Pnr.	
6 Oct–23 Dec 1943	Finisterres I	AUS-Inf-9. 12. 24. 58. 59. 60.	
27 Dec 1943	Shaggy Ridge	AUS-Inf-9. 10. 12. 14. 16. 25. 27. 31. 33. 2 Pnr.	
1–28 Feb 1944	Finisterres II	AUS-Inf-9. 12. 24. 58. 59. 60.	
18 Mar 1944	Barum	AUS-Inf-58. 59.	
13 Apr 1944	Bogadjim	AUS-Inf-60.	
24 Apr 1944	Madang	AUS-Inf-30.	
3 Dec 1943	Kalueng River	AUS-Inf-22.	
9–17 Dec 1943	Wareo – Lakona	AUS-LH-1. Inf-22. 24.	
3–20 Dec 1943	Gusika – Fortification Point	AUS-LH-1. Inf-22. 29. 46. 52.	
1943	Ramu Valley	AUS-Inf-14. 16. 25. 27. 31. 33. 2 Pnr.	
21 Dec 1943– 15 Jan 1944	Sio	AUS-Inf-13. 15. 17.	
25 Jan–19 Jun 1944	Sio – Sepik River	AUS-Inf-30. 35. PIR.	
17 Dec 1944– 2 Jan 1945	Matapau	AUS-Inf-11.	
3–4 Jan 1945	Perembil	AUS-Inf-5.	
5–7 Jan 1945	Abau – Malin	AUS-LH-6. Inf-8. 11.	
19 Jan–19 Feb 1945	Nambut Ridge	AUS-Inf-1. 3. 3 MG.	
18 Jan–6 Feb 1945	Balif	AUS-Inf-5.	
4–9 Mar 1945	Anumb River	AUS-LH-6. Inf-3 MG.	
16 Mar–5 Apr 1945	But Dagua	AUS-Inf-1. 2. 3. Inf-3 MG.	
8 Mar–24 Apr 1945	Maprik	AUS-LH-6. Inf-6. 7.	

Dates	Honoured or *Non-Honoured* Battle	Honour awarded to or *Participants in* Battle	Remarks
9–29 Apr 1945	**Hawain River**	AUS-**LH-4.** Inf-**1. 2. 3.**	
8–11 May 1945	**Wewak**	AUS-**LH-4. 6.** Inf-**4. 11.**	
11–15 May 1945	**Wirui Mission**	AUS-**LH-4. 6.** Inf-**4. 11.**	
28 May–5 Jul 1945	**Mount Shiburangu – Mount Tazaki**	AUS-Inf-**4. 8.**	
3 May–14 Jul 1945	**Yamil – Ulupu**	AUS-Inf-**5. 6. 7.**	
15 Jul–8 Aug 1945	**Kaboibus – Kiarivu**	AUS-Inf-**5. 6. 7. PIR.**	
17 Jan–9 Feb 1945	**Tsimba Ridge**	AUS-Inf-**31. 51.**	
7–11 Jun 1945	**Bonis – Porton**	AUS-Inf-**26. 31. 51. PIR.**	
18 Dec 1944	**Artillery Hill**	AUS-Inf-**9.**	
30 Dec 1944	**Pearl Ridge**	AUS-Inf-**25.**	
19–29 Dec 1944	**Adele River**	AUS-Inf-**15.**	
4–17 Jan 1945	**Mawaraka**	AUS-Inf-**15. 25. 42. 47.**	
2–15 Feb 1945	**Mosigetta**	AUS-Inf-**9. 25. 61.**	
25 Jan–26 Feb 1945	**Purlata River**	AUS-Inf-**9. 25. 61.**	
16–19 Feb 1945	**Darara**	AUS-Inf-**25.**	
28 Mar–6 Apr 1945	**Slater's Knoll**	AUS-**LH-4.** Inf-**25.**	
17 Apr–7 May 1945	**Hongorai River**	AUS-**LH-4.** Inf-**9. 24. 58. 59. 60.**	
13–22 May 1945	**Egan's Ridge – Hongorai Ford**	AUS-**LH-4.** Inf-**24. 58. 59.**	
17–28 May 1945	**Commando Road**	AUS-Inf-**60.**	
2–7 Jun 1945	**Hari River**	AUS-**LH-4.** Inf-**24. 58. 59. 60.**	
13–16 Jun 1945	**Ogorata River**	AUS-Inf-**24. 58. 59. 60.**	
16–25 Jun 1945	**Mobiai River**	AUS-Inf-**58. 59. 60.**	
26–30 Jun 1945	**Mivo River**	AUS-**LH-4.** Inf-**15. 24. 58. 59. 60.**	
2–9 Jul 1945	**Mivo Ford**	AUS-Inf-**42. 47.**	
5–7 Mar 1945	**Waitavolo**	AUS-Inf-**14. 16. 19. 32.**	
1 May–15 Aug 1945	**Borneo**	AUS-**LH-1. 7. 9.** Inf-**9. 10. 12. 13. 14. 15. 16. 17. 23. 24. 25. 27. 28. 31. 32. 33. 43. 48. MG-1. 2. Pnr-1. 3. 4.**	
1 May–15 Aug 1945	**Tarakan**	AUS-**LH-9.** Inf-**23. 24. 48. 3 Pnr.**	
10 Jun–8 Aug 1945	**Brunei**	AUS-Inf-**13. 15. 17. 2 MG.**	
10–21 Jun 1945	**Labuan**	AUS-**LH-9.** Inf-**28. 43. 2 MG.**	
17–30 Jun 1945	**Beaufort**	AUS-Inf-**28. 32. 43.**	
10–23 Jun 1945.	**Miri**	AUS-INF-**13. 15. 17.**	
1–9 Jul 1945	**Balikpapan**	AUS-**LH-1. 7.** Inf-**9. 12. 14. 16. 25. 27. 31. 33. 1 MG.**	
10–22 Jul 1945	**Milford Highway**	AUS-**LH-1. 7.** Inf-**25. 31. 33. 1 MG.**	

Dates	**Honoured** or *Non-Honoured* Battle	**Honour awarded** to or *Participants in* Battle	Remarks
20 Feb 1942– 15 Aug 1945	**South West Pacific 1942–45**	AUS-**LH-1. 4. 6. 7. 8. 9. 20. Inf-1. 2. 3. 4. 5. 6. 7. 8. 9. 10. 11. 12. 13. 14. 15. 16. 17. 19. 21. 22. 23. 24. 25. 26. 27. 28. 29. 30. 31. 32. 33. 35. 36. 39. 40. 42. 43. 46. 47. 48. 49. 51. 52. 53. 58. 59. 60. 61. 62. PIR. PNG. MG-1. 2. 3. 7. Pnr-1. 2. 3. 4.**	

WORLD WAR II: SOUTH PACIFIC
Medals awarded: British War Medal 1939–45. 1939–45 Star. Pacific Star.

7 Aug 1942– 20 Mar 1944	**Solomons**	NZ-Inf-**1. 3. 4. 5. 6. 7. 8. 9. 11. 12. 15. 16. 34. 35.**	
31 Aug–9 Oct 1943	**Vella Lavella**	NZ-Inf-**1. 4. 8. 12. 35.**	
27 Oct–12 Nov 1943	**Treasury Islands**	NZ-Inf-**3. 5. 6. 7. 9. 11. 15. 16. 34.**	
30 Jan–23 Feb 1944	**Green Islands**	NZ-Inf-**1. 4. 8. 12. 35.**	
7 Aug 1942– 25 Jun 1944	**South Pacific 1942–44**	NZ-**MR-2. 6. 9. NZ Scot. Inf-1. 3. 4. 5. 6. 7. 8. 9. 11. 12. 15. 16. 34. 35. Ruahine.**	

WORLD WAR II: SOUTH EAST ASIA
Medals awarded: British War Medal 1939–45. 1939–45 Star. GSM (Army and RAF) 1918–64 with clasp for 1945–46.

1942	**Java 1942**	AUS-**3 MG. 2 Pnr.**	
1939–40	*North West Frontier india 1939–40*	IND-Cav-*13.*	
Sep 1945–Nov 1946	*Malaya & Java 1945–46*(clasp)	Inf-*3. 14. 24. 72. Para.* IND-Cav-*13.*	

PALESTINE 1945–8
Medals awarded: GSM (Army and RAF) 1918–64 with clasp.

Sep 1945–Jun 1948	*Palestine 1945–48*	*LG. 1 DG. 4/7 DG. 3 H. 9 L. 12 L. 15/19 H. 17/21 L. RTR. Inf-GG. CG. IG. WG. 1. 2. 6. 8. 10. 12. 15. 20. 22. 24. 25. 31. 32. 33. 34. 35. 37. 40. 43. 45. 47. 57. 60. 64. 71. 83. 87. 91. Para.*	

MALAYA 1948–60
Medals awarded: GSM (Army and RAF) 1918–64 with clasp.

Jun 1948–Jul 1960	*Malaya 1948–60*	*1 DG. 1 D. 4 H. 11 H. 12 L. 13/18 H. 15/19 H. Inf-GG. CG. SG. 2. 10. 11. 12. 13. 14. 15. 19. 21. 22. 23. 24. 25. 26. 27. 29. 37. 45. 47. 50. 51. 62. 63. 72. 75. RB. SAS.*	

KOREA
Medals awarded: Korea Medal. UN Medal with clasp **Korea**.

16–25 Sep 1950	**Naktong Bridgehead**	Inf-**57.** Inf-*91.*	
17–18 Oct 1950	**Sariwon**	AUS-Inf-**RAR.**	
21–22 Oct 1950	**Yongyu**	AUS-Inf-**RAR.**	
23–30 Oct 1950	**Chongju**	Inf-**57.** AUS-Inf-**RAR.**	
4–5 Nov 1950	**Pakchon**	Inf-**91.** AUS-Inf-**RAR.**	
23–30 Nov 1950	**Chong Chon II**	Inf-**57.**	
1 Jan 1951	**Uijongbu**	AUS-Inf-**RAR.**	

Dates	Honoured or Non-Honoured Battle	Honour awarded to or Participants in Battle	Remarks
2–4 Jan 1951	**Seoul**	**8 H.** Inf-**5. 83.**	
14–17 Feb 1951	**Chuam-Ni**	Inf-**57.** AUS-Inf-**RAR.**	
16–20 Feb 1951	**Hill 327**	**8 H.** Inf-**28.**	
7–12 Mar 1951	**Maehwa-San**	AUS-Inf-**RAR.**	
3–16 Apr 1951	**Kapyong-Chon**	Inf-**57.**	
22–25 Apr 1951	**The Imjin**	**8 H.** Inf-**5. 28. 83.**	28 (Royal Gloucestershire Regiment) and 170 Battery awarded USA Presidential Citation. Also **Imjin** Battery.
22–25 Apr 1951	**Kapyong**	Inf-**57.** AUS-Inf-**RAR.** CDN-Inf-**PPCLI.**	
3–12 Oct 1951	**Kowang-San**	**8 H.** Inf-**5. 25. 53.** AUS-Inf-**RAR.**	
4–6 Nov 1951	**Maryang-San**	Inf-**17. 25.**	
17–19 Nov 1951	**Hill 227 I**	Inf-**53.**	
18–19 Nov 1952	**The Hook 1952**	**5 DG.** Inf-**42.**	
28–29 May 1953	**The Hook 1953**	Inf-**8. 33.**	
24–26 Jul 1953	**The Samichon**	AUS-Inf-**RAR.**	
1 Aug 1950–26 Jul 1953	**Korea 1950–53**	**5 DG. 8 H. RTR.** Inf-**5. 7. 8. 9. 17. 25. 28. 33. 41. 42. 53. 57. 68. 83. 91.** AUS-Inf-**RAR.** CDN-Cav-**Strathcona.** Inf-**RCR. PPCLI. R22R.**	

KENYA
Medals awarded: Africa GSM 1902–56 with clasp.

Dates	Honoured or Non-Honoured Battle	Honour awarded to or Participants in Battle	Remarks
Oct 1952–Nov 1956	*Kenya*	Inf-*3. 5. 11. 20. 27. 28. 42. 51. 53. 87. RB.* AF-*KAR. Kenya.*	

CYPRUS
Medals awarded: GSM (Army and RAF) 1918–64 with clasp.

Dates	Honoured or Non-Honoured Battle	Honour awarded to or Participants in Battle	Remarks
Apr 1955–Apr 1959	*Cyprus*	*LG. RHG.* Inf-*GG. IG. 1. 3. 6. 9. 11. 12. 13. 14. 17. 19. 20. 21. 23. 27. 28. 31. 33. 38. 39. 41. 42. 43. 49. 50. 51. 57. 62. 68. 71. 83. 91. Para.*	

SUEZ
Medals awarded: GSM (Army and RAF) 1918–64 with clasp **Near East**.

Dates	Honoured or Non-Honoured Battle	Honour awarded to or Participants in Battle	Remarks
Oct–Dec 1956	*Suez*	*RTR.* Inf-*GG. CG. 1. 7. 14. 50. 65. 91. Para.*	

SOUTH ARABIA
Medals awarded: GSM (Army and RAF) 1918–64 with clasp. Campaign Service Medal with clasps for **Radfan** and **South Arabia**.

Dates	Honoured or Non-Honoured Battle	Honour awarded to or Participants in Battle	Remarks
Jan 1957–Jun 1960	*Arabian Peninsula*	*LG. 13/18 H. 15/19 H.* Inf-*3. 6. 10. 14. 21. 28. 48. 53. 65. 79.*	Aden, Muscat, Oman, Persian Gulf.
Aug 1964	*Radfan*	*10 H. RTR.* Inf-*CG. IG. 1. 9. 25. 35. Para. SAS.*	
Aug 1964–Nov 1967	*South Arabia*	*1 DG. 4/7 DG. 5 DG. 3 H. 10 H. RTR.* Inf-*CG. IG. WG. 1. 5. 9. 13. 14. 16. 24. 25. 26. 28. 35. 47. 51. 87. 91. Para. SAS.*	Mainly Aden

Dates	**Honoured** or *Non-Honoured* Battle	**Honour awarded** to or *Participants in* Battle	Remarks

NORTH BORNEO & MALAYA

Medals awarded: GSM (Army and RAF) 1918–64 with clasp **Brunei**. Campaign Service Medal with clasps **Borneo** and **Malay Peninsula**.

Dates	Battle	Participants	Remarks
Dec 1962–64	*Brunei*	Inf-*43. 51. 72.*	
Dec 1962–64	*Borneo*	*4 H. RTR.* Inf-*SG. 17. 43. 51. 83. 91. RB.*	
Aug 1964–Jun 1965	*Malay Peninsula*	*LG.* Inf-*SG. 25. 43. 72.*	

FALKLAND ISLANDS 1982

Medals awarded: Campaign Service Medal with clasp.

Dates	Battle	Participants	Remarks
28–29 May 1982	**Goose Green**	**Para.**	
11–12 Jun 1982	**Mount Longdon**	**Para.**	
13–14 Jun 1982	**Tumbledown Mountain**	Inf-**SG.**	
13–14 Jun 1982	**Wireless Ridge**	**Para.**	
2 Apr–14 Jun 1982	**Falkland Islands 1982**	**Blues & Royals.** Inf-**SG. WG. 7 GR. Para. SAS.**	

HONOURS AWARDED TO VOLUNTEER BNS OF BRITISH REGIMENTS – 2nd BOER WAR 1899–1902

South Africa
1900–1
6(Rifle)/8. 9/8. 4/11. 5(POW)-11. 4/13. 5/13. 4/15. 5/21. 7(Merioneth & Montgomery)/23. Brecknockshire/24. 7/29. 4/32. 5/32. 8(IOW Rifles)/37. 4/39. 5/40. 4/43. 5(Buchan & Formatin)/75. 28 LR(Artists Rifles). 1 Cambs. Inns of Court.

1900–2
4/1. 5/1. 7/1. 4/2. 5/2. 4/3. 5(Weald of Kent)/3. 4/4. 5/4. 4/5. 5/5. 6/5. 5/6. 6/6. 7/6. 1 CLR/7. 2 CLR/7. 3 CLR/7. 5/8. 7/8. 8(Irish)/8. 4/9. 5/9. 4/10. 5/10. 4/12. 5/12. 5/14. 6/14. 7&8(Leeds Rifles)/14. 5/16. 4/17. 5/17. 5/19. 5/20. 6/20. 7/20. 8/20. 4/21. 5(Earl of Chester's)/22. 6/22. 4(Denbighshire)-23. 5(Flintshire)/23. 6(Caernarvon & Anglesey)/23. 4(The Border)/25. 5(Dumfries & Galloway)/25. 5/26. 6/26. 7/26. 8/26. 4(City of Bristol)/28. 5/28. 8/29. 4/30. 5/30. 5/31. 6/31. 4/33. 5/33. 6/33. 7/33. 4(Cumberland & Westmoreland)/34. 4/35. 5(Cinque Ports)/35. 4/37. 5/37. 6(Duke of Connaught's)/37. 5/38. 6/38. 4/40. 5/41. 6(Glamorgan)-41. 4(City of Dundee)/42. 5(Angus & Dundee)/42. 6(Perthshire)/42. 7(Fife)/42. Buckingham Bn/43. 4/44. 5/44. 6/44. 7/44. 5/45. 6/45. 7. (Robin Hood)/45. 8/45. 4/47. 5/47. 4/48. 4/49. 4/50. 5/50. 4/51. 5/51. 4/53. 7/57. 8/57. 9/57. 4/62. 5/63. 6/63. 7/63. 8(Ardwick)/63. 9/63. 5/64. 6/64. 4(Hallamshire)/65. 5/65. 5/68. 6/68. 7/68. 8/68. 9/68. 5/71. 6(City of Glasgow)/71. 7(Blythswood)/71. 8(Lanark)/71. 9(Glasgow Highland)/71. 4(Ross Highland)/72. 5(Sutherland & Caithness)/72. 6(Morayshire)/72. 4/75. 6(Banff & Donside)/75. 4/79. 5(Renfrew)/91. 6(Renfrew)/91. 7/91. 8(Argyllshire)/91. 9(Dumbartonshire)/91. 1 Mon. 2 Mon. 3 Mon.

1901
8/1.

1901–2
6/1. 9(Highlanders)/1. 10(Cyclist)/1. 4/22. 5(Cumberland)/34. 10/63.

1902
10(Scottish)/8.

PART IV
Maps and Indexes

Above: The landing of troops from HMT *River Clyde* at Sedd-el-Bahr, Gallipoli, 25 April 1915. Photogravure from a painting by Charles Dixon. *NAM*

Introduction

The purpose of this part of the book is to locate all battles, honoured and non-honoured, and other place names referred to in the narrative, as accurately as possible on maps within the constraints of scale. In respect of the battles the place name given in the honour title, or ascribed to non-honoured battles, has been located; it is not necessarily exactly where the fighting, which sometimes covered a wide area, took place.

On the maps, as in the narrative and the chronological list, names shown in bold type are of honoured battles, names in italics of non-honoured battles, and those in Roman type of Place Names.

Indexes

There are two indexes, one of battles and the other of places. All the battles listed in Part III are shown in the index and located on the maps, and the converse is also true; this applies also to the place names appearing in Part II and the index.

The Index of Battles shows after each name the page numbers where the description appears in Part II and the name in Part III, followed by the map sheet number and the grid reference on each map, and the latitude and longitude in parenthesis to help those readers who wish to locate the places on larger scale maps. For example the entry '176, 292; 12a5 (35/14)' after a name would mean that the battle appears in the narrative (Part II) on page 176, in the chronological list (Part III) on page 292, on map sheet 12, grid reference square 'a5', and is within the square of latitude 35 and longitude 14. The Index of Place Names omits the second number, ie the page in Part III.

The Index of Battles has been cross-referenced where the title of the honour is a qualified place name, eg **Advance on Tripoli** and **Tripoli, Advance on**, and also where the place name of the honour is preceded by a foreign language prefix, eg **Alamein, El** and **El Alamein**, but not where it is prefixed by 'The'.

Where hyphenated double names appear in the index they are frequently two separate places, often quite close together and linked in the honour, and both places are shown separately on the maps. These double names are also cross-referenced.

Except in a few necessary places, dates are not included on the maps. Where a date appears in the Index after a name in the same type it is part of the honour title. Dates in parenthesis, eg **Aden** (1839) are shown to distinguish

between two or more battles which have occurred at the same place, sometimes at widely different dates, and where no date has been included in the title of either honour. In some cases 'I' or 'II' are shown after the name as part of the title of the honour, normally to indicate two different battles at the same place in the same year, eg **Cassino I** and **Cassino II**. Such places only occur once on the maps, as do places which are the title of more than one honour at the same place distinguished by different dates as part of the title, eg **Kut al Amara 1915** and **Kut al Amara 1917**.

In a very few cases an honoured name appears twice in the index without any date or other distinction. This is because the two battles occurred in places in different countries which happened to have the same name, and reference to the narrative will make this clear, eg **The Moro**, which in one case is a battle in 1762 at a fort of that name near Havana in Cuba and the other is a battle in 1943 at a river of the same name in Italy.

The Maps

A map of the world is included on the end-pages of the book. On it are outlined the numbered individual area map sheets, without the detailed insets. Also shown on it are a number of battles, honoured and non-honoured, and place names which do not fit conveniently on to the area map sheets; some of these are isolated campaigns, but some are related to specific campaigns on the area maps.

The area maps are not limited to specific campaigns but show all the locations of battles and places within the geographical area, and will help the reader to see how some areas, for example Flanders, had a number of campaigns fought over them throughout the history of the British Army. The exact location of names shown only on the world map and associated with a particular campaign should be easily related to places on the area maps by reference to the world map. A number of the area maps have insets included on them, showing in larger scale and more detail some areas where too many battles have been honoured to be clearly shown on the smaller scale maps.

Where the name of a campaign is that of a country or a limited geographical area it is shown on the map in the appropriate type, but in many cases the campaign name, eg 1st Afghan War, is not shown on the map although Afghanistan is shown in Roman type. In the case of some countries a name is given in bold or italic type and also in Roman type; this has been done where the name of the country or area has changed, and indicates that an honour, or ascribed non-honour, has been awarded in the original name of the country at the time of the campaign. An example is **Bechuanaland** and Botswana.

All countries are named, and these names and their boundaries are those of the present day, except for those of the old Indian states which are shown as they were at the time of the campaigns because they are mentioned in the text and, being no longer used, are of help in understanding the course of the campaign.

There are many instances where for battles of the same name but at different times some have been honoured and some were not honoured, eg Martinique. These titles are shown on the maps in bold type to indicate that one at least was honoured. In a few cases country campaign titles have been shown more than once on the maps, eg **China**, and this indicates that different campaigns occurred in quite different areas of a large country.

Finally an apology. The author and the publisher both fully realise that pull-out maps, which can be read alongside the narrative without the need for continued turning over of pages, or a slip case of separate maps, would be of considerable advantage to the reader. It was with much regret, however, that these ideas had to be abandoned on the basis of the exigencies of production and the significant extra cost to an already expensive book.

North-West Europe.

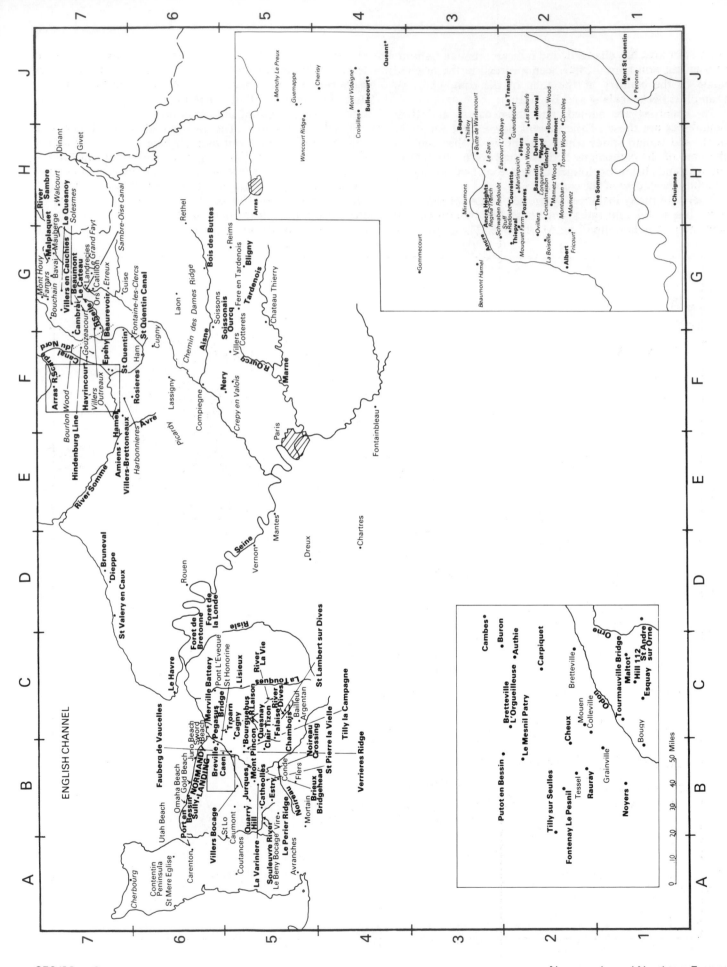

Normandy and Northern France.

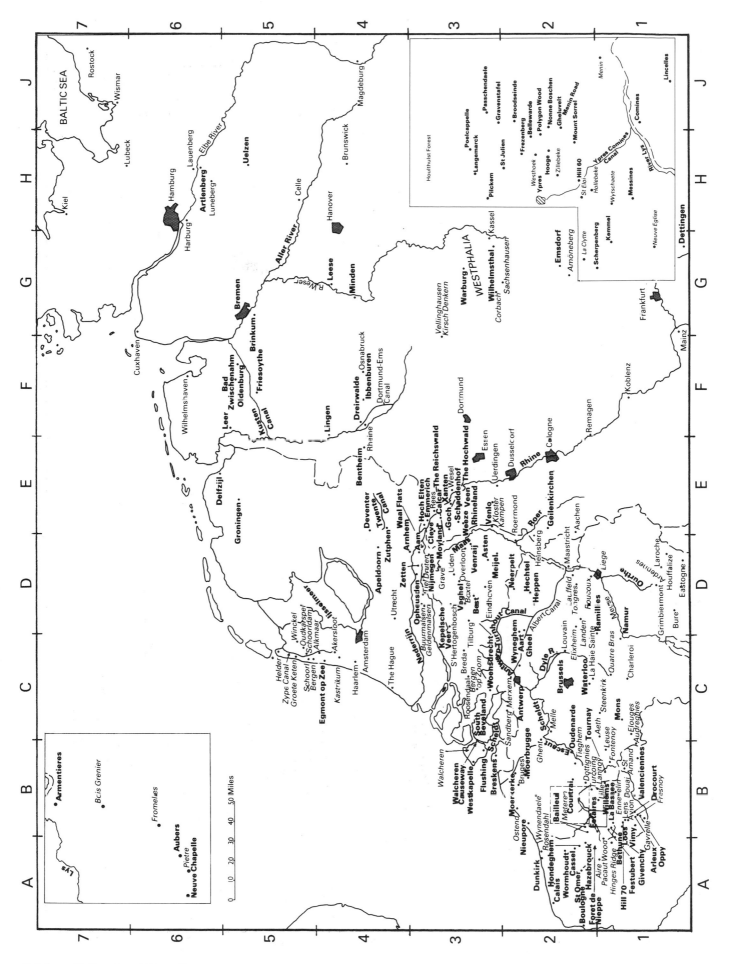

Belgium, Holland and West Germany.

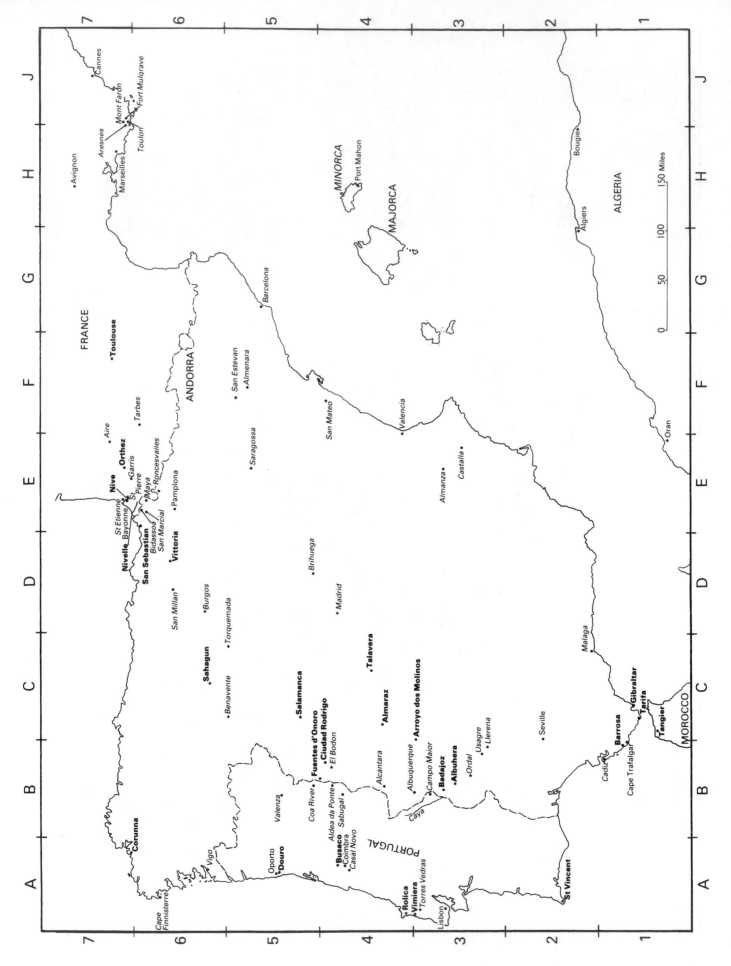

The Iberian Peninsula and the Western Mediterranean.

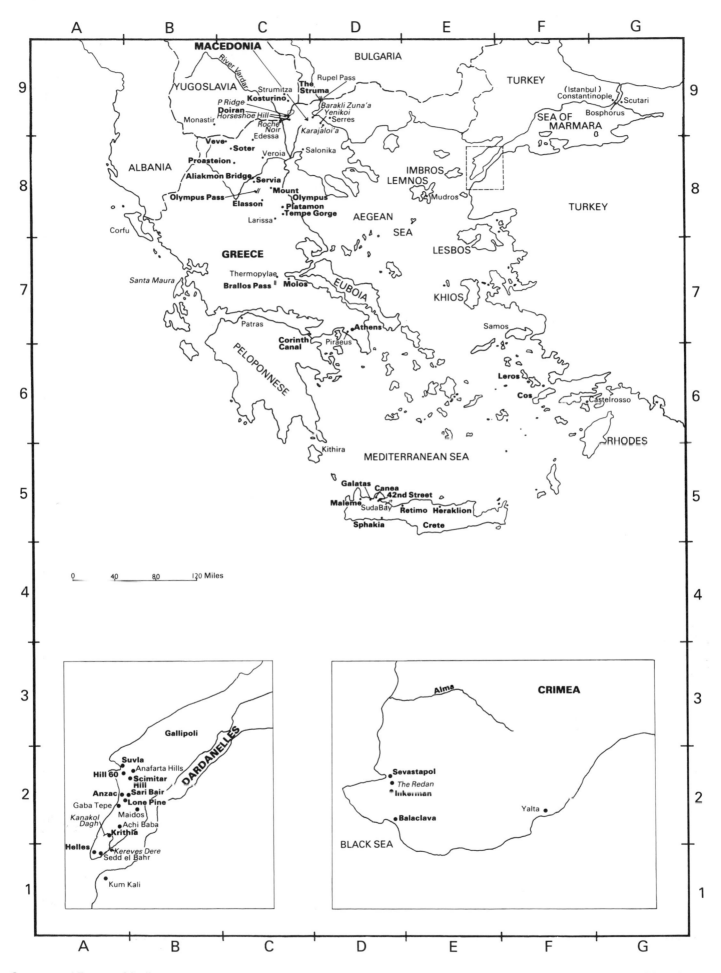

Main Map Labels

MACEDONIA
BULGARIA
River Vardar
Rupel Pass
YUGOSLAVIA
Strumitza
The Struma
Kosturino
(Istanbul) Constantinople
Scutari
P Ridge
Barakli Zuna'a
Yenikoi
Doiran
Horseshoe Hill
SEA OF MARMARA
Bosphorus
Monastir
Roche Noir
*Serres
Karajaloi'a
Edessa
Veve
Soter
Veroia
Salonika
IMBROS
LEMNOS
TURKEY
Proasteion
ALBANIA
Aliakmon Bridge
Servia
Mudros
Olympus Pass
Mount Olympus
Elasson
Platamon
Larissa
Tempe Gorge
AEGEAN SEA
Corfu
LESBOS
GREECE
KHIOS
Santa Maura
Thermopylae
Brallos Pass
Molos
EUBOIA
Samos
Athens
Patras
Piraeus
Corinth Canal
Leros
PELOPONNESE
Cos
Castelrosso
Kithira
RHODES
MEDITERRANEAN SEA
Galatas
Canea
42nd Street
Maleme
SudaBay
Retimo
Heraklion
Sphakia
Crete

Scale: 0 40 80 120 Miles

Gallipoli Inset

Gallipoli
DARDANELLES
Suvla
Anafarta Hills
Hill 60
Scimitar Hill
Sari Bair
Anzac
Lone Pine
Gaba Tepe
Maidos
Kanakol Dagh
Achi Baba
Krithia
Helles
Kereves Dere
Sedd el Bahr
Kum Kali

Crimea Inset

CRIMEA
Alma
Sevastapol
The Redan
Inkerman
Yalta
Balaclava
BLACK SEA

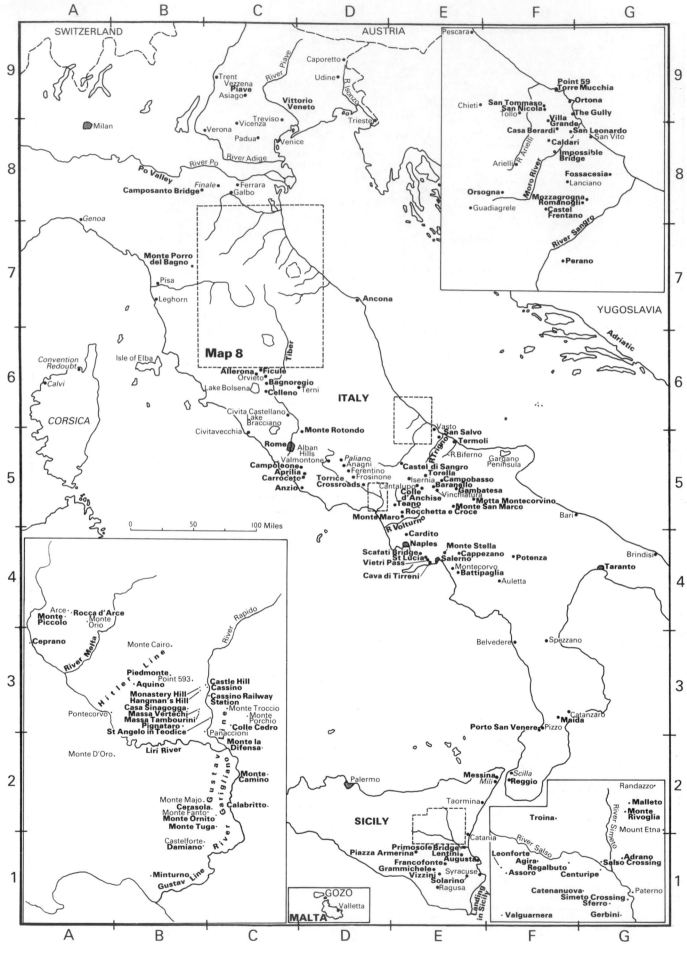

AUSTRIA

Pescara

9

Milan

Trent
Vezzena
Piave
Asiago

Caporetto

Udine

Point 59
Torre Mucchia

Chieti
San Tommaso
San Nicola
Tollo
Ortona
The Gully

Treviso
Verona
Vicenza
Padua
Vittorio
Veneto
Venice
Trieste

Casa Berardi
Villa
Grande
San Leonardo
San Vito

Caldari

Arielli
R Arielli
Impossible
Bridge

8

Po Valley
River Po
River Adige

Ferrara
Galbo

Camposanto Bridge
Finale

Orsogna
Moro River
Fossacesia
Lanciano

Guadiagrele
Mozzagrogna
Romanogli
Castel
Frentano

Genoa

Monte Porro
del Bagno

7

Pisa

Leghorn

River Sangro

Perano

YUGOSLAVIA

Ancona

6

Convention
Redoubt

Calvi

Isle of Elba

Tiber

Map 8

Adriatic

CORSICA

Allerona **Ficule**
Orvieto
Bagnoregio
Lake Bolsena
Celleno
Terni

ITALY

Civita Castellano
Lake
Bracciano

Monte Rotondo

Vasto
San Salvo
Termoli
R Trigno
R.Biferno
Gargano
Peninsula

5

Civitavecchia

Rome
Alban
Hills
Valmontone

Paliano
Anagni
Ferentino
Frosinone

Campoleone
Aprilia
Carroceto
Anzio

Torrice
Crossroads

Castel di Sangro
Torella
Isernia
Campobasso
Cantalupo
Barangllo
Gambatesa
Colle
d'Anchise
Vinchiatura
Motta Montecorvino
Teano
Rocchetta e Croce
Monte San Marco

Monte Maro
R Volturno

Bari

4

0   50   100 Miles

Cardito

Naples

Monte Stella
Cappezano
Scafati Bridge
St Lucia
Salerno
Vietri Pass
Montecorvo
Cava di Tirreni
Battipaglia
Auletta

Potenza

Brindisi

Taranto

Arce
Rocca d'Arce
Monte
Piccolo
Monte
Orio

River Rapido

Belvedere
Spezzano

3

Ceprano

River Melfa
Hitler Line

Monte Cairo.

Piedmonte
Aquino
Point 593.
Castle Hill
Cassino
Cassino Railway
Station

Monastery Hill
Hangman's Hill
Casa Sinagogga
Massa Vertechi
Massa Tambourini
Pignataro
St Angelo in Teodice

Monte Troccio
Monte
Colle Cedro
Porchio
Panaccioni

Catanzaro
Maida

Pontecorvo

Monte la
Difensa

Porto San Venere
Pizzo

2

Monte D'Oro.
Liri River

Gustav Line
River Garigliano

Monte
Camino

Palermo

Monte Majo.
Cerasola.
Monte Fanto.
Monte Ornito.
Monte Tuga.
Castelforte.
Damiano.

Calabritto

Messina
Scilla
Mili
Reggio

Randazzo
Malleto
Monte
Rivoglia

Taormina

SICILY

Catania
River Salso
River Simeto
Mount Etna

1

Minturno
Gustav Line

Primosole Bridge
Piazza Armerina
Lentini
Augusta
Francofonte
Grammichele
Vizzini
Solarino
Syracuse
Ragusa

Troina
Leonforte
Agira
Regalbuto
Assoro
Centuripe
Salso
Crossing
Adrano
Paterno

GOZO
Valletta

MALTA

Landing in Sicily

Catenanuova-
Simeto Crossing.
Sferro
Valguarnera
Gerbini

Italy and Sicily.

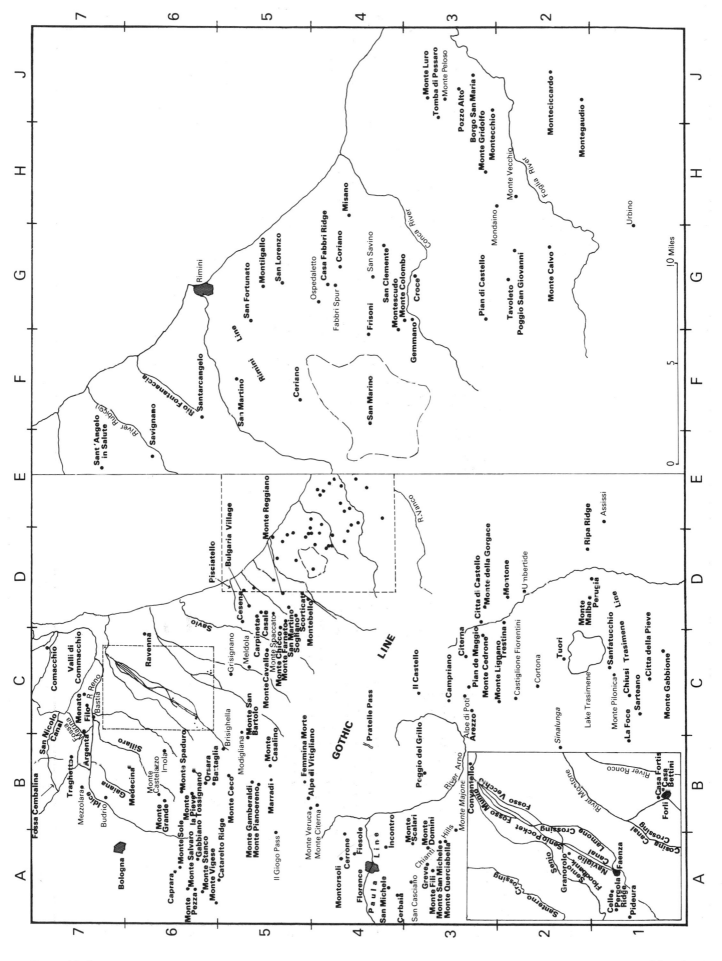

Central Italy.

Map 8/361

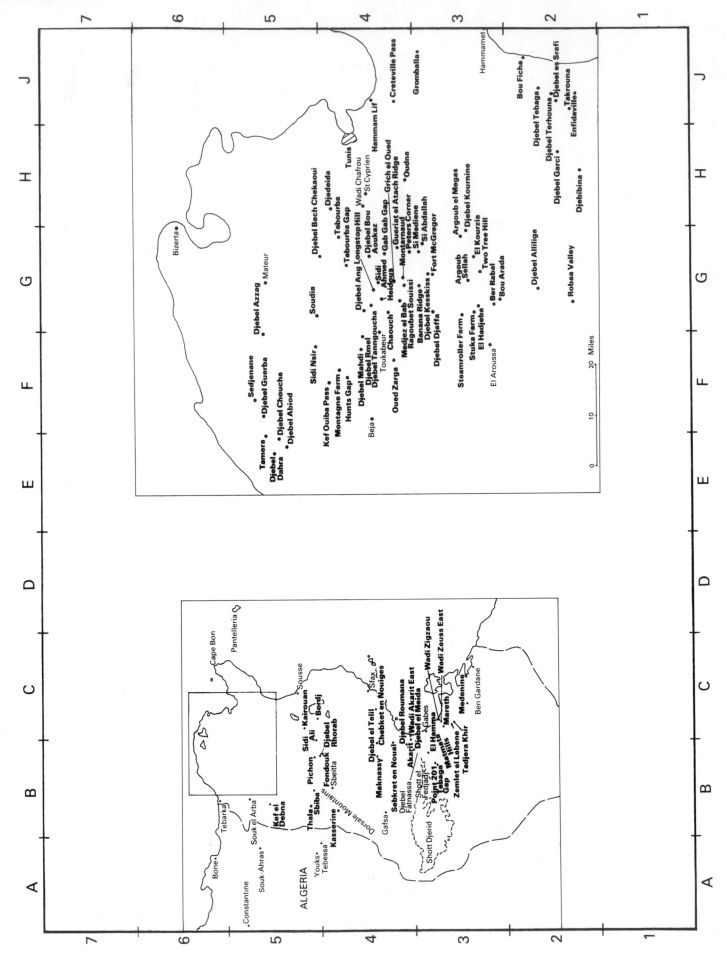

Tunisia.

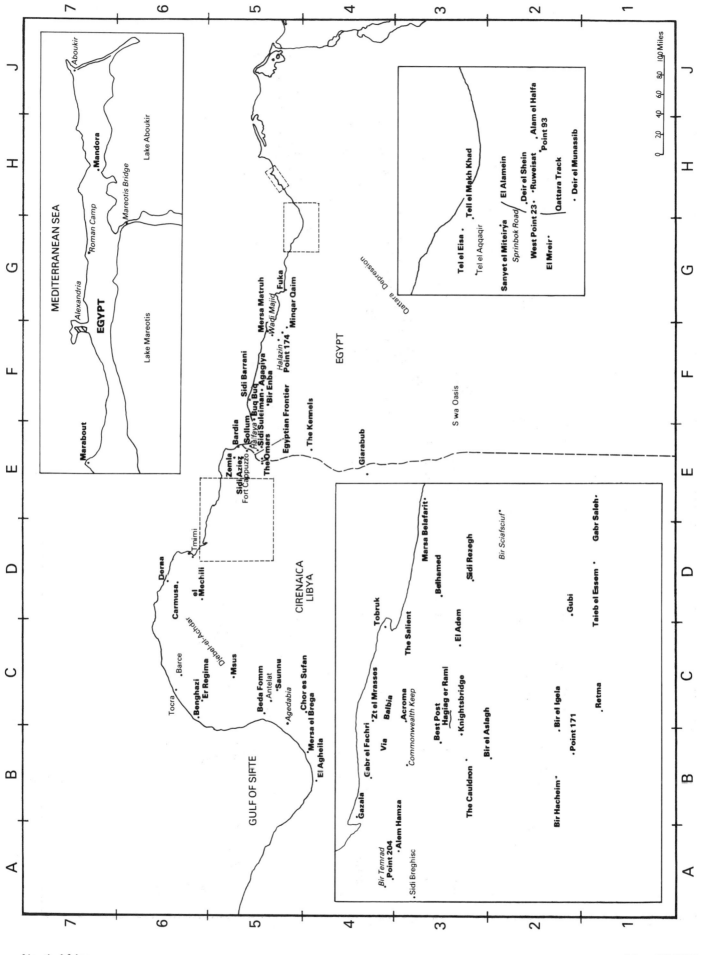

North Africa.

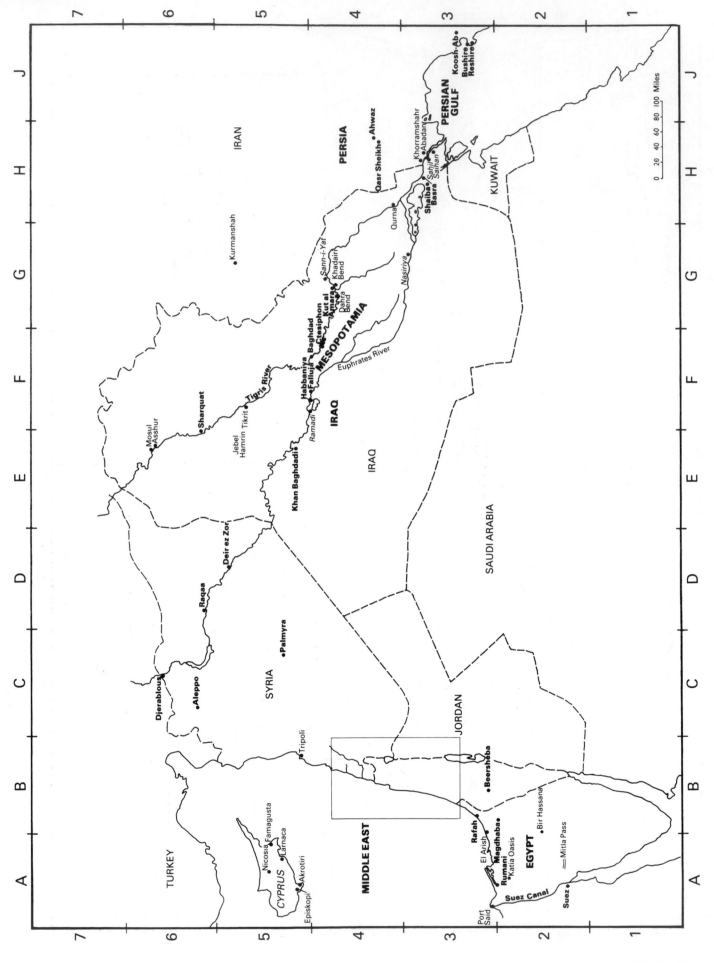

The Middle East.

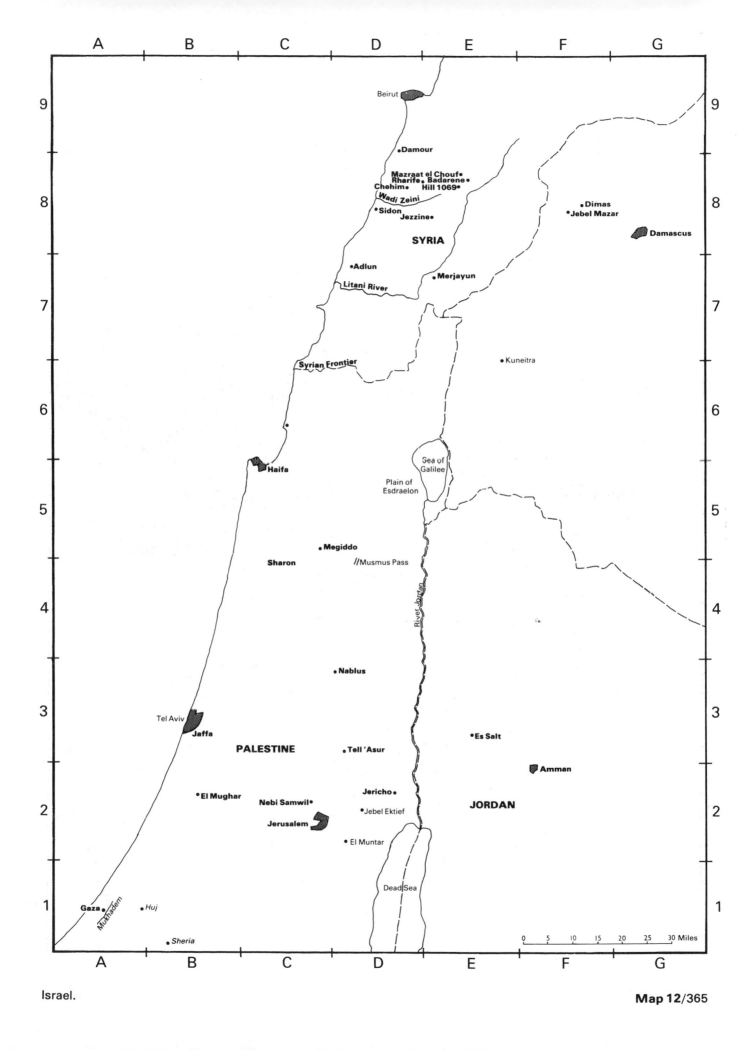

Israel.

Map **12**/365

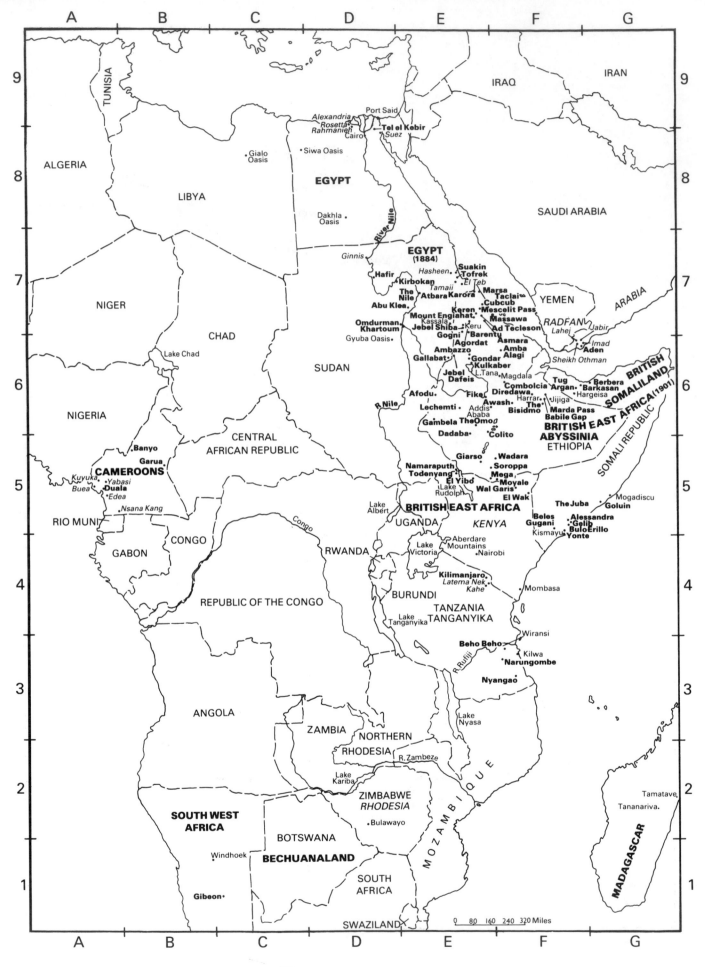

	A	B	C	D	E	F	G	
9					IRAQ		IRAN	**9**
8	ALGERIA	TUNISIA	LIBYA	Port Said	Alexandria Rosetta Rahmanieh Cairo **Tel el Kebir** *Suez*	SAUDI ARABIA		**8**
				Gialo Oasis *Siwa Oasis*	**EGYPT**			
7		NIGER	CHAD	Dakhla Oasis	**EGYPT (1884)** *Ginnis* *Hasheen* **Suakin** **Tofrek** *El Teb* **Hafir** **Kirbokan** *Tamaii* **Marsa** **Taclai** **The Nile** **Atbara** **Karora** **Cubcub** **Abu Klea** **Mescelit Pass** **Massawa** **Mount Engiahat** *Keren* **Ad Tecleson** *Kassala* **Omdurman** **Jebel Shiba** *Keru* **Barentu** **Khartoum** **Gogni** **Asmara** *Gyuba Oasis* **Agordat** **Ambazzo** **Amba Alagi** **Gallabat** *Gondar* **Kulkaber**	YEMEN *ARABIA* *RADFAN* *Lahej* *Jabir* *Imad* **Aden** *Sheikh Othman*		**7**
6	NIGERIA	Lake Chad	CENTRAL AFRICAN REPUBLIC	**Jebel Dafeis** *L.Tana* **R Nile** **Afodu** *Magdala* **Combolcia** **Fika** **Diredawa** **Lechemti** **Awash** *Harrar* **The Bisidmo** *Addis Ababa* **Marda Pass** **Gambela** **TheOmo** **Babile Gap** **Dadaba** **Colito**	**Tug Argan** **Berbera** **Barkasan** *Hargeisa* *Jijiga* **BRITISH SOMALILAND** **BRITISH EAST AFRICA** (1901) **ABYSSINIA** SOMALI REPUBLIC ETHIOPIA		**6**
5	**Banyo** **Garua** *Kuyuka* **CAMEROONS** *Yabasi* *Buea* **Duala** *Edea* RIO MUNI *Nsana Kang*		CONGO	ANGOLA	*Giarso* • *Wadara* **Namaraputh** **Soroppa** **Todenyang** **Mega** **El Yibo** **Moyale** *Lake Rudolph* **Wal Garis** **BRITISH EAST AFRICA** **El Wak** **The Juba** **Goluin** UGANDA *KENYA* **Beles** **Alessandra** **Gugani** **Gelib** *Kismayu* **Bulo Erillo** **Yonte** *Mogadiscu*		**5**
4	GABON	REPUBLIC OF THE CONGO	*Congo* RWANDA	Lake Albert Lake Victoria Aberdare Mountains *Nairobi* **Kilimanjaro** *Latema Nek* *Kahe* BURUNDI TANZANIA TANGANYIKA Lake Tanganyika	*Mombasa* *Wiransi*		**4**
3			ANGOLA	ZAMBIA **Beho Beho** *Kilwa* **Narungombe** *R.Rufiji* **Nyangao** Lake Nyasa		MADAGASCAR	**3**
2		**SOUTH WEST AFRICA**	BOTSWANA **BECHUANALAND** *Windhoek*	NORTHERN RHODESIA *R. Zambeze* Lake Kariba **ZIMBABWE** *RHODESIA* *Bulawayo*	MOZAMBIQUE	Tamatave Tananariva.	**2**
1			*Gibeon*	SOUTH AFRICA SWAZILAND	0 80 160 240 320 Miles		**1**
	A	B	C	D	E	F	G	

Africa.

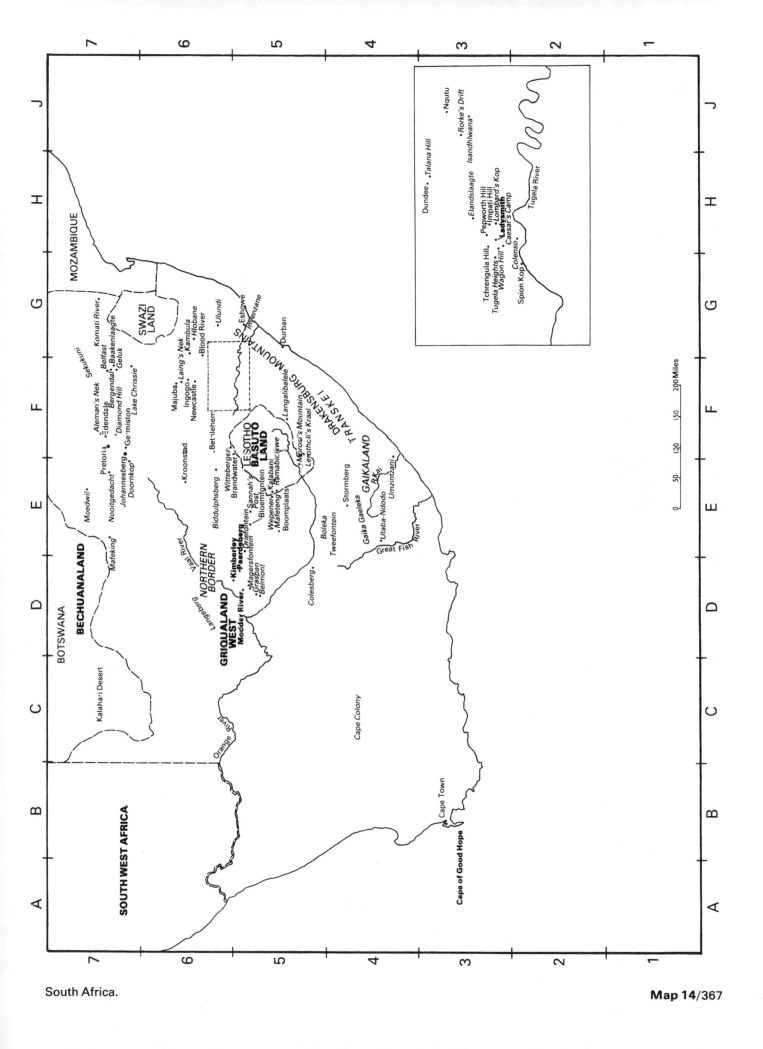

South Africa.

Map 14/367

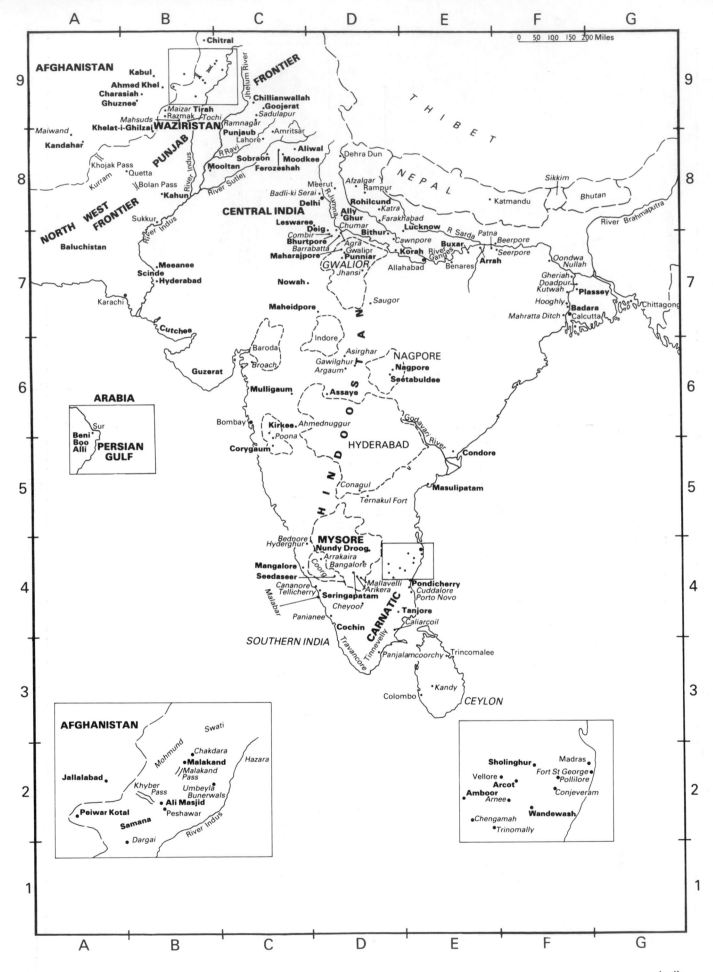

A B C D E F G

AFGHANISTAN

•Chitral

9

Kabul•
Ahmed Khel
Charasiah•
Ghuznee•

Maizar **Tirah**
Mahsuds• Razmak• **Tochi**

FRONTIER

•Chillianwallah
Goojerat•
•Sadulapur

Ramnagar

Jhelum River

Maiwand•
Kandahar•
Khelat-i-Ghilzai•
WAZIRISTAN
Punjaub
Lahore•
•Amritsar

Dehra Dun

THIBET

Sikkim

9

Khojak Pass
Kurram
•Quetta
||Bolan Pass
Sukkur

PUNJAB
Mooltan
Sobraon
Ferozeshah
Moodkee
•**Aliwal**

Afzalgar
•Rampur

NEPAL

•Katmandu

Bhutan

8

NORTH WEST FRONTIER

Baluchistan

River Indus
•Kahun

R.Ravi
River Sutlej

Meerut
Badli-ki Serai
R.Jumna
Delhi
Ally
Ghur
Chumar

Rohilcund
•Katra
Farakhabad•
Lucknow

R.Sarda
•Patna
•Beerpore

River Brahmaputra

8

CENTRAL INDIA
Leswaree
Combir **Deig**
Bhurtpore
Barrabatta
Maharajpore
Agra•
Gwalior•

Bithur
•Cawnpore
Korah
River Ganges
Buxar
•Seerpore
Arrah

•Oondwa Nullah

7

Scinde
Meeanee•
•**Hyderabad**

Karachi•

Punniar
GWALIOR
Jhansi•

•Saugor

Allahabad•
•Benares

Gheriah•
Doadpur•
Kutwah•
Hooghly
Mahratta Ditch

•Plassey
Badara
•Calcutta

•Chittagong

7

Cutchee•

Maheidpore•

Indore•

Nowah•

6

ARABIA
Sur
Beni Boo Alli
PERSIAN GULF

Baroda•
Broach•
Guzerat

Mulligaum•

Asirghar•
Gawilghur•
Argaum•

H
I
N
D
O
O
S
T
A
N

NAGPORE
•**Nagpore**
Seetabuldee•

6

5

Bombay•

Kirkee•
•Poona

Corygaum•

Ahmednuggur•
Assaye•

Godavery River

HYDERABAD

•**Condore**

5

Conagul•

Masulipatam•

Ternakul Fort•

4

Bednore•
Hyderghur•

MYSORE
Nundy Droog•
Arrakaira•
Bangalore•

Coorg

Mallavelli•
Arikera•

Pondicherry
Cuddalore•
Porto Novo

4

Mangalore•
Seedaseer•

Cananore•
Tellicherry•
Malabar

Seringapatam•
Cheyoor•

Tanjore•
Caliarcoil•

Panianee•

Cochin•
CARNATIC

Trincomalee•

3

SOUTHERN INDIA

Travancore
Tinnevelly
Panjalamcoorchy•

•Kandy

Colombo•

CEYLON

3

2

AFGHANISTAN

Swati
Mohmund
•Chakdara
Malakand•
Malakand Pass//
Hazara

Jallalabad•

Khyber Pass
Umbeyla
Bunerwals
Ali Masjid•
Peshawar•

Sholinghur•
Vellore•
Arcot
Amboor•
Arnee•

Madras•
Fort St George•
Pollilore•
Conjeveram•

Peiwar Kotal•
Samana
Dargai•

River Indus

Chengamah•
•Trinomally

Wandewash•

2

1

A B C D E F G

1

India.

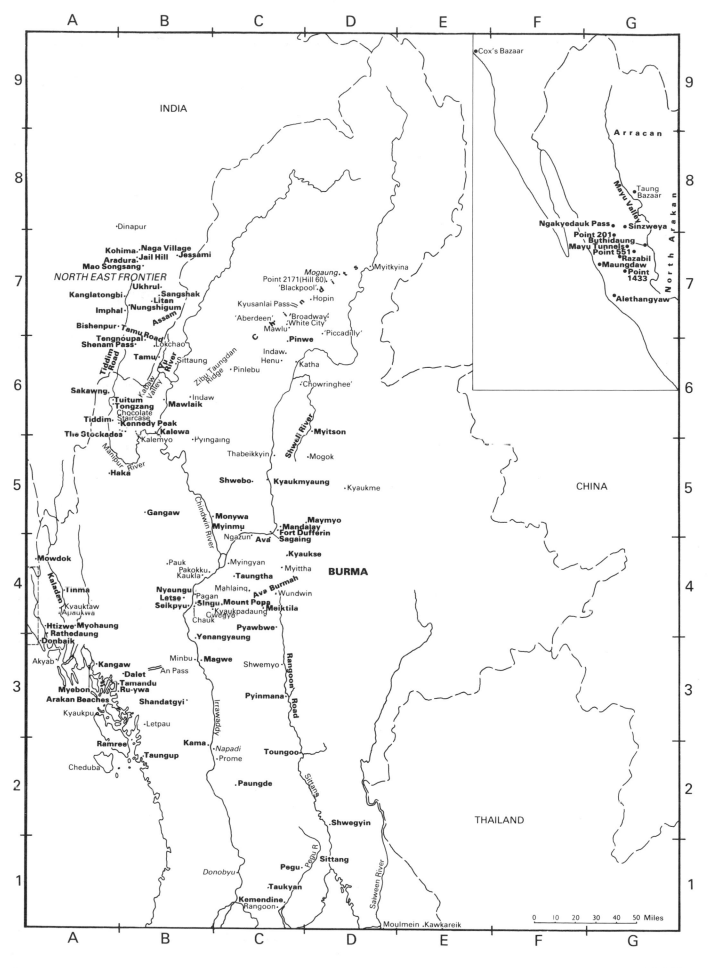

A   **B**   **C**   **D**   **E**   **F**   **G**

9

INDIA

Cox's Bazaar

A r r a c a n

Taung
Bazaar

•Dinapur

8

Mayu Valley

North Arakan

Ngakyedauk Pass
Point 201 •Sinzweya
Buthidaung
Mayu Tunnels•
Point 551 •Razabil
•Maungdaw •Point
1433

Kohima• •Naga Village
Aradura• •Jail Hill •Jessami
Mao Songsang•

NORTH EAST FRONTIER
Ukhrul•

Point 2171(Hill 60)•
Mogaung.• '• *t s*
'Blackpool'• •Myitkyina
•Hopin

•Alethangyaw

7

Kanglatongbi• •Sangshak
•Litan
Imphal• •Nungshigum
Bishenpur• *Assam*
Tengnoupal• Tamu Road •Lokchao
Shenam Pass•
Tiddim Tamu•

Kyusanlai Pass•
'Aberdeen'• •'Broadway'
•White City
Mawlu• •'Piccadilly'
•Pinwe
Indaw•
Henu• •Katha

Sakawng•
Tuitum•
Tongzang• Chocolate •Mawlaik
Tiddim• Staircase
•Kennedy Peak •Kalewa
The Stockades•

'Chowringhee'•

•Indaw

•Pyingaing

Shweli River
Myitson•

6

•Pinlebu

Zibu Taungdan
Ridge

5

•Haka

Thabeikkyin• •Mogok

Shwebo• •Kyaukmyaung
•Kyaukme

CHINA

•Gangaw

Chindwin River

Monywa• •Maymyo
Myinmu• •Mandalay
Ngazun• •Fort Dufferin
Ava• Sagaing

Mowdok•

•Pauk
Pakokku•
Kaukla•

•Kyaukse

•Myittha

BURMA

4

•Tinma

Kaladan

Kyauktaw•
Apaukwa•

Nyaungu• •Myingyan
Letse• •Taungtha
Seikpyu• •Singu •Mount Popa
•Pagan •Meiktila
Chauk• Kyaukpadaung
Gwegyo• •Wundwin

Mahlaing•

Ava Burmah

Htizwe• •Myohaung
Rathedaung•
Donbaik•
Akyab•

Pyawbwe•

•Yenangyaung

3

Kangaw•
•Dalet
Myebon• •Tamandu
•Ru-ywa
Arakan Beaches•
Kyaukpu•

Minbu• •Magwe
An Pass

Shwemyo•

Rangoon Road

Irrawaddy

•Letpau

Shandatgyi•

Pyinmana•

2

Ramree• •Taungup

Kama•

Cheduba•

•Napadi
•Prome

Toungoo•

Sittang

•Paungde

THAILAND

1

Salween River

Pegu R

•Shwegyin

Donobyu
Pegu• Sittang•

•Taukyan
Kemendine•
Rangoon•

Moulmein• •Kawkareik

0 10 20 30 40 50 Miles

A   **B**   **C**   **D**   **E**   **F**   **G**

Burma.

Map 16/369

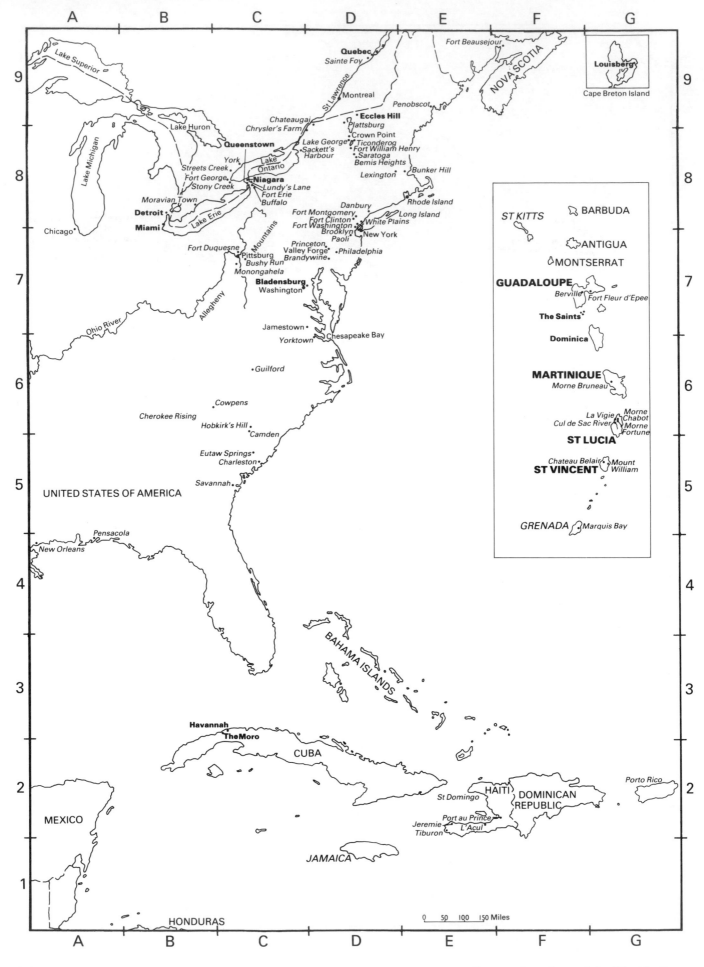

Eastern America and the West Indies.

Map labels:

A B C D E F G

Lake Superior
Fort Beausejour
NOVA SCOTIA
Louisberg
Cape Breton Island
Quebec
Sainte Foy
Lake Huron
Montreal
St Lawrence
Penobscot
Chateaugai
Chrysler's Farm
Eccles Hill
Plattsburg
Crown Point
Queenstown
Lake George
Sackett's Harbour
Ticonderog
Fort William Henry
Saratoga
Bemis Heights
York
Lake Ontario
Streets Creek
Fort George
Stony Creek
Niagara
Lundy's Lane
Fort Erie
Buffalo
Lexington
Bunker Hill
Moravian Town
Lake Erie
Danbury
Rhode Island
Long Island
Detroit
Fort Montgomery
Fort Clinton
White Plains
Miami
Fort Washington
Brooklyn
New York
Chicago
Mountains
Paoli
Fort Duquesne
Princeton
Valley Forge
Brandywine
Philadelphia
Pittsburg
Bushy Run
Monongahela
Bladensburg
Washington
Allegheny
Jamestown
Ohio River
Yorktown
Chesapeake Bay
Guilford
Cowpens
Cherokee Rising
Hobkirk's Hill
Camden
Eutaw Springs
Charleston
Savannah
UNITED STATES OF AMERICA
Pensacola
New Orleans
BAHAMA ISLANDS
MEXICO
Havannah
The Moro
CUBA
Porto Rico
HAITI
DOMINICAN REPUBLIC
St Domingo
Port au Prince
L'Acul
Jeremie
Tiburon
JAMAICA
HONDURAS

Inset key (West Indies):
ST KITTS
BARBUDA
ANTIGUA
MONTSERRAT
GUADALOUPE
Berville
Fort Fleur d'Epee
The Saints
Dominica
MARTINIQUE
Morne Bruneau
La Vigie
Morne Chabot
Cul de Sac River
Morne Fortune
ST LUCIA
Chateau Belair
Mount William
ST VINCENT
GRENADA
Marquis Bay

0 50 100 150 Miles

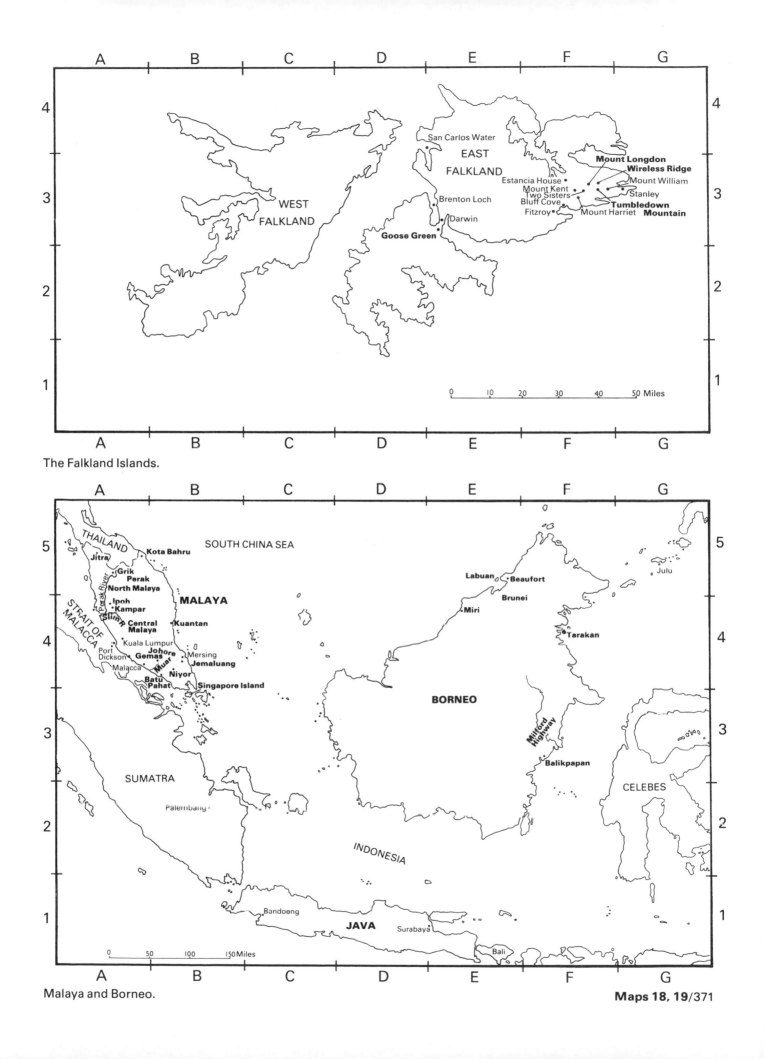

The Falkland Islands.

West Falkland
East Falkland
San Carlos Water
Estancia House
Mount Kent
Two Sisters
Bluff Cove
Fitzroy
Brenton Loch
Darwin
Goose Green
Mount Longdon
Wireless Ridge
Mount William
Stanley
Tumbledown Mountain
Mount Harriet

Malaya and Borneo.

THAILAND
SOUTH CHINA SEA
Jitra
Kota Bahru
Grik
Perak
North Malaya
Peak River
STRAIT OF MALACCA
Ipoh
Kampar
Slim
Central Malaya
Kuantan
MALAYA
Kuala Lumpur
Port Dickson
Johore
Gemas
Mersing
Malacca
Muar
Jemaluang
Batu Pahat
Niyor
Singapore Island
SUMATRA
Palembang
Labuan
Beaufort
Brunei
Miri
Tarakan
BORNEO
Milford Highway
Balikpapan
CELEBES
Julu
INDONESIA
Bandoeng
JAVA
Surabaya
Bali

Maps 18, 19/371

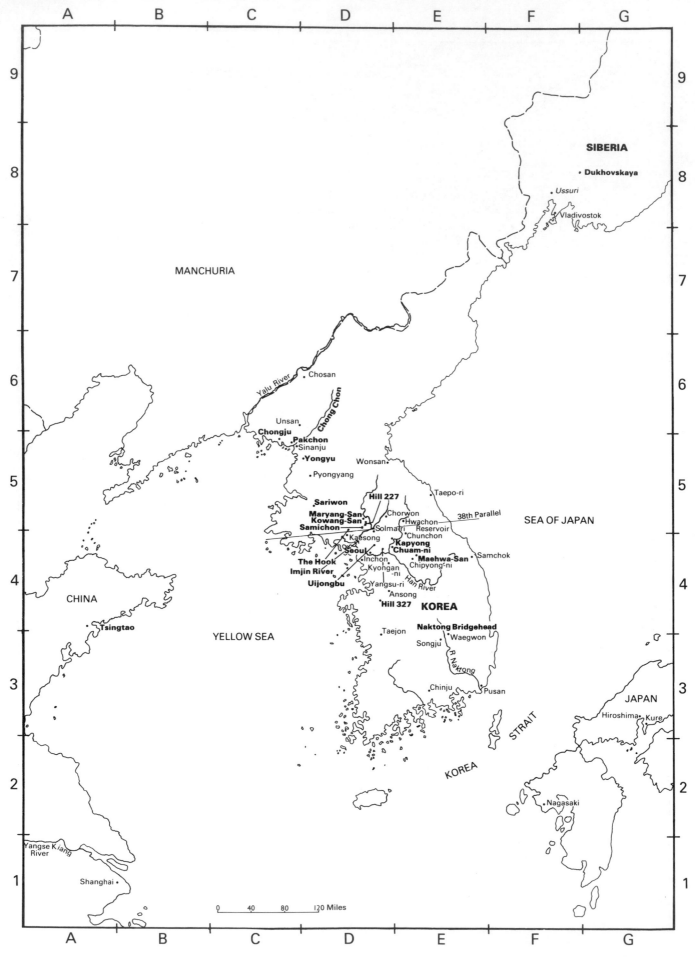

SIBERIA

• **Dukhovskaya**

• *Ussuri*

• Vladivostok

MANCHURIA

Yalu River • Chosan

Chong Chon

Unsan

Chongju
Pakchon
•Sinanju

Yongyu

•Wonsan

• Pyongyang

• Taepo-ri

Hill 227

Sariwon

Maryang-San
Kowang-San Chorwon
Samichon •Solma-ri •Hwachon 38th Parallel
      Reservoir

SEA OF JAPAN

•Kaesong •Chunchon

Seoul• **Kapyong**
  Chuam-ni

•Samchok

The Hook •Inchon **Maehwa-San**
Imjin River •Kyonggan •Chipyong-ni
   -ni *Han River*
Uijongbu •Yangsu-ri
   •Ansong

CHINA **Hill 327** **KOREA**

• **Tsingtao**

YELLOW SEA **Naktong Bridgehead**
   •Taejon •Waegwon
    Songju *R Naktong*

JAPAN

Hiroshima• •Kure

  •Chinju •Pusan

STRAIT

KOREA

•Nagasaki

Yangse Kiang
River

• Shanghai

0 40 80 120 Miles

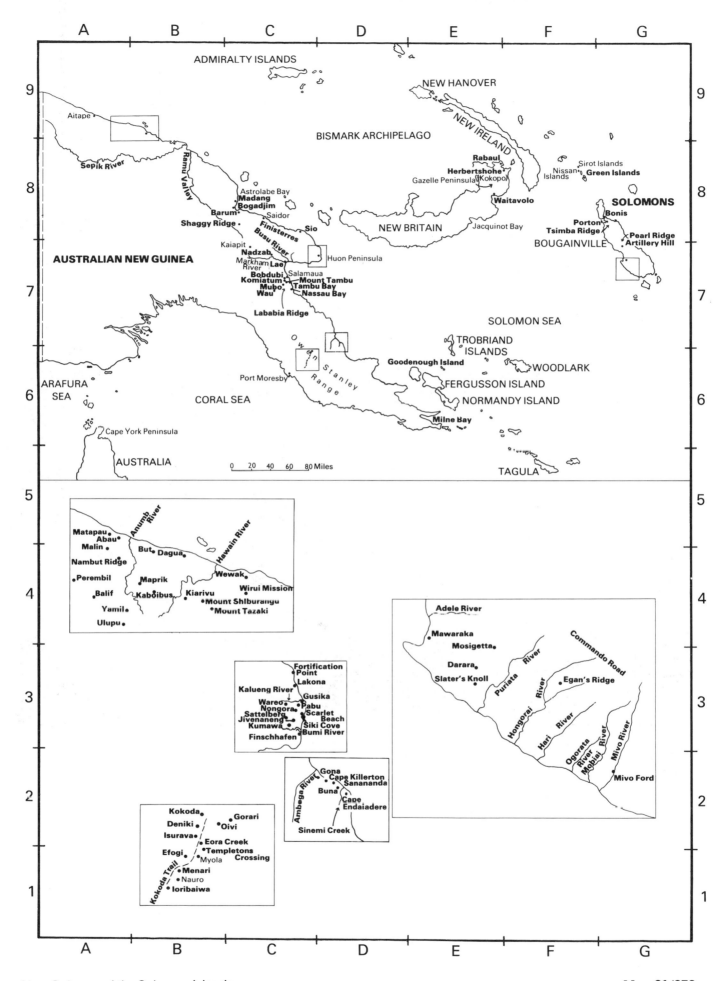

New Guinea and the Solomon Islands.

Map 21/373

Storming the Dargai Ridge during the Tirah Expedition on the
North West Frontier. *NAM*

Index of Battles

387

Index of Place Names

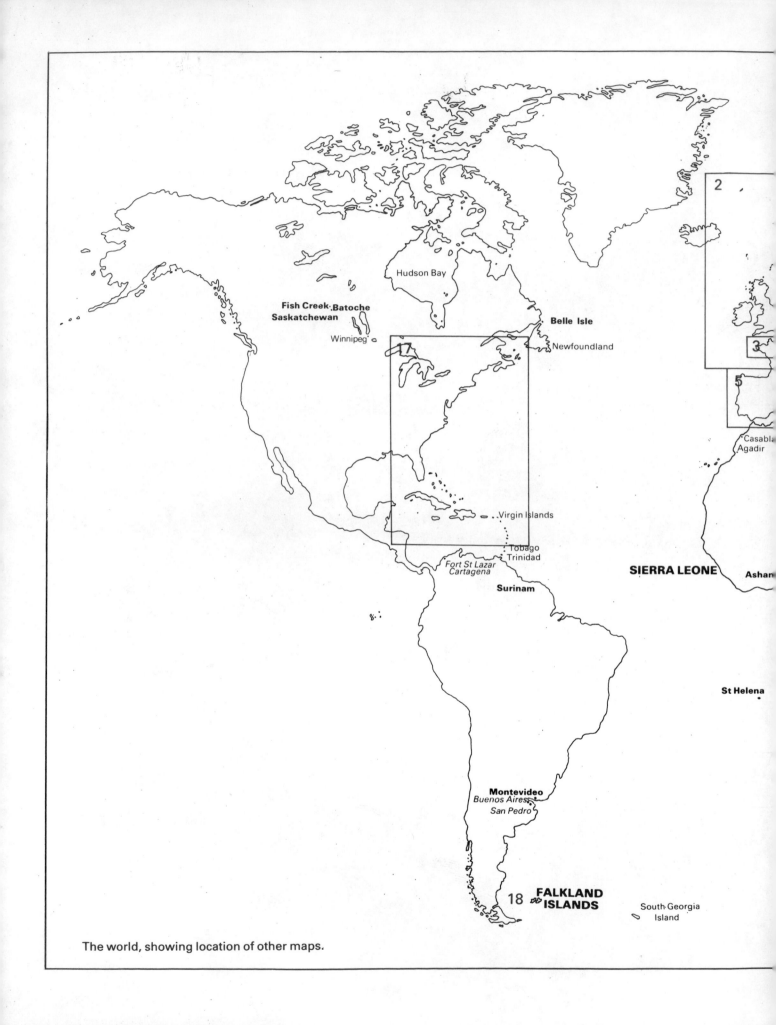

The world, showing location of other maps.